LENA FINKLE'S MAGIC BARREL

A GRAPHIC NOVEL BY ANYA ULINICH

Penguin Books

PENGUIN BOOKS

Published by the Penguin Group
Penguin Group (USA) LLC
375 Hudson Street
New York, New York 10014

USA | Canada | UK | Ireland | Australia | New Zealand | India | South Africa | China
penguin.com
A Penguin Random House Company

First published in Penguin Books 2014

ISBN 978-0-14-312524-2

Printed in the United States of America

1   3   5   7   9   10   8   6   4   2

FOR EFFIE AND EMILY

●

WITH APOLOGIES TO
BERNARD MALAMUD

PART ONE

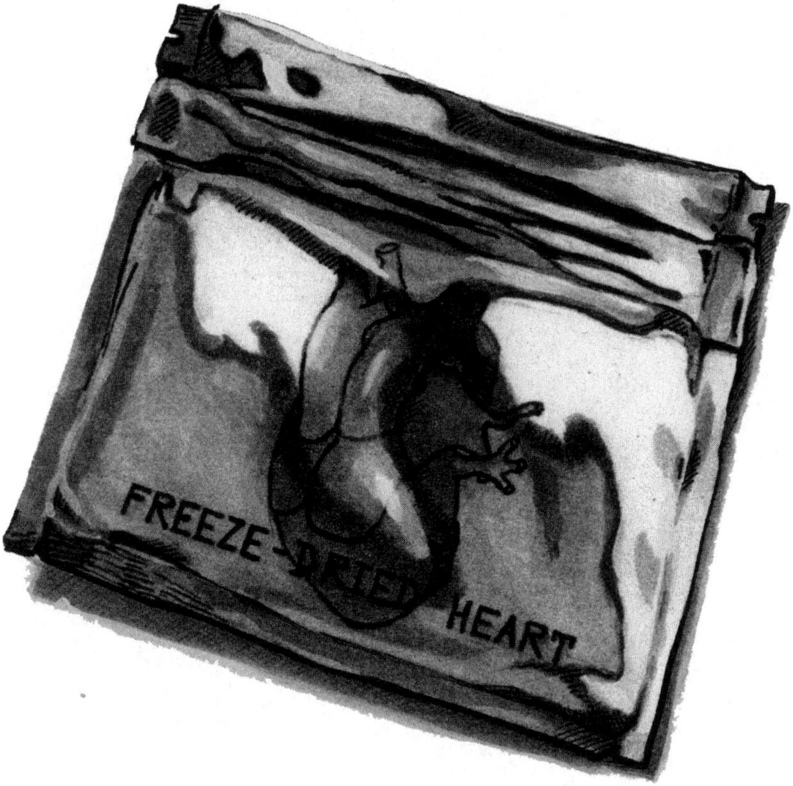
FREEZE-DRIED HEART

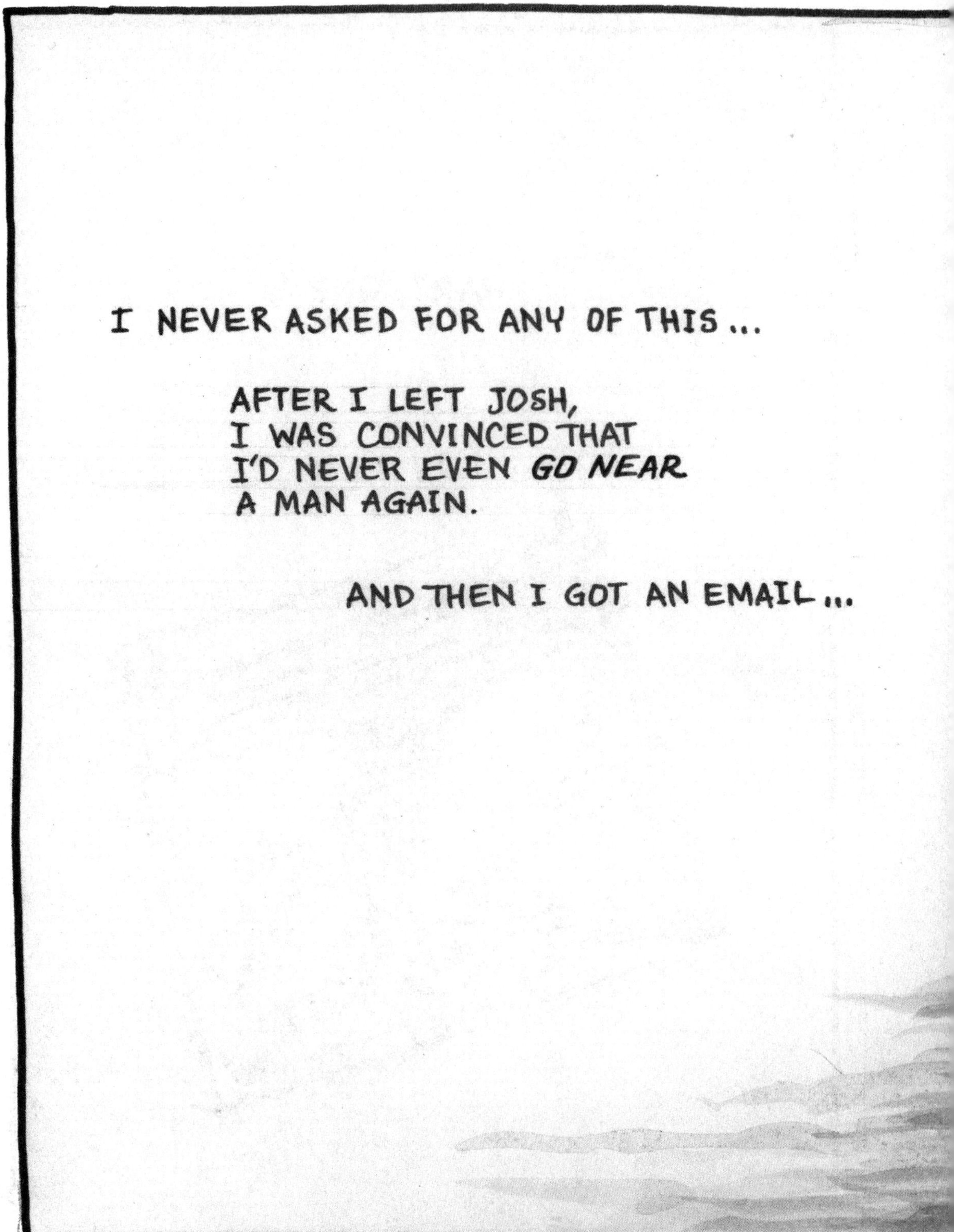
I NEVER ASKED FOR ANY OF THIS...
AFTER I LEFT JOSH, I WAS CONVINCED THAT I'D NEVER EVEN *GO NEAR* A MAN AGAIN.
AND THEN I GOT AN EMAIL...

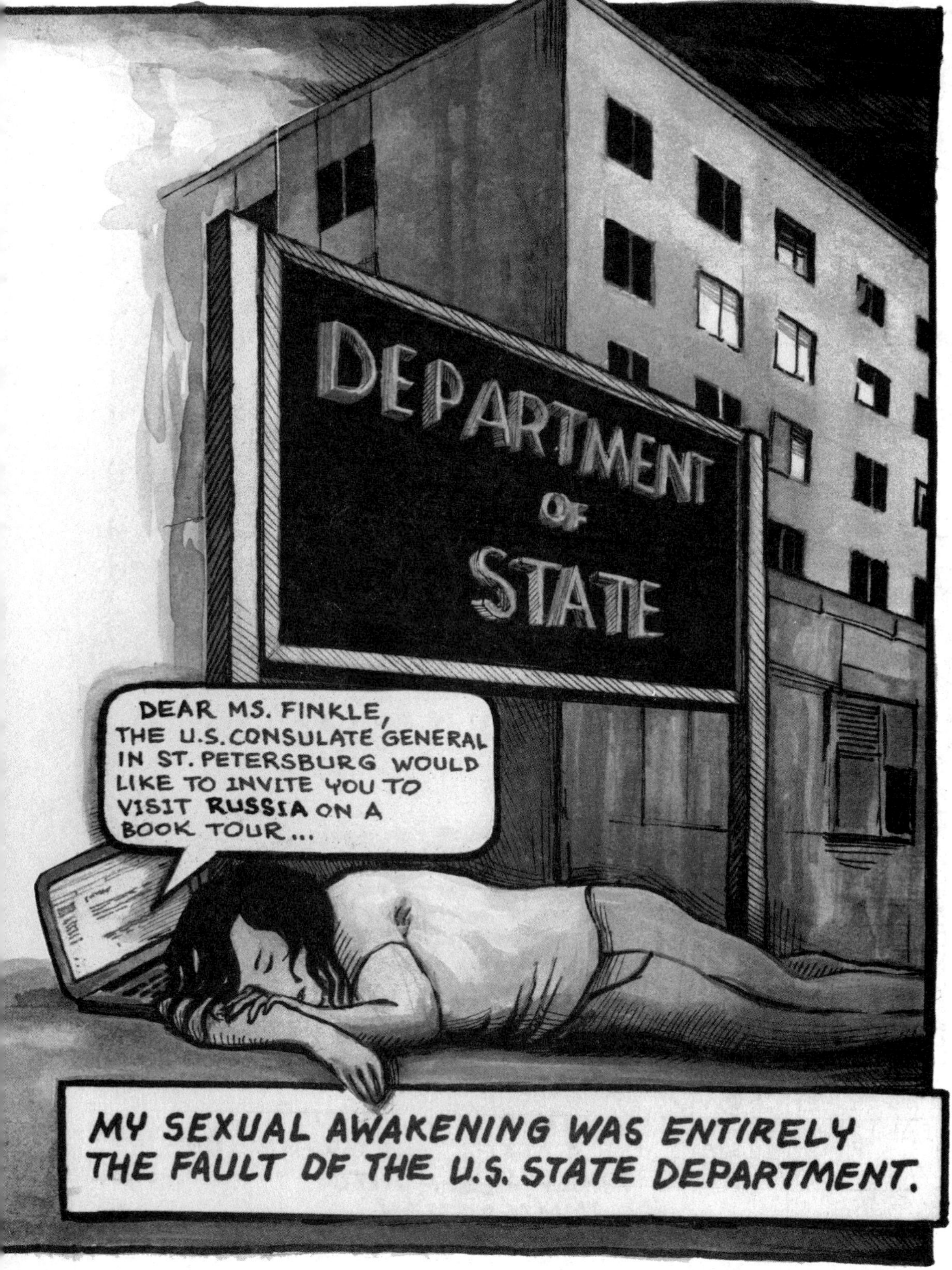
DEPARTMENT OF STATE
DEAR MS. FINKLE, THE U.S. CONSULATE GENERAL IN ST. PETERSBURG WOULD LIKE TO INVITE YOU TO VISIT RUSSIA ON A BOOK TOUR...
MY SEXUAL AWAKENING WAS ENTIRELY THE FAULT OF THE U.S. STATE DEPARTMENT.

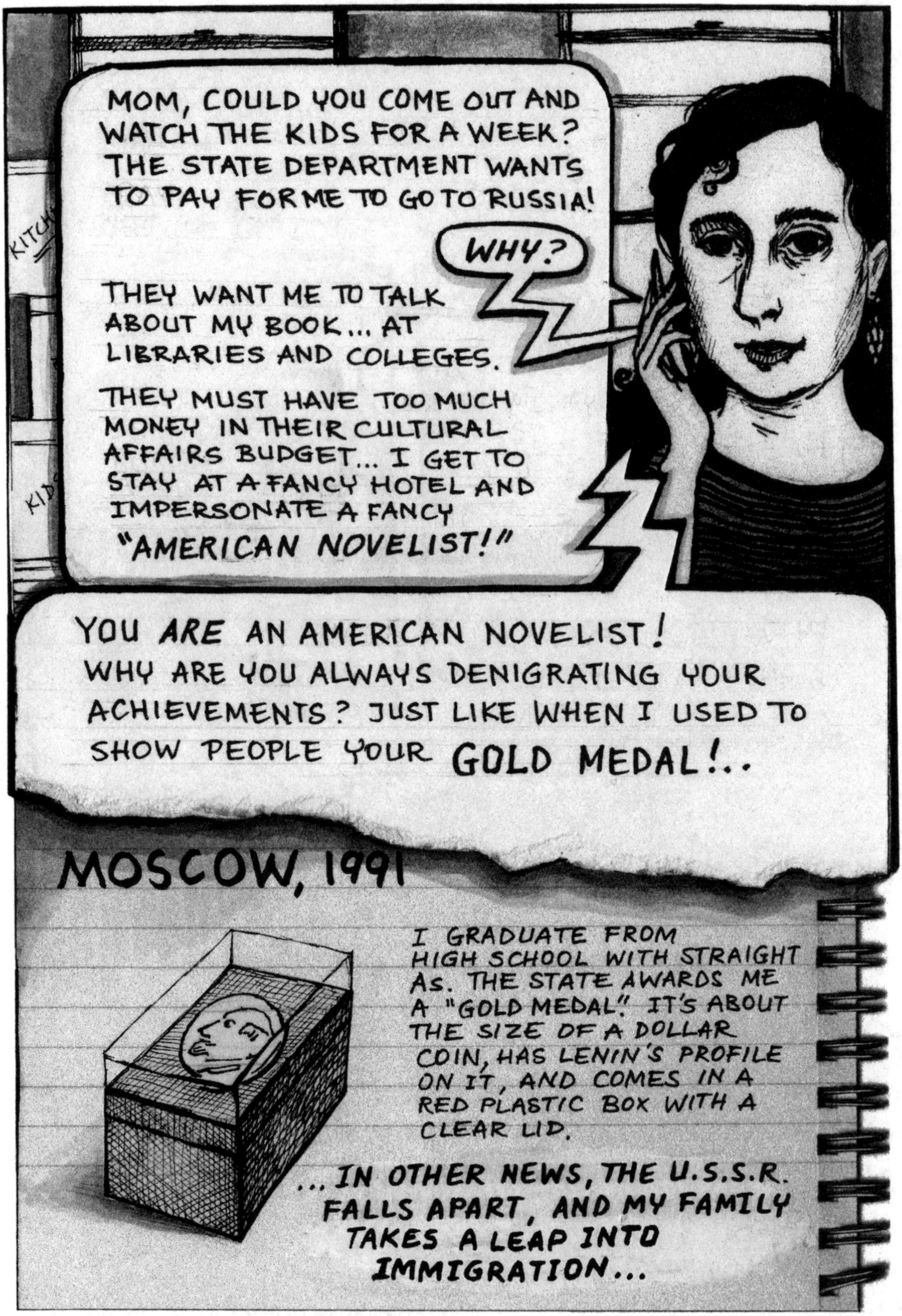

MOM, COULD YOU COME OUT AND WATCH THE KIDS FOR A WEEK? THE STATE DEPARTMENT WANTS TO PAY FOR ME TO GO TO RUSSIA!

WHY?

THEY WANT ME TO TALK ABOUT MY BOOK... AT LIBRARIES AND COLLEGES.

THEY MUST HAVE TOO MUCH MONEY IN THEIR CULTURAL AFFAIRS BUDGET... I GET TO STAY AT A FANCY HOTEL AND IMPERSONATE A FANCY "AMERICAN NOVELIST!"

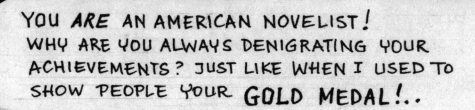

YOU **ARE** AN AMERICAN NOVELIST! WHY ARE YOU ALWAYS DENIGRATING YOUR ACHIEVEMENTS? JUST LIKE WHEN I USED TO SHOW PEOPLE YOUR **GOLD MEDAL!**..

MOSCOW, 1991

I GRADUATE FROM HIGH SCHOOL WITH STRAIGHT A's. THE STATE AWARDS ME A "GOLD MEDAL." IT'S ABOUT THE SIZE OF A DOLLAR COIN, HAS LENIN'S PROFILE ON IT, AND COMES IN A RED PLASTIC BOX WITH A CLEAR LID.

... IN OTHER NEWS, THE U.S.S.R. FALLS APART, AND MY FAMILY TAKES A LEAP INTO IMMIGRATION...

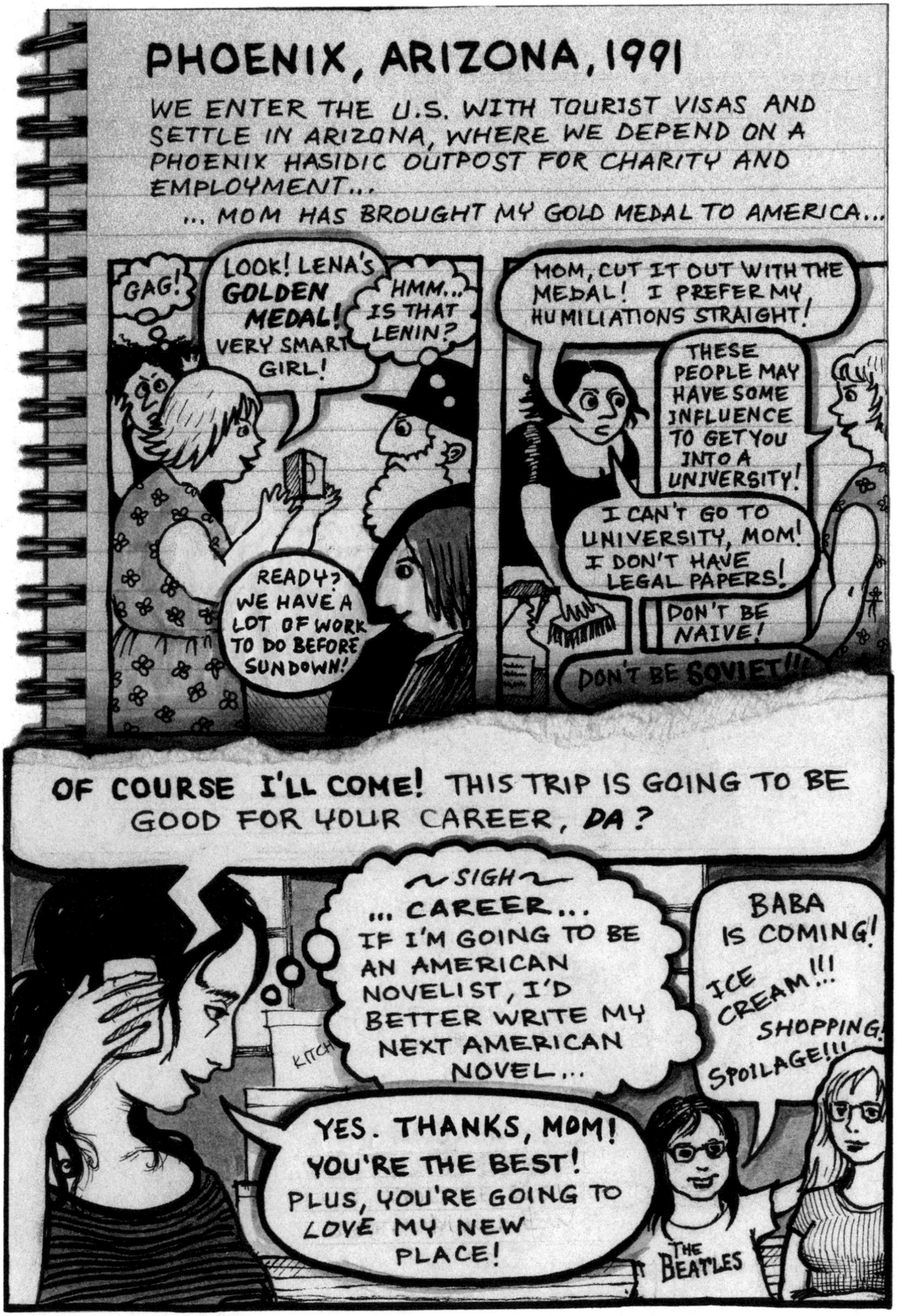
PHOENIX, ARIZONA, 1991
WE ENTER THE U.S. WITH TOURIST VISAS AND SETTLE IN ARIZONA, WHERE WE DEPEND ON A PHOENIX HASIDIC OUTPOST FOR CHARITY AND EMPLOYMENT...
... MOM HAS BROUGHT MY GOLD MEDAL TO AMERICA...
GAG!
LOOK! LENA'S GOLDEN MEDAL! VERY SMART GIRL!
HMM... IS THAT LENIN?
READY? WE HAVE A LOT OF WORK TO DO BEFORE SUNDOWN!
MOM, CUT IT OUT WITH THE MEDAL! I PREFER MY HUMILIATIONS STRAIGHT!
THESE PEOPLE MAY HAVE SOME INFLUENCE TO GET YOU INTO A UNIVERSITY!
I CAN'T GO TO UNIVERSITY, MOM! I DON'T HAVE LEGAL PAPERS!
DON'T BE NAIVE!
DON'T BE SOVIET!!!
OF COURSE I'LL COME! THIS TRIP IS GOING TO BE GOOD FOR YOUR CAREER, DA?
~SIGH~
... CAREER... IF I'M GOING TO BE AN AMERICAN NOVELIST, I'D BETTER WRITE MY NEXT AMERICAN NOVEL...
BABA IS COMING!
ICE CREAM!!!
SHOPPING!
SPOILAGE!!!
YES. THANKS, MOM! YOU'RE THE BEST! PLUS, YOU'RE GOING TO LOVE MY NEW PLACE!
THE BEATLES

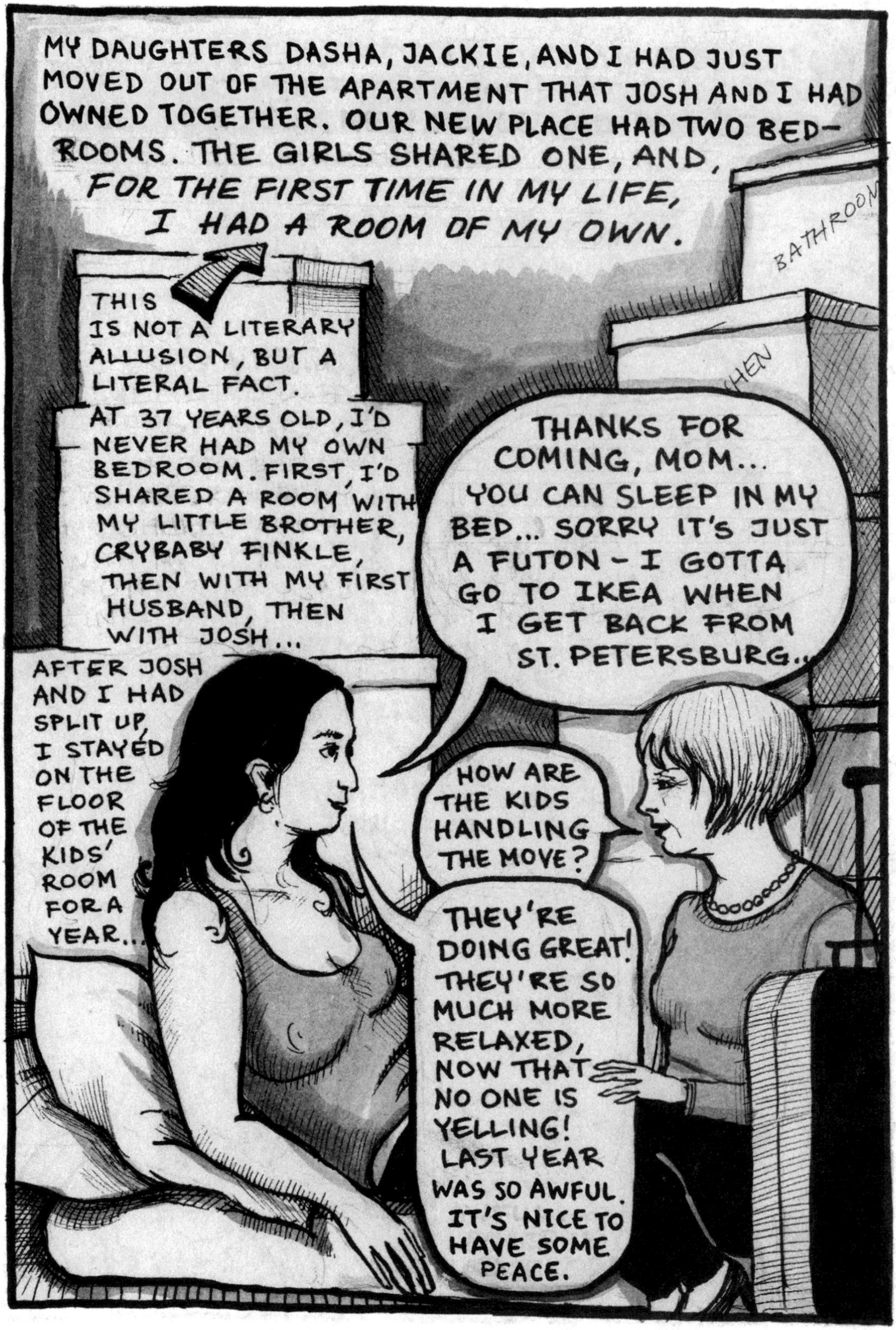
MY DAUGHTERS DASHA, JACKIE, AND I HAD JUST MOVED OUT OF THE APARTMENT THAT JOSH AND I HAD OWNED TOGETHER. OUR NEW PLACE HAD TWO BED-ROOMS. THE GIRLS SHARED ONE, AND, FOR THE FIRST TIME IN MY LIFE, I HAD A ROOM OF MY OWN.
BATHROOM
THIS IS NOT A LITERARY ALLUSION, BUT A LITERAL FACT.
AT 37 YEARS OLD, I'D NEVER HAD MY OWN BEDROOM. FIRST, I'D SHARED A ROOM WITH MY LITTLE BROTHER, CRYBABY FINKLE, THEN WITH MY FIRST HUSBAND, THEN WITH JOSH...
THANKS FOR COMING, MOM... YOU CAN SLEEP IN MY BED... SORRY IT'S JUST A FUTON - I GOTTA GO TO IKEA WHEN I GET BACK FROM ST. PETERSBURG...
AFTER JOSH AND I HAD SPLIT UP, I STAYED ON THE FLOOR OF THE KIDS' ROOM FOR A YEAR...
HOW ARE THE KIDS HANDLING THE MOVE?
THEY'RE DOING GREAT! THEY'RE SO MUCH MORE RELAXED, NOW THAT NO ONE IS YELLING! LAST YEAR WAS SO AWFUL. IT'S NICE TO HAVE SOME PEACE.

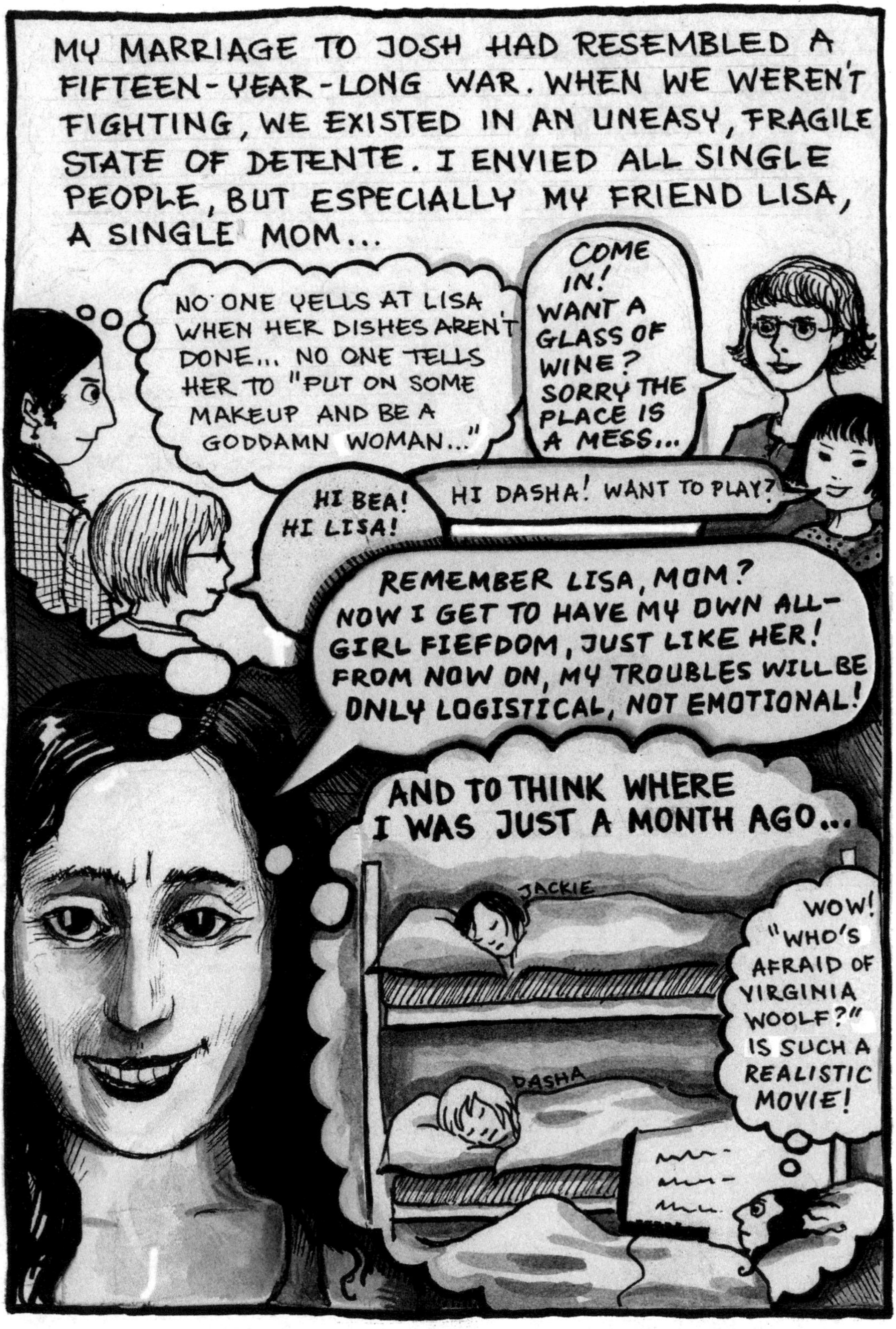
MY MARRIAGE TO JOSH HAD RESEMBLED A FIFTEEN-YEAR-LONG WAR. WHEN WE WEREN'T FIGHTING, WE EXISTED IN AN UNEASY, FRAGILE STATE OF DETENTE. I ENVIED ALL SINGLE PEOPLE, BUT ESPECIALLY MY FRIEND LISA, A SINGLE MOM...
NO ONE YELLS AT LISA WHEN HER DISHES AREN'T DONE... NO ONE TELLS HER TO "PUT ON SOME MAKEUP AND BE A GODDAMN WOMAN..."
COME IN! WANT A GLASS OF WINE? SORRY THE PLACE IS A MESS...
HI BEA! HI LISA!
HI DASHA! WANT TO PLAY?
REMEMBER LISA, MOM? NOW I GET TO HAVE MY OWN ALL-GIRL FIEFDOM, JUST LIKE HER! FROM NOW ON, MY TROUBLES WILL BE ONLY LOGISTICAL, NOT EMOTIONAL!
AND TO THINK WHERE I WAS JUST A MONTH AGO...
JACKIE
DASHA
WOW! "WHO'S AFRAID OF VIRGINIA WOOLF?" IS SUCH A REALISTIC MOVIE!

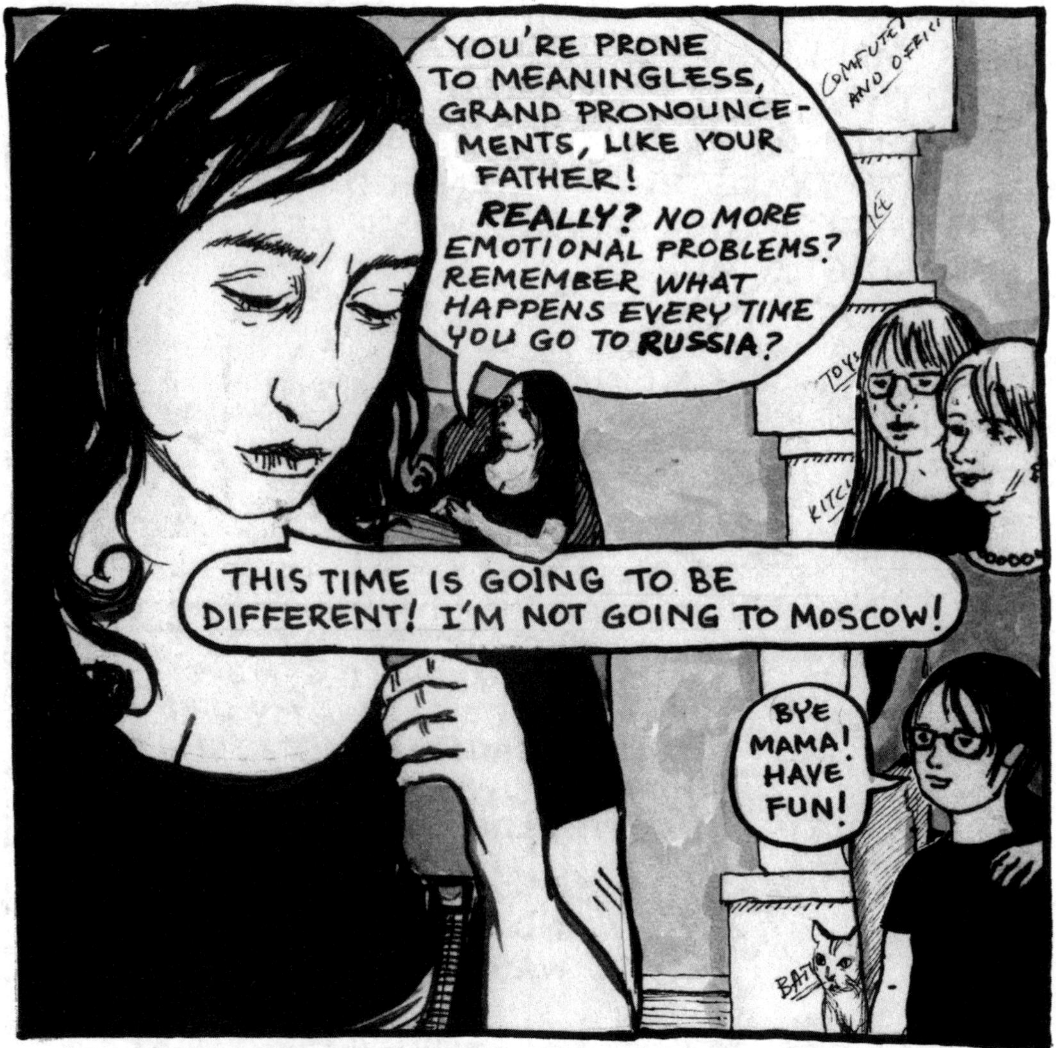
YOU'RE PRONE TO MEANINGLESS, GRAND PRONOUNCEMENTS, LIKE YOUR FATHER!
REALLY? NO MORE EMOTIONAL PROBLEMS? REMEMBER WHAT HAPPENS EVERY TIME YOU GO TO RUSSIA?
THIS TIME IS GOING TO BE DIFFERENT! I'M NOT GOING TO MOSCOW!
BYE MAMA! HAVE FUN!

I'M AN IMMIGRANT, *NOT* AN EXPATRIATE.

I NEVER MANAGED TO HAVE A BI-CONTINENTAL LIFE, LIKE SOME OF MY RUSSIAN FRIENDS...

MY GRANDPARENTS WERE DEAD, MY PARENTS LIVED IN ARIZONA, AND I NO LONGER HAD CLOSE FAMILY IN RUSSIA... I'D SPENT HALF MY LIFE BEING MARRIED TO JOSH, AN ARIZONA NATIVE, AND OUR KIDS DIDN'T SPEAK RUSSIAN...

... I'D GONE BACK TO MOSCOW JUST TWICE IN THE LAST TWENTY YEARS...

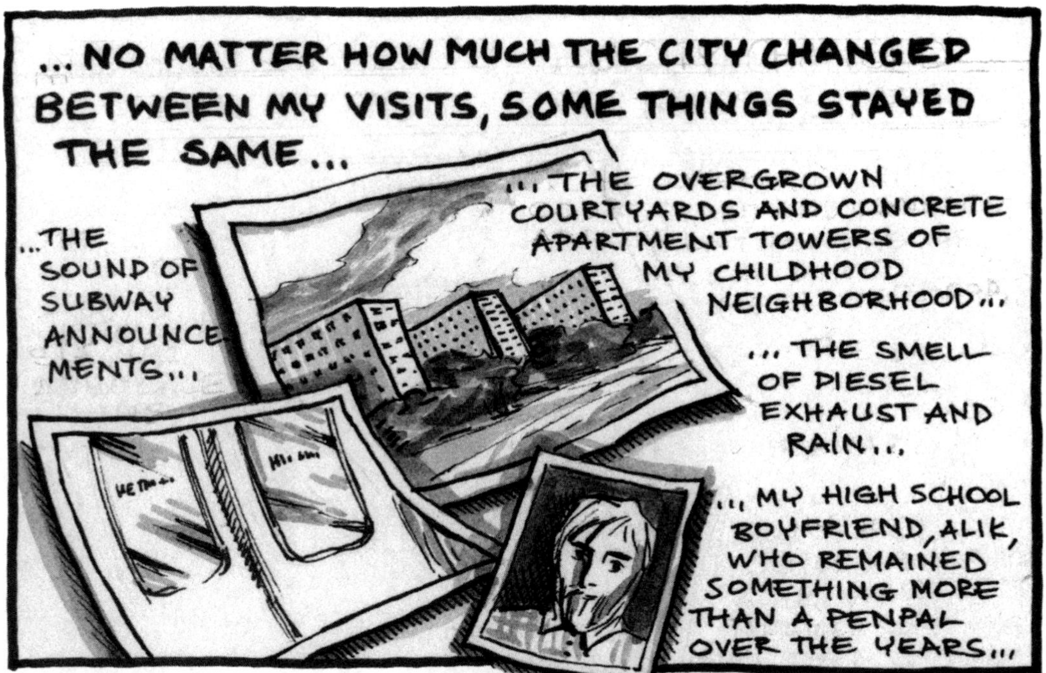
...NO MATTER HOW MUCH THE CITY CHANGED BETWEEN MY VISITS, SOME THINGS STAYED THE SAME...
...THE SOUND OF SUBWAY ANNOUNCEMENTS...
...THE OVERGROWN COURTYARDS AND CONCRETE APARTMENT TOWERS OF MY CHILDHOOD NEIGHBORHOOD...
...THE SMELL OF DIESEL EXHAUST AND RAIN...
...MY HIGH SCHOOL BOYFRIEND, ALIK, WHO REMAINED SOMETHING MORE THAN A PENPAL OVER THE YEARS...

...EVERY TIME I RETURNED HOME, MOSCOW WEDGED ITSELF BETWEEN ME AND MY LIFE.

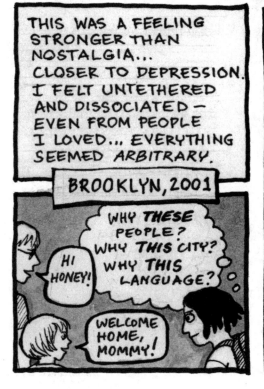

THIS WAS A FEELING STRONGER THAN NOSTALGIA... CLOSER TO DEPRESSION. I FELT UNTETHERED AND DISSOCIATED—EVEN FROM PEOPLE I LOVED... EVERYTHING SEEMED *ARBITRARY*.

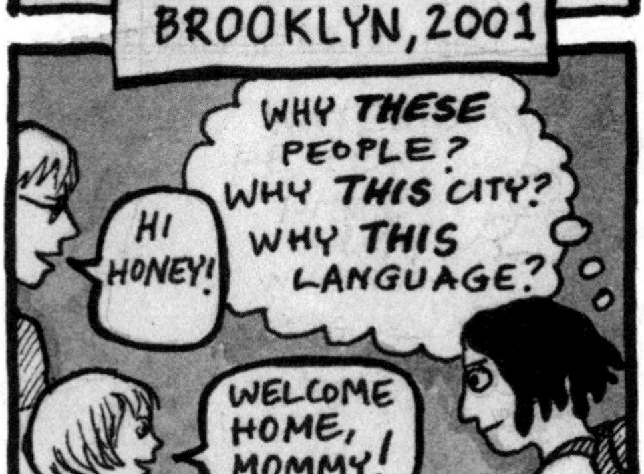
BROOKLYN, 2001
WHY THESE PEOPLE? WHY THIS CITY? WHY THIS LANGUAGE?
HI HONEY!
WELCOME HOME, MOMMY!

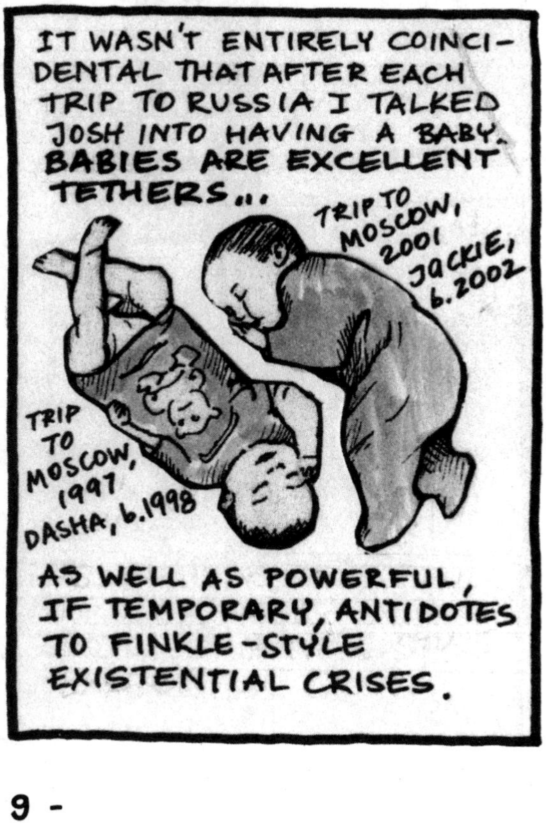
IT WASN'T ENTIRELY COINCIDENTAL THAT AFTER EACH TRIP TO RUSSIA I TALKED JOSH INTO HAVING A BABY. BABIES ARE EXCELLENT TETHERS...
TRIP TO MOSCOW, 2001
JACKIE, 6.2002
TRIP TO MOSCOW, 1997
DASHA, 6.1998
AS WELL AS POWERFUL, IF TEMPORARY, ANTIDOTES TO FINKLE-STYLE EXISTENTIAL CRISES.

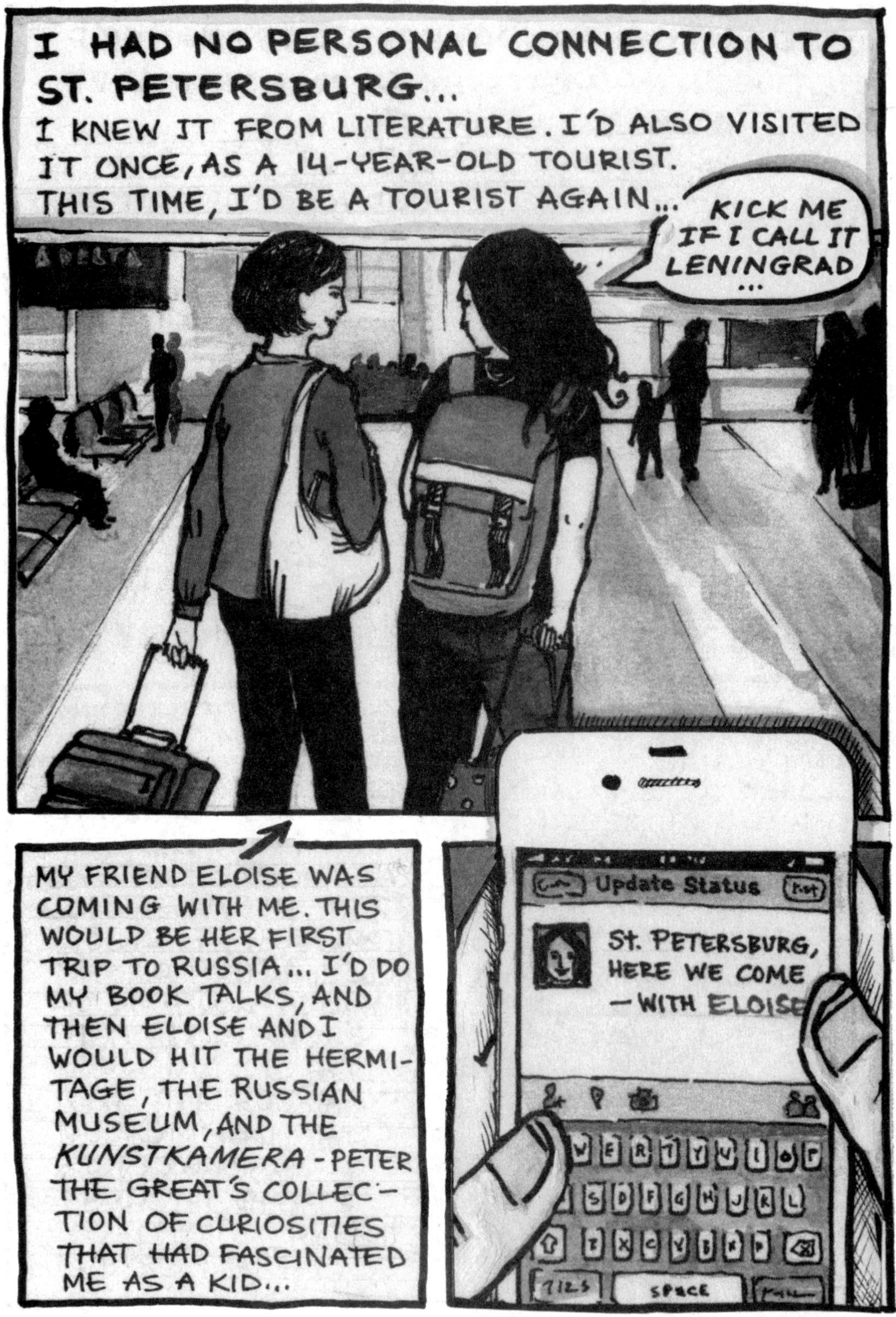
I HAD NO PERSONAL CONNECTION TO ST. PETERSBURG...
I KNEW IT FROM LITERATURE. I'D ALSO VISITED IT ONCE, AS A 14-YEAR-OLD TOURIST.
THIS TIME, I'D BE A TOURIST AGAIN...
KICK ME IF I CALL IT LENINGRAD...
MY FRIEND ELOISE WAS COMING WITH ME. THIS WOULD BE HER FIRST TRIP TO RUSSIA... I'D DO MY BOOK TALKS, AND THEN ELOISE AND I WOULD HIT THE HERMITAGE, THE RUSSIAN MUSEUM, AND THE *KUNSTKAMERA* - PETER THE GREAT'S COLLECTION OF CURIOSITIES THAT HAD FASCINATED ME AS A KID...
Update Status
St. PETERSBURG, HERE WE COME —WITH ELOISE
SPACE

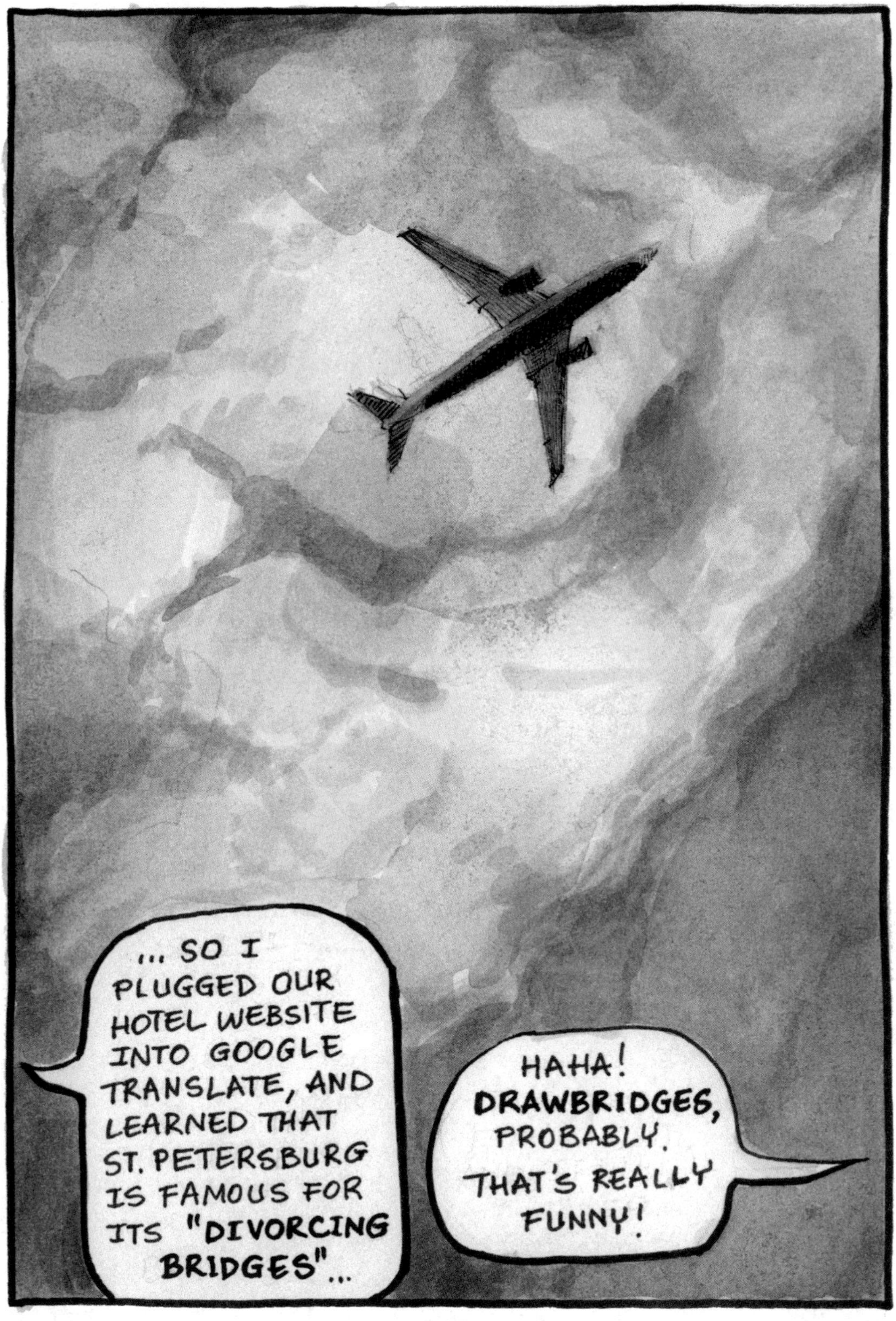
... SO I PLUGGED OUR HOTEL WEBSITE INTO GOOGLE TRANSLATE, AND LEARNED THAT ST. PETERSBURG IS FAMOUS FOR ITS "DIVORCING BRIDGES"...
HAHA! DRAWBRIDGES, PROBABLY. THAT'S REALLY FUNNY!

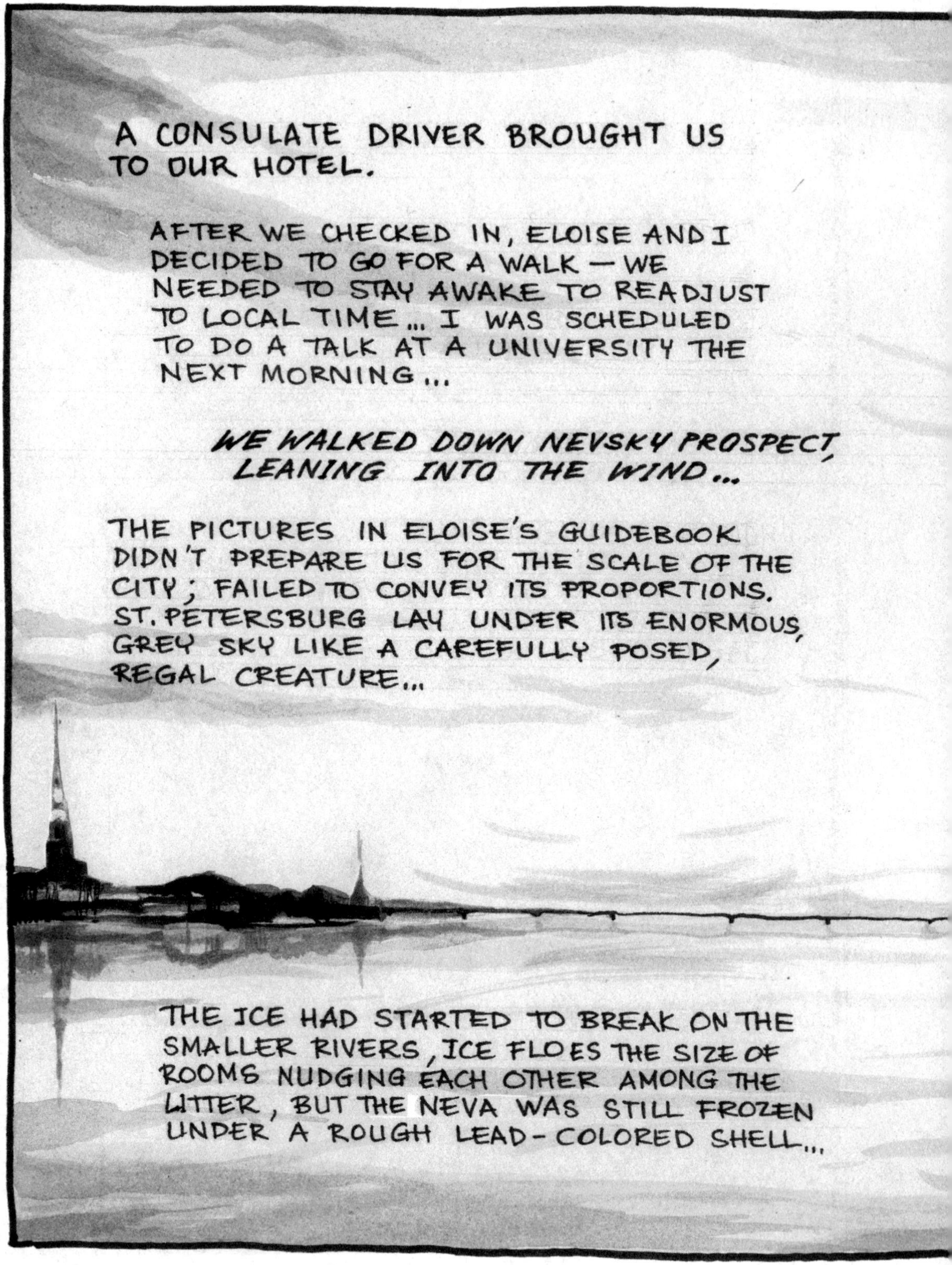
A CONSULATE DRIVER BROUGHT US TO OUR HOTEL.
AFTER WE CHECKED IN, ELOISE AND I DECIDED TO GO FOR A WALK — WE NEEDED TO STAY AWAKE TO READJUST TO LOCAL TIME... I WAS SCHEDULED TO DO A TALK AT A UNIVERSITY THE NEXT MORNING...
WE WALKED DOWN NEVSKY PROSPECT, LEANING INTO THE WIND...
THE PICTURES IN ELOISE'S GUIDEBOOK DIDN'T PREPARE US FOR THE SCALE OF THE CITY; FAILED TO CONVEY ITS PROPORTIONS. ST. PETERSBURG LAY UNDER ITS ENORMOUS, GREY SKY LIKE A CAREFULLY POSED, REGAL CREATURE...
THE ICE HAD STARTED TO BREAK ON THE SMALLER RIVERS, ICE FLOES THE SIZE OF ROOMS NUDGING EACH OTHER AMONG THE LITTER, BUT THE NEVA WAS STILL FROZEN UNDER A ROUGH LEAD-COLORED SHELL...

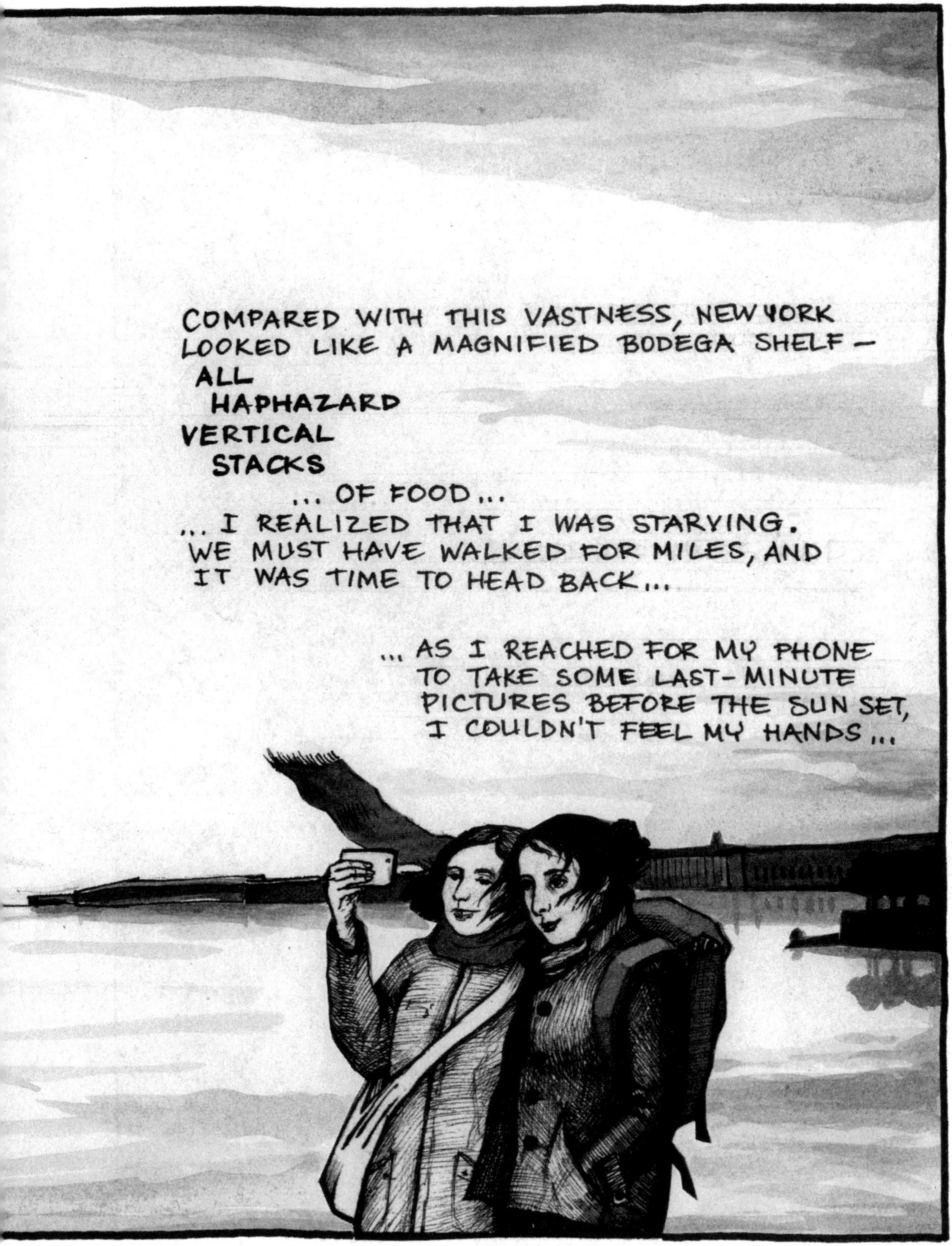
COMPARED WITH THIS VASTNESS, NEW YORK LOOKED LIKE A MAGNIFIED BODEGA SHELF —
ALL
HAPHAZARD
VERTICAL
STACKS
... OF FOOD...
... I REALIZED THAT I WAS STARVING. WE MUST HAVE WALKED FOR MILES, AND IT WAS TIME TO HEAD BACK...
... AS I REACHED FOR MY PHONE TO TAKE SOME LAST-MINUTE PICTURES BEFORE THE SUN SET, I COULDN'T FEEL MY HANDS...

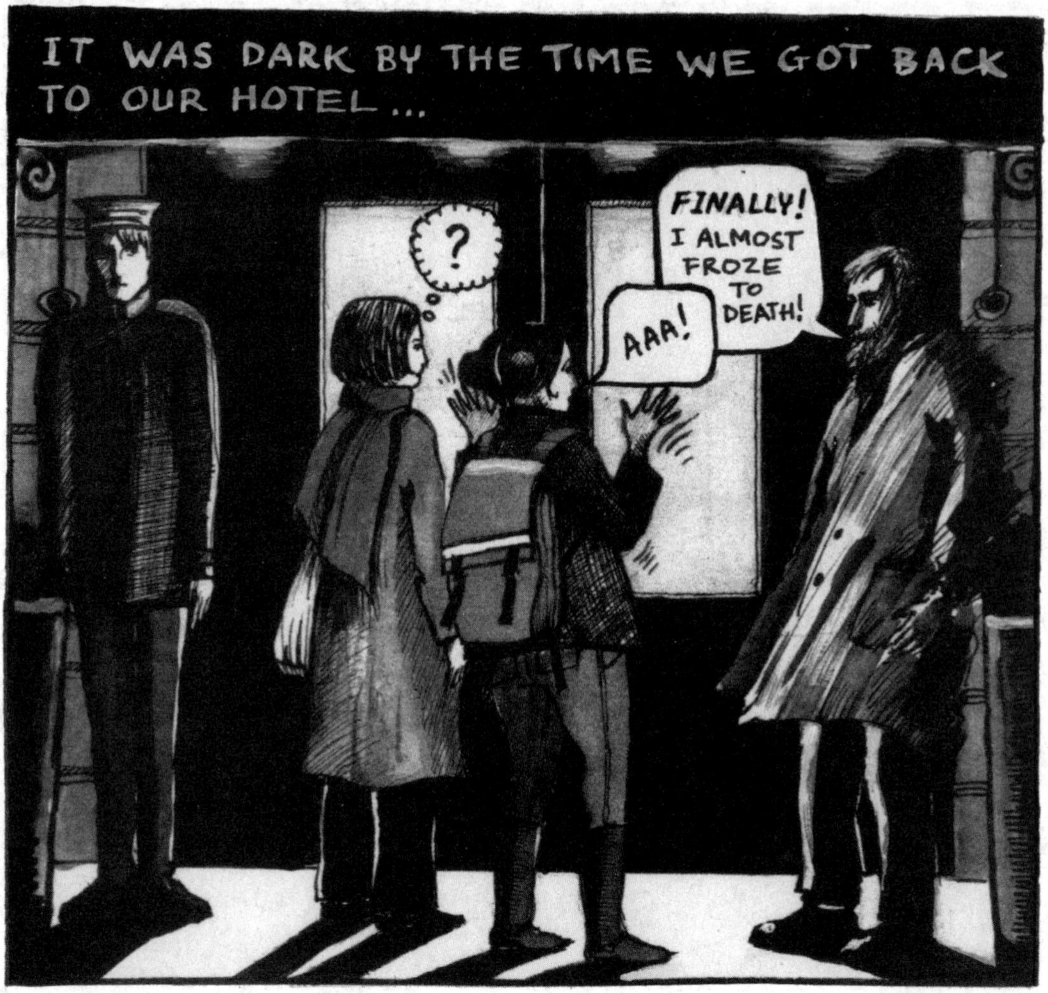
IT WAS DARK BY THE TIME WE GOT BACK TO OUR HOTEL...
?
FINALLY! I ALMOST FROZE TO DEATH!
AAA!

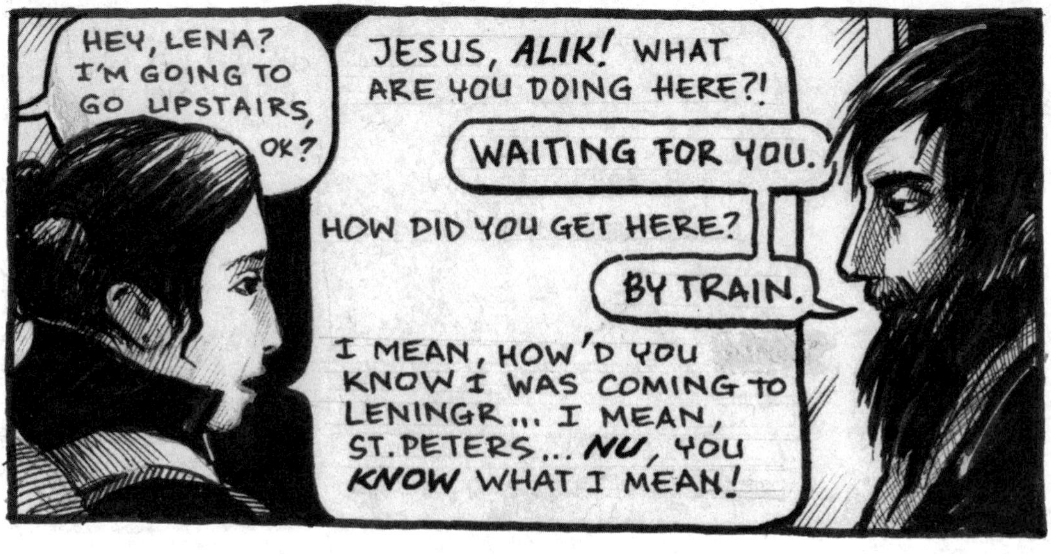
HEY, LENA? I'M GOING TO GO UPSTAIRS, OK?
JESUS, ALIK! WHAT ARE YOU DOING HERE?!
WAITING FOR YOU.
HOW DID YOU GET HERE?
BY TRAIN.
I MEAN, HOW'D YOU KNOW I WAS COMING TO LENINGR... I MEAN, ST. PETERS... NU, YOU KNOW WHAT I MEAN!

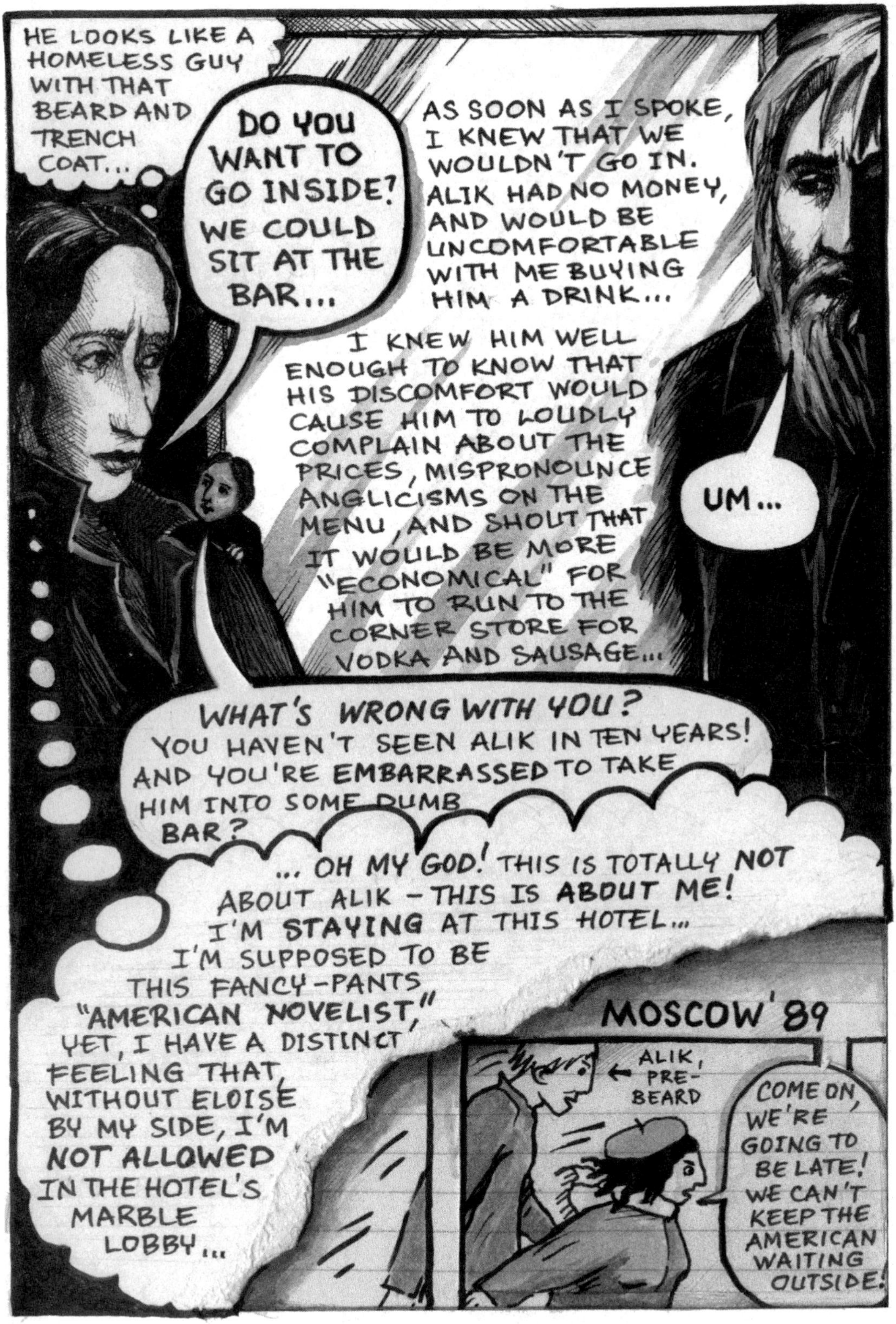
HE LOOKS LIKE A HOMELESS GUY WITH THAT BEARD AND TRENCH COAT...
DO YOU WANT TO GO INSIDE? WE COULD SIT AT THE BAR...
AS SOON AS I SPOKE, I KNEW THAT WE WOULDN'T GO IN. ALIK HAD NO MONEY, AND WOULD BE UNCOMFORTABLE WITH ME BUYING HIM A DRINK...
I KNEW HIM WELL ENOUGH TO KNOW THAT HIS DISCOMFORT WOULD CAUSE HIM TO LOUDLY COMPLAIN ABOUT THE PRICES, MISPRONOUNCE ANGLICISMS ON THE MENU, AND SHOUT THAT IT WOULD BE MORE "ECONOMICAL" FOR HIM TO RUN TO THE CORNER STORE FOR VODKA AND SAUSAGE...
UM...
WHAT'S WRONG WITH YOU? YOU HAVEN'T SEEN ALIK IN TEN YEARS! AND YOU'RE EMBARRASSED TO TAKE HIM INTO SOME DUMB BAR?
... OH MY GOD! THIS IS TOTALLY NOT ABOUT ALIK - THIS IS ABOUT ME! I'M STAYING AT THIS HOTEL... I'M SUPPOSED TO BE THIS FANCY-PANTS "AMERICAN NOVELIST," YET, I HAVE A DISTINCT FEELING THAT, WITHOUT ELOISE BY MY SIDE, I'M NOT ALLOWED IN THE HOTEL'S MARBLE LOBBY...
MOSCOW '89
ALIK, PRE-BEARD
COME ON, WE'RE GOING TO BE LATE! WE CAN'T KEEP THE AMERICAN WAITING OUTSIDE!

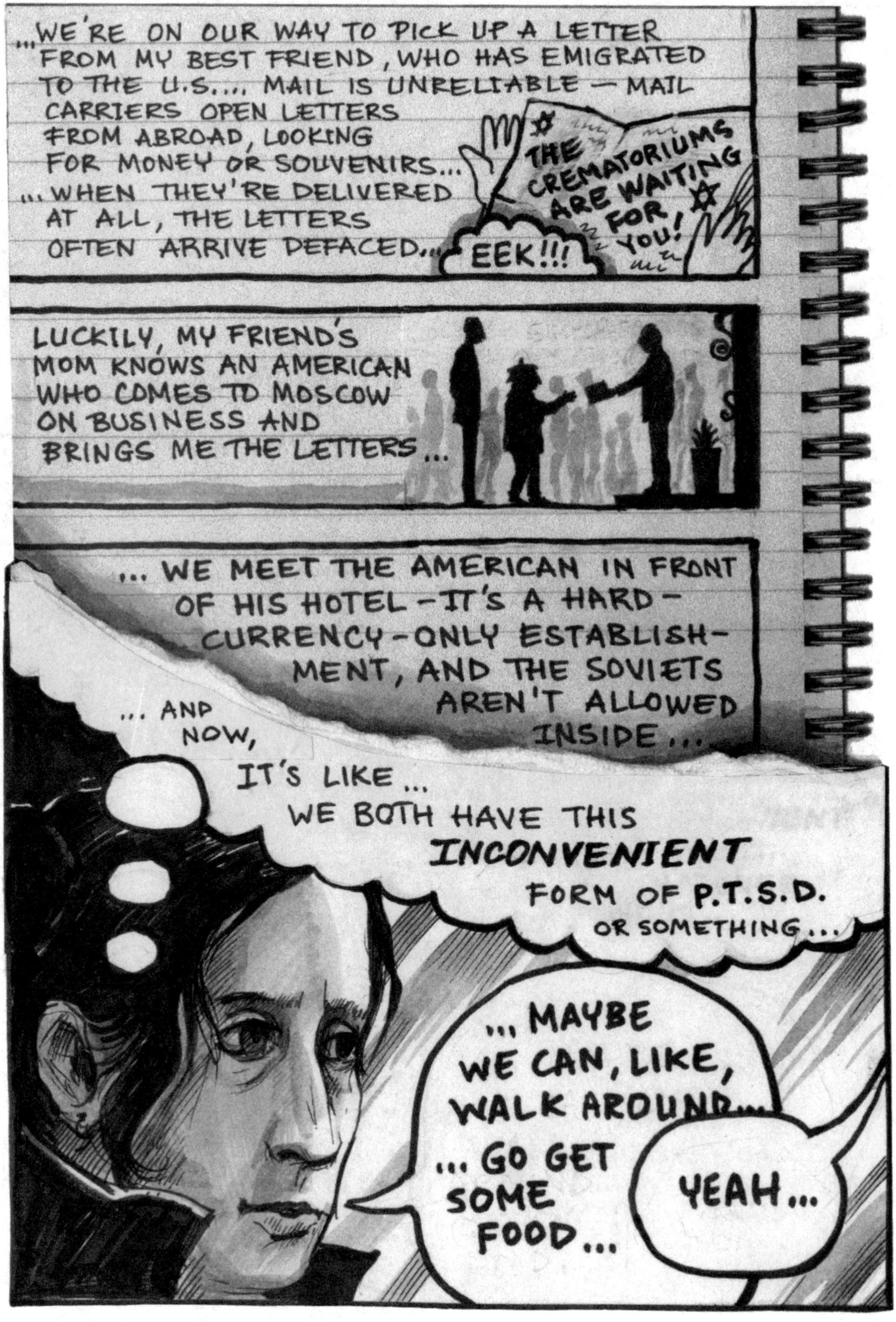

...WE'RE ON OUR WAY TO PICK UP A LETTER FROM MY BEST FRIEND, WHO HAS EMIGRATED TO THE U.S.... MAIL IS UNRELIABLE — MAIL CARRIERS OPEN LETTERS FROM ABROAD, LOOKING FOR MONEY OR SOUVENIRS...
...WHEN THEY'RE DELIVERED AT ALL, THE LETTERS OFTEN ARRIVE DEFACED...
THE CREMATORIUMS ARE WAITING FOR YOU!
EEK!!!
LUCKILY, MY FRIEND'S MOM KNOWS AN AMERICAN WHO COMES TO MOSCOW ON BUSINESS AND BRINGS ME THE LETTERS...
... WE MEET THE AMERICAN IN FRONT OF HIS HOTEL - IT'S A HARD-CURRENCY-ONLY ESTABLISHMENT, AND THE SOVIETS AREN'T ALLOWED INSIDE...
... AND NOW, IT'S LIKE... WE BOTH HAVE THIS INCONVENIENT FORM OF P.T.S.D. OR SOMETHING...
... MAYBE WE CAN, LIKE, WALK AROUND...
... GO GET SOME FOOD...
YEAH...

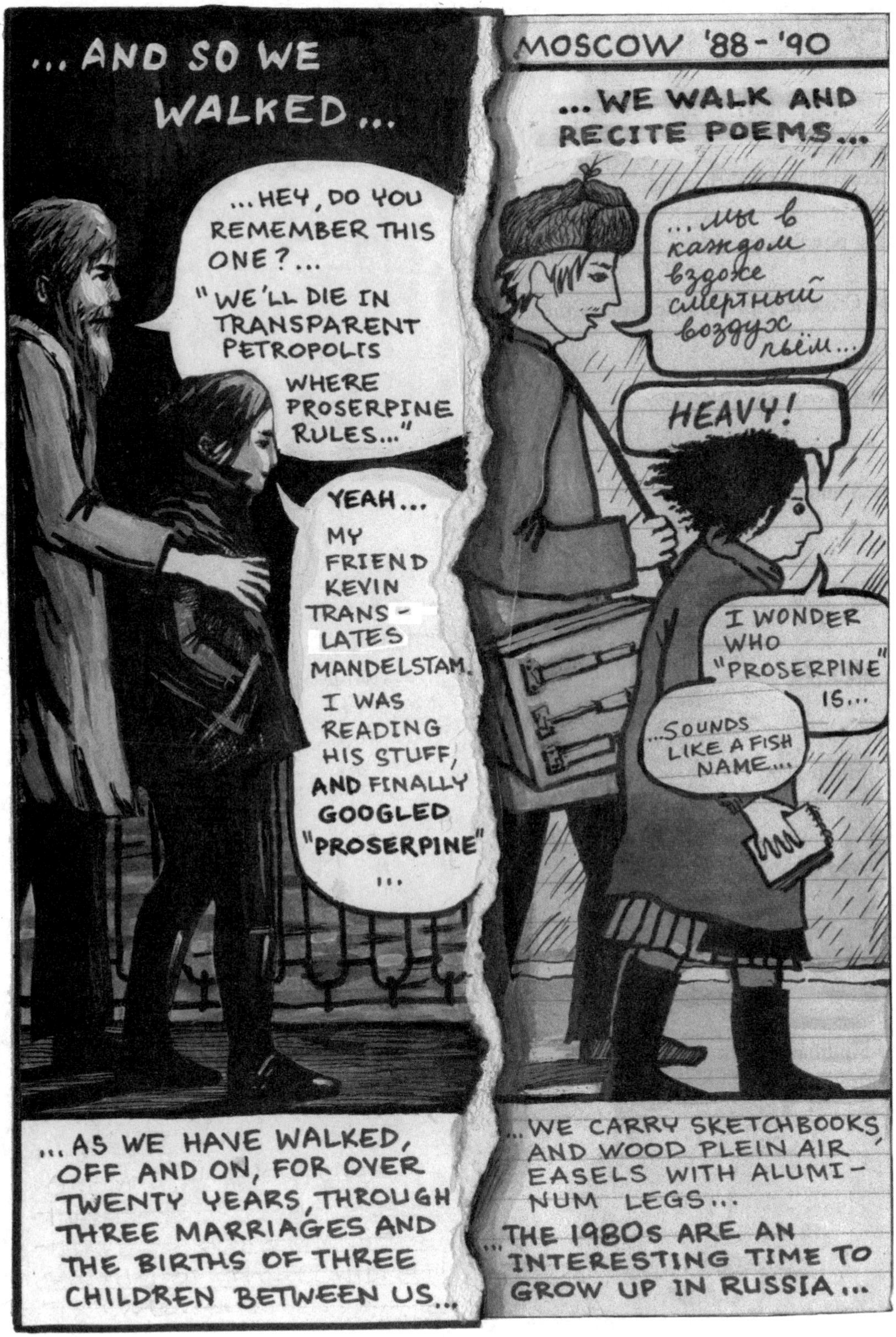
...AND SO WE WALKED...
...HEY, DO YOU REMEMBER THIS ONE?... "WE'LL DIE IN TRANSPARENT PETROPOLIS WHERE PROSERPINE RULES..."
YEAH... MY FRIEND KEVIN TRANS-LATES MANDELSTAM. I WAS READING HIS STUFF, AND FINALLY GOOGLED "PROSERPINE"...
...AS WE HAVE WALKED, OFF AND ON, FOR OVER TWENTY YEARS, THROUGH THREE MARRIAGES AND THE BIRTHS OF THREE CHILDREN BETWEEN US...
MOSCOW '88-'90
...WE WALK AND RECITE POEMS...
...мы в каждом вздохе смертный воздух пьём...
HEAVY!
I WONDER WHO "PROSERPINE" IS...
...SOUNDS LIKE A FISH NAME...
...WE CARRY SKETCHBOOKS AND WOOD PLEIN AIR EASELS WITH ALUMI-NUM LEGS...
...THE 1980s ARE AN INTERESTING TIME TO GROW UP IN RUSSIA...

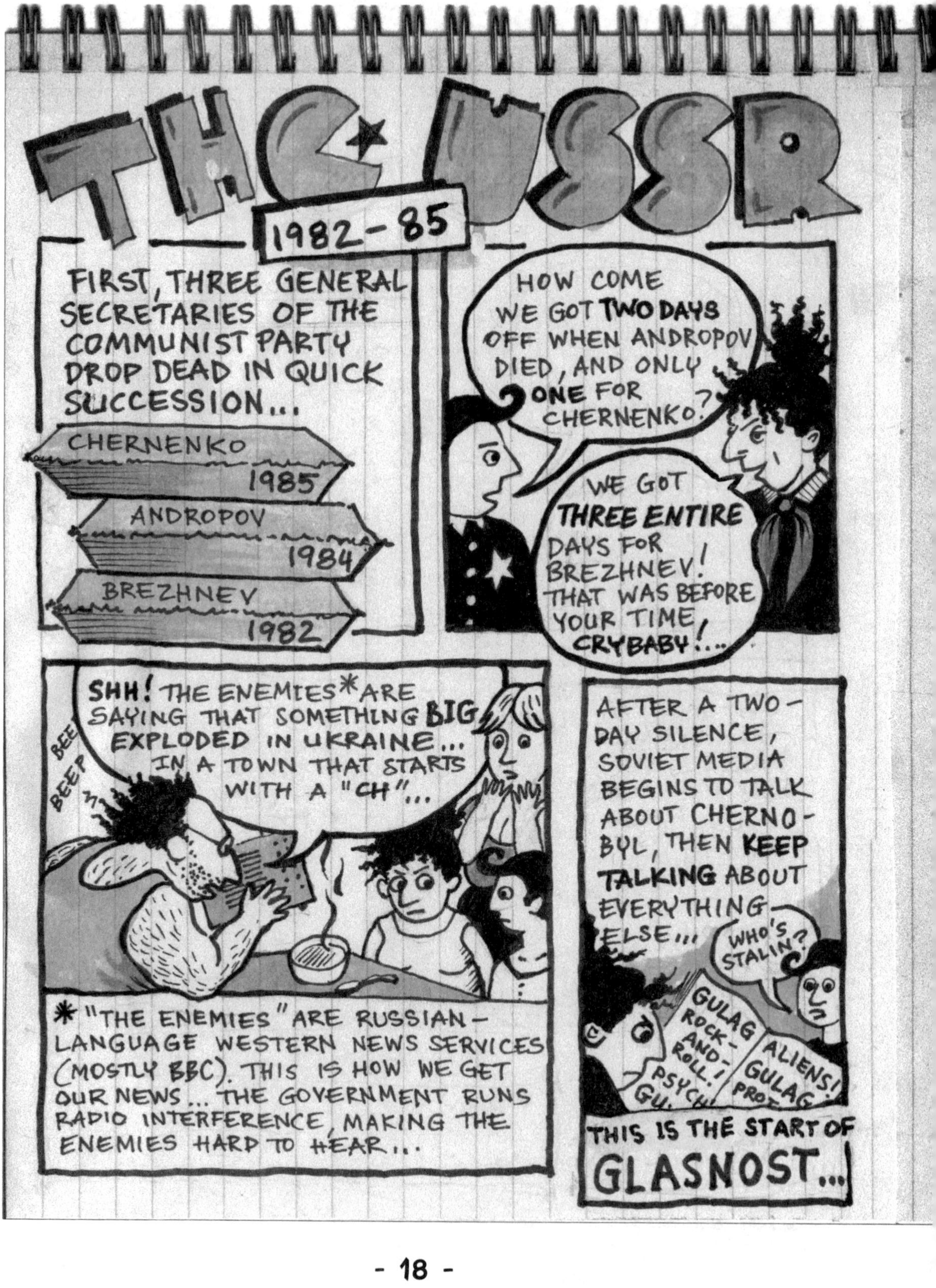
THE USSR
1982-85
FIRST, THREE GENERAL SECRETARIES OF THE COMMUNIST PARTY DROP DEAD IN QUICK SUCCESSION...
CHERNENKO 1985
ANDROPOV 1984
BREZHNEV 1982
HOW COME WE GOT TWO DAYS OFF WHEN ANDROPOV DIED, AND ONLY ONE FOR CHERNENKO?
WE GOT THREE ENTIRE DAYS FOR BREZHNEV! THAT WAS BEFORE YOUR TIME, CRYBABY!...
SHH! THE ENEMIES* ARE SAYING THAT SOMETHING BIG EXPLODED IN UKRAINE... IN A TOWN THAT STARTS WITH A "CH"...
BEE BEEP
* "THE ENEMIES" ARE RUSSIAN-LANGUAGE WESTERN NEWS SERVICES (MOSTLY BBC). THIS IS HOW WE GET OUR NEWS... THE GOVERNMENT RUNS RADIO INTERFERENCE, MAKING THE ENEMIES HARD TO HEAR...
AFTER A TWO-DAY SILENCE, SOVIET MEDIA BEGINS TO TALK ABOUT CHERNOBYL, THEN KEEP TALKING ABOUT EVERYTHING ELSE...
WHO'S STALIN?
GULAG ROCK-AND-ROLL! PSYCH GU
ALIENS! GULAG PROT
THIS IS THE START OF GLASNOST...

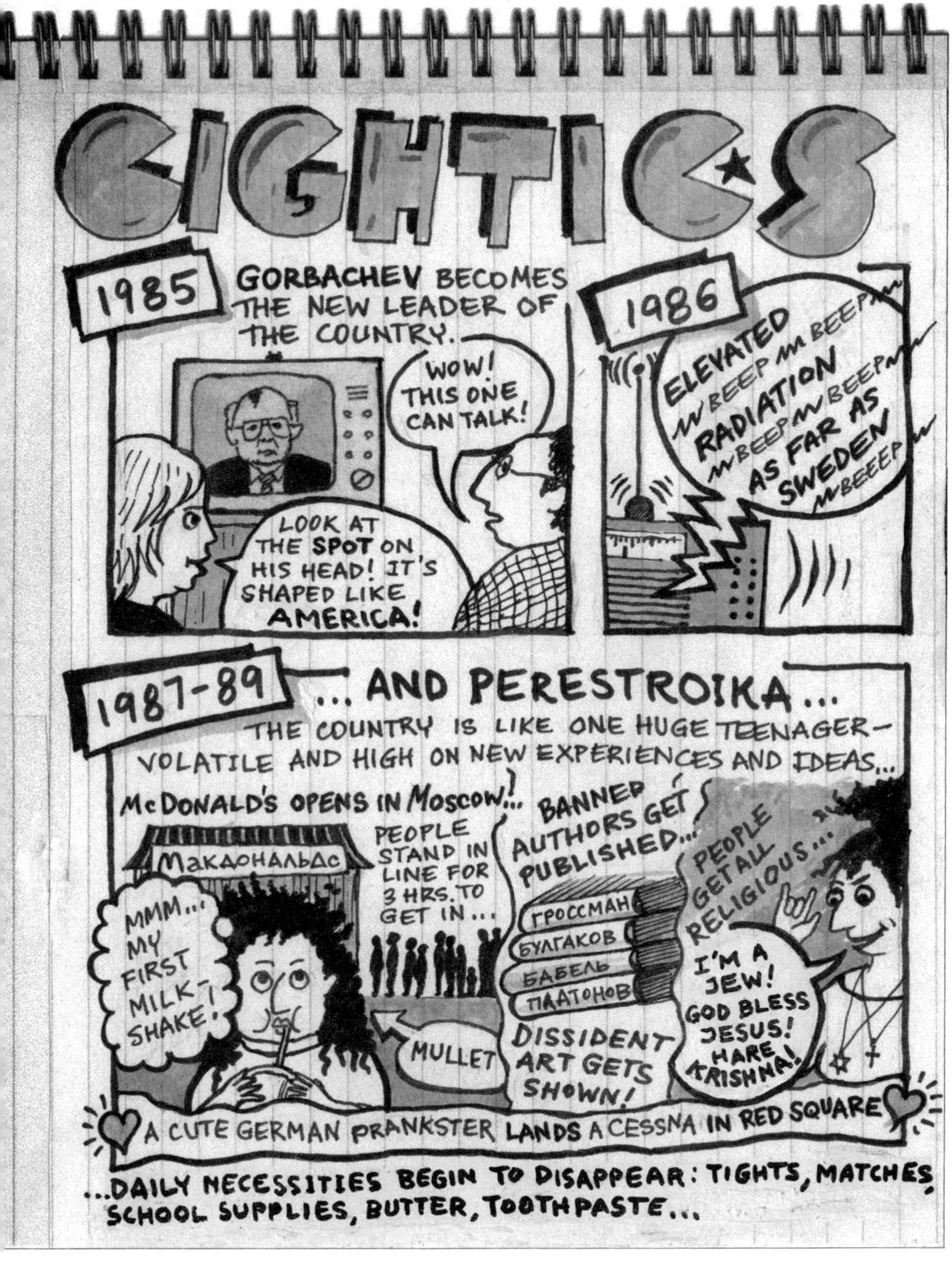
EIGHTIES
1985
GORBACHEV BECOMES THE NEW LEADER OF THE COUNTRY.
WOW! THIS ONE CAN TALK!
LOOK AT THE SPOT ON HIS HEAD! IT'S SHAPED LIKE AMERICA!
1986
ELEVATED BEEP BEEP RADIATION BEEP BEEP AS FAR AS SWEDEN BEEEP
1987-89
... AND PERESTROIKA...
THE COUNTRY IS LIKE ONE HUGE TEENAGER— VOLATILE AND HIGH ON NEW EXPERIENCES AND IDEAS...
McDONALD'S OPENS IN Moscow!...
Макдональдс
PEOPLE STAND IN LINE FOR 3 HRS. TO GET IN...
MMM... MY FIRST MILK-SHAKE!
MULLET
BANNED AUTHORS GET PUBLISHED...
ГРОССМАН
БУЛГАКОВ
БАБЕЛЬ
ПЛАТОНОВ
DISSIDENT ART GETS SHOWN!
PEOPLE GET ALL RELIGIOUS...
I'M A JEW! GOD BLESS JESUS! HARE KRISHNA!
A CUTE GERMAN PRANKSTER LANDS A CESSNA IN RED SQUARE
...DAILY NECESSITIES BEGIN TO DISAPPEAR: TIGHTS, MATCHES, SCHOOL SUPPLIES, BUTTER, TOOTHPASTE...

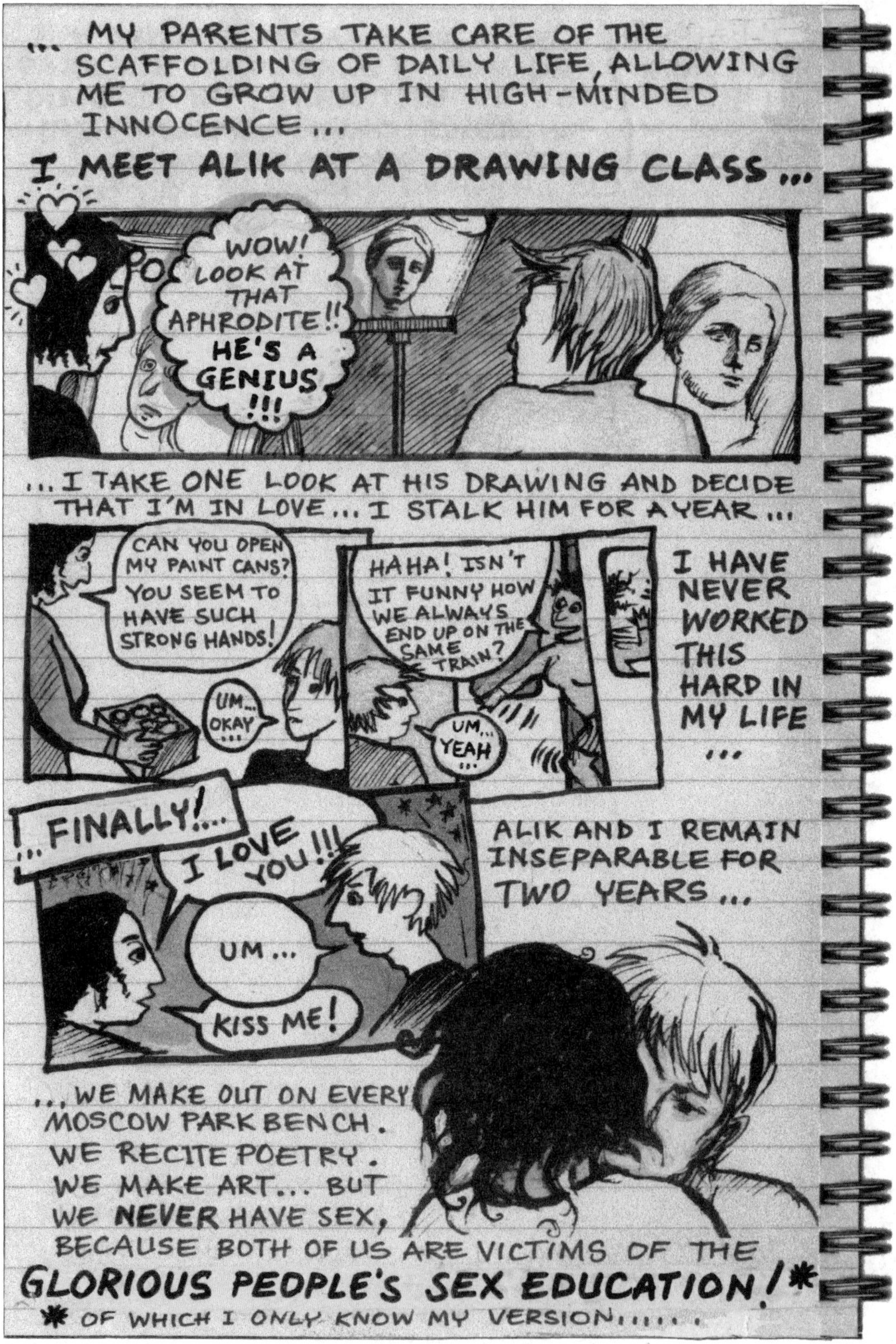
... MY PARENTS TAKE CARE OF THE SCAFFOLDING OF DAILY LIFE, ALLOWING ME TO GROW UP IN HIGH-MINDED INNOCENCE...
I MEET ALIK AT A DRAWING CLASS...
WOW! LOOK AT THAT APHRODITE!!
HE'S A GENIUS !!!
...I TAKE ONE LOOK AT HIS DRAWING AND DECIDE THAT I'M IN LOVE... I STALK HIM FOR A YEAR...
CAN YOU OPEN MY PAINT CANS? YOU SEEM TO HAVE SUCH STRONG HANDS!
UM... OKAY...
HAHA! ISN'T IT FUNNY HOW WE ALWAYS END UP ON THE SAME TRAIN?
UM... YEAH...
I HAVE NEVER WORKED THIS HARD IN MY LIFE ...
...FINALLY!...
I LOVE YOU!!!
UM...
KISS ME!
ALIK AND I REMAIN INSEPARABLE FOR TWO YEARS...
...WE MAKE OUT ON EVERY MOSCOW PARK BENCH. WE RECITE POETRY. WE MAKE ART... BUT WE NEVER HAVE SEX, BECAUSE BOTH OF US ARE VICTIMS OF THE
GLORIOUS PEOPLE'S SEX EDUCATION!*
* OF WHICH I ONLY KNOW MY VERSION......

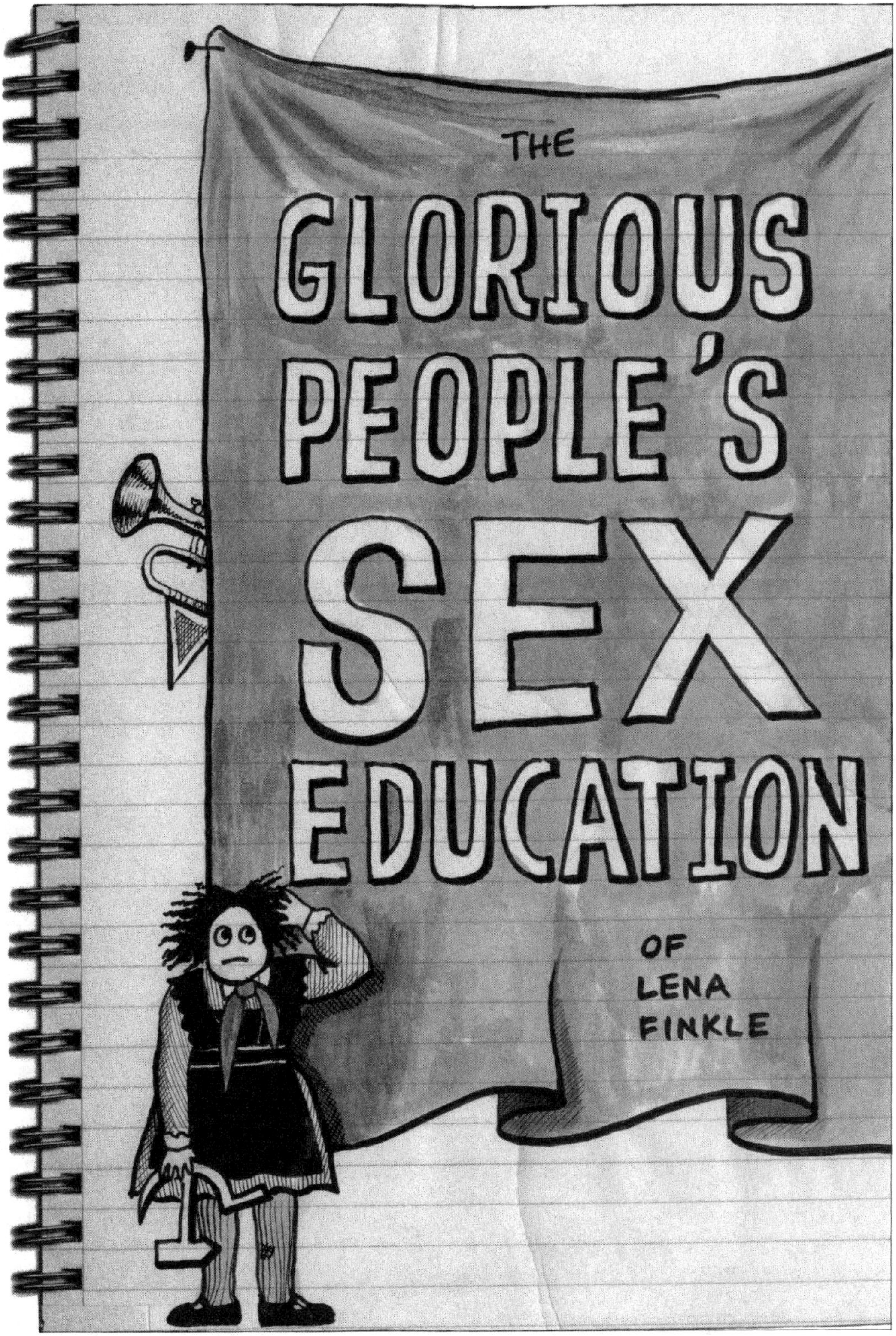
THE
GLORIOUS PEOPLE'S SEX EDUCATION
OF
LENA
FINKLE

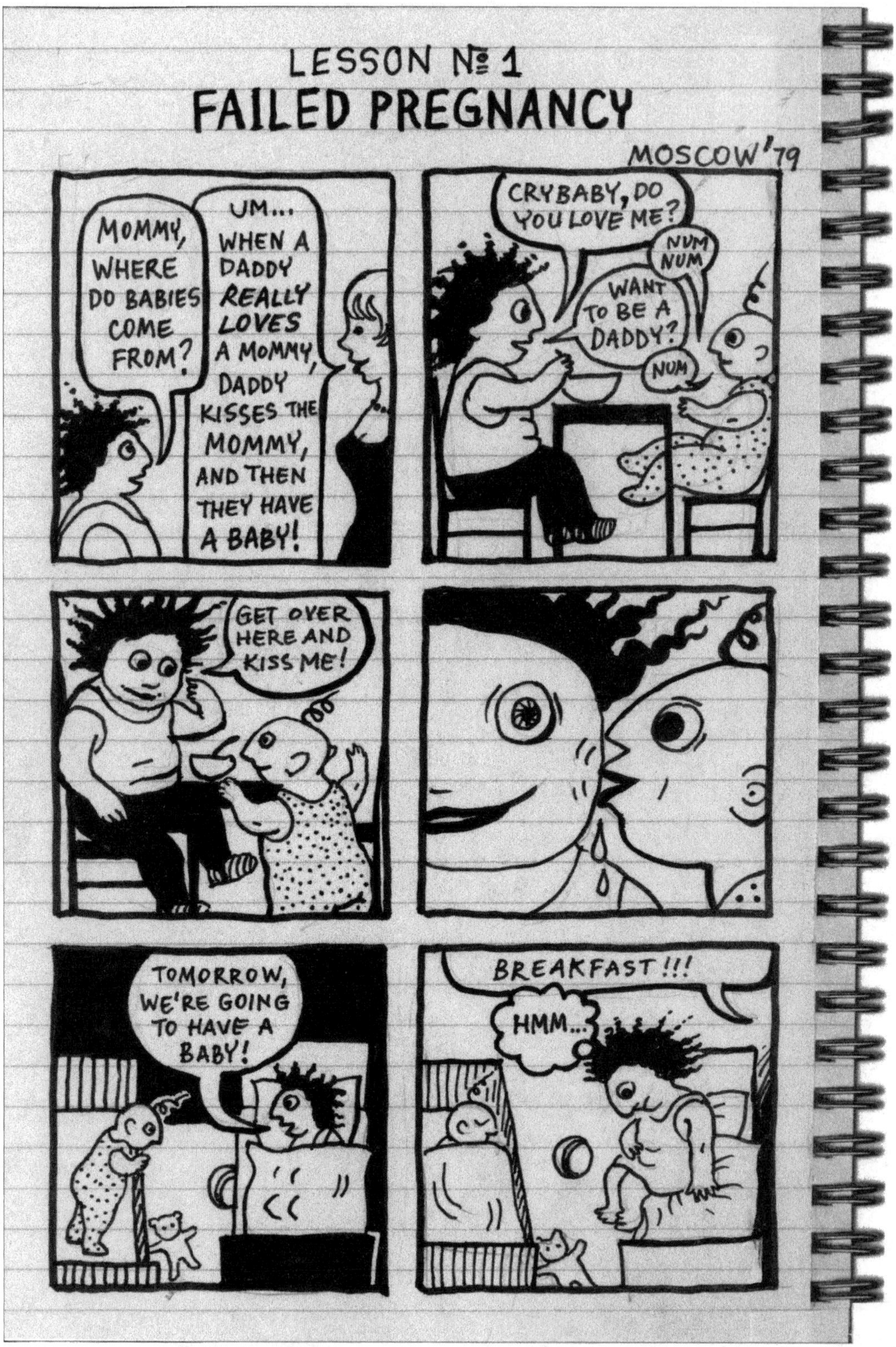
LESSON № 1
FAILED PREGNANCY
MOSCOW '79
MOMMY, WHERE DO BABIES COME FROM?
UM... WHEN A DADDY REALLY LOVES A MOMMY, DADDY KISSES THE MOMMY, AND THEN THEY HAVE A BABY!
CRYBABY, DO YOU LOVE ME?
NUM NUM
WANT TO BE A DADDY?
NUM
GET OVER HERE AND KISS ME!
TOMORROW, WE'RE GOING TO HAVE A BABY!
BREAKFAST!!!
HMM...

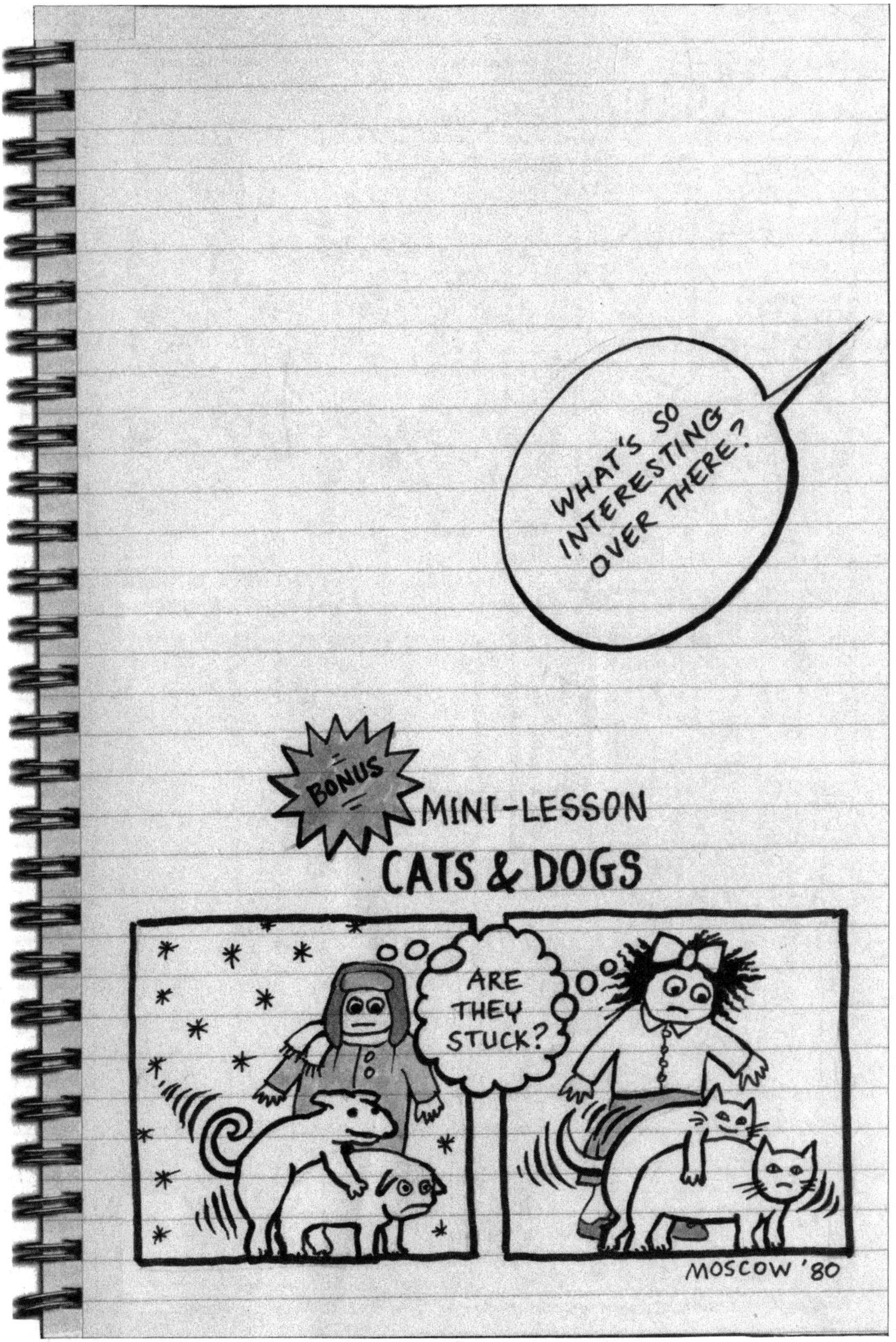
WHAT'S SO INTERESTING OVER THERE?
BONUS
MINI-LESSON
CATS & DOGS
ARE THEY STUCK?
MOSCOW '80

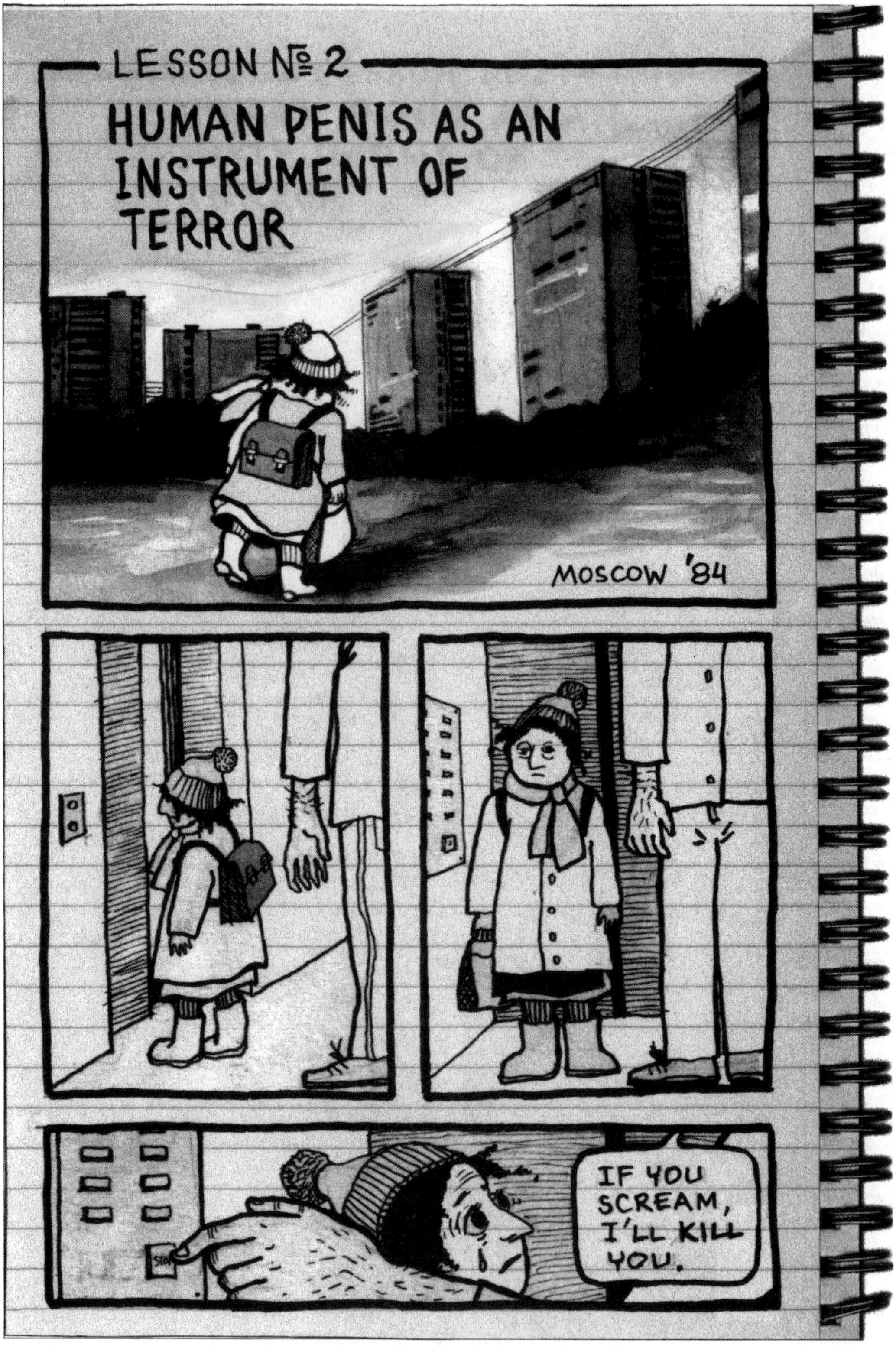
LESSON № 2
HUMAN PENIS AS AN INSTRUMENT OF TERROR
MOSCOW '84
IF YOU SCREAM, I'LL KILL YOU.

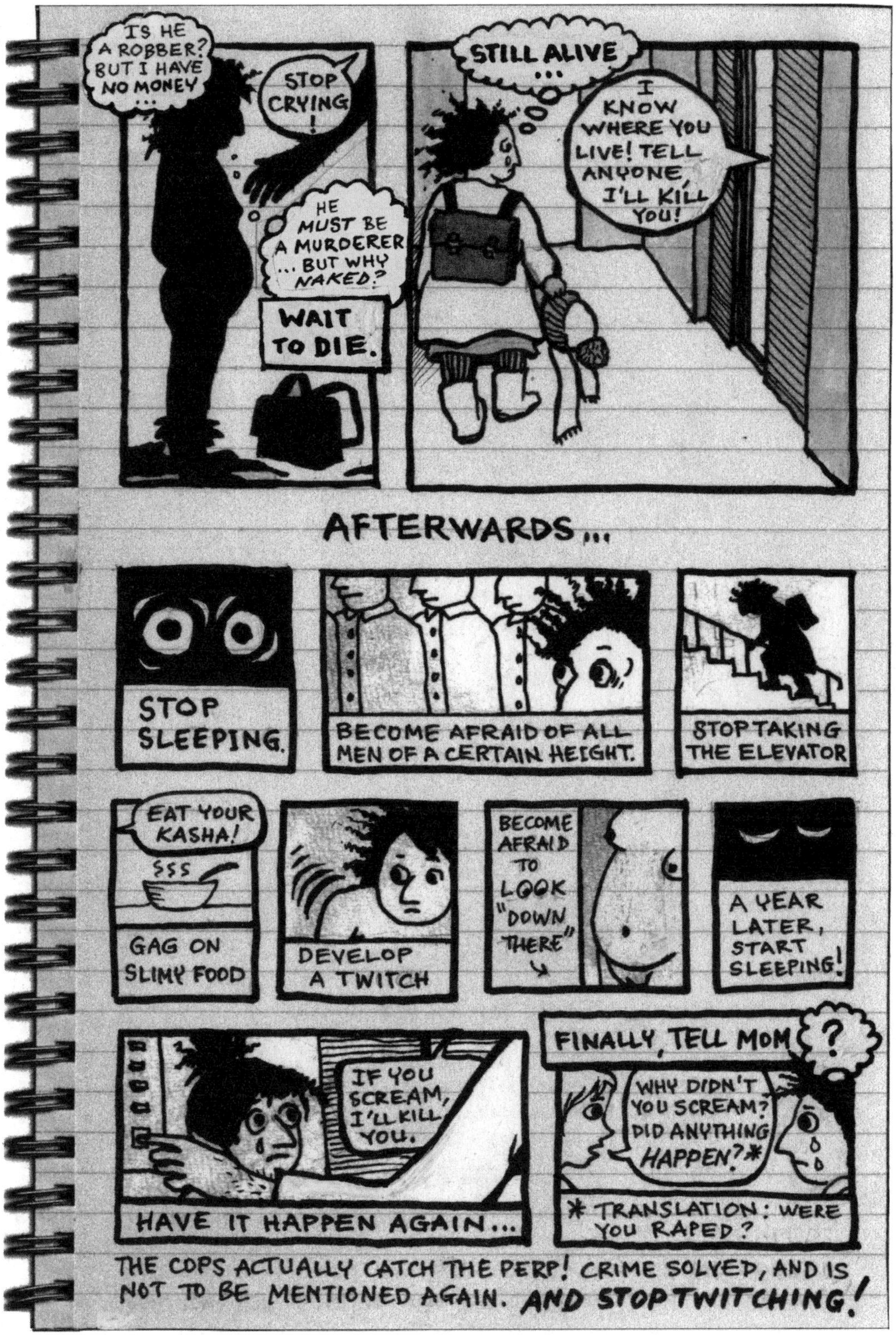
IS HE A ROBBER? BUT I HAVE NO MONEY ...
STOP CRYING!
HE MUST BE A MURDERER ... BUT WHY NAKED?
WAIT TO DIE.
STILL ALIVE ...
I KNOW WHERE YOU LIVE! TELL ANYONE, I'LL KILL YOU!
AFTERWARDS...
STOP SLEEPING.
BECOME AFRAID OF ALL MEN OF A CERTAIN HEIGHT.
STOP TAKING THE ELEVATOR
EAT YOUR KASHA!
SSS
GAG ON SLIMY FOOD
DEVELOP A TWITCH
BECOME AFRAID TO LOOK "DOWN THERE"
A YEAR LATER, START SLEEPING!
IF YOU SCREAM, I'LL KILL YOU.
HAVE IT HAPPEN AGAIN...
FINALLY, TELL MOM
?
WHY DIDN'T YOU SCREAM? DID ANYTHING HAPPEN?*
* TRANSLATION: WERE YOU RAPED?
THE COPS ACTUALLY CATCH THE PERP! CRIME SOLVED, AND IS NOT TO BE MENTIONED AGAIN. AND STOP TWITCHING!

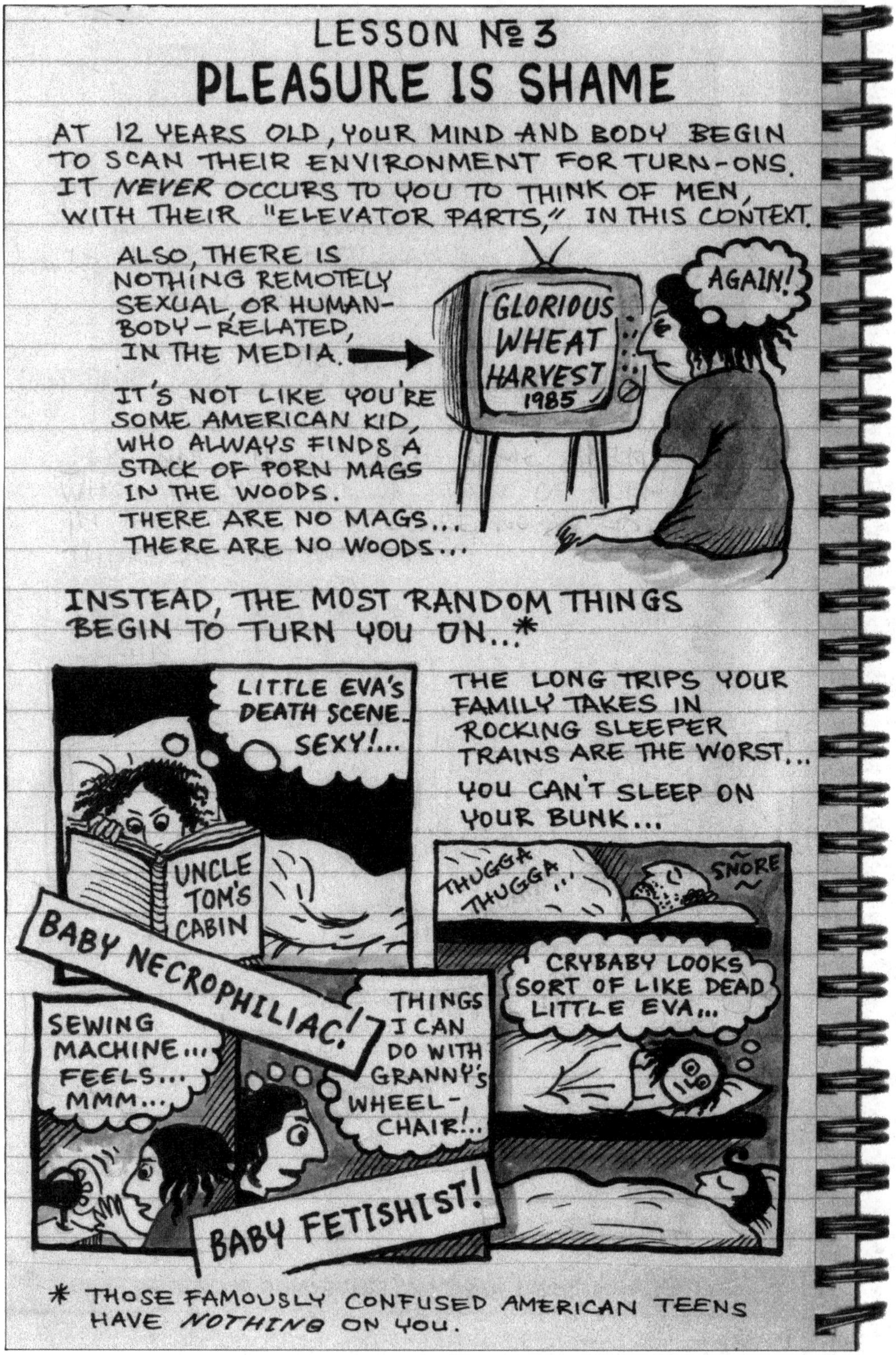
LESSON № 3
PLEASURE IS SHAME
AT 12 YEARS OLD, YOUR MIND AND BODY BEGIN TO SCAN THEIR ENVIRONMENT FOR TURN-ONS. IT *NEVER* OCCURS TO YOU TO THINK OF MEN, WITH THEIR "ELEVATOR PARTS," IN THIS CONTEXT.
ALSO, THERE IS NOTHING REMOTELY SEXUAL, OR HUMAN-BODY-RELATED, IN THE MEDIA.
GLORIOUS WHEAT HARVEST 1985
AGAIN!
IT'S NOT LIKE YOU'RE SOME AMERICAN KID, WHO ALWAYS FINDS A STACK OF PORN MAGS IN THE WOODS.
THERE ARE NO MAGS...
THERE ARE NO WOODS...
INSTEAD, THE MOST RANDOM THINGS BEGIN TO TURN YOU ON...*
LITTLE EVA'S DEATH SCENE. SEXY!...
UNCLE TOM'S CABIN
BABY NECROPHILIAC!
SEWING MACHINE... FEELS... MMM...
THINGS I CAN DO WITH GRANNY'S WHEEL-CHAIR!..
BABY FETISHIST!
THE LONG TRIPS YOUR FAMILY TAKES IN ROCKING SLEEPER TRAINS ARE THE WORST...
YOU CAN'T SLEEP ON YOUR BUNK...
THUGGA THUGGA
SNORE
CRYBABY LOOKS SORT OF LIKE DEAD LITTLE EVA...
* THOSE FAMOUSLY CONFUSED AMERICAN TEENS HAVE *NOTHING* ON YOU.

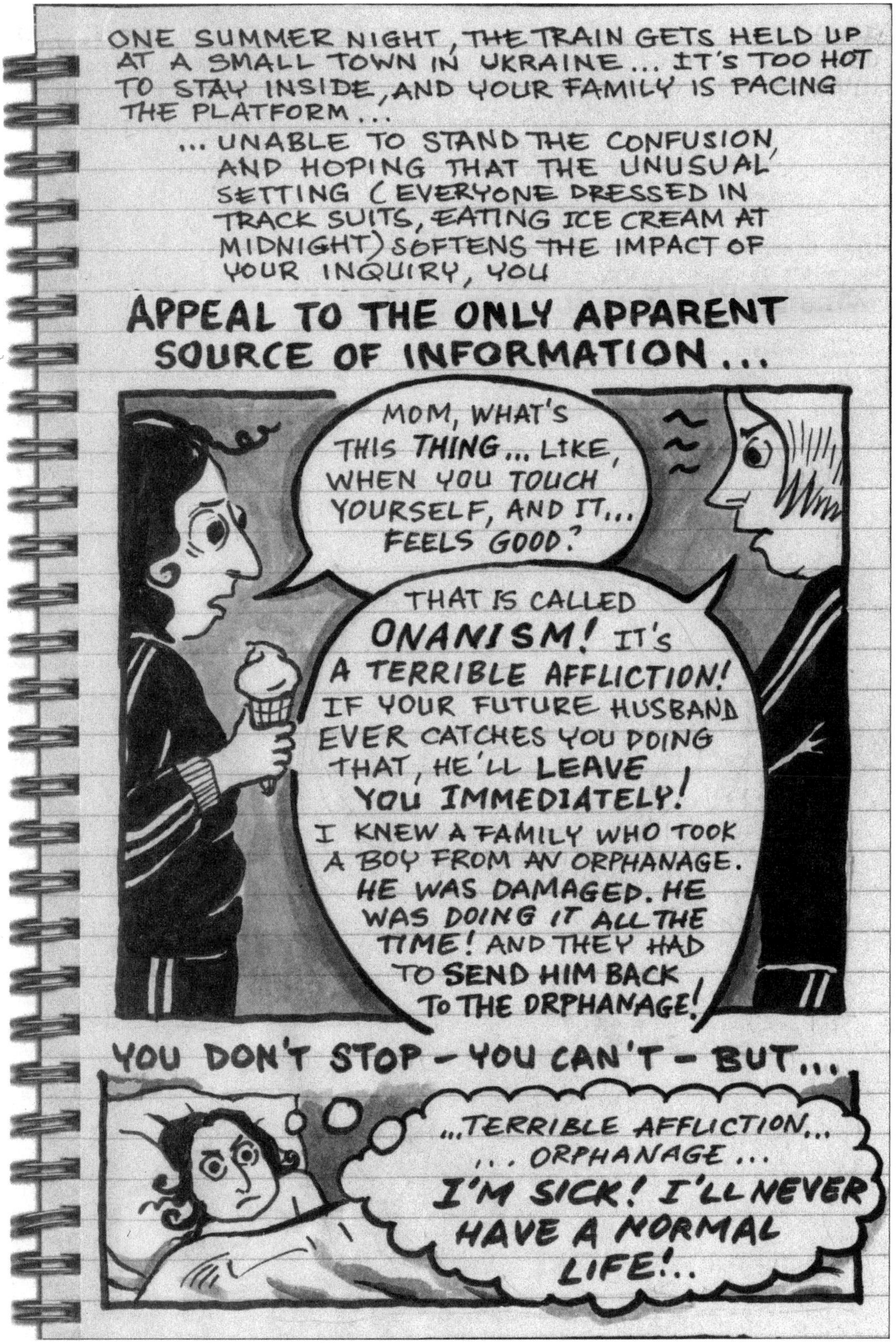
ONE SUMMER NIGHT, THE TRAIN GETS HELD UP AT A SMALL TOWN IN UKRAINE... IT'S TOO HOT TO STAY INSIDE, AND YOUR FAMILY IS PACING THE PLATFORM...
...UNABLE TO STAND THE CONFUSION, AND HOPING THAT THE UNUSUAL SETTING (EVERYONE DRESSED IN TRACK SUITS, EATING ICE CREAM AT MIDNIGHT) SOFTENS THE IMPACT OF YOUR INQUIRY, YOU
APPEAL TO THE ONLY APPARENT SOURCE OF INFORMATION...
MOM, WHAT'S THIS THING... LIKE, WHEN YOU TOUCH YOURSELF, AND IT... FEELS GOOD?
THAT IS CALLED ONANISM! IT'S A TERRIBLE AFFLICTION! IF YOUR FUTURE HUSBAND EVER CATCHES YOU DOING THAT, HE'LL LEAVE YOU IMMEDIATELY! I KNEW A FAMILY WHO TOOK A BOY FROM AN ORPHANAGE. HE WAS DAMAGED. HE WAS DOING IT ALL THE TIME! AND THEY HAD TO SEND HIM BACK TO THE ORPHANAGE!
YOU DON'T STOP - YOU CAN'T - BUT...
...TERRIBLE AFFLICTION... ...ORPHANAGE... I'M SICK! I'LL NEVER HAVE A NORMAL LIFE!..

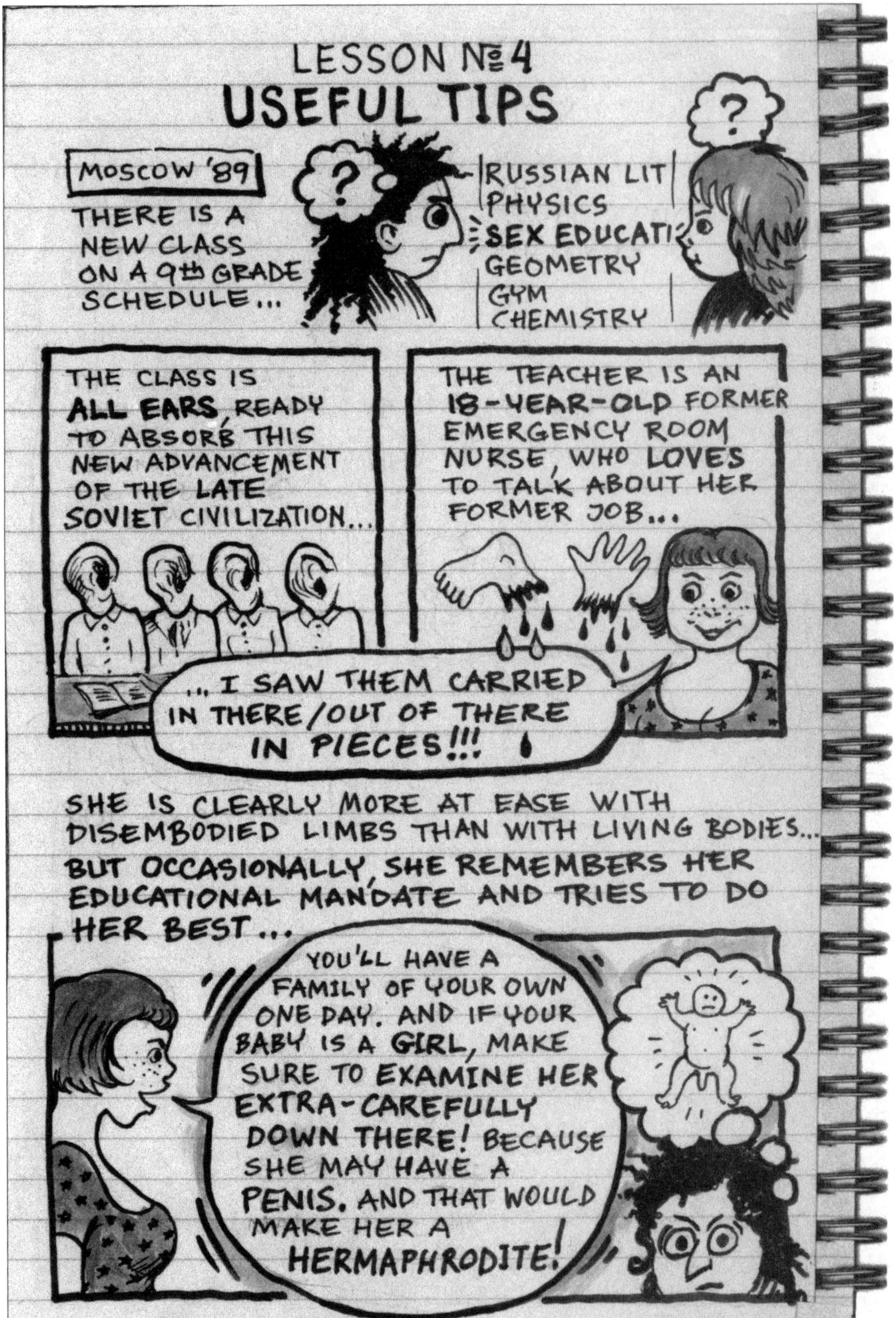
LESSON № 4
USEFUL TIPS
MOSCOW '89
THERE IS A NEW CLASS ON A 9th GRADE SCHEDULE...
RUSSIAN LIT
PHYSICS
SEX EDUCATI
GEOMETRY
GYM
CHEMISTRY
THE CLASS IS ALL EARS, READY TO ABSORB THIS NEW ADVANCEMENT OF THE LATE SOVIET CIVILIZATION...
THE TEACHER IS AN 18-YEAR-OLD FORMER EMERGENCY ROOM NURSE, WHO LOVES TO TALK ABOUT HER FORMER JOB...
...I SAW THEM CARRIED IN THERE/OUT OF THERE IN PIECES!!!
SHE IS CLEARLY MORE AT EASE WITH DISEMBODIED LIMBS THAN WITH LIVING BODIES... BUT OCCASIONALLY, SHE REMEMBERS HER EDUCATIONAL MANDATE AND TRIES TO DO HER BEST...
YOU'LL HAVE A FAMILY OF YOUR OWN ONE DAY. AND IF YOUR BABY IS A GIRL, MAKE SURE TO EXAMINE HER EXTRA-CAREFULLY DOWN THERE! BECAUSE SHE MAY HAVE A PENIS. AND THAT WOULD MAKE HER A HERMAPHRODITE!

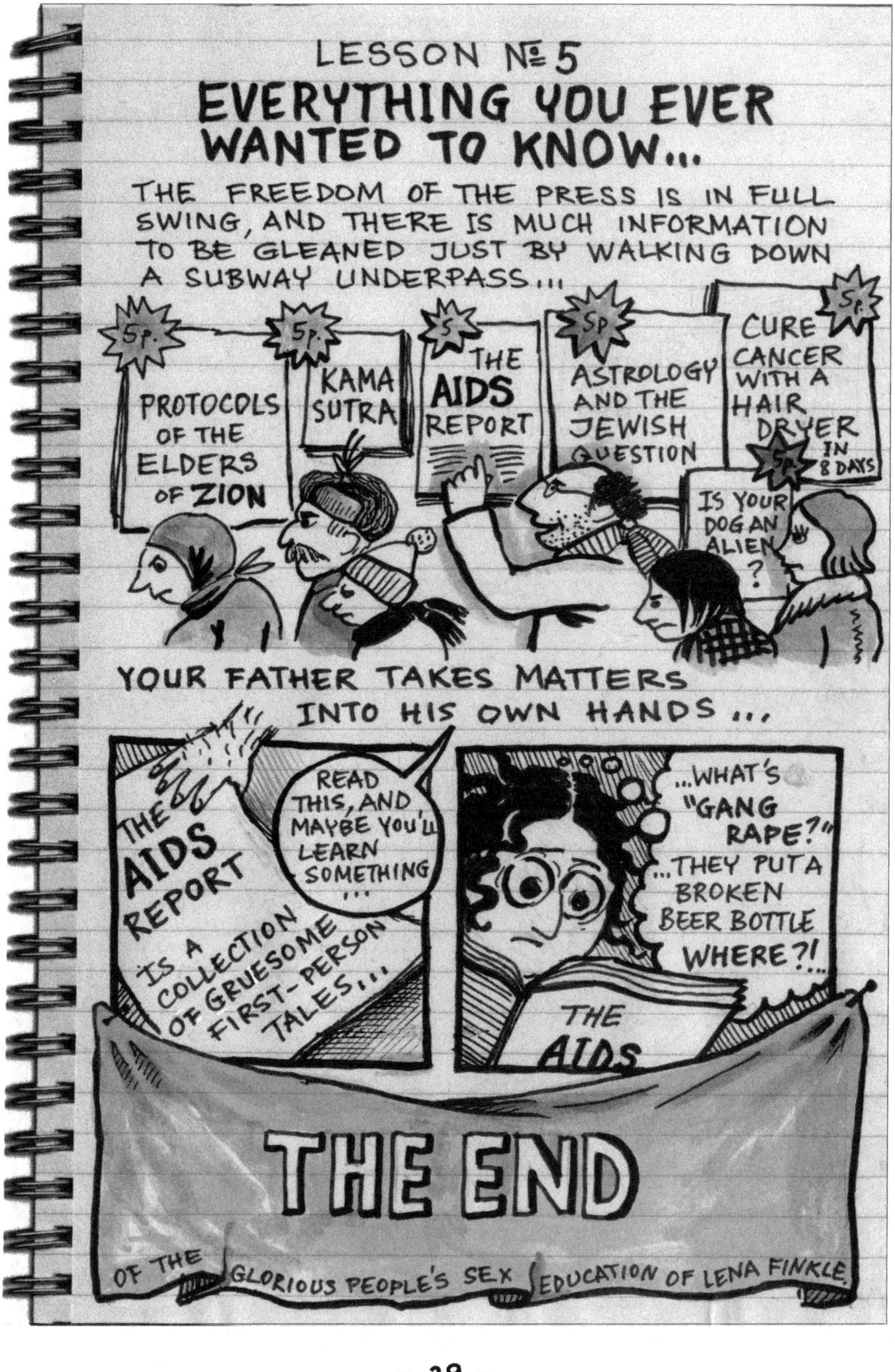
LESSON № 5
EVERYTHING YOU EVER WANTED TO KNOW...
THE FREEDOM OF THE PRESS IS IN FULL SWING, AND THERE IS MUCH INFORMATION TO BE GLEANED JUST BY WALKING DOWN A SUBWAY UNDERPASS...
5p.
PROTOCOLS OF THE ELDERS OF ZION
5p.
KAMA SUTRA
5
THE AIDS REPORT
5p.
ASTROLOGY AND THE JEWISH QUESTION
5p.
CURE CANCER WITH A HAIR DRYER IN 8 DAYS
5p.
IS YOUR DOG AN ALIEN?
YOUR FATHER TAKES MATTERS INTO HIS OWN HANDS...
THE AIDS REPORT
READ THIS, AND MAYBE YOU'LL LEARN SOMETHING...
IS A COLLECTION OF GRUESOME FIRST-PERSON TALES...
...WHAT'S "GANG RAPE?" ...THEY PUT A BROKEN BEER BOTTLE WHERE?!...
THE AIDS
THE END
OF THE GLORIOUS PEOPLE'S SEX EDUCATION OF LENA FINKLE.

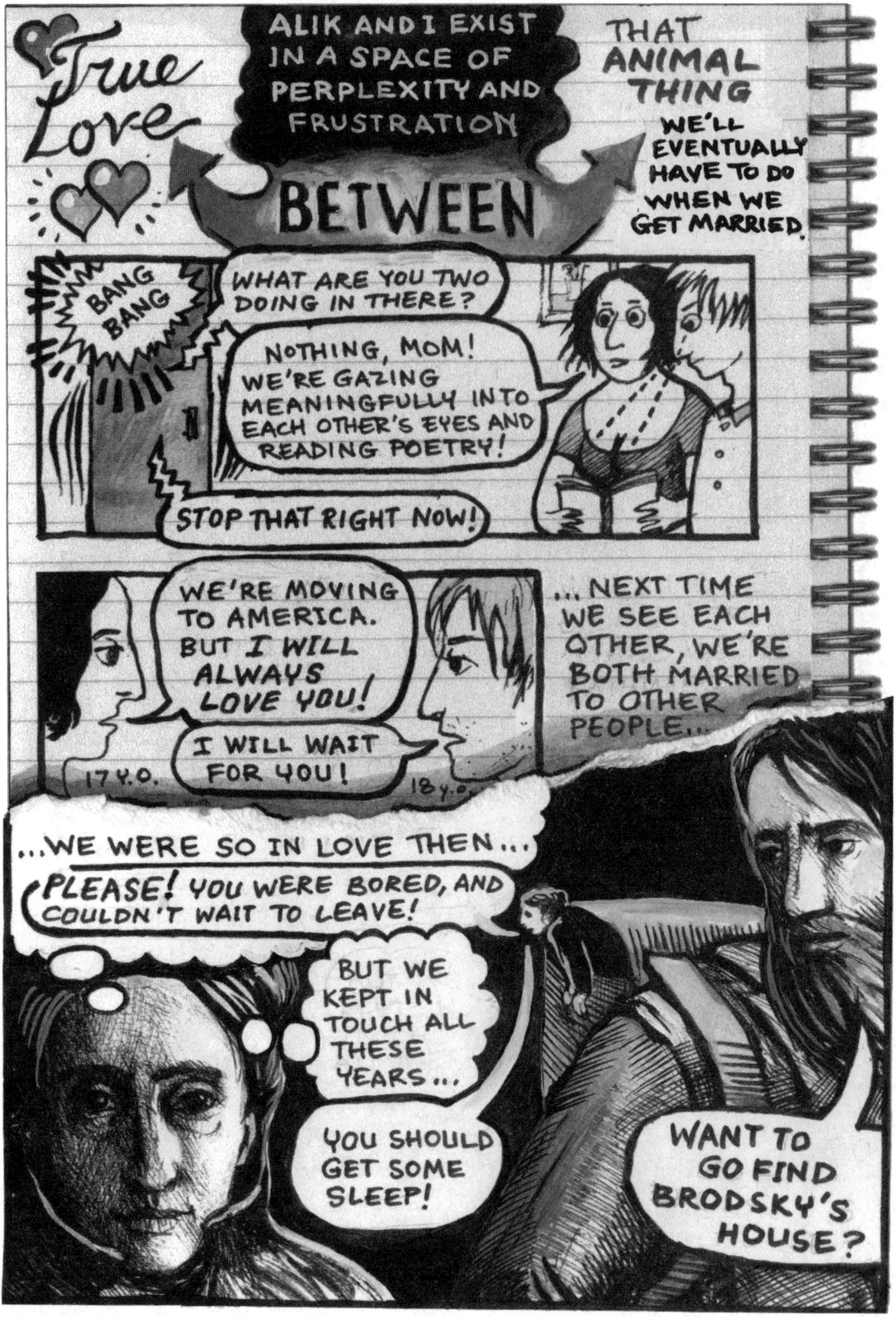
True Love
ALIK AND I EXIST IN A SPACE OF PERPLEXITY AND FRUSTRATION
BETWEEN
THAT ANIMAL THING
WE'LL EVENTUALLY HAVE TO DO WHEN WE GET MARRIED
BANG BANG
WHAT ARE YOU TWO DOING IN THERE?
NOTHING, MOM! WE'RE GAZING MEANINGFULLY INTO EACH OTHER'S EYES AND READING POETRY!
STOP THAT RIGHT NOW!
WE'RE MOVING TO AMERICA. BUT I WILL ALWAYS LOVE YOU!
I WILL WAIT FOR YOU!
17 Y.O.
18 Y.O.
...NEXT TIME WE SEE EACH OTHER, WE'RE BOTH MARRIED TO OTHER PEOPLE...
...WE WERE SO IN LOVE THEN...
PLEASE! YOU WERE BORED, AND COULDN'T WAIT TO LEAVE!
BUT WE KEPT IN TOUCH ALL THESE YEARS...
YOU SHOULD GET SOME SLEEP!
WANT TO GO FIND BRODSKY'S HOUSE?

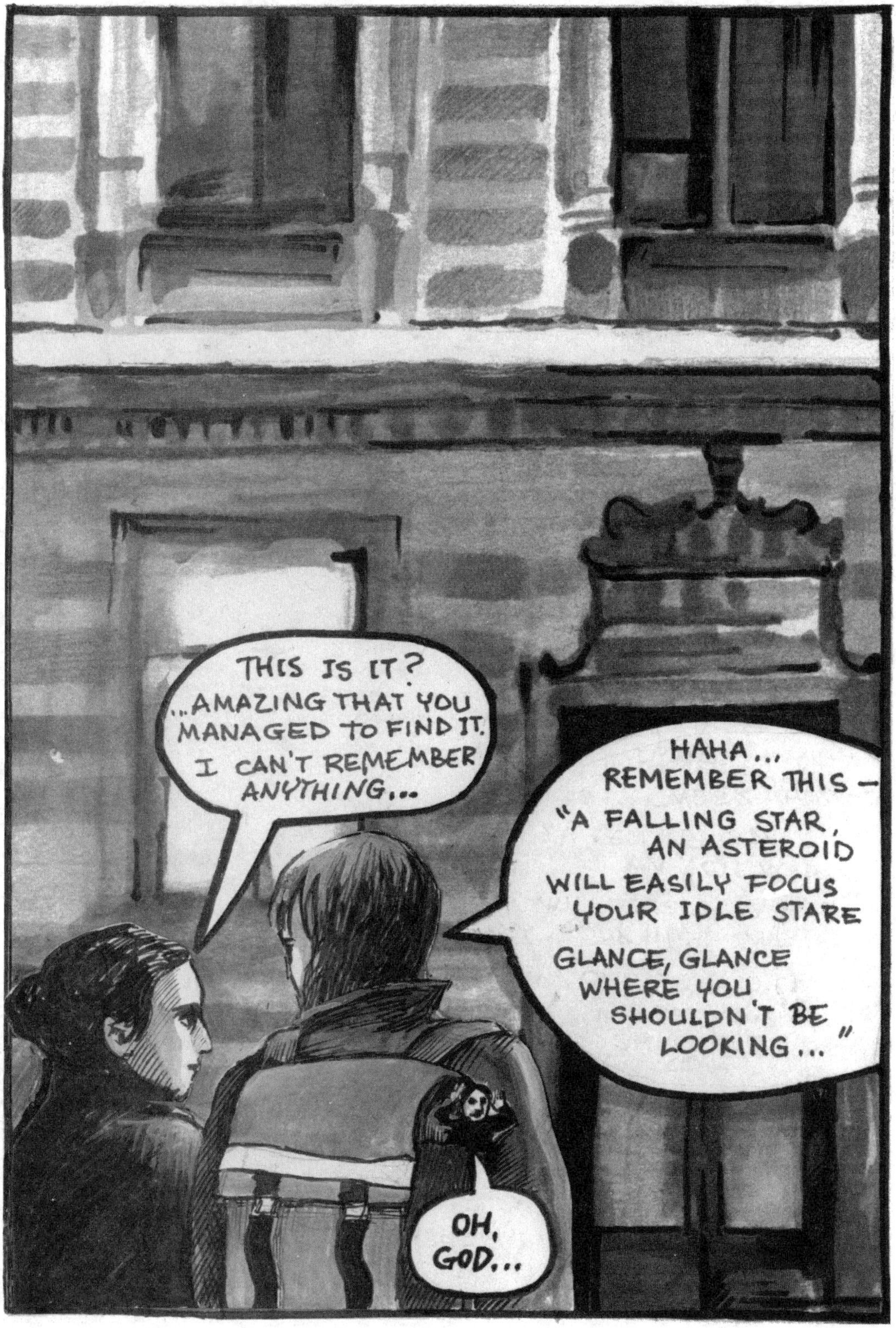
THIS IS IT? ...AMAZING THAT YOU MANAGED TO FIND IT. I CAN'T REMEMBER ANYTHING...
HAHA... REMEMBER THIS— "A FALLING STAR, AN ASTEROID WILL EASILY FOCUS YOUR IDLE STARE GLANCE, GLANCE WHERE YOU SHOULDN'T BE LOOKING..."
OH, GOD...

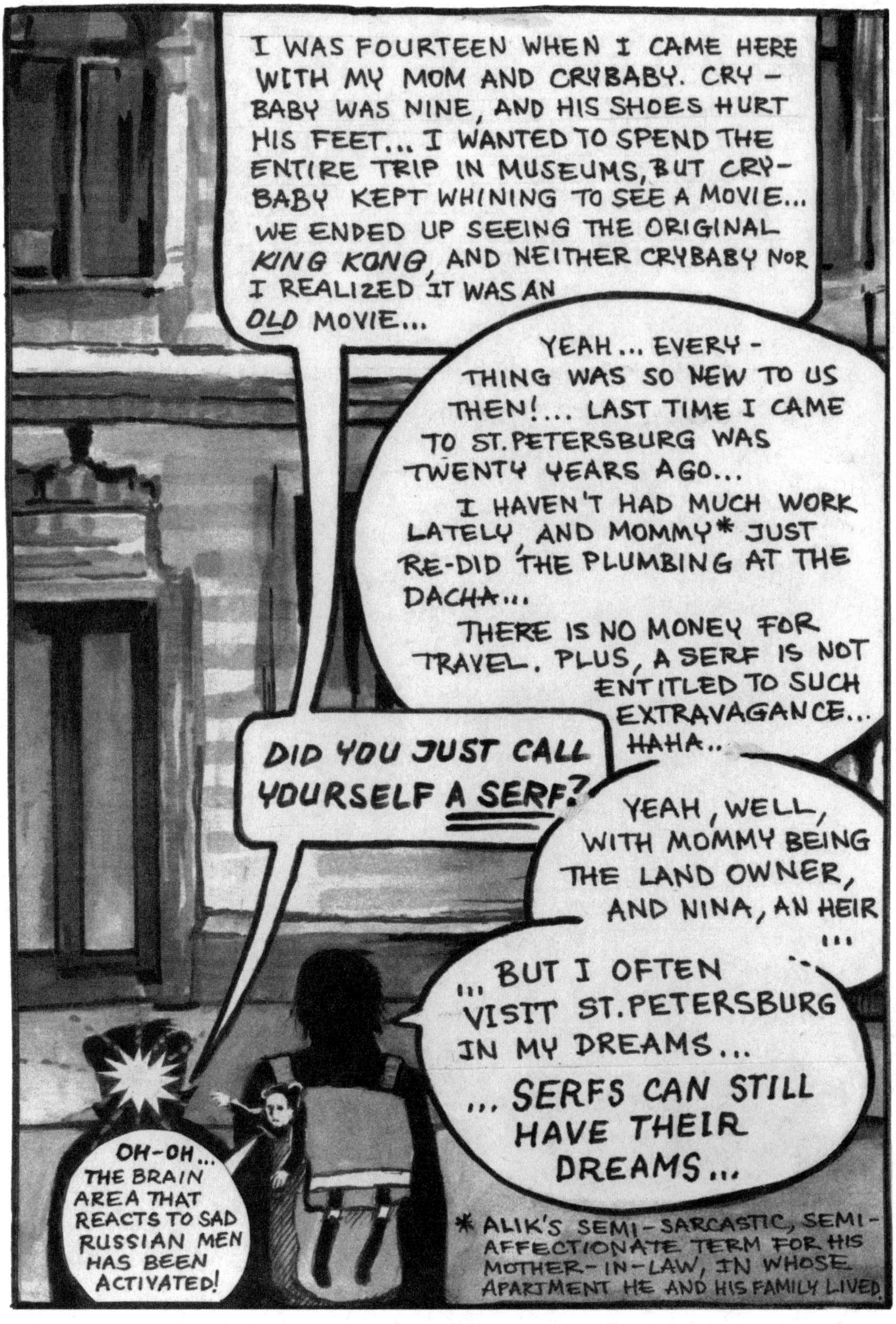
I WAS FOURTEEN WHEN I CAME HERE WITH MY MOM AND CRYBABY. CRY-BABY WAS NINE, AND HIS SHOES HURT HIS FEET... I WANTED TO SPEND THE ENTIRE TRIP IN MUSEUMS, BUT CRY-BABY KEPT WHINING TO SEE A MOVIE... WE ENDED UP SEEING THE ORIGINAL *KING KONG*, AND NEITHER CRYBABY NOR I REALIZED IT WAS AN OLD MOVIE...
YEAH... EVERY-THING WAS SO NEW TO US THEN!... LAST TIME I CAME TO ST. PETERSBURG WAS TWENTY YEARS AGO...
I HAVEN'T HAD MUCH WORK LATELY, AND MOMMY* JUST RE-DID THE PLUMBING AT THE DACHA...
THERE IS NO MONEY FOR TRAVEL. PLUS, A SERF IS NOT ENTITLED TO SUCH EXTRAVAGANCE... HAHA..
DID YOU JUST CALL YOURSELF A SERF?
YEAH, WELL, WITH MOMMY BEING THE LAND OWNER, AND NINA, AN HEIR ...
... BUT I OFTEN VISIT ST. PETERSBURG IN MY DREAMS...
... SERFS CAN STILL HAVE THEIR DREAMS...
OH-OH... THE BRAIN AREA THAT REACTS TO SAD RUSSIAN MEN HAS BEEN ACTIVATED!
* ALIK'S SEMI-SARCASTIC, SEMI-AFFECTIONATE TERM FOR HIS MOTHER-IN-LAW, IN WHOSE APARTMENT HE AND HIS FAMILY LIVED.

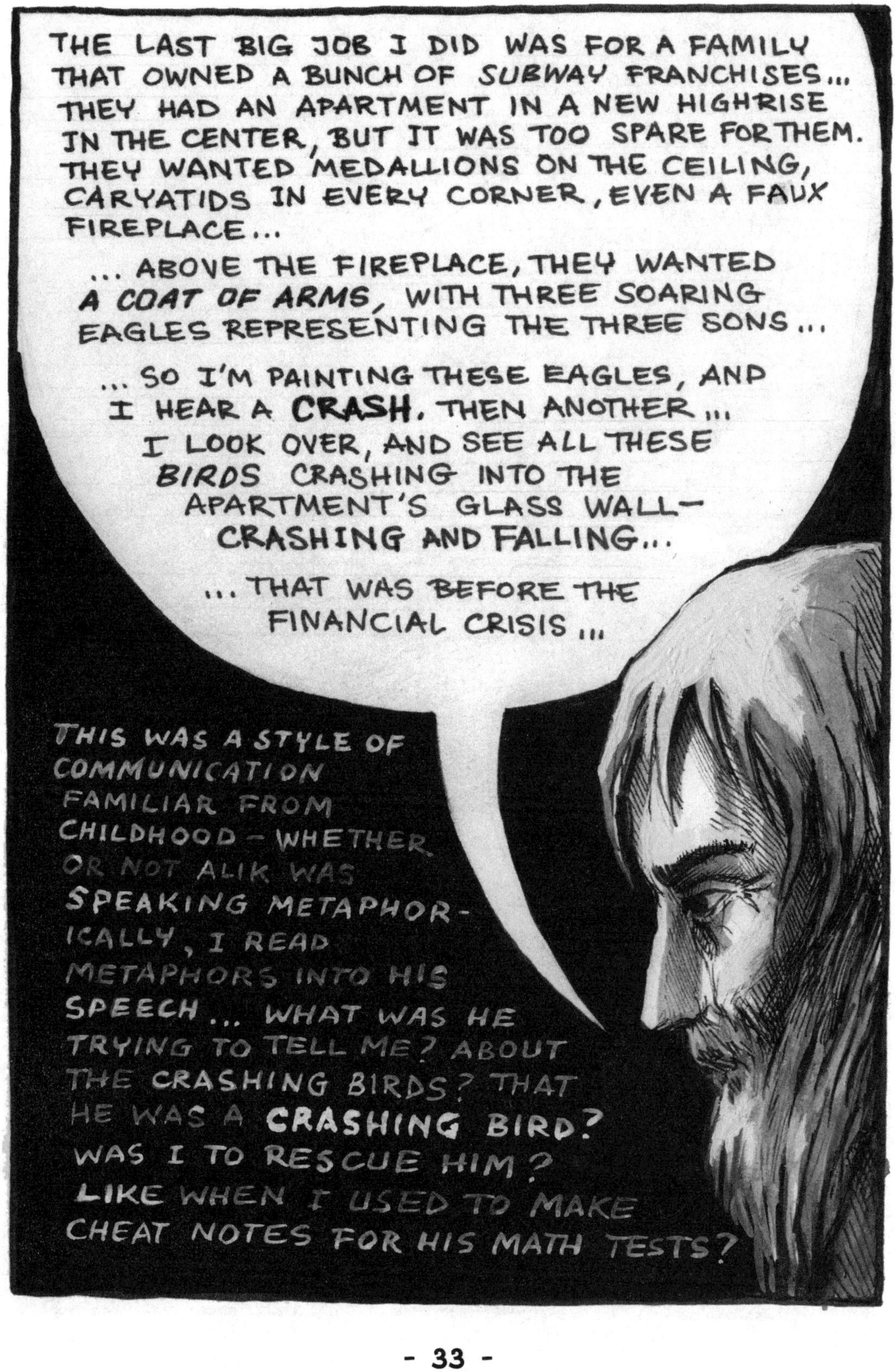
THE LAST BIG JOB I DID WAS FOR A FAMILY THAT OWNED A BUNCH OF SUBWAY FRANCHISES... THEY HAD AN APARTMENT IN A NEW HIGHRISE IN THE CENTER, BUT IT WAS TOO SPARE FOR THEM. THEY WANTED MEDALLIONS ON THE CEILING, CARYATIDS IN EVERY CORNER, EVEN A FAUX FIREPLACE...
... ABOVE THE FIREPLACE, THEY WANTED A COAT OF ARMS, WITH THREE SOARING EAGLES REPRESENTING THE THREE SONS...
... SO I'M PAINTING THESE EAGLES, AND I HEAR A CRASH. THEN ANOTHER... I LOOK OVER, AND SEE ALL THESE BIRDS CRASHING INTO THE APARTMENT'S GLASS WALL— CRASHING AND FALLING...
... THAT WAS BEFORE THE FINANCIAL CRISIS...
THIS WAS A STYLE OF COMMUNICATION FAMILIAR FROM CHILDHOOD – WHETHER OR NOT ALIK WAS SPEAKING METAPHORICALLY, I READ METAPHORS INTO HIS SPEECH ... WHAT WAS HE TRYING TO TELL ME? ABOUT THE CRASHING BIRDS? THAT HE WAS A CRASHING BIRD? WAS I TO RESCUE HIM? LIKE WHEN I USED TO MAKE CHEAT NOTES FOR HIS MATH TESTS?

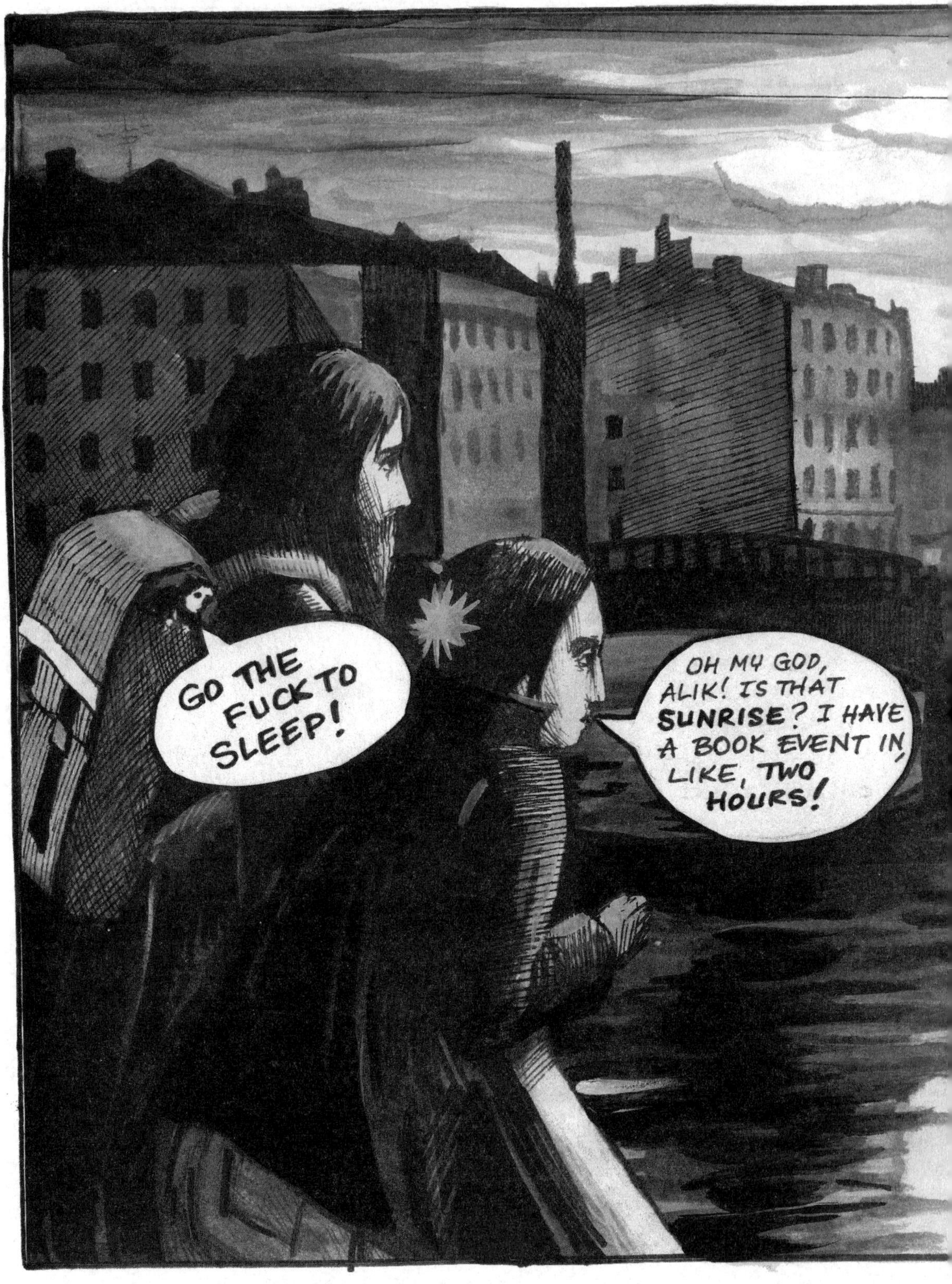
OH MY GOD, ALIK! IS THAT SUNRISE? I HAVE A BOOK EVENT IN, LIKE, TWO HOURS!
GO THE FUCK TO SLEEP!

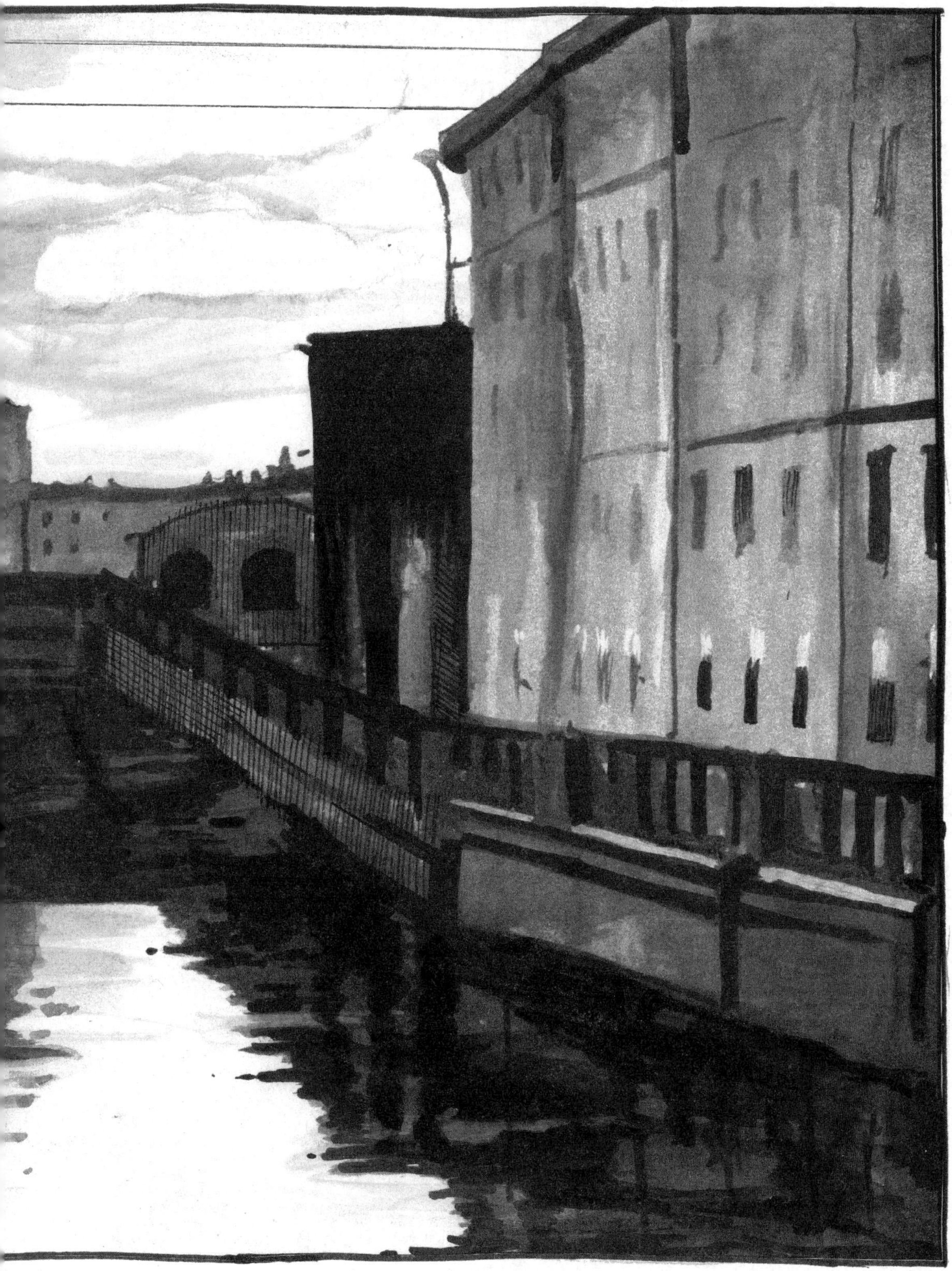

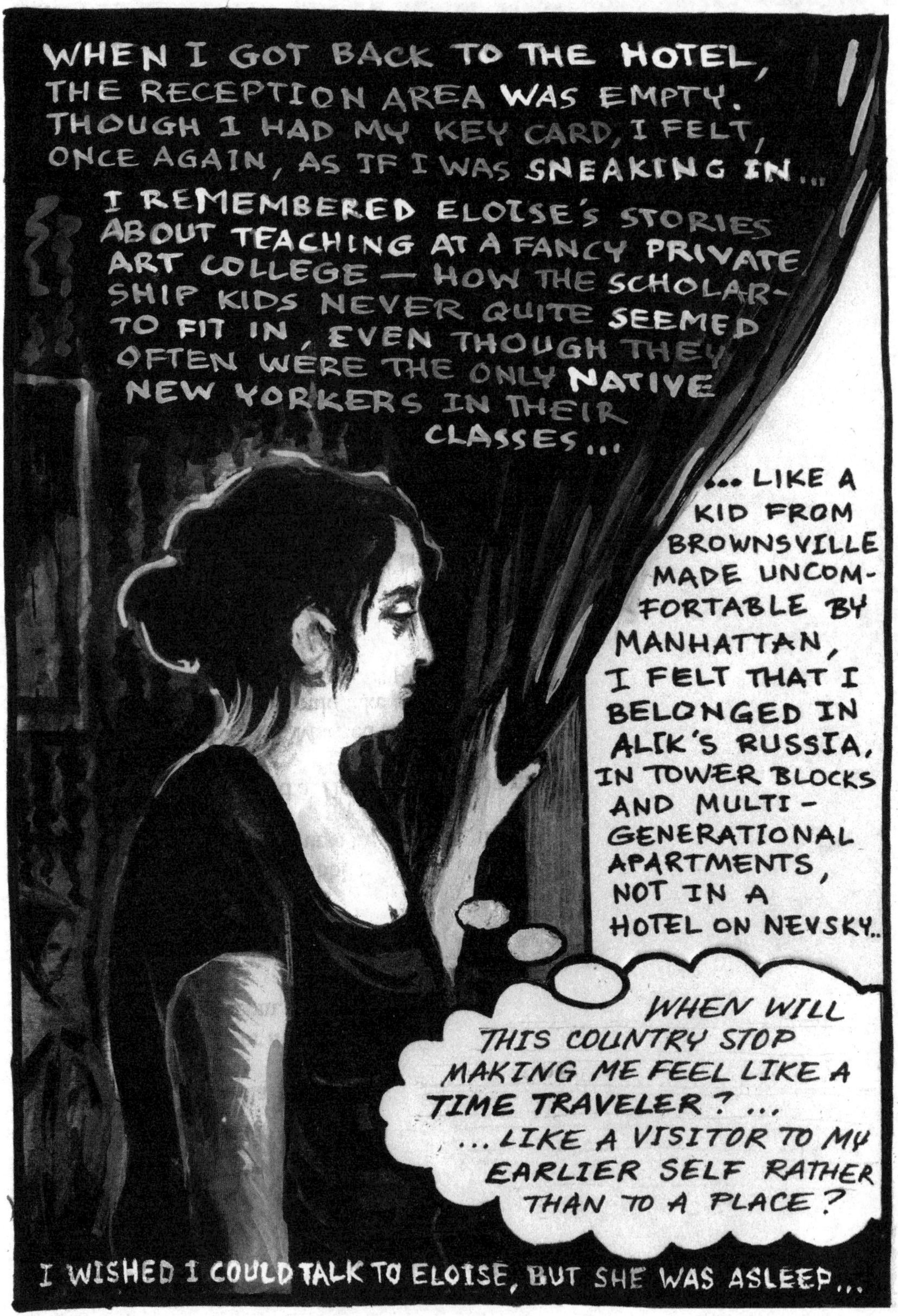
WHEN I GOT BACK TO THE HOTEL, THE RECEPTION AREA WAS EMPTY. THOUGH I HAD MY KEY CARD, I FELT, ONCE AGAIN, AS IF I WAS SNEAKING IN...
I REMEMBERED ELOISE'S STORIES ABOUT TEACHING AT A FANCY PRIVATE ART COLLEGE — HOW THE SCHOLARSHIP KIDS NEVER QUITE SEEMED TO FIT IN, EVEN THOUGH THEY OFTEN WERE THE ONLY NATIVE NEW YORKERS IN THEIR CLASSES...
...LIKE A KID FROM BROWNSVILLE MADE UNCOMFORTABLE BY MANHATTAN, I FELT THAT I BELONGED IN ALIK'S RUSSIA, IN TOWER BLOCKS AND MULTI-GENERATIONAL APARTMENTS, NOT IN A HOTEL ON NEVSKY...
WHEN WILL THIS COUNTRY STOP MAKING ME FEEL LIKE A TIME TRAVELER? ... ...LIKE A VISITOR TO MY EARLIER SELF RATHER THAN TO A PLACE?
I WISHED I COULD TALK TO ELOISE, BUT SHE WAS ASLEEP...

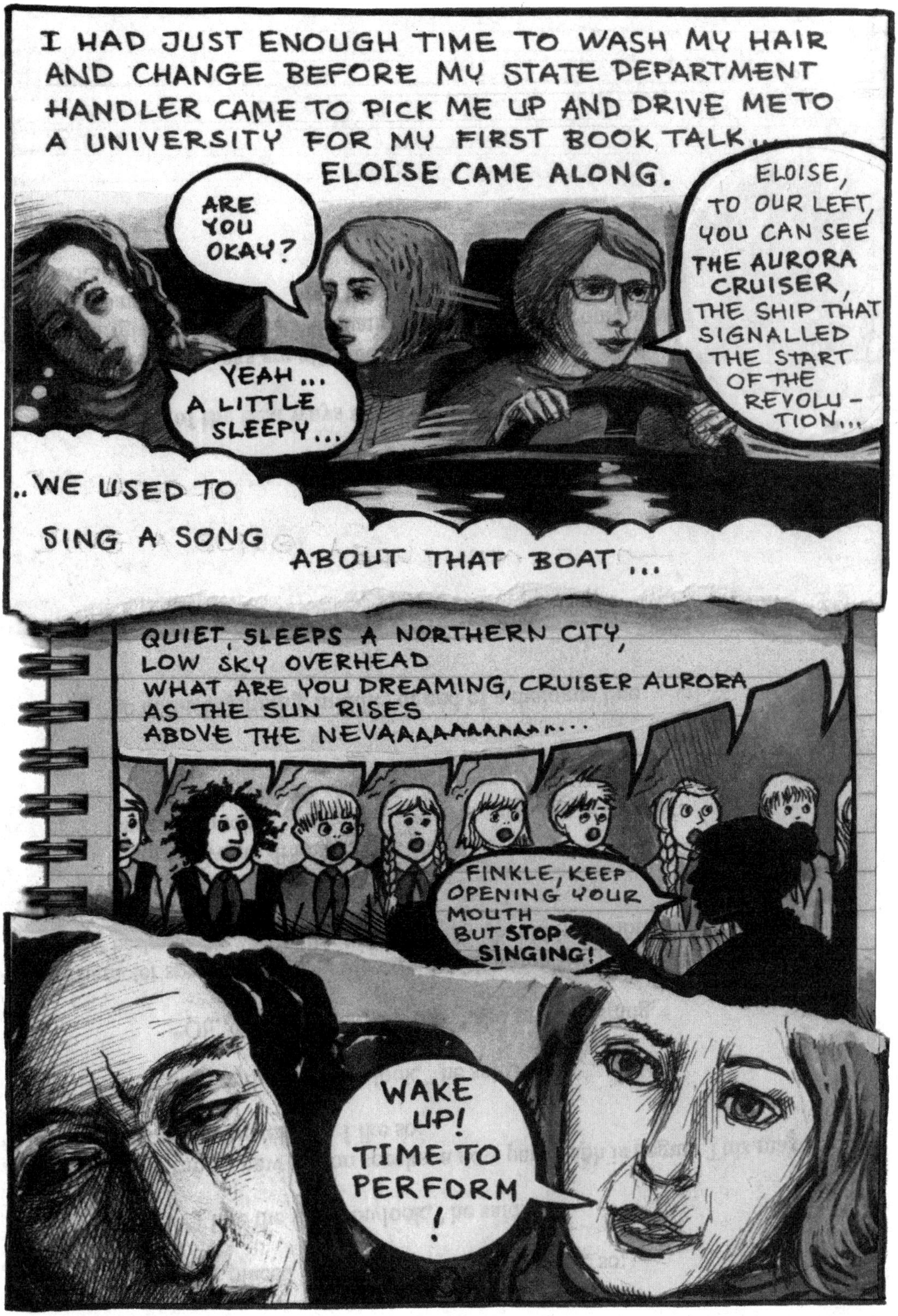
I HAD JUST ENOUGH TIME TO WASH MY HAIR AND CHANGE BEFORE MY STATE DEPARTMENT HANDLER CAME TO PICK ME UP AND DRIVE ME TO A UNIVERSITY FOR MY FIRST BOOK TALK...
ELOISE CAME ALONG.
ARE YOU OKAY?
ELOISE, TO OUR LEFT, YOU CAN SEE THE AURORA CRUISER, THE SHIP THAT SIGNALLED THE START OF THE REVOLU-TION...
YEAH... A LITTLE SLEEPY...
..WE USED TO SING A SONG ABOUT THAT BOAT...
QUIET, SLEEPS A NORTHERN CITY,
LOW SKY OVERHEAD
WHAT ARE YOU DREAMING, CRUISER AURORA
AS THE SUN RISES
ABOVE THE NEVAAAAAAAAAA...
FINKLE, KEEP OPENING YOUR MOUTH BUT STOP SINGING!
WAKE UP! TIME TO PERFORM!

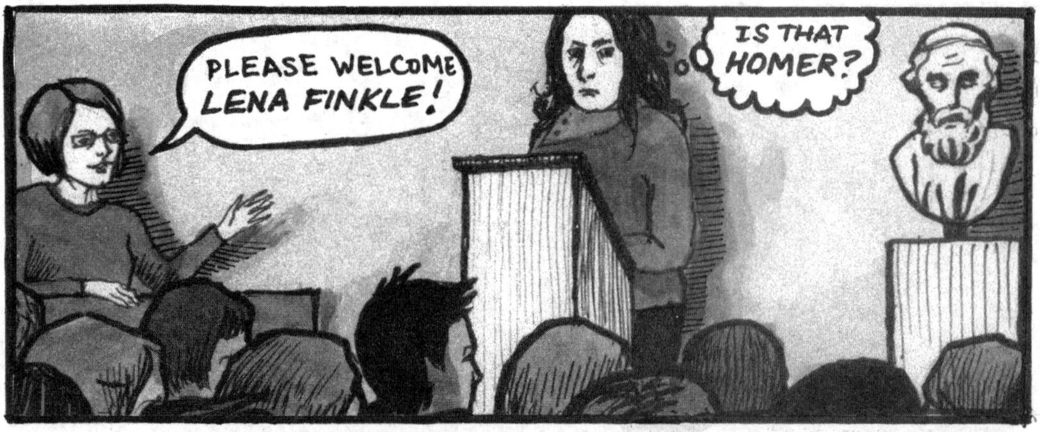
PLEASE WELCOME LENA FINKLE!
IS THAT HOMER?

THE UNIVERSITY REQUESTED THAT I SPEAK ENGLISH. AS I TOLD THE STUDENTS ABOUT MY NOVEL, I NOTICED VARYING DEGREES OF INCOMPREHENSION IN THEIR EYES. I REMEMBERED A SIMILAR TALK I'D GIVEN TO AN ESL CLASS AT A BROOKLYN HIGH SCHOOL. AFTERWARDS, THE KIDS HAD ASKED QUESTIONS THAT THEY'D PREPARED IN ADVANCE. A RECURRENT ONE HAD BEEN: "DO YOU MAKE A GOOD LIVING?"

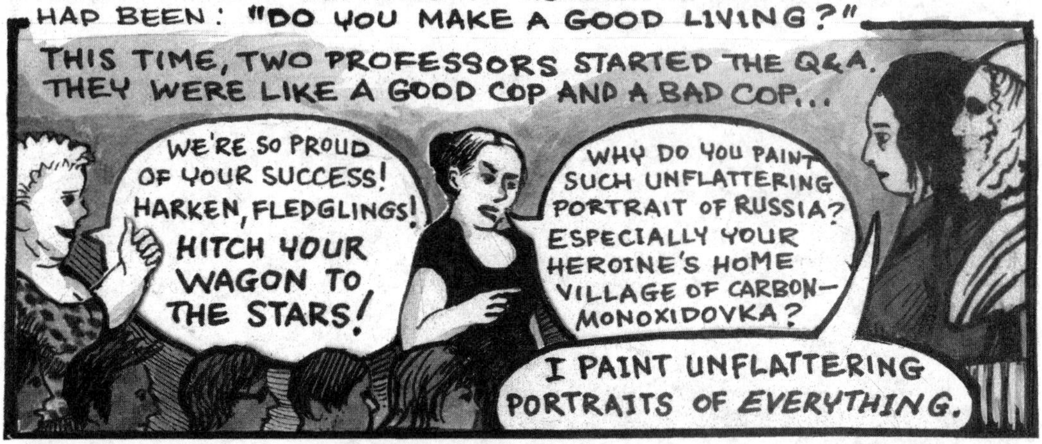
THIS TIME, TWO PROFESSORS STARTED THE Q&A. THEY WERE LIKE A GOOD COP AND A BAD COP...
WE'RE SO PROUD OF YOUR SUCCESS! HARKEN, FLEDGLINGS! HITCH YOUR WAGON TO THE STARS!
WHY DO YOU PAINT SUCH UNFLATTERING PORTRAIT OF RUSSIA? ESPECIALLY YOUR HEROINE'S HOME VILLAGE OF CARBON-MONOXIDOVKA?
I PAINT UNFLATTERING PORTRAITS OF EVERYTHING.

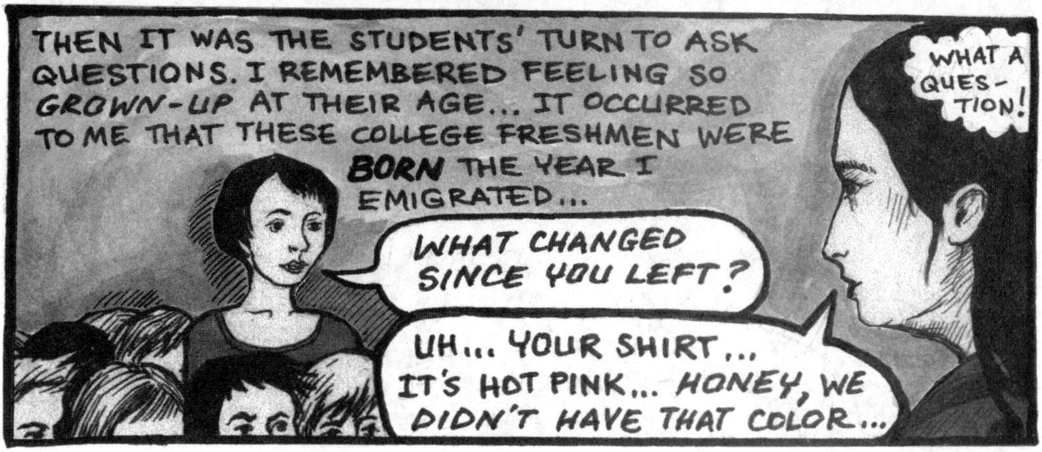
THEN IT WAS THE STUDENTS' TURN TO ASK QUESTIONS. I REMEMBERED FEELING SO GROWN-UP AT THEIR AGE... IT OCCURRED TO ME THAT THESE COLLEGE FRESHMEN WERE BORN THE YEAR I EMIGRATED...
WHAT A QUES-TION!
WHAT CHANGED SINCE YOU LEFT?
UH... YOUR SHIRT... IT'S HOT PINK... HONEY, WE DIDN'T HAVE THAT COLOR...

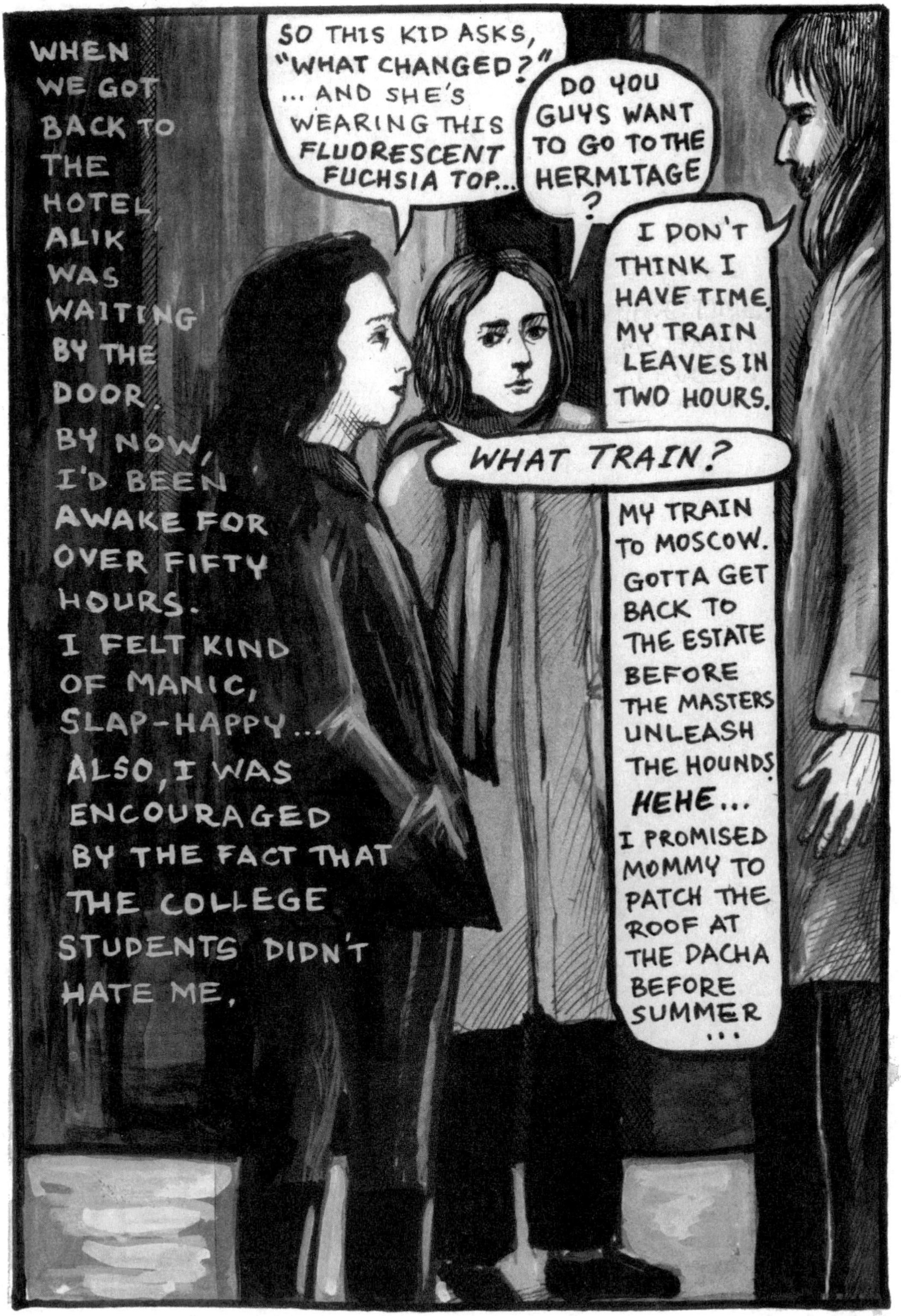
WHEN WE GOT BACK TO THE HOTEL, ALIK WAS WAITING BY THE DOOR. BY NOW, I'D BEEN AWAKE FOR OVER FIFTY HOURS. I FELT KIND OF MANIC, SLAP-HAPPY... ALSO, I WAS ENCOURAGED BY THE FACT THAT THE COLLEGE STUDENTS DIDN'T HATE ME.
SO THIS KID ASKS, "WHAT CHANGED?" ... AND SHE'S WEARING THIS FLUORESCENT FUCHSIA TOP...
DO YOU GUYS WANT TO GO TO THE HERMITAGE?
I DON'T THINK I HAVE TIME. MY TRAIN LEAVES IN TWO HOURS.
WHAT TRAIN?
MY TRAIN TO MOSCOW. GOTTA GET BACK TO THE ESTATE BEFORE THE MASTERS UNLEASH THE HOUNDS. HEHE... I PROMISED MOMMY TO PATCH THE ROOF AT THE DACHA BEFORE SUMMER...

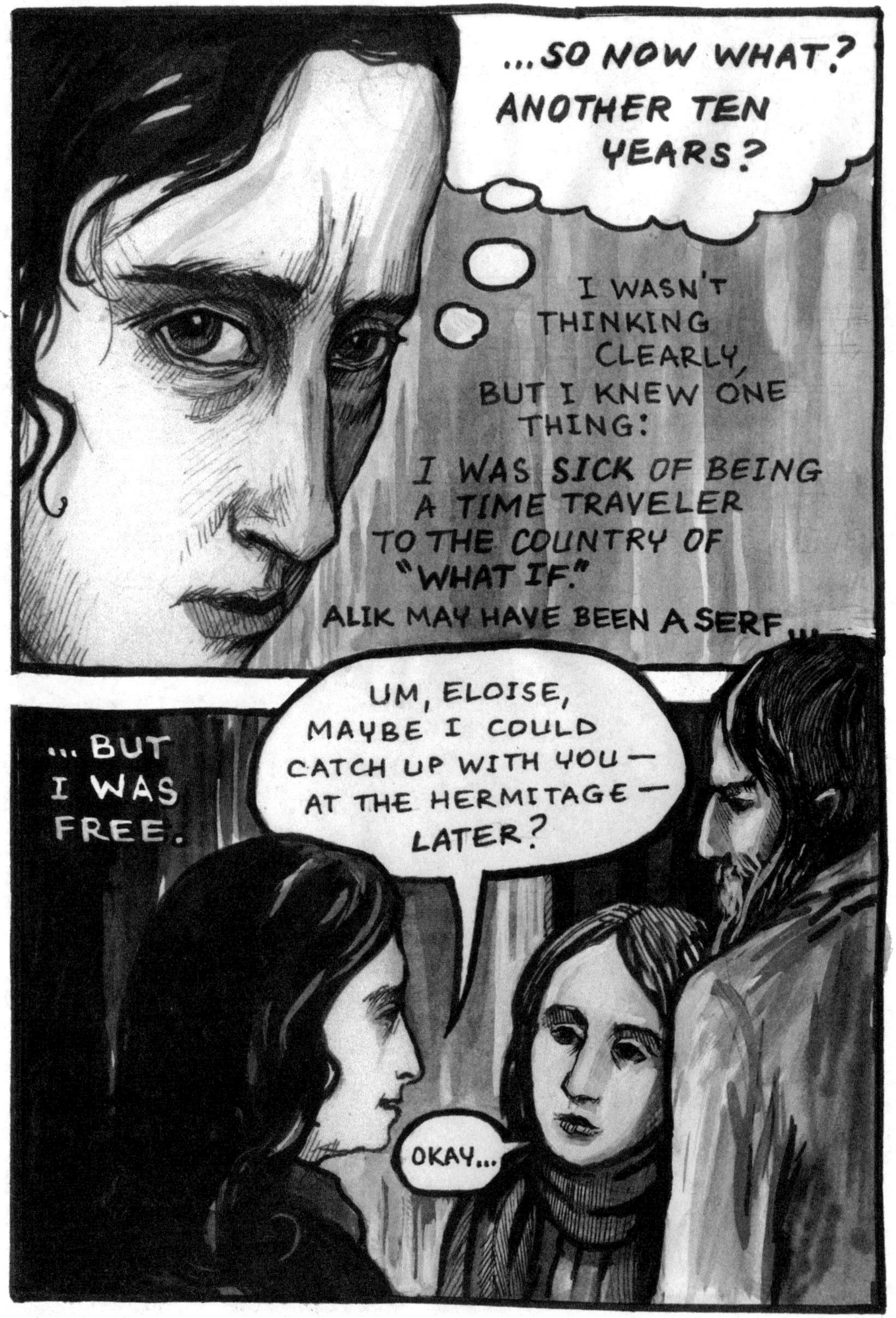

...SO NOW WHAT? ANOTHER TEN YEARS?
I WASN'T THINKING CLEARLY, BUT I KNEW ONE THING:
I WAS SICK OF BEING A TIME TRAVELER TO THE COUNTRY OF "WHAT IF."
ALIK MAY HAVE BEEN A SERF...
...BUT I WAS FREE.
UM, ELOISE, MAYBE I COULD CATCH UP WITH YOU— AT THE HERMITAGE— LATER?
OKAY...

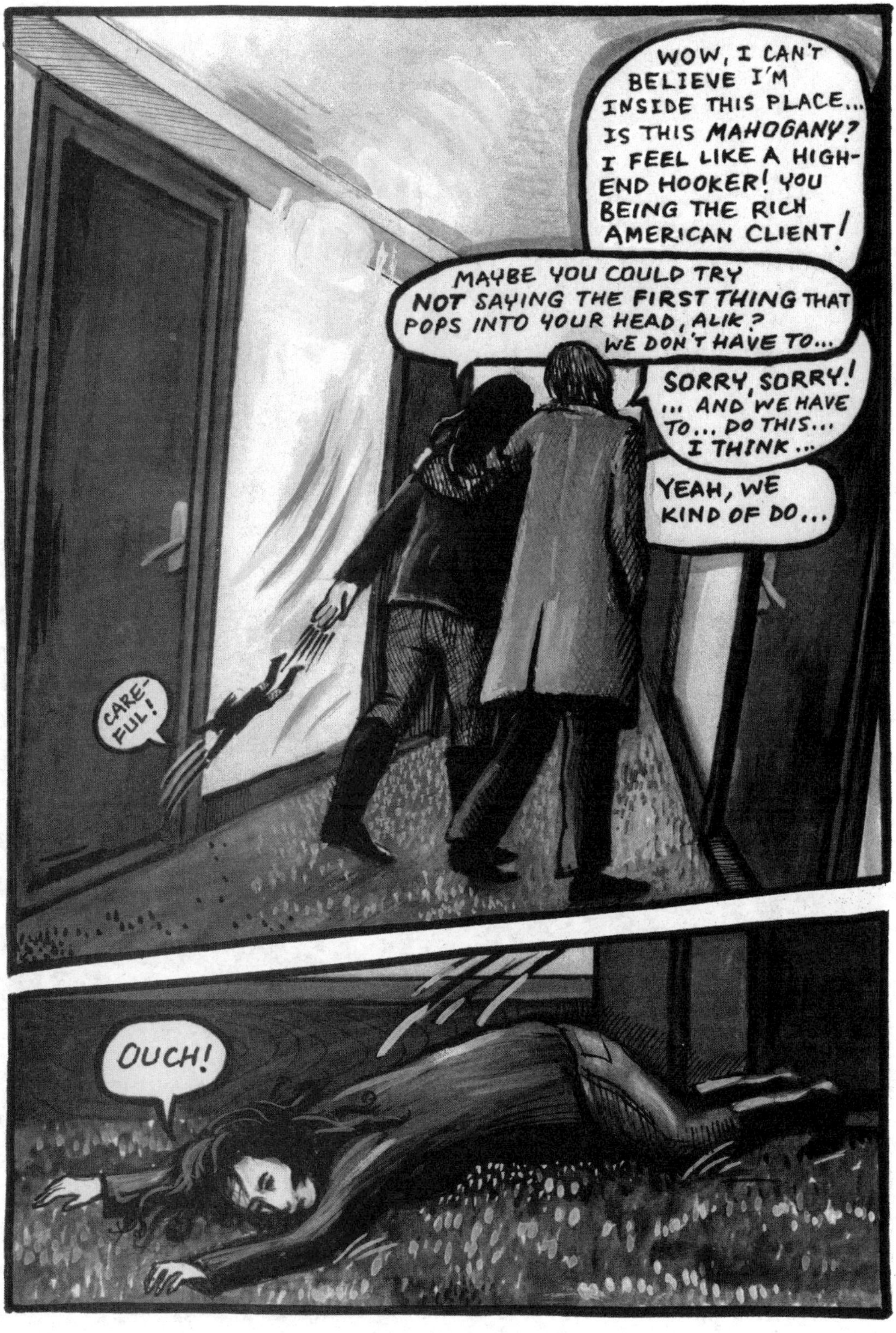
WOW, I CAN'T BELIEVE I'M INSIDE THIS PLACE... IS THIS MAHOGANY? I FEEL LIKE A HIGH-END HOOKER! YOU BEING THE RICH AMERICAN CLIENT!
MAYBE YOU COULD TRY NOT SAYING THE FIRST THING THAT POPS INTO YOUR HEAD, ALIK? WE DON'T HAVE TO...
SORRY, SORRY! ... AND WE HAVE TO... DO THIS... I THINK...
YEAH, WE KIND OF DO...
CARE-FUL!
OUCH!

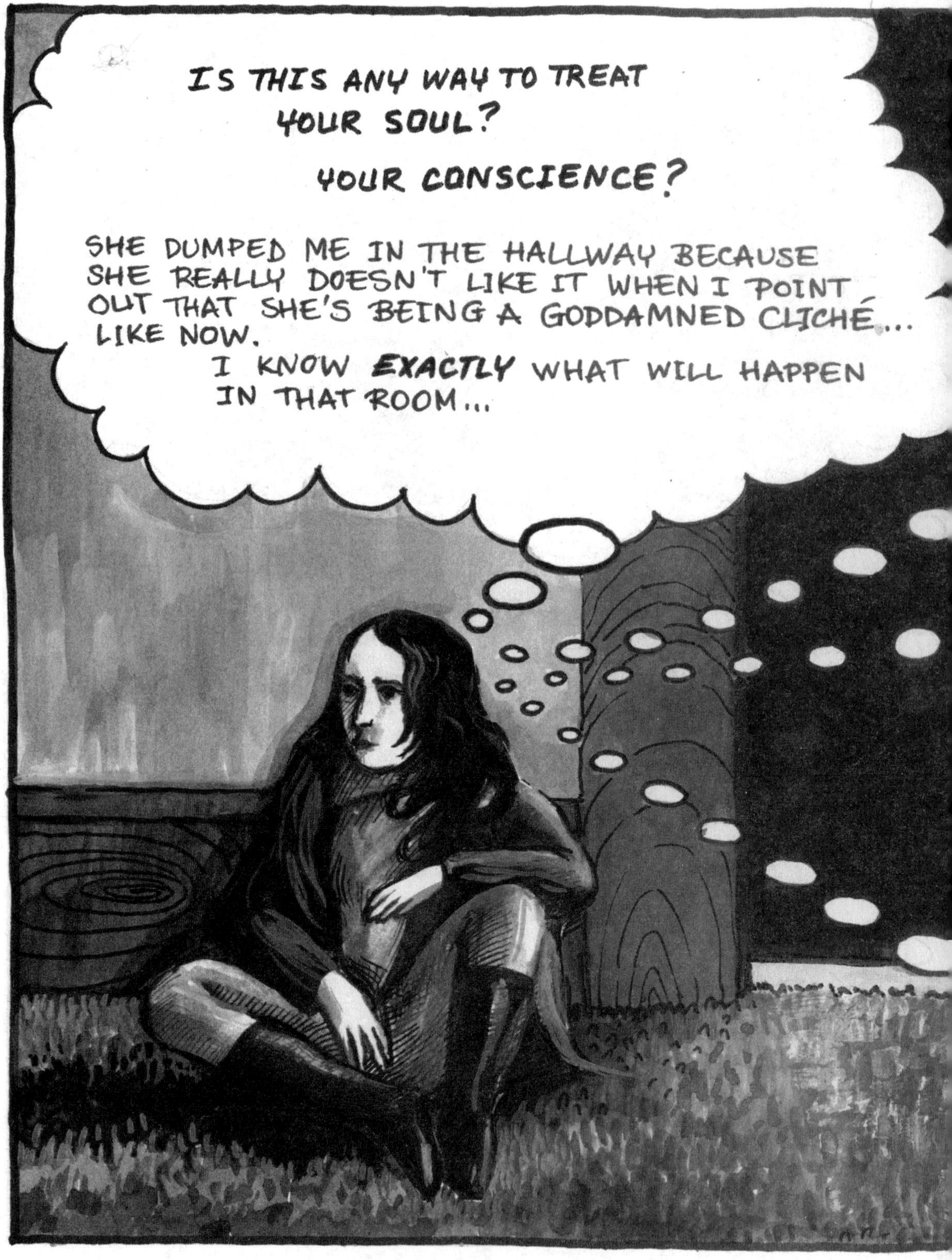
IS THIS ANY WAY TO TREAT YOUR SOUL? YOUR CONSCIENCE?
SHE DUMPED ME IN THE HALLWAY BECAUSE SHE REALLY DOESN'T LIKE IT WHEN I POINT OUT THAT SHE'S BEING A GODDAMNED CLICHÉ... LIKE NOW.
I KNOW EXACTLY WHAT WILL HAPPEN IN THAT ROOM...

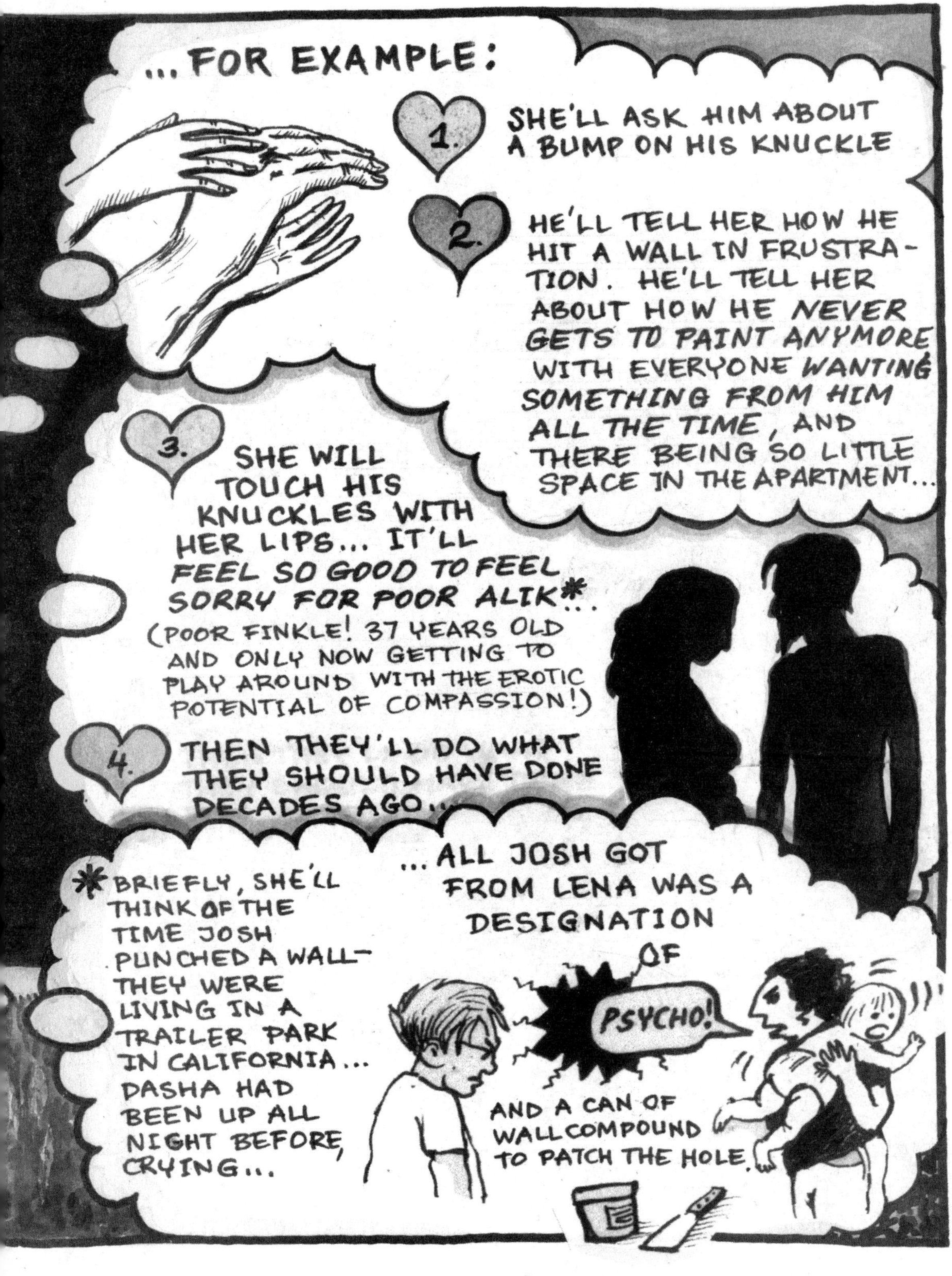
...FOR EXAMPLE:
1. SHE'LL ASK HIM ABOUT A BUMP ON HIS KNUCKLE
2. HE'LL TELL HER HOW HE HIT A WALL IN FRUSTRATION. HE'LL TELL HER ABOUT HOW HE NEVER GETS TO PAINT ANYMORE WITH EVERYONE WANTING SOMETHING FROM HIM ALL THE TIME, AND THERE BEING SO LITTLE SPACE IN THE APARTMENT...
3. SHE WILL TOUCH HIS KNUCKLES WITH HER LIPS... IT'LL FEEL SO GOOD TO FEEL SORRY FOR POOR ALIK*...
(POOR FINKLE! 37 YEARS OLD AND ONLY NOW GETTING TO PLAY AROUND WITH THE EROTIC POTENTIAL OF COMPASSION!)
4. THEN THEY'LL DO WHAT THEY SHOULD HAVE DONE DECADES AGO...
* BRIEFLY, SHE'LL THINK OF THE TIME JOSH PUNCHED A WALL— THEY WERE LIVING IN A TRAILER PARK IN CALIFORNIA... DASHA HAD BEEN UP ALL NIGHT BEFORE, CRYING...
...ALL JOSH GOT FROM LENA WAS A DESIGNATION OF
PSYCHO!
AND A CAN OF WALLCOMPOUND TO PATCH THE HOLE.

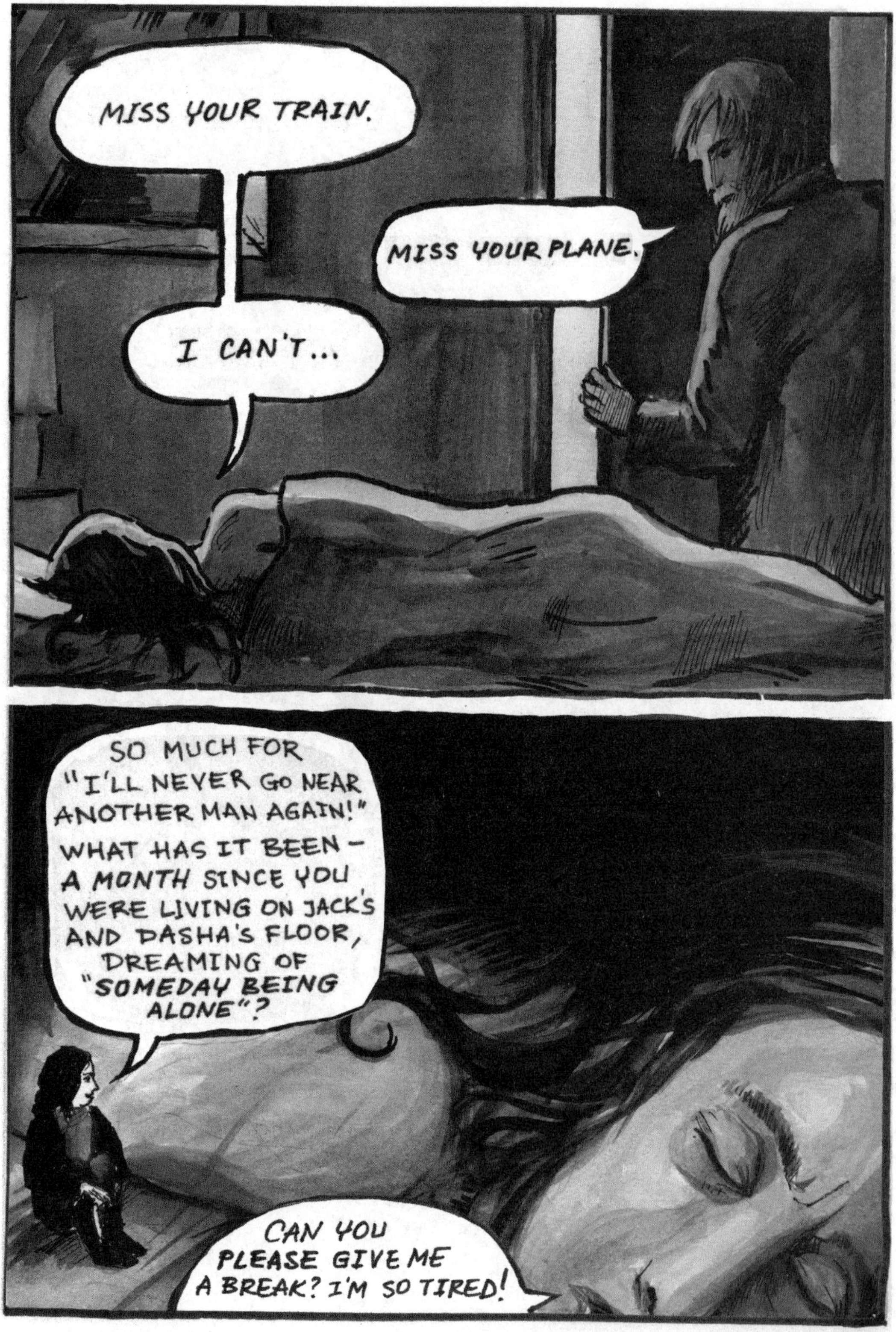
MISS YOUR TRAIN.
MISS YOUR PLANE.
I CAN'T...
SO MUCH FOR "I'LL NEVER GO NEAR ANOTHER MAN AGAIN!" WHAT HAS IT BEEN – A MONTH SINCE YOU WERE LIVING ON JACK'S AND DASHA'S FLOOR, DREAMING OF "SOMEDAY BEING ALONE"?
CAN YOU PLEASE GIVE ME A BREAK? I'M SO TIRED!

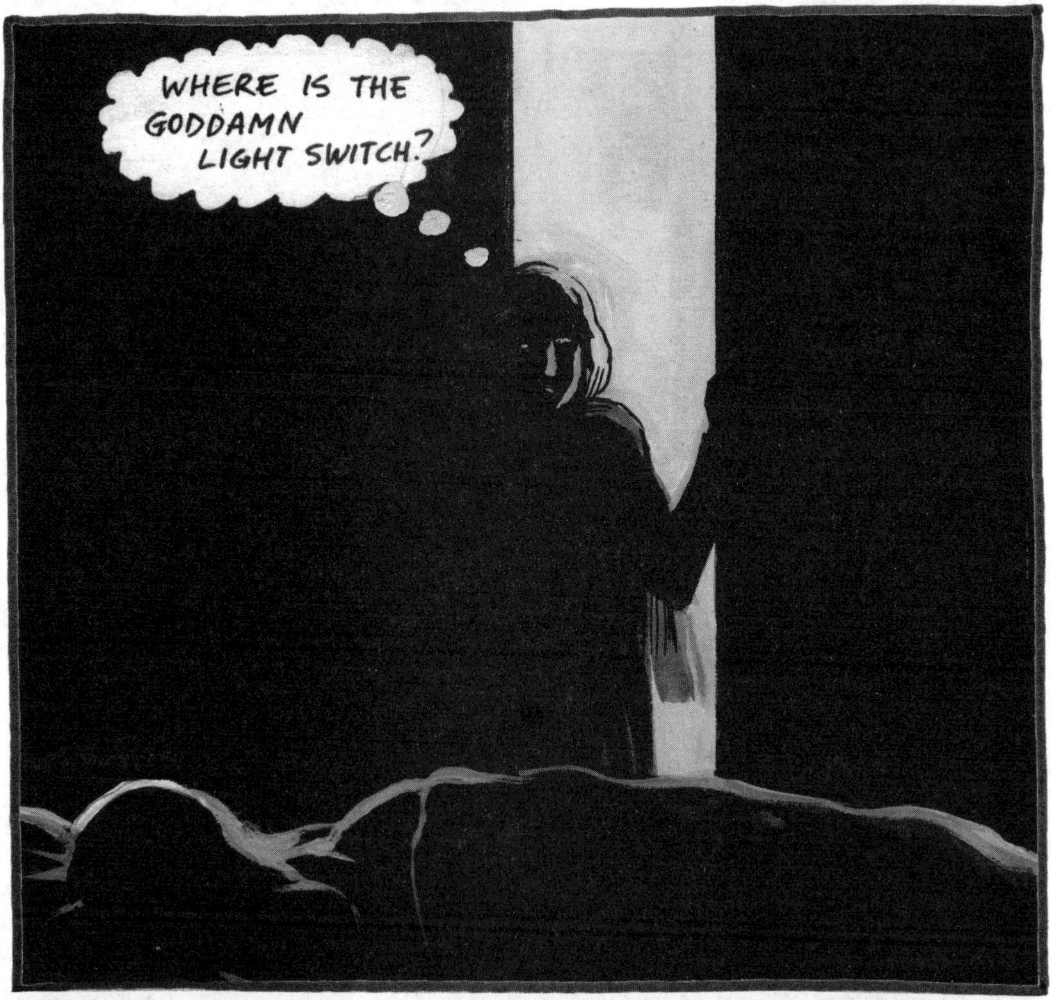
WHERE IS THE GODDAMN LIGHT SWITCH?

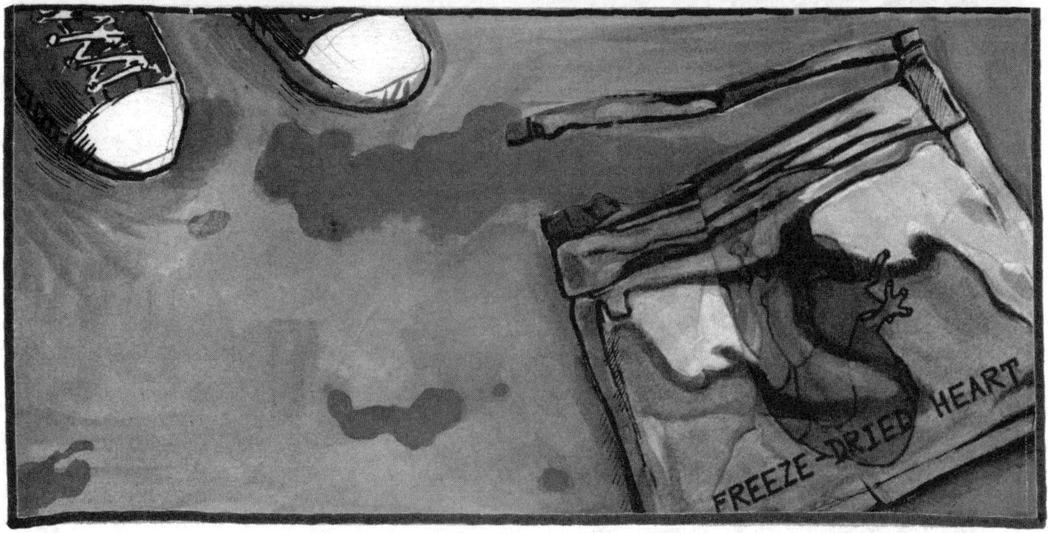
FREEZE-DRIED HEART

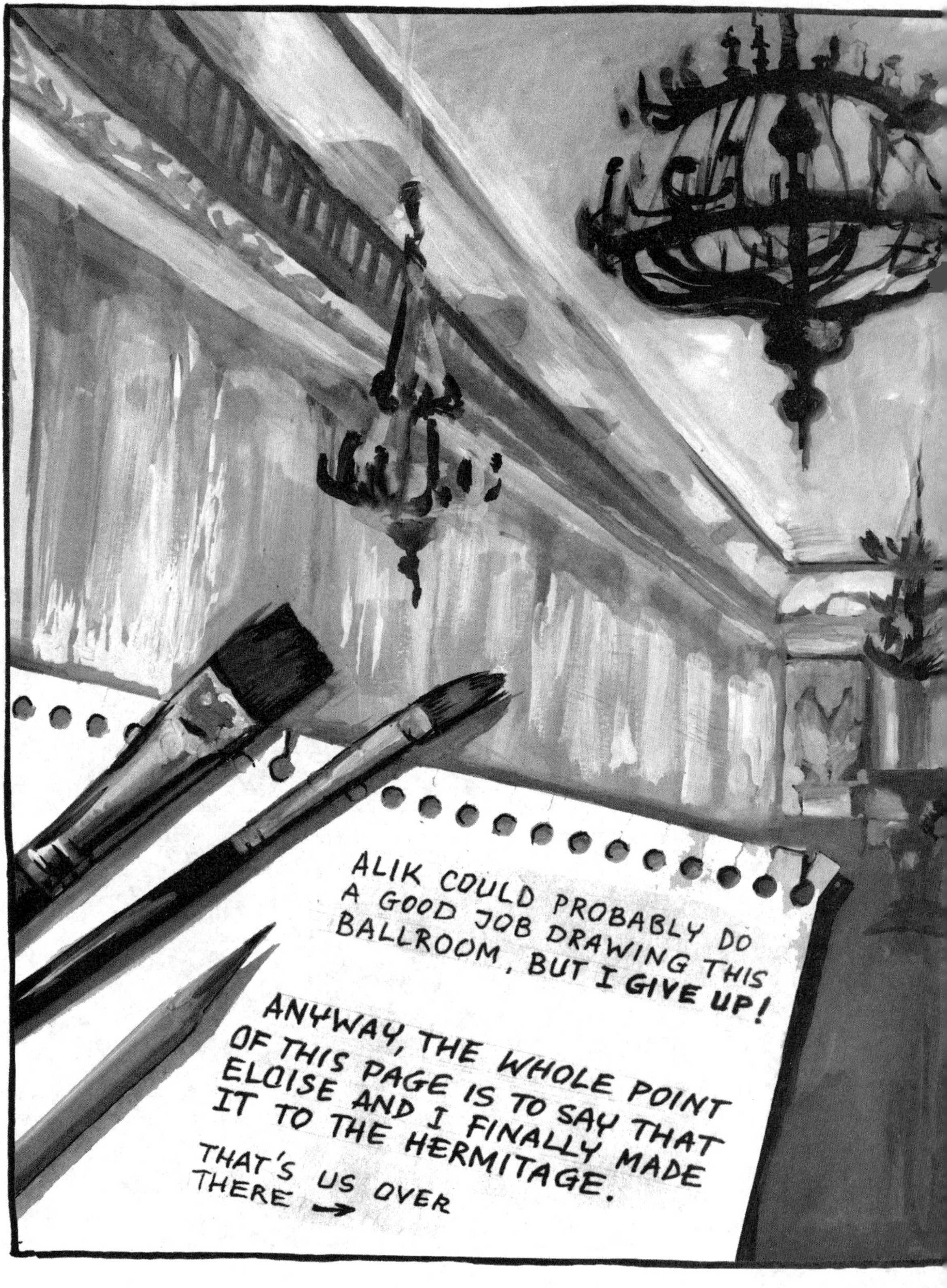
ALIK COULD PROBABLY DO A GOOD JOB DRAWING THIS BALLROOM, BUT I GIVE UP!
ANYWAY, THE WHOLE POINT OF THIS PAGE IS TO SAY THAT ELOISE AND I FINALLY MADE IT TO THE HERMITAGE.
THAT'S US OVER THERE →

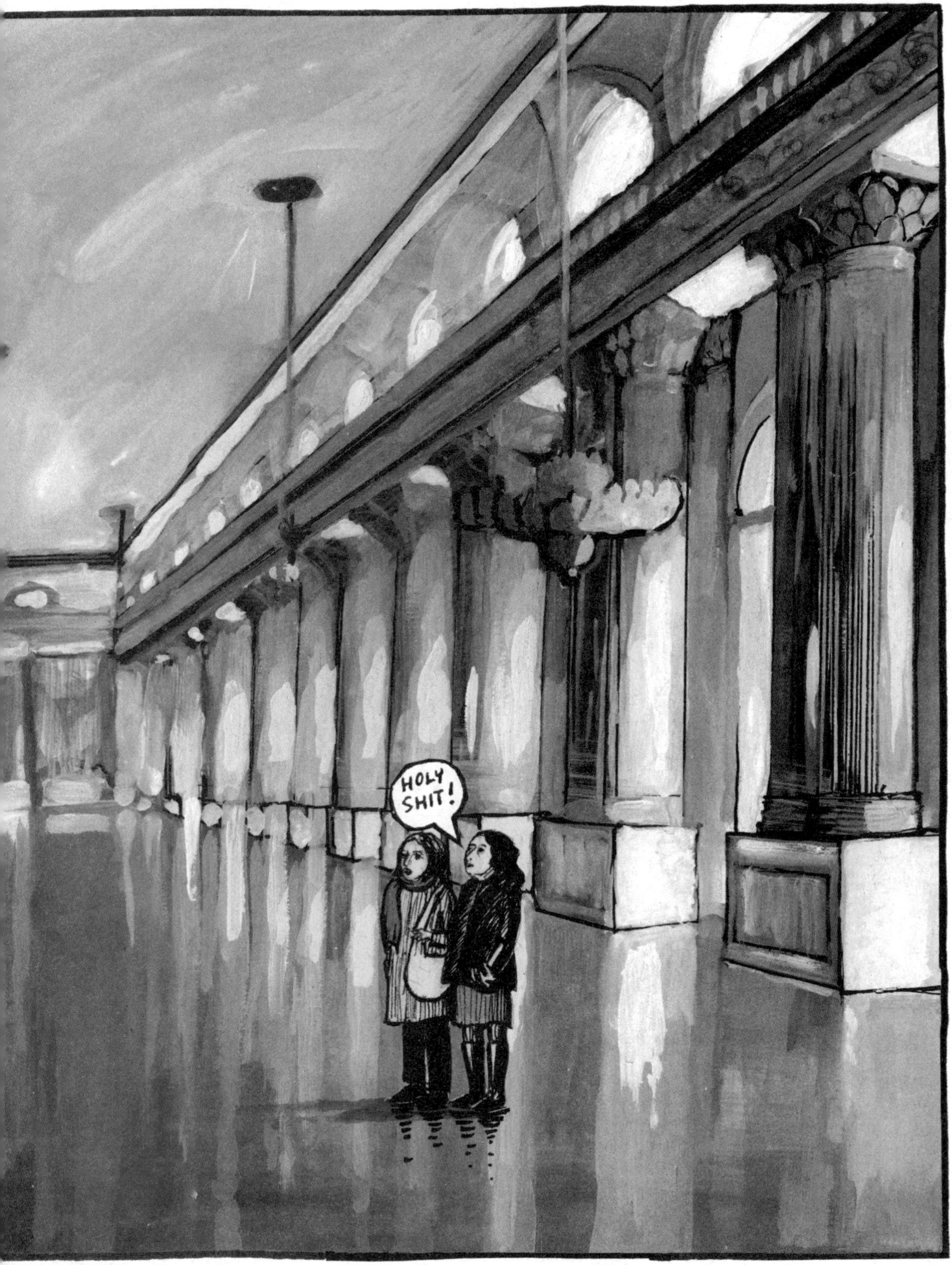
HOLY SHIT!

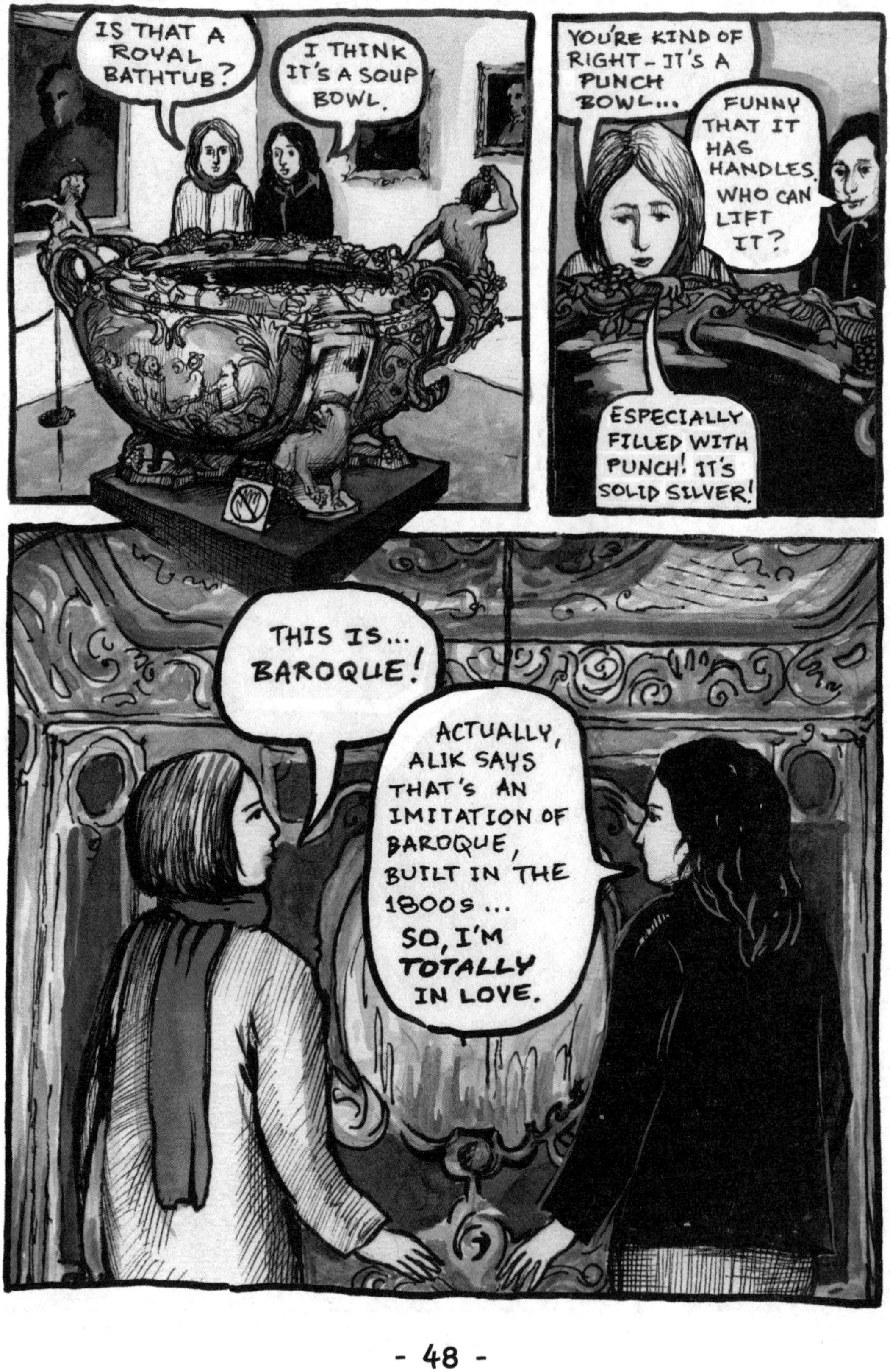
IS THAT A ROYAL BATHTUB?
I THINK IT'S A SOUP BOWL.
YOU'RE KIND OF RIGHT – IT'S A PUNCH BOWL...
FUNNY THAT IT HAS HANDLES. WHO CAN LIFT IT?
ESPECIALLY FILLED WITH PUNCH! IT'S SOLID SILVER!
THIS IS... BAROQUE!
ACTUALLY, ALIK SAYS THAT'S AN IMITATION OF BAROQUE, BUILT IN THE 1800s... SO, I'M *TOTALLY* IN LOVE.

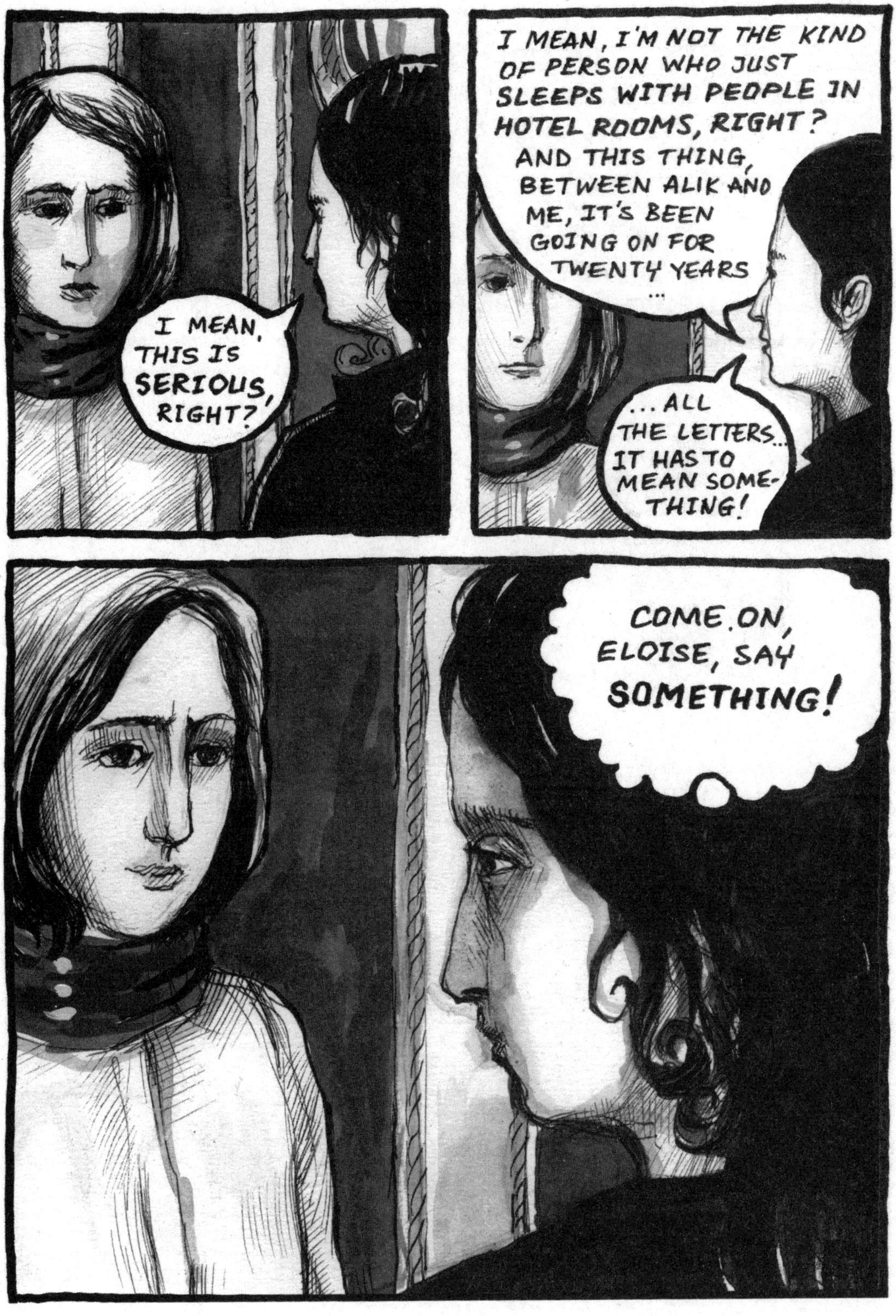
I MEAN, THIS IS SERIOUS, RIGHT?
I MEAN, I'M NOT THE KIND OF PERSON WHO JUST SLEEPS WITH PEOPLE IN HOTEL ROOMS, RIGHT? AND THIS THING, BETWEEN ALIK AND ME, IT'S BEEN GOING ON FOR TWENTY YEARS ...
... ALL THE LETTERS... IT HAS TO MEAN SOMETHING!
COME ON, ELOISE, SAY SOMETHING!

THE THING ABOUT ELOISE

... WAS THAT SHE WASN'T SIMPLY A FRIEND ... SHE WAS MORE LIKE AN OLDER SISTER TO ME, OR EVEN (SORRY, ELOISE!) A COOL, SUPPORTIVE, UNDERSTANDING, *NON-IMMIGRANT* MOM! SORRY! 1)) SORRY! SORRY!

ELOISE WAS EIGHTEEN YEARS OLDER THAN ME, AND I RELIED ON HER TO HAVE THE ANSWERS TO MY QUESTIONS.

WHEN JOSH AND I MOVED TO BROOKLYN AND SENT DASHA TO PRESCHOOL, WE DISCOVERED THAT NEW YORKERS OF A CERTAIN SOCIAL CLASS DIDN'T PROCREATE BEFORE THEIR MID-THIRTIES, AND THAT WE WERE HALF A GENERATION YOUNGER AND IMMEASURABLY MORE SQUARE THAN THE PARENTS OF DASHA'S PLAYMATES...

THESE WERE PEOPLE WITH SORDID PASTS AND OUTSIZE ACCOMPLISHMENTS, ROUNDS OF IVF AND PUBLISHED NOVELS, REAL FURNITURE AND DINNER PARTIES *WITH WINE* ...

... TO WHICH, TO MY AMAZE-MENT, JOSH AND I WERE OFTEN INVITED !!! ...

U-HAUL U-HAUL

DASHA IN A NON-BRITISH STROLLER WITH AN UGLY DISNEY CREATURE ON IT →

TRAILER FULL OF HUGE PAINTINGS I'D MADE IN ART SCHOOL IN CALI-FORNIA, WHERE THE PROFESSORS ENCOURAGED ME TO "WORK BIG."

BROOKLYN, 2000

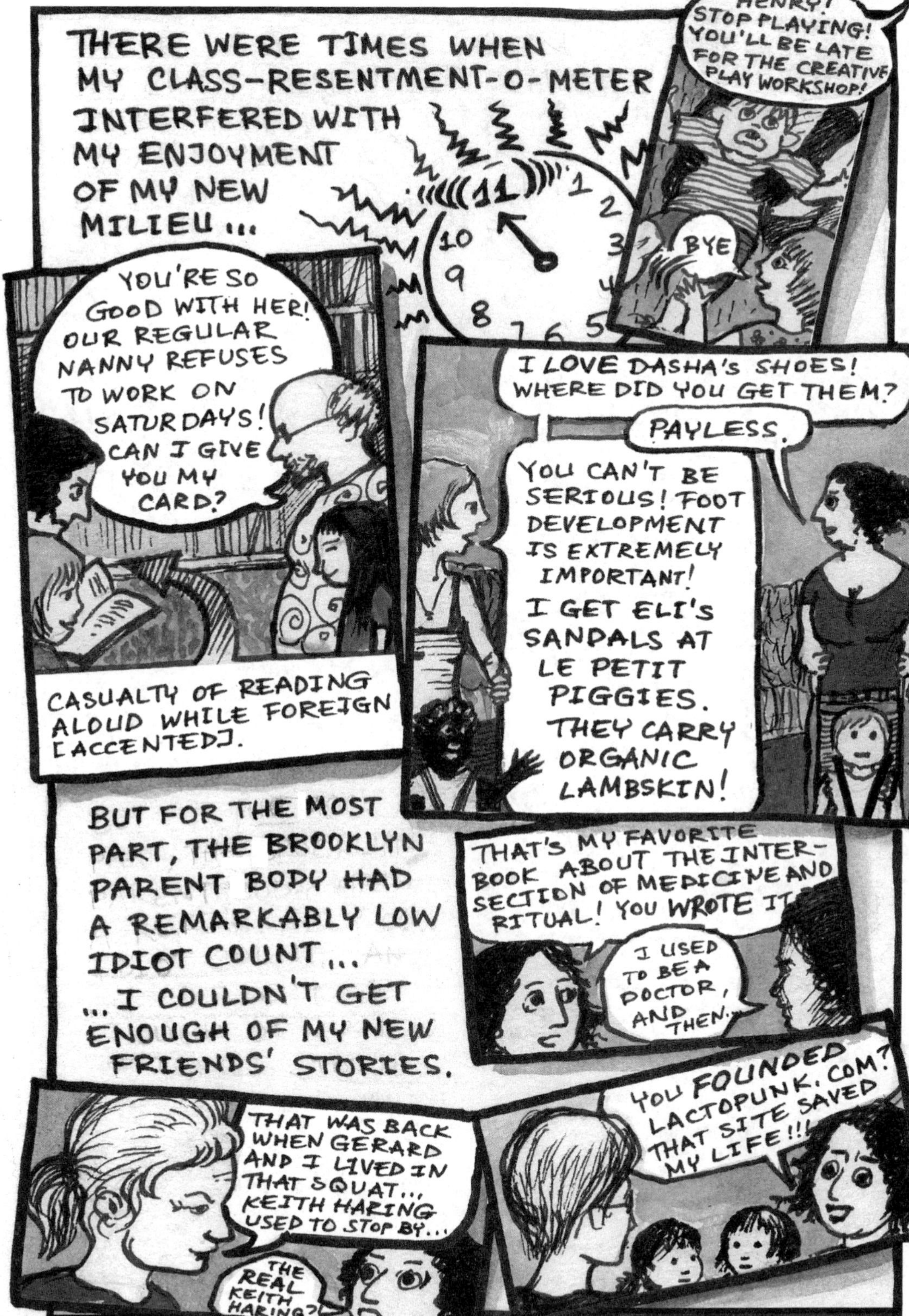
THERE WERE TIMES WHEN MY CLASS-RESENTMENT-O-METER INTERFERED WITH MY ENJOYMENT OF MY NEW MILIEU...
HENRY! STOP PLAYING! YOU'LL BE LATE FOR THE CREATIVE PLAY WORKSHOP!
BYE
YOU'RE SO GOOD WITH HER! OUR REGULAR NANNY REFUSES TO WORK ON SATURDAYS! CAN I GIVE YOU MY CARD?
CASUALTY OF READING ALOUD WHILE FOREIGN [ACCENTED].
I LOVE DASHA'S SHOES! WHERE DID YOU GET THEM?
PAYLESS.
YOU CAN'T BE SERIOUS! FOOT DEVELOPMENT IS EXTREMELY IMPORTANT! I GET ELI'S SANDALS AT LE PETIT PIGGIES. THEY CARRY ORGANIC LAMBSKIN!
BUT FOR THE MOST PART, THE BROOKLYN PARENT BODY HAD A REMARKABLY LOW IDIOT COUNT... ...I COULDN'T GET ENOUGH OF MY NEW FRIENDS' STORIES.
THAT'S MY FAVORITE BOOK ABOUT THE INTERSECTION OF MEDICINE AND RITUAL! YOU WROTE IT!
I USED TO BE A DOCTOR, AND THEN...
THAT WAS BACK WHEN GERARD AND I LIVED IN THAT SQUAT... KEITH HARING USED TO STOP BY...
THE REAL KEITH HARING?
YOU FOUNDED LACTOPUNK.COM? THAT SITE SAVED MY LIFE!!!

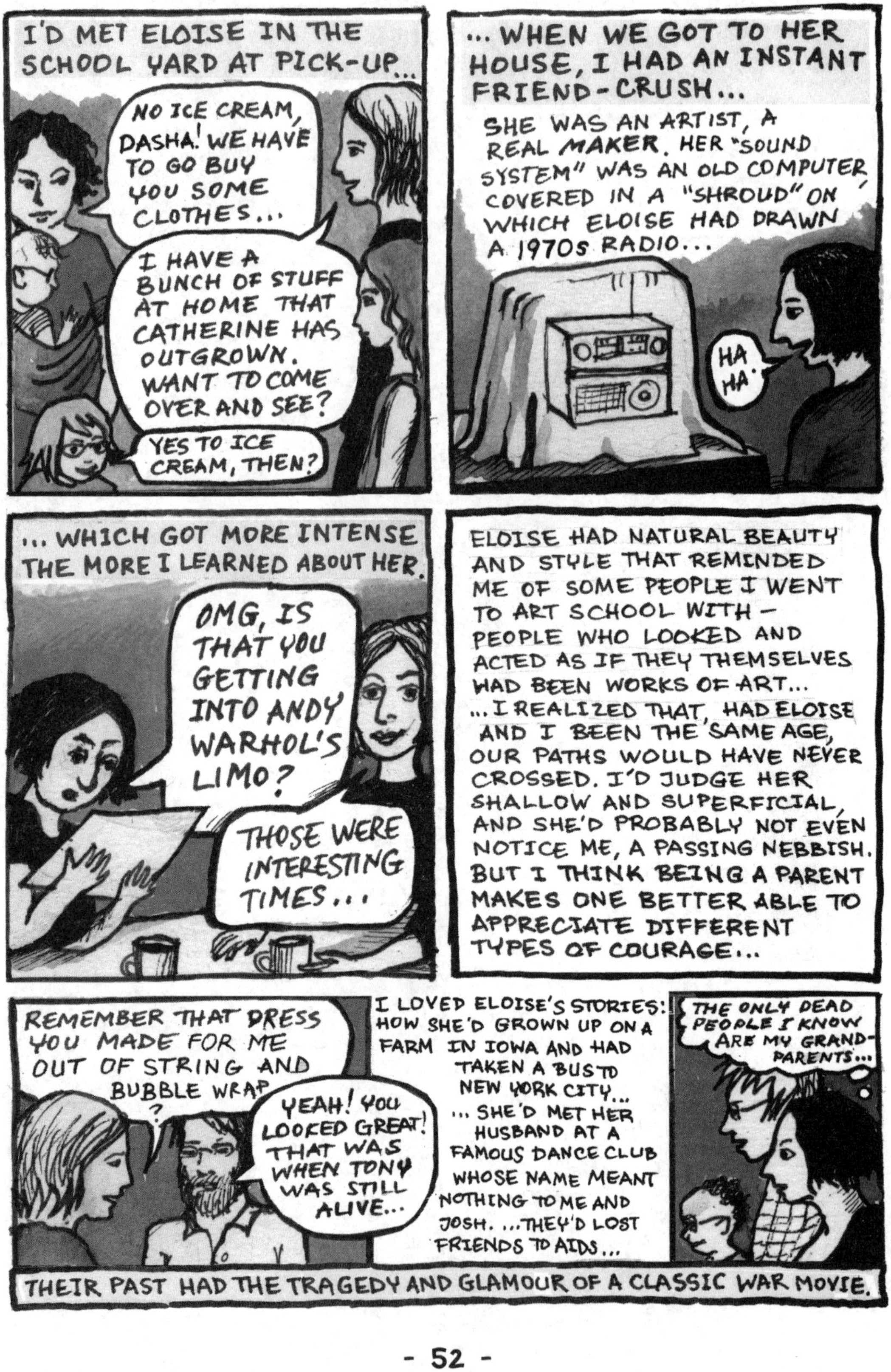
I'D MET ELOISE IN THE SCHOOL YARD AT PICK-UP...
NO ICE CREAM, DASHA! WE HAVE TO GO BUY YOU SOME CLOTHES...
I HAVE A BUNCH OF STUFF AT HOME THAT CATHERINE HAS OUTGROWN. WANT TO COME OVER AND SEE?
YES TO ICE CREAM, THEN?
... WHEN WE GOT TO HER HOUSE, I HAD AN INSTANT FRIEND-CRUSH...
SHE WAS AN ARTIST, A REAL MAKER. HER "SOUND SYSTEM" WAS AN OLD COMPUTER COVERED IN A "SHROUD" ON WHICH ELOISE HAD DRAWN A 1970s RADIO...
HA HA
... WHICH GOT MORE INTENSE THE MORE I LEARNED ABOUT HER.
OMG, IS THAT YOU GETTING INTO ANDY WARHOL'S LIMO?
THOSE WERE INTERESTING TIMES...
ELOISE HAD NATURAL BEAUTY AND STYLE THAT REMINDED ME OF SOME PEOPLE I WENT TO ART SCHOOL WITH - PEOPLE WHO LOOKED AND ACTED AS IF THEY THEMSELVES HAD BEEN WORKS OF ART... ... I REALIZED THAT, HAD ELOISE AND I BEEN THE SAME AGE, OUR PATHS WOULD HAVE NEVER CROSSED. I'D JUDGE HER SHALLOW AND SUPERFICIAL, AND SHE'D PROBABLY NOT EVEN NOTICE ME, A PASSING NEBBISH. BUT I THINK BEING A PARENT MAKES ONE BETTER ABLE TO APPRECIATE DIFFERENT TYPES OF COURAGE...
REMEMBER THAT DRESS YOU MADE FOR ME OUT OF STRING AND BUBBLE WRAP?
YEAH! YOU LOOKED GREAT! THAT WAS WHEN TONY WAS STILL ALIVE...
I LOVED ELOISE'S STORIES: HOW SHE'D GROWN UP ON A FARM IN IOWA AND HAD TAKEN A BUS TO NEW YORK CITY... ... SHE'D MET HER HUSBAND AT A FAMOUS DANCE CLUB WHOSE NAME MEANT NOTHING TO ME AND JOSH. ... THEY'D LOST FRIENDS TO AIDS...
THE ONLY DEAD PEOPLE I KNOW ARE MY GRANDPARENTS...
THEIR PAST HAD THE TRAGEDY AND GLAMOUR OF A CLASSIC WAR MOVIE.

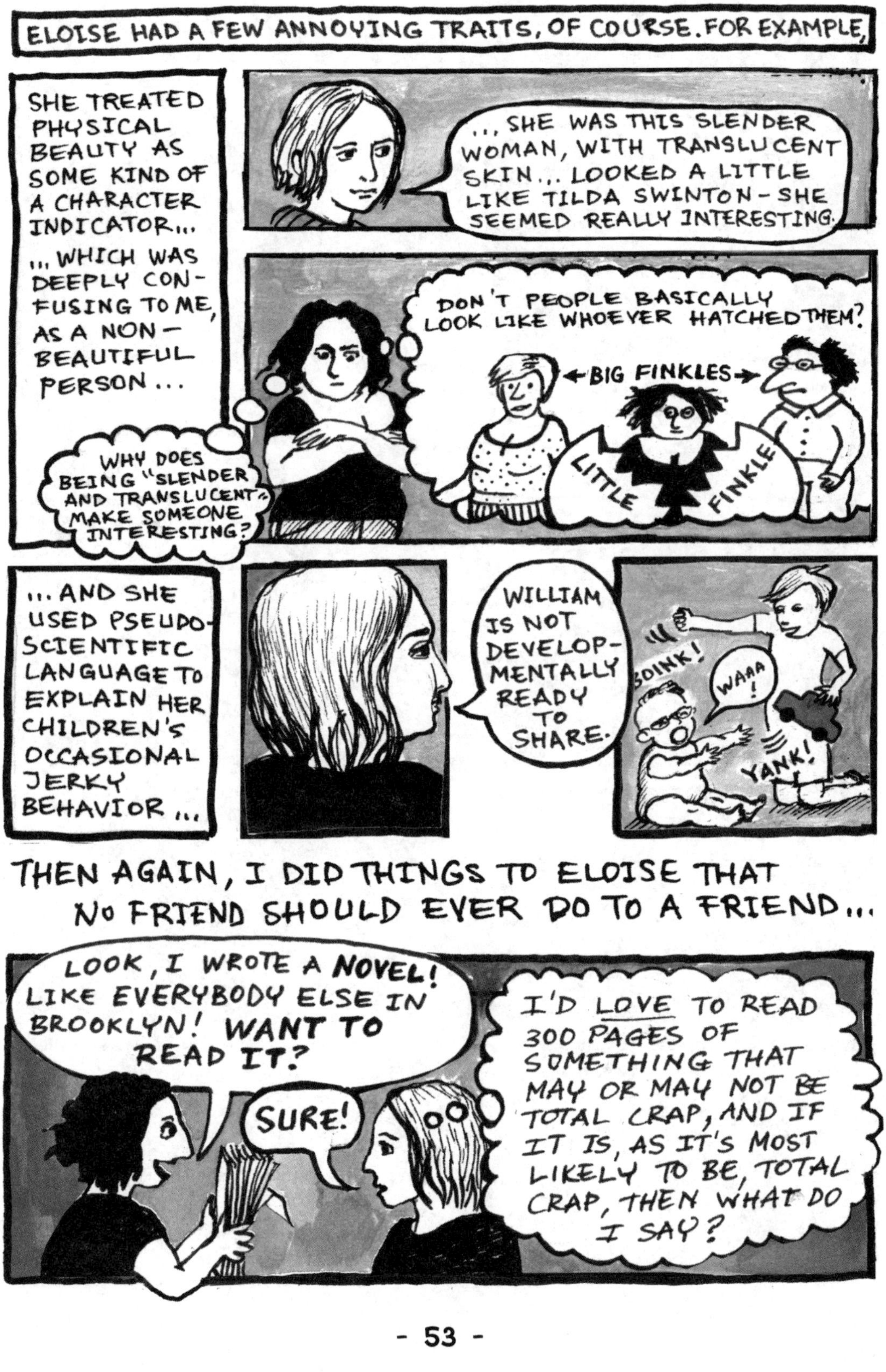
ELOISE HAD A FEW ANNOYING TRAITS, OF COURSE. FOR EXAMPLE,
SHE TREATED PHYSICAL BEAUTY AS SOME KIND OF A CHARACTER INDICATOR...
..., SHE WAS THIS SLENDER WOMAN, WITH TRANSLUCENT SKIN... LOOKED A LITTLE LIKE TILDA SWINTON - SHE SEEMED REALLY INTERESTING.
... WHICH WAS DEEPLY CONFUSING TO ME, AS A NON-BEAUTIFUL PERSON...
DON'T PEOPLE BASICALLY LOOK LIKE WHOEVER HATCHED THEM?
BIG FINKLES
LITTLE FINKLE
WHY DOES BEING "SLENDER AND TRANSLUCENT" MAKE SOMEONE INTERESTING?
... AND SHE USED PSEUDO-SCIENTIFIC LANGUAGE TO EXPLAIN HER CHILDREN'S OCCASIONAL JERKY BEHAVIOR...
WILLIAM IS NOT DEVELOPMENTALLY READY TO SHARE.
BOINK!
WAAA!
YANK!
THEN AGAIN, I DID THINGS TO ELOISE THAT NO FRIEND SHOULD EVER DO TO A FRIEND...
LOOK, I WROTE A NOVEL! LIKE EVERYBODY ELSE IN BROOKLYN! WANT TO READ IT?
SURE!
I'D LOVE TO READ 300 PAGES OF SOMETHING THAT MAY OR MAY NOT BE TOTAL CRAP, AND IF IT IS, AS IT'S MOST LIKELY TO BE, TOTAL CRAP, THEN WHAT DO I SAY?

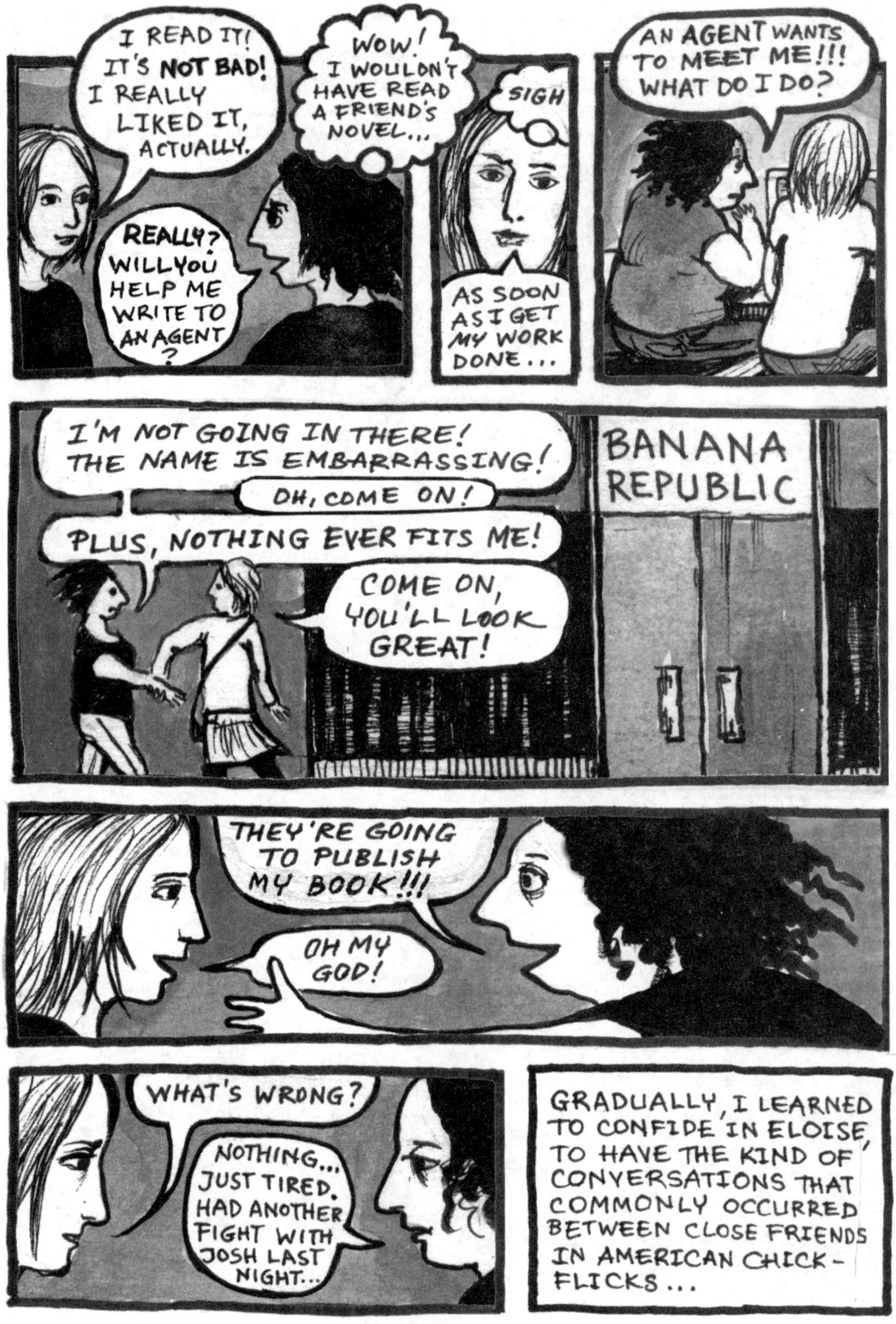
I READ IT! IT'S NOT BAD! I REALLY LIKED IT, ACTUALLY.
REALLY? WILL YOU HELP ME WRITE TO AN AGENT?
WOW! I WOULDN'T HAVE READ A FRIEND'S NOVEL...
SIGH
AS SOON AS I GET MY WORK DONE...
AN AGENT WANTS TO MEET ME!!! WHAT DO I DO?
I'M NOT GOING IN THERE! THE NAME IS EMBARRASSING!
OH, COME ON!
PLUS, NOTHING EVER FITS ME!
COME ON, YOU'LL LOOK GREAT!
BANANA REPUBLIC
THEY'RE GOING TO PUBLISH MY BOOK!!!
OH MY GOD!
WHAT'S WRONG?
NOTHING... JUST TIRED. HAD ANOTHER FIGHT WITH JOSH LAST NIGHT...
GRADUALLY, I LEARNED TO CONFIDE IN ELOISE, TO HAVE THE KIND OF CONVERSATIONS THAT COMMONLY OCCURRED BETWEEN CLOSE FRIENDS IN AMERICAN CHICK-FLICKS...

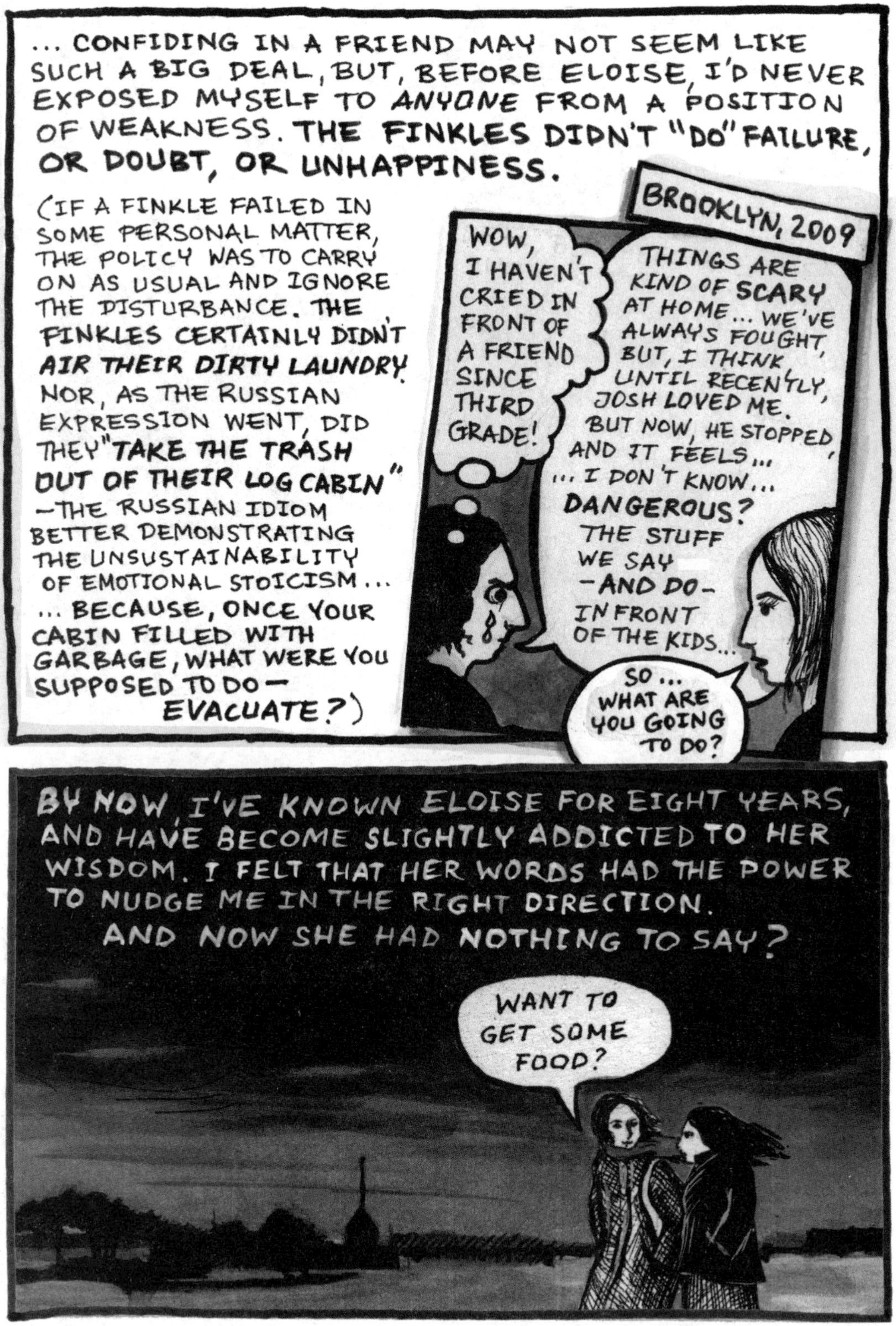
... CONFIDING IN A FRIEND MAY NOT SEEM LIKE SUCH A BIG DEAL, BUT, BEFORE ELOISE, I'D NEVER EXPOSED MYSELF TO ANYONE FROM A POSITION OF WEAKNESS. THE FINKLES DIDN'T "DO" FAILURE, OR DOUBT, OR UNHAPPINESS.
(IF A FINKLE FAILED IN SOME PERSONAL MATTER, THE POLICY WAS TO CARRY ON AS USUAL AND IGNORE THE DISTURBANCE. THE FINKLES CERTAINLY DIDN'T AIR THEIR DIRTY LAUNDRY. NOR, AS THE RUSSIAN EXPRESSION WENT, DID THEY "TAKE THE TRASH OUT OF THEIR LOG CABIN" —THE RUSSIAN IDIOM BETTER DEMONSTRATING THE UNSUSTAINABILITY OF EMOTIONAL STOICISM ...
... BECAUSE, ONCE YOUR CABIN FILLED WITH GARBAGE, WHAT WERE YOU SUPPOSED TO DO— EVACUATE?)
BROOKLYN, 2009
WOW, I HAVEN'T CRIED IN FRONT OF A FRIEND SINCE THIRD GRADE!
THINGS ARE KIND OF SCARY AT HOME... WE'VE ALWAYS FOUGHT, BUT, I THINK, UNTIL RECENTLY, JOSH LOVED ME. BUT NOW, HE STOPPED, AND IT FEELS... ... I DON'T KNOW... DANGEROUS? THE STUFF WE SAY —AND DO— IN FRONT OF THE KIDS...
SO... WHAT ARE YOU GOING TO DO?
BY NOW, I'VE KNOWN ELOISE FOR EIGHT YEARS, AND HAVE BECOME SLIGHTLY ADDICTED TO HER WISDOM. I FELT THAT HER WORDS HAD THE POWER TO NUDGE ME IN THE RIGHT DIRECTION.
AND NOW SHE HAD NOTHING TO SAY?
WANT TO GET SOME FOOD?

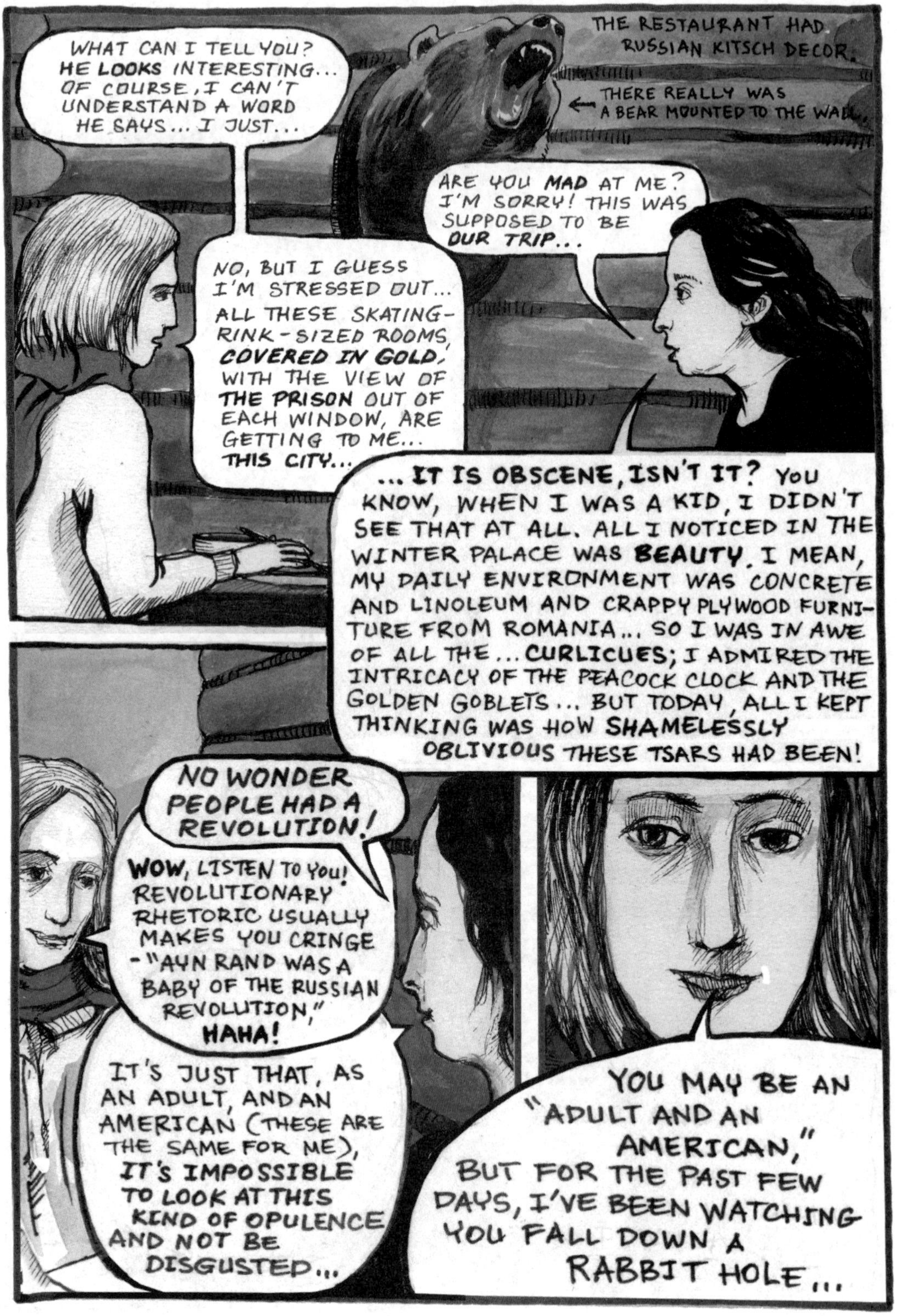
THE RESTAURANT HAD RUSSIAN KITSCH DECOR.
THERE REALLY WAS A BEAR MOUNTED TO THE WALL.
WHAT CAN I TELL YOU? HE LOOKS INTERESTING... OF COURSE, I CAN'T UNDERSTAND A WORD HE SAYS... I JUST...
ARE YOU MAD AT ME? I'M SORRY! THIS WAS SUPPOSED TO BE OUR TRIP...
NO, BUT I GUESS I'M STRESSED OUT... ALL THESE SKATING-RINK-SIZED ROOMS, COVERED IN GOLD, WITH THE VIEW OF THE PRISON OUT OF EACH WINDOW, ARE GETTING TO ME... THIS CITY...
...IT IS OBSCENE, ISN'T IT? YOU KNOW, WHEN I WAS A KID, I DIDN'T SEE THAT AT ALL. ALL I NOTICED IN THE WINTER PALACE WAS BEAUTY. I MEAN, MY DAILY ENVIRONMENT WAS CONCRETE AND LINOLEUM AND CRAPPY PLYWOOD FURNITURE FROM ROMANIA... SO I WAS IN AWE OF ALL THE... CURLICUES; I ADMIRED THE INTRICACY OF THE PEACOCK CLOCK AND THE GOLDEN GOBLETS... BUT TODAY, ALL I KEPT THINKING WAS HOW SHAMELESSLY OBLIVIOUS THESE TSARS HAD BEEN!
NO WONDER PEOPLE HAD A REVOLUTION!
WOW, LISTEN TO YOU! REVOLUTIONARY RHETORIC USUALLY MAKES YOU CRINGE - "AYN RAND WAS A BABY OF THE RUSSIAN REVOLUTION," HAHA!
IT'S JUST THAT, AS AN ADULT, AND AN AMERICAN (THESE ARE THE SAME FOR ME), IT'S IMPOSSIBLE TO LOOK AT THIS KIND OF OPULENCE AND NOT BE DISGUSTED...
YOU MAY BE AN "ADULT AND AN AMERICAN," BUT FOR THE PAST FEW DAYS, I'VE BEEN WATCHING YOU FALL DOWN A RABBIT HOLE...

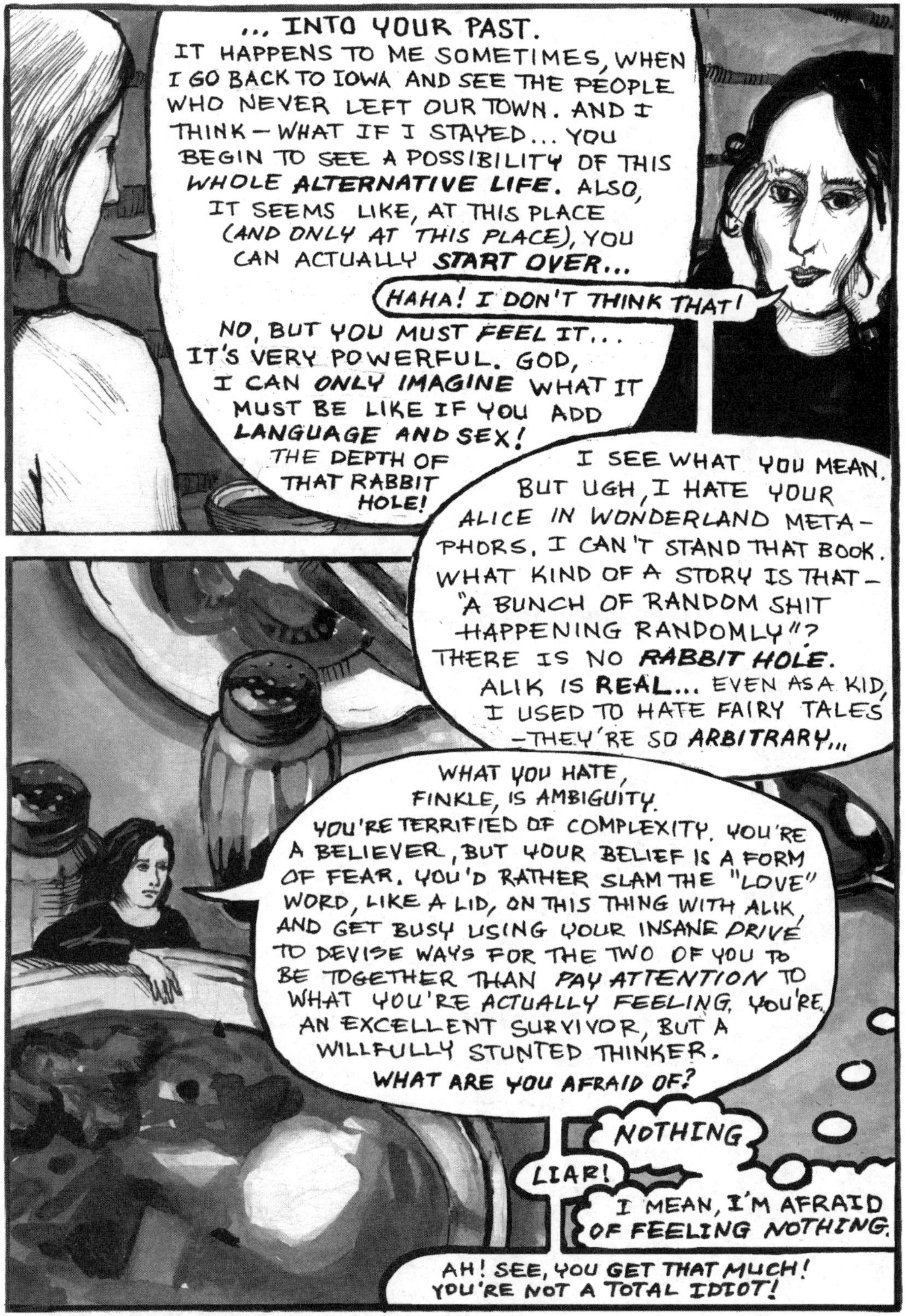

... INTO YOUR PAST. IT HAPPENS TO ME SOMETIMES, WHEN I GO BACK TO IOWA AND SEE THE PEOPLE WHO NEVER LEFT OUR TOWN. AND I THINK — WHAT IF I STAYED... YOU BEGIN TO SEE A POSSIBILITY OF THIS WHOLE ALTERNATIVE LIFE. ALSO, IT SEEMS LIKE, AT THIS PLACE (AND ONLY AT THIS PLACE), YOU CAN ACTUALLY START OVER...
HAHA! I DON'T THINK THAT!
NO, BUT YOU MUST FEEL IT... IT'S VERY POWERFUL. GOD, I CAN ONLY IMAGINE WHAT IT MUST BE LIKE IF YOU ADD LANGUAGE AND SEX! THE DEPTH OF THAT RABBIT HOLE!
I SEE WHAT YOU MEAN. BUT UGH, I HATE YOUR ALICE IN WONDERLAND META-PHORS. I CAN'T STAND THAT BOOK. WHAT KIND OF A STORY IS THAT — "A BUNCH OF RANDOM SHIT HAPPENING RANDOMLY"? THERE IS NO RABBIT HOLE. ALIK IS REAL... EVEN AS A KID, I USED TO HATE FAIRY TALES — THEY'RE SO ARBITRARY...
WHAT YOU HATE, FINKLE, IS AMBIGUITY. YOU'RE TERRIFIED OF COMPLEXITY. YOU'RE A BELIEVER, BUT YOUR BELIEF IS A FORM OF FEAR. YOU'D RATHER SLAM THE "LOVE" WORD, LIKE A LID, ON THIS THING WITH ALIK, AND GET BUSY USING YOUR INSANE DRIVE TO DEVISE WAYS FOR THE TWO OF YOU TO BE TOGETHER THAN PAY ATTENTION TO WHAT YOU'RE ACTUALLY FEELING. YOU'RE AN EXCELLENT SURVIVOR, BUT A WILLFULLY STUNTED THINKER. WHAT ARE YOU AFRAID OF?
NOTHING
LIAR!
I MEAN, I'M AFRAID OF FEELING NOTHING.
AH! SEE, YOU GET THAT MUCH! YOU'RE NOT A TOTAL IDIOT!

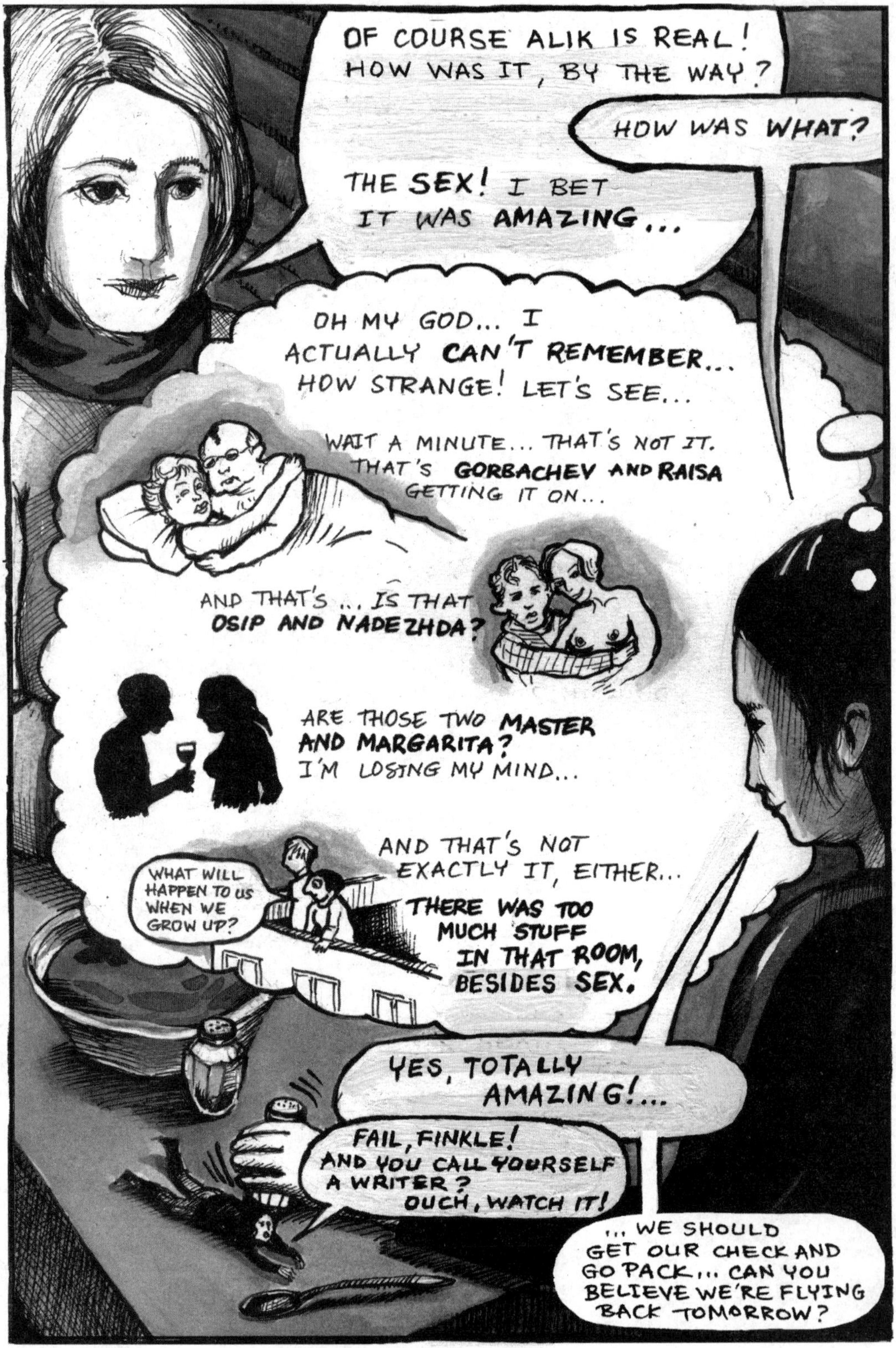
OF COURSE ALIK IS REAL! HOW WAS IT, BY THE WAY?
HOW WAS WHAT?
THE SEX! I BET IT WAS AMAZING...
OH MY GOD... I ACTUALLY CAN'T REMEMBER... HOW STRANGE! LET'S SEE...
WAIT A MINUTE... THAT'S NOT IT. THAT'S GORBACHEV AND RAISA GETTING IT ON...
AND THAT'S ... IS THAT OSIP AND NADEZHDA?
ARE THOSE TWO MASTER AND MARGARITA? I'M LOSING MY MIND...
AND THAT'S NOT EXACTLY IT, EITHER...
WHAT WILL HAPPEN TO US WHEN WE GROW UP?
THERE WAS TOO MUCH STUFF IN THAT ROOM, BESIDES SEX.
YES, TOTALLY AMAZING!...
FAIL, FINKLE! AND YOU CALL YOURSELF A WRITER? OUCH, WATCH IT!
... WE SHOULD GET OUR CHECK AND GO PACK... CAN YOU BELIEVE WE'RE FLYING BACK TOMORROW?

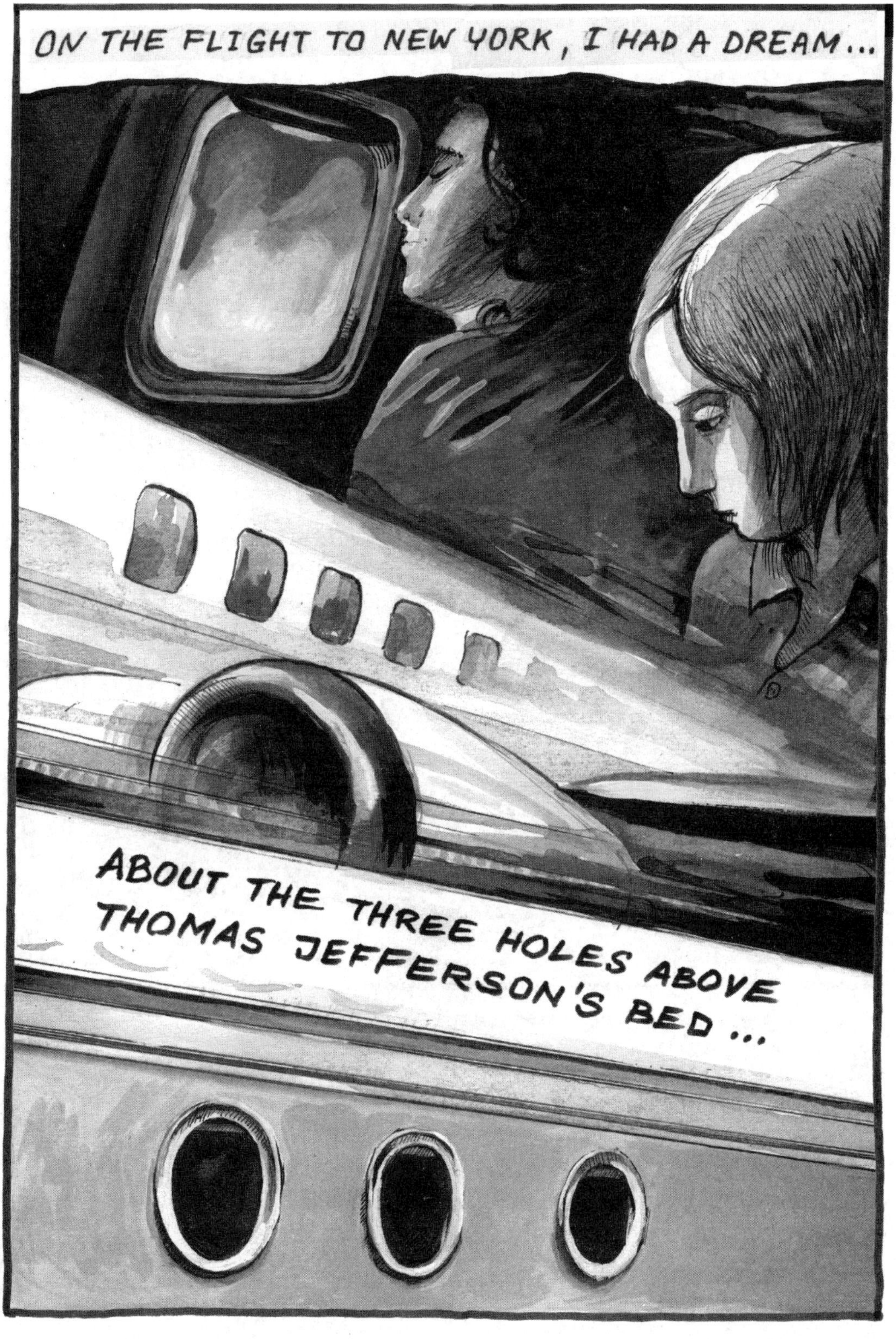
ON THE FLIGHT TO NEW YORK, I HAD A DREAM...
ABOUT THE THREE HOLES ABOVE THOMAS JEFFERSON'S BED...

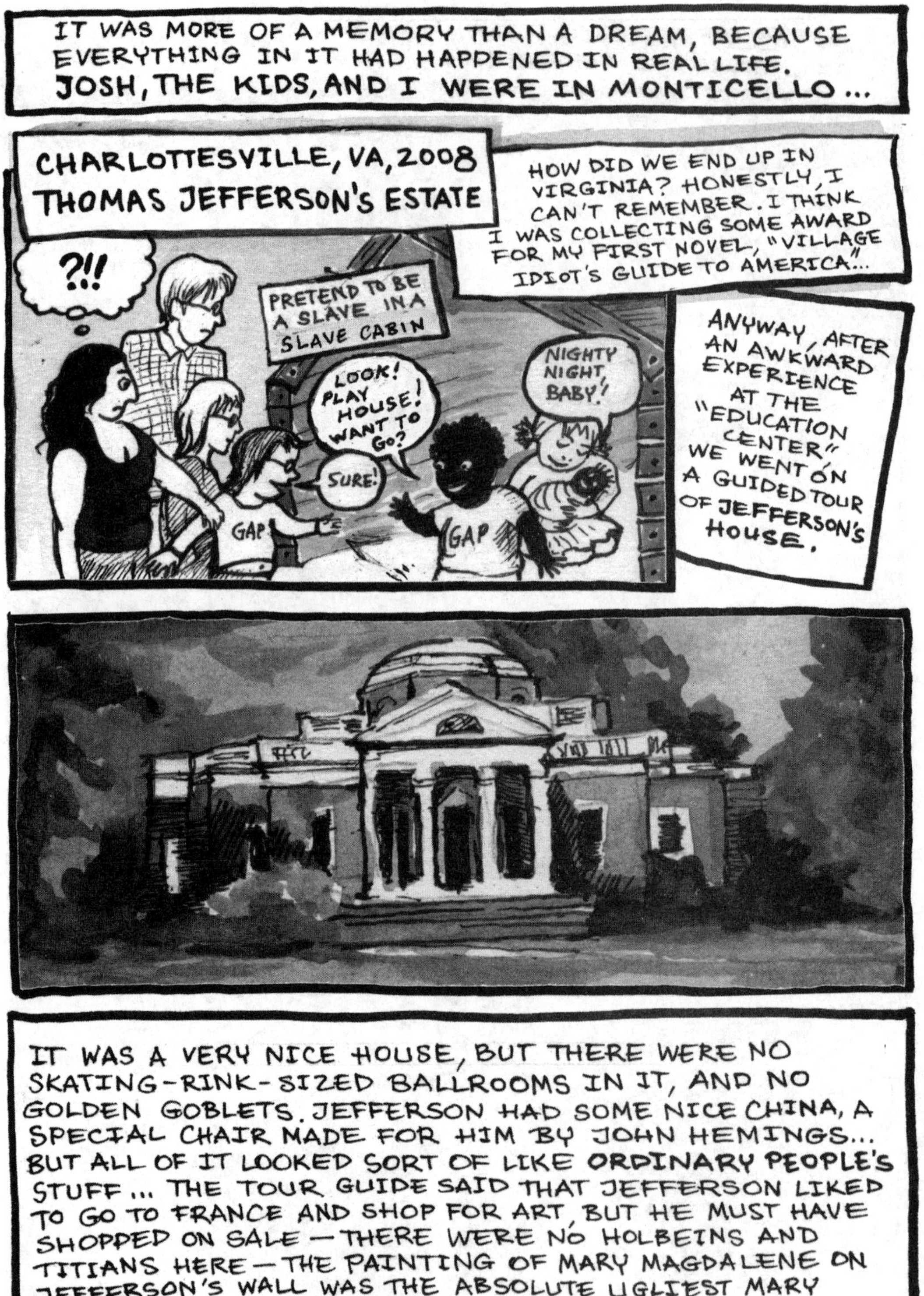
IT WAS MORE OF A MEMORY THAN A DREAM, BECAUSE EVERYTHING IN IT HAD HAPPENED IN REAL LIFE. JOSH, THE KIDS, AND I WERE IN MONTICELLO...
CHARLOTTESVILLE, VA, 2008
THOMAS JEFFERSON'S ESTATE
HOW DID WE END UP IN VIRGINIA? HONESTLY, I CAN'T REMEMBER. I THINK I WAS COLLECTING SOME AWARD FOR MY FIRST NOVEL, "VILLAGE IDIOT'S GUIDE TO AMERICA"...
?!!
PRETEND TO BE A SLAVE IN A SLAVE CABIN
LOOK! PLAY HOUSE! WANT TO GO?
SURE!
NIGHTY NIGHT, BABY!
GAP
GAP
ANYWAY, AFTER AN AWKWARD EXPERIENCE AT THE "EDUCATION CENTER" WE WENT ON A GUIDED TOUR OF JEFFERSON'S HOUSE.
IT WAS A VERY NICE HOUSE, BUT THERE WERE NO SKATING-RINK-SIZED BALLROOMS IN IT, AND NO GOLDEN GOBLETS. JEFFERSON HAD SOME NICE CHINA, A SPECIAL CHAIR MADE FOR HIM BY JOHN HEMINGS... BUT ALL OF IT LOOKED SORT OF LIKE ORDINARY PEOPLE'S STUFF... THE TOUR GUIDE SAID THAT JEFFERSON LIKED TO GO TO FRANCE AND SHOP FOR ART, BUT HE MUST HAVE SHOPPED ON SALE — THERE WERE NO HOLBEINS AND TITIANS HERE — THE PAINTING OF MARY MAGDALENE ON JEFFERSON'S WALL WAS THE ABSOLUTE UGLIEST MARY MAGDALENE I'D EVER SEEN...

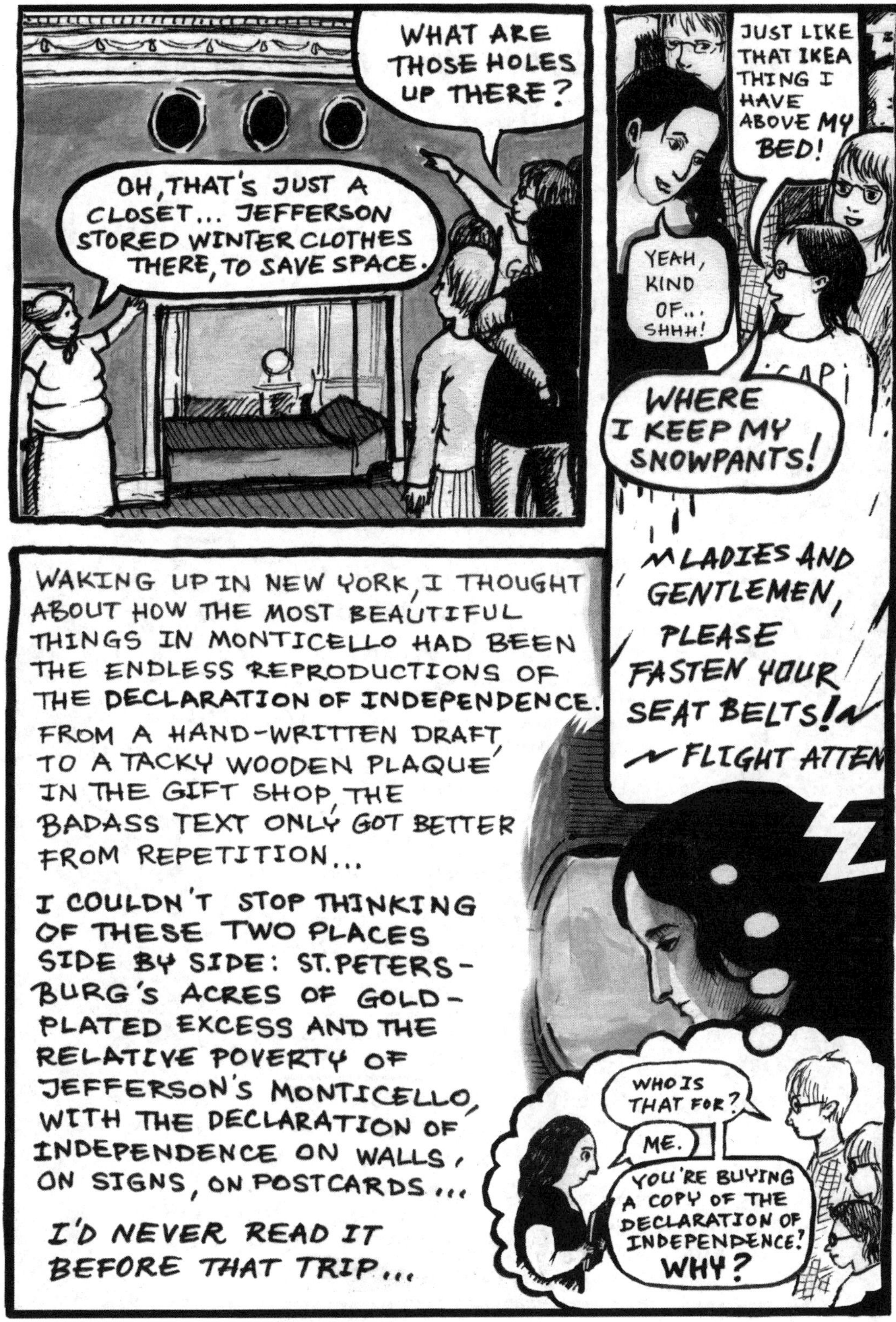
WHAT ARE THOSE HOLES UP THERE?
OH, THAT'S JUST A CLOSET... JEFFERSON STORED WINTER CLOTHES THERE, TO SAVE SPACE.
JUST LIKE THAT IKEA THING I HAVE ABOVE MY BED!
YEAH, KIND OF... SHHH!
WHERE I KEEP MY SNOWPANTS!
WAKING UP IN NEW YORK, I THOUGHT ABOUT HOW THE MOST BEAUTIFUL THINGS IN MONTICELLO HAD BEEN THE ENDLESS REPRODUCTIONS OF THE DECLARATION OF INDEPENDENCE.
FROM A HAND-WRITTEN DRAFT TO A TACKY WOODEN PLAQUE IN THE GIFT SHOP, THE BADASS TEXT ONLY GOT BETTER FROM REPETITION...
I COULDN'T STOP THINKING OF THESE TWO PLACES SIDE BY SIDE: ST. PETERSBURG'S ACRES OF GOLD-PLATED EXCESS AND THE RELATIVE POVERTY OF JEFFERSON'S MONTICELLO, WITH THE DECLARATION OF INDEPENDENCE ON WALLS, ON SIGNS, ON POSTCARDS...
I'D NEVER READ IT BEFORE THAT TRIP...
LADIES AND GENTLEMEN, PLEASE FASTEN YOUR SEAT BELTS!
FLIGHT ATTEN
WHO IS THAT FOR?
ME.
YOU'RE BUYING A COPY OF THE DECLARATION OF INDEPENDENCE? WHY?

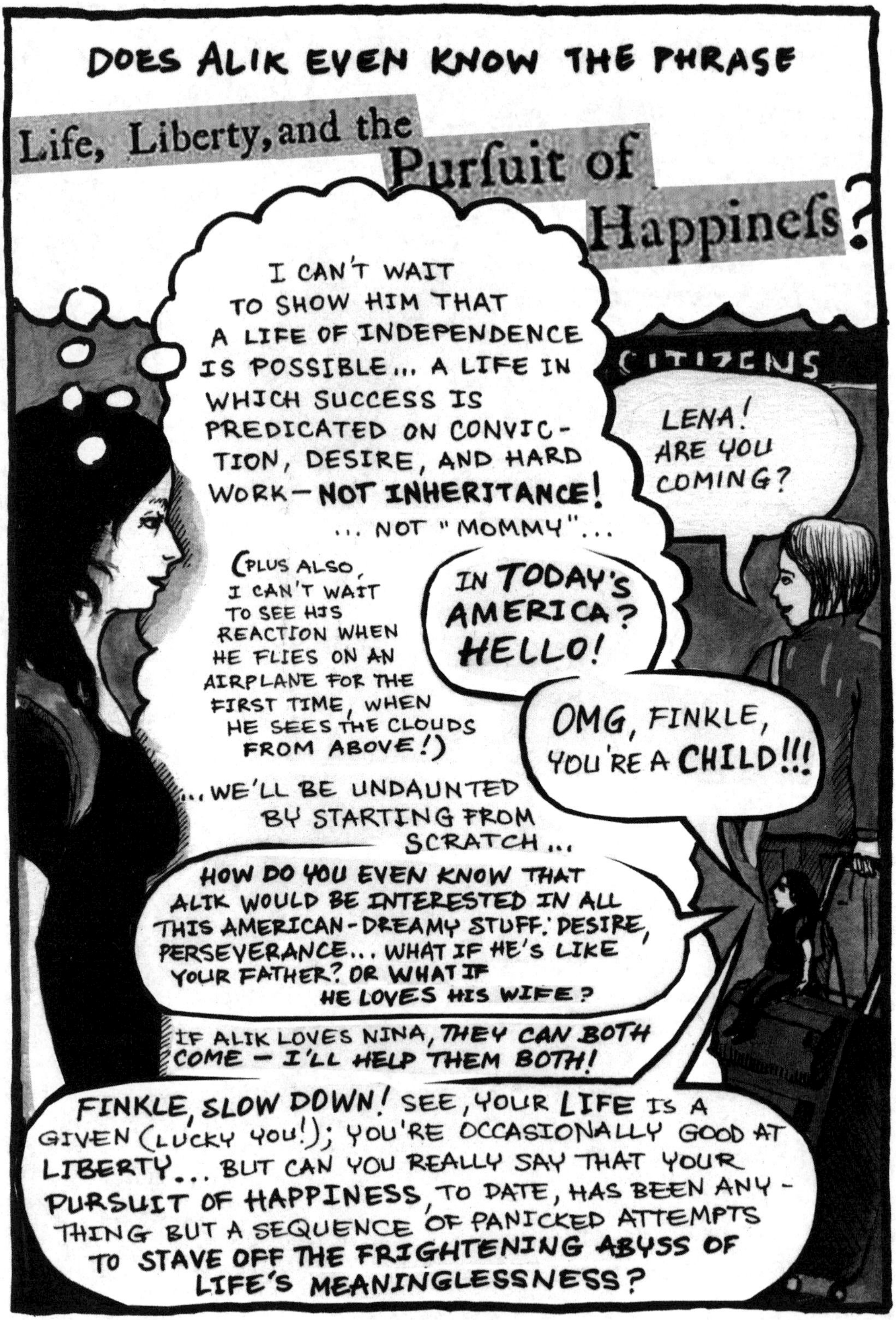
DOES ALIK EVEN KNOW THE PHRASE
Life, Liberty, and the Purſuit of Happineſs?
I CAN'T WAIT TO SHOW HIM THAT A LIFE OF INDEPENDENCE IS POSSIBLE... A LIFE IN WHICH SUCCESS IS PREDICATED ON CONVICTION, DESIRE, AND HARD WORK—NOT INHERITANCE! ... NOT "MOMMY"...
(PLUS ALSO, I CAN'T WAIT TO SEE HIS REACTION WHEN HE FLIES ON AN AIRPLANE FOR THE FIRST TIME, WHEN HE SEES THE CLOUDS FROM ABOVE!)
...WE'LL BE UNDAUNTED BY STARTING FROM SCRATCH...
CITIZENS
LENA! ARE YOU COMING?
IN TODAY'S AMERICA? HELLO!
OMG, FINKLE, YOU'RE A CHILD!!!
HOW DO YOU EVEN KNOW THAT ALIK WOULD BE INTERESTED IN ALL THIS AMERICAN-DREAMY STUFF: DESIRE, PERSEVERANCE... WHAT IF HE'S LIKE YOUR FATHER? OR WHAT IF HE LOVES HIS WIFE?
IF ALIK LOVES NINA, THEY CAN BOTH COME—I'LL HELP THEM BOTH!
FINKLE, SLOW DOWN! SEE, YOUR LIFE IS A GIVEN (LUCKY YOU!); YOU'RE OCCASIONALLY GOOD AT LIBERTY... BUT CAN YOU REALLY SAY THAT YOUR PURSUIT OF HAPPINESS, TO DATE, HAS BEEN ANYTHING BUT A SEQUENCE OF PANICKED ATTEMPTS TO STAVE OFF THE FRIGHTENING ABYSS OF LIFE'S MEANINGLESSNESS?

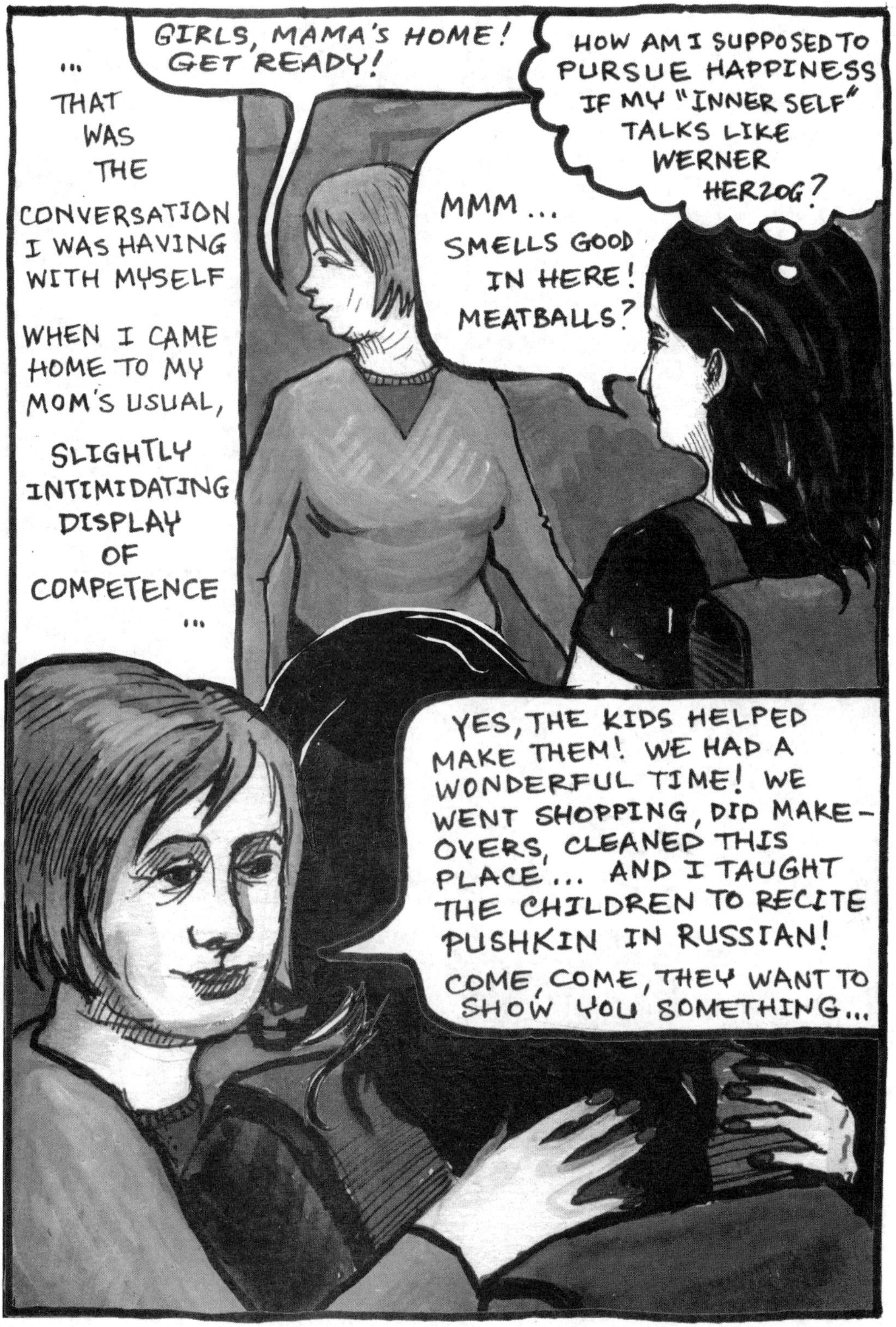
... THAT WAS THE CONVERSATION I WAS HAVING WITH MYSELF
GIRLS, MAMA'S HOME! GET READY!
HOW AM I SUPPOSED TO PURSUE HAPPINESS IF MY "INNER SELF" TALKS LIKE WERNER HERZOG?
MMM... SMELLS GOOD IN HERE! MEATBALLS?
WHEN I CAME HOME TO MY MOM'S USUAL,
SLIGHTLY INTIMIDATING DISPLAY OF COMPETENCE ...
YES, THE KIDS HELPED MAKE THEM! WE HAD A WONDERFUL TIME! WE WENT SHOPPING, DID MAKE-OVERS, CLEANED THIS PLACE... AND I TAUGHT THE CHILDREN TO RECITE PUSHKIN IN RUSSIAN!
COME, COME, THEY WANT TO SHOW YOU SOMETHING...

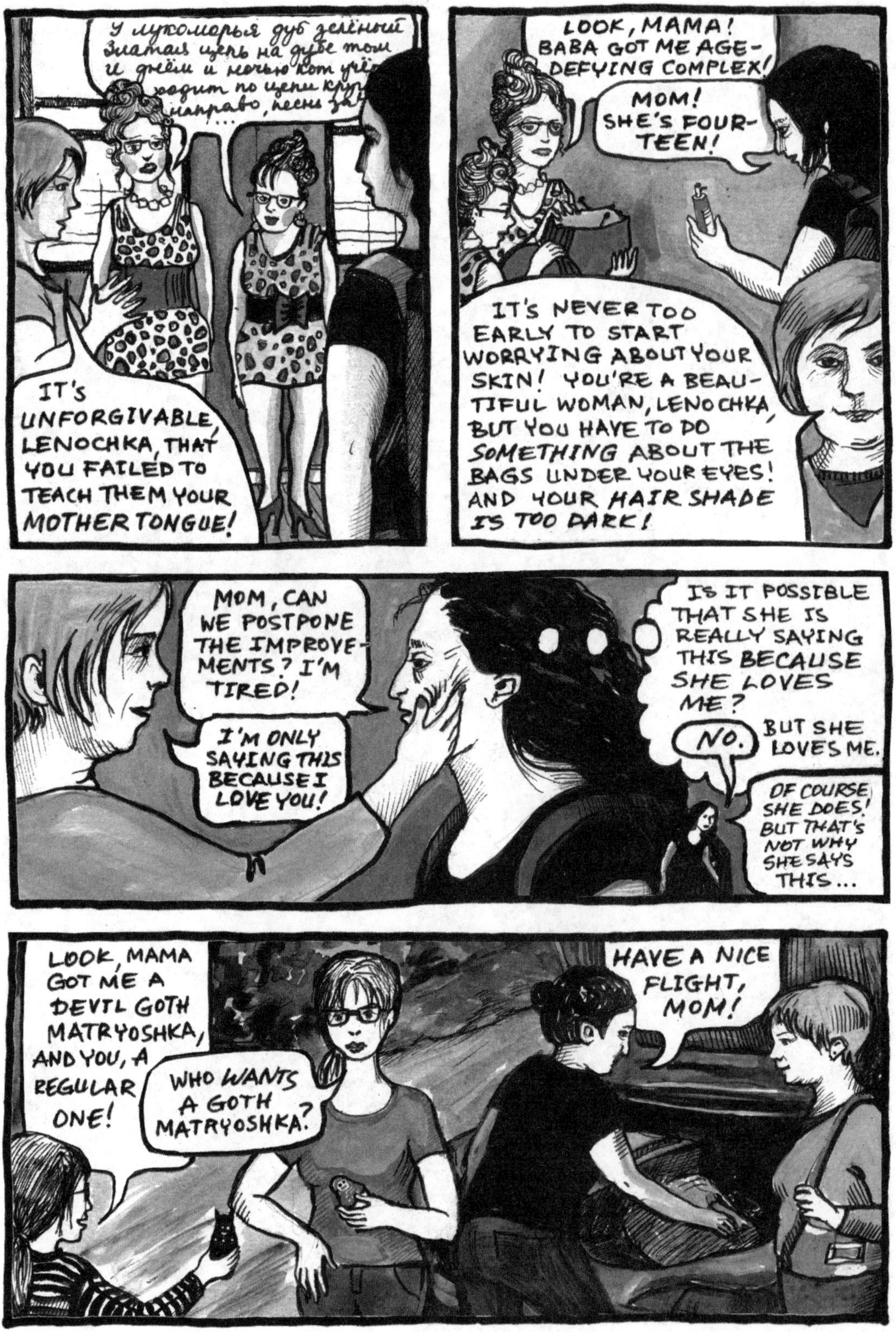

У лукоморья дуб зелёный Златая цепь на дубе том И днём и ночью кот уч ходит по цепи кр направо, песнь з ...
IT'S UNFORGIVABLE, LENOCHKA, THAT YOU FAILED TO TEACH THEM YOUR MOTHER TONGUE!
LOOK, MAMA! BABA GOT ME AGE-DEFYING COMPLEX!
MOM! SHE'S FOURTEEN!
IT'S NEVER TOO EARLY TO START WORRYING ABOUT YOUR SKIN! YOU'RE A BEAUTIFUL WOMAN, LENOCHKA, BUT YOU HAVE TO DO *SOMETHING* ABOUT THE BAGS UNDER YOUR EYES! AND YOUR *HAIR SHADE* IS TOO DARK!
MOM, CAN WE POSTPONE THE IMPROVEMENTS? I'M TIRED!
I'M ONLY SAYING THIS BECAUSE I LOVE YOU!
IS IT POSSIBLE THAT SHE IS REALLY SAYING THIS BECAUSE SHE LOVES ME?
NO.
BUT SHE LOVES ME.
OF COURSE SHE DOES! BUT THAT'S NOT WHY SHE SAYS THIS...
LOOK, MAMA GOT ME A DEVIL GOTH MATRYOSHKA, AND YOU, A REGULAR ONE!
WHO *WANTS* A GOTH MATRYOSHKA?
HAVE A NICE FLIGHT, MOM!

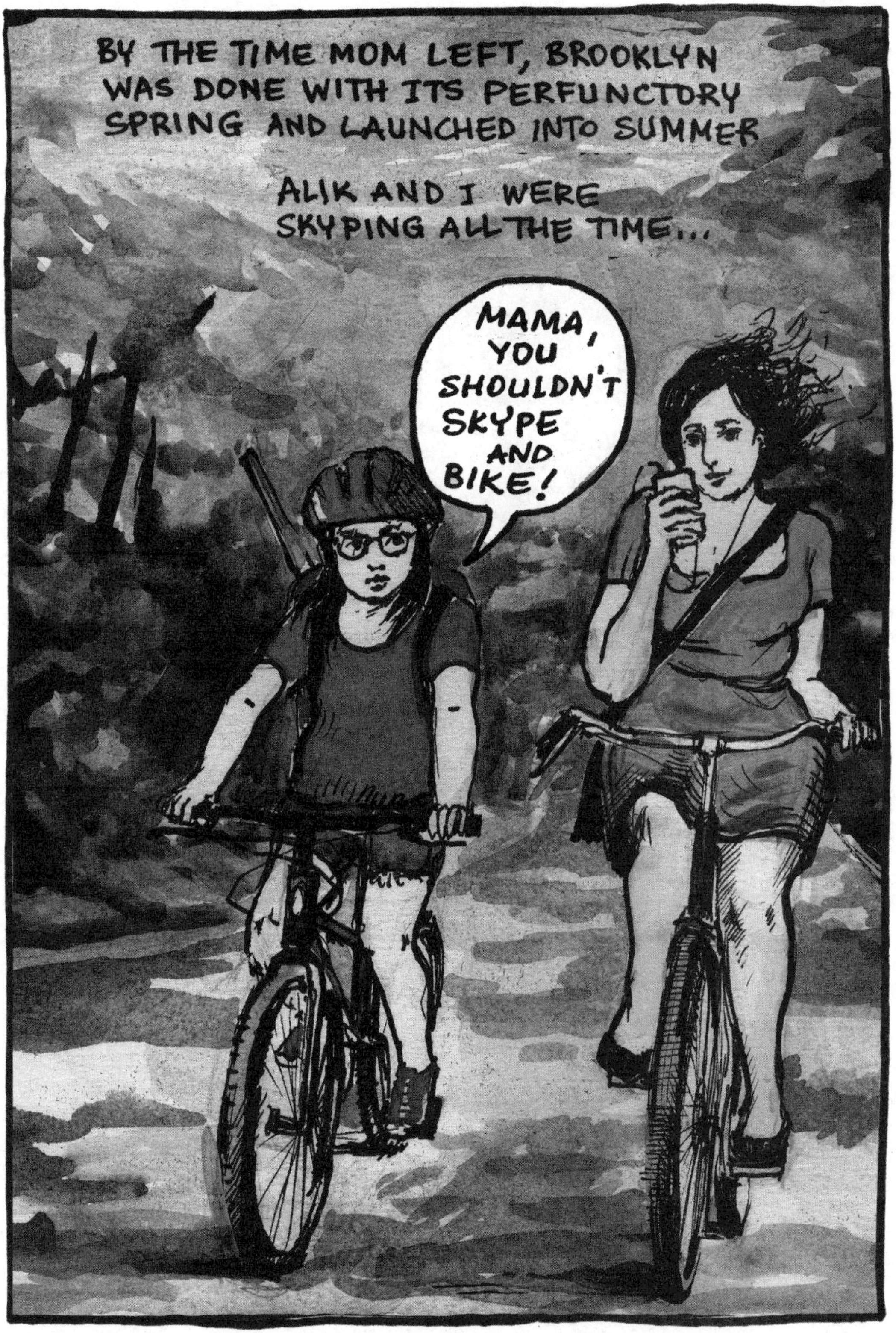
BY THE TIME MOM LEFT, BROOKLYN WAS DONE WITH ITS PERFUNCTORY SPRING AND LAUNCHED INTO SUMMER
ALIK AND I WERE SKYPING ALL THE TIME...
MAMA, YOU SHOULDN'T SKYPE AND BIKE!

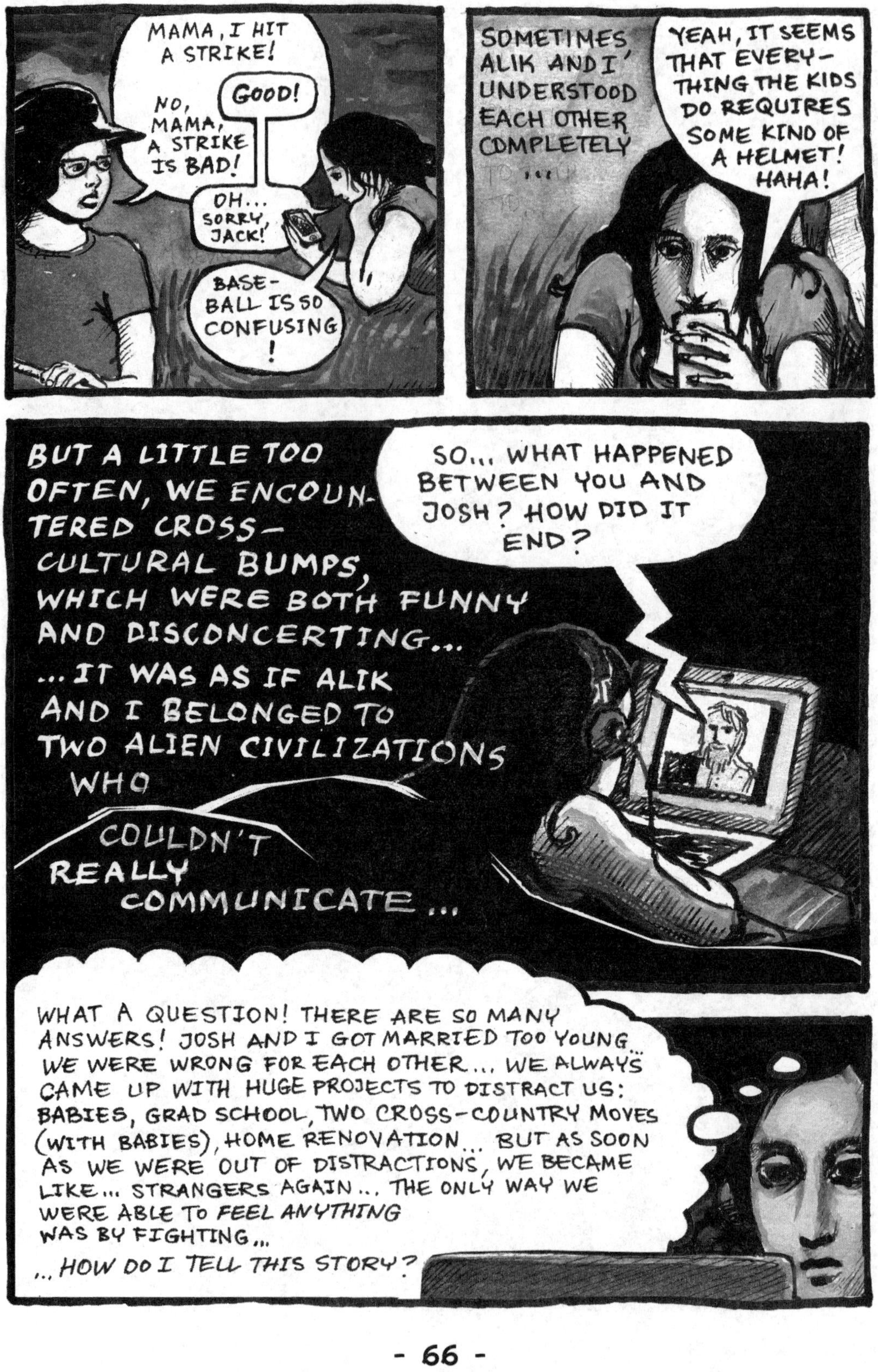

MAMA, I HIT A STRIKE!
GOOD!
NO, MAMA, A STRIKE IS BAD!
OH... SORRY, JACK!
BASE-BALL IS SO CONFUSING!
SOMETIMES ALIK AND I UNDERSTOOD EACH OTHER COMPLETELY
YEAH, IT SEEMS THAT EVERY-THING THE KIDS DO REQUIRES SOME KIND OF A HELMET! HAHA!
BUT A LITTLE TOO OFTEN, WE ENCOUN-TERED CROSS-CULTURAL BUMPS, WHICH WERE BOTH FUNNY AND DISCONCERTING...
...IT WAS AS IF ALIK AND I BELONGED TO TWO ALIEN CIVILIZATIONS WHO
COULDN'T REALLY COMMUNICATE...
SO... WHAT HAPPENED BETWEEN YOU AND JOSH? HOW DID IT END?
WHAT A QUESTION! THERE ARE SO MANY ANSWERS! JOSH AND I GOT MARRIED TOO YOUNG... WE WERE WRONG FOR EACH OTHER... WE ALWAYS CAME UP WITH HUGE PROJECTS TO DISTRACT US: BABIES, GRAD SCHOOL, TWO CROSS-COUNTRY MOVES (WITH BABIES), HOME RENOVATION... BUT AS SOON AS WE WERE OUT OF DISTRACTIONS, WE BECAME LIKE... STRANGERS AGAIN... THE ONLY WAY WE WERE ABLE TO *FEEL ANYTHING* WAS BY FIGHTING...
...HOW DO I TELL THIS STORY?

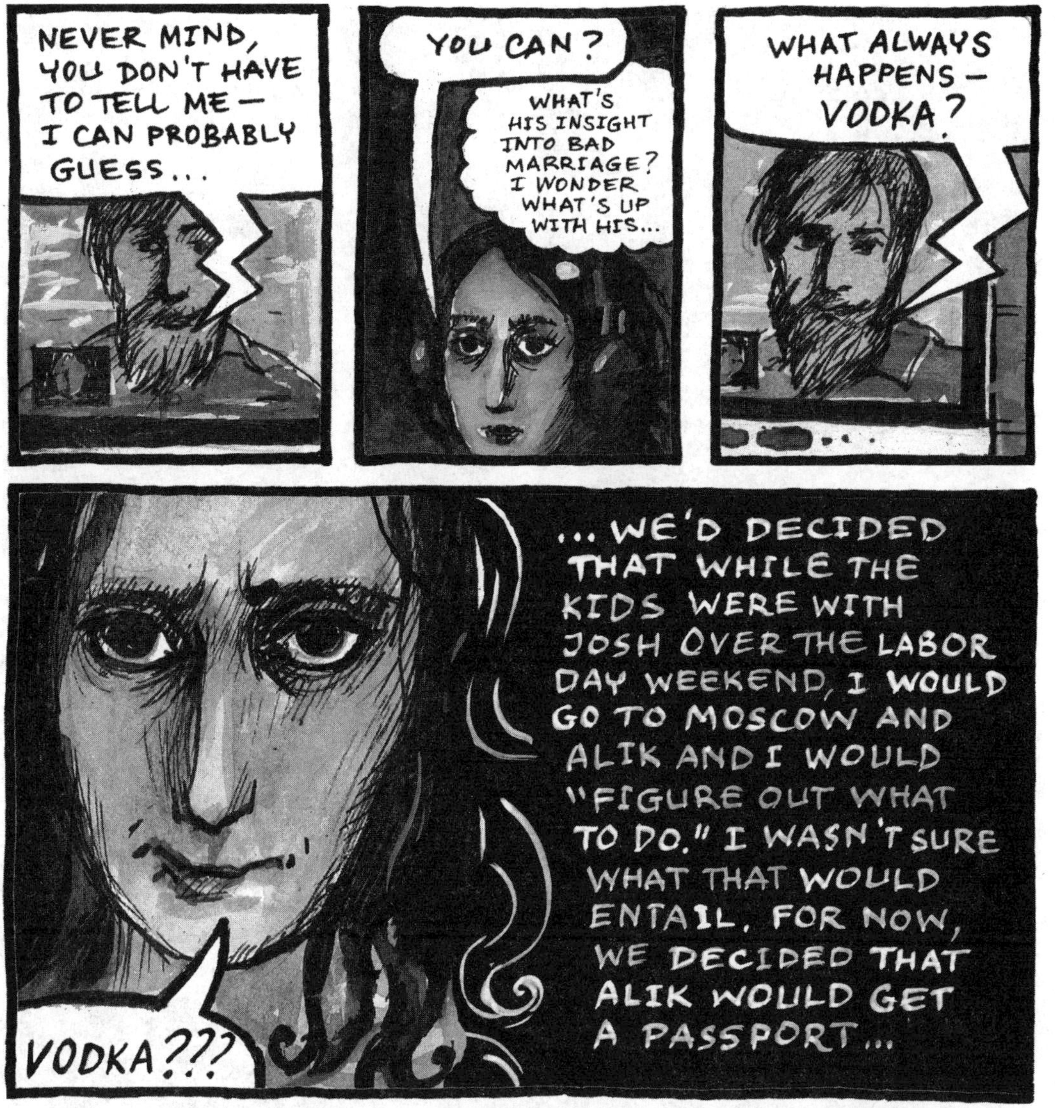
NEVER MIND, YOU DON'T HAVE TO TELL ME — I CAN PROBABLY GUESS...
YOU CAN?
WHAT'S HIS INSIGHT INTO BAD MARRIAGE? I WONDER WHAT'S UP WITH HIS...
WHAT ALWAYS HAPPENS — VODKA?
...WE'D DECIDED THAT WHILE THE KIDS WERE WITH JOSH OVER THE LABOR DAY WEEKEND, I WOULD GO TO MOSCOW AND ALIK AND I WOULD "FIGURE OUT WHAT TO DO." I WASN'T SURE WHAT THAT WOULD ENTAIL. FOR NOW, WE DECIDED THAT ALIK WOULD GET A PASSPORT...
VODKA???

...BUT EVERY TIME I TRIED TO TALK ABOUT THAT, HE VEERED INTO SOME PRETTY BUT VAGUE METAPHOR... A WAY OF TALKING THAT SEEMED SO CHARMING IN ST. PETERSBURG WAS SLIGHTLY IRRITATING OVER SKYPE.

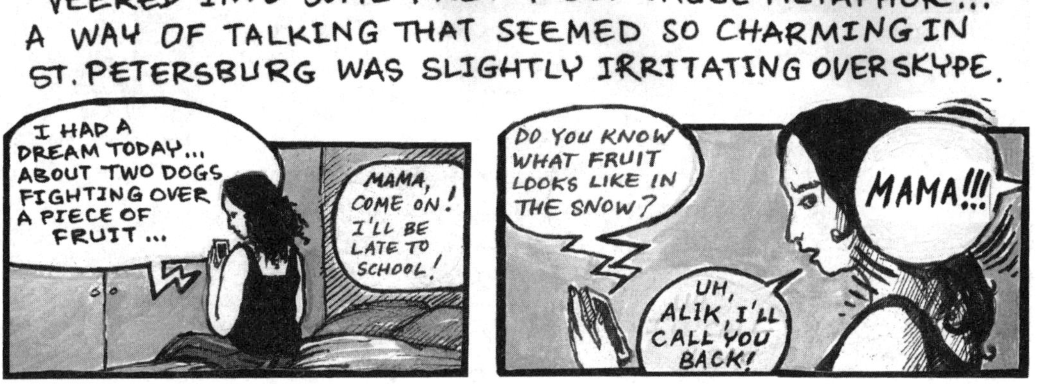
I HAD A DREAM TODAY... ABOUT TWO DOGS FIGHTING OVER A PIECE OF FRUIT...
MAMA, COME ON! I'LL BE LATE TO SCHOOL!
DO YOU KNOW WHAT FRUIT LOOKS LIKE IN THE SNOW?
MAMA!!!
UH, ALIK, I'LL CALL YOU BACK!

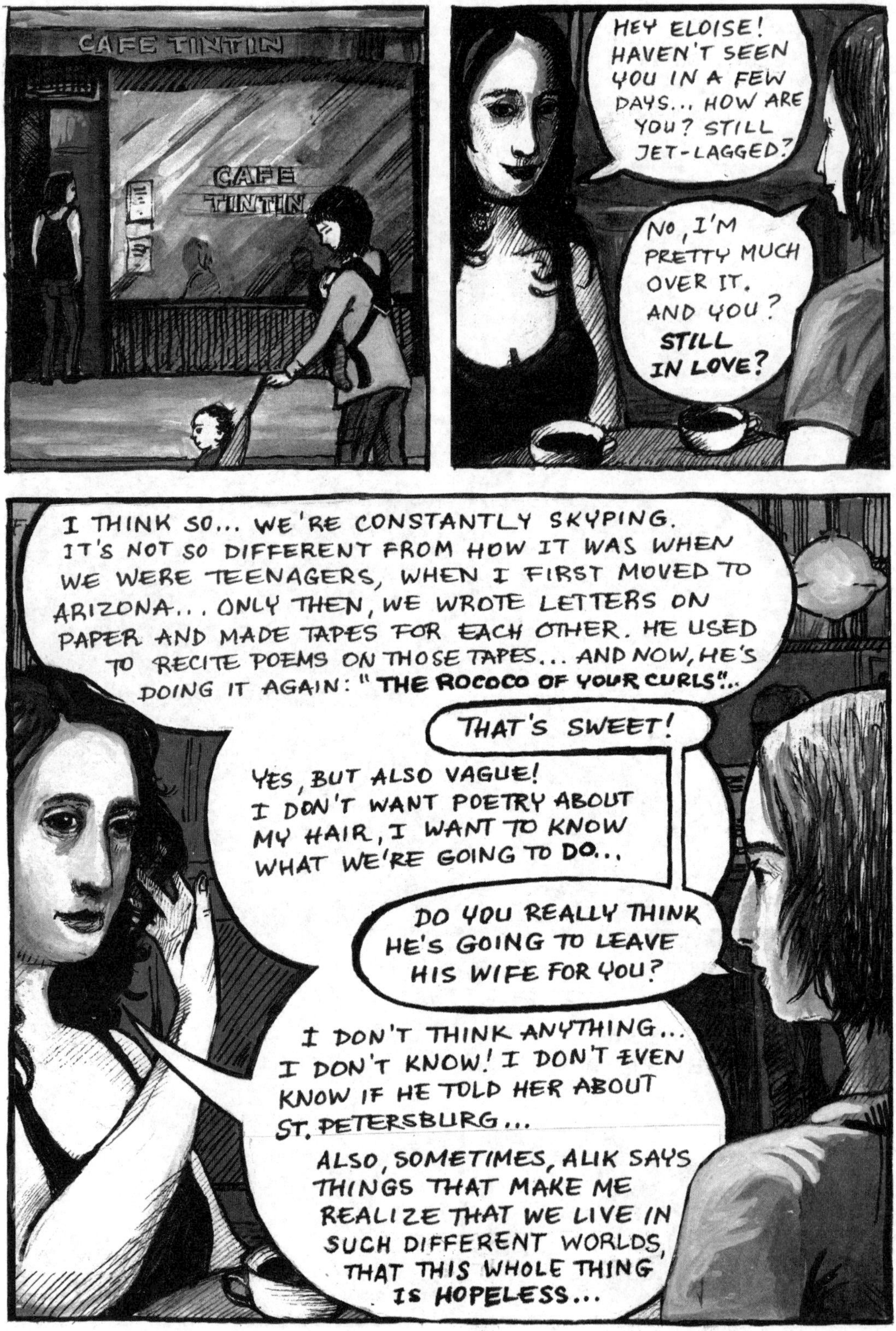
CAFE TINTIN
CAFE TINTIN
HEY ELOISE! HAVEN'T SEEN YOU IN A FEW DAYS... HOW ARE YOU? STILL JET-LAGGED?
NO, I'M PRETTY MUCH OVER IT. AND YOU? STILL IN LOVE?
I THINK SO... WE'RE CONSTANTLY SKYPING. IT'S NOT SO DIFFERENT FROM HOW IT WAS WHEN WE WERE TEENAGERS, WHEN I FIRST MOVED TO ARIZONA... ONLY THEN, WE WROTE LETTERS ON PAPER AND MADE TAPES FOR EACH OTHER. HE USED TO RECITE POEMS ON THOSE TAPES... AND NOW, HE'S DOING IT AGAIN: "THE ROCOCO OF YOUR CURLS"..
THAT'S SWEET!
YES, BUT ALSO VAGUE! I DON'T WANT POETRY ABOUT MY HAIR, I WANT TO KNOW WHAT WE'RE GOING TO DO...
DO YOU REALLY THINK HE'S GOING TO LEAVE HIS WIFE FOR YOU?
I DON'T THINK ANYTHING... I DON'T KNOW! I DON'T EVEN KNOW IF HE TOLD HER ABOUT ST. PETERSBURG...
ALSO, SOMETIMES, ALIK SAYS THINGS THAT MAKE ME REALIZE THAT WE LIVE IN SUCH DIFFERENT WORLDS, THAT THIS WHOLE THING IS HOPELESS...

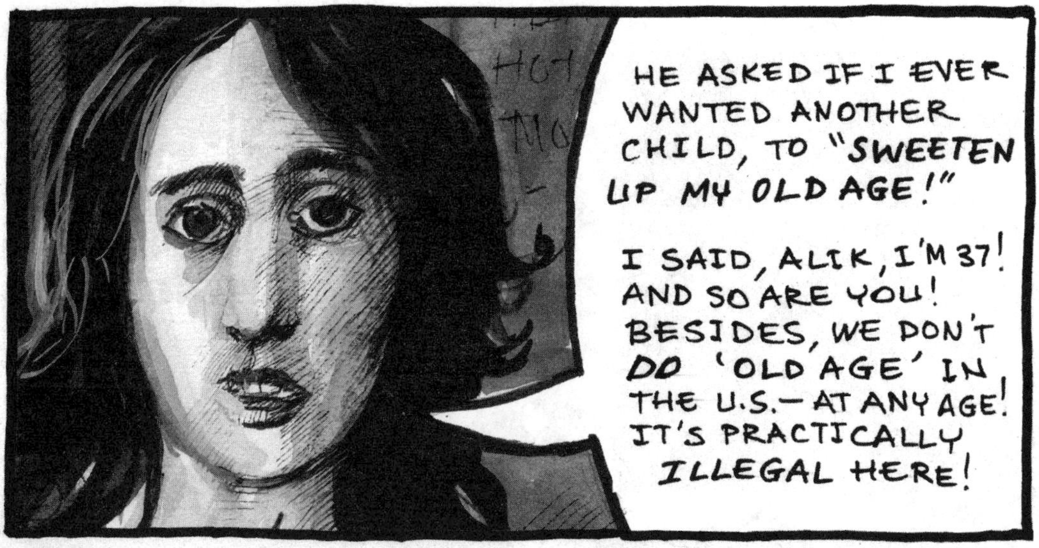
HE ASKED IF I EVER WANTED ANOTHER CHILD, TO "SWEETEN UP MY OLD AGE!"
I SAID, ALIK, I'M 37! AND SO ARE YOU! BESIDES, WE DON'T DO 'OLD AGE' IN THE U.S.– AT ANY AGE! IT'S PRACTICALLY ILLEGAL HERE!

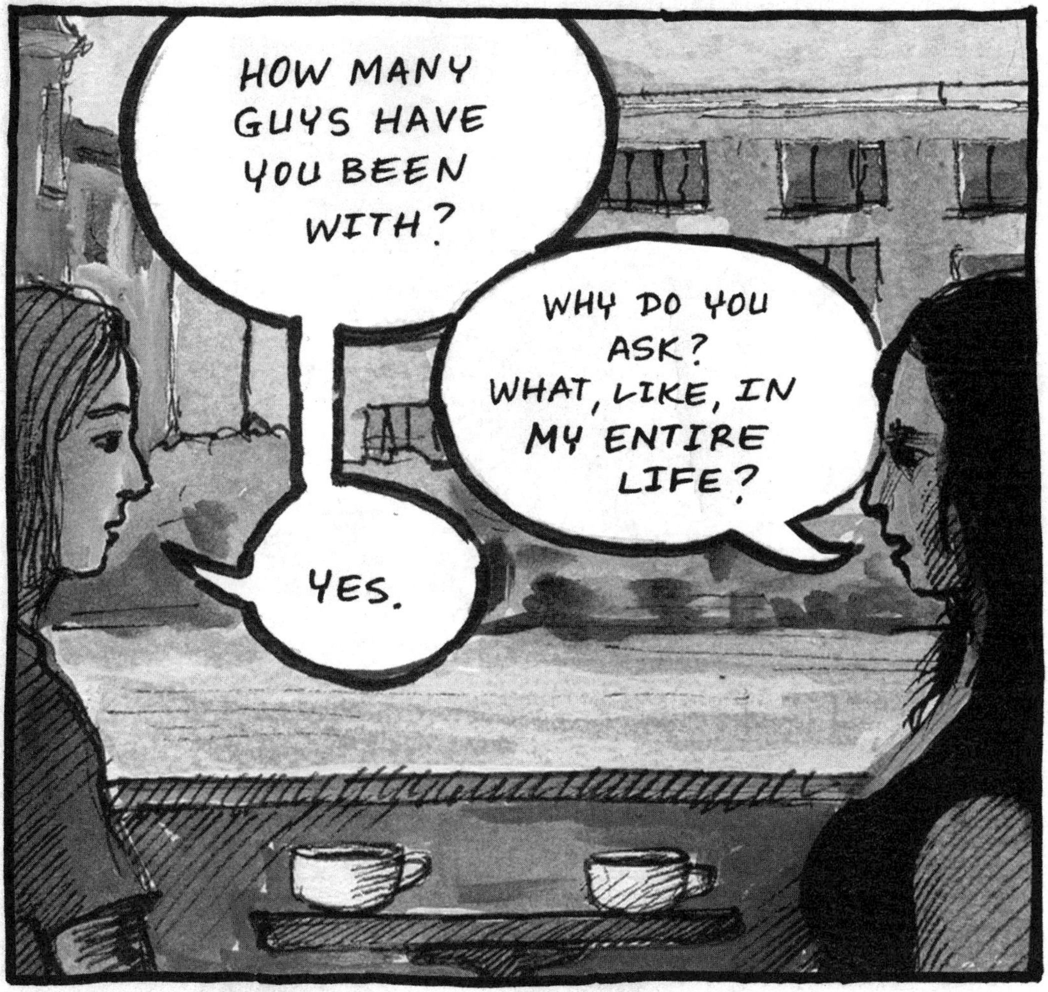
HOW MANY GUYS HAVE YOU BEEN WITH?
WHY DO YOU ASK? WHAT, LIKE, IN MY ENTIRE LIFE?
YES.

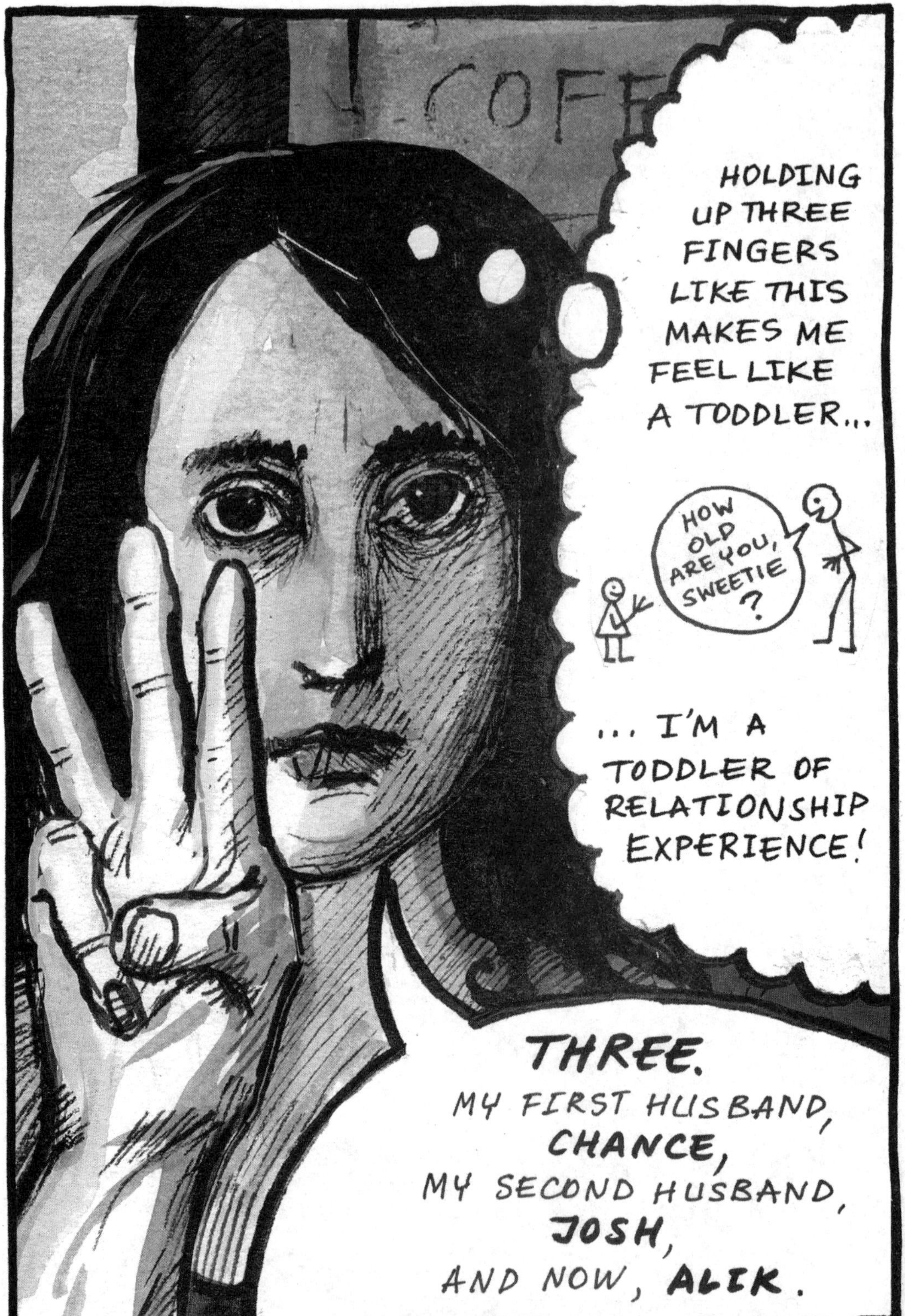
COFF
HOLDING UP THREE FINGERS LIKE THIS MAKES ME FEEL LIKE A TODDLER...
HOW OLD ARE YOU, SWEETIE?
... I'M A TODDLER OF RELATIONSHIP EXPERIENCE!
THREE.
MY FIRST HUSBAND, CHANCE, MY SECOND HUSBAND, JOSH, AND NOW, ALIK.

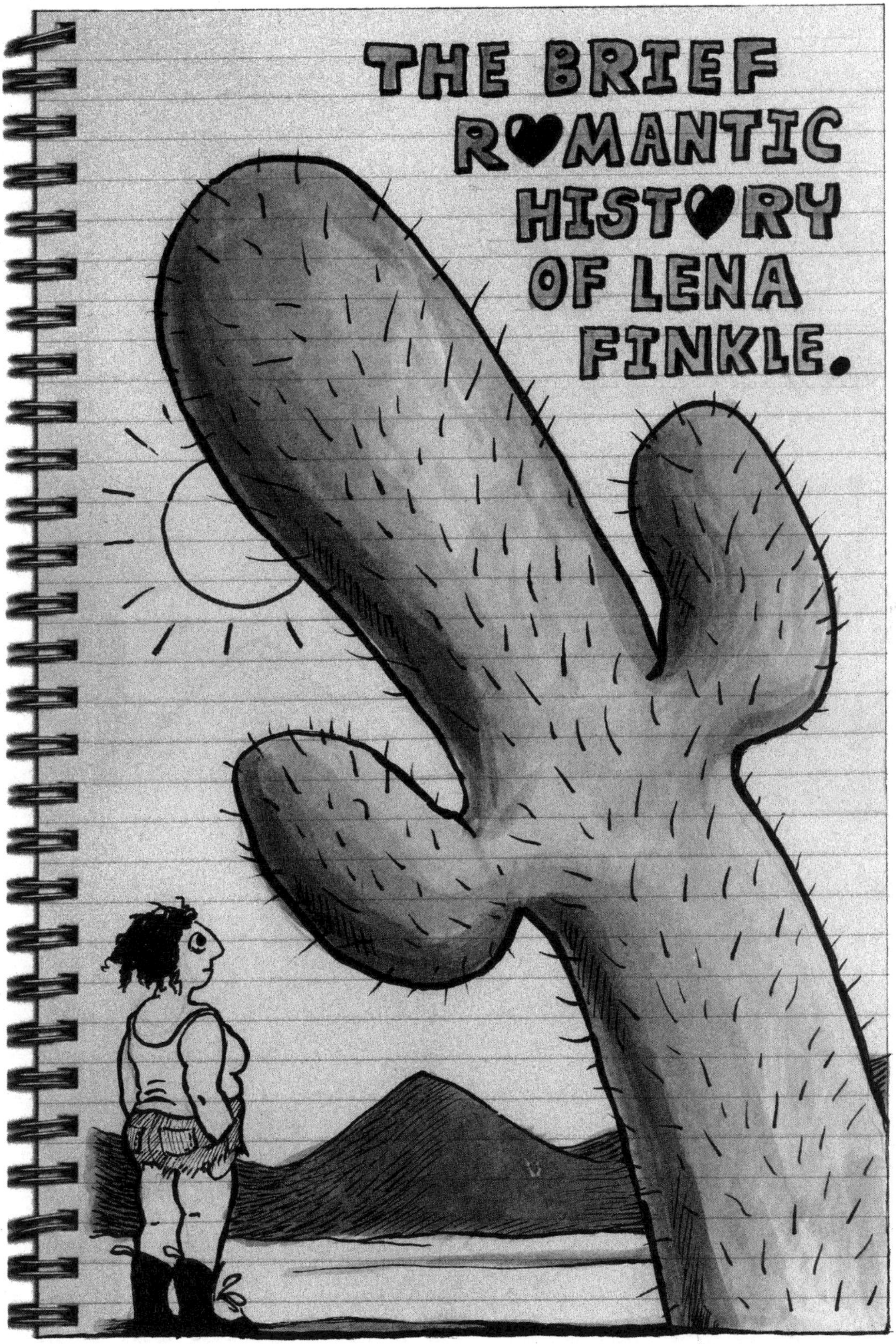
THE BRIEF
ROMANTIC
HISTORY
OF LENA
FINKLE.

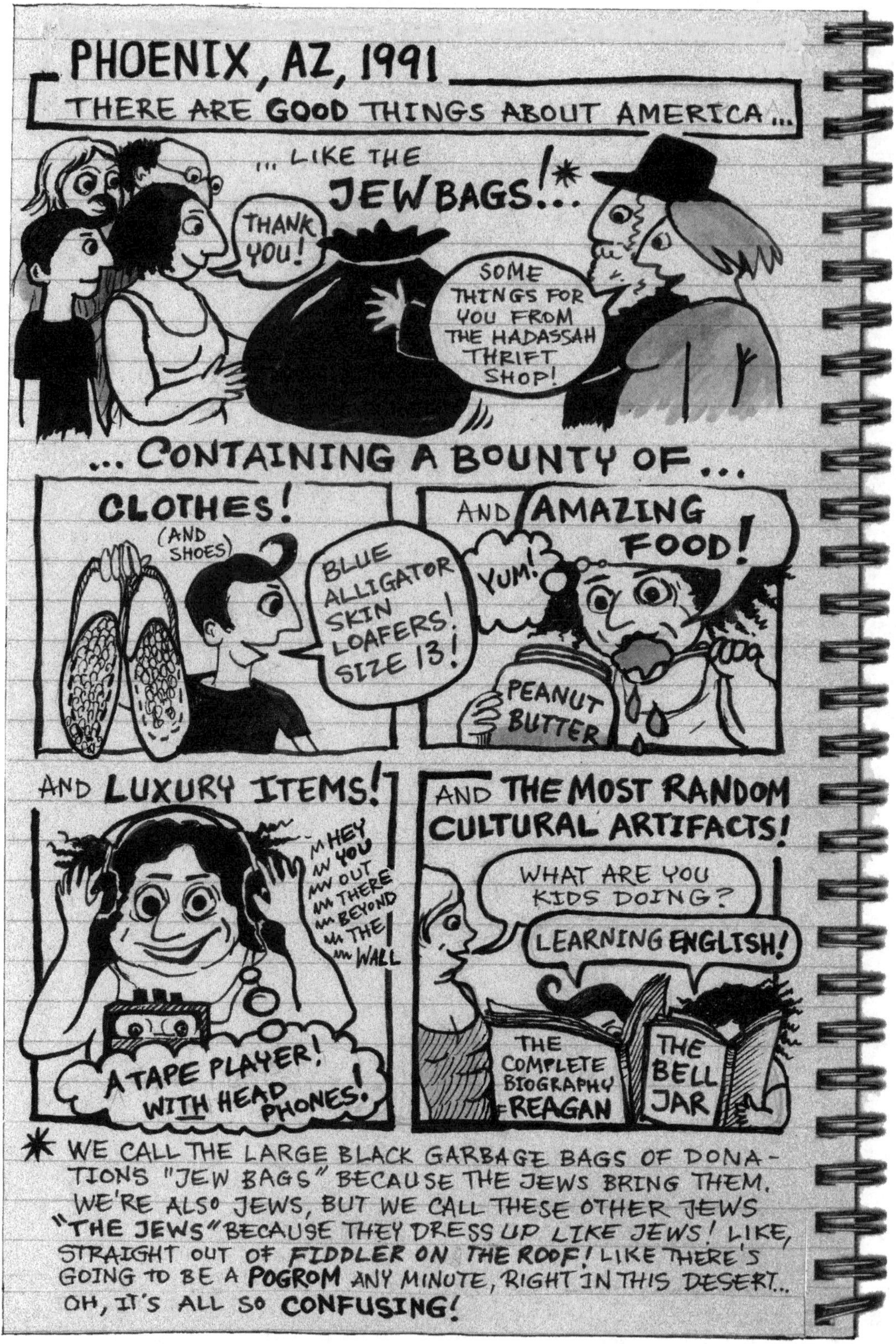
PHOENIX, AZ, 1991
THERE ARE GOOD THINGS ABOUT AMERICA...
... LIKE THE JEW BAGS!*...
THANK YOU!
SOME THINGS FOR YOU FROM THE HADASSAH THRIFT SHOP!
... CONTAINING A BOUNTY OF ...
CLOTHES! (AND SHOES)
BLUE ALLIGATOR SKIN LOAFERS! SIZE 13!
AND AMAZING FOOD!
YUM!
PEANUT BUTTER
AND LUXURY ITEMS!
HEY YOU OUT THERE BEYOND THE WALL
A TAPE PLAYER! WITH HEAD PHONES!
AND THE MOST RANDOM CULTURAL ARTIFACTS!
WHAT ARE YOU KIDS DOING?
LEARNING ENGLISH!
THE COMPLETE BIOGRAPHY OF REAGAN
THE BELL JAR
* WE CALL THE LARGE BLACK GARBAGE BAGS OF DONATIONS "JEW BAGS" BECAUSE THE JEWS BRING THEM. WE'RE ALSO JEWS, BUT WE CALL THESE OTHER JEWS "THE JEWS" BECAUSE THEY DRESS UP LIKE JEWS! LIKE, STRAIGHT OUT OF FIDDLER ON THE ROOF! LIKE THERE'S GOING TO BE A POGROM ANY MINUTE, RIGHT IN THIS DESERT... OH, IT'S ALL SO CONFUSING!

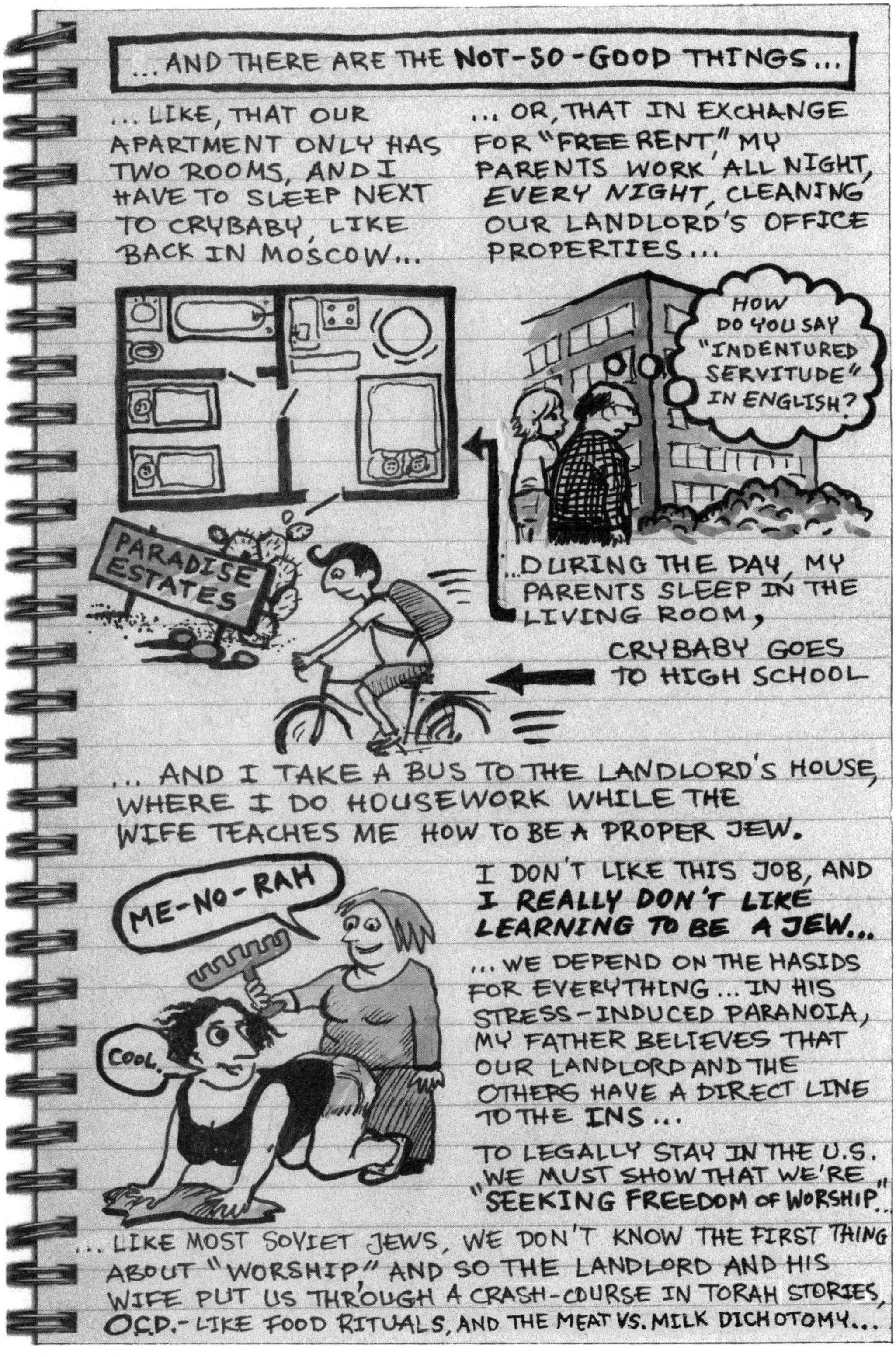
...AND THERE ARE THE NOT-SO-GOOD THINGS...
...LIKE, THAT OUR APARTMENT ONLY HAS TWO ROOMS, AND I HAVE TO SLEEP NEXT TO CRYBABY, LIKE BACK IN MOSCOW...
...OR, THAT IN EXCHANGE FOR "FREE RENT," MY PARENTS WORK ALL NIGHT, EVERY NIGHT, CLEANING OUR LANDLORD'S OFFICE PROPERTIES...
HOW DO YOU SAY "INDENTURED SERVITUDE" IN ENGLISH?
PARADISE ESTATES
...DURING THE DAY, MY PARENTS SLEEP IN THE LIVING ROOM,
CRYBABY GOES TO HIGH SCHOOL
...AND I TAKE A BUS TO THE LANDLORD'S HOUSE, WHERE I DO HOUSEWORK WHILE THE WIFE TEACHES ME HOW TO BE A PROPER JEW.
ME-NO-RAH
COOL.
I DON'T LIKE THIS JOB, AND I REALLY DON'T LIKE LEARNING TO BE A JEW...
...WE DEPEND ON THE HASIDS FOR EVERYTHING... IN HIS STRESS-INDUCED PARANOIA, MY FATHER BELIEVES THAT OUR LANDLORD AND THE OTHERS HAVE A DIRECT LINE TO THE INS...
TO LEGALLY STAY IN THE U.S. WE MUST SHOW THAT WE'RE "SEEKING FREEDOM OF WORSHIP"...
...LIKE MOST SOVIET JEWS, WE DON'T KNOW THE FIRST THING ABOUT "WORSHIP," AND SO THE LANDLORD AND HIS WIFE PUT US THROUGH A CRASH-COURSE IN TORAH STORIES, O.C.D.-LIKE FOOD RITUALS, AND THE MEAT VS. MILK DICHOTOMY...

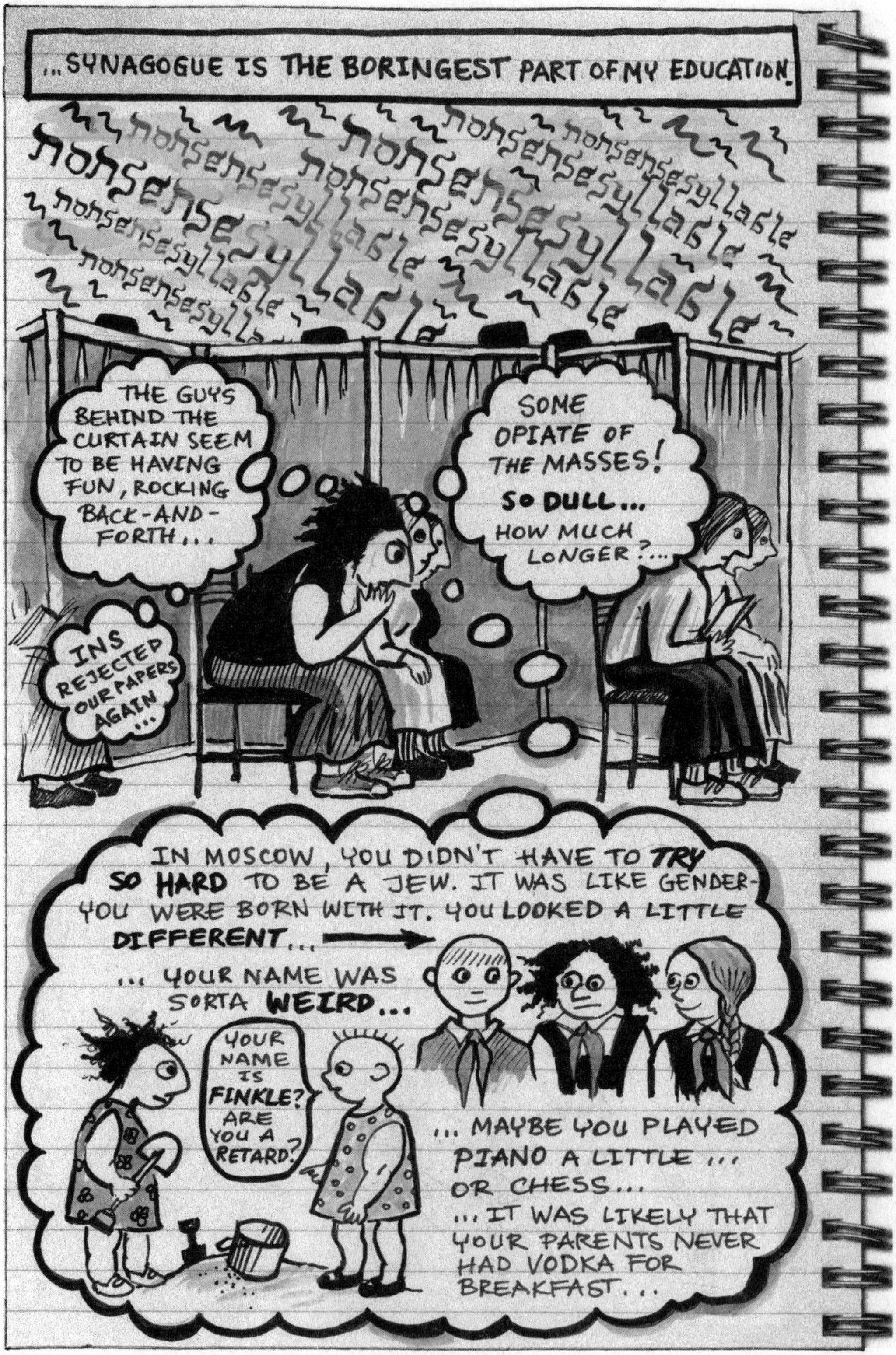
...SYNAGOGUE IS THE BORINGEST PART OF MY EDUCATION.
nonsensesyllable nonsensesyllable nonsensesyllable nonsensesyllable nonsensesyllable nonsensesyllable
THE GUYS BEHIND THE CURTAIN SEEM TO BE HAVING FUN, ROCKING BACK-AND-FORTH...
SOME OPIATE OF THE MASSES! SO DULL... HOW MUCH LONGER?...
INS REJECTED OUR PAPERS AGAIN...
IN MOSCOW, YOU DIDN'T HAVE TO TRY SO HARD TO BE A JEW. IT WAS LIKE GENDER- YOU WERE BORN WITH IT. YOU LOOKED A LITTLE DIFFERENT...
... YOUR NAME WAS SORTA WEIRD...
YOUR NAME IS FINKLE? ARE YOU A RETARD?
... MAYBE YOU PLAYED PIANO A LITTLE ... OR CHESS...
... IT WAS LIKELY THAT YOUR PARENTS NEVER HAD VODKA FOR BREAKFAST...

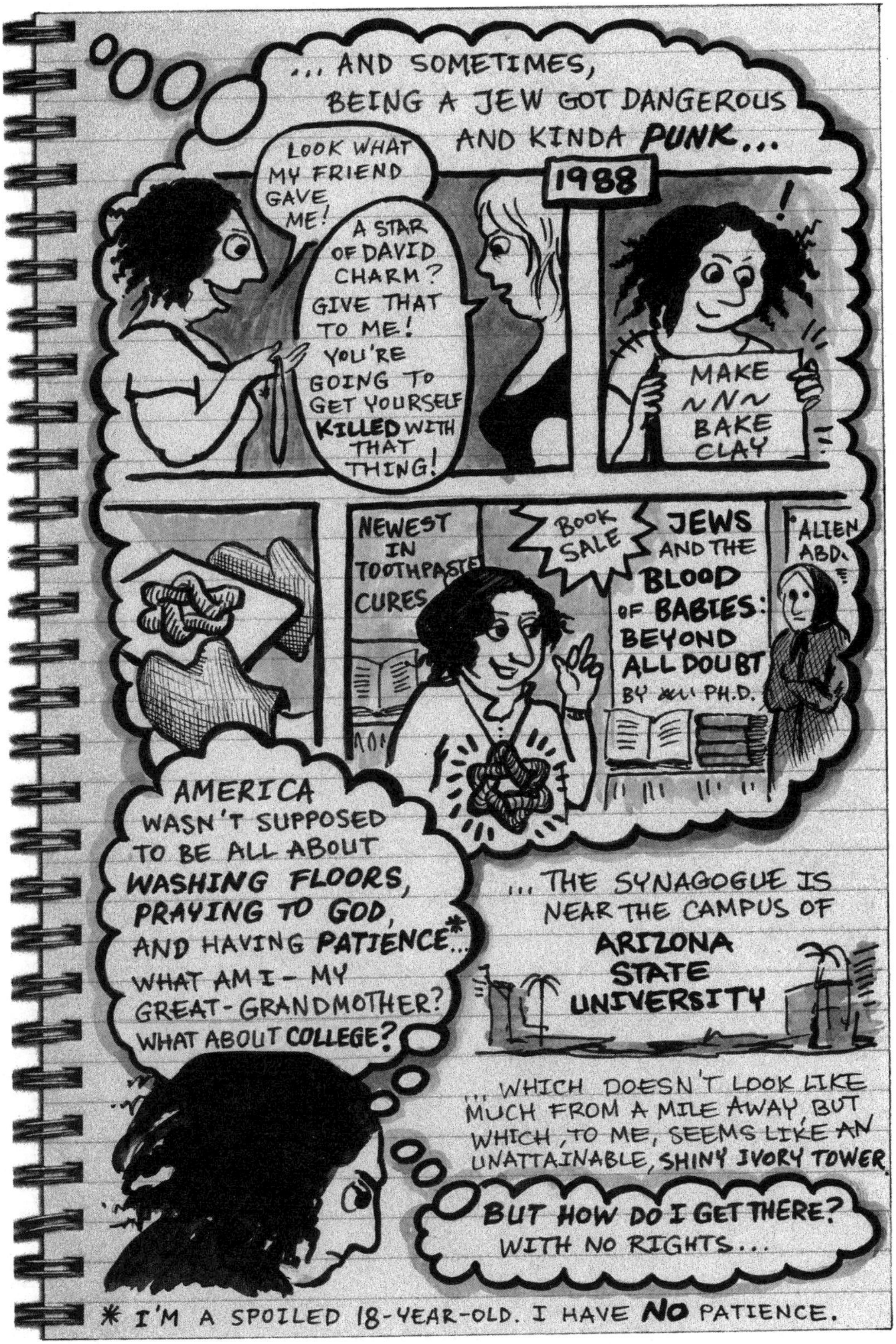
...AND SOMETIMES, BEING A JEW GOT DANGEROUS AND KINDA PUNK...
1988
LOOK WHAT MY FRIEND GAVE ME!
A STAR OF DAVID CHARM? GIVE THAT TO ME! YOU'RE GOING TO GET YOURSELF KILLED WITH THAT THING!
!
MAKE BAKE CLAY
NEWEST IN TOOTHPASTE CURES
BOOK SALE
JEWS AND THE BLOOD OF BABIES: BEYOND ALL DOUBT
ALIEN ABD
AMERICA WASN'T SUPPOSED TO BE ALL ABOUT WASHING FLOORS, PRAYING TO GOD, AND HAVING PATIENCE*... WHAT AM I – MY GREAT-GRANDMOTHER? WHAT ABOUT COLLEGE?
...THE SYNAGOGUE IS NEAR THE CAMPUS OF ARIZONA STATE UNIVERSITY
...WHICH DOESN'T LOOK LIKE MUCH FROM A MILE AWAY, BUT WHICH, TO ME, SEEMS LIKE AN UNATTAINABLE, SHINY IVORY TOWER.
BUT HOW DO I GET THERE? WITH NO RIGHTS...
* I'M A SPOILED 18-YEAR-OLD. I HAVE NO PATIENCE.

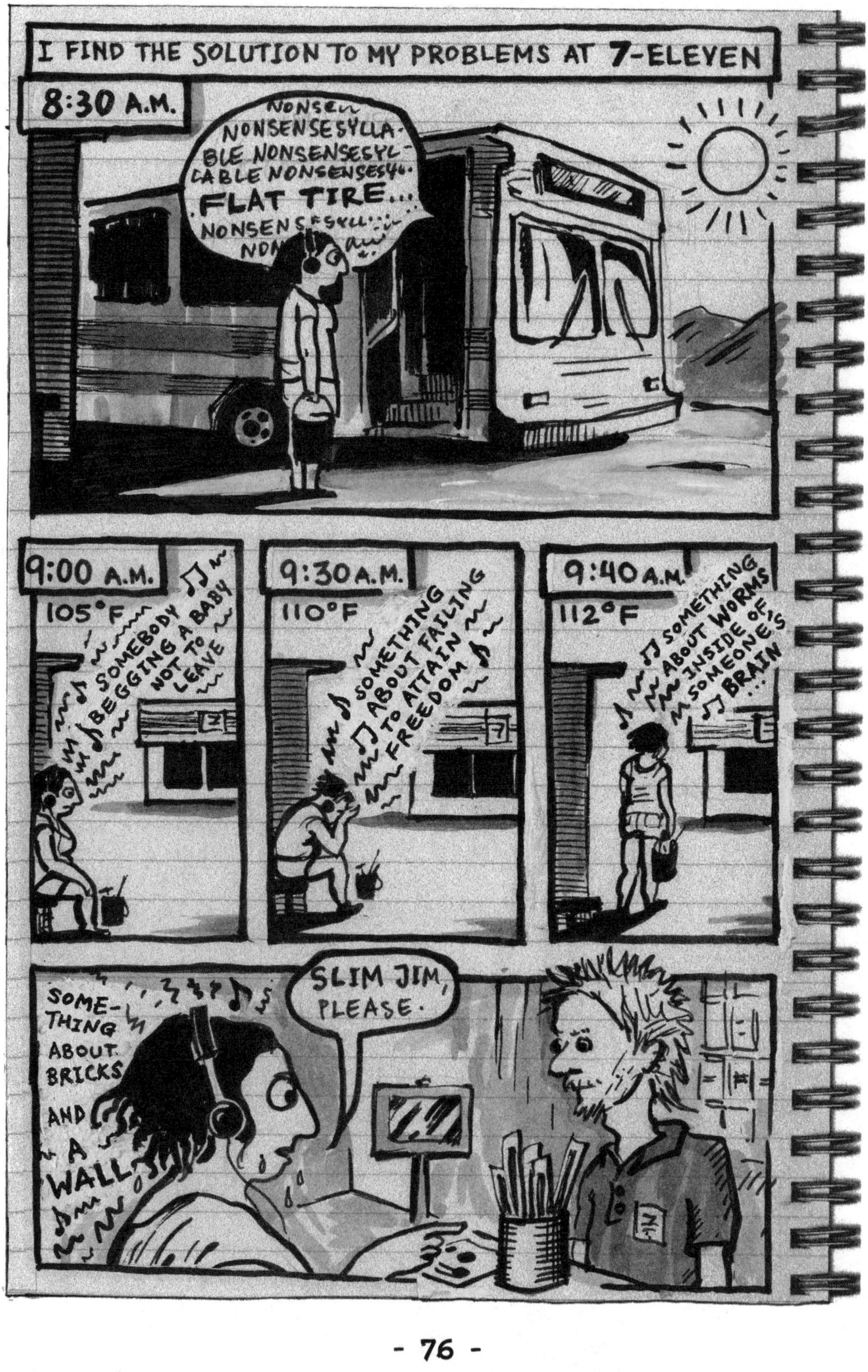
I FIND THE SOLUTION TO MY PROBLEMS AT 7-ELEVEN
8:30 A.M.
NONSEN NONSENSESYLLA-BLE NONSENSESYL-LABLE NONSENSESYL... FLAT TIRE... NONSENSESYLL...
9:00 A.M.
105°F
SOMEBODY BEGGING A BABY NOT TO LEAVE
9:30 A.M.
110°F
SOMETHING ABOUT FAILING TO ATTAIN FREEDOM
9:40 A.M.
112°F
SOMETHING ABOUT WORMS INSIDE OF SOMEONE'S BRAIN...
SOME-THING ABOUT BRICKS AND A WALL
SLIM JIM, PLEASE.

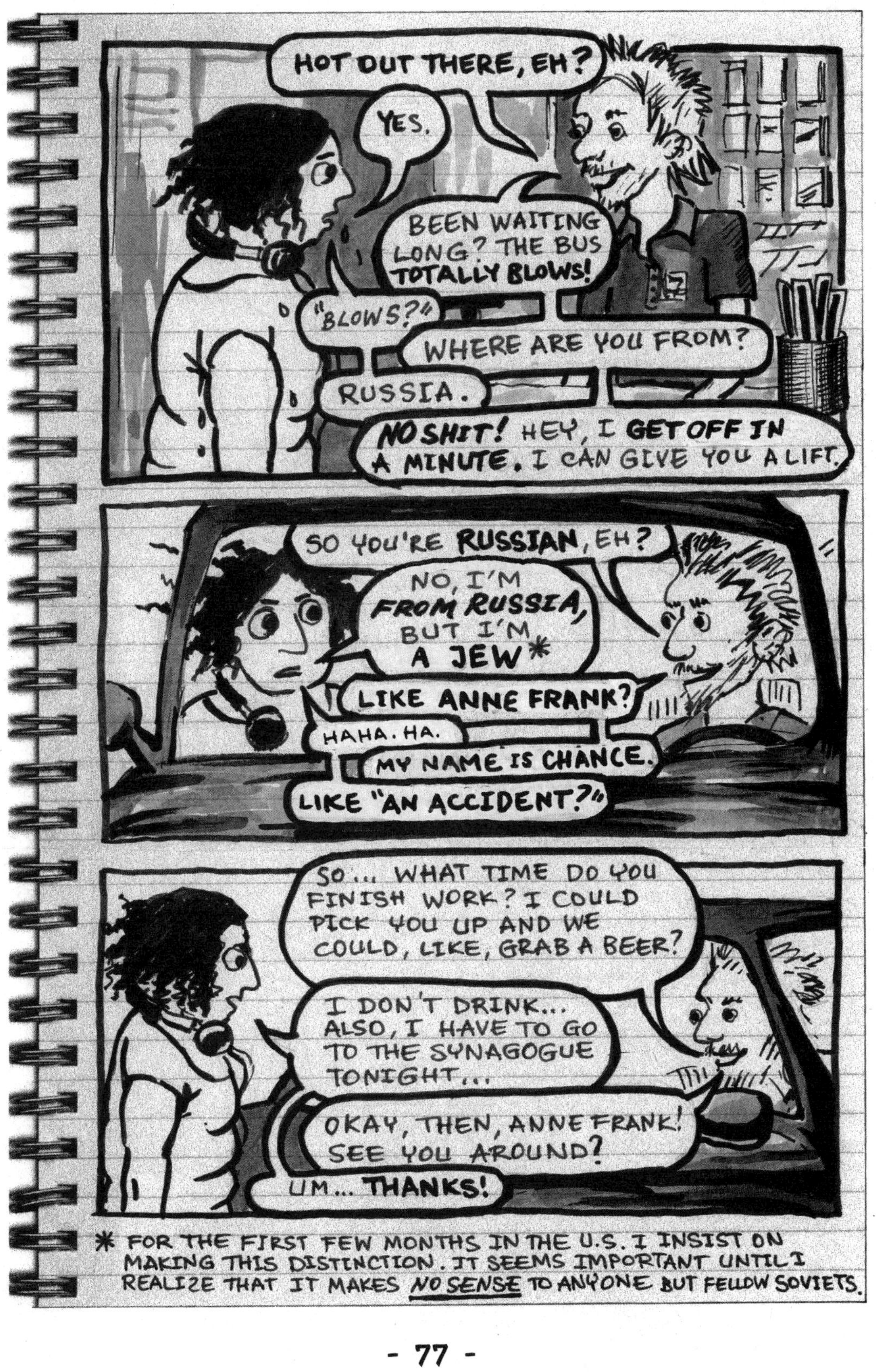
HOT OUT THERE, EH?
YES.
BEEN WAITING LONG? THE BUS TOTALLY BLOWS!
"BLOWS?"
WHERE ARE YOU FROM?
RUSSIA.
NO SHIT! HEY, I GET OFF IN A MINUTE. I CAN GIVE YOU A LIFT.
SO YOU'RE RUSSIAN, EH?
NO, I'M FROM RUSSIA, BUT I'M A JEW*
LIKE ANNE FRANK?
HAHA. HA.
MY NAME IS CHANCE.
LIKE "AN ACCIDENT?"
SO... WHAT TIME DO YOU FINISH WORK? I COULD PICK YOU UP AND WE COULD, LIKE, GRAB A BEER?
I DON'T DRINK... ALSO, I HAVE TO GO TO THE SYNAGOGUE TONIGHT...
OKAY, THEN, ANNE FRANK! SEE YOU AROUND?
UM... THANKS!

* FOR THE FIRST FEW MONTHS IN THE U.S. I INSIST ON MAKING THIS DISTINCTION. IT SEEMS IMPORTANT UNTIL I REALIZE THAT IT MAKES <u>NO SENSE</u> TO ANYONE BUT FELLOW SOVIETS.

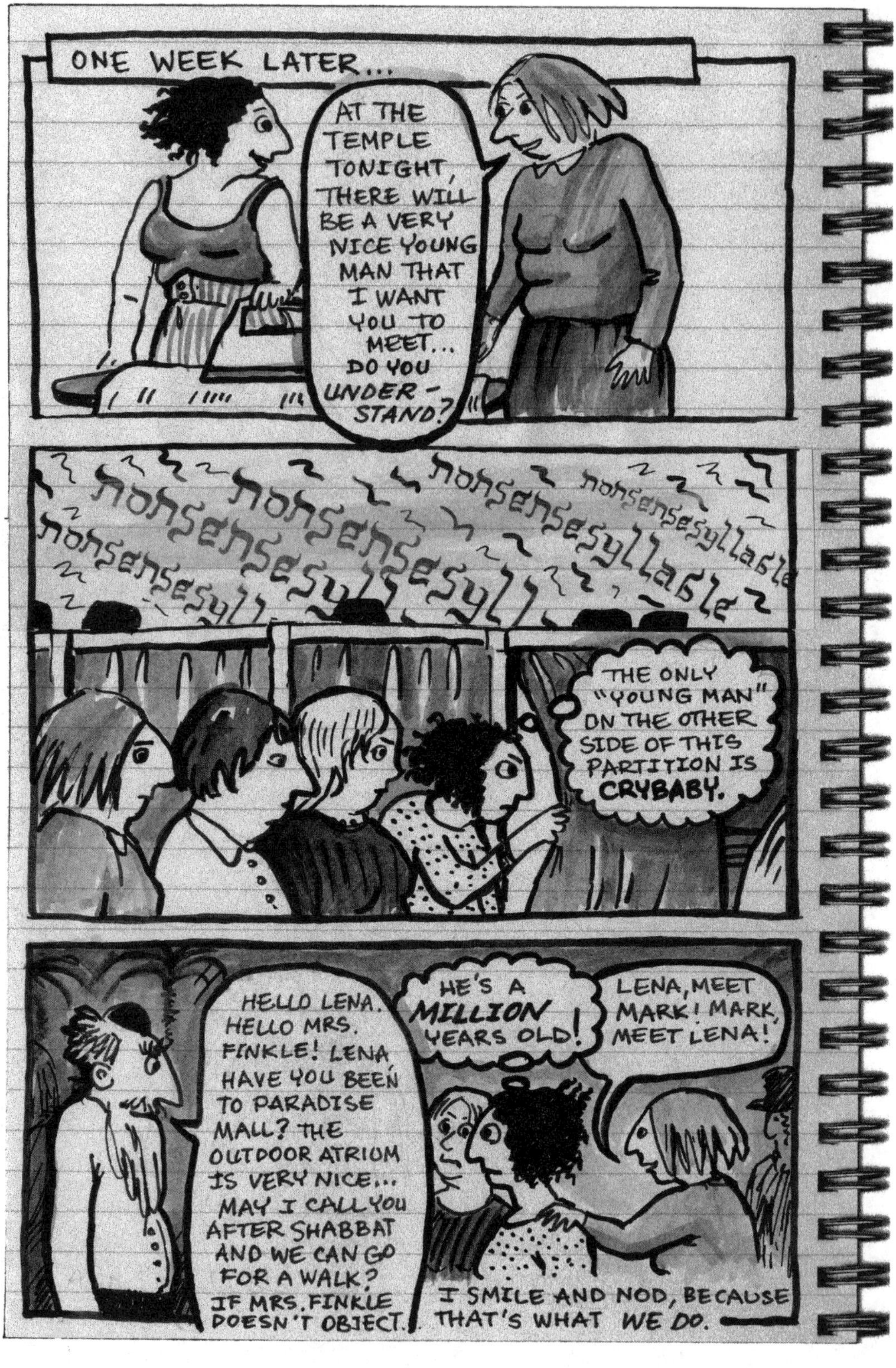
ONE WEEK LATER...
AT THE TEMPLE TONIGHT, THERE WILL BE A VERY NICE YOUNG MAN THAT I WANT YOU TO MEET... DO YOU UNDER-STAND?
nonsensesyllable nonsensesyllable nonsensesyll nonsensesyll nonsensesyll nonsensesyll
THE ONLY "YOUNG MAN" ON THE OTHER SIDE OF THIS PARTITION IS CRYBABY.
HELLO LENA. HELLO MRS. FINKLE! LENA HAVE YOU BEEN TO PARADISE MALL? THE OUTDOOR ATRIUM IS VERY NICE... MAY I CALL YOU AFTER SHABBAT AND WE CAN GO FOR A WALK? IF MRS. FINKLE DOESN'T OBJECT.
HE'S A MILLION YEARS OLD!
LENA, MEET MARK! MARK, MEET LENA!
I SMILE AND NOD, BECAUSE THAT'S WHAT WE DO.

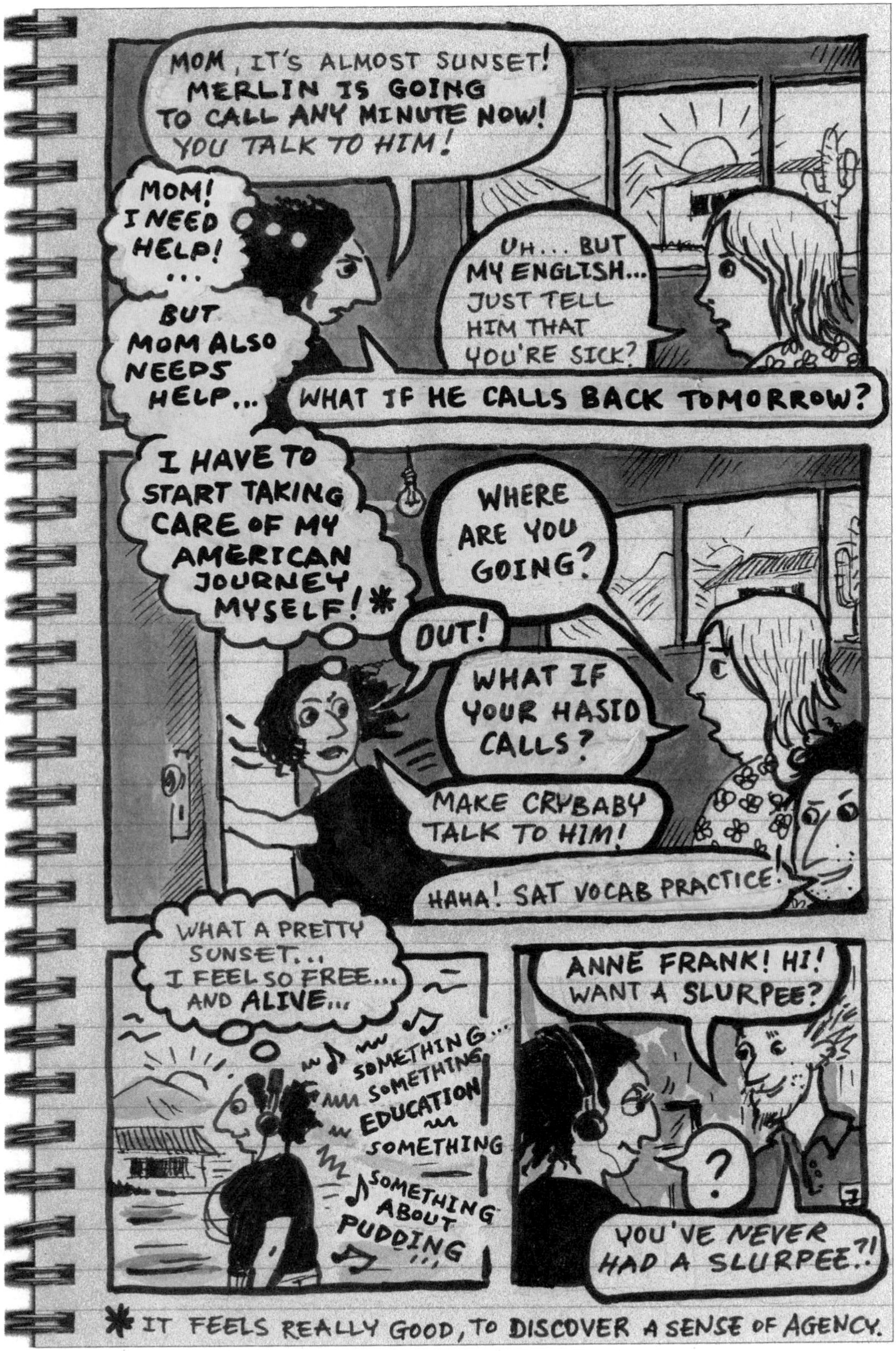
MOM, IT'S ALMOST SUNSET! MERLIN IS GOING TO CALL ANY MINUTE NOW! YOU TALK TO HIM!
MOM! I NEED HELP! ...
BUT MOM ALSO NEEDS HELP...
UH... BUT MY ENGLISH... JUST TELL HIM THAT YOU'RE SICK?
WHAT IF HE CALLS BACK TOMORROW?
I HAVE TO START TAKING CARE OF MY AMERICAN JOURNEY MYSELF! *
WHERE ARE YOU GOING?
OUT!
WHAT IF YOUR HASID CALLS?
MAKE CRYBABY TALK TO HIM!
HAHA! SAT VOCAB PRACTICE!
WHAT A PRETTY SUNSET... I FEEL SO FREE... AND ALIVE...
SOMETHING... SOMETHING SOMETHING EDUCATION SOMETHING SOMETHING ABOUT PUDDING
ANNE FRANK! HI! WANT A SLURPEE?
?
YOU'VE NEVER HAD A SLURPEE?!

* IT FEELS REALLY GOOD, TO DISCOVER A SENSE OF AGENCY.

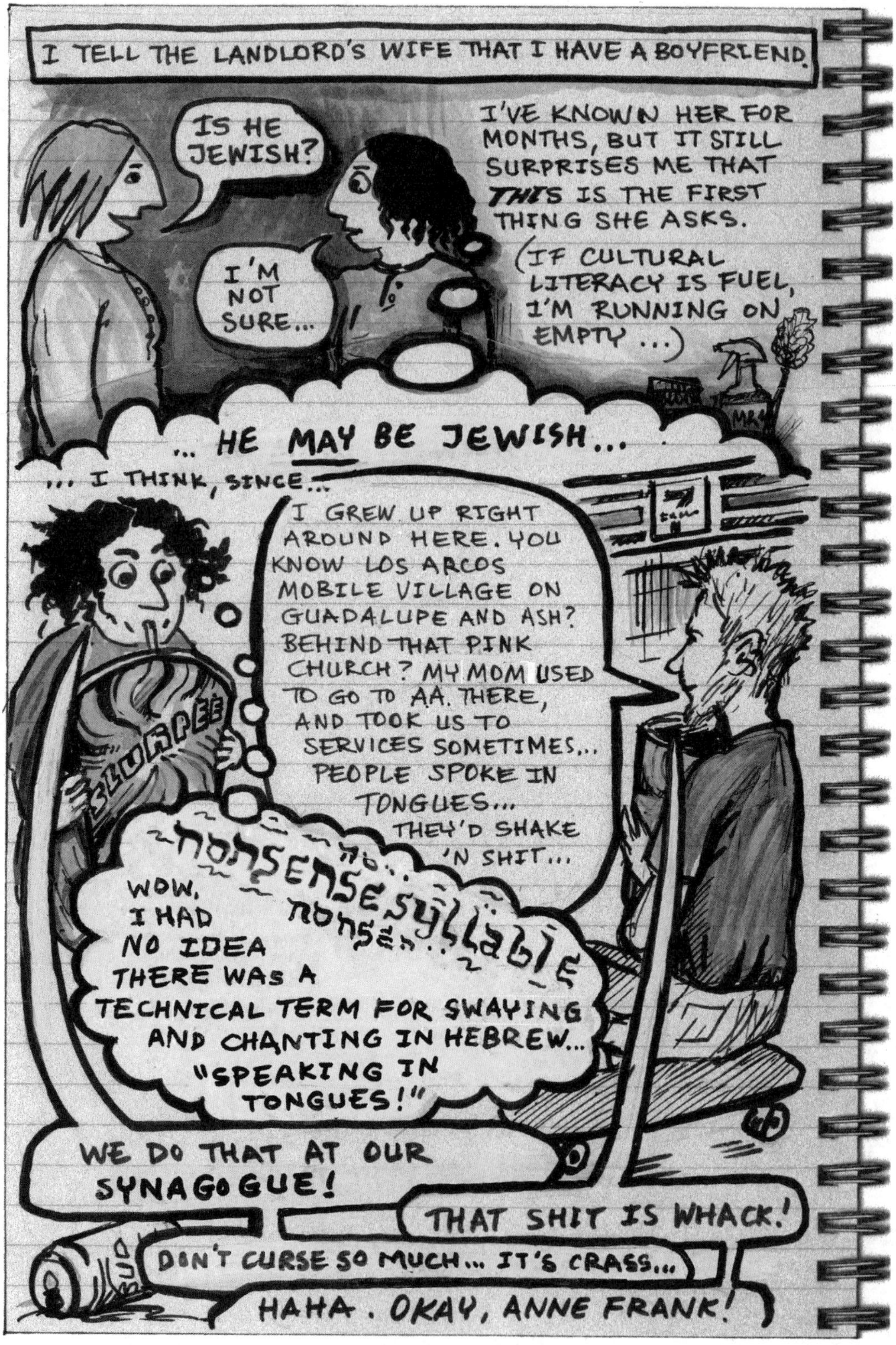
I TELL THE LANDLORD'S WIFE THAT I HAVE A BOYFRIEND.
IS HE JEWISH?
I'M NOT SURE...
I'VE KNOWN HER FOR MONTHS, BUT IT STILL SURPRISES ME THAT THIS IS THE FIRST THING SHE ASKS.
(IF CULTURAL LITERACY IS FUEL, I'M RUNNING ON EMPTY...)
... HE MAY BE JEWISH...
... I THINK, SINCE...
I GREW UP RIGHT AROUND HERE. YOU KNOW LOS ARCOS MOBILE VILLAGE ON GUADALUPE AND ASH? BEHIND THAT PINK CHURCH? MY MOM USED TO GO TO A.A. THERE, AND TOOK US TO SERVICES SOMETIMES... PEOPLE SPOKE IN TONGUES... THEY'D SHAKE 'N SHIT...
SLURPEE
NONSENSE SYLLABLE
WOW. I HAD NO IDEA THERE WAS A TECHNICAL TERM FOR SWAYING AND CHANTING IN HEBREW... "SPEAKING IN TONGUES!"
WE DO THAT AT OUR SYNAGOGUE!
THAT SHIT IS WHACK!
DON'T CURSE SO MUCH... IT'S CRASS...
HAHA. OKAY, ANNE FRANK!

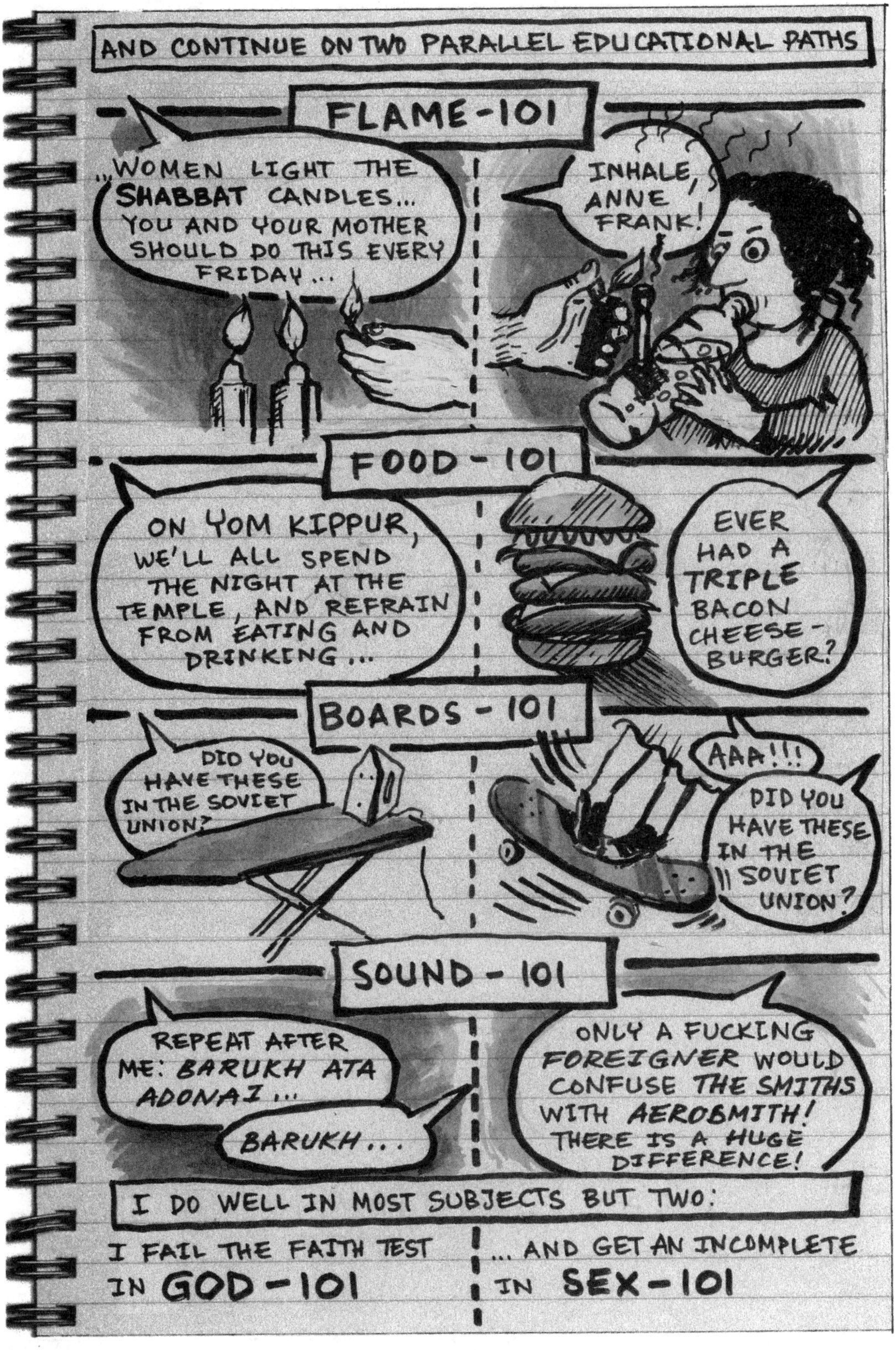
AND CONTINUE ON TWO PARALLEL EDUCATIONAL PATHS
FLAME-101
...WOMEN LIGHT THE SHABBAT CANDLES... YOU AND YOUR MOTHER SHOULD DO THIS EVERY FRIDAY...
INHALE, ANNE FRANK!
FOOD-101
ON YOM KIPPUR, WE'LL ALL SPEND THE NIGHT AT THE TEMPLE, AND REFRAIN FROM EATING AND DRINKING...
EVER HAD A TRIPLE BACON CHEESE-BURGER?
BOARDS-101
DID YOU HAVE THESE IN THE SOVIET UNION?
AAA!!!
DID YOU HAVE THESE IN THE SOVIET UNION?
SOUND-101
REPEAT AFTER ME: BARUKH ATA ADONAI...
BARUKH...
ONLY A FUCKING FOREIGNER WOULD CONFUSE THE SMITHS WITH AEROSMITH! THERE IS A HUGE DIFFERENCE!
I DO WELL IN MOST SUBJECTS BUT TWO:
I FAIL THE FAITH TEST IN GOD-101
... AND GET AN INCOMPLETE IN SEX-101

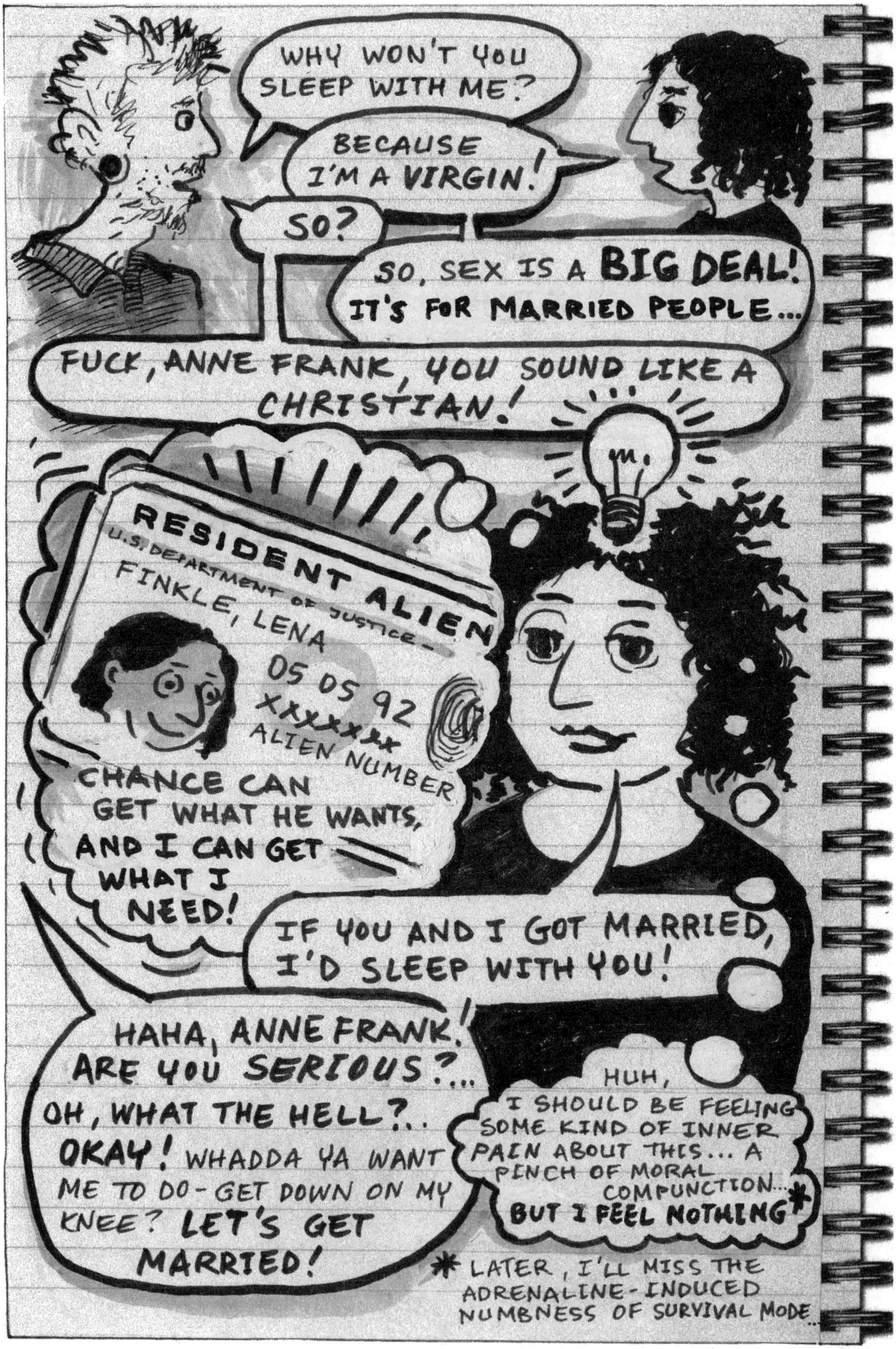
WHY WON'T YOU SLEEP WITH ME?
BECAUSE I'M A VIRGIN!
SO?
SO, SEX IS A BIG DEAL! IT'S FOR MARRIED PEOPLE...
FUCK, ANNE FRANK, YOU SOUND LIKE A CHRISTIAN!
RESIDENT ALIEN
U.S. DEPARTMENT OF JUSTICE
FINKLE, LENA
05 05 92
ALIEN NUMBER
CHANCE CAN GET WHAT HE WANTS, AND I CAN GET WHAT I NEED!
IF YOU AND I GOT MARRIED, I'D SLEEP WITH YOU!
HAHA, ANNE FRANK! ARE YOU SERIOUS?... OH, WHAT THE HELL?.. OKAY! WHADDA YA WANT ME TO DO - GET DOWN ON MY KNEE? LET'S GET MARRIED!
HUH, I SHOULD BE FEELING SOME KIND OF INNER PAIN ABOUT THIS... A PINCH OF MORAL COMPUNCTION... BUT I FEEL NOTHING*
* LATER, I'LL MISS THE ADRENALINE-INDUCED NUMBNESS OF SURVIVAL MODE...

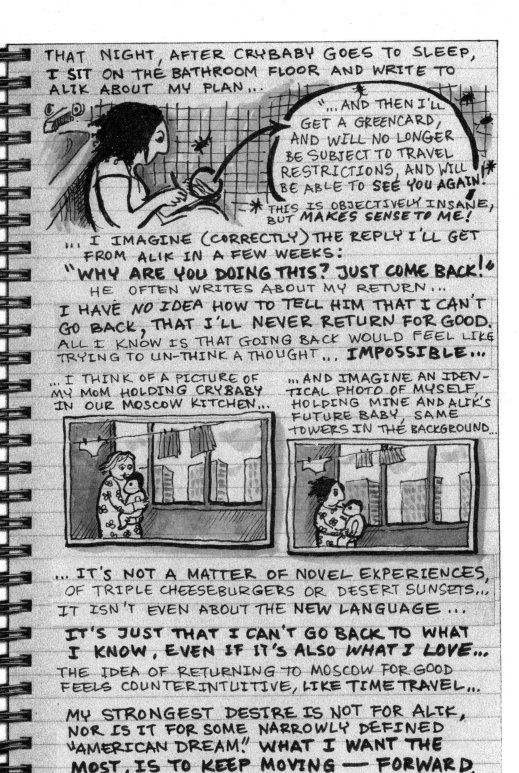

THAT NIGHT, AFTER CRYBABY GOES TO SLEEP, I SIT ON THE BATHROOM FLOOR AND WRITE TO ALIK ABOUT MY PLAN...

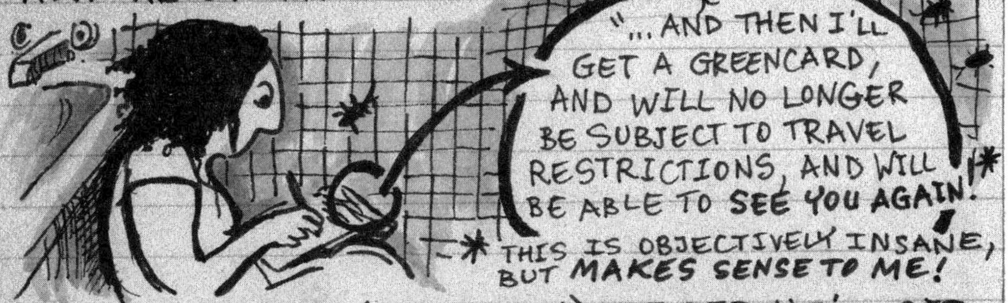
"...AND THEN I'LL GET A GREENCARD, AND WILL NO LONGER BE SUBJECT TO TRAVEL RESTRICTIONS, AND WILL BE ABLE TO **SEE YOU AGAIN!***
*THIS IS OBJECTIVELY INSANE, BUT **MAKES SENSE TO ME!**

... I IMAGINE (CORRECTLY) THE REPLY I'LL GET FROM ALIK IN A FEW WEEKS:

"WHY ARE YOU DOING THIS? JUST COME BACK!"

HE OFTEN WRITES ABOUT MY RETURN...

I HAVE *NO IDEA* HOW TO TELL HIM THAT I CAN'T GO BACK, THAT I'LL NEVER RETURN FOR GOOD.

ALL I KNOW IS THAT GOING BACK WOULD FEEL LIKE TRYING TO UN-THINK A THOUGHT... **IMPOSSIBLE...**

... I THINK OF A PICTURE OF MY MOM HOLDING CRYBABY IN OUR MOSCOW KITCHEN...

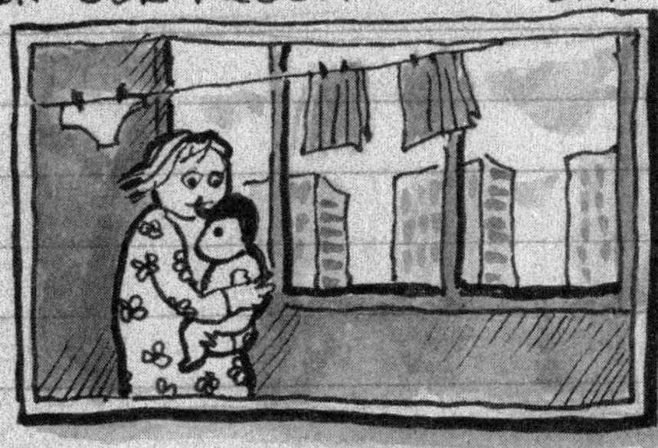

... AND IMAGINE AN IDENTICAL PHOTO OF MYSELF, HOLDING MINE AND ALIK'S FUTURE BABY, SAME TOWERS IN THE BACKGROUND...

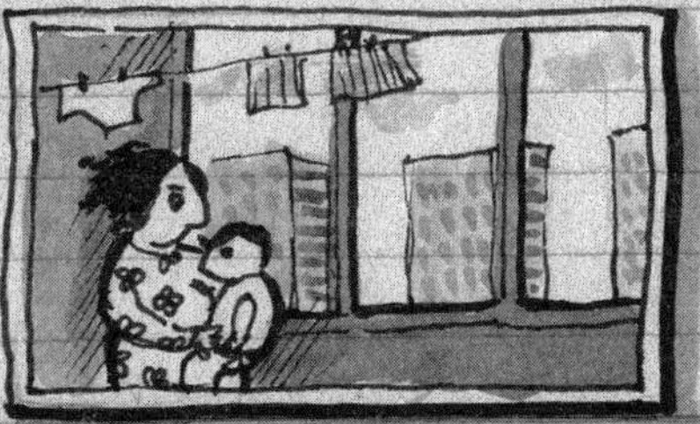

... IT'S NOT A MATTER OF NOVEL EXPERIENCES, OF TRIPLE CHEESEBURGERS OR DESERT SUNSETS... IT ISN'T EVEN ABOUT THE **NEW LANGUAGE**...

IT'S JUST THAT I CAN'T GO BACK TO WHAT I KNOW, EVEN IF IT'S ALSO *WHAT I LOVE...*

THE IDEA OF RETURNING TO MOSCOW FOR GOOD FEELS COUNTERINTUITIVE, LIKE TIME TRAVEL...

MY STRONGEST DESIRE IS NOT FOR ALIK, NOR IS IT FOR SOME NARROWLY DEFINED "AMERICAN DREAM." **WHAT I WANT THE MOST, IS TO KEEP MOVING — FORWARD, TOWARD THE UNKNOWN...**

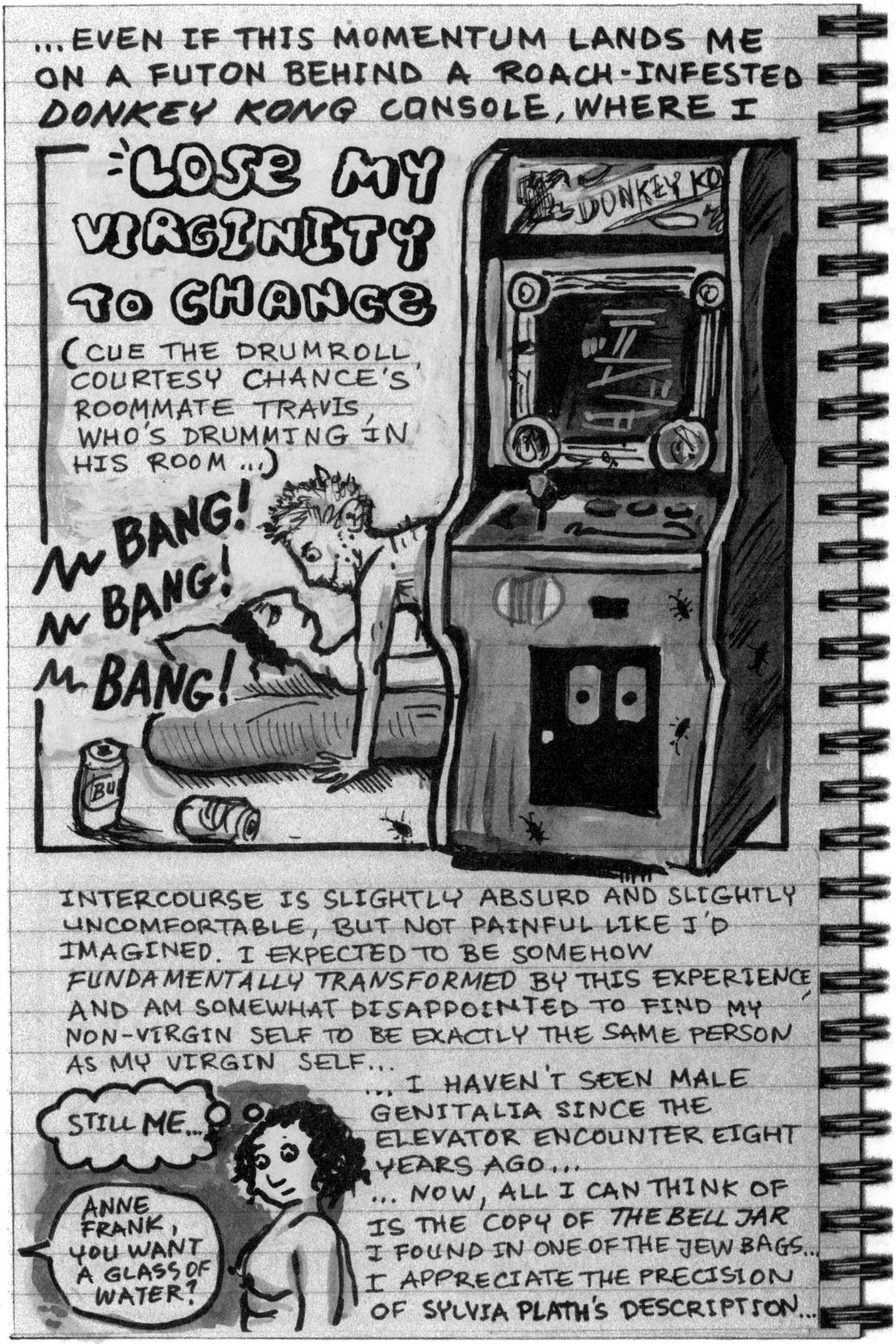
...EVEN IF THIS MOMENTUM LANDS ME ON A FUTON BEHIND A ROACH-INFESTED DONKEY KONG CONSOLE, WHERE I
LOSE MY VIRGINITY TO CHANCE
(CUE THE DRUMROLL, COURTESY CHANCE'S ROOMMATE TRAVIS, WHO'S DRUMMING IN HIS ROOM...)
DONKEY KO
BANG!
BANG!
BANG!
INTERCOURSE IS SLIGHTLY ABSURD AND SLIGHTLY UNCOMFORTABLE, BUT NOT PAINFUL LIKE I'D IMAGINED. I EXPECTED TO BE SOMEHOW FUNDAMENTALLY TRANSFORMED BY THIS EXPERIENCE, AND AM SOMEWHAT DISAPPOINTED TO FIND MY NON-VIRGIN SELF TO BE EXACTLY THE SAME PERSON AS MY VIRGIN SELF...
STILL ME...
...I HAVEN'T SEEN MALE GENITALIA SINCE THE ELEVATOR ENCOUNTER EIGHT YEARS AGO...
...NOW, ALL I CAN THINK OF IS THE COPY OF THE BELL JAR I FOUND IN ONE OF THE JEW BAGS... I APPRECIATE THE PRECISION OF SYLVIA PLATH'S DESCRIPTION...
ANNE FRANK, YOU WANT A GLASS OF WATER?

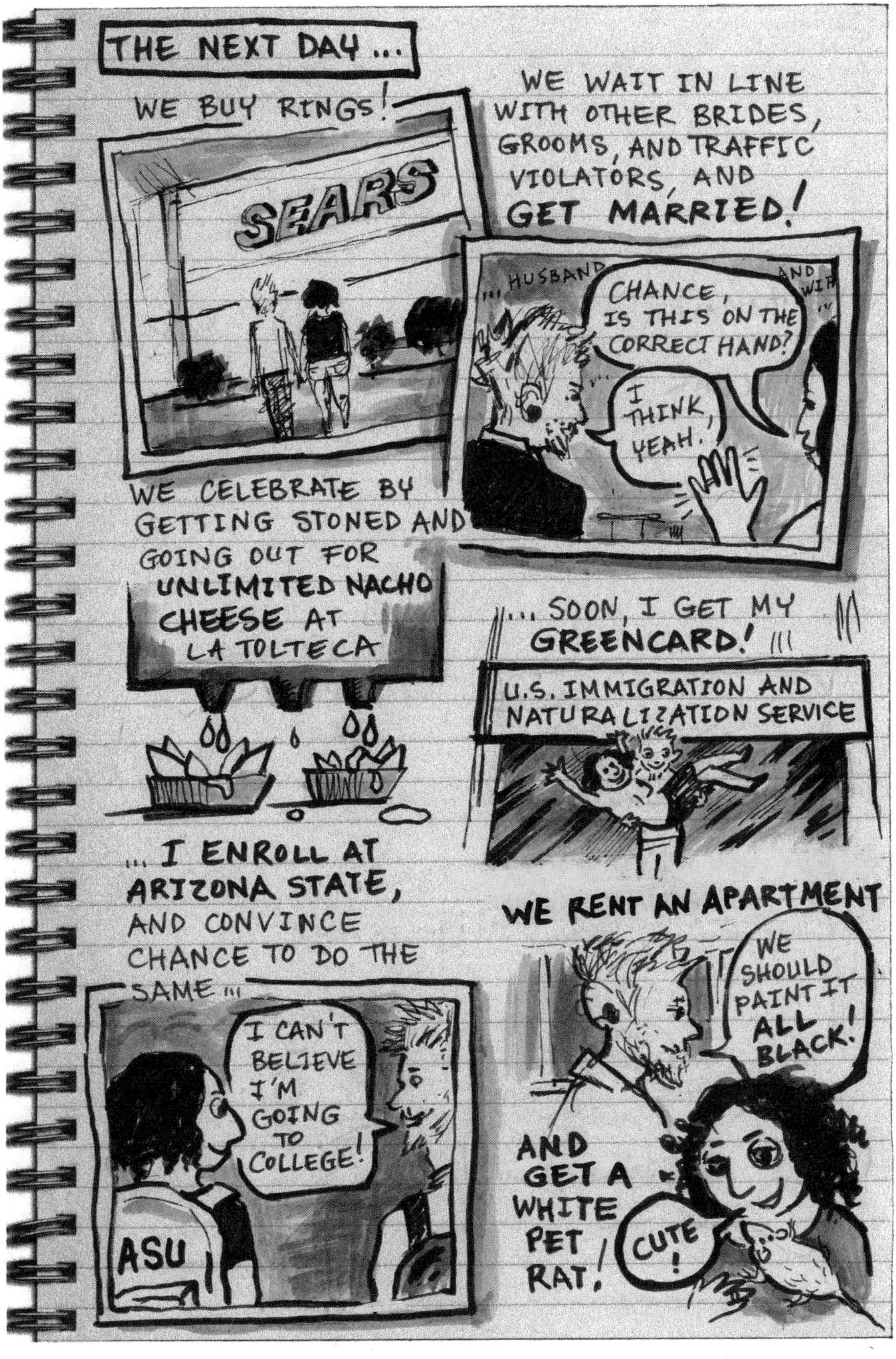
THE NEXT DAY ...
WE BUY RINGS!
SEARS
WE WAIT IN LINE WITH OTHER BRIDES, GROOMS, AND TRAFFIC VIOLATORS, AND GET MARRIED!
... HUSBAND
AND WIFE
CHANCE, IS THIS ON THE CORRECT HAND?
I THINK, YEAH.
WE CELEBRATE BY GETTING STONED AND GOING OUT FOR UNLIMITED NACHO CHEESE AT LA TOLTECA
... SOON, I GET MY GREENCARD!
U.S. IMMIGRATION AND NATURALIZATION SERVICE
... I ENROLL AT ARIZONA STATE, AND CONVINCE CHANCE TO DO THE SAME ...
I CAN'T BELIEVE I'M GOING TO COLLEGE!
ASU
WE RENT AN APARTMENT
WE SHOULD PAINT IT ALL BLACK!
AND GET A WHITE PET RAT!
CUTE!

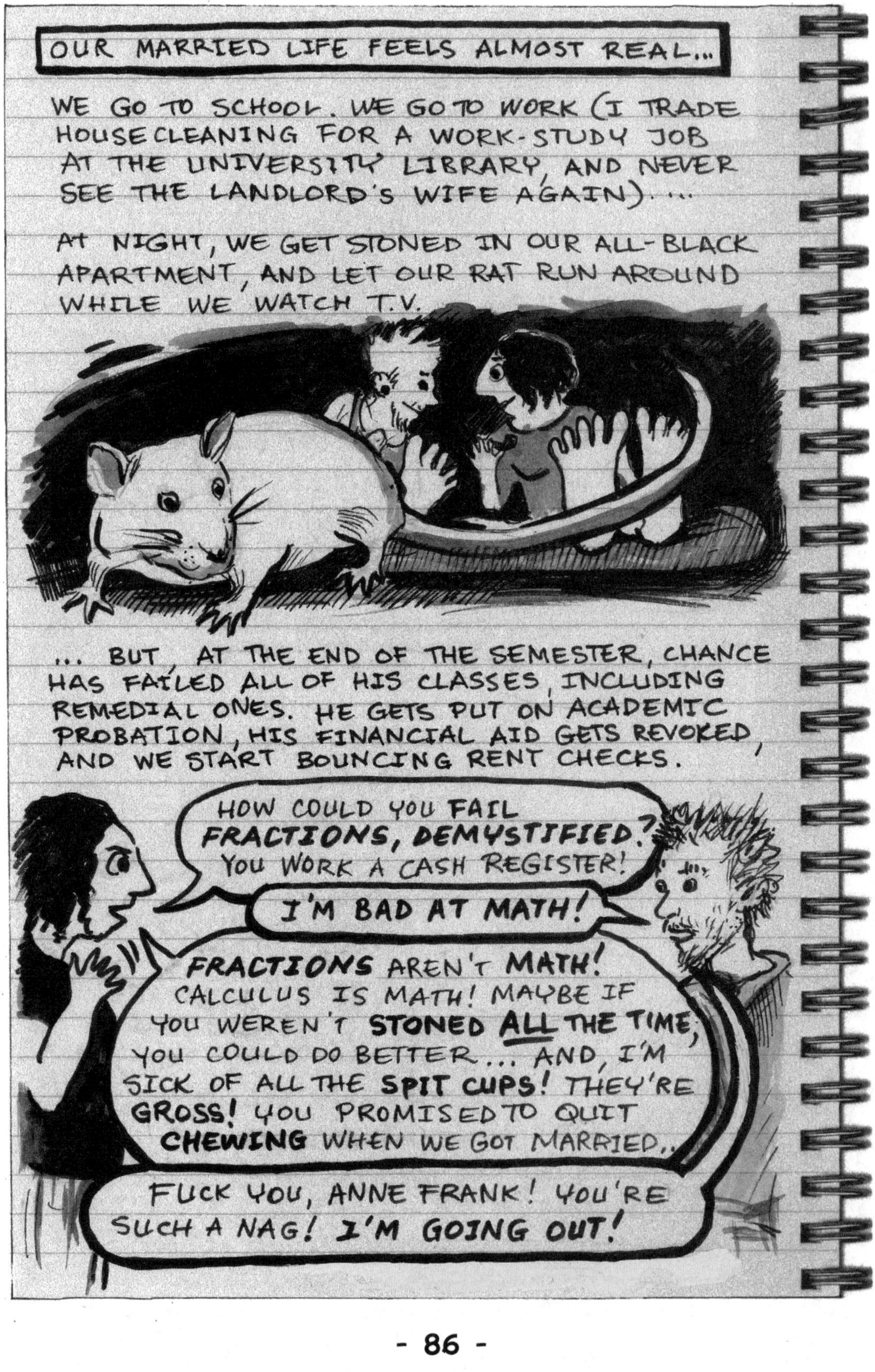
OUR MARRIED LIFE FEELS ALMOST REAL...
WE GO TO SCHOOL. WE GO TO WORK (I TRADE HOUSECLEANING FOR A WORK-STUDY JOB AT THE UNIVERSITY LIBRARY, AND NEVER SEE THE LANDLORD'S WIFE AGAIN)...
AT NIGHT, WE GET STONED IN OUR ALL-BLACK APARTMENT, AND LET OUR RAT RUN AROUND WHILE WE WATCH T.V.
... BUT, AT THE END OF THE SEMESTER, CHANCE HAS FAILED ALL OF HIS CLASSES, INCLUDING REMEDIAL ONES. HE GETS PUT ON ACADEMIC PROBATION, HIS FINANCIAL AID GETS REVOKED, AND WE START BOUNCING RENT CHECKS.
HOW COULD YOU FAIL FRACTIONS, DEMYSTIFIED? YOU WORK A CASH REGISTER!
I'M BAD AT MATH!
FRACTIONS AREN'T MATH! CALCULUS IS MATH! MAYBE IF YOU WEREN'T STONED ALL THE TIME, YOU COULD DO BETTER... AND, I'M SICK OF ALL THE SPIT CUPS! THEY'RE GROSS! YOU PROMISED TO QUIT CHEWING WHEN WE GOT MARRIED...
FUCK YOU, ANNE FRANK! YOU'RE SUCH A NAG! I'M GOING OUT!

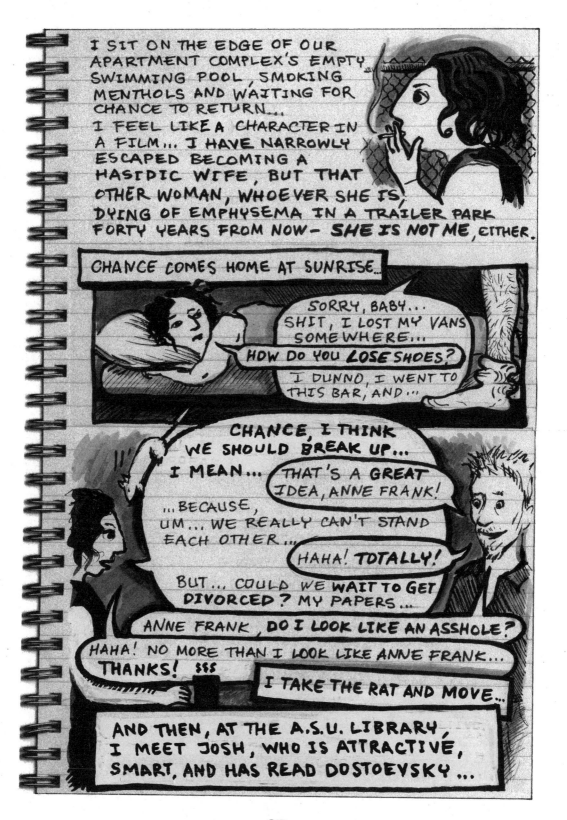

I SIT ON THE EDGE OF OUR APARTMENT COMPLEX'S EMPTY SWIMMING POOL, SMOKING MENTHOLS AND WAITING FOR CHANCE TO RETURN... I FEEL LIKE A CHARACTER IN A FILM... I HAVE NARROWLY ESCAPED BECOMING A HASIDIC WIFE, BUT THAT OTHER WOMAN, WHOEVER SHE IS, DYING OF EMPHYSEMA IN A TRAILER PARK FORTY YEARS FROM NOW— SHE IS NOT ME, EITHER.

CHANCE COMES HOME AT SUNRISE...

SORRY, BABY... SHIT, I LOST MY VANS SOMEWHERE...

HOW DO YOU LOSE SHOES?

I DUNNO, I WENT TO THIS BAR, AND...

CHANCE, I THINK WE SHOULD BREAK UP... I MEAN...

THAT'S A GREAT IDEA, ANNE FRANK!

...BECAUSE, UM... WE REALLY CAN'T STAND EACH OTHER...

HAHA! TOTALLY!

BUT... COULD WE WAIT TO GET DIVORCED? MY PAPERS...

ANNE FRANK, DO I LOOK LIKE AN ASSHOLE?

HAHA! NO MORE THAN I LOOK LIKE ANNE FRANK... THANKS! $$$

I TAKE THE RAT AND MOVE...

AND THEN, AT THE A.S.U. LIBRARY, I MEET JOSH, WHO IS ATTRACTIVE, SMART, AND HAS READ DOSTOEVSKY...

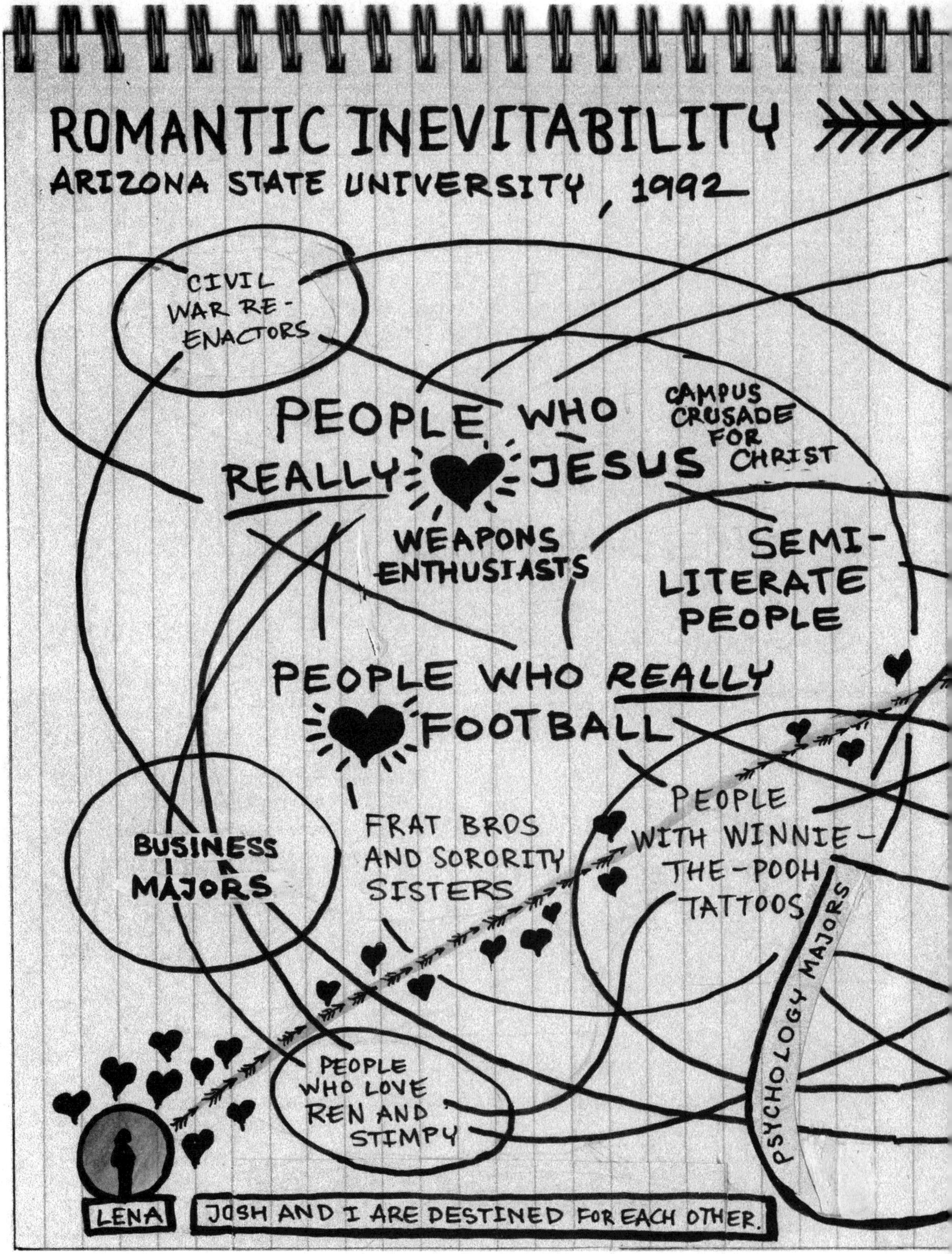
ROMANTIC INEVITABILITY
ARIZONA STATE UNIVERSITY, 1992
CIVIL WAR RE-ENACTORS
PEOPLE WHO REALLY ♥ JESUS
CAMPUS CRUSADE FOR CHRIST
WEAPONS ENTHUSIASTS
SEMI-LITERATE PEOPLE
PEOPLE WHO REALLY ♥ FOOTBALL
BUSINESS MAJORS
FRAT BROS AND SORORITY SISTERS
PEOPLE WITH WINNIE-THE-POOH TATTOOS
PSYCHOLOGY MAJORS
PEOPLE WHO LOVE REN AND STIMPY
LENA
JOSH AND I ARE DESTINED FOR EACH OTHER.

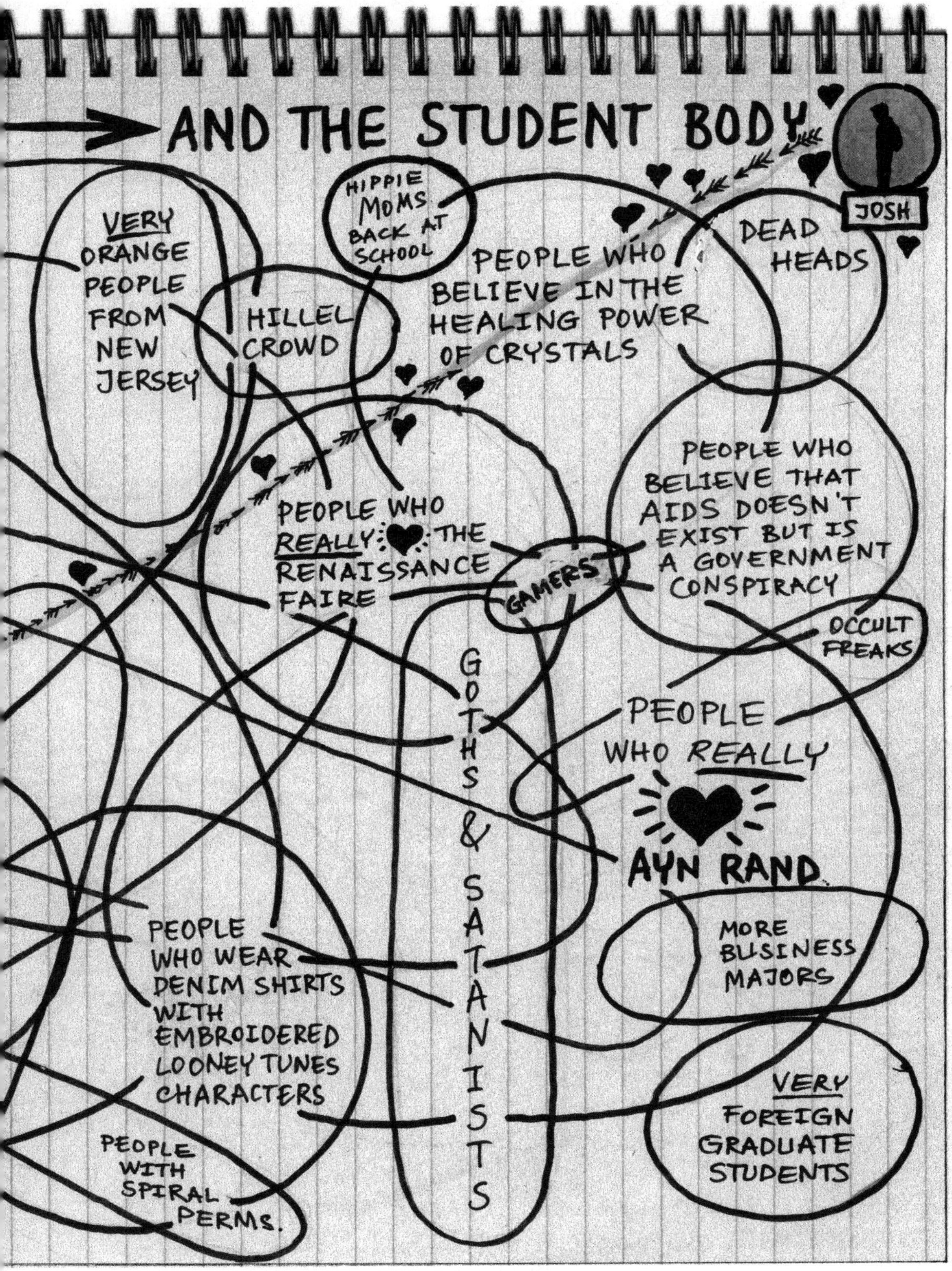

AND THE STUDENT BODY
JOSH
HIPPIE MOMS BACK AT SCHOOL
VERY ORANGE PEOPLE FROM NEW JERSEY
HILLEL CROWD
PEOPLE WHO BELIEVE IN THE HEALING POWER OF CRYSTALS
DEAD HEADS
PEOPLE WHO REALLY ♥ THE RENAISSANCE FAIRE
GAMERS
PEOPLE WHO BELIEVE THAT AIDS DOESN'T EXIST BUT IS A GOVERNMENT CONSPIRACY
OCCULT FREAKS
GOTHS & SATANISTS
PEOPLE WHO REALLY ♥ AYN RAND
MORE BUSINESS MAJORS
PEOPLE WHO WEAR DENIM SHIRTS WITH EMBROIDERED LOONEY TUNES CHARACTERS
VERY FOREIGN GRADUATE STUDENTS
PEOPLE WITH SPIRAL PERMS.

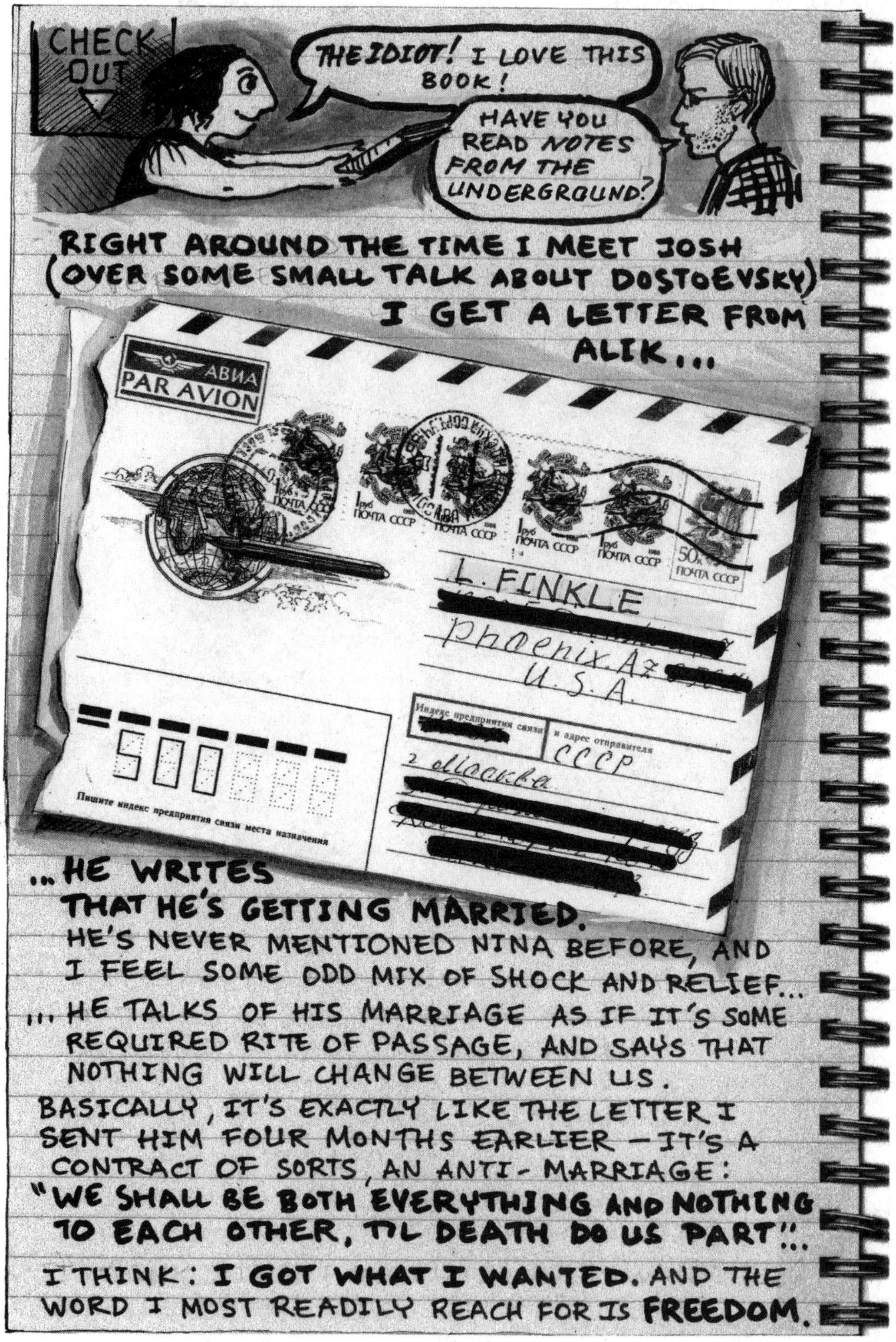
CHECK OUT
THE IDIOT! I LOVE THIS BOOK!
HAVE YOU READ NOTES FROM THE UNDERGROUND?
RIGHT AROUND THE TIME I MEET JOSH (OVER SOME SMALL TALK ABOUT DOSTOEVSKY) I GET A LETTER FROM ALIK...
АВИА
PAR AVION
ПОЧТА СССР
50к ПОЧТА СССР
L. FINKLE
[redacted]
Phoenix Az [redacted]
U.S.A.
Индекс предприятия связи
[redacted]
и адрес отправителя
СССР
г Москва
[redacted]
500
Пишите индекс предприятия связи места назначения
...HE WRITES THAT HE'S GETTING MARRIED.
HE'S NEVER MENTIONED NINA BEFORE, AND I FEEL SOME ODD MIX OF SHOCK AND RELIEF...
...HE TALKS OF HIS MARRIAGE AS IF IT'S SOME REQUIRED RITE OF PASSAGE, AND SAYS THAT NOTHING WILL CHANGE BETWEEN US.
BASICALLY, IT'S EXACTLY LIKE THE LETTER I SENT HIM FOUR MONTHS EARLIER — IT'S A CONTRACT OF SORTS, AN ANTI-MARRIAGE:
"WE SHALL BE BOTH EVERYTHING AND NOTHING TO EACH OTHER, TIL DEATH DO US PART"...
I THINK: I GOT WHAT I WANTED. AND THE WORD I MOST READILY REACH FOR IS FREEDOM.

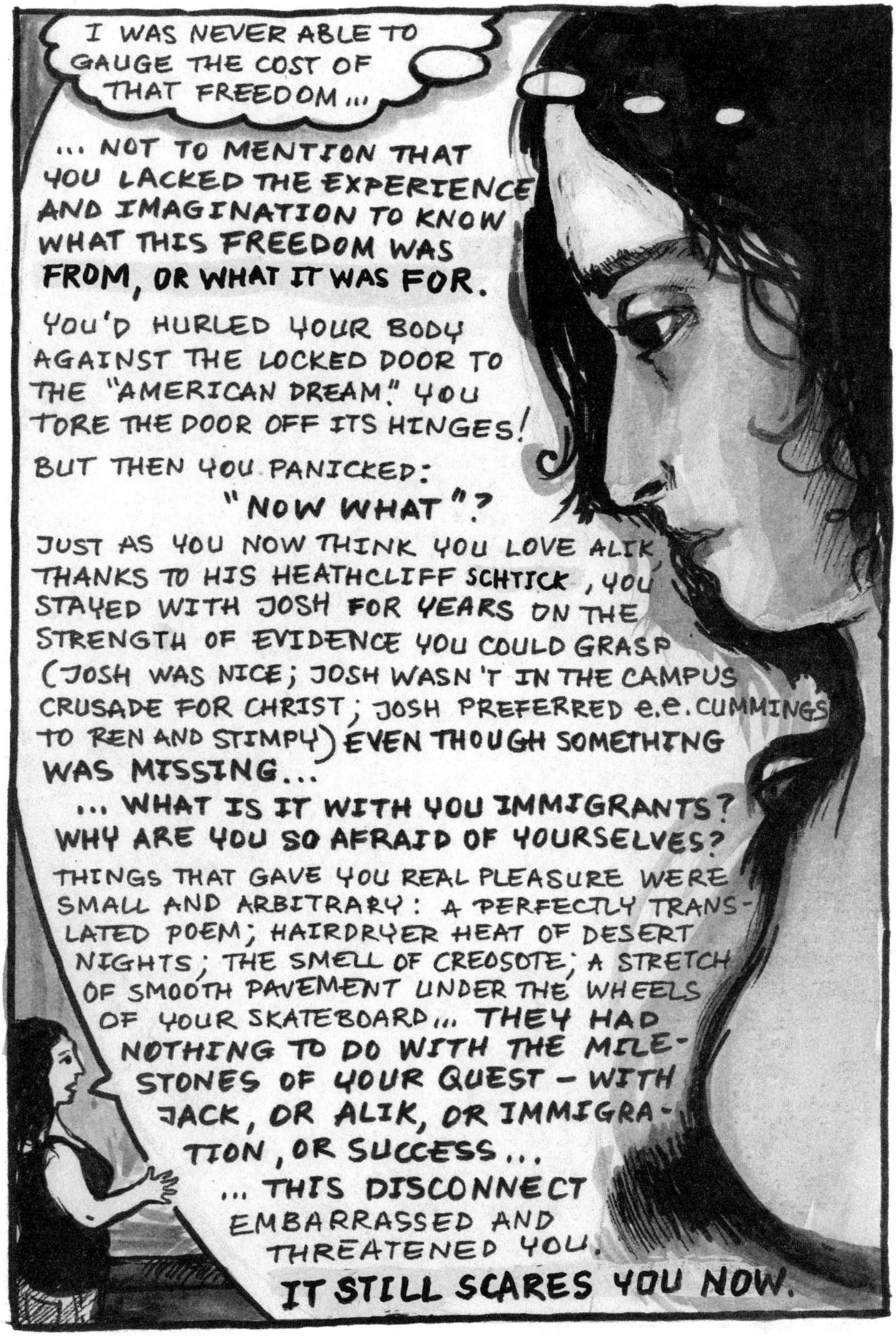
I WAS NEVER ABLE TO GAUGE THE COST OF THAT FREEDOM...
... NOT TO MENTION THAT YOU LACKED THE EXPERIENCE AND IMAGINATION TO KNOW WHAT THIS FREEDOM WAS FROM, OR WHAT IT WAS FOR.
YOU'D HURLED YOUR BODY AGAINST THE LOCKED DOOR TO THE "AMERICAN DREAM." YOU TORE THE DOOR OFF ITS HINGES!
BUT THEN YOU PANICKED:
"NOW WHAT"?
JUST AS YOU NOW THINK YOU LOVE ALIK THANKS TO HIS HEATHCLIFF SCHTICK, YOU STAYED WITH JOSH FOR YEARS ON THE STRENGTH OF EVIDENCE YOU COULD GRASP (JOSH WAS NICE; JOSH WASN'T IN THE CAMPUS CRUSADE FOR CHRIST; JOSH PREFERRED e.e. CUMMINGS TO REN AND STIMPY) EVEN THOUGH SOMETHING WAS MISSING...
... WHAT IS IT WITH YOU IMMIGRANTS? WHY ARE YOU SO AFRAID OF YOURSELVES?
THINGS THAT GAVE YOU REAL PLEASURE WERE SMALL AND ARBITRARY: A PERFECTLY TRANSLATED POEM; HAIRDRYER HEAT OF DESERT NIGHTS; THE SMELL OF CREOSOTE; A STRETCH OF SMOOTH PAVEMENT UNDER THE WHEELS OF YOUR SKATEBOARD... THEY HAD NOTHING TO DO WITH THE MILESTONES OF YOUR QUEST – WITH JACK, OR ALIK, OR IMMIGRATION, OR SUCCESS...
... THIS DISCONNECT EMBARRASSED AND THREATENED YOU.
IT STILL SCARES YOU NOW.

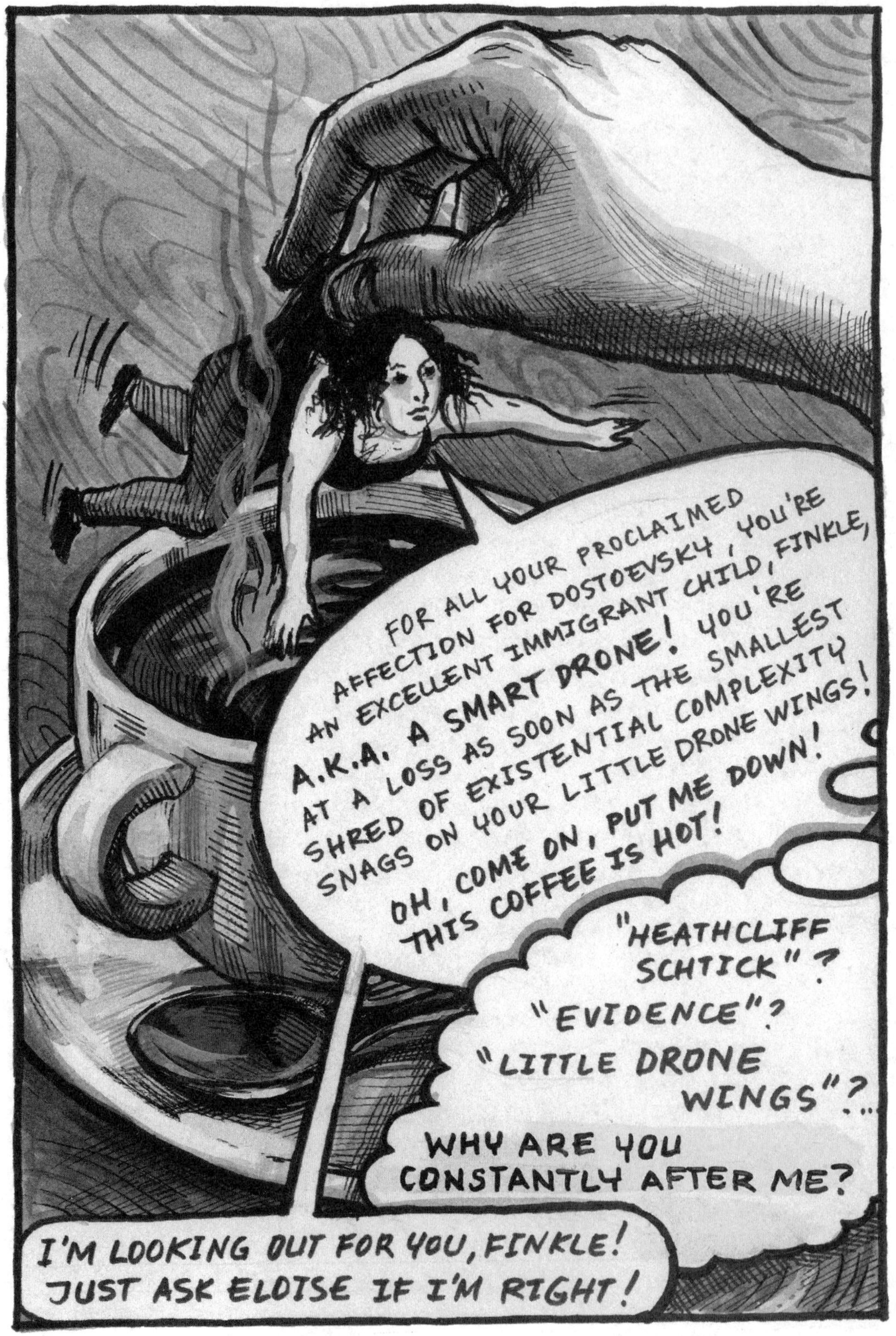
FOR ALL YOUR PROCLAIMED AFFECTION FOR DOSTOEVSKY, YOU'RE AN EXCELLENT IMMIGRANT CHILD, FINKLE, A.K.A. A SMART DRONE! YOU'RE AT A LOSS AS SOON AS THE SMALLEST SHRED OF EXISTENTIAL COMPLEXITY SNAGS ON YOUR LITTLE DRONE WINGS!
OH, COME ON, PUT ME DOWN! THIS COFFEE IS HOT!
"HEATHCLIFF SCHTICK"? "EVIDENCE"? "LITTLE DRONE WINGS"?... WHY ARE YOU CONSTANTLY AFTER ME?
I'M LOOKING OUT FOR YOU, FINKLE! JUST ASK ELOISE IF I'M RIGHT!

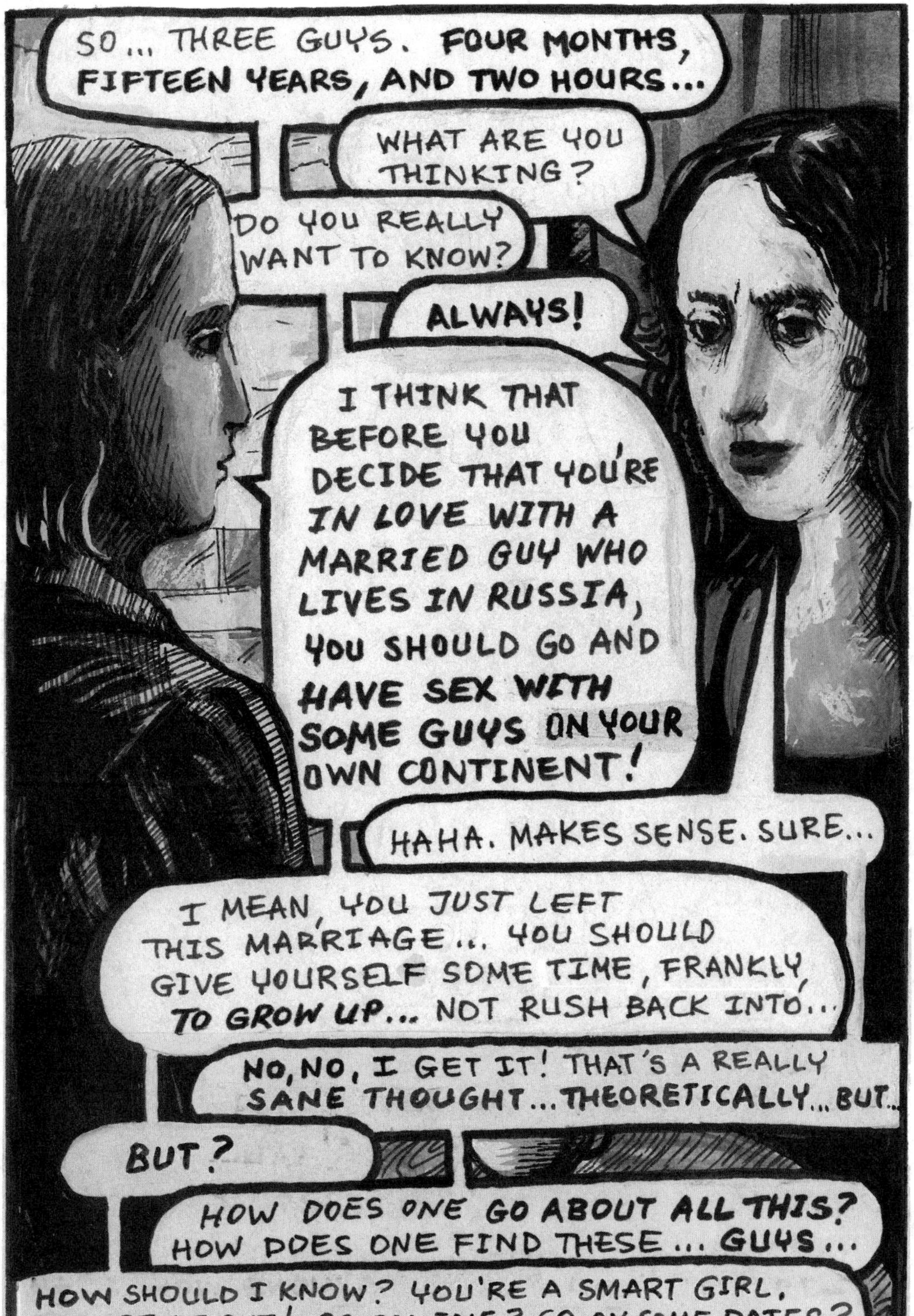
SO... THREE GUYS. FOUR MONTHS, FIFTEEN YEARS, AND TWO HOURS...
WHAT ARE YOU THINKING?
DO YOU REALLY WANT TO KNOW?
ALWAYS!
I THINK THAT BEFORE YOU DECIDE THAT YOU'RE IN LOVE WITH A MARRIED GUY WHO LIVES IN RUSSIA, YOU SHOULD GO AND HAVE SEX WITH SOME GUYS ON YOUR OWN CONTINENT!
HAHA. MAKES SENSE. SURE...
I MEAN, YOU JUST LEFT THIS MARRIAGE... YOU SHOULD GIVE YOURSELF SOME TIME, FRANKLY, TO GROW UP... NOT RUSH BACK INTO...
NO, NO, I GET IT! THAT'S A REALLY SANE THOUGHT... THEORETICALLY... BUT...
BUT?
HOW DOES ONE GO ABOUT ALL THIS? HOW DOES ONE FIND THESE... GUYS...
HOW SHOULD I KNOW? YOU'RE A SMART GIRL, FIGURE IT OUT! GO ONLINE? GO ON SOME DATES?

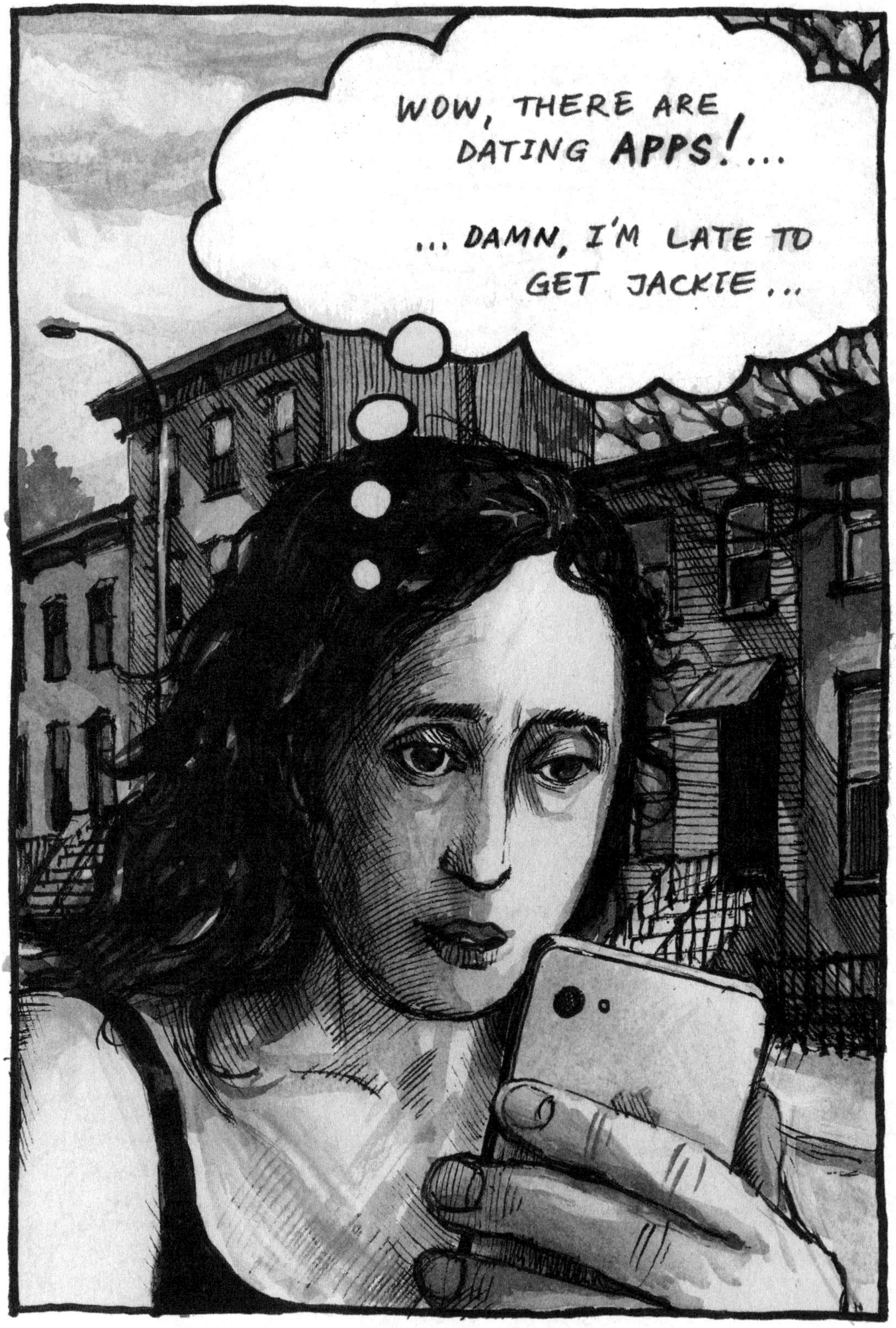
WOW, THERE ARE DATING APPS!...
... DAMN, I'M LATE TO GET JACKIE...

PART TWO

anthropology
Brooklyn, New York
My self-summary
Honest man who doesn't play Games. Scrabble enthusiast.
!

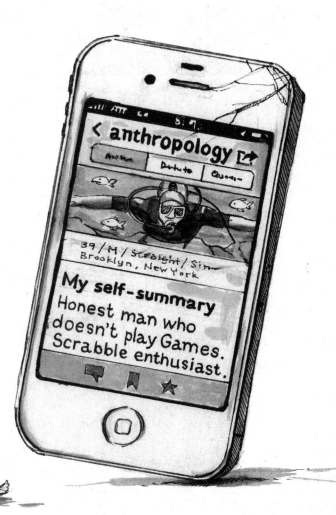

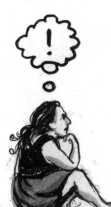

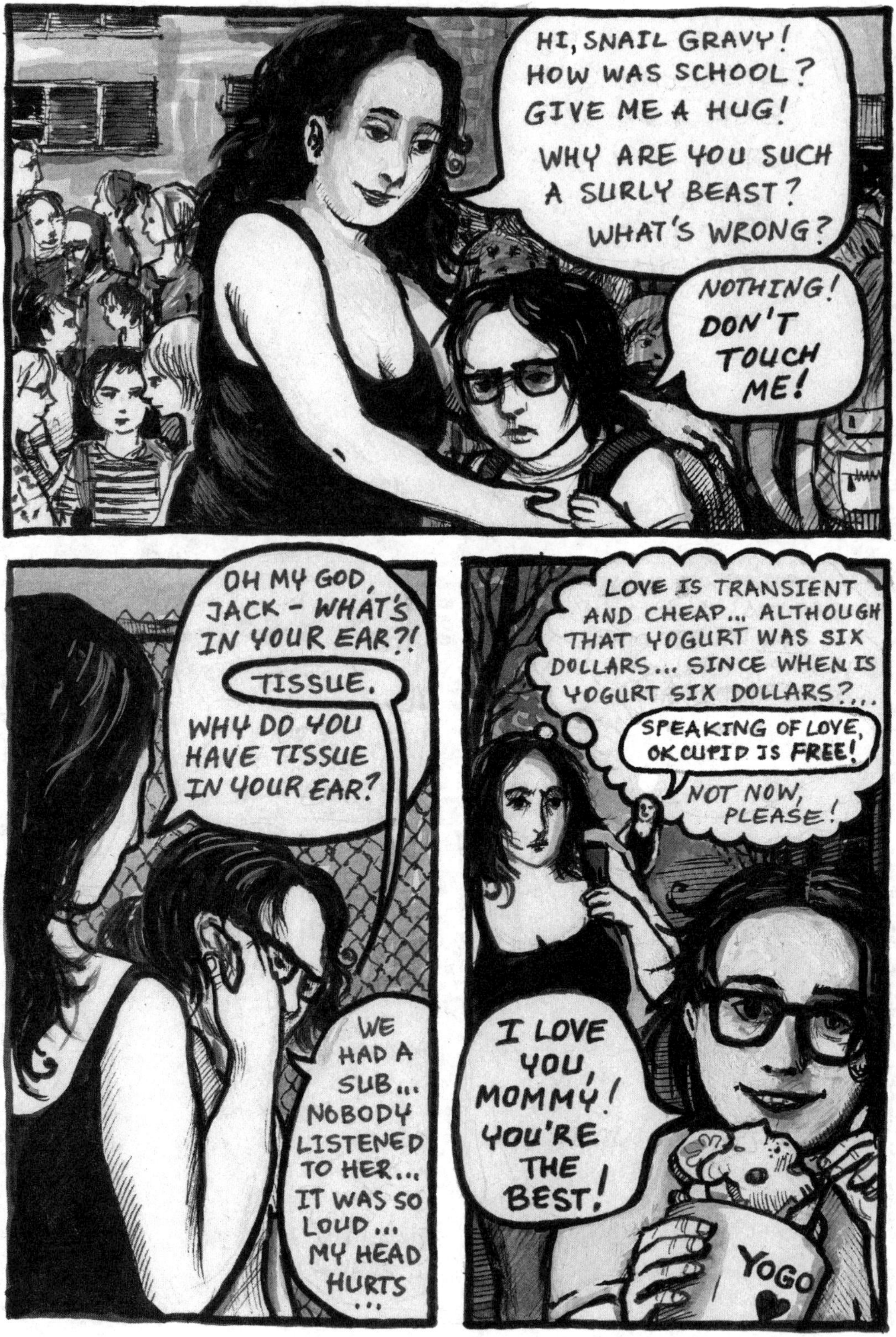
HI, SNAIL GRAVY! HOW WAS SCHOOL? GIVE ME A HUG! WHY ARE YOU SUCH A SURLY BEAST? WHAT'S WRONG?
NOTHING! DON'T TOUCH ME!
OH MY GOD, JACK - WHAT'S IN YOUR EAR?!
TISSUE.
WHY DO YOU HAVE TISSUE IN YOUR EAR?
WE HAD A SUB... NOBODY LISTENED TO HER... IT WAS SO LOUD... MY HEAD HURTS...
LOVE IS TRANSIENT AND CHEAP... ALTHOUGH THAT YOGURT WAS SIX DOLLARS... SINCE WHEN IS YOGURT SIX DOLLARS?...
SPEAKING OF LOVE, OKCUPID IS FREE!
NOT NOW, PLEASE!
I LOVE YOU, MOMMY! YOU'RE THE BEST!
YOGO

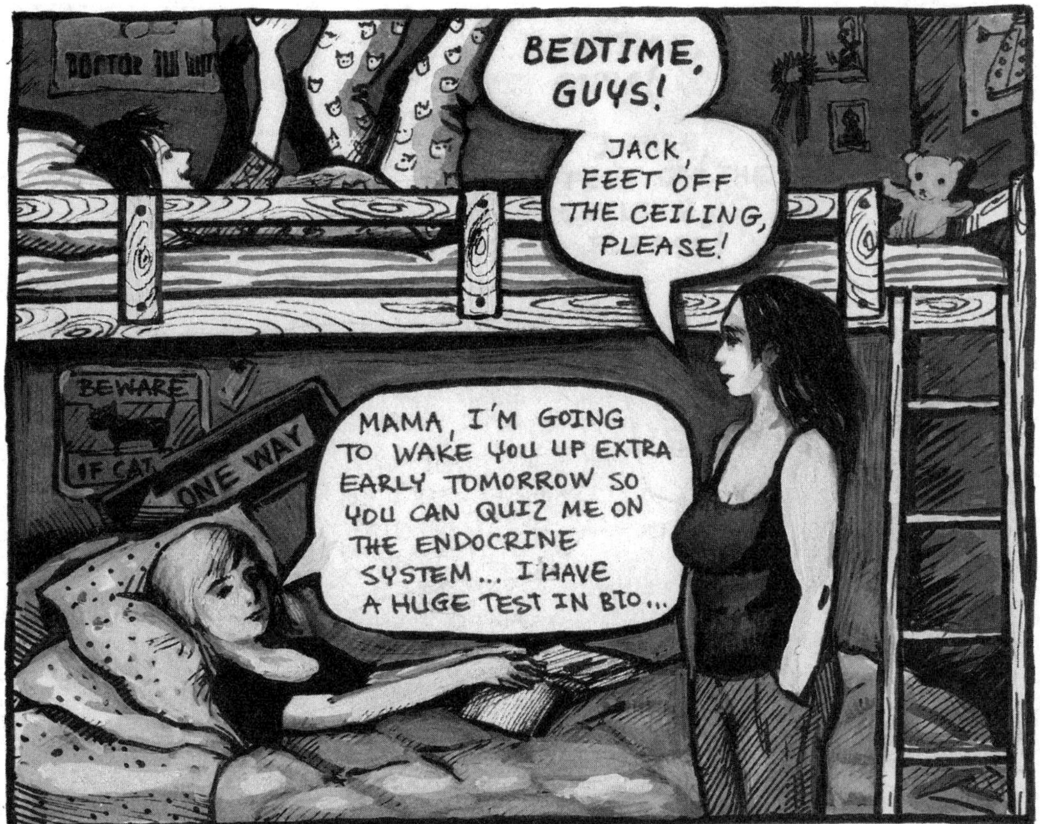
BEDTIME, GUYS!
JACK, FEET OFF THE CEILING, PLEASE!
BEWARE OF CAT
ONE WAY
MAMA, I'M GOING TO WAKE YOU UP EXTRA EARLY TOMORROW SO YOU CAN QUIZ ME ON THE ENDOCRINE SYSTEM... I HAVE A HUGE TEST IN BIO...

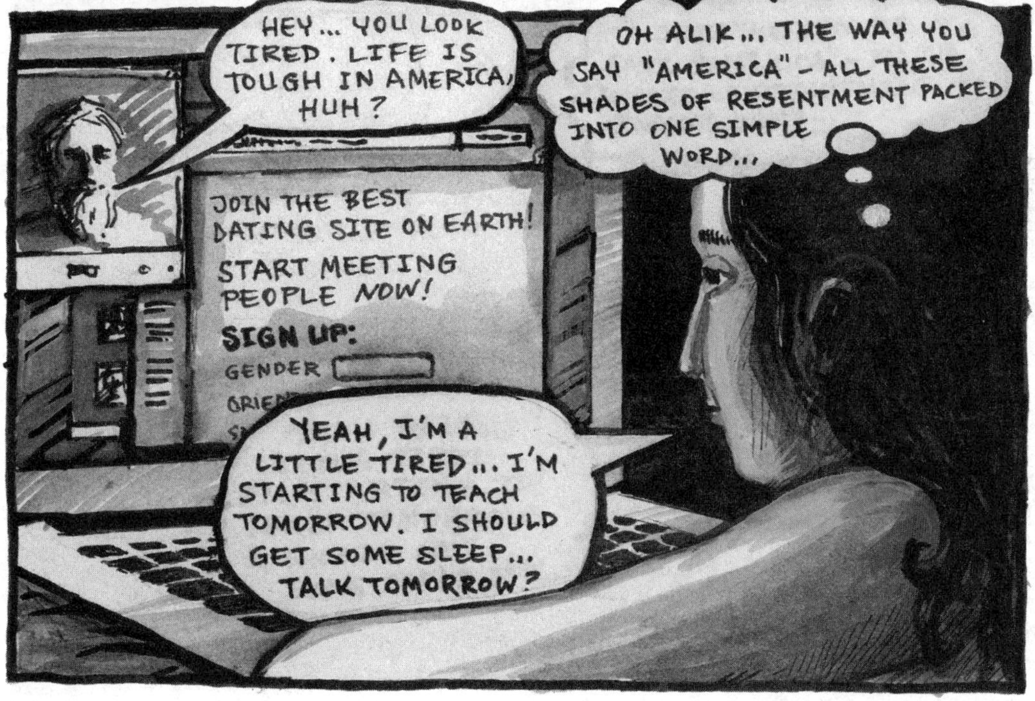
HEY... YOU LOOK TIRED. LIFE IS TOUGH IN AMERICA, HUH?
OH ALIK... THE WAY YOU SAY "AMERICA" - ALL THESE SHADES OF RESENTMENT PACKED INTO ONE SIMPLE WORD...
JOIN THE BEST DATING SITE ON EARTH!
START MEETING PEOPLE NOW!
SIGN UP:
GENDER
YEAH, I'M A LITTLE TIRED... I'M STARTING TO TEACH TOMORROW. I SHOULD GET SOME SLEEP... TALK TOMORROW?

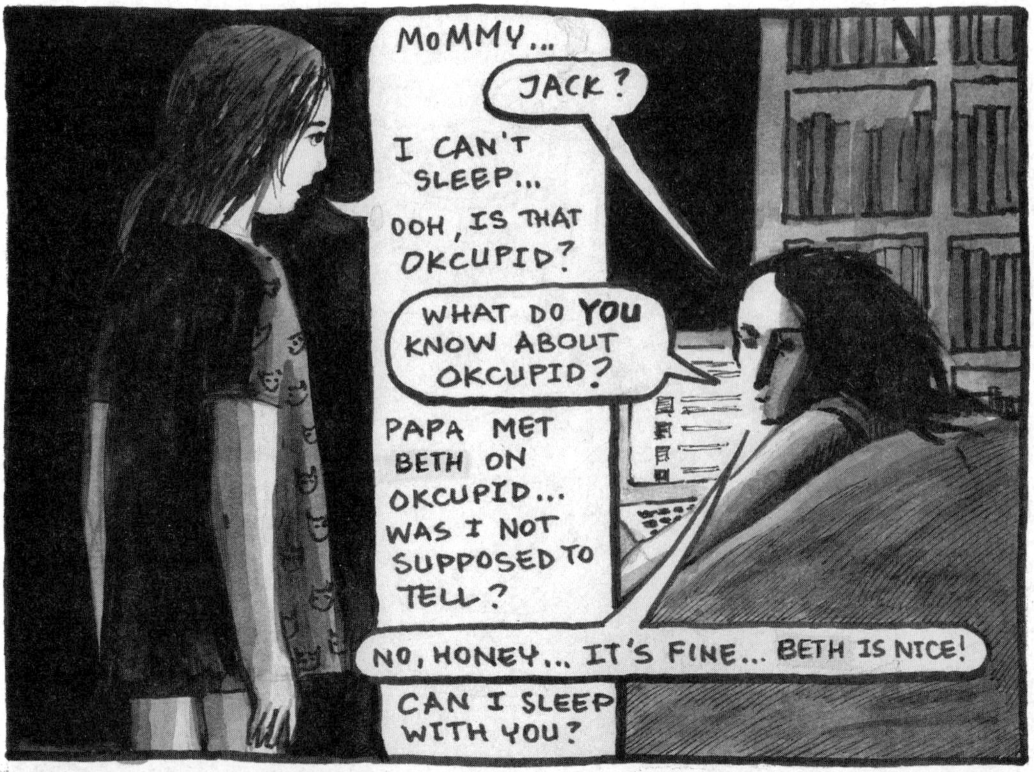
MOMMY...
JACK?
I CAN'T SLEEP...
OOH, IS THAT OKCUPID?
WHAT DO YOU KNOW ABOUT OKCUPID?
PAPA MET BETH ON OKCUPID... WAS I NOT SUPPOSED TO TELL?
NO, HONEY... IT'S FINE... BETH IS NICE!
CAN I SLEEP WITH YOU?

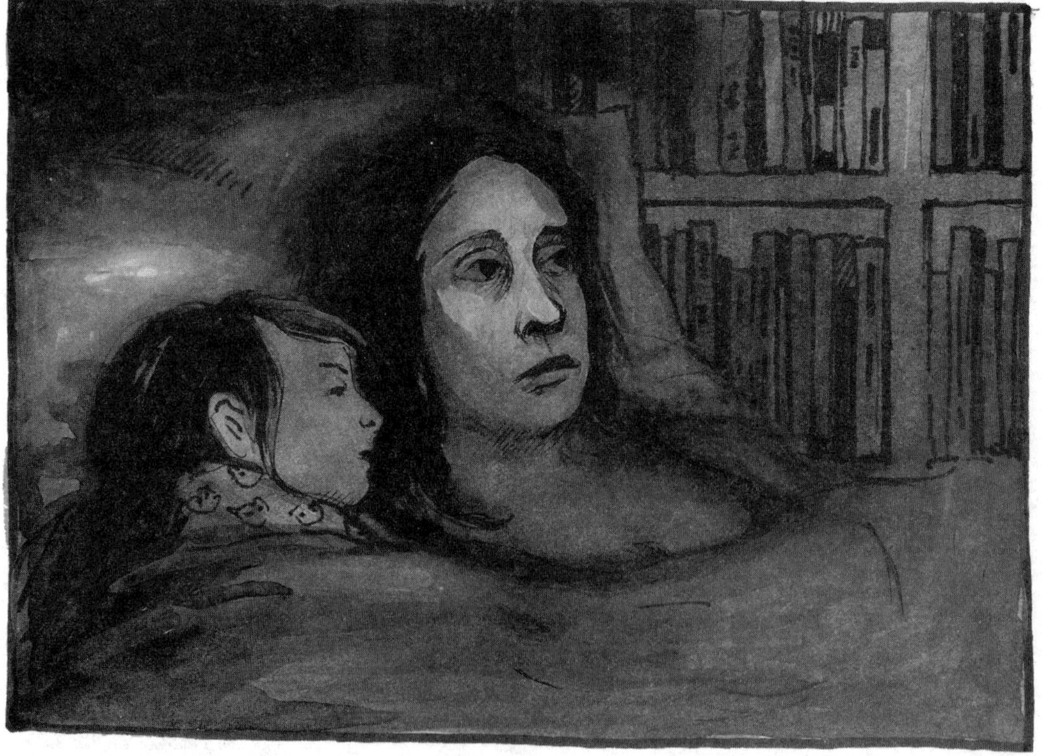

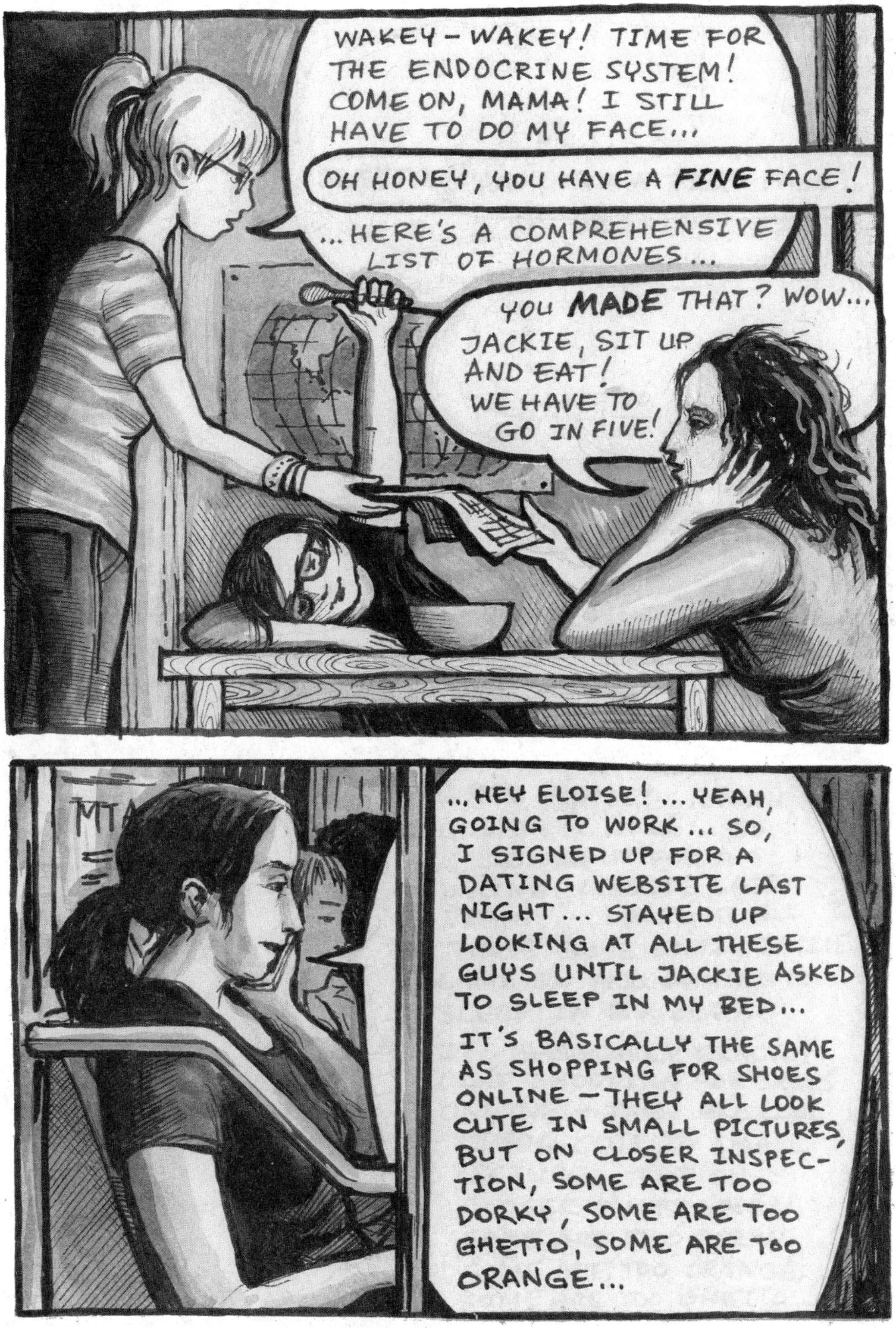
WAKEY-WAKEY! TIME FOR THE ENDOCRINE SYSTEM! COME ON, MAMA! I STILL HAVE TO DO MY FACE...
OH HONEY, YOU HAVE A FINE FACE!
...HERE'S A COMPREHENSIVE LIST OF HORMONES...
YOU MADE THAT? WOW... JACKIE, SIT UP AND EAT! WE HAVE TO GO IN FIVE!
MTA
...HEY ELOISE! ...YEAH, GOING TO WORK... SO, I SIGNED UP FOR A DATING WEBSITE LAST NIGHT... STAYED UP LOOKING AT ALL THESE GUYS UNTIL JACKIE ASKED TO SLEEP IN MY BED...
IT'S BASICALLY THE SAME AS SHOPPING FOR SHOES ONLINE — THEY ALL LOOK CUTE IN SMALL PICTURES, BUT ON CLOSER INSPECTION, SOME ARE TOO DORKY, SOME ARE TOO GHETTO, SOME ARE TOO ORANGE...

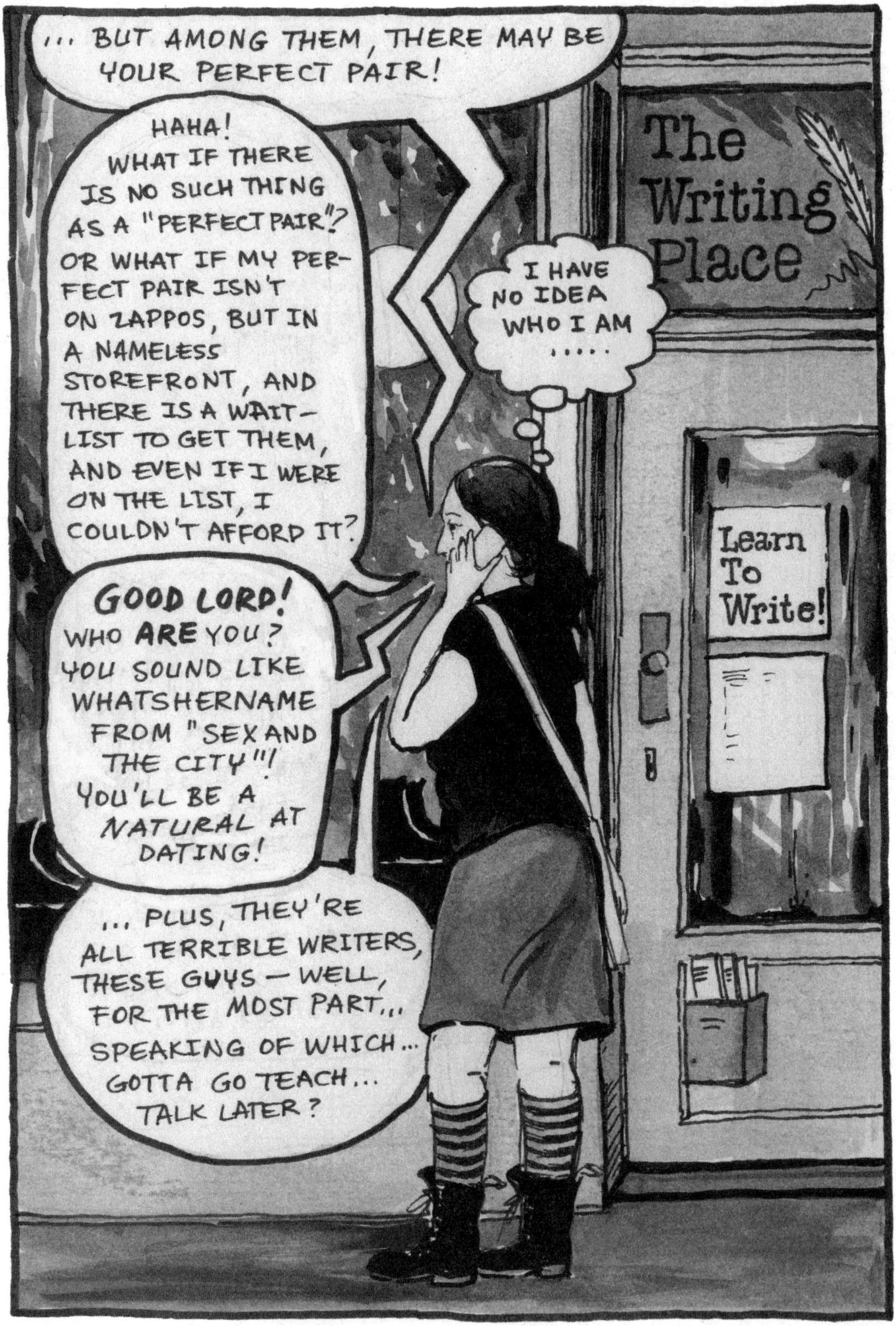
... BUT AMONG THEM, THERE MAY BE YOUR PERFECT PAIR!
HAHA! WHAT IF THERE IS NO SUCH THING AS A "PERFECT PAIR"? OR WHAT IF MY PERFECT PAIR ISN'T ON ZAPPOS, BUT IN A NAMELESS STOREFRONT, AND THERE IS A WAIT-LIST TO GET THEM, AND EVEN IF I WERE ON THE LIST, I COULDN'T AFFORD IT?
I HAVE NO IDEA WHO I AM .....
The Writing Place
Learn To Write!
GOOD LORD! WHO ARE YOU? YOU SOUND LIKE WHATSHERNAME FROM "SEX AND THE CITY"! YOU'LL BE A NATURAL AT DATING!
... PLUS, THEY'RE ALL TERRIBLE WRITERS, THESE GUYS — WELL, FOR THE MOST PART... SPEAKING OF WHICH... GOTTA GO TEACH... TALK LATER?

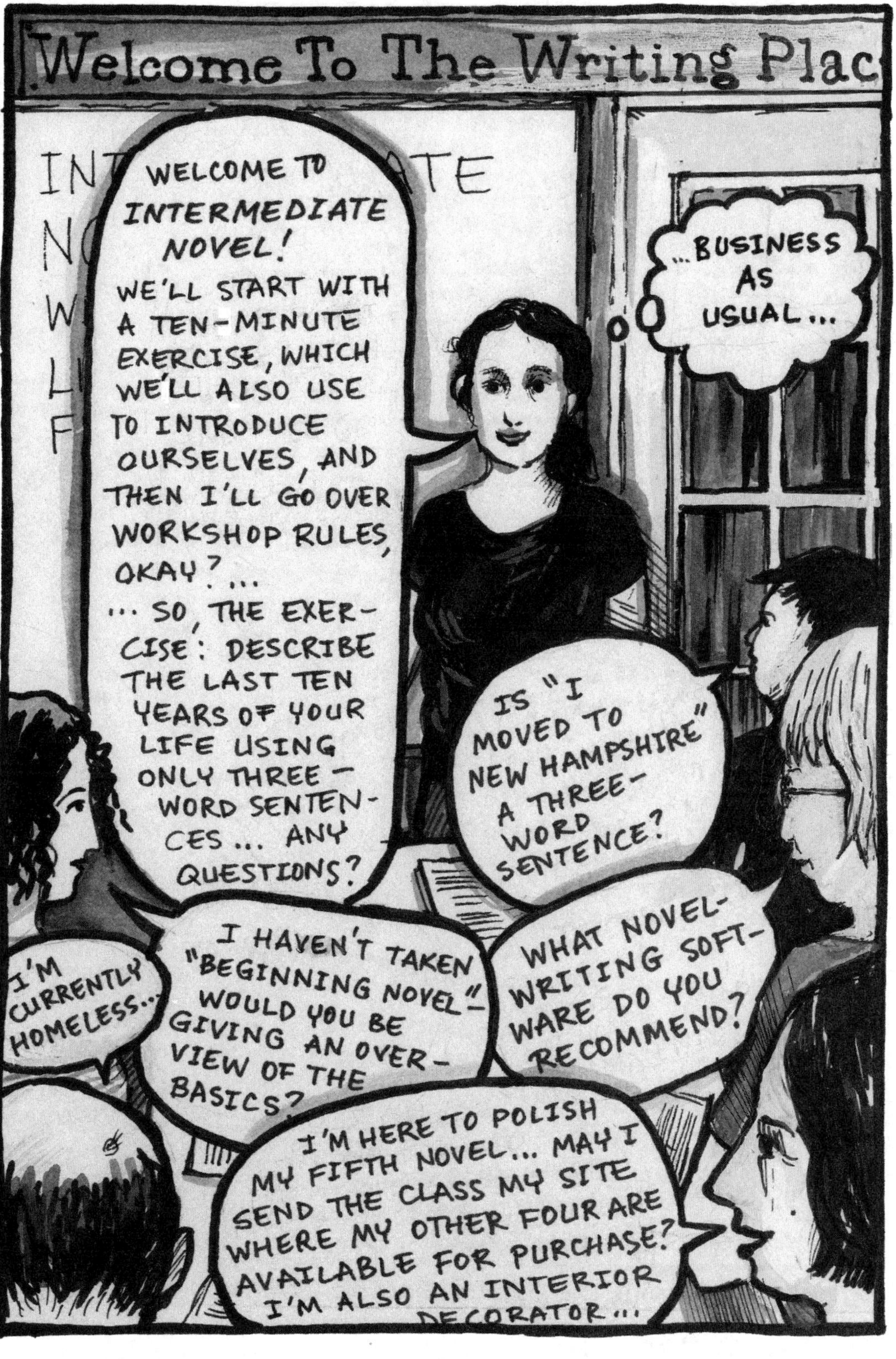

Welcome To The Writing Plac
WELCOME TO INTERMEDIATE NOVEL! WE'LL START WITH A TEN-MINUTE EXERCISE, WHICH WE'LL ALSO USE TO INTRODUCE OURSELVES, AND THEN I'LL GO OVER WORKSHOP RULES, OKAY? ... ... SO, THE EXERCISE: DESCRIBE THE LAST TEN YEARS OF YOUR LIFE USING ONLY THREE-WORD SENTENCES... ANY QUESTIONS?
...BUSINESS AS USUAL...
IS "I MOVED TO NEW HAMPSHIRE" A THREE-WORD SENTENCE?
I'M CURRENTLY HOMELESS...
I HAVEN'T TAKEN "BEGINNING NOVEL"- WOULD YOU BE GIVING AN OVERVIEW OF THE BASICS?
WHAT NOVEL-WRITING SOFTWARE DO YOU RECOMMEND?
I'M HERE TO POLISH MY FIFTH NOVEL... MAY I SEND THE CLASS MY SITE WHERE MY OTHER FOUR ARE AVAILABLE FOR PURCHASE? I'M ALSO AN INTERIOR DECORATOR...

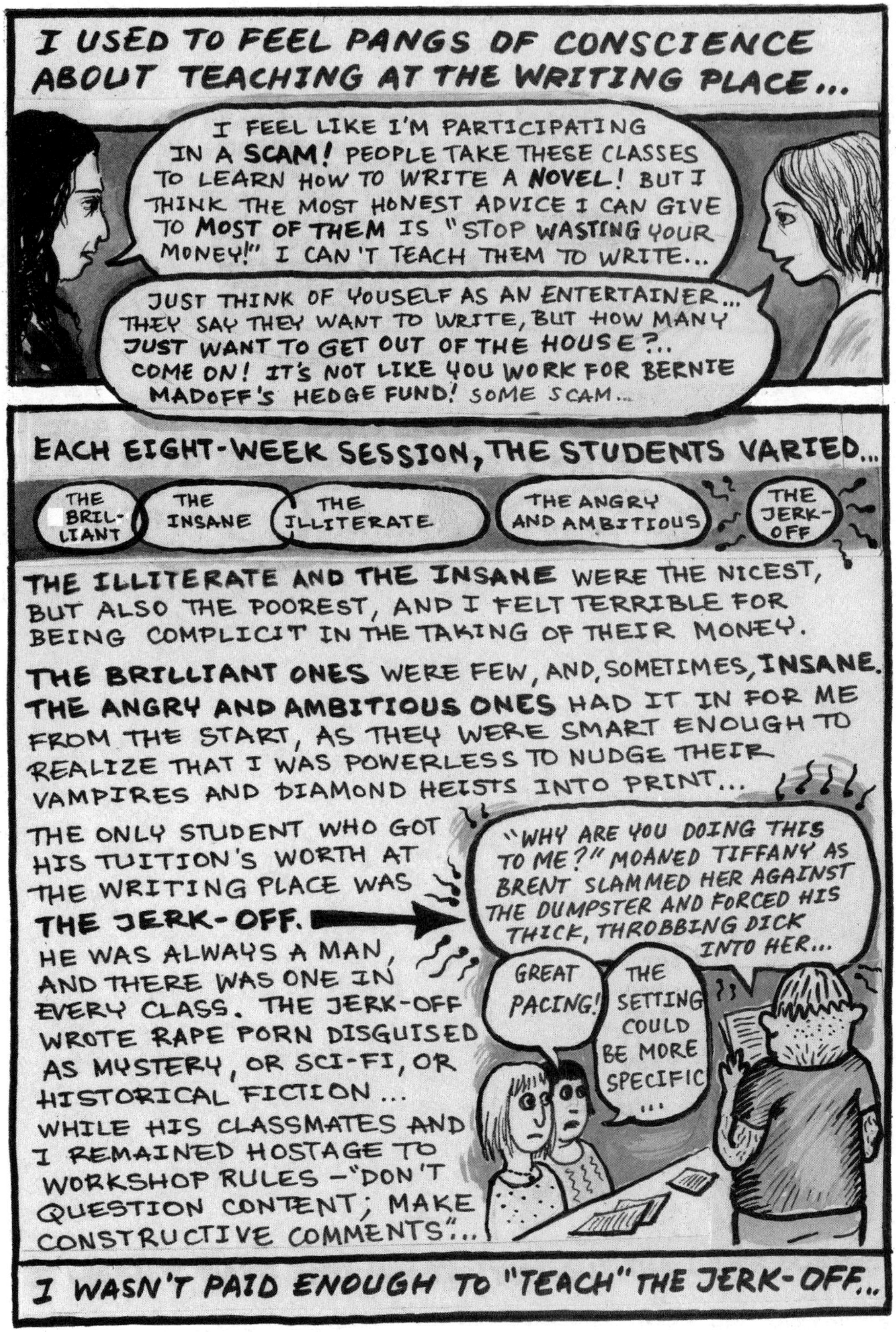

I USED TO FEEL PANGS OF CONSCIENCE ABOUT TEACHING AT THE WRITING PLACE...
I FEEL LIKE I'M PARTICIPATING IN A SCAM! PEOPLE TAKE THESE CLASSES TO LEARN HOW TO WRITE A NOVEL! BUT I THINK THE MOST HONEST ADVICE I CAN GIVE TO MOST OF THEM IS "STOP WASTING YOUR MONEY!" I CAN'T TEACH THEM TO WRITE...
JUST THINK OF YOUSELF AS AN ENTERTAINER... THEY SAY THEY WANT TO WRITE, BUT HOW MANY JUST WANT TO GET OUT OF THE HOUSE?.. COME ON! IT'S NOT LIKE YOU WORK FOR BERNIE MADOFF'S HEDGE FUND! SOME SCAM...
EACH EIGHT-WEEK SESSION, THE STUDENTS VARIED...
THE BRIL-LIANT
THE INSANE
THE ILLITERATE
THE ANGRY AND AMBITIOUS
THE JERK-OFF
THE ILLITERATE AND THE INSANE WERE THE NICEST, BUT ALSO THE POOREST, AND I FELT TERRIBLE FOR BEING COMPLICIT IN THE TAKING OF THEIR MONEY.
THE BRILLIANT ONES WERE FEW, AND, SOMETIMES, INSANE. THE ANGRY AND AMBITIOUS ONES HAD IT IN FOR ME FROM THE START, AS THEY WERE SMART ENOUGH TO REALIZE THAT I WAS POWERLESS TO NUDGE THEIR VAMPIRES AND DIAMOND HEISTS INTO PRINT...
THE ONLY STUDENT WHO GOT HIS TUITION'S WORTH AT THE WRITING PLACE WAS THE JERK-OFF.
"WHY ARE YOU DOING THIS TO ME?" MOANED TIFFANY AS BRENT SLAMMED HER AGAINST THE DUMPSTER AND FORCED HIS THICK, THROBBING DICK INTO HER...
HE WAS ALWAYS A MAN, AND THERE WAS ONE IN EVERY CLASS. THE JERK-OFF WROTE RAPE PORN DISGUISED AS MYSTERY, OR SCI-FI, OR HISTORICAL FICTION... WHILE HIS CLASSMATES AND I REMAINED HOSTAGE TO WORKSHOP RULES —"DON'T QUESTION CONTENT; MAKE CONSTRUCTIVE COMMENTS"...
GREAT PACING!
THE SETTING COULD BE MORE SPECIFIC...
I WASN'T PAID ENOUGH TO "TEACH" THE JERK-OFF...

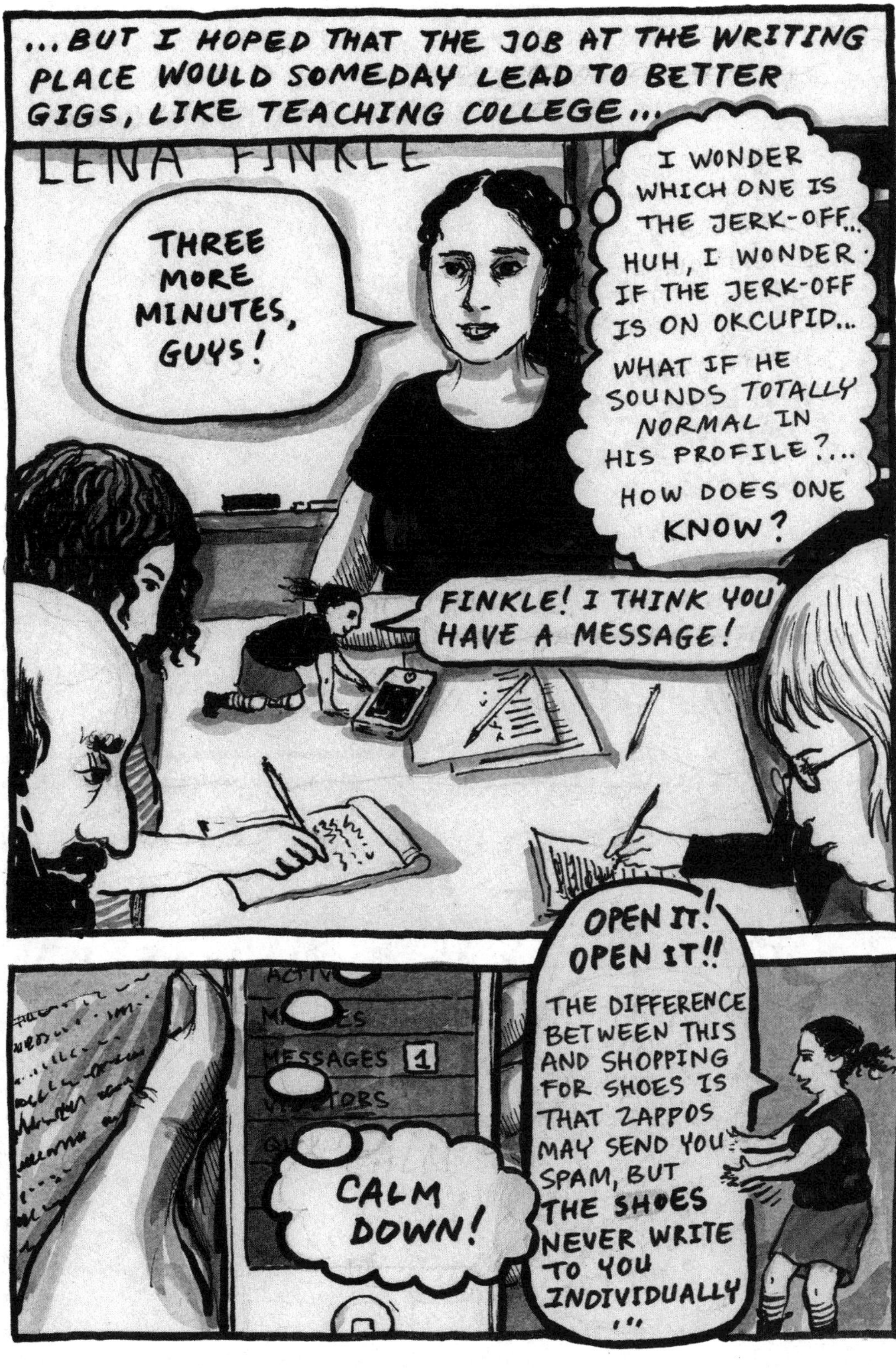
...BUT I HOPED THAT THE JOB AT THE WRITING PLACE WOULD SOMEDAY LEAD TO BETTER GIGS, LIKE TEACHING COLLEGE...
LENA FINKLE
THREE MORE MINUTES, GUYS!
I WONDER WHICH ONE IS THE JERK-OFF... HUH, I WONDER IF THE JERK-OFF IS ON OKCUPID... WHAT IF HE SOUNDS TOTALLY NORMAL IN HIS PROFILE?... HOW DOES ONE KNOW?
FINKLE! I THINK YOU HAVE A MESSAGE!
MESSAGES 1
VISITORS
OPEN IT! OPEN IT!! THE DIFFERENCE BETWEEN THIS AND SHOPPING FOR SHOES IS THAT ZAPPOS MAY SEND YOU SPAM, BUT THE SHOES NEVER WRITE TO YOU INDIVIDUALLY!"
CALM DOWN!

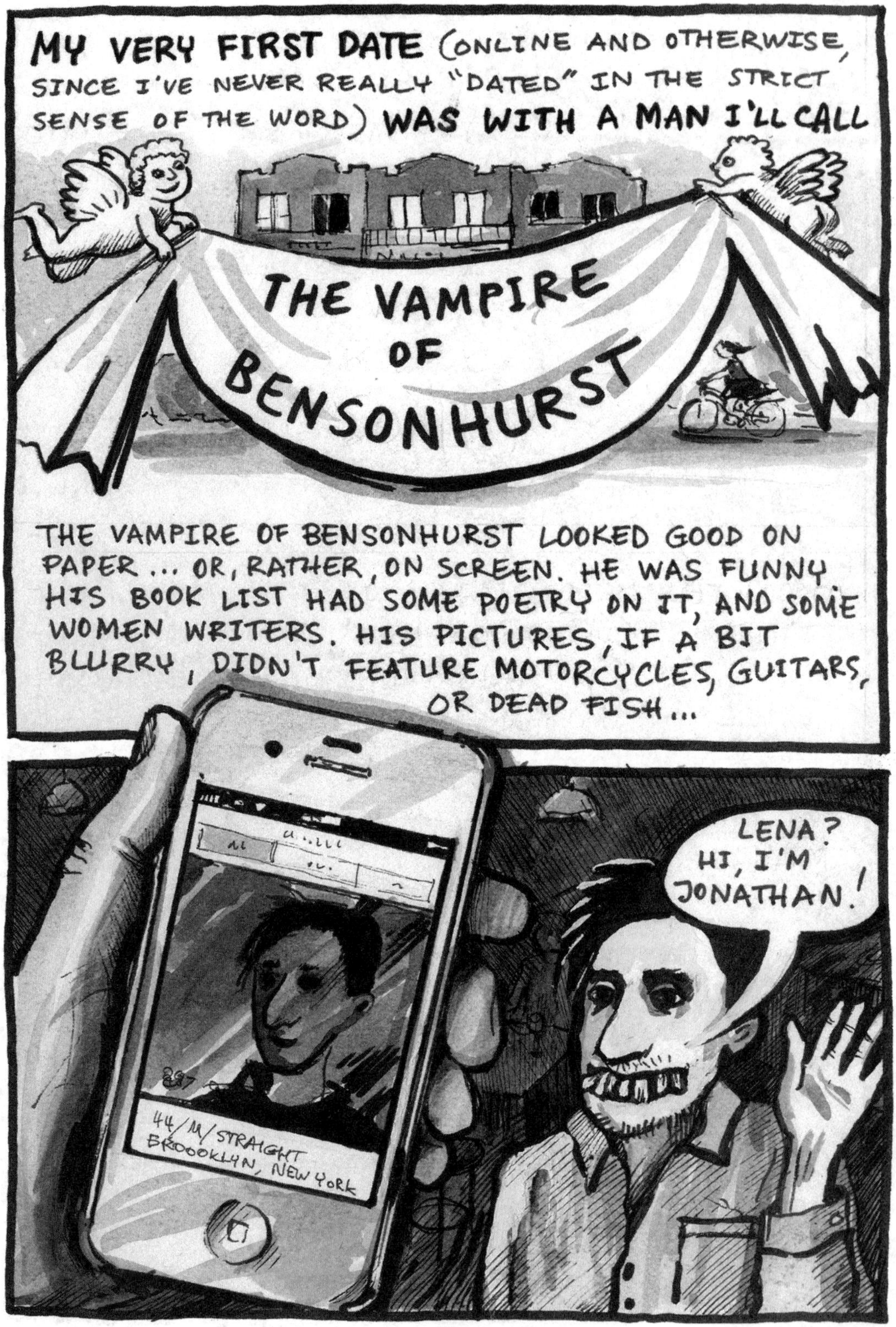

MY VERY FIRST DATE (ONLINE AND OTHERWISE, SINCE I'VE NEVER REALLY "DATED" IN THE STRICT SENSE OF THE WORD) WAS WITH A MAN I'LL CALL
THE VAMPIRE OF BENSONHURST
THE VAMPIRE OF BENSONHURST LOOKED GOOD ON PAPER... OR, RATHER, ON SCREEN. HE WAS FUNNY HIS BOOK LIST HAD SOME POETRY ON IT, AND SOME WOMEN WRITERS. HIS PICTURES, IF A BIT BLURRY, DIDN'T FEATURE MOTORCYCLES, GUITARS, OR DEAD FISH...
44/M/STRAIGHT
BROOOKLYN, NEW YORK
LENA? HI, I'M JONATHAN!

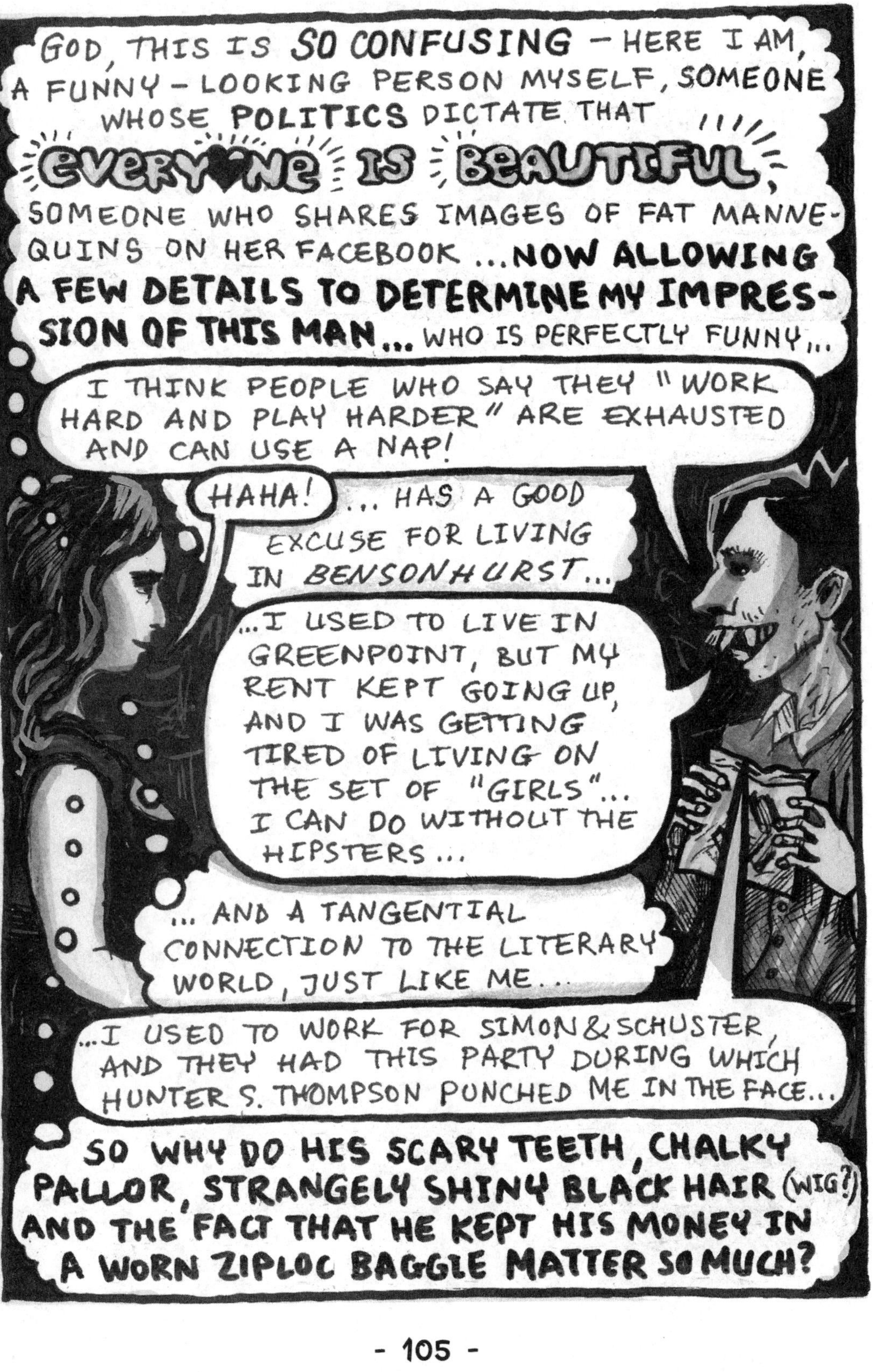
GOD, THIS IS SO CONFUSING — HERE I AM, A FUNNY-LOOKING PERSON MYSELF, SOMEONE WHOSE POLITICS DICTATE THAT EVERYONE IS BEAUTIFUL, SOMEONE WHO SHARES IMAGES OF FAT MANNEQUINS ON HER FACEBOOK ...NOW ALLOWING A FEW DETAILS TO DETERMINE MY IMPRESSION OF THIS MAN... WHO IS PERFECTLY FUNNY...
I THINK PEOPLE WHO SAY THEY "WORK HARD AND PLAY HARDER" ARE EXHAUSTED AND CAN USE A NAP!
HAHA!
... HAS A GOOD EXCUSE FOR LIVING IN BENSONHURST...
...I USED TO LIVE IN GREENPOINT, BUT MY RENT KEPT GOING UP, AND I WAS GETTING TIRED OF LIVING ON THE SET OF "GIRLS"... I CAN DO WITHOUT THE HIPSTERS...
... AND A TANGENTIAL CONNECTION TO THE LITERARY WORLD, JUST LIKE ME...
...I USED TO WORK FOR SIMON & SCHUSTER, AND THEY HAD THIS PARTY DURING WHICH HUNTER S. THOMPSON PUNCHED ME IN THE FACE...
SO WHY DO HIS SCARY TEETH, CHALKY PALLOR, STRANGELY SHINY BLACK HAIR (WIG?) AND THE FACT THAT HE KEPT HIS MONEY IN A WORN ZIPLOC BAGGIE MATTER SO MUCH?

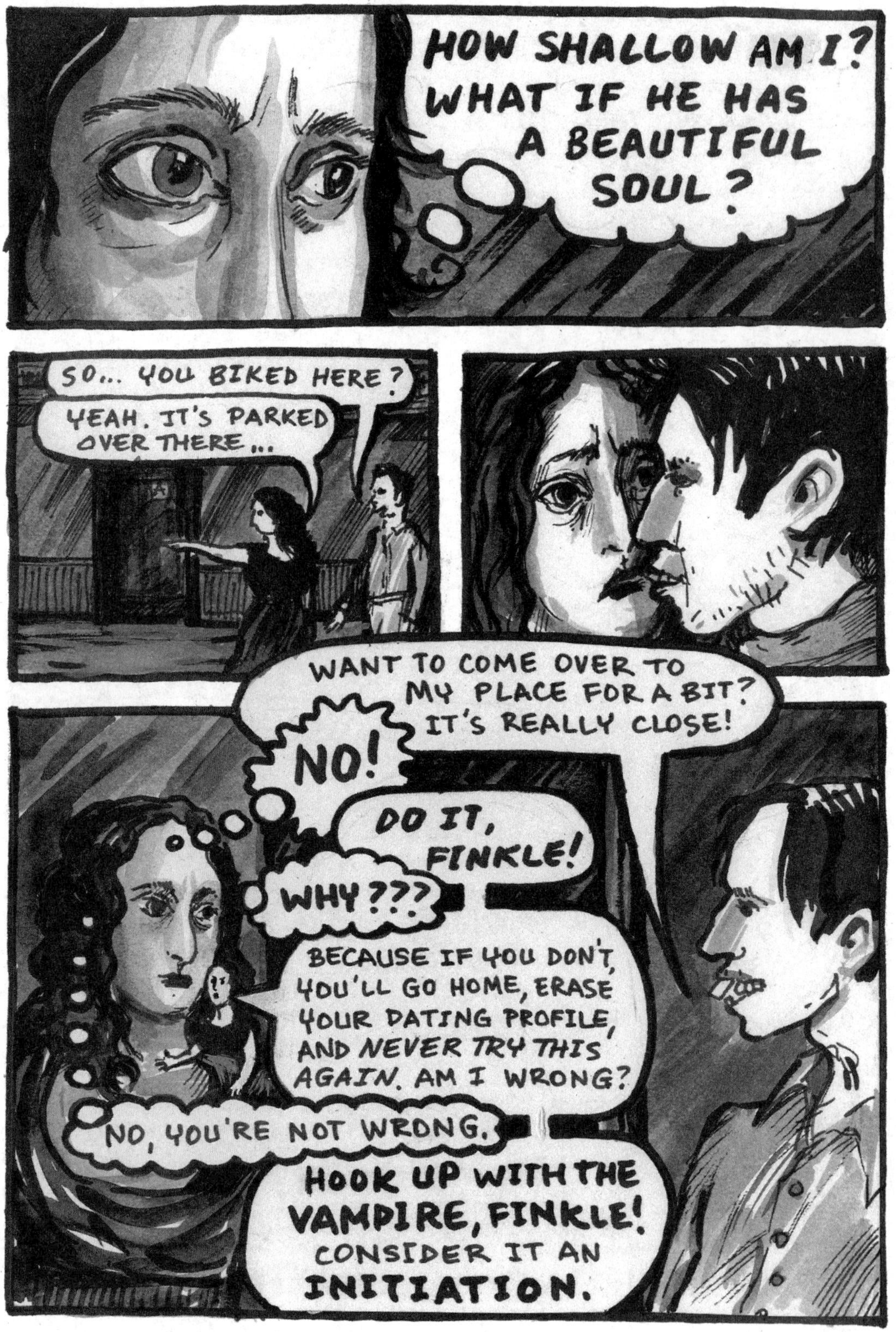
HOW SHALLOW AM I? WHAT IF HE HAS A BEAUTIFUL SOUL?
SO... YOU BIKED HERE?
YEAH. IT'S PARKED OVER THERE...
WANT TO COME OVER TO MY PLACE FOR A BIT? IT'S REALLY CLOSE!
NO!
DO IT, FINKLE!
WHY???
BECAUSE IF YOU DON'T, YOU'LL GO HOME, ERASE YOUR DATING PROFILE, AND *NEVER TRY THIS AGAIN*. AM I WRONG?
NO, YOU'RE NOT WRONG.
HOOK UP WITH THE VAMPIRE, FINKLE! CONSIDER IT AN INITIATION.

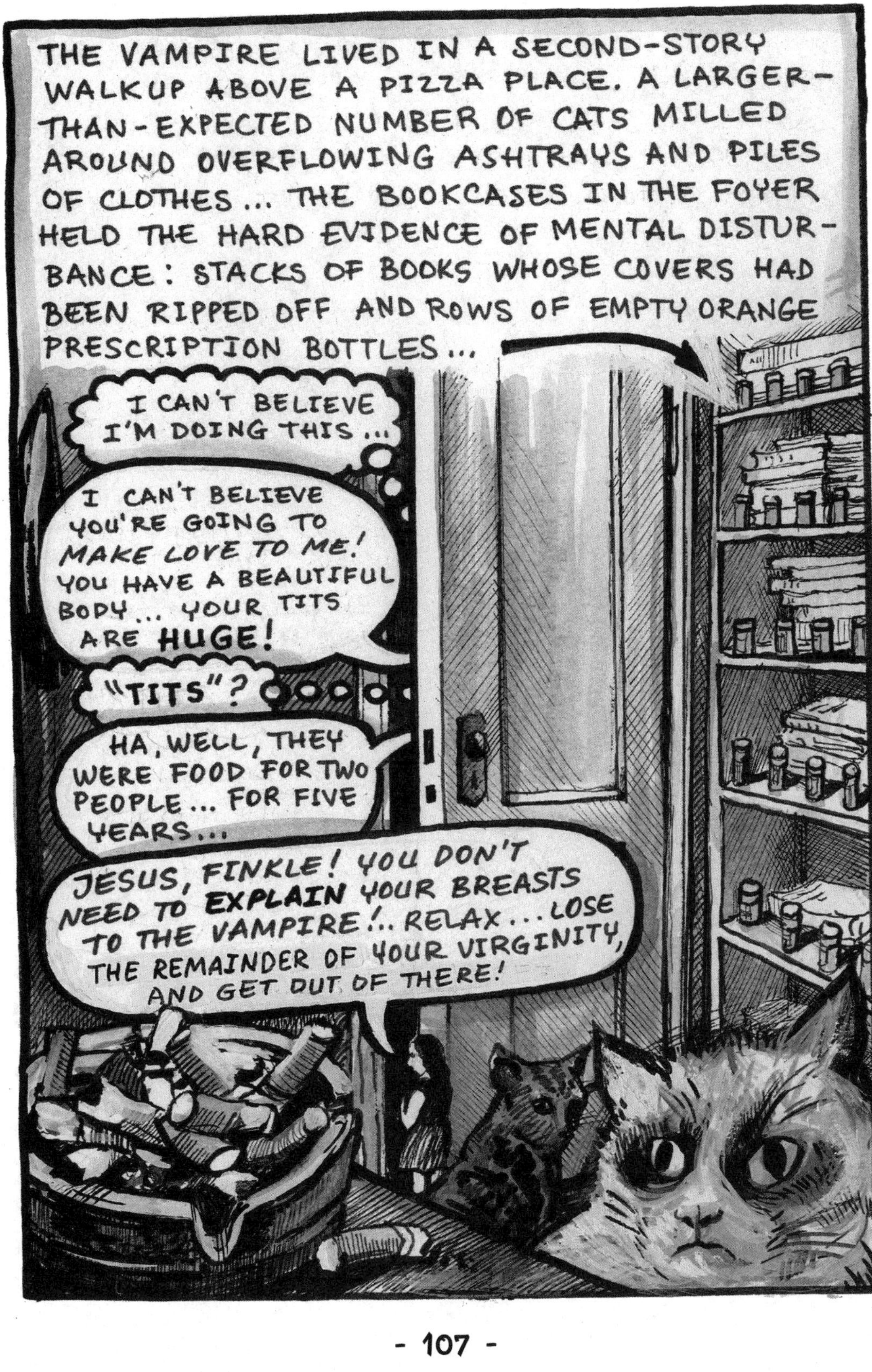
THE VAMPIRE LIVED IN A SECOND-STORY WALKUP ABOVE A PIZZA PLACE. A LARGER-THAN-EXPECTED NUMBER OF CATS MILLED AROUND OVERFLOWING ASHTRAYS AND PILES OF CLOTHES... THE BOOKCASES IN THE FOYER HELD THE HARD EVIDENCE OF MENTAL DISTURBANCE: STACKS OF BOOKS WHOSE COVERS HAD BEEN RIPPED OFF AND ROWS OF EMPTY ORANGE PRESCRIPTION BOTTLES...
I CAN'T BELIEVE I'M DOING THIS...
I CAN'T BELIEVE YOU'RE GOING TO MAKE LOVE TO ME! YOU HAVE A BEAUTIFUL BODY... YOUR TITS ARE HUGE!
"TITS"?
HA, WELL, THEY WERE FOOD FOR TWO PEOPLE... FOR FIVE YEARS...
JESUS, FINKLE! YOU DON'T NEED TO EXPLAIN YOUR BREASTS TO THE VAMPIRE!.. RELAX... LOSE THE REMAINDER OF YOUR VIRGINITY, AND GET OUT OF THERE!

YOU CAN STAY...
NO, I CAN'T...
WILL I SEE YOU AGAIN?
THIS WAS... MORE OF A... TRAINING SESSION FOR ME... I'M SORRY...
I CAN'T BELIEVE I SLEPT WITH THE VAMPIRE!
JUST THINK ABOUT THOSE ITALIAN NEO-REALIST MOVIES WHERE A BOY GOES TO A BROTHEL AND GETS DEFLOWERED BY AN UGLY OLD WHORE...
AM I THE BOY OR THE WHORE IN THIS SCENARIO?
DON'T PLAY DUMB! YOU'RE THE BOY. NOW THAT YOU WENT AND HAD SEX WITH SOMEONE YOU HAVEN'T KNOWN FOR TWENTY YEARS, THE NEXT TIME WILL BE EASIER!
THERE WON'T BE A NEXT TIME.

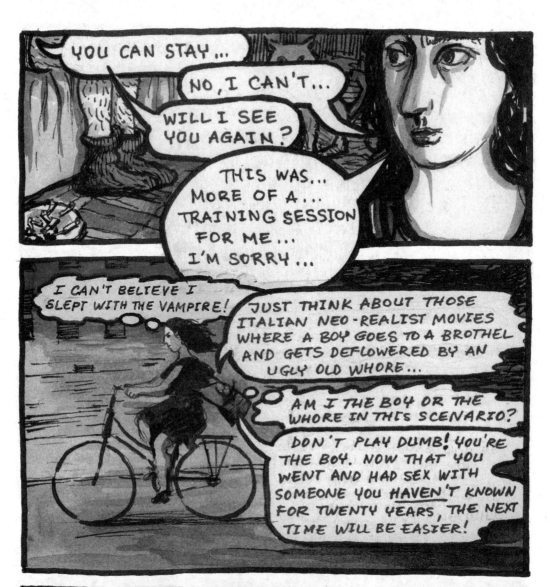

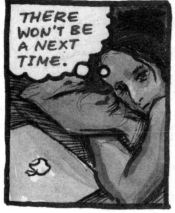

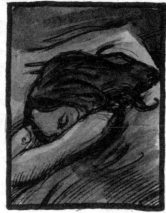

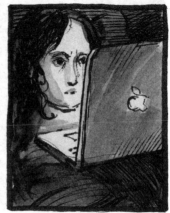

READER, I WENT BACK ONLINE. AFTER I GOT SOME SLEEP AND WASHED THE CIGARETTE SMELL OF VAMPIRE'S LAIR OUT OF MY HAIR, I LOOKED BACK ON MY NIGHT WITH HIM AS A SUCCESSFULLY COMPLETED MISSION...

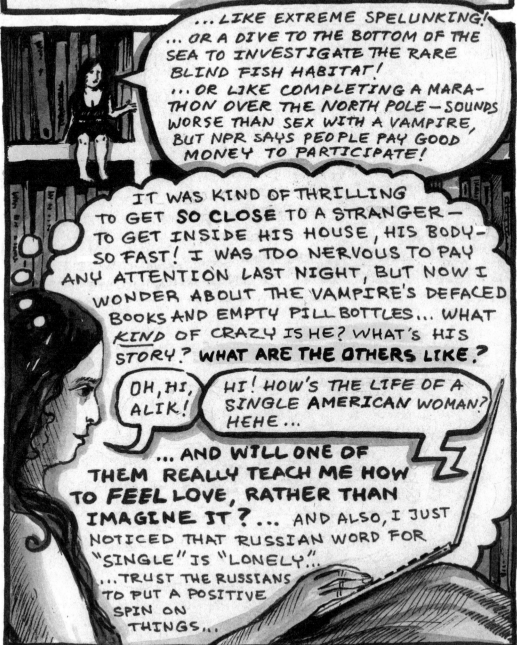

...LIKE EXTREME SPELUNKING! ...OR A DIVE TO THE BOTTOM OF THE SEA TO INVESTIGATE THE RARE BLIND FISH HABITAT! ...OR LIKE COMPLETING A MARATHON OVER THE NORTH POLE—SOUNDS WORSE THAN SEX WITH A VAMPIRE, BUT NPR SAYS PEOPLE PAY GOOD MONEY TO PARTICIPATE!

IT WAS KIND OF THRILLING TO GET **SO CLOSE** TO A STRANGER— TO GET INSIDE HIS HOUSE, HIS BODY— SO FAST! I WAS TOO NERVOUS TO PAY ANY ATTENTION LAST NIGHT, BUT NOW I WONDER ABOUT THE VAMPIRE'S DEFACED BOOKS AND EMPTY PILL BOTTLES... WHAT _KIND_ OF CRAZY IS HE? WHAT'S HIS STORY? **WHAT ARE THE OTHERS LIKE?**

OH, HI, ALIK!

HI! HOW'S THE LIFE OF A SINGLE AMERICAN WOMAN? HEHE...

...AND WILL ONE OF THEM REALLY TEACH ME HOW TO **FEEL** LOVE, RATHER THAN IMAGINE IT? ... AND ALSO, I JUST NOTICED THAT RUSSIAN WORD FOR "SINGLE" IS "LONELY."... ...TRUST THE RUSSIANS TO PUT A POSITIVE SPIN ON THINGS...

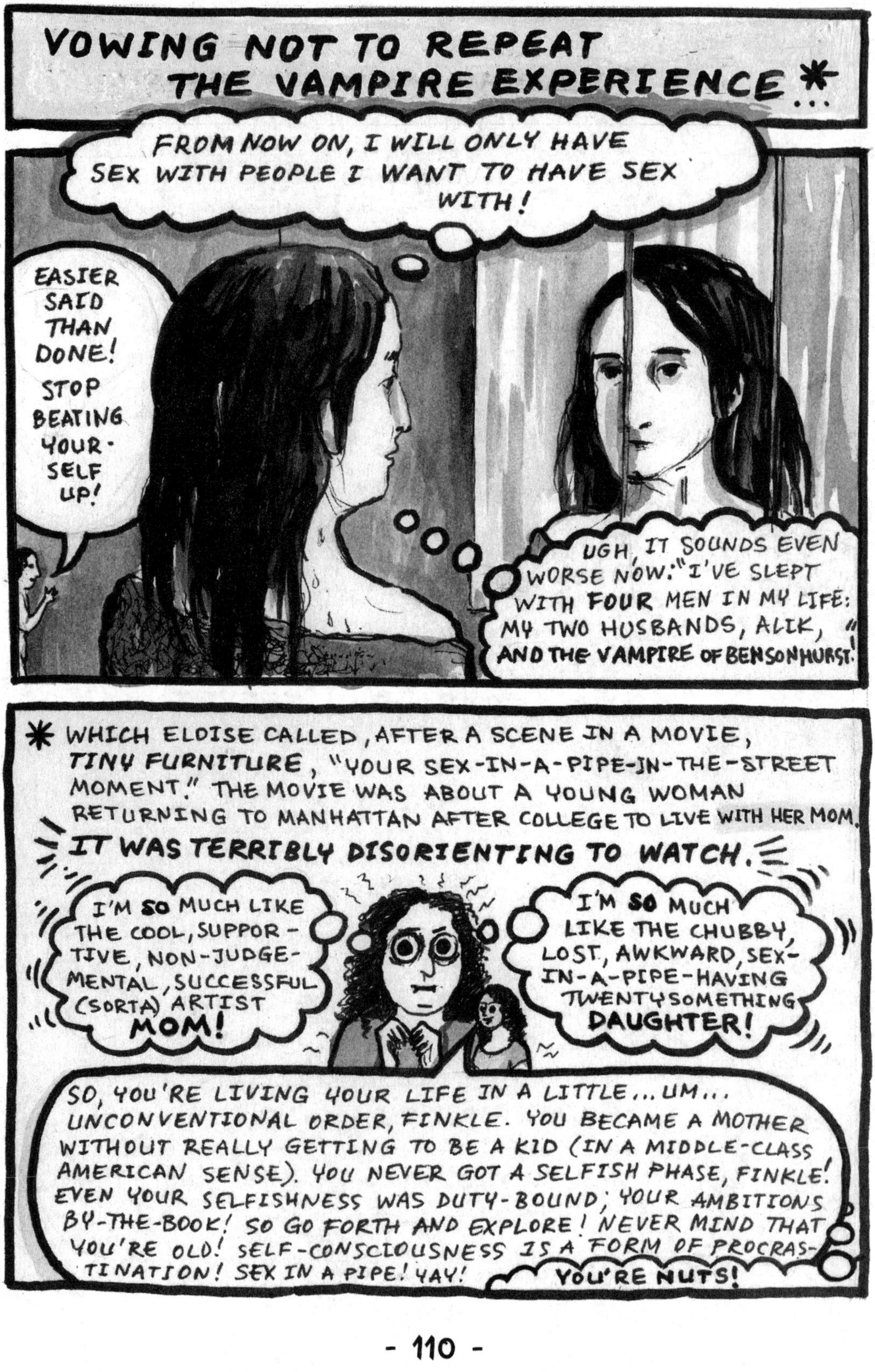
VOWING NOT TO REPEAT THE VAMPIRE EXPERIENCE*...
FROM NOW ON, I WILL ONLY HAVE SEX WITH PEOPLE I WANT TO HAVE SEX WITH!
EASIER SAID THAN DONE! STOP BEATING YOURSELF UP!
UGH, IT SOUNDS EVEN WORSE NOW: "I'VE SLEPT WITH FOUR MEN IN MY LIFE: MY TWO HUSBANDS, ALIK, AND THE VAMPIRE OF BENSONHURST."
* WHICH ELOISE CALLED, AFTER A SCENE IN A MOVIE, TINY FURNITURE, "YOUR SEX-IN-A-PIPE-IN-THE-STREET MOMENT." THE MOVIE WAS ABOUT A YOUNG WOMAN RETURNING TO MANHATTAN AFTER COLLEGE TO LIVE WITH HER MOM. IT WAS TERRIBLY DISORIENTING TO WATCH.
I'M SO MUCH LIKE THE COOL, SUPPORTIVE, NON-JUDGEMENTAL, SUCCESSFUL (SORTA) ARTIST MOM!
I'M SO MUCH LIKE THE CHUBBY, LOST, AWKWARD, SEX-IN-A-PIPE-HAVING TWENTYSOMETHING DAUGHTER!
SO, YOU'RE LIVING YOUR LIFE IN A LITTLE... UM... UNCONVENTIONAL ORDER, FINKLE. YOU BECAME A MOTHER WITHOUT REALLY GETTING TO BE A KID (IN A MIDDLE-CLASS AMERICAN SENSE). YOU NEVER GOT A SELFISH PHASE, FINKLE! EVEN YOUR SELFISHNESS WAS DUTY-BOUND; YOUR AMBITIONS BY-THE-BOOK! SO GO FORTH AND EXPLORE! NEVER MIND THAT YOU'RE OLD! SELF-CONSCIOUSNESS IS A FORM OF PROCRASTINATION! SEX IN A PIPE! YAY!
YOU'RE NUTS!

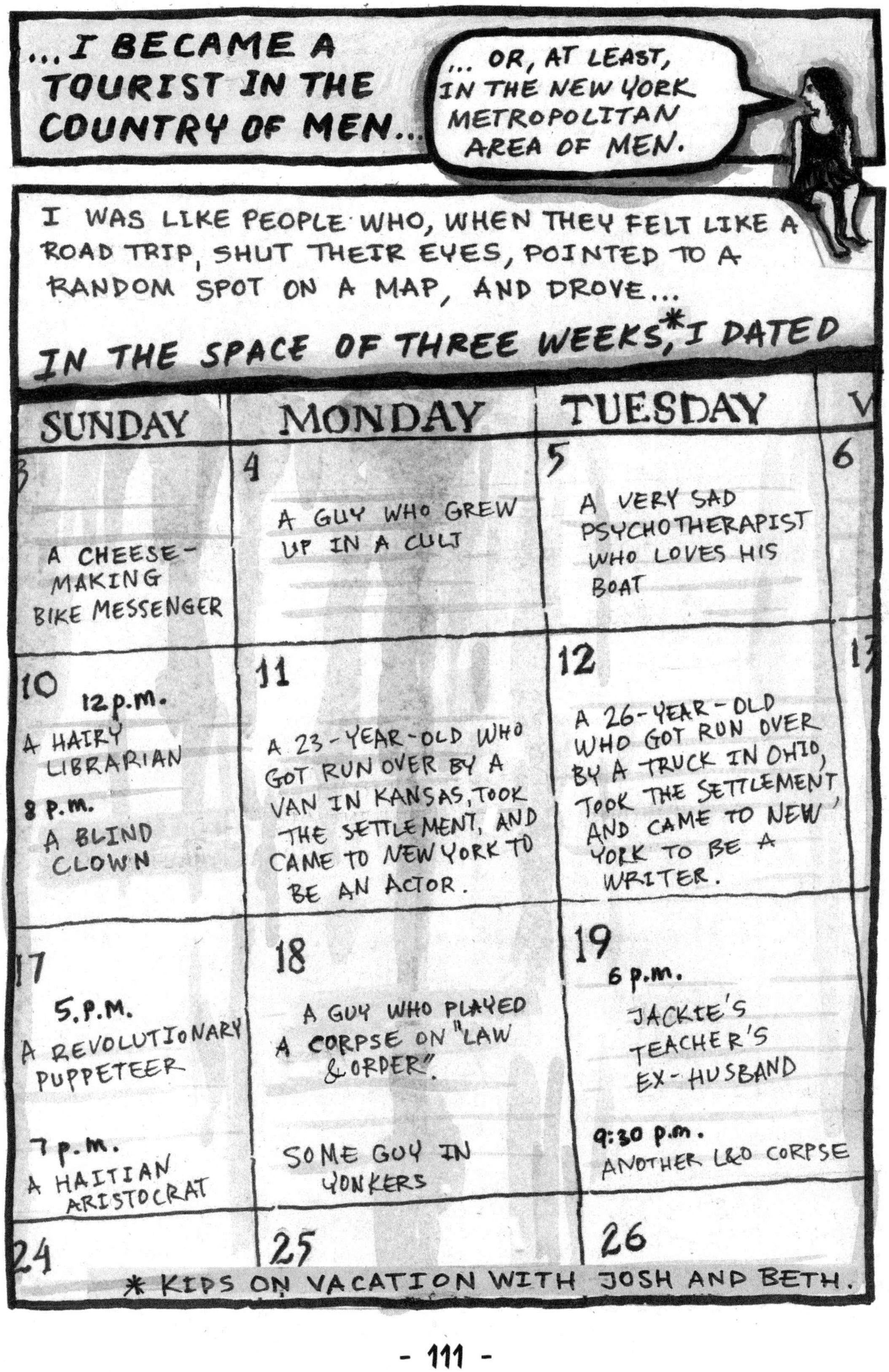

...I BECAME A TOURIST IN THE COUNTRY OF MEN...

...OR, AT LEAST, IN THE NEW YORK METROPOLITAN AREA OF MEN.

I WAS LIKE PEOPLE WHO, WHEN THEY FELT LIKE A ROAD TRIP, SHUT THEIR EYES, POINTED TO A RANDOM SPOT ON A MAP, AND DROVE...

IN THE SPACE OF THREE WEEKS,* I DATED

SUNDAY	MONDAY	TUESDAY	V
3 A CHEESE-MAKING BIKE MESSENGER	4 A GUY WHO GREW UP IN A CULT	5 A VERY SAD PSYCHOTHERAPIST WHO LOVES HIS BOAT	6
10 12 p.m. A HAIRY LIBRARIAN 8 p.m. A BLIND CLOWN	11 A 23-YEAR-OLD WHO GOT RUN OVER BY A VAN IN KANSAS, TOOK THE SETTLEMENT, AND CAME TO NEW YORK TO BE AN ACTOR.	12 A 26-YEAR-OLD WHO GOT RUN OVER BY A TRUCK IN OHIO, TOOK THE SETTLEMENT AND CAME TO NEW YORK TO BE A WRITER.	13
17 5 P.M. A REVOLUTIONARY PUPPETEER 7 p.m. A HAITIAN ARISTOCRAT	18 A GUY WHO PLAYED A CORPSE ON "LAW & ORDER". SOME GUY IN YONKERS	19 6 p.m. JACKIE'S TEACHER'S EX-HUSBAND 9:30 p.m. ANOTHER L&O CORPSE	
24	25	26	

* KIDS ON VACATION WITH JOSH AND BETH.

- 111 -

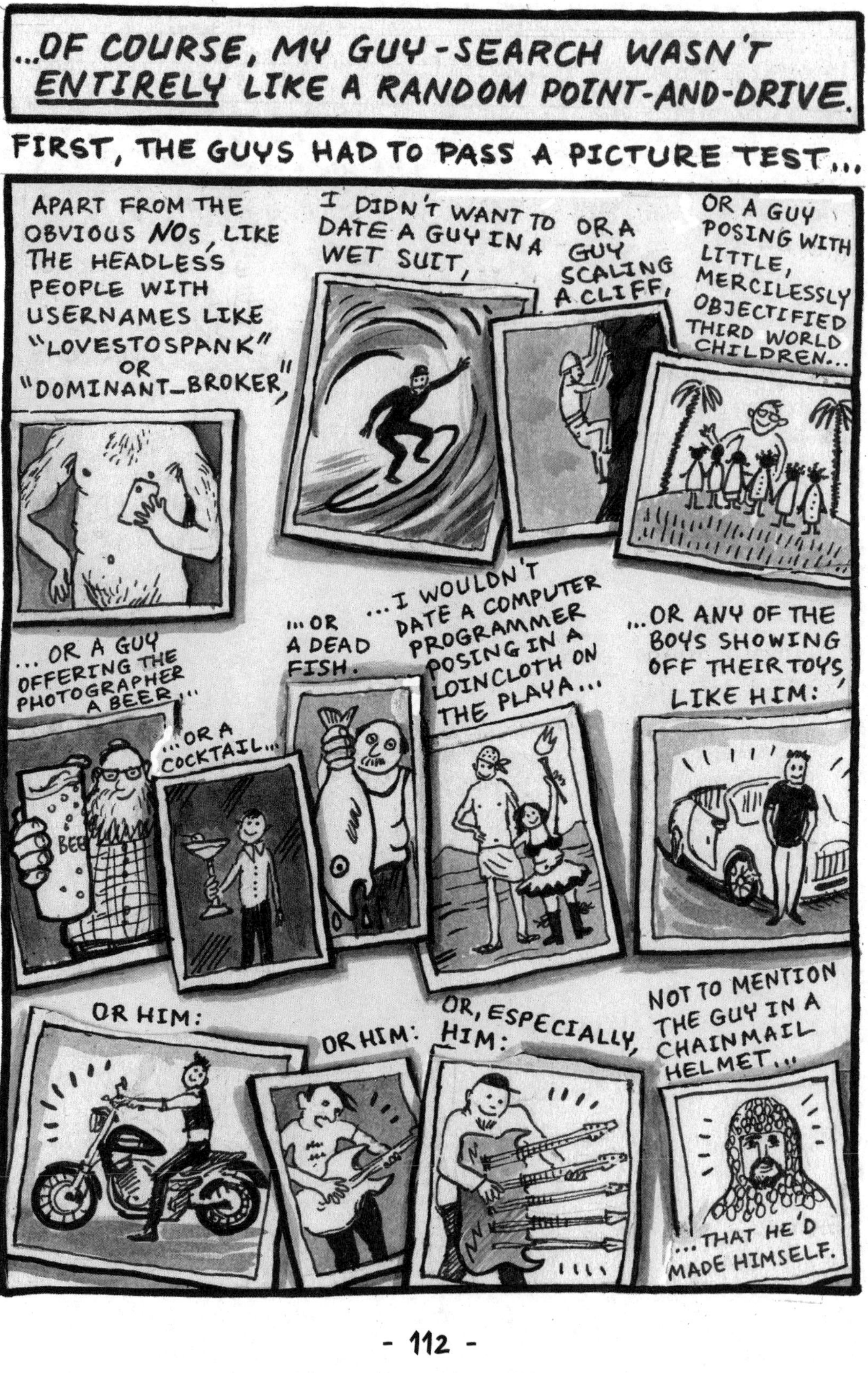
...OF COURSE, MY GUY-SEARCH WASN'T ENTIRELY LIKE A RANDOM POINT-AND-DRIVE.
FIRST, THE GUYS HAD TO PASS A PICTURE TEST...
APART FROM THE OBVIOUS NOs, LIKE THE HEADLESS PEOPLE WITH USERNAMES LIKE "LOVESTOSPANK" OR "DOMINANT_BROKER,"
I DIDN'T WANT TO DATE A GUY IN A WET SUIT,
OR A GUY SCALING A CLIFF,
OR A GUY POSING WITH LITTLE, MERCILESSLY OBJECTIFIED THIRD WORLD CHILDREN...
... OR A GUY OFFERING THE PHOTOGRAPHER A BEER...
...OR A COCKTAIL...
...OR A DEAD FISH.
...I WOULDN'T DATE A COMPUTER PROGRAMMER POSING IN A LOINCLOTH ON THE PLAYA...
...OR ANY OF THE BOYS SHOWING OFF THEIR TOYS, LIKE HIM:
OR HIM:
OR HIM:
OR, ESPECIALLY, HIM:
NOT TO MENTION THE GUY IN A CHAINMAIL HELMET...
...THAT HE'D MADE HIMSELF.

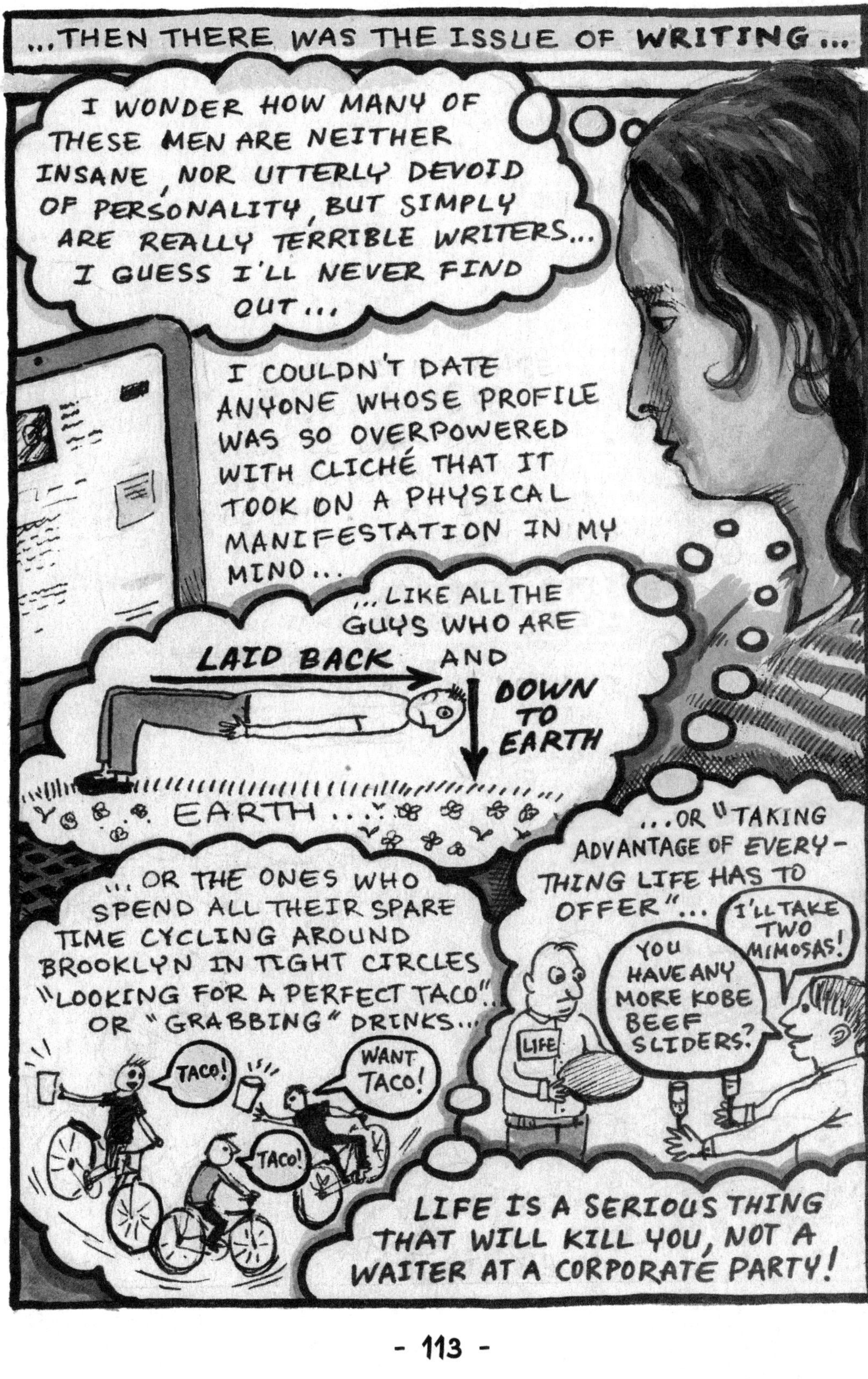
...THEN THERE WAS THE ISSUE OF WRITING...
I WONDER HOW MANY OF THESE MEN ARE NEITHER INSANE, NOR UTTERLY DEVOID OF PERSONALITY, BUT SIMPLY ARE REALLY TERRIBLE WRITERS... I GUESS I'LL NEVER FIND OUT...
I COULDN'T DATE ANYONE WHOSE PROFILE WAS SO OVERPOWERED WITH CLICHÉ THAT IT TOOK ON A PHYSICAL MANIFESTATION IN MY MIND...
...LIKE ALL THE GUYS WHO ARE LAID BACK AND DOWN TO EARTH
EARTH...
...OR THE ONES WHO SPEND ALL THEIR SPARE TIME CYCLING AROUND BROOKLYN IN TIGHT CIRCLES "LOOKING FOR A PERFECT TACO"... OR "GRABBING" DRINKS...
TACO!
WANT TACO!
TACO!
...OR "TAKING ADVANTAGE OF EVERYTHING LIFE HAS TO OFFER"...
LIFE
YOU HAVE ANY MORE KOBE BEEF SLIDERS?
I'LL TAKE TWO MIMOSAS!
LIFE IS A SERIOUS THING THAT WILL KILL YOU, NOT A WAITER AT A CORPORATE PARTY!

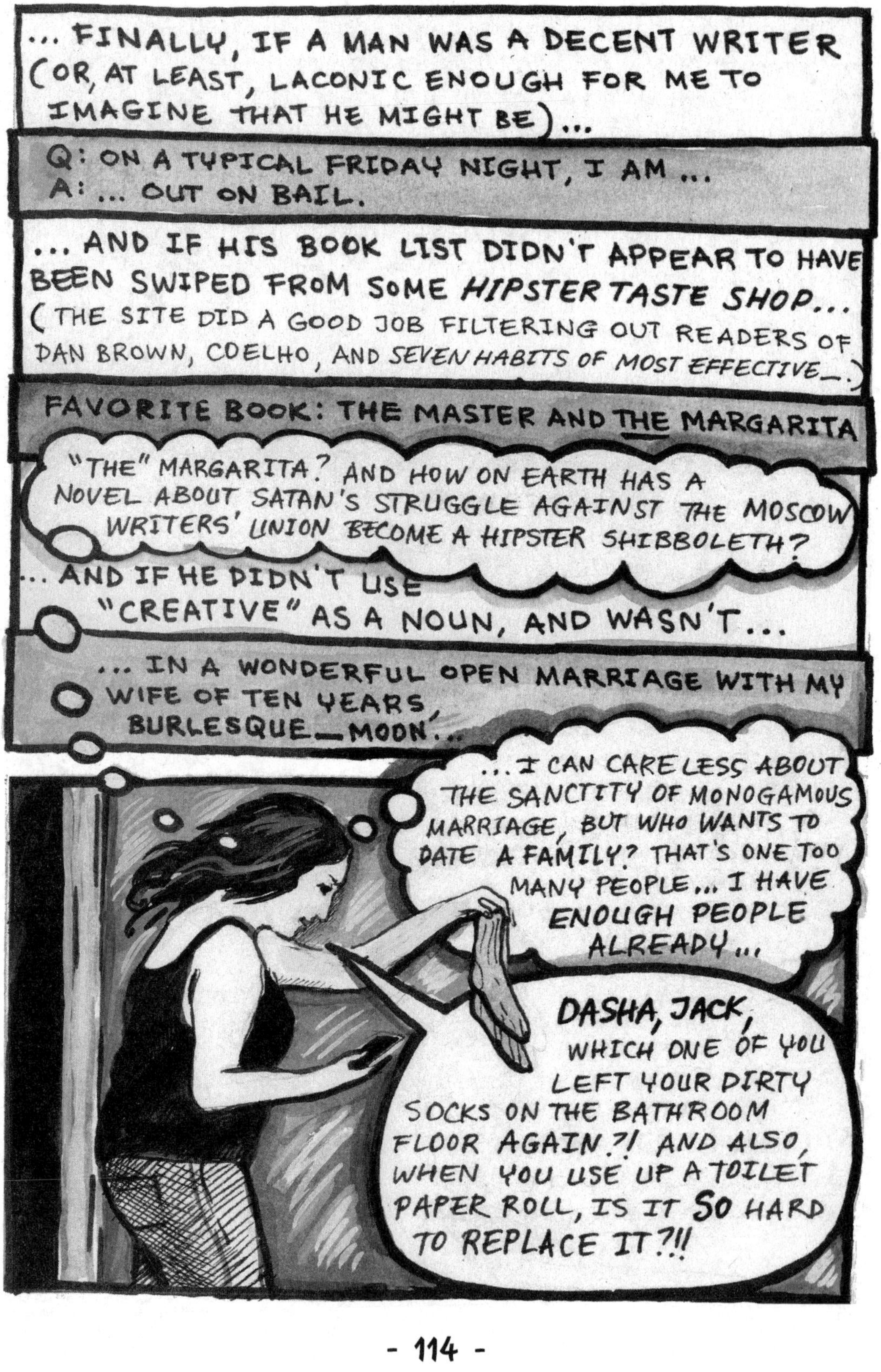
... FINALLY, IF A MAN WAS A DECENT WRITER (OR, AT LEAST, LACONIC ENOUGH FOR ME TO IMAGINE THAT HE MIGHT BE)...
Q: ON A TYPICAL FRIDAY NIGHT, I AM ...
A: ... OUT ON BAIL.
... AND IF HIS BOOK LIST DIDN'T APPEAR TO HAVE BEEN SWIPED FROM SOME HIPSTER TASTE SHOP... (THE SITE DID A GOOD JOB FILTERING OUT READERS OF DAN BROWN, COELHO, AND SEVEN HABITS OF MOST EFFECTIVE_.)
FAVORITE BOOK: THE MASTER AND THE MARGARITA
"THE" MARGARITA? AND HOW ON EARTH HAS A NOVEL ABOUT SATAN'S STRUGGLE AGAINST THE MOSCOW WRITERS' UNION BECOME A HIPSTER SHIBBOLETH?
... AND IF HE DIDN'T USE "CREATIVE" AS A NOUN, AND WASN'T...
... IN A WONDERFUL OPEN MARRIAGE WITH MY WIFE OF TEN YEARS, BURLESQUE_MOON'...
... I CAN CARE LESS ABOUT THE SANCTITY OF MONOGAMOUS MARRIAGE, BUT WHO WANTS TO DATE A FAMILY? THAT'S ONE TOO MANY PEOPLE... I HAVE ENOUGH PEOPLE ALREADY...
DASHA, JACK, WHICH ONE OF YOU LEFT YOUR DIRTY SOCKS ON THE BATHROOM FLOOR AGAIN?! AND ALSO, WHEN YOU USE UP A TOILET PAPER ROLL, IS IT SO HARD TO REPLACE IT?!!

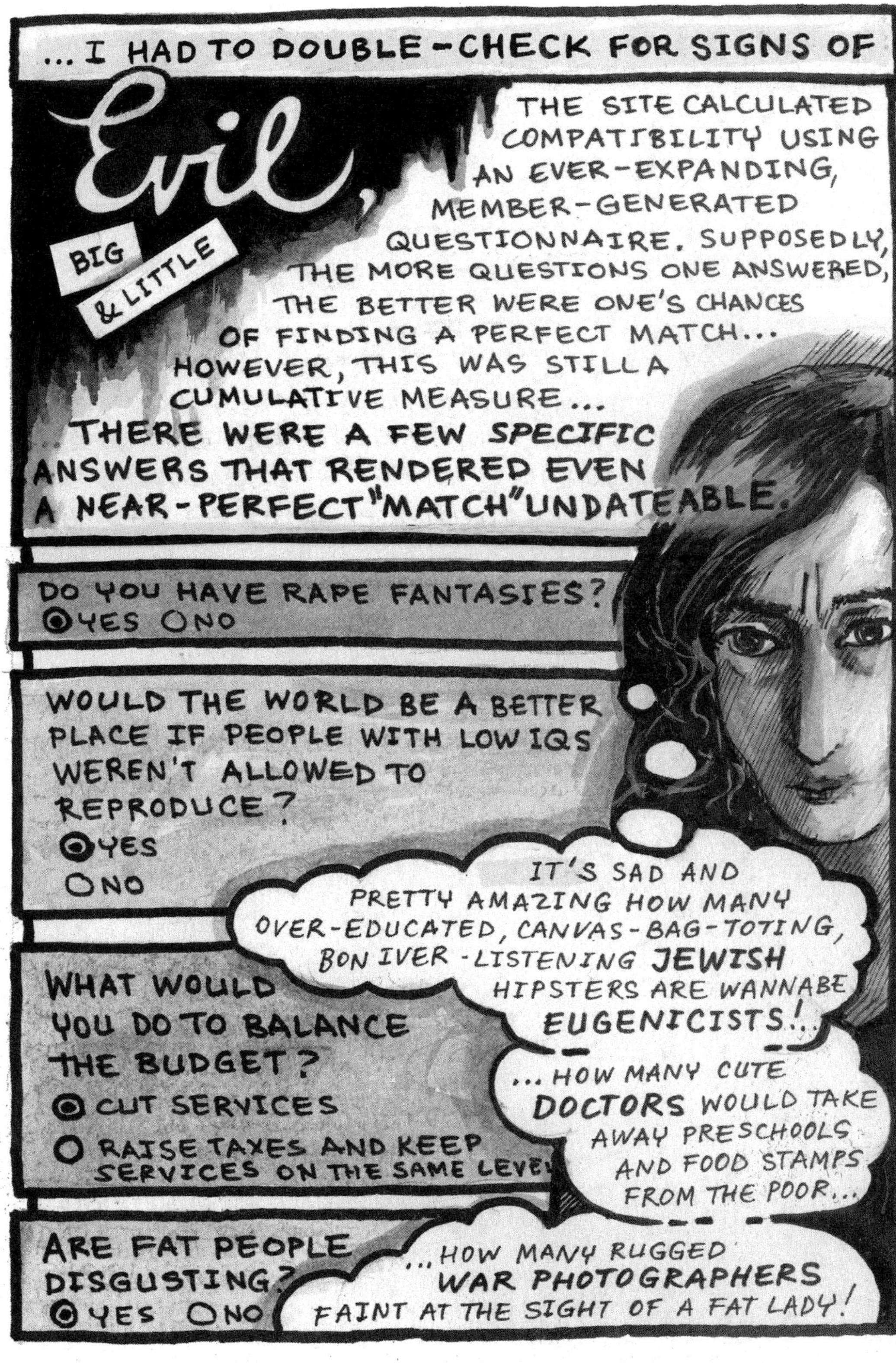

...I HAD TO DOUBLE-CHECK FOR SIGNS OF
Evil,
BIG & LITTLE
THE SITE CALCULATED COMPATIBILITY USING AN EVER-EXPANDING, MEMBER-GENERATED QUESTIONNAIRE. SUPPOSEDLY, THE MORE QUESTIONS ONE ANSWERED, THE BETTER WERE ONE'S CHANCES OF FINDING A PERFECT MATCH... HOWEVER, THIS WAS STILL A CUMULATIVE MEASURE... THERE WERE A FEW SPECIFIC ANSWERS THAT RENDERED EVEN A NEAR-PERFECT "MATCH" UNDATEABLE.
DO YOU HAVE RAPE FANTASIES? ◉YES ○NO
WOULD THE WORLD BE A BETTER PLACE IF PEOPLE WITH LOW IQS WEREN'T ALLOWED TO REPRODUCE? ◉YES ○NO
IT'S SAD AND PRETTY AMAZING HOW MANY OVER-EDUCATED, CANVAS-BAG-TOTING, BON IVER-LISTENING JEWISH HIPSTERS ARE WANNABE EUGENICISTS!..
WHAT WOULD YOU DO TO BALANCE THE BUDGET? ◉CUT SERVICES ○RAISE TAXES AND KEEP SERVICES ON THE SAME LEVEL
...HOW MANY CUTE DOCTORS WOULD TAKE AWAY PRESCHOOLS AND FOOD STAMPS FROM THE POOR...
ARE FAT PEOPLE DISGUSTING? ◉YES ○NO
...HOW MANY RUGGED WAR PHOTOGRAPHERS FAINT AT THE SIGHT OF A FAT LADY!

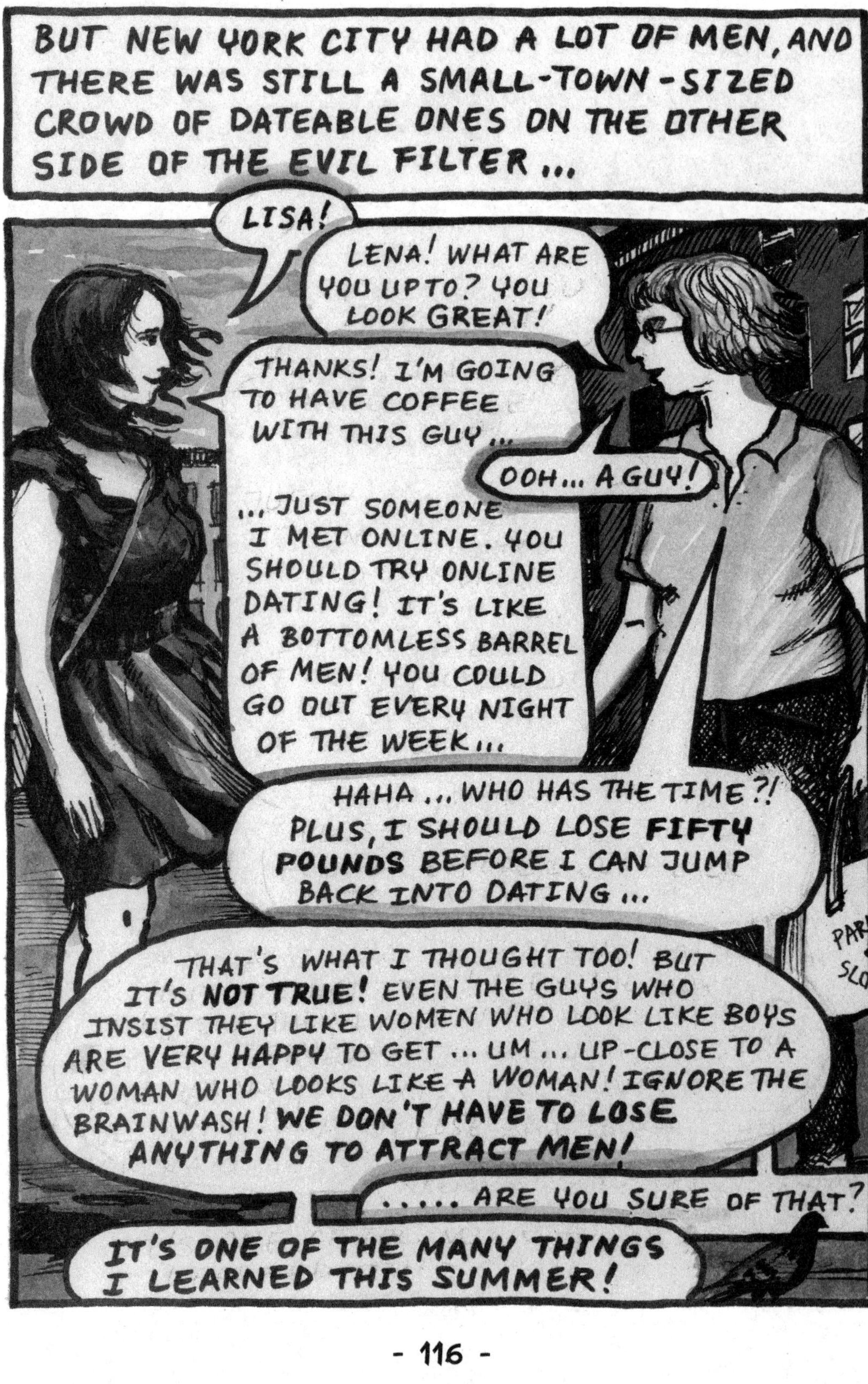
BUT NEW YORK CITY HAD A LOT OF MEN, AND THERE WAS STILL A SMALL-TOWN-SIZED CROWD OF DATEABLE ONES ON THE OTHER SIDE OF THE EVIL FILTER ...
LISA!
LENA! WHAT ARE YOU UPTO? YOU LOOK GREAT!
THANKS! I'M GOING TO HAVE COFFEE WITH THIS GUY...
OOH... A GUY!
... JUST SOMEONE I MET ONLINE. YOU SHOULD TRY ONLINE DATING! IT'S LIKE A BOTTOMLESS BARREL OF MEN! YOU COULD GO OUT EVERY NIGHT OF THE WEEK...
HAHA ... WHO HAS THE TIME?! PLUS, I SHOULD LOSE **FIFTY POUNDS** BEFORE I CAN JUMP BACK INTO DATING...
THAT'S WHAT I THOUGHT TOO! BUT IT'S **NOT TRUE!** EVEN THE GUYS WHO INSIST THEY LIKE WOMEN WHO LOOK LIKE BOYS ARE VERY HAPPY TO GET ... UM ... UP-CLOSE TO A WOMAN WHO LOOKS LIKE A WOMAN! IGNORE THE BRAINWASH! **WE DON'T HAVE TO LOSE ANYTHING TO ATTRACT MEN!**
..... ARE YOU SURE OF THAT?
IT'S ONE OF THE MANY THINGS I LEARNED THIS SUMMER!

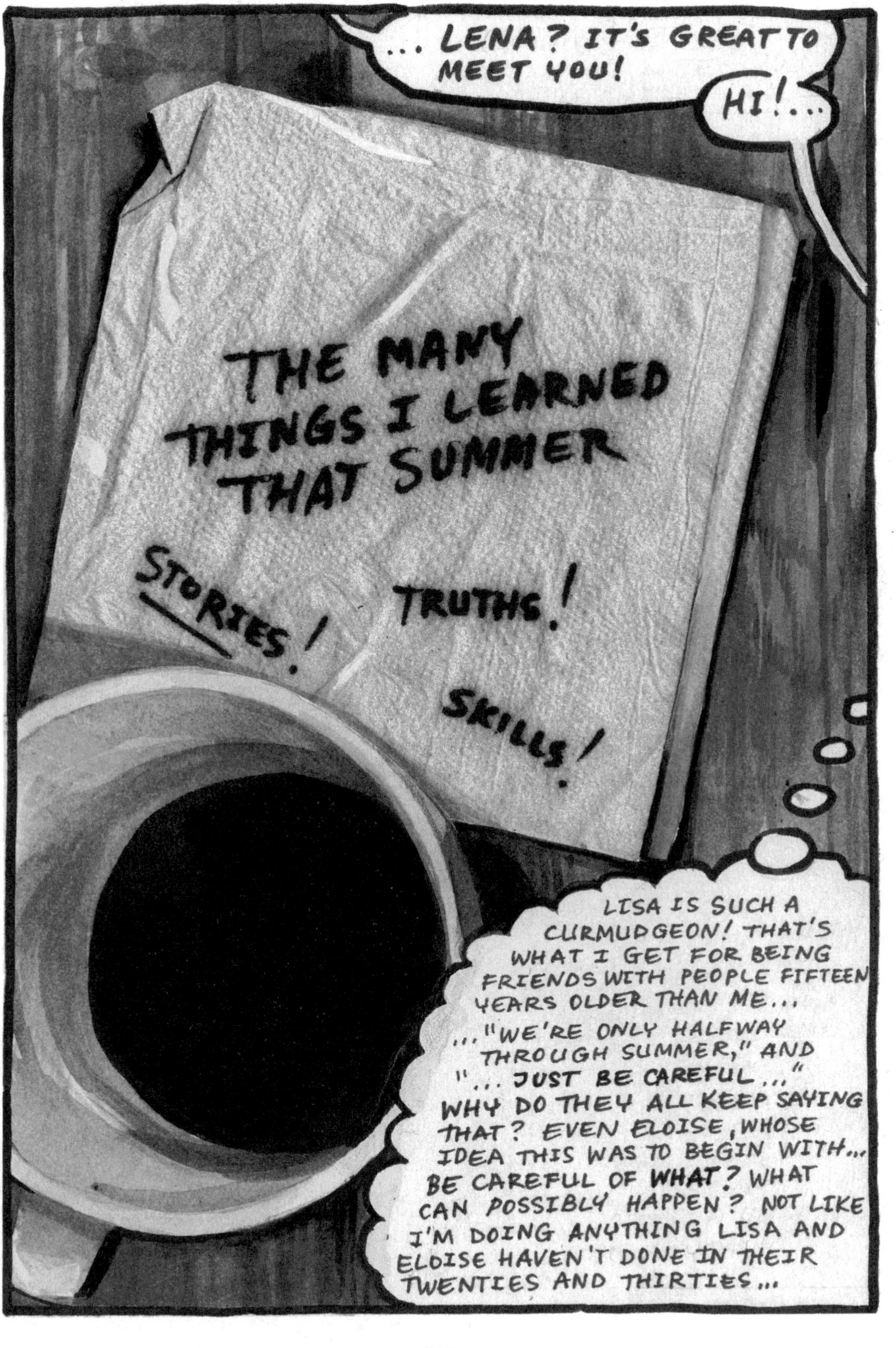
... LENA? IT'S GREAT TO MEET YOU!
HI!...
THE MANY THINGS I LEARNED THAT SUMMER
STORIES!
TRUTHS!
SKILLS!
LISA IS SUCH A CURMUDGEON! THAT'S WHAT I GET FOR BEING FRIENDS WITH PEOPLE FIFTEEN YEARS OLDER THAN ME... ..."WE'RE ONLY HALFWAY THROUGH SUMMER," AND "... JUST BE CAREFUL..." WHY DO THEY ALL KEEP SAYING THAT? EVEN ELOISE, WHOSE IDEA THIS WAS TO BEGIN WITH... BE CAREFUL OF WHAT? WHAT CAN POSSIBLY HAPPEN? NOT LIKE I'M DOING ANYTHING LISA AND ELOISE HAVEN'T DONE IN THEIR TWENTIES AND THIRTIES...

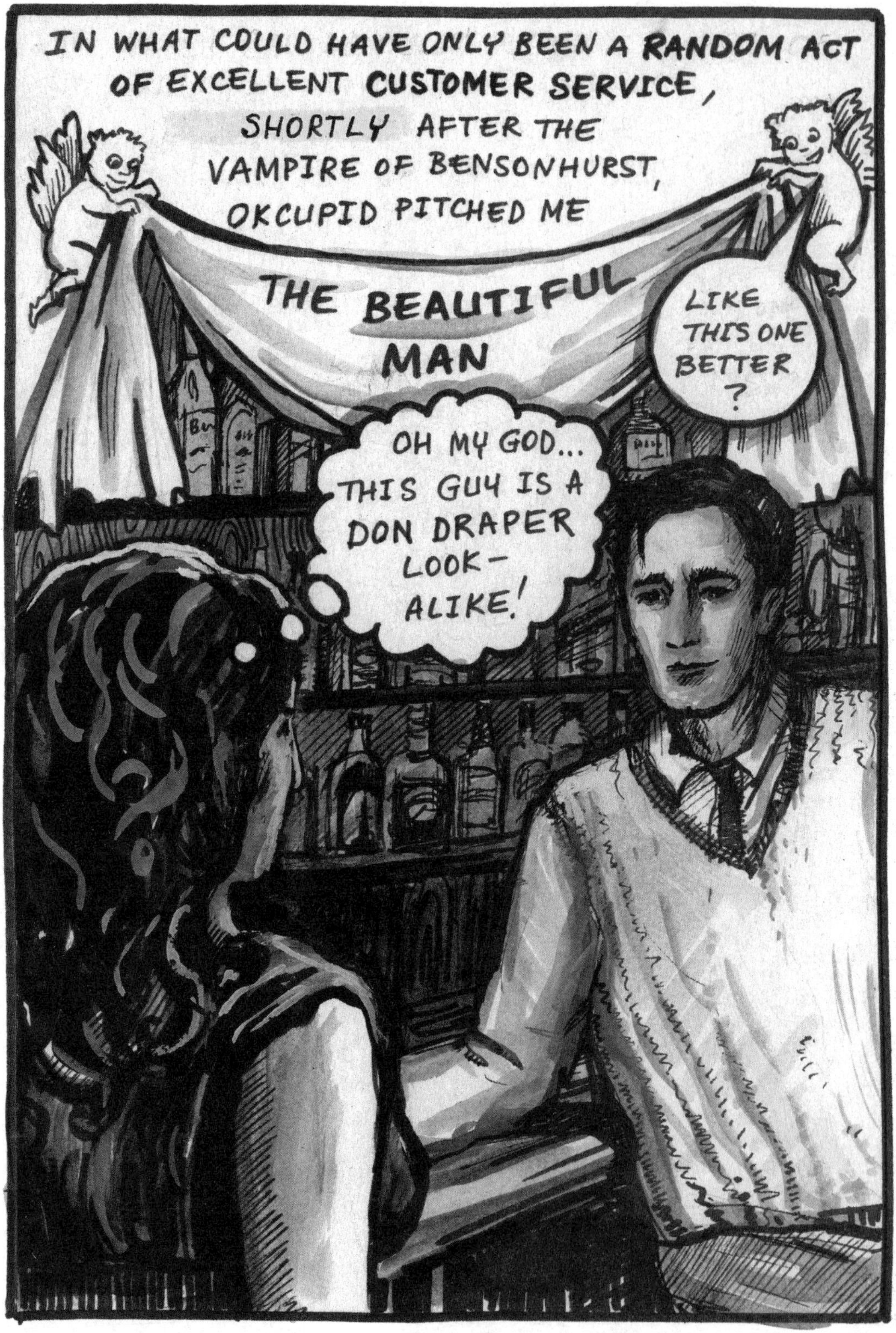
IN WHAT COULD HAVE ONLY BEEN A RANDOM ACT OF EXCELLENT CUSTOMER SERVICE, SHORTLY AFTER THE VAMPIRE OF BENSONHURST, OKCUPID PITCHED ME
THE BEAUTIFUL MAN
LIKE THIS ONE BETTER?
OH MY GOD... THIS GUY IS A DON DRAPER LOOK-ALIKE!

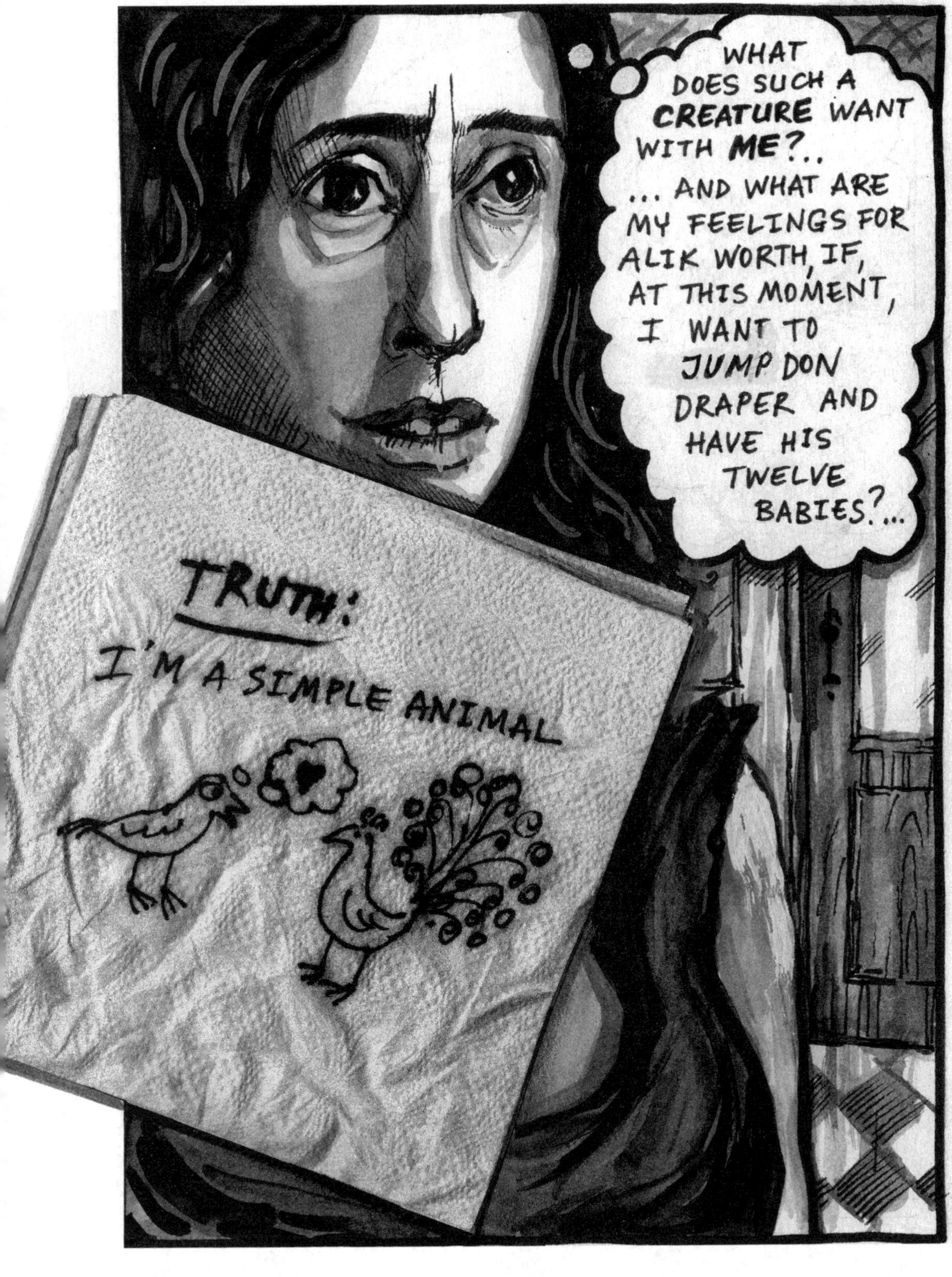
WHAT DOES SUCH A CREATURE WANT WITH ME?.. ... AND WHAT ARE MY FEELINGS FOR ALIK WORTH, IF, AT THIS MOMENT, I WANT TO JUMP DON DRAPER AND HAVE HIS TWELVE BABIES?...
TRUTH:
I'M A SIMPLE ANIMAL

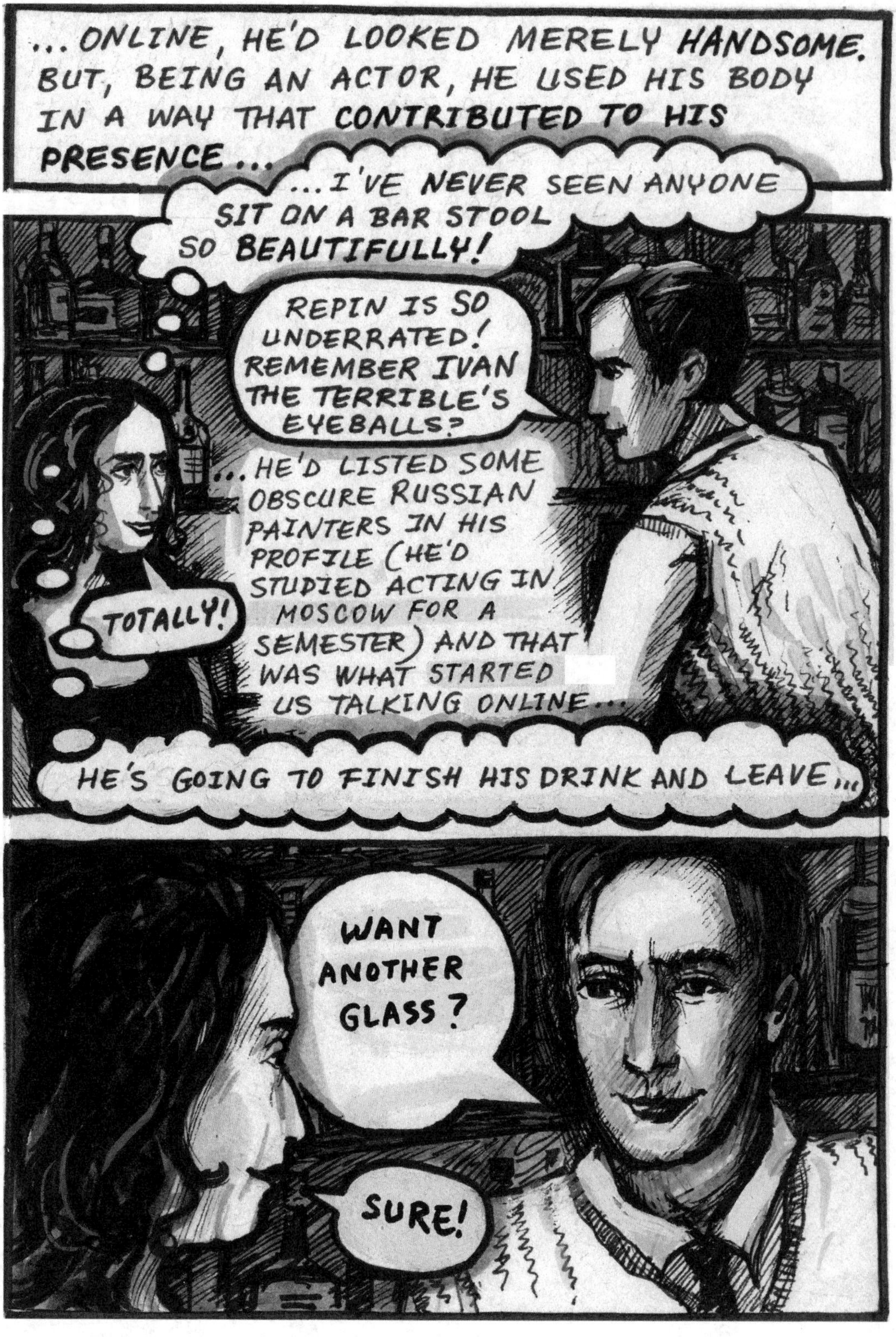
...ONLINE, HE'D LOOKED MERELY HANDSOME. BUT, BEING AN ACTOR, HE USED HIS BODY IN A WAY THAT CONTRIBUTED TO HIS PRESENCE...
...I'VE NEVER SEEN ANYONE SIT ON A BAR STOOL SO BEAUTIFULLY!
REPIN IS SO UNDERRATED! REMEMBER IVAN THE TERRIBLE'S EYEBALLS?
...HE'D LISTED SOME OBSCURE RUSSIAN PAINTERS IN HIS PROFILE (HE'D STUDIED ACTING IN MOSCOW FOR A SEMESTER) AND THAT WAS WHAT STARTED US TALKING ONLINE...
TOTALLY!
HE'S GOING TO FINISH HIS DRINK AND LEAVE...
WANT ANOTHER GLASS?
SURE!

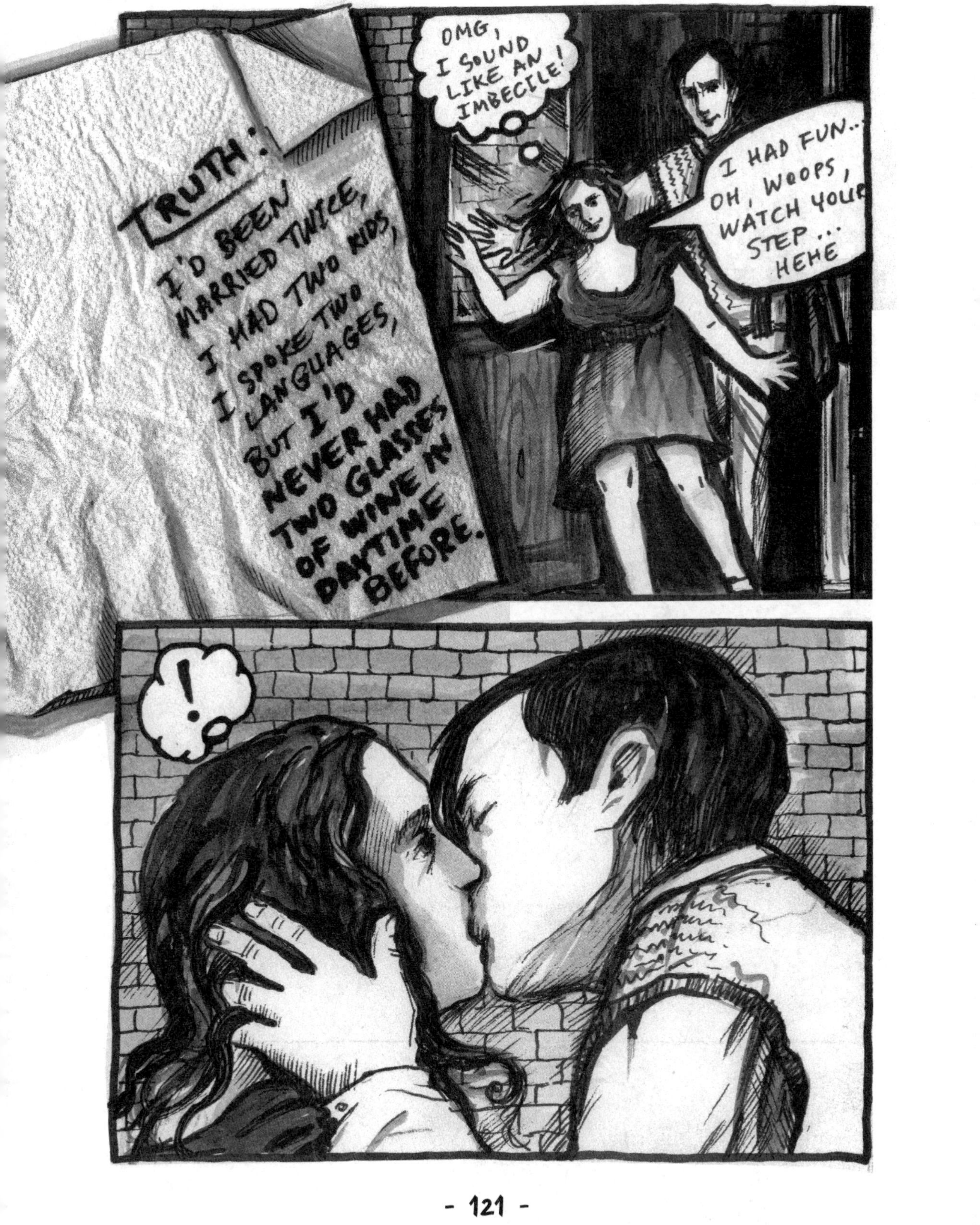
TRUTH:
I'D BEEN MARRIED TWICE, I HAD TWO KIDS, I SPOKE TWO LANGUAGES, BUT I'D NEVER HAD TWO GLASSES OF WINE IN DAYTIME BEFORE.
OMG, I SOUND LIKE AN IMBECILE!
I HAD FUN... OH, WOOPS, WATCH YOUR STEP... HEHE
!

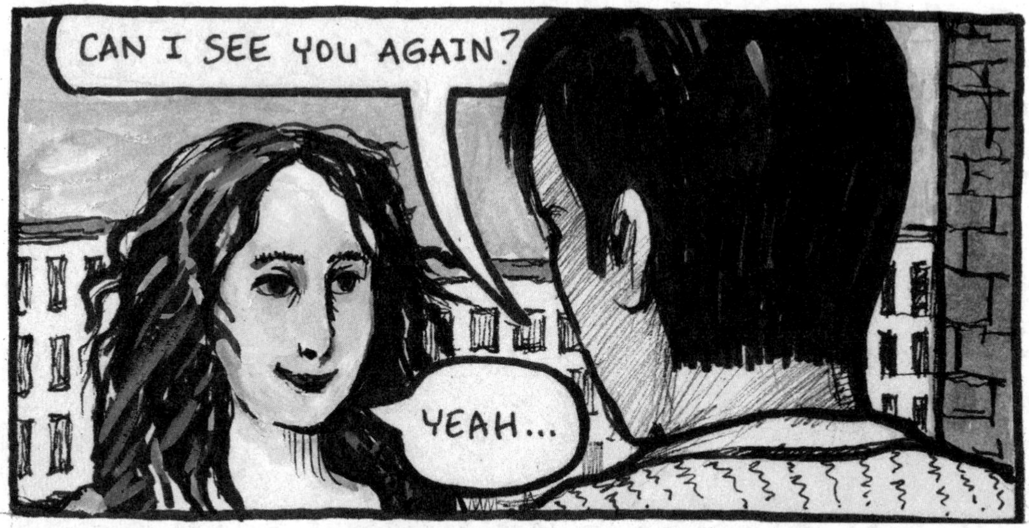
CAN I SEE YOU AGAIN?
YEAH...

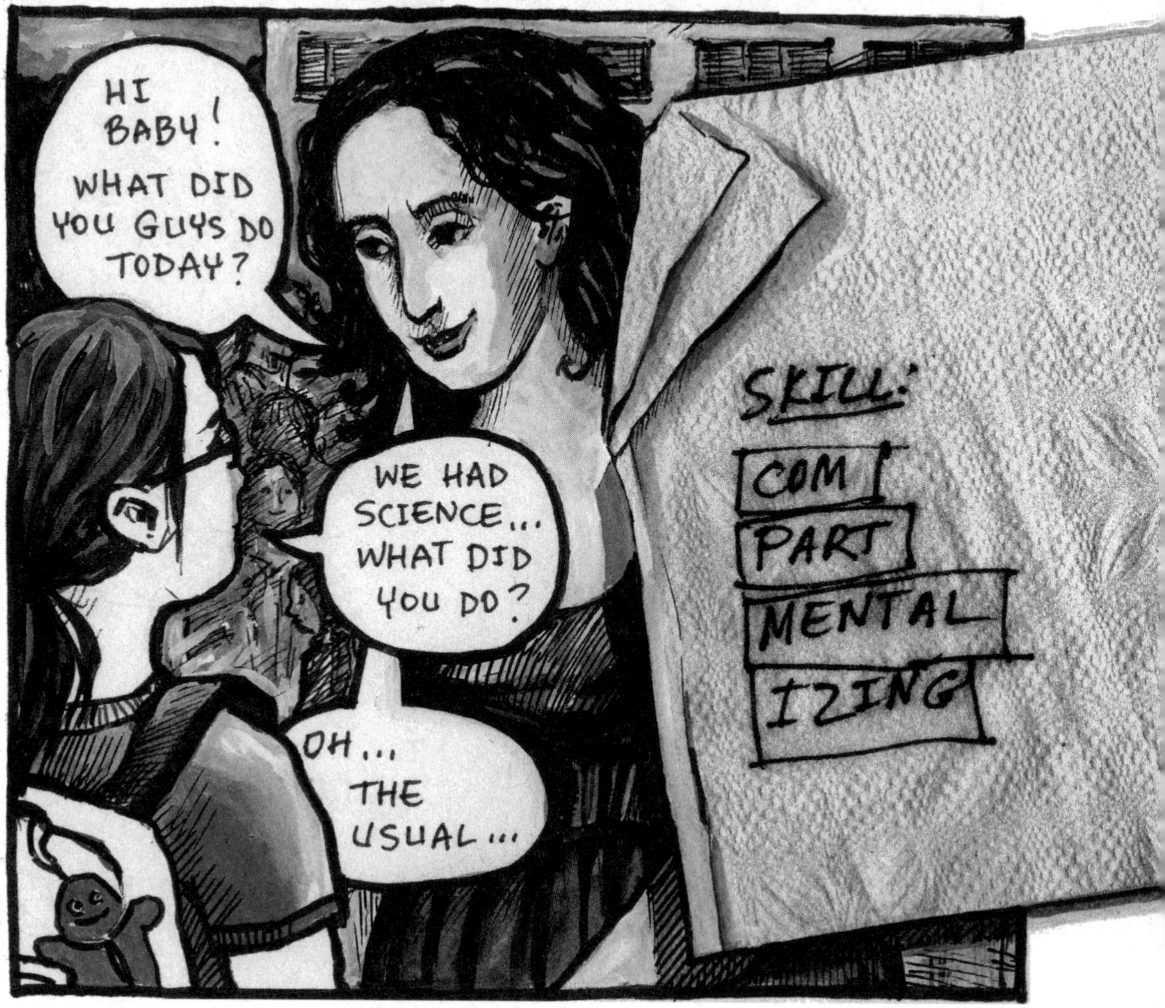
HI BABY! WHAT DID YOU GUYS DO TODAY?
WE HAD SCIENCE... WHAT DID YOU DO?
OH... THE USUAL...
SKILL:
COM
PART
MENTAL
IZING

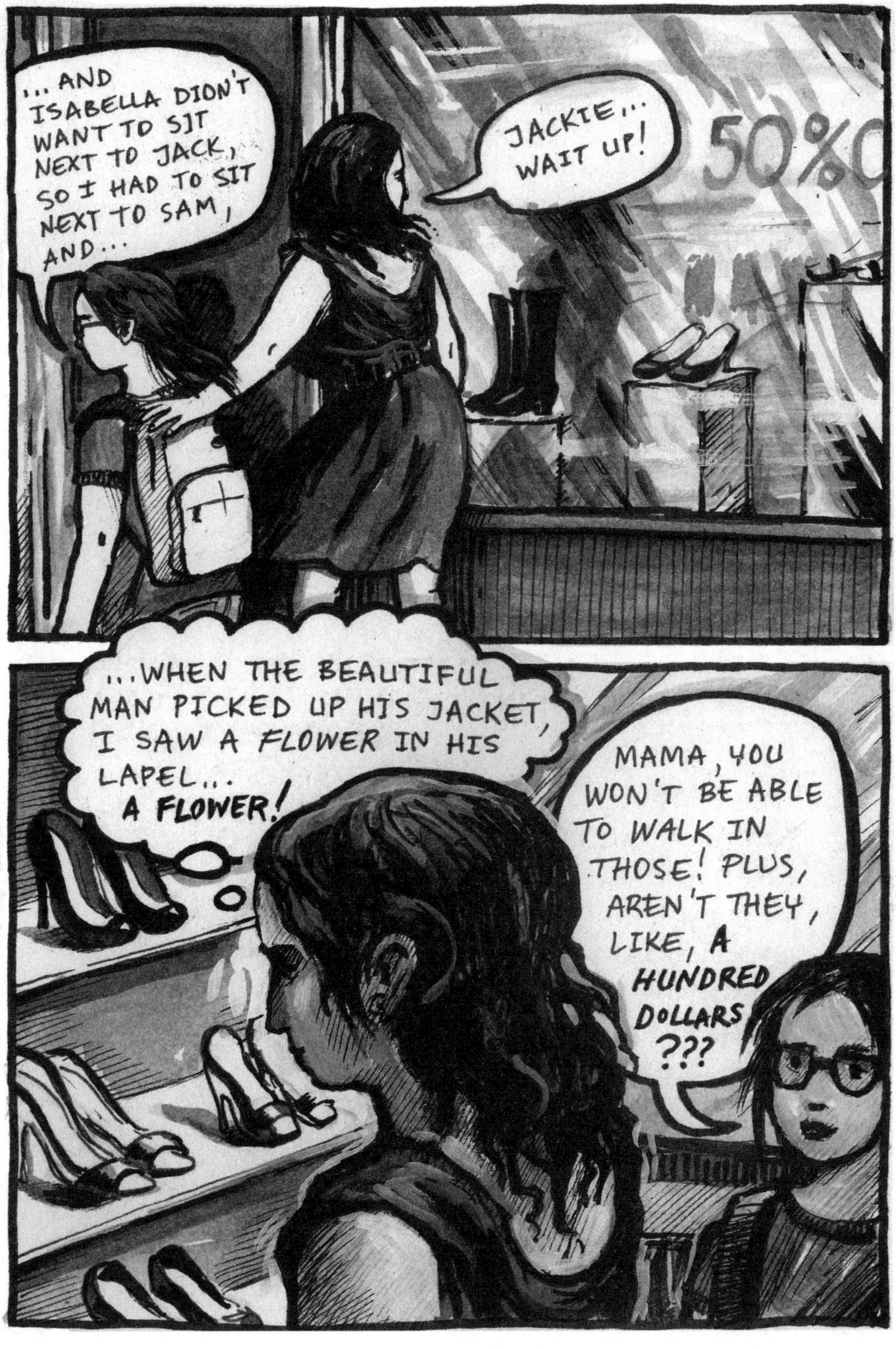
... AND ISABELLA DIDN'T WANT TO SIT NEXT TO JACK, SO I HAD TO SIT NEXT TO SAM, AND...
JACKIE... WAIT UP!
50%
...WHEN THE BEAUTIFUL MAN PICKED UP HIS JACKET, I SAW A *FLOWER* IN HIS LAPEL... **A FLOWER!**
MAMA, YOU WON'T BE ABLE TO WALK IN THOSE! PLUS, AREN'T THEY, LIKE, **A HUNDRED DOLLARS???**

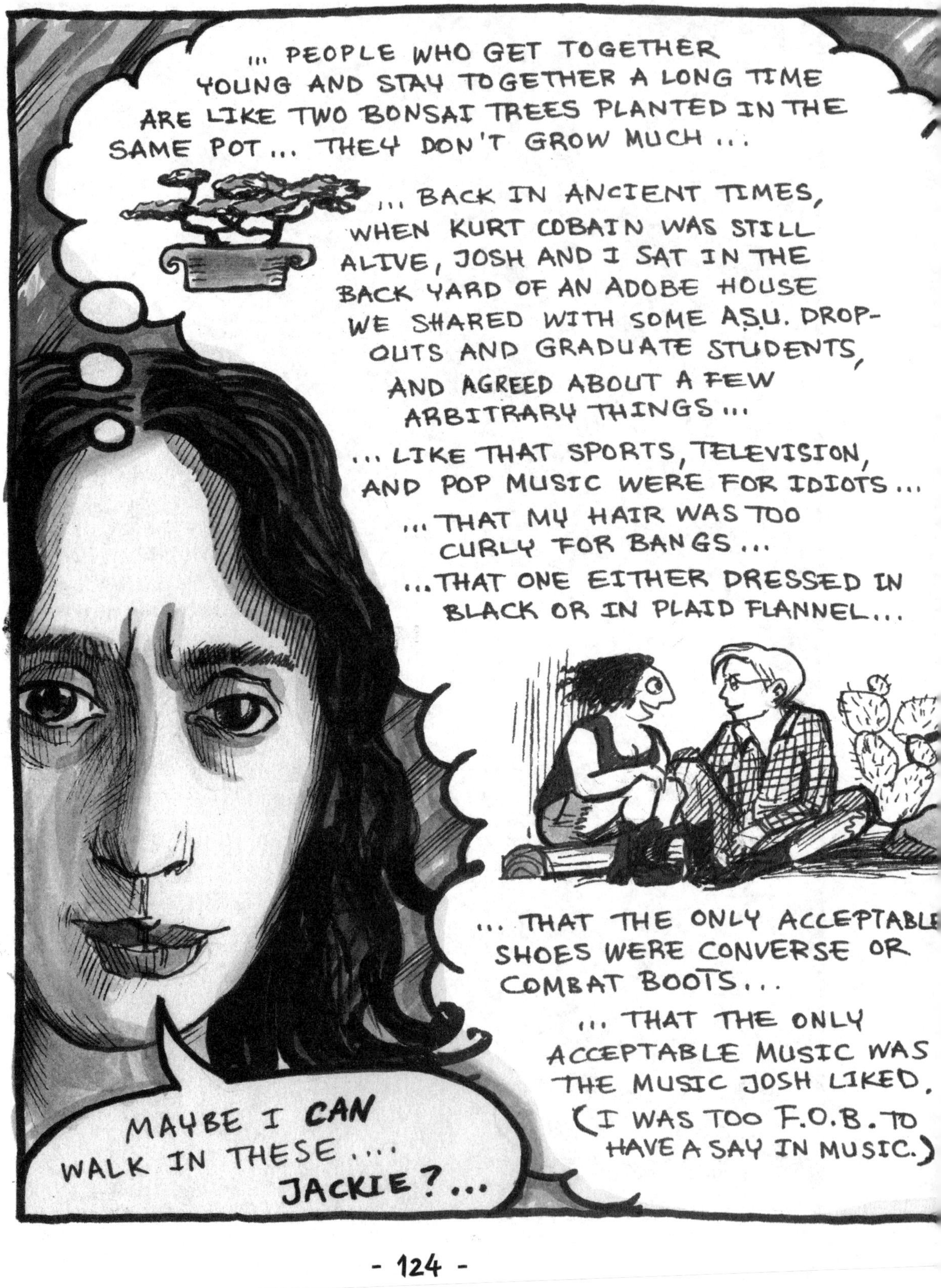
... PEOPLE WHO GET TOGETHER YOUNG AND STAY TOGETHER A LONG TIME ARE LIKE TWO BONSAI TREES PLANTED IN THE SAME POT... THEY DON'T GROW MUCH...
... BACK IN ANCIENT TIMES, WHEN KURT COBAIN WAS STILL ALIVE, JOSH AND I SAT IN THE BACK YARD OF AN ADOBE HOUSE WE SHARED WITH SOME A.S.U. DROP-OUTS AND GRADUATE STUDENTS, AND AGREED ABOUT A FEW ARBITRARY THINGS...
... LIKE THAT SPORTS, TELEVISION, AND POP MUSIC WERE FOR IDIOTS...
... THAT MY HAIR WAS TOO CURLY FOR BANGS...
... THAT ONE EITHER DRESSED IN BLACK OR IN PLAID FLANNEL...
... THAT THE ONLY ACCEPTABLE SHOES WERE CONVERSE OR COMBAT BOOTS...
... THAT THE ONLY ACCEPTABLE MUSIC WAS THE MUSIC JOSH LIKED.
(I WAS TOO F.O.B. TO HAVE A SAY IN MUSIC.)
MAYBE I **CAN** WALK IN THESE.... JACKIE?...

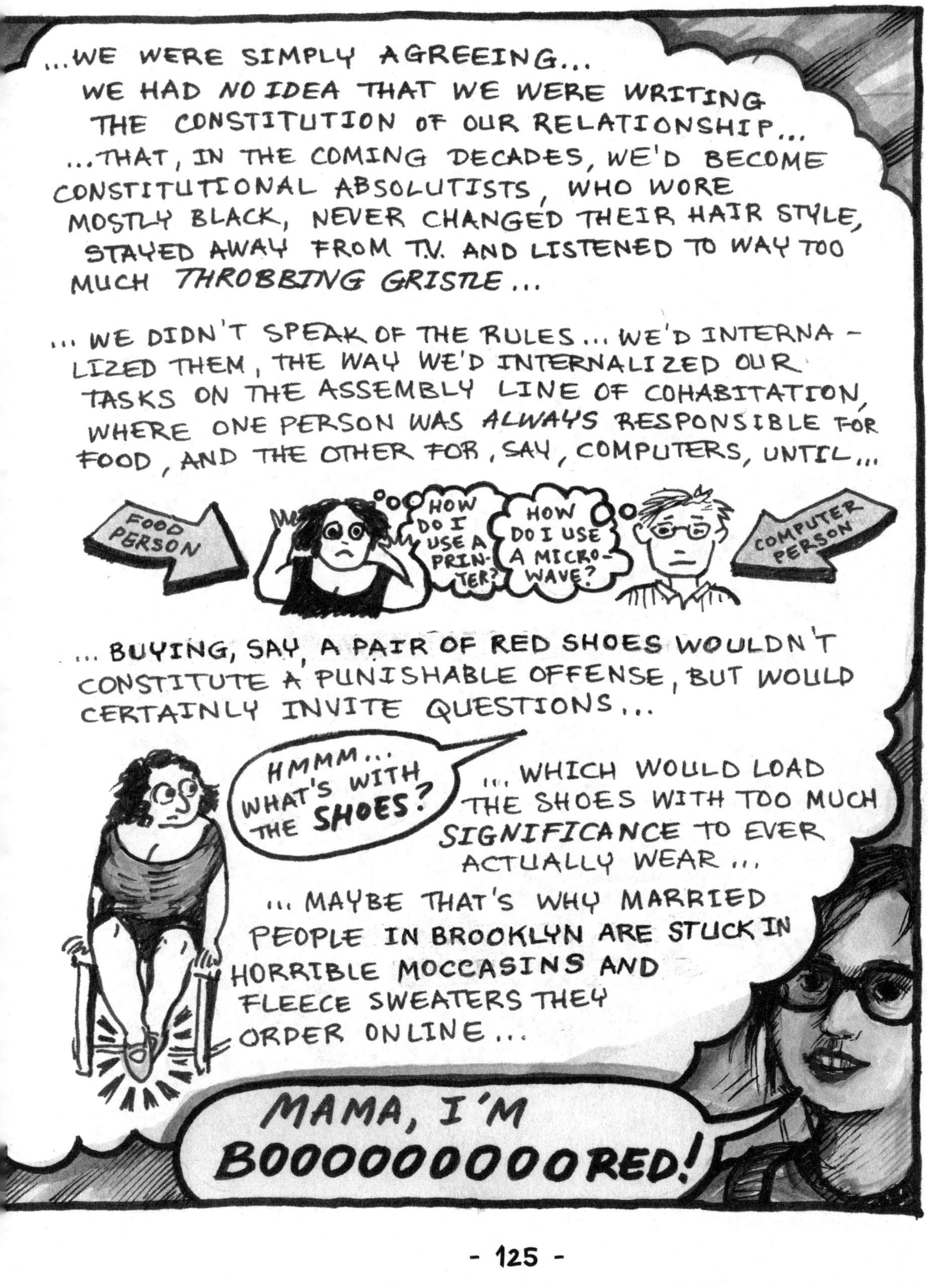
...WE WERE SIMPLY AGREEING...
WE HAD NO IDEA THAT WE WERE WRITING THE CONSTITUTION OF OUR RELATIONSHIP...
...THAT, IN THE COMING DECADES, WE'D BECOME CONSTITUTIONAL ABSOLUTISTS, WHO WORE MOSTLY BLACK, NEVER CHANGED THEIR HAIR STYLE, STAYED AWAY FROM T.V. AND LISTENED TO WAY TOO MUCH THROBBING GRISTLE...
...WE DIDN'T SPEAK OF THE RULES... WE'D INTERNALIZED THEM, THE WAY WE'D INTERNALIZED OUR TASKS ON THE ASSEMBLY LINE OF COHABITATION, WHERE ONE PERSON WAS ALWAYS RESPONSIBLE FOR FOOD, AND THE OTHER FOR, SAY, COMPUTERS, UNTIL...
FOOD PERSON
HOW DO I USE A PRINTER?
HOW DO I USE A MICROWAVE?
COMPUTER PERSON
...BUYING, SAY, A PAIR OF RED SHOES WOULDN'T CONSTITUTE A PUNISHABLE OFFENSE, BUT WOULD CERTAINLY INVITE QUESTIONS...
HMMM... WHAT'S WITH THE SHOES?
...WHICH WOULD LOAD THE SHOES WITH TOO MUCH SIGNIFICANCE TO EVER ACTUALLY WEAR...
...MAYBE THAT'S WHY MARRIED PEOPLE IN BROOKLYN ARE STUCK IN HORRIBLE MOCCASINS AND FLEECE SWEATERS THEY ORDER ONLINE...
MAMA, I'M BOOOOOOOOOOREDǃ

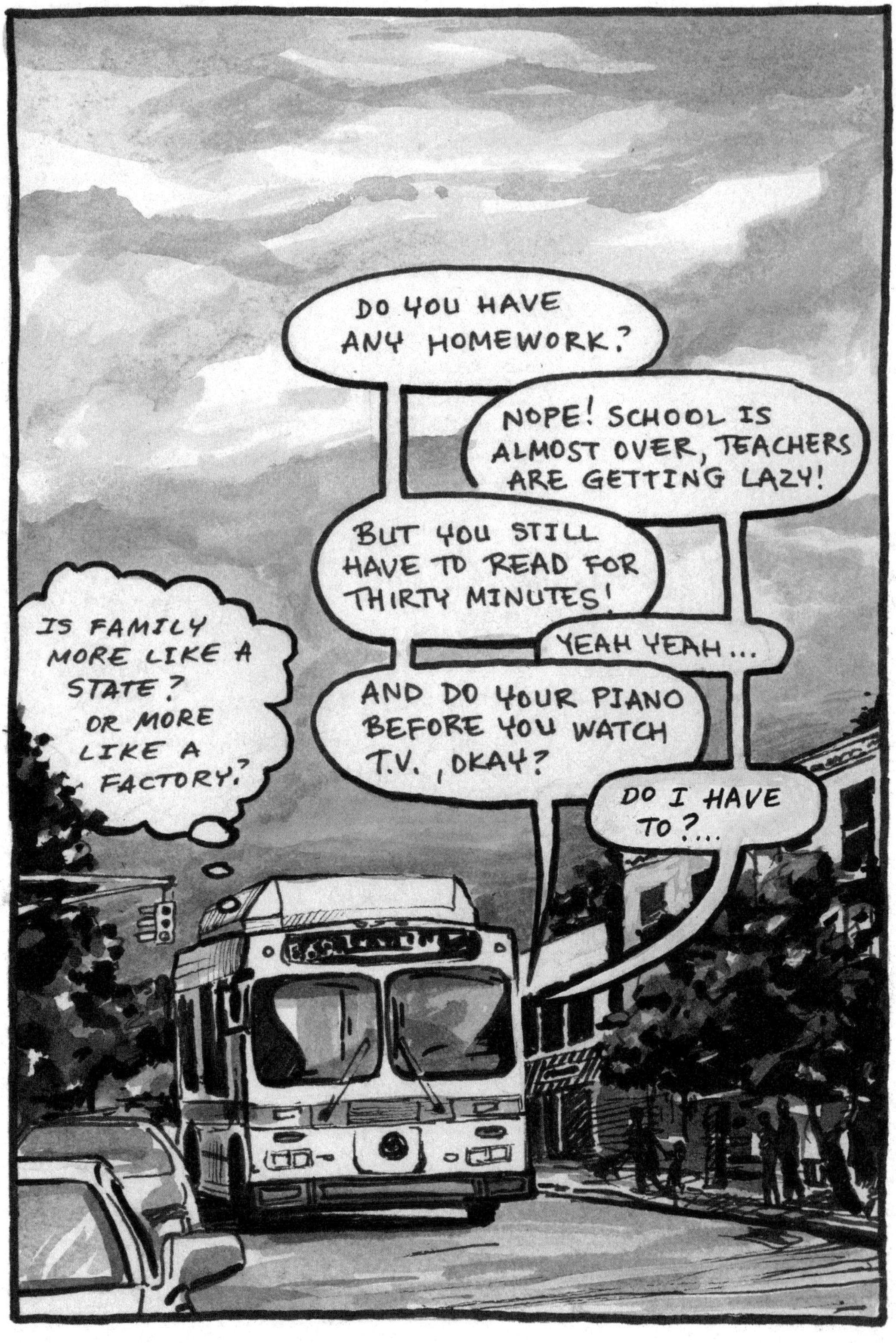
DO YOU HAVE ANY HOMEWORK?
NOPE! SCHOOL IS ALMOST OVER, TEACHERS ARE GETTING LAZY!
BUT YOU STILL HAVE TO READ FOR THIRTY MINUTES!
YEAH YEAH...
AND DO YOUR PIANO BEFORE YOU WATCH T.V., OKAY?
DO I HAVE TO?...
IS FAMILY MORE LIKE A STATE? OR MORE LIKE A FACTORY?

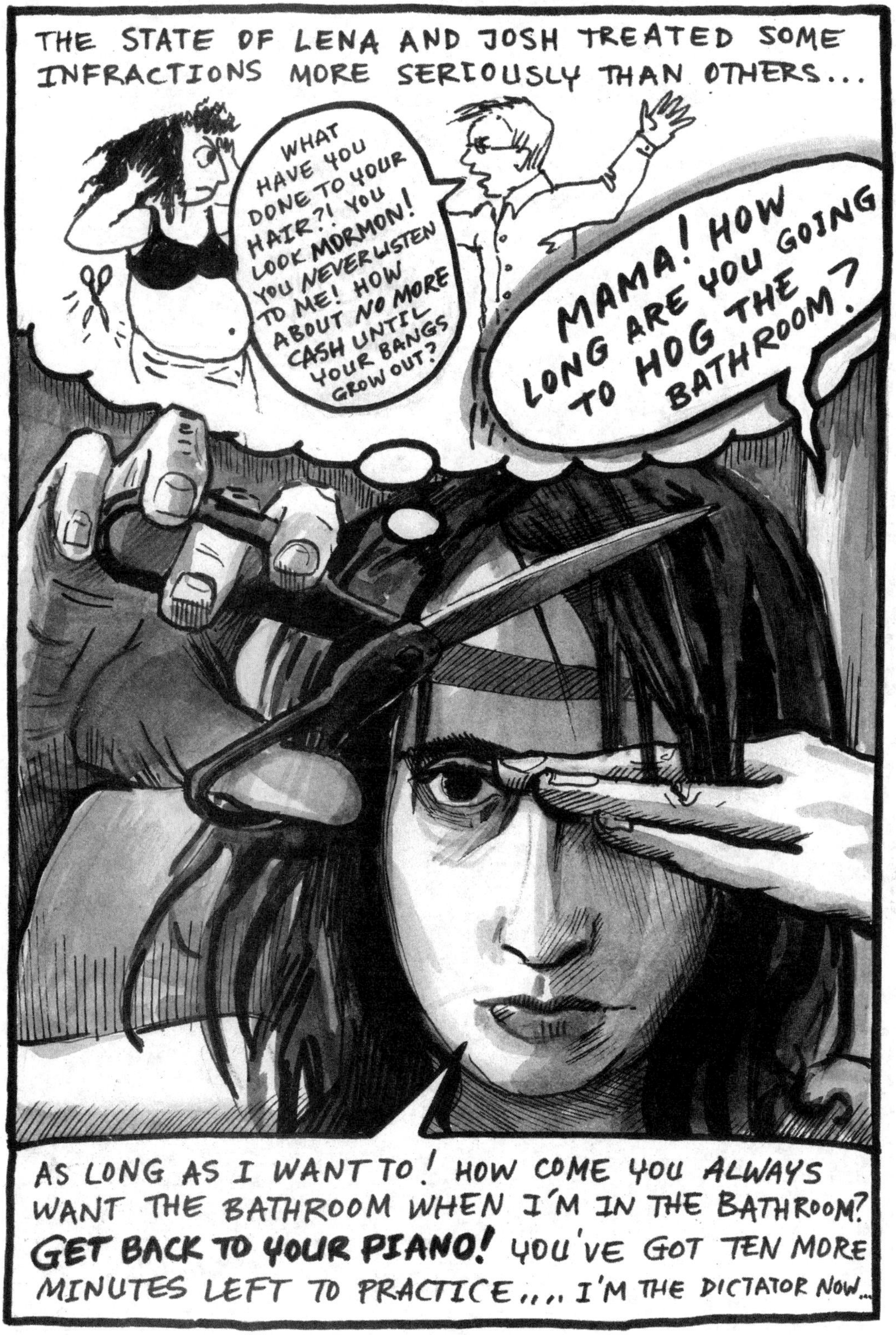
THE STATE OF LENA AND JOSH TREATED SOME INFRACTIONS MORE SERIOUSLY THAN OTHERS...
WHAT HAVE YOU DONE TO YOUR HAIR?! YOU LOOK MORMON! YOU NEVER LISTEN TO ME! HOW ABOUT NO MORE CASH UNTIL YOUR BANGS GROW OUT?
MAMA! HOW LONG ARE YOU GOING TO HOG THE BATHROOM?
AS LONG AS I WANT TO! HOW COME YOU ALWAYS WANT THE BATHROOM WHEN I'M IN THE BATHROOM? GET BACK TO YOUR PIANO! YOU'VE GOT TEN MORE MINUTES LEFT TO PRACTICE.... I'M THE DICTATOR NOW...

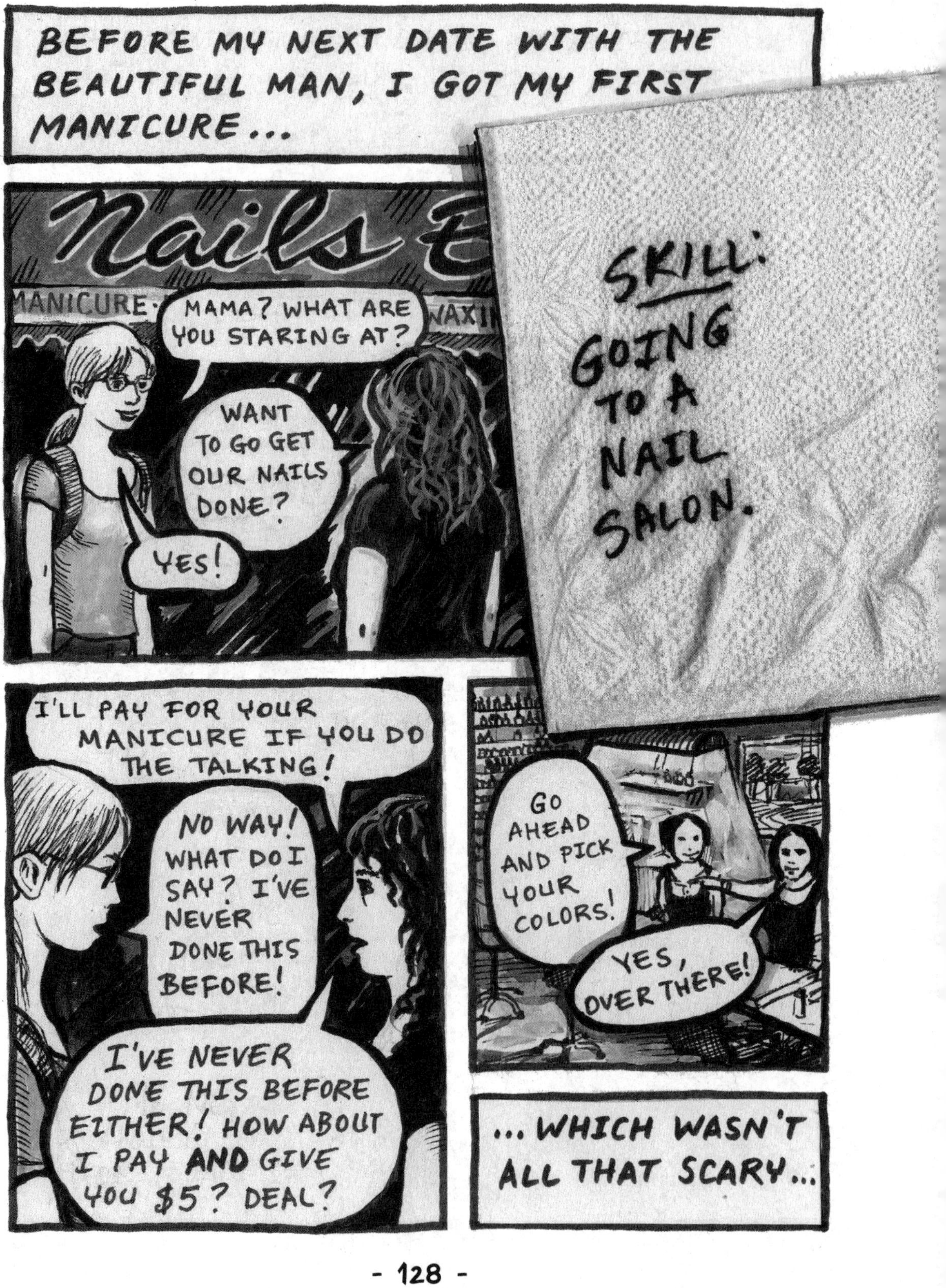

BEFORE MY NEXT DATE WITH THE BEAUTIFUL MAN, I GOT MY FIRST MANICURE...
Nails
MANICURE
WAXI
MAMA? WHAT ARE YOU STARING AT?
WANT TO GO GET OUR NAILS DONE?
YES!
SKILL: GOING TO A NAIL SALON.
I'LL PAY FOR YOUR MANICURE IF YOU DO THE TALKING!
NO WAY! WHAT DO I SAY? I'VE NEVER DONE THIS BEFORE!
I'VE NEVER DONE THIS BEFORE EITHER! HOW ABOUT I PAY AND GIVE YOU $5? DEAL?
GO AHEAD AND PICK YOUR COLORS!
YES, OVER THERE!
...WHICH WASN'T ALL THAT SCARY...

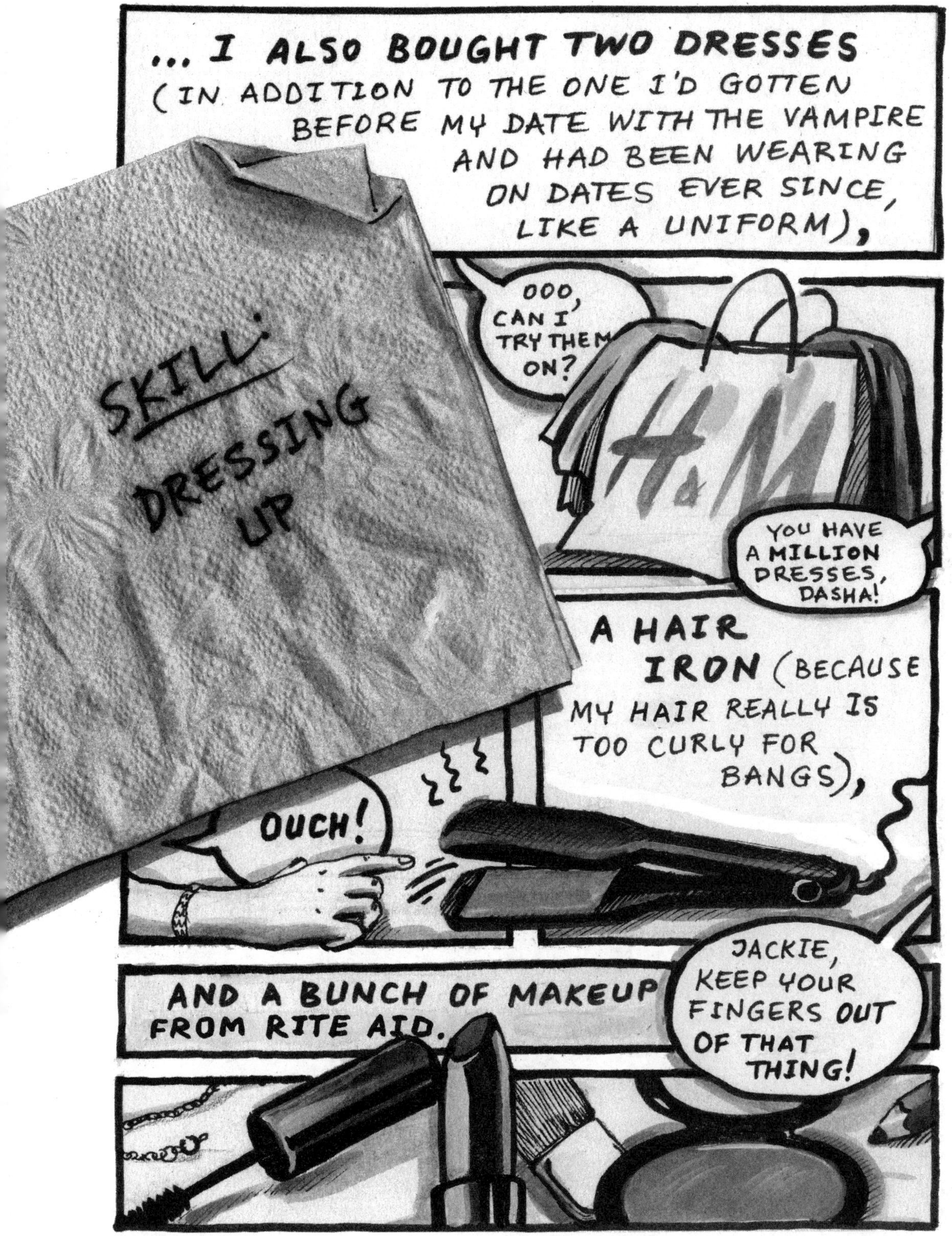
... I ALSO BOUGHT TWO DRESSES (IN ADDITION TO THE ONE I'D GOTTEN BEFORE MY DATE WITH THE VAMPIRE AND HAD BEEN WEARING ON DATES EVER SINCE, LIKE A UNIFORM),
SKILL: DRESSING UP
OOO, CAN I TRY THEM ON?
H&M
YOU HAVE A MILLION DRESSES, DASHA!
A HAIR IRON (BECAUSE MY HAIR REALLY IS TOO CURLY FOR BANGS),
OUCH!
AND A BUNCH OF MAKEUP FROM RITE AID.
JACKIE, KEEP YOUR FINGERS OUT OF THAT THING!

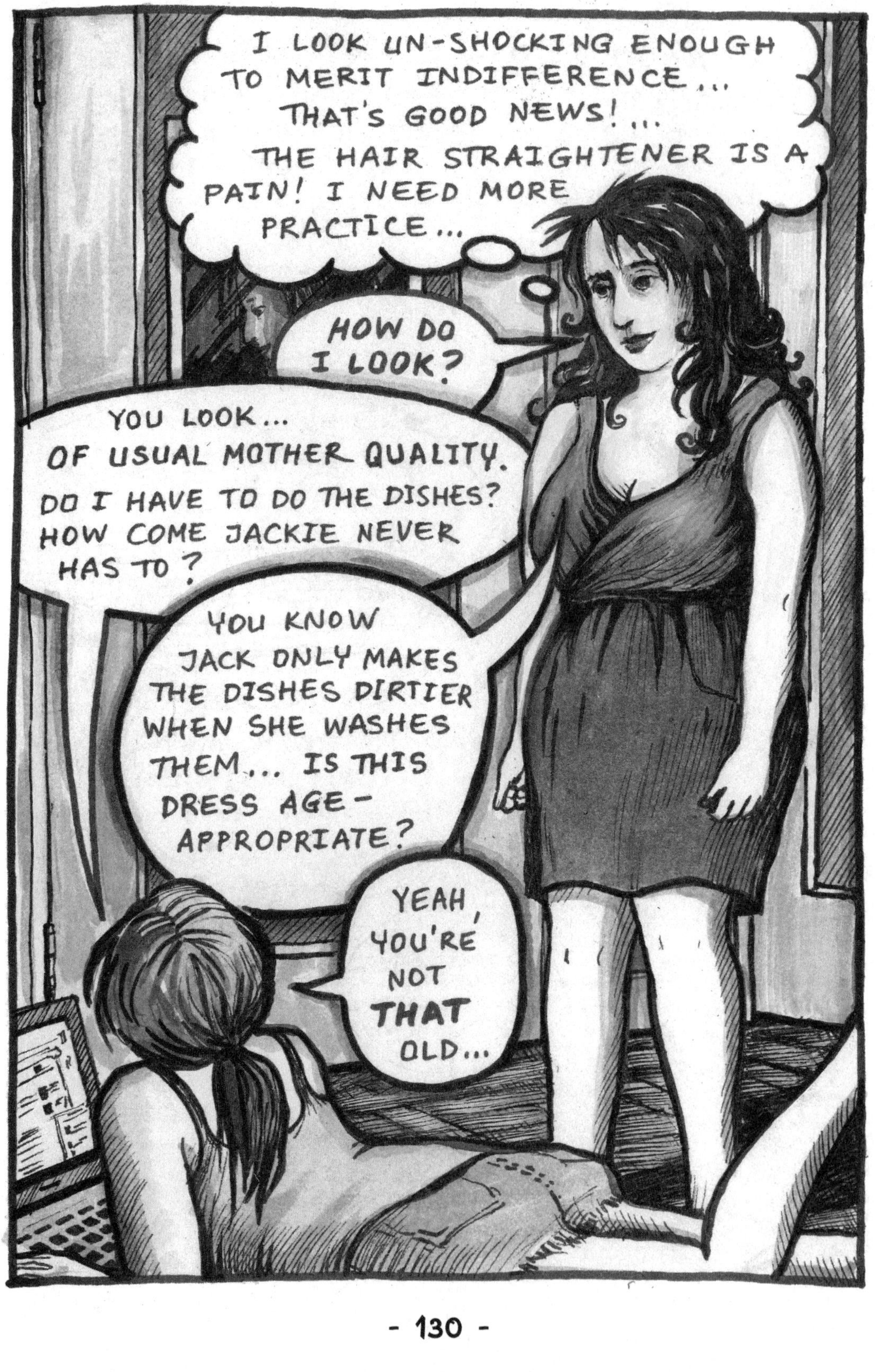
I LOOK UN-SHOCKING ENOUGH TO MERIT INDIFFERENCE... THAT'S GOOD NEWS!... THE HAIR STRAIGHTENER IS A PAIN! I NEED MORE PRACTICE...
HOW DO I LOOK?
YOU LOOK... OF USUAL MOTHER QUALITY. DO I HAVE TO DO THE DISHES? HOW COME JACKIE NEVER HAS TO?
YOU KNOW JACK ONLY MAKES THE DISHES DIRTIER WHEN SHE WASHES THEM... IS THIS DRESS AGE-APPROPRIATE?
YEAH, YOU'RE NOT **THAT** OLD...

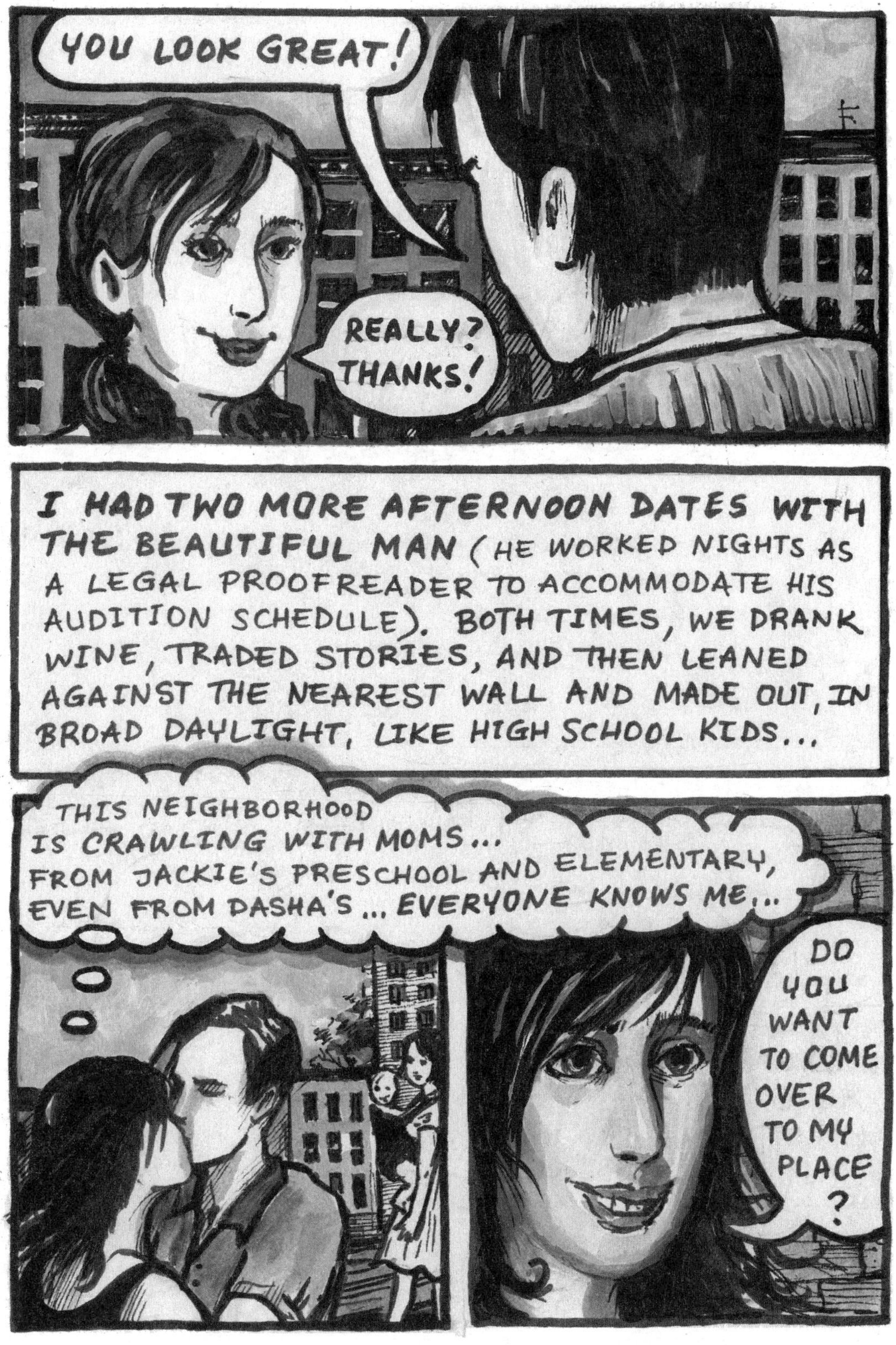
YOU LOOK GREAT!
REALLY? THANKS!
I HAD TWO MORE AFTERNOON DATES WITH THE BEAUTIFUL MAN (HE WORKED NIGHTS AS A LEGAL PROOFREADER TO ACCOMMODATE HIS AUDITION SCHEDULE). BOTH TIMES, WE DRANK WINE, TRADED STORIES, AND THEN LEANED AGAINST THE NEAREST WALL AND MADE OUT, IN BROAD DAYLIGHT, LIKE HIGH SCHOOL KIDS...
THIS NEIGHBORHOOD IS CRAWLING WITH MOMS... FROM JACKIE'S PRESCHOOL AND ELEMENTARY, EVEN FROM DASHA'S... EVERYONE KNOWS ME...
DO YOU WANT TO COME OVER TO MY PLACE ?

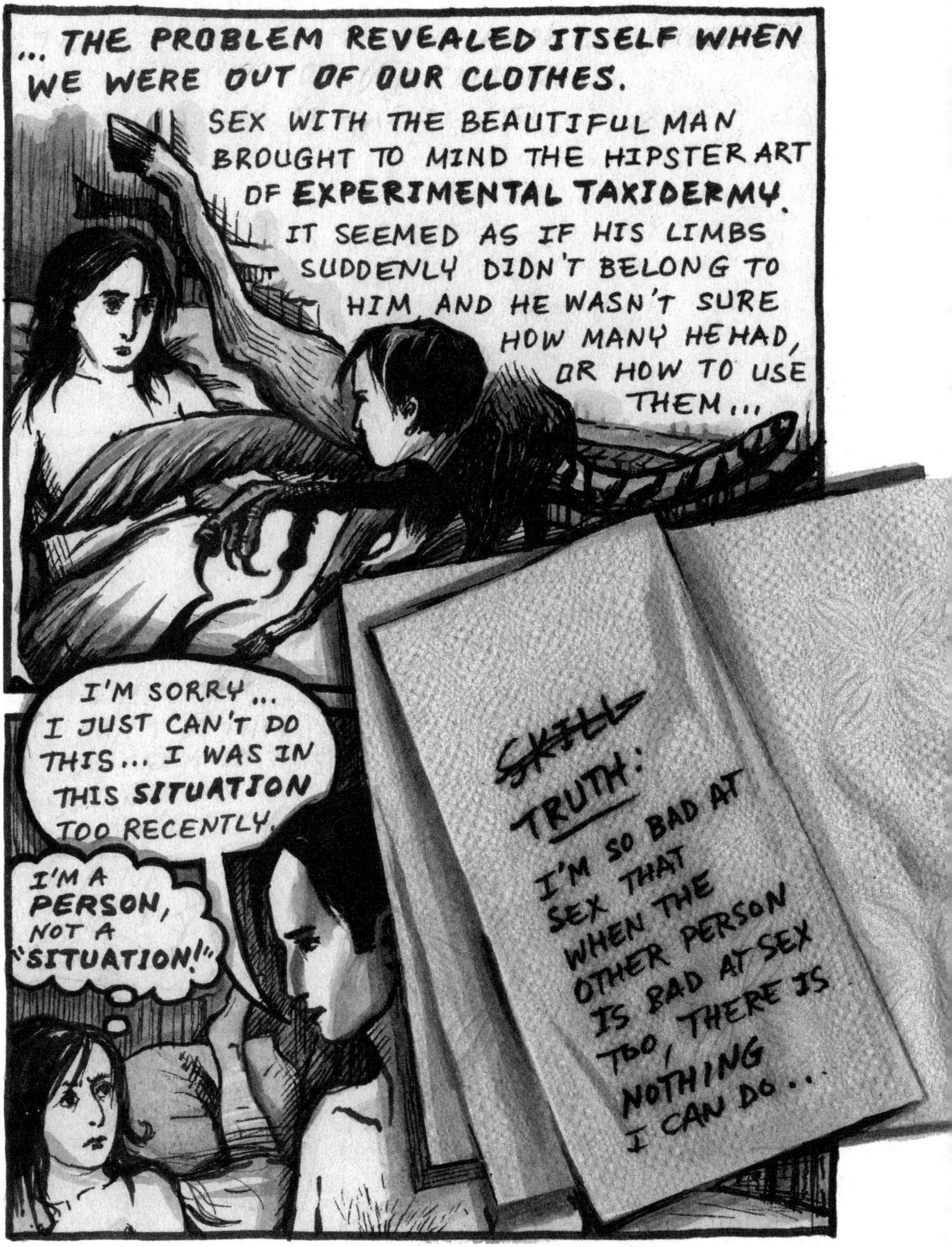
... THE PROBLEM REVEALED ITSELF WHEN WE WERE OUT OF OUR CLOTHES.
SEX WITH THE BEAUTIFUL MAN BROUGHT TO MIND THE HIPSTER ART OF EXPERIMENTAL TAXIDERMY.
IT SEEMED AS IF HIS LIMBS SUDDENLY DIDN'T BELONG TO HIM, AND HE WASN'T SURE HOW MANY HE HAD, OR HOW TO USE THEM...
I'M SORRY... I JUST CAN'T DO THIS... I WAS IN THIS SITUATION TOO RECENTLY.
I'M A PERSON, NOT A "SITUATION!"
~~SKILL~~
TRUTH:
I'M SO BAD AT SEX THAT WHEN THE OTHER PERSON IS BAD AT SEX TOO, THERE IS NOTHING I CAN DO...

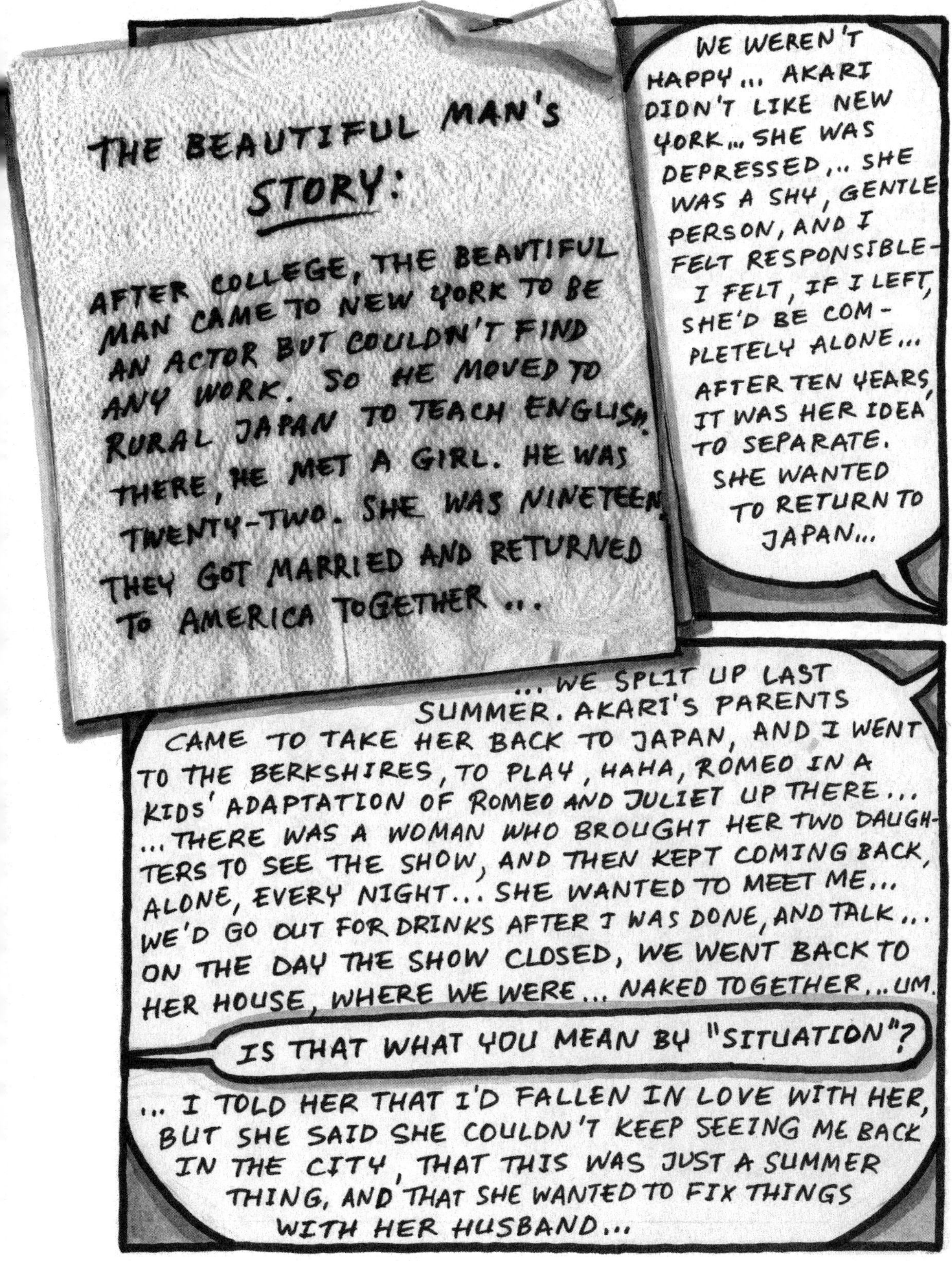
THE BEAUTIFUL MAN'S STORY:
AFTER COLLEGE, THE BEAUTIFUL MAN CAME TO NEW YORK TO BE AN ACTOR BUT COULDN'T FIND ANY WORK. SO HE MOVED TO RURAL JAPAN TO TEACH ENGLISH. THERE, HE MET A GIRL. HE WAS TWENTY-TWO. SHE WAS NINETEEN. THEY GOT MARRIED AND RETURNED TO AMERICA TOGETHER...
WE WEREN'T HAPPY... AKARI DIDN'T LIKE NEW YORK... SHE WAS DEPRESSED... SHE WAS A SHY, GENTLE PERSON, AND I FELT RESPONSIBLE- I FELT, IF I LEFT, SHE'D BE COMPLETELY ALONE... AFTER TEN YEARS, IT WAS HER IDEA TO SEPARATE. SHE WANTED TO RETURN TO JAPAN...
... WE SPLIT UP LAST SUMMER. AKARI'S PARENTS CAME TO TAKE HER BACK TO JAPAN, AND I WENT TO THE BERKSHIRES, TO PLAY, HAHA, ROMEO IN A KIDS' ADAPTATION OF ROMEO AND JULIET UP THERE... ... THERE WAS A WOMAN WHO BROUGHT HER TWO DAUGHTERS TO SEE THE SHOW, AND THEN KEPT COMING BACK, ALONE, EVERY NIGHT... SHE WANTED TO MEET ME... WE'D GO OUT FOR DRINKS AFTER I WAS DONE, AND TALK... ON THE DAY THE SHOW CLOSED, WE WENT BACK TO HER HOUSE, WHERE WE WERE... NAKED TOGETHER... UM.
IS THAT WHAT YOU MEAN BY "SITUATION"?
... I TOLD HER THAT I'D FALLEN IN LOVE WITH HER, BUT SHE SAID SHE COULDN'T KEEP SEEING ME BACK IN THE CITY, THAT THIS WAS JUST A SUMMER THING, AND THAT SHE WANTED TO FIX THINGS WITH HER HUSBAND...

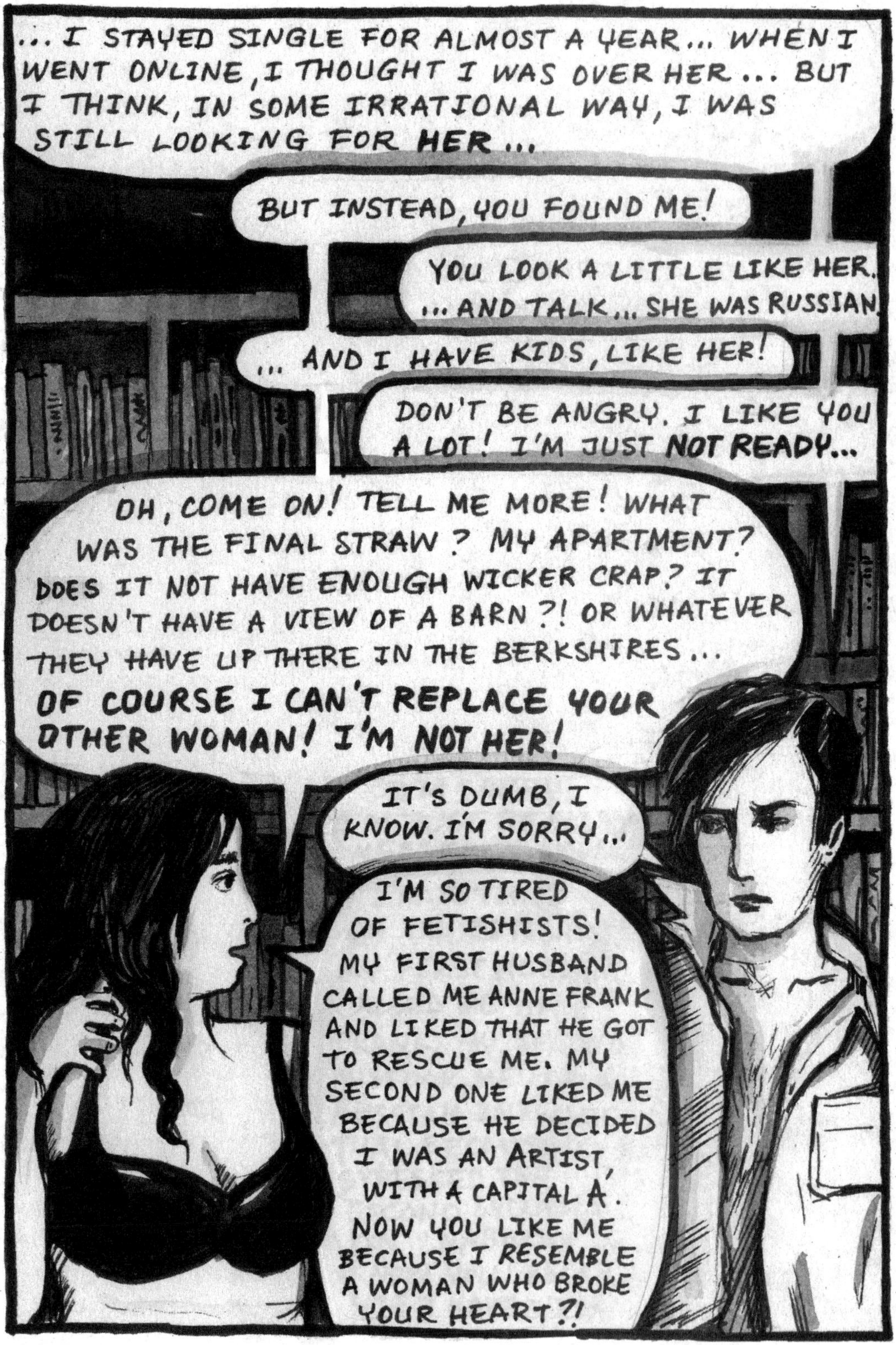
... I STAYED SINGLE FOR ALMOST A YEAR... WHEN I WENT ONLINE, I THOUGHT I WAS OVER HER... BUT I THINK, IN SOME IRRATIONAL WAY, I WAS STILL LOOKING FOR HER...
BUT INSTEAD, YOU FOUND ME!
YOU LOOK A LITTLE LIKE HER. ... AND TALK... SHE WAS RUSSIAN.
... AND I HAVE KIDS, LIKE HER!
DON'T BE ANGRY. I LIKE YOU A LOT! I'M JUST NOT READY...
OH, COME ON! TELL ME MORE! WHAT WAS THE FINAL STRAW? MY APARTMENT? DOES IT NOT HAVE ENOUGH WICKER CRAP? IT DOESN'T HAVE A VIEW OF A BARN?! OR WHATEVER THEY HAVE UP THERE IN THE BERKSHIRES... OF COURSE I CAN'T REPLACE YOUR OTHER WOMAN! I'M NOT HER!
IT'S DUMB, I KNOW. I'M SORRY...
I'M SO TIRED OF FETISHISTS! MY FIRST HUSBAND CALLED ME ANNE FRANK AND LIKED THAT HE GOT TO RESCUE ME. MY SECOND ONE LIKED ME BECAUSE HE DECIDED I WAS AN ARTIST, WITH A CAPITAL A. NOW YOU LIKE ME BECAUSE I RESEMBLE A WOMAN WHO BROKE YOUR HEART?!

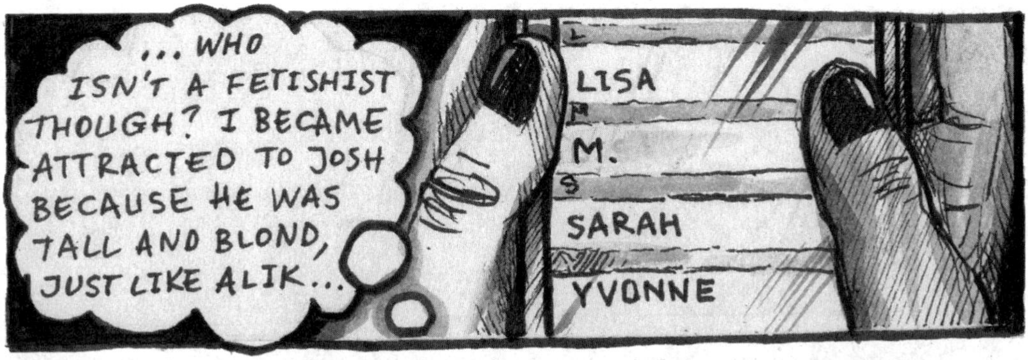
... WHO ISN'T A FETISHIST THOUGH? I BECAME ATTRACTED TO JOSH BECAUSE HE WAS TALL AND BLOND, JUST LIKE ALIK...
LISA
M.
SARAH
YVONNE

MY WISE FRIENDS RAN A STEAMROLLER OVER THE BEAUTIFUL MAN'S HEARTBREAK TALE

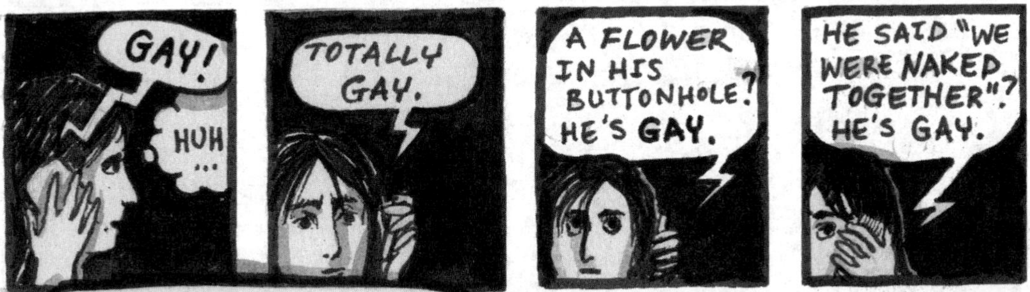
GAY!
HUH...
TOTALLY GAY.
A FLOWER IN HIS BUTTONHOLE? HE'S GAY.
HE SAID "WE WERE NAKED TOGETHER"? HE'S GAY.

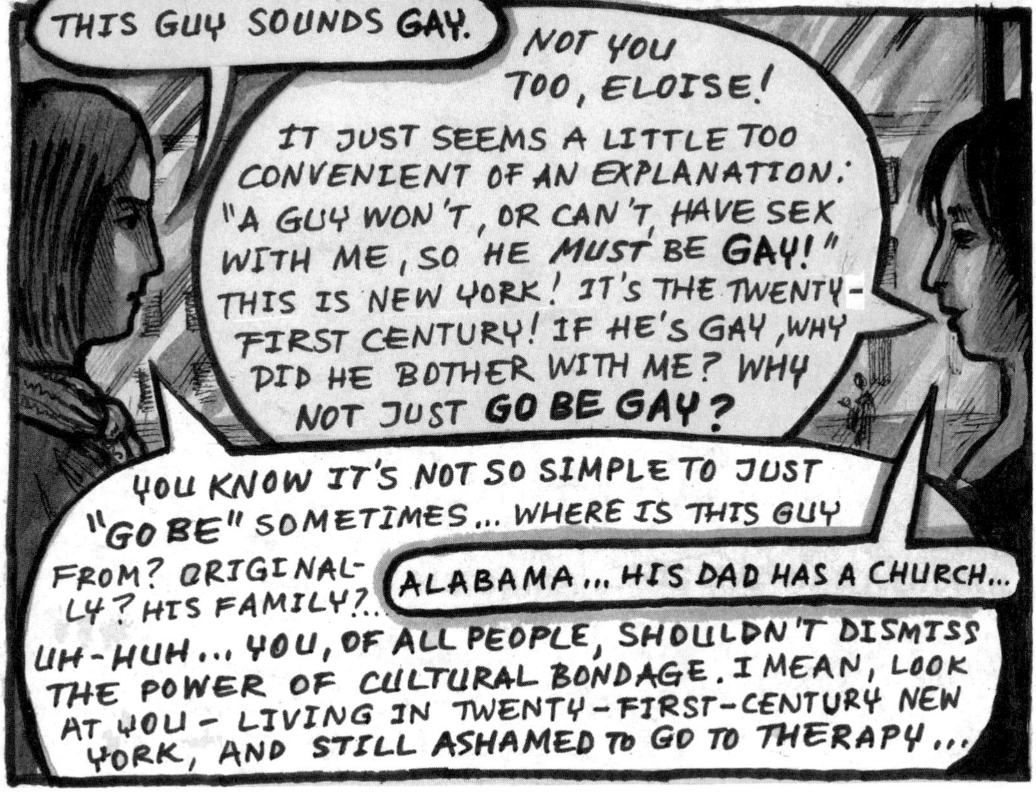
THIS GUY SOUNDS GAY.
NOT YOU TOO, ELOISE!
IT JUST SEEMS A LITTLE TOO CONVENIENT OF AN EXPLANATION: "A GUY WON'T, OR CAN'T, HAVE SEX WITH ME, SO HE MUST BE GAY!" THIS IS NEW YORK! IT'S THE TWENTY-FIRST CENTURY! IF HE'S GAY, WHY DID HE BOTHER WITH ME? WHY NOT JUST GO BE GAY?
YOU KNOW IT'S NOT SO SIMPLE TO JUST "GO BE" SOMETIMES... WHERE IS THIS GUY FROM? ORIGINAL-LY? HIS FAMILY?...
ALABAMA... HIS DAD HAS A CHURCH...
UH-HUH... YOU, OF ALL PEOPLE, SHOULDN'T DISMISS THE POWER OF CULTURAL BONDAGE. I MEAN, LOOK AT YOU - LIVING IN TWENTY-FIRST-CENTURY NEW YORK, AND STILL ASHAMED TO GO TO THERAPY...

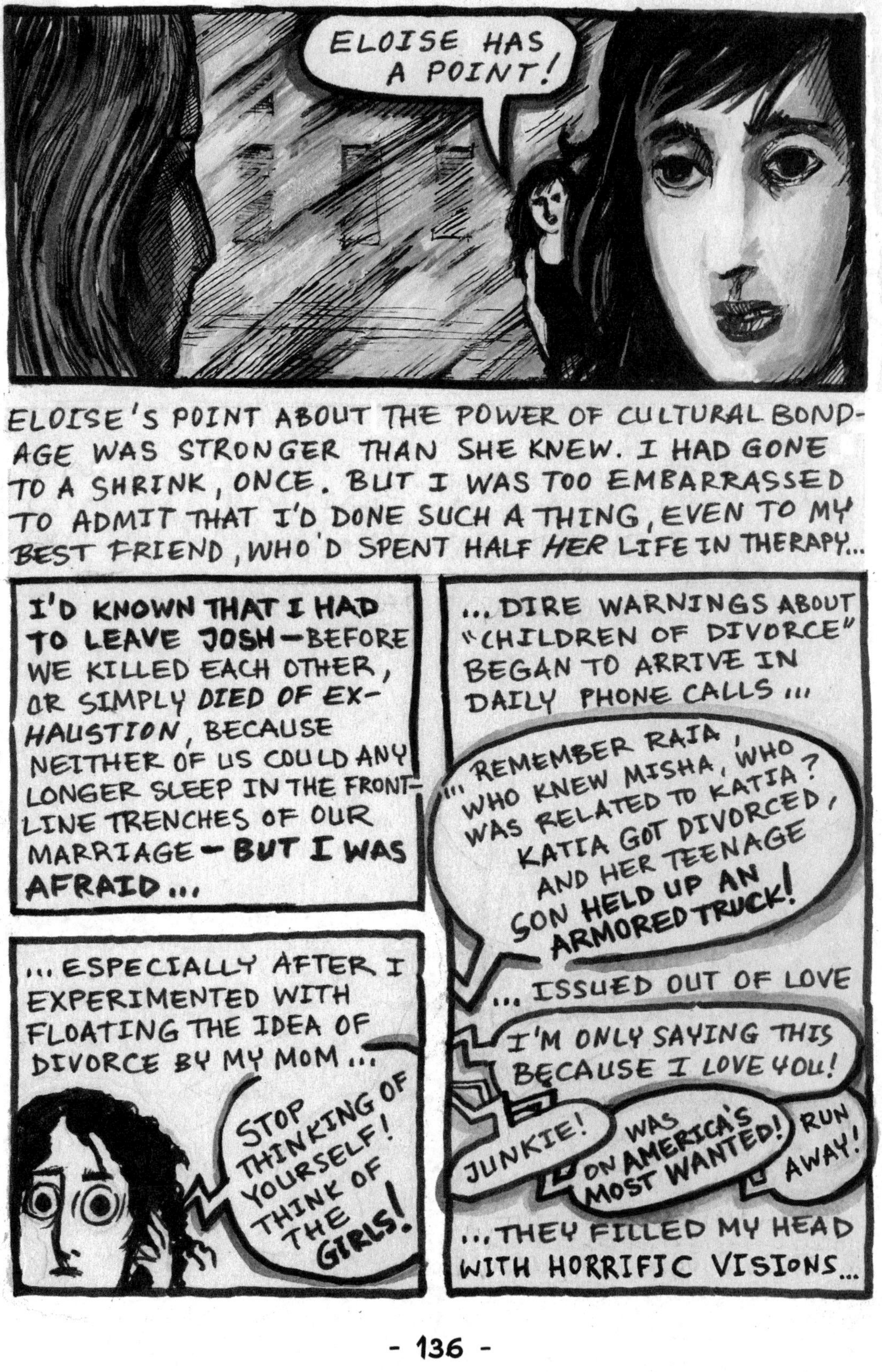
ELOISE HAS A POINT!
ELOISE'S POINT ABOUT THE POWER OF CULTURAL BONDAGE WAS STRONGER THAN SHE KNEW. I HAD GONE TO A SHRINK, ONCE. BUT I WAS TOO EMBARRASSED TO ADMIT THAT I'D DONE SUCH A THING, EVEN TO MY BEST FRIEND, WHO'D SPENT HALF HER LIFE IN THERAPY...
I'D KNOWN THAT I HAD TO LEAVE JOSH—BEFORE WE KILLED EACH OTHER, OR SIMPLY DIED OF EXHAUSTION, BECAUSE NEITHER OF US COULD ANY LONGER SLEEP IN THE FRONT-LINE TRENCHES OF OUR MARRIAGE—BUT I WAS AFRAID...
...ESPECIALLY AFTER I EXPERIMENTED WITH FLOATING THE IDEA OF DIVORCE BY MY MOM...
STOP THINKING OF YOURSELF! THINK OF THE GIRLS!
...DIRE WARNINGS ABOUT "CHILDREN OF DIVORCE" BEGAN TO ARRIVE IN DAILY PHONE CALLS...
...REMEMBER RAIA, WHO KNEW MISHA, WHO WAS RELATED TO KATIA? KATIA GOT DIVORCED, AND HER TEENAGE SON HELD UP AN ARMORED TRUCK!
...ISSUED OUT OF LOVE
I'M ONLY SAYING THIS BECAUSE I LOVE YOU!
JUNKIE!
WAS ON AMERICA'S MOST WANTED!
RUN AWAY!
...THEY FILLED MY HEAD WITH HORRIFIC VISIONS...

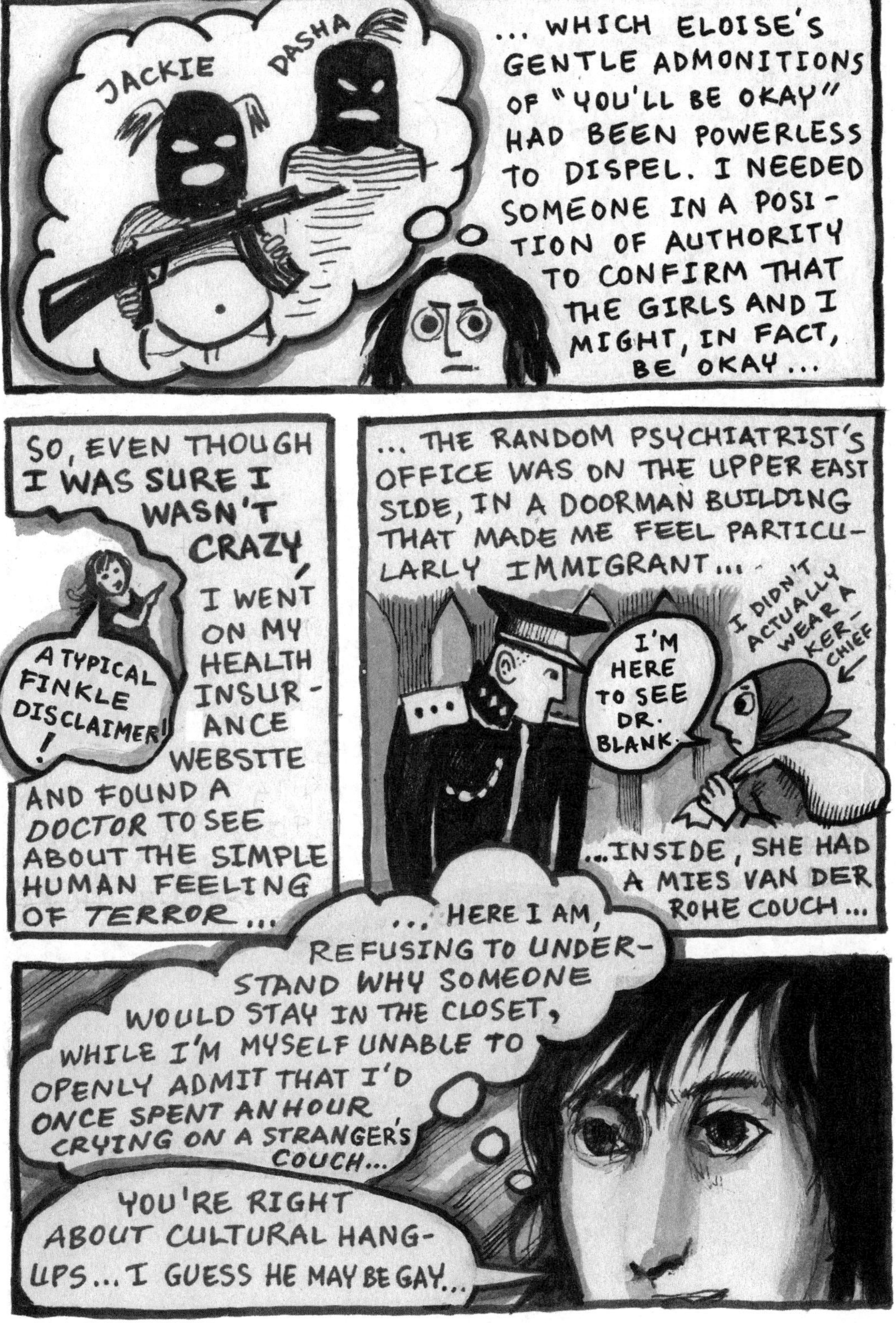
JACKIE
DASHA
... WHICH ELOISE'S GENTLE ADMONITIONS OF "YOU'LL BE OKAY" HAD BEEN POWERLESS TO DISPEL. I NEEDED SOMEONE IN A POSITION OF AUTHORITY TO CONFIRM THAT THE GIRLS AND I MIGHT, IN FACT, BE OKAY...
SO, EVEN THOUGH I WAS SURE I WASN'T CRAZY,
A TYPICAL FINKLE DISCLAIMER!
I WENT ON MY HEALTH INSURANCE WEBSITE AND FOUND A DOCTOR TO SEE ABOUT THE SIMPLE HUMAN FEELING OF TERROR...
... THE RANDOM PSYCHIATRIST'S OFFICE WAS ON THE UPPER EAST SIDE, IN A DOORMAN BUILDING THAT MADE ME FEEL PARTICULARLY IMMIGRANT...
I'M HERE TO SEE DR. BLANK.
I DIDN'T ACTUALLY WEAR A KERCHIEF
...INSIDE, SHE HAD A MIES VAN DER ROHE COUCH...
... HERE I AM, REFUSING TO UNDERSTAND WHY SOMEONE WOULD STAY IN THE CLOSET, WHILE I'M MYSELF UNABLE TO OPENLY ADMIT THAT I'D ONCE SPENT AN HOUR CRYING ON A STRANGER'S COUCH...
YOU'RE RIGHT ABOUT CULTURAL HANG-UPS... I GUESS HE MAY BE GAY...

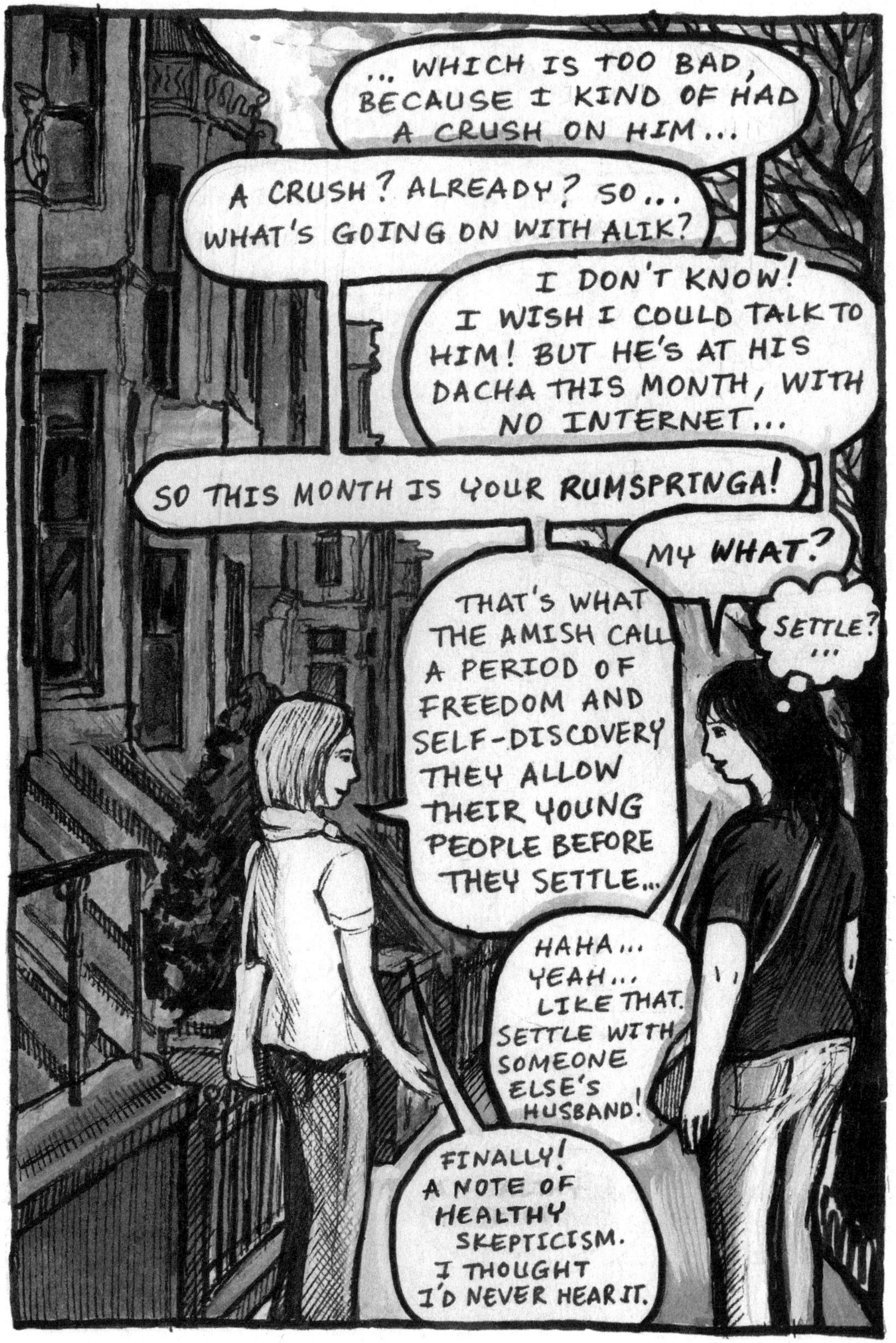
... WHICH IS TOO BAD, BECAUSE I KIND OF HAD A CRUSH ON HIM...
A CRUSH? ALREADY? SO... WHAT'S GOING ON WITH ALIK?
I DON'T KNOW! I WISH I COULD TALK TO HIM! BUT HE'S AT HIS DACHA THIS MONTH, WITH NO INTERNET...
SO THIS MONTH IS YOUR RUMSPRINGA!
MY WHAT?
THAT'S WHAT THE AMISH CALL A PERIOD OF FREEDOM AND SELF-DISCOVERY THEY ALLOW THEIR YOUNG PEOPLE BEFORE THEY SETTLE...
SETTLE? ...
HAHA... YEAH... LIKE THAT. SETTLE WITH SOMEONE ELSE'S HUSBAND!
FINALLY! A NOTE OF HEALTHY SKEPTICISM. I THOUGHT I'D NEVER HEAR IT.

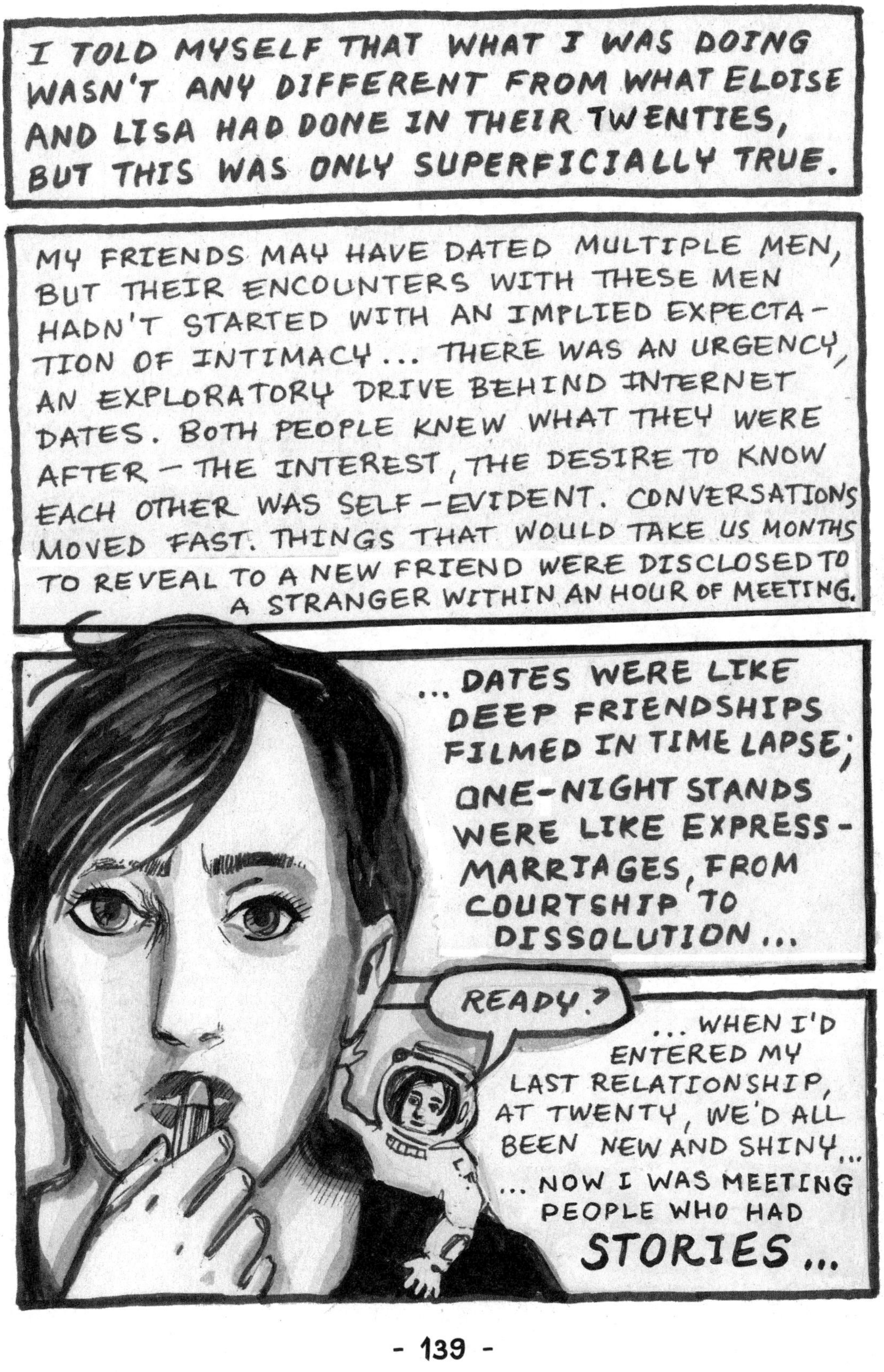
I TOLD MYSELF THAT WHAT I WAS DOING WASN'T ANY DIFFERENT FROM WHAT ELOISE AND LISA HAD DONE IN THEIR TWENTIES, BUT THIS WAS ONLY SUPERFICIALLY TRUE.
MY FRIENDS MAY HAVE DATED MULTIPLE MEN, BUT THEIR ENCOUNTERS WITH THESE MEN HADN'T STARTED WITH AN IMPLIED EXPECTATION OF INTIMACY... THERE WAS AN URGENCY, AN EXPLORATORY DRIVE BEHIND INTERNET DATES. BOTH PEOPLE KNEW WHAT THEY WERE AFTER—THE INTEREST, THE DESIRE TO KNOW EACH OTHER WAS SELF-EVIDENT. CONVERSATIONS MOVED FAST. THINGS THAT WOULD TAKE US MONTHS TO REVEAL TO A NEW FRIEND WERE DISCLOSED TO A STRANGER WITHIN AN HOUR OF MEETING.
...DATES WERE LIKE DEEP FRIENDSHIPS FILMED IN TIME LAPSE; ONE-NIGHT STANDS WERE LIKE EXPRESS-MARRIAGES, FROM COURTSHIP TO DISSOLUTION...
READY?
...WHEN I'D ENTERED MY LAST RELATIONSHIP, AT TWENTY, WE'D ALL BEEN NEW AND SHINY...
...NOW I WAS MEETING PEOPLE WHO HAD STORIES...

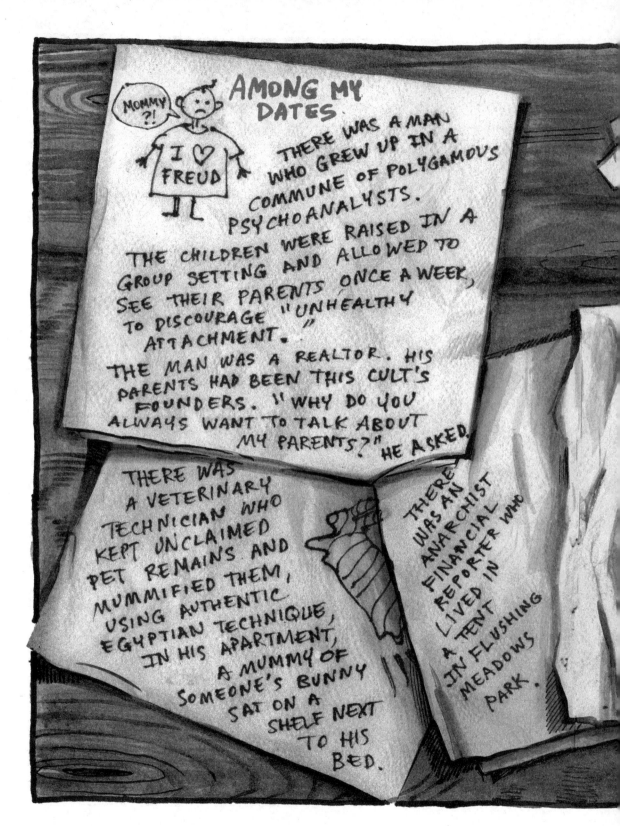

AMONG MY DATES

Mommy?!
I ♡ FREUD

THERE WAS A MAN WHO GREW UP IN A COMMUNE OF POLYGAMOUS PSYCHOANALYSTS.

THE CHILDREN WERE RAISED IN A GROUP SETTING AND ALLOWED TO SEE THEIR PARENTS ONCE A WEEK, TO DISCOURAGE "UNHEALTHY ATTACHMENT."

THE MAN WAS A REALTOR. HIS PARENTS HAD BEEN THIS CULT'S FOUNDERS. "WHY DO YOU ALWAYS WANT TO TALK ABOUT MY PARENTS?" HE ASKED.

THERE WAS A VETERINARY TECHNICIAN WHO KEPT UNCLAIMED PET REMAINS AND MUMMIFIED THEM, USING AUTHENTIC EGYPTIAN TECHNIQUE, IN HIS APARTMENT. A MUMMY OF SOMEONE'S BUNNY SAT ON A SHELF NEXT TO HIS BED.

THERE WAS AN ANARCHIST FINANCIAL REPORTER WHO LIVED IN A TENT IN FLUSHING MEADOWS PARK.

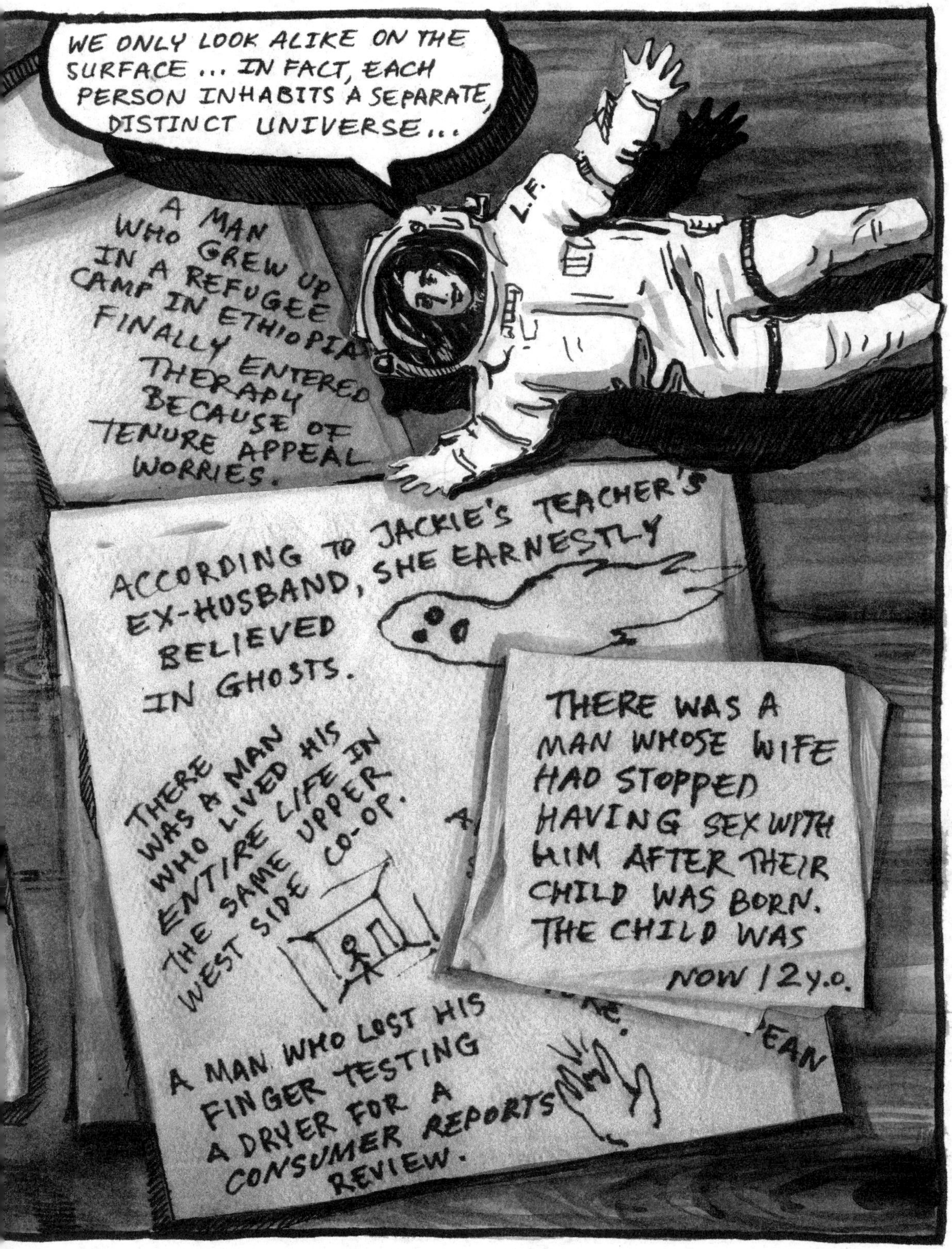
WE ONLY LOOK ALIKE ON THE SURFACE ... IN FACT, EACH PERSON INHABITS A SEPARATE, DISTINCT UNIVERSE...
L.F.
A MAN WHO GREW UP IN A REFUGEE CAMP IN ETHIOPIA FINALLY ENTERED THERAPY BECAUSE OF TENURE APPEAL WORRIES.
ACCORDING TO JACKIE'S TEACHER'S EX-HUSBAND, SHE EARNESTLY BELIEVED IN GHOSTS.
THERE WAS A MAN WHO LIVED HIS ENTIRE LIFE IN THE SAME UPPER WEST SIDE CO-OP.
THERE WAS A MAN WHOSE WIFE HAD STOPPED HAVING SEX WITH HIM AFTER THEIR CHILD WAS BORN. THE CHILD WAS NOW 12 y.o.
A MAN WHO LOST HIS FINGER TESTING A DRYER FOR A CONSUMER REPORTS REVIEW.

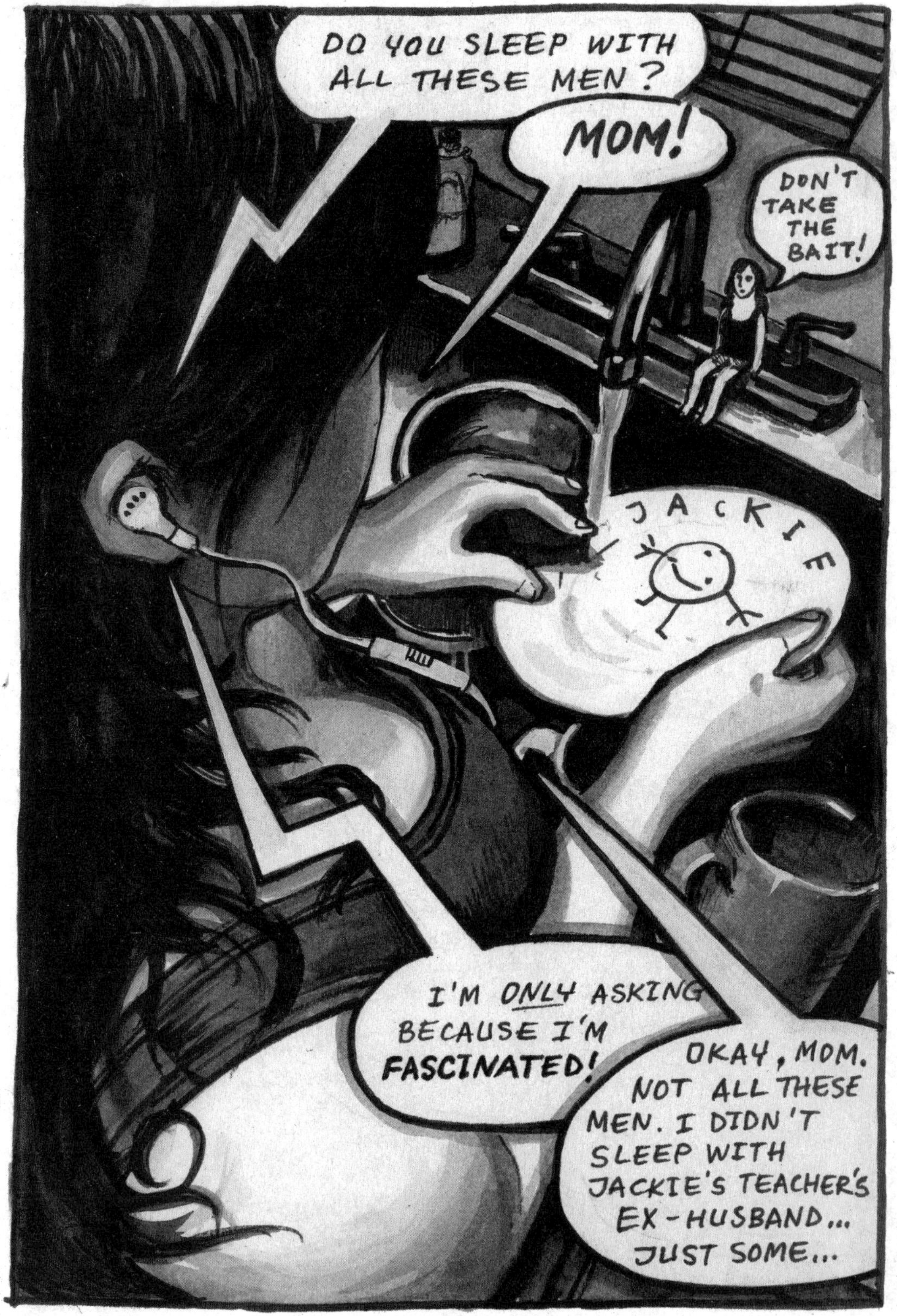
DO YOU SLEEP WITH ALL THESE MEN?
MOM!
DON'T TAKE THE BAIT!
JACKIE
I'M ONLY ASKING BECAUSE I'M FASCINATED!
OKAY, MOM. NOT ALL THESE MEN. I DIDN'T SLEEP WITH JACKIE'S TEACHER'S EX-HUSBAND... JUST SOME...

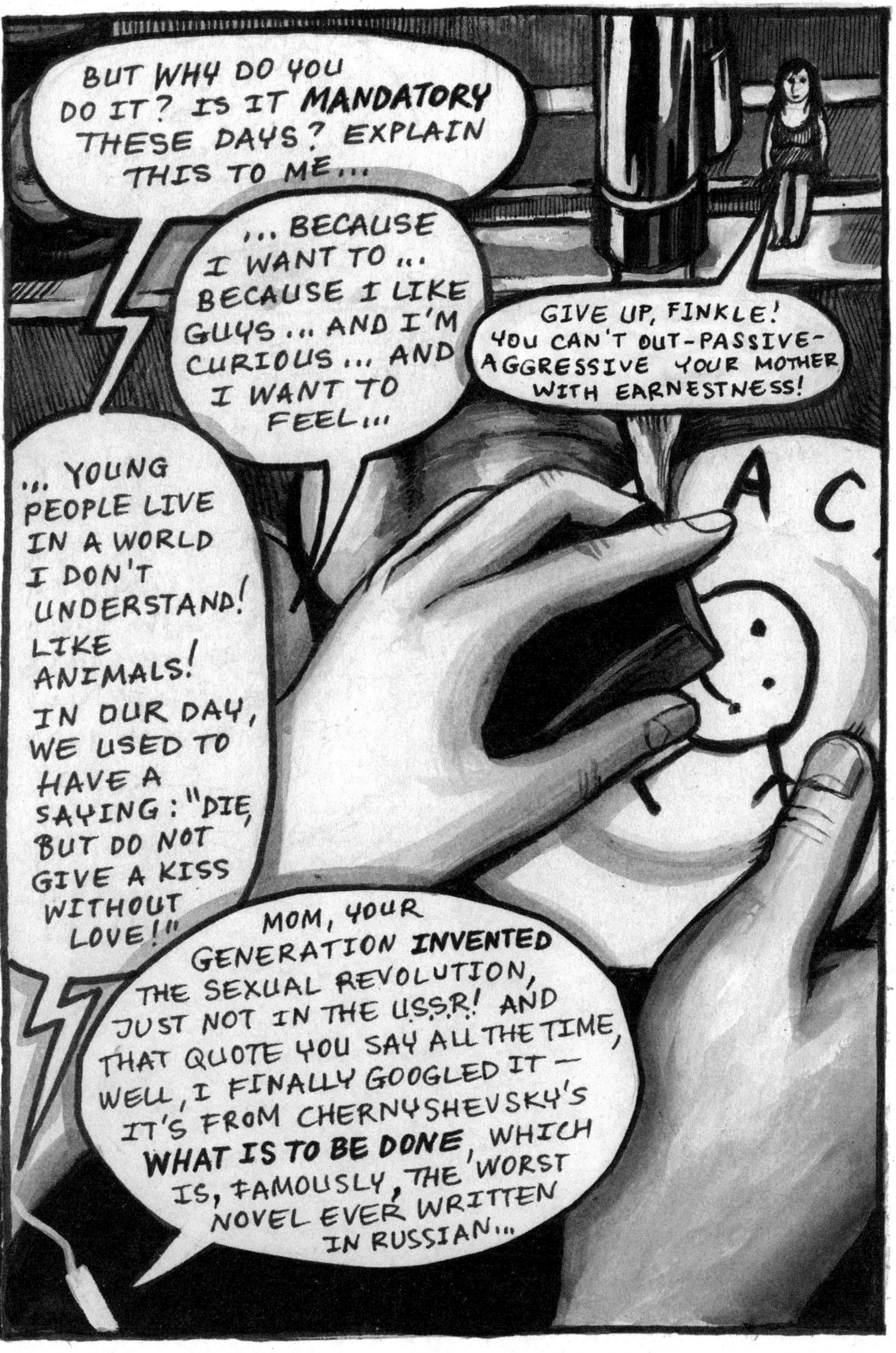
BUT WHY DO YOU DO IT? IS IT MANDATORY THESE DAYS? EXPLAIN THIS TO ME...
... BECAUSE I WANT TO... BECAUSE I LIKE GUYS... AND I'M CURIOUS... AND I WANT TO FEEL...
GIVE UP, FINKLE! YOU CAN'T OUT-PASSIVE-AGGRESSIVE YOUR MOTHER WITH EARNESTNESS!
A C
... YOUNG PEOPLE LIVE IN A WORLD I DON'T UNDERSTAND! LIKE ANIMALS! IN OUR DAY, WE USED TO HAVE A SAYING: "DIE, BUT DO NOT GIVE A KISS WITHOUT LOVE!"
MOM, YOUR GENERATION INVENTED THE SEXUAL REVOLUTION, JUST NOT IN THE U.S.S.R! AND THAT QUOTE YOU SAY ALL THE TIME, WELL, I FINALLY GOOGLED IT — IT'S FROM CHERNYSHEVSKY'S WHAT IS TO BE DONE, WHICH IS, FAMOUSLY, THE WORST NOVEL EVER WRITTEN IN RUSSIAN...

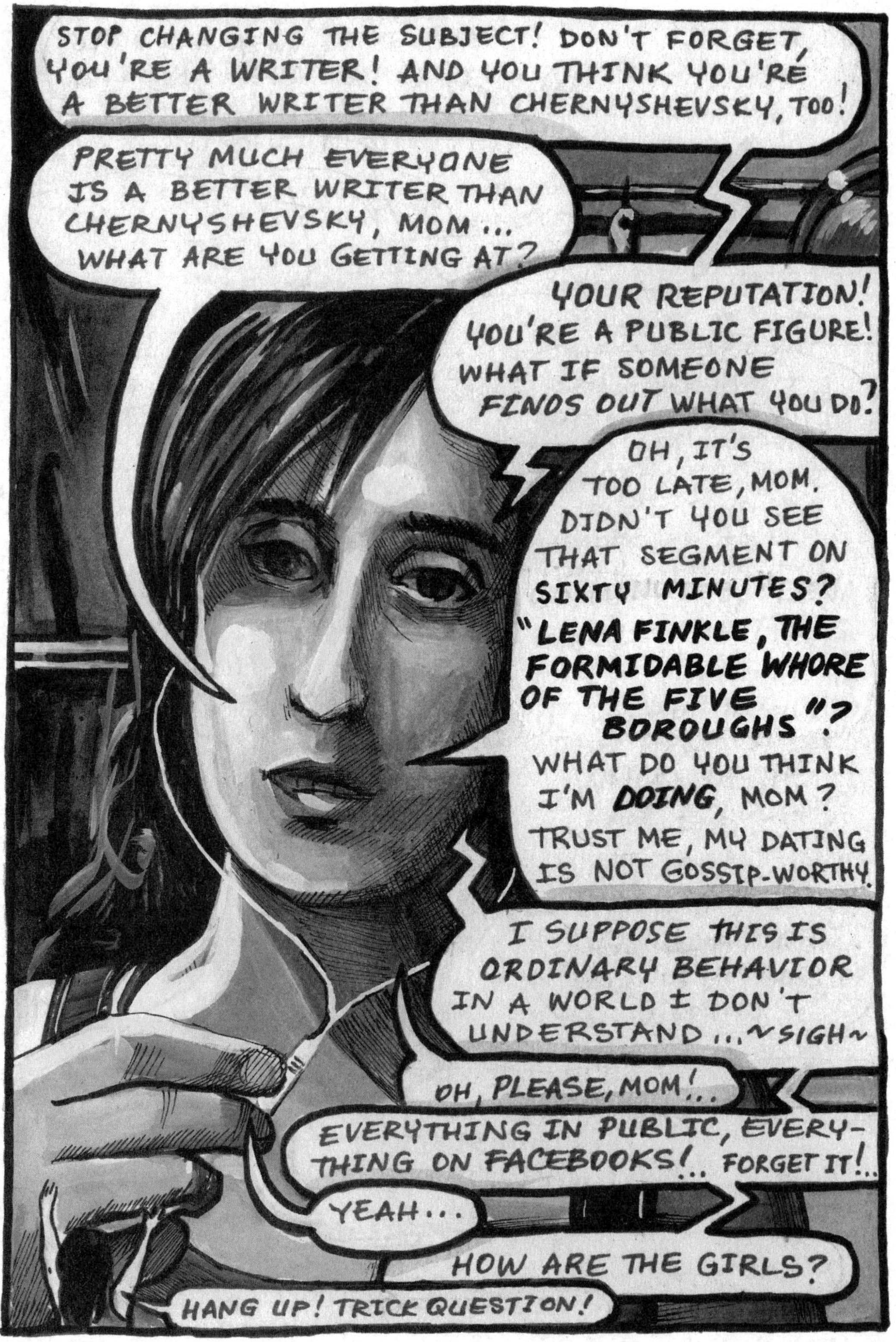
STOP CHANGING THE SUBJECT! DON'T FORGET, YOU'RE A WRITER! AND YOU THINK YOU'RE A BETTER WRITER THAN CHERNYSHEVSKY, TOO!
PRETTY MUCH EVERYONE IS A BETTER WRITER THAN CHERNYSHEVSKY, MOM... WHAT ARE YOU GETTING AT?
YOUR REPUTATION! YOU'RE A PUBLIC FIGURE! WHAT IF SOMEONE FINDS OUT WHAT YOU DO?
OH, IT'S TOO LATE, MOM. DIDN'T YOU SEE THAT SEGMENT ON SIXTY MINUTES? "LENA FINKLE, THE FORMIDABLE WHORE OF THE FIVE BOROUGHS"? WHAT DO YOU THINK I'M DOING, MOM? TRUST ME, MY DATING IS NOT GOSSIP-WORTHY.
I SUPPOSE THIS IS ORDINARY BEHAVIOR IN A WORLD I DON'T UNDERSTAND... ~SIGH~
OH, PLEASE, MOM!..
EVERYTHING IN PUBLIC, EVERYTHING ON FACEBOOKS!.. FORGET IT!..
YEAH...
HOW ARE THE GIRLS?
HANG UP! TRICK QUESTION!

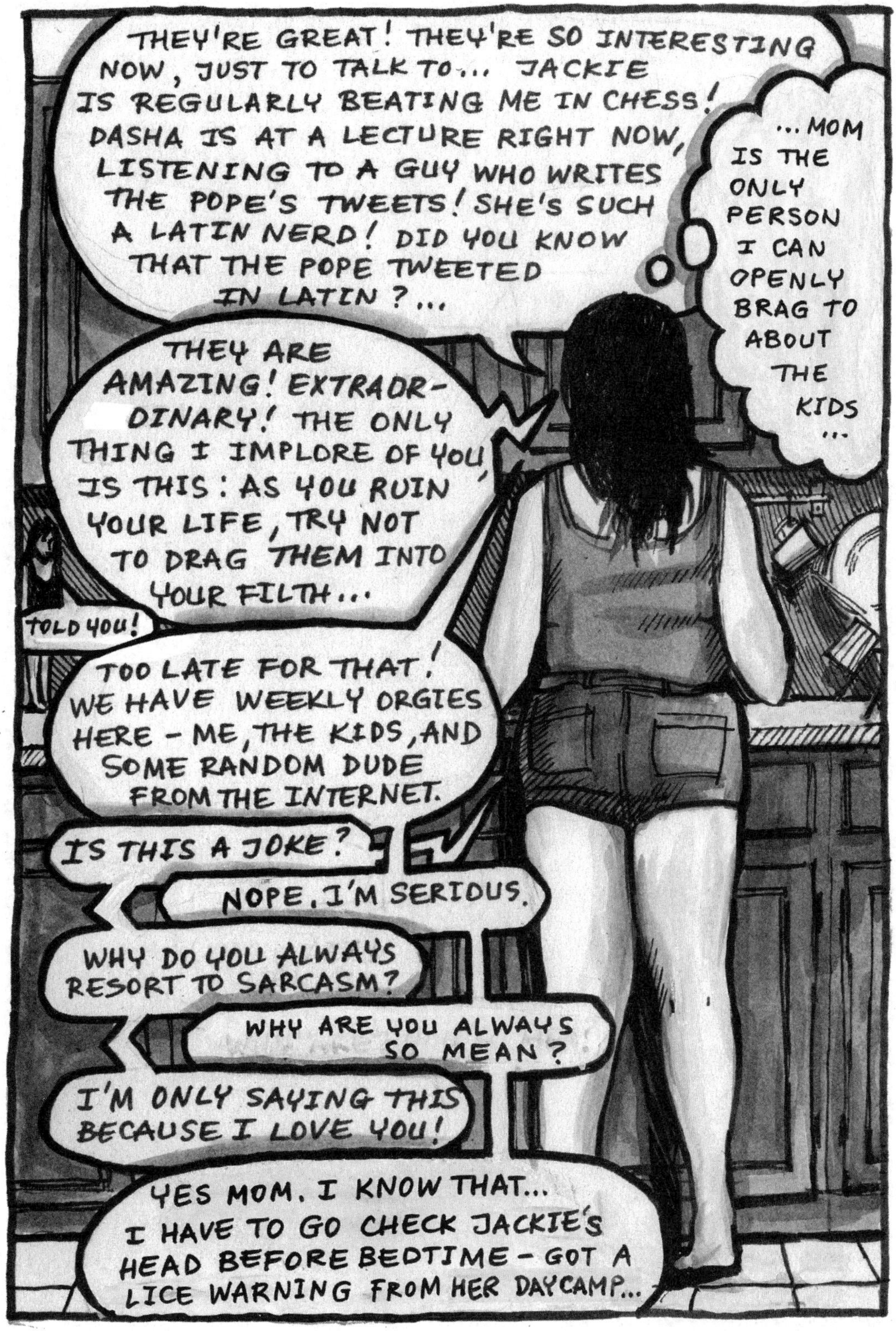
THEY'RE GREAT! THEY'RE SO INTERESTING NOW, JUST TO TALK TO... JACKIE IS REGULARLY BEATING ME IN CHESS! DASHA IS AT A LECTURE RIGHT NOW, LISTENING TO A GUY WHO WRITES THE POPE'S TWEETS! SHE'S SUCH A LATIN NERD! DID YOU KNOW THAT THE POPE TWEETED IN LATIN?...
...MOM IS THE ONLY PERSON I CAN OPENLY BRAG TO ABOUT THE KIDS...
THEY ARE AMAZING! EXTRAORDINARY! THE ONLY THING I IMPLORE OF YOU, IS THIS: AS YOU RUIN YOUR LIFE, TRY NOT TO DRAG THEM INTO YOUR FILTH...
TOLD YOU!
TOO LATE FOR THAT! WE HAVE WEEKLY ORGIES HERE - ME, THE KIDS, AND SOME RANDOM DUDE FROM THE INTERNET.
IS THIS A JOKE?
NOPE. I'M SERIOUS.
WHY DO YOU ALWAYS RESORT TO SARCASM?
WHY ARE YOU ALWAYS SO MEAN?
I'M ONLY SAYING THIS BECAUSE I LOVE YOU!
YES MOM. I KNOW THAT... I HAVE TO GO CHECK JACKIE'S HEAD BEFORE BEDTIME - GOT A LICE WARNING FROM HER DAYCAMP...

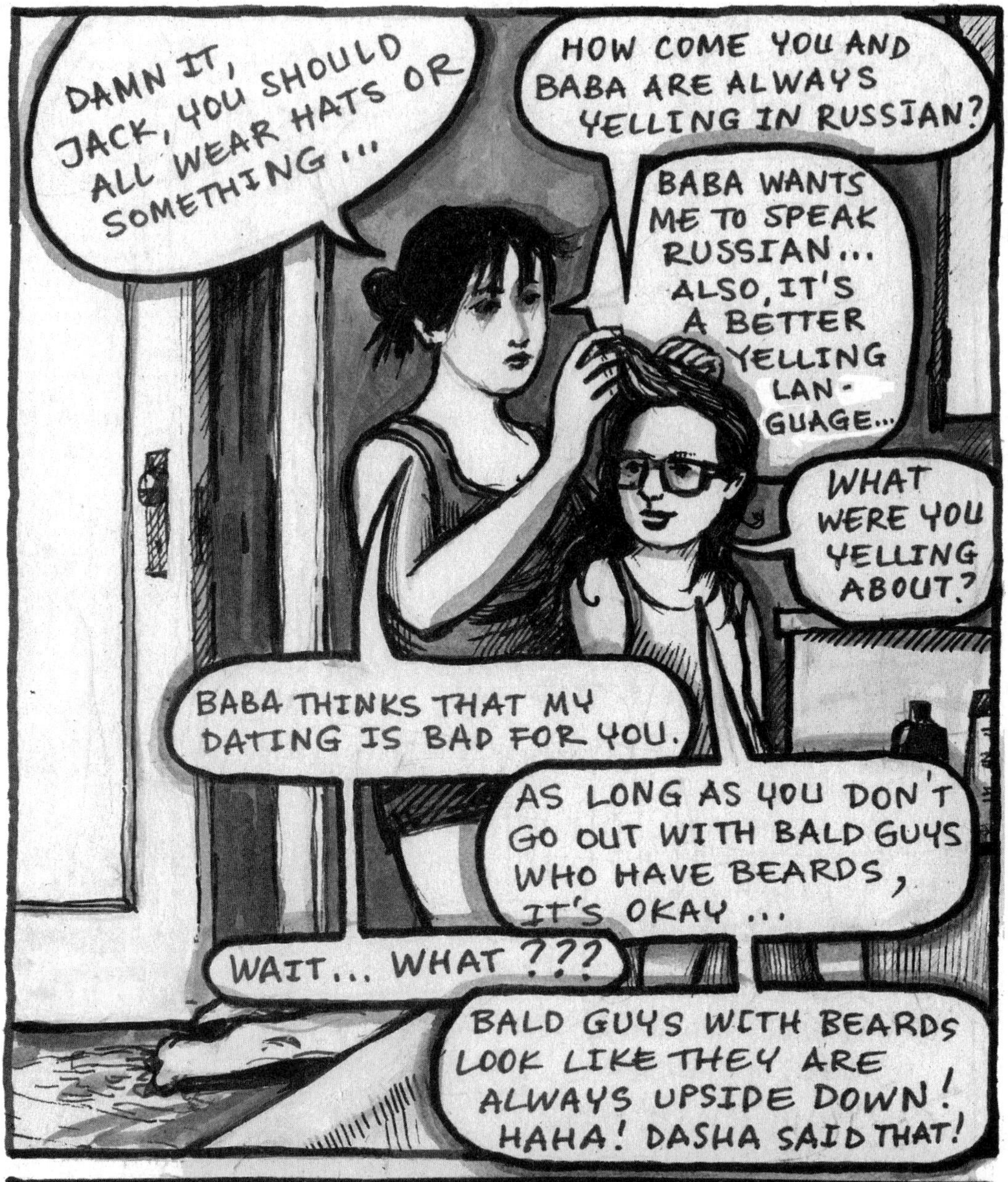
DAMN IT, JACK, YOU SHOULD ALL WEAR HATS OR SOMETHING...
HOW COME YOU AND BABA ARE ALWAYS YELLING IN RUSSIAN?
BABA WANTS ME TO SPEAK RUSSIAN... ALSO, IT'S A BETTER YELLING LAN-GUAGE...
WHAT WERE YOU YELLING ABOUT?
BABA THINKS THAT MY DATING IS BAD FOR YOU.
AS LONG AS YOU DON'T GO OUT WITH BALD GUYS WHO HAVE BEARDS, IT'S OKAY...
WAIT... WHAT???
BALD GUYS WITH BEARDS LOOK LIKE THEY ARE ALWAYS UPSIDE DOWN! HAHA! DASHA SAID THAT!

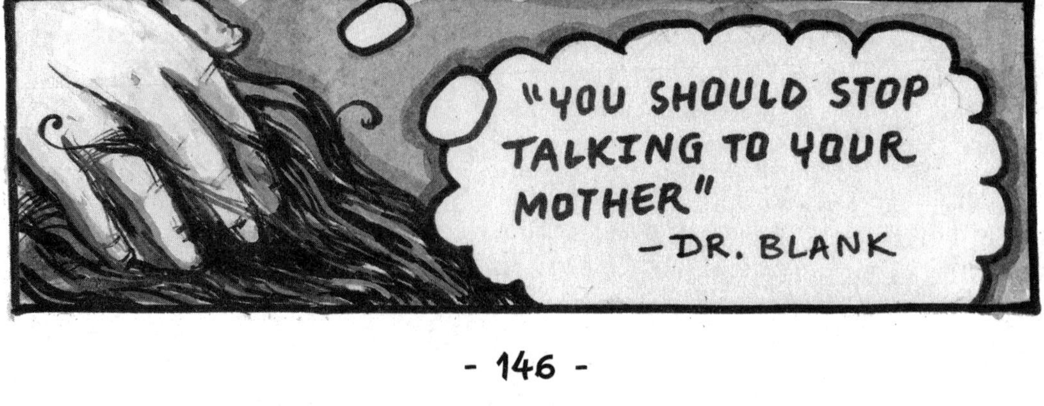
"YOU SHOULD STOP TALKING TO YOUR MOTHER"
—DR. BLANK

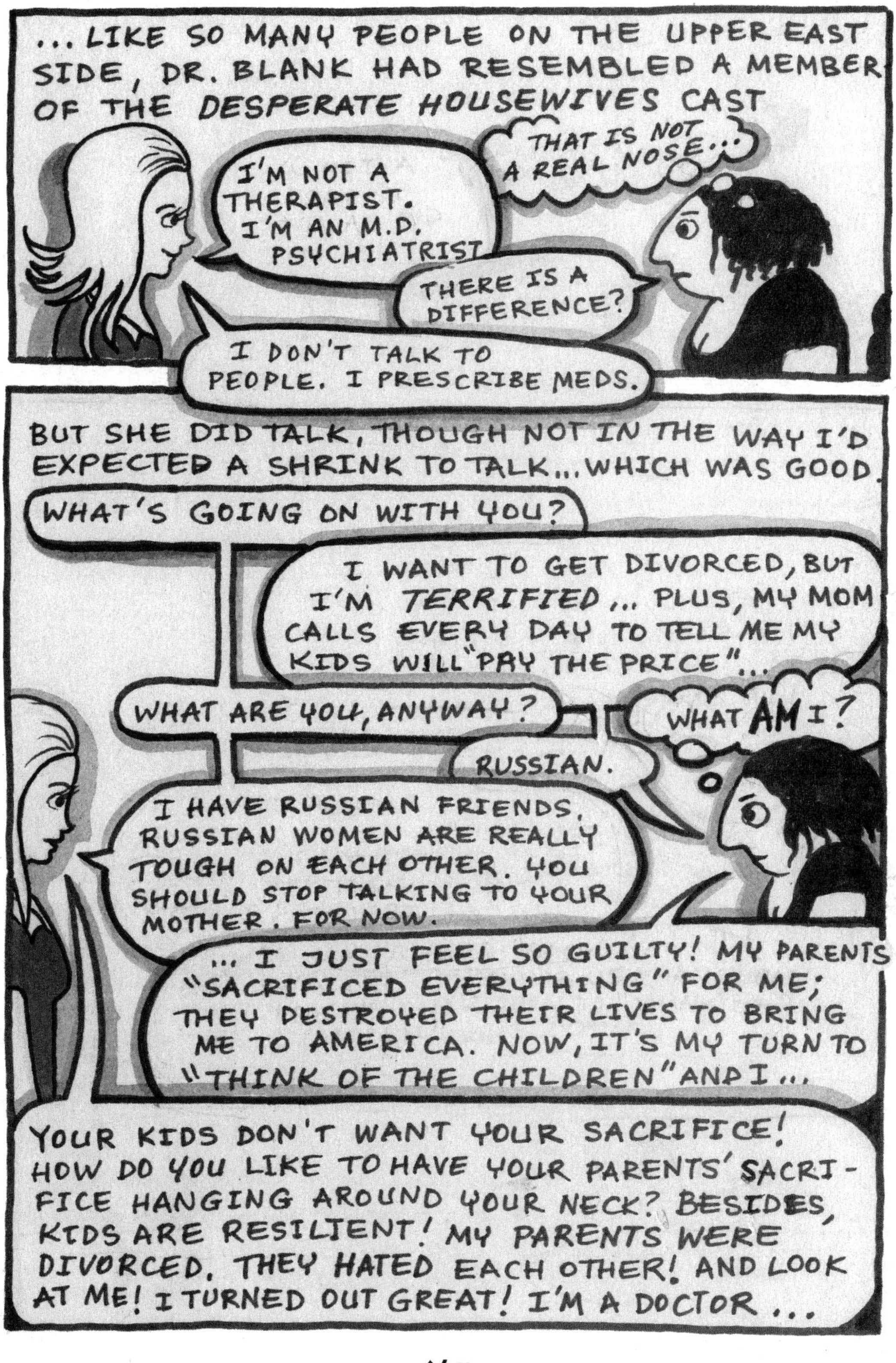
...LIKE SO MANY PEOPLE ON THE UPPER EAST SIDE, DR. BLANK HAD RESEMBLED A MEMBER OF THE *DESPERATE HOUSEWIVES* CAST
I'M NOT A THERAPIST. I'M AN M.D. PSYCHIATRIST
THAT IS NOT A REAL NOSE...
THERE IS A DIFFERENCE?
I DON'T TALK TO PEOPLE. I PRESCRIBE MEDS.
BUT SHE DID TALK, THOUGH NOT IN THE WAY I'D EXPECTED A SHRINK TO TALK... WHICH WAS GOOD.
WHAT'S GOING ON WITH YOU?
I WANT TO GET DIVORCED, BUT I'M *TERRIFIED*... PLUS, MY MOM CALLS EVERY DAY TO TELL ME MY KIDS WILL "PAY THE PRICE"...
WHAT ARE YOU, ANYWAY?
WHAT **AM** I?
RUSSIAN.
I HAVE RUSSIAN FRIENDS. RUSSIAN WOMEN ARE REALLY TOUGH ON EACH OTHER. YOU SHOULD STOP TALKING TO YOUR MOTHER. FOR NOW.
... I JUST FEEL SO GUILTY! MY PARENTS "SACRIFICED EVERYTHING" FOR ME; THEY DESTROYED THEIR LIVES TO BRING ME TO AMERICA. NOW, IT'S MY TURN TO "THINK OF THE CHILDREN" AND I...
YOUR KIDS DON'T WANT YOUR SACRIFICE! HOW DO YOU LIKE TO HAVE YOUR PARENTS' SACRIFICE HANGING AROUND YOUR NECK? BESIDES, KIDS ARE RESILIENT! MY PARENTS WERE DIVORCED. THEY HATED EACH OTHER! AND LOOK AT ME! I TURNED OUT GREAT! I'M A DOCTOR...

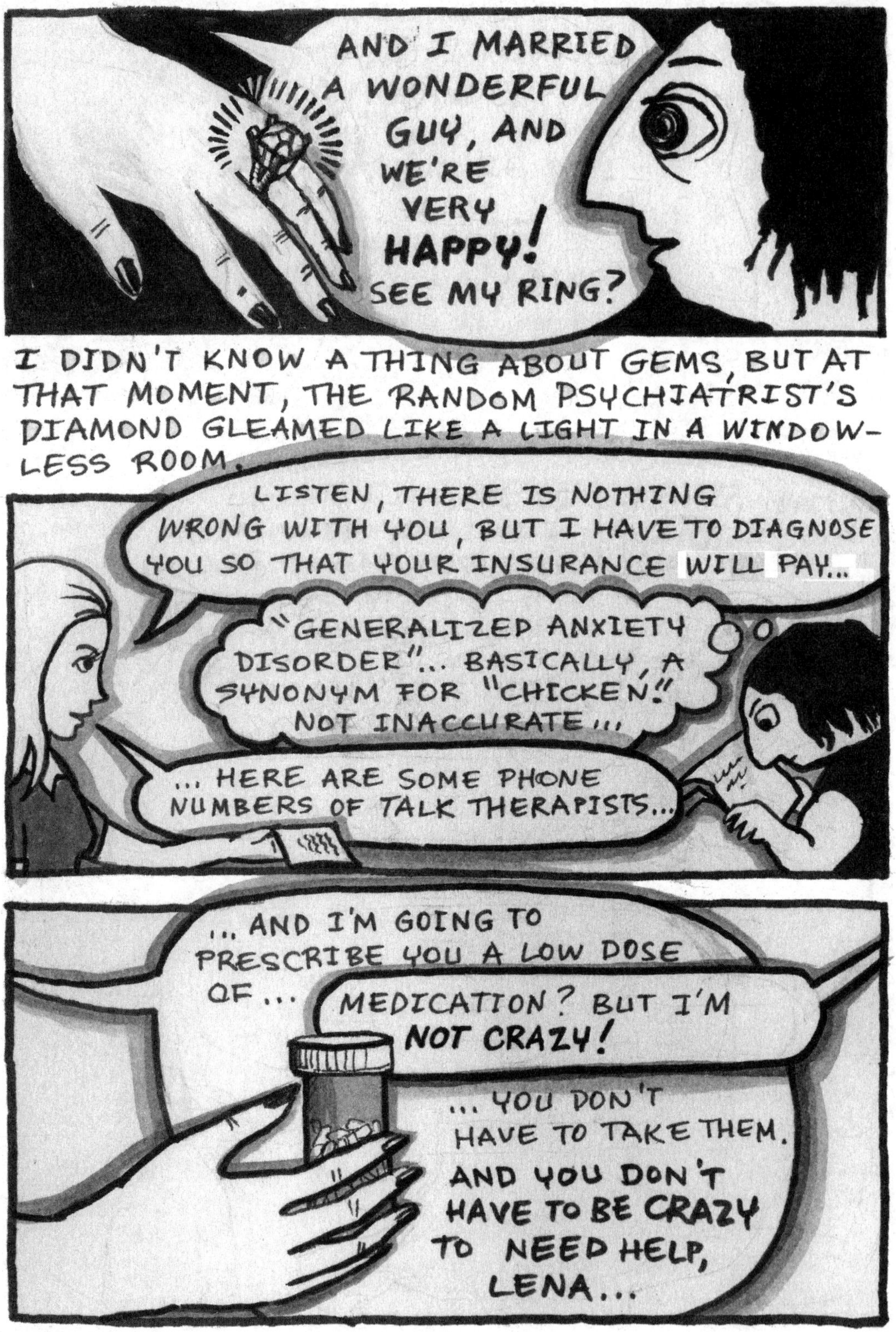
AND I MARRIED A WONDERFUL GUY, AND WE'RE VERY HAPPY! SEE MY RING?
I DIDN'T KNOW A THING ABOUT GEMS, BUT AT THAT MOMENT, THE RANDOM PSYCHIATRIST'S DIAMOND GLEAMED LIKE A LIGHT IN A WINDOW-LESS ROOM.
LISTEN, THERE IS NOTHING WRONG WITH YOU, BUT I HAVE TO DIAGNOSE YOU SO THAT YOUR INSURANCE WILL PAY...
"GENERALIZED ANXIETY DISORDER"... BASICALLY, A SYNONYM FOR "CHICKEN!" NOT INACCURATE...
... HERE ARE SOME PHONE NUMBERS OF TALK THERAPISTS...
... AND I'M GOING TO PRESCRIBE YOU A LOW DOSE OF...
MEDICATION? BUT I'M NOT CRAZY!
... YOU DON'T HAVE TO TAKE THEM.
AND YOU DON'T HAVE TO BE CRAZY TO NEED HELP, LENA...

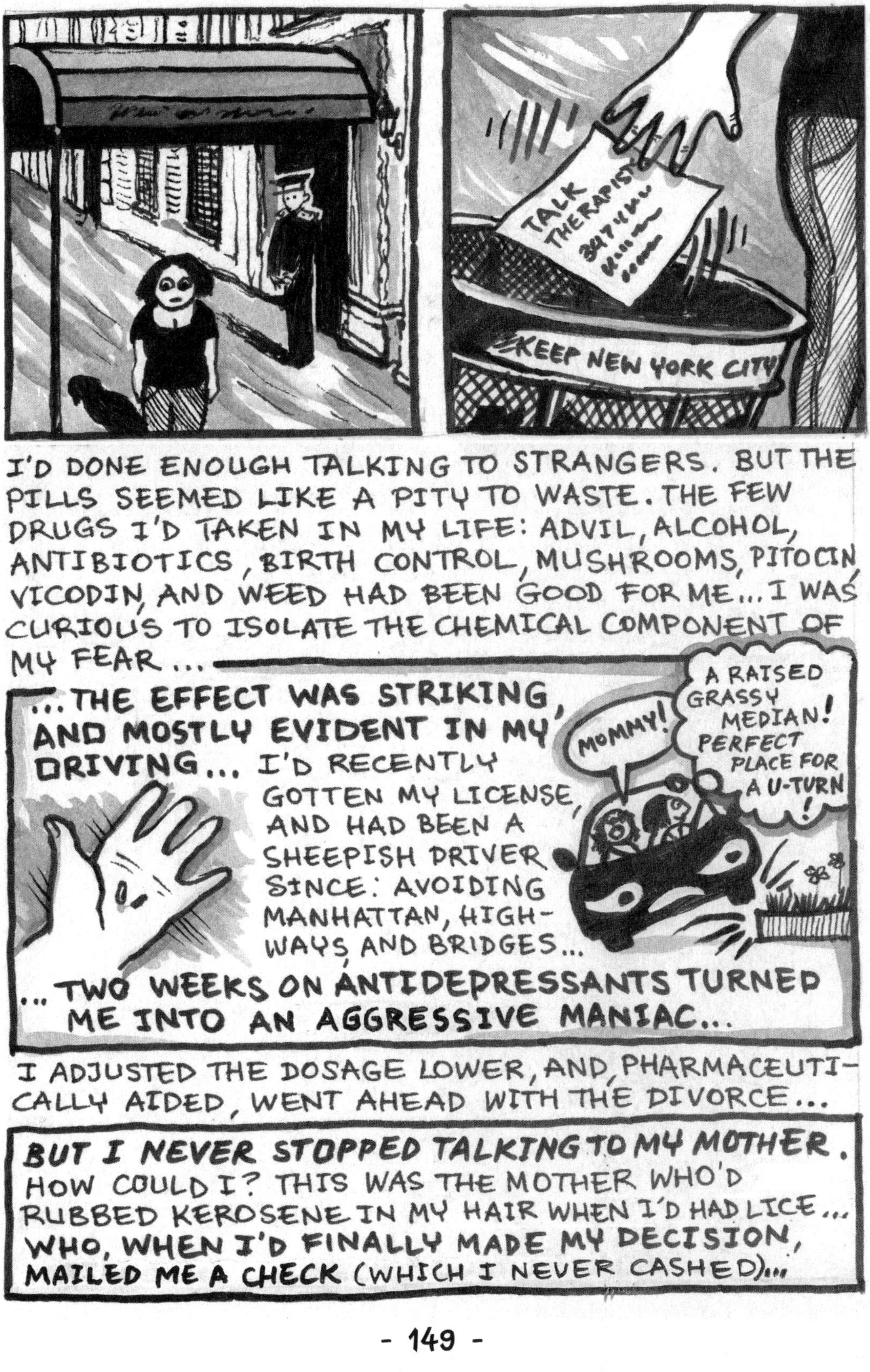
TALK THERAPIST
KEEP NEW YORK CITY
I'D DONE ENOUGH TALKING TO STRANGERS. BUT THE PILLS SEEMED LIKE A PITY TO WASTE. THE FEW DRUGS I'D TAKEN IN MY LIFE: ADVIL, ALCOHOL, ANTIBIOTICS, BIRTH CONTROL, MUSHROOMS, PITOCIN, VICODIN, AND WEED HAD BEEN GOOD FOR ME... I WAS CURIOUS TO ISOLATE THE CHEMICAL COMPONENT OF MY FEAR...
...THE EFFECT WAS STRIKING, AND MOSTLY EVIDENT IN MY DRIVING... I'D RECENTLY GOTTEN MY LICENSE, AND HAD BEEN A SHEEPISH DRIVER SINCE: AVOIDING MANHATTAN, HIGHWAYS, AND BRIDGES...
MOMMY!
A RAISED GRASSY MEDIAN! PERFECT PLACE FOR A U-TURN!
...TWO WEEKS ON ANTIDEPRESSANTS TURNED ME INTO AN AGGRESSIVE MANIAC...
I ADJUSTED THE DOSAGE LOWER, AND, PHARMACEUTICALLY AIDED, WENT AHEAD WITH THE DIVORCE...
BUT I NEVER STOPPED TALKING TO MY MOTHER. HOW COULD I? THIS WAS THE MOTHER WHO'D RUBBED KEROSENE IN MY HAIR WHEN I'D HAD LICE... WHO, WHEN I'D FINALLY MADE MY DECISION, MAILED ME A CHECK (WHICH I NEVER CASHED)...

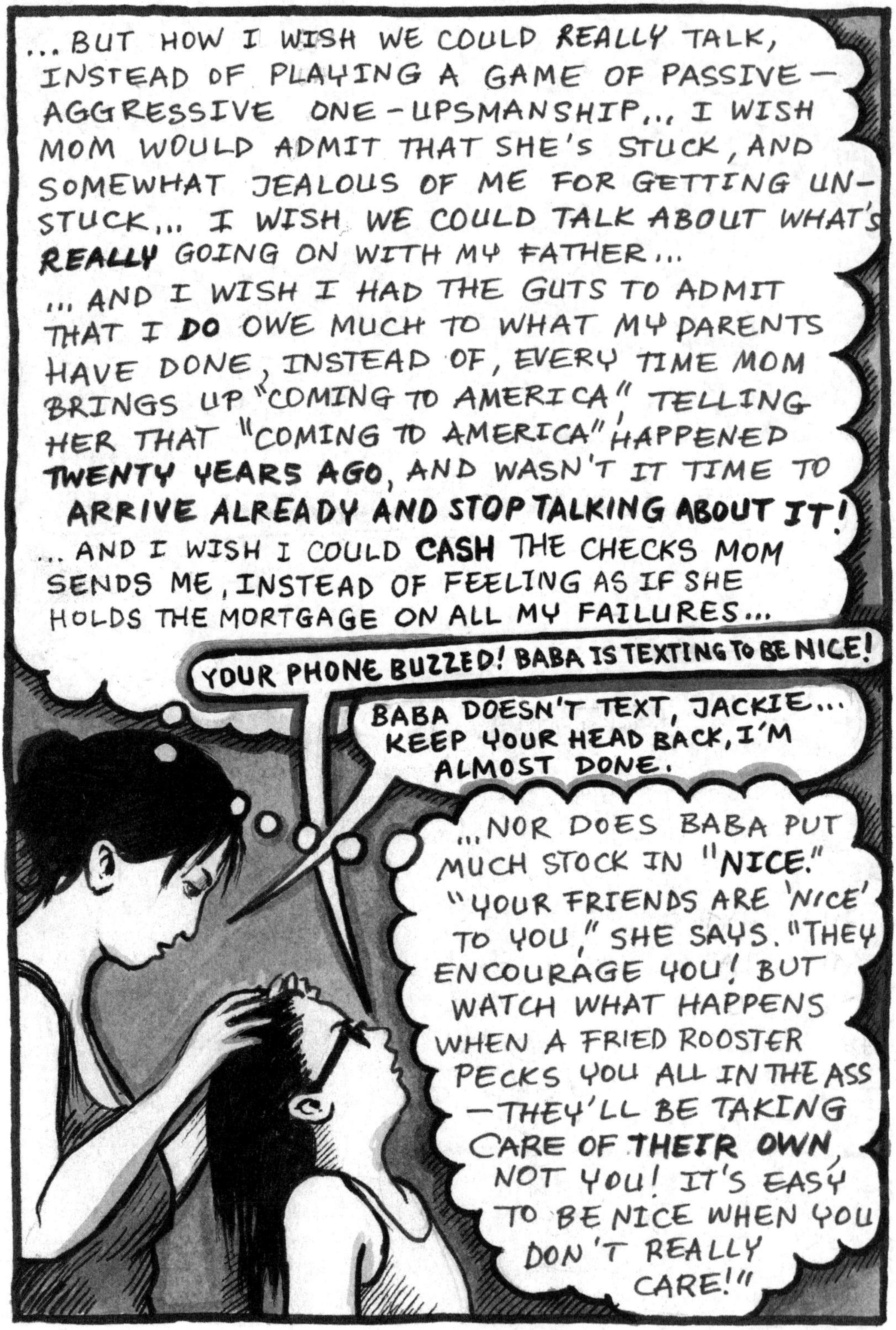
...BUT HOW I WISH WE COULD REALLY TALK, INSTEAD OF PLAYING A GAME OF PASSIVE-AGGRESSIVE ONE-UPSMANSHIP... I WISH MOM WOULD ADMIT THAT SHE'S STUCK, AND SOMEWHAT JEALOUS OF ME FOR GETTING UN-STUCK... I WISH WE COULD TALK ABOUT WHAT'S REALLY GOING ON WITH MY FATHER...
...AND I WISH I HAD THE GUTS TO ADMIT THAT I DO OWE MUCH TO WHAT MY PARENTS HAVE DONE, INSTEAD OF, EVERY TIME MOM BRINGS UP "COMING TO AMERICA," TELLING HER THAT "COMING TO AMERICA" HAPPENED TWENTY YEARS AGO, AND WASN'T IT TIME TO ARRIVE ALREADY AND STOP TALKING ABOUT IT!
...AND I WISH I COULD CASH THE CHECKS MOM SENDS ME, INSTEAD OF FEELING AS IF SHE HOLDS THE MORTGAGE ON ALL MY FAILURES...
YOUR PHONE BUZZED! BABA IS TEXTING TO BE NICE!
BABA DOESN'T TEXT, JACKIE... KEEP YOUR HEAD BACK, I'M ALMOST DONE.
...NOR DOES BABA PUT MUCH STOCK IN "NICE." "YOUR FRIENDS ARE 'NICE' TO YOU," SHE SAYS. "THEY ENCOURAGE YOU! BUT WATCH WHAT HAPPENS WHEN A FRIED ROOSTER PECKS YOU ALL IN THE ASS—THEY'LL BE TAKING CARE OF THEIR OWN, NOT YOU! IT'S EASY TO BE NICE WHEN YOU DON'T REALLY CARE!"

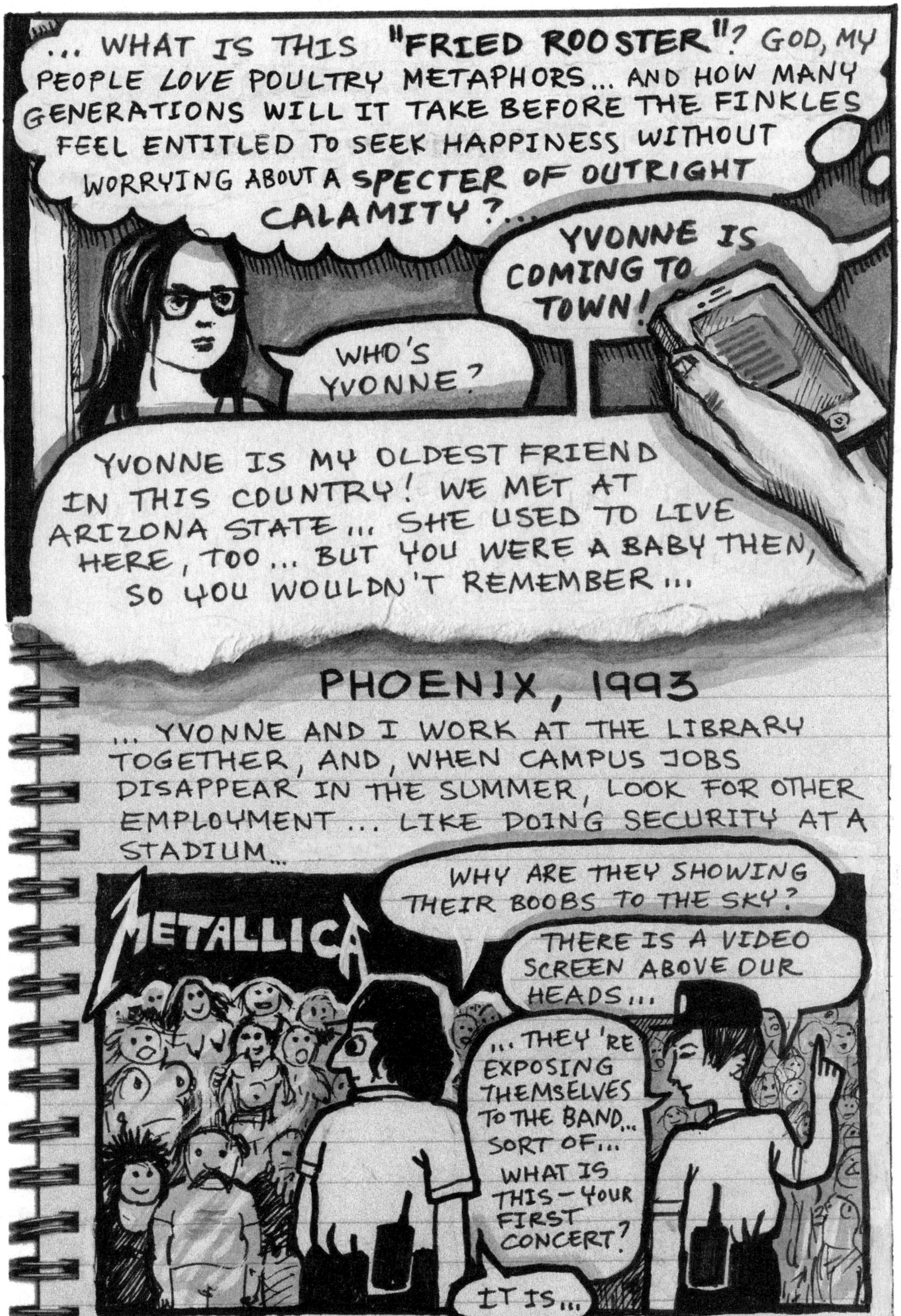
... WHAT IS THIS "FRIED ROOSTER"? GOD, MY PEOPLE LOVE POULTRY METAPHORS... AND HOW MANY GENERATIONS WILL IT TAKE BEFORE THE FINKLES FEEL ENTITLED TO SEEK HAPPINESS WITHOUT WORRYING ABOUT A SPECTER OF OUTRIGHT CALAMITY?...
YVONNE IS COMING TO TOWN!
WHO'S YVONNE?
YVONNE IS MY OLDEST FRIEND IN THIS COUNTRY! WE MET AT ARIZONA STATE... SHE USED TO LIVE HERE, TOO... BUT YOU WERE A BABY THEN, SO YOU WOULDN'T REMEMBER...
PHOENIX, 1993
... YVONNE AND I WORK AT THE LIBRARY TOGETHER, AND, WHEN CAMPUS JOBS DISAPPEAR IN THE SUMMER, LOOK FOR OTHER EMPLOYMENT... LIKE DOING SECURITY AT A STADIUM...
METALLICA
WHY ARE THEY SHOWING THEIR BOOBS TO THE SKY?
THERE IS A VIDEO SCREEN ABOVE OUR HEADS...
... THEY'RE EXPOSING THEMSELVES TO THE BAND... SORT OF... WHAT IS THIS — YOUR FIRST CONCERT?
IT IS...

I'M AN ART MAJOR. YVONNE MAJORS IN POLIT-
ICAL SCIENCE. I LIVE WITH JOSH AND THE
HIPPIES NEAR THE UNIVERSITY. YVONNE LIVES
AT HOME, IN A PART OF SUBURBAN PHOENIX
THAT LOOKS LIKE A BORDER TOWN...

...YVONNE'S MOM IS HMONG, AND
HER FATHER IS MEXICAN. YVONNE
IS THE FIRST PERSON IN HER FAMI-
LY TO GO TO COLLEGE... YVONNE
DOESN'T INVITE ME TO HER HOUSE. SHE
DOESN'T EVEN TELL ME WHICH HOUSE
ALONG THE UNPAVED LANE IS HERS... I WAIT
FOR HER AT THE END OF THE BLOCK...

... I ADMIRE YVONNE VERY MUCH — FOR HER
MEANINGFUL PIERCINGS, AND HER SELF-IMPOSED
AUSTERITY (SHE IS VEGAN; SHE WEARS ONLY
BLACK, WHITE, AND RED). THOUGH SHE WAS BORN
IN AMERICA AND HAS A CAR, I SUSPECT HER
LIFE IS HARDER THAN MINE... YVONNE EXUDES
DISCIPLINE... I FEEL SHAPELESS NEXT TO HER,
LIKE AN AMOEBA... I WANT TO LEARN FROM HER.

...I'D LOST TOUCH WITH YVONNE WHEN JOSH AND I LEFT ARIZONA. WE RECONNECTED AGAIN IN NEW YORK YEARS LATER. YVONNE WAS GETTING HER PH.D. AT COLUMBIA. SHE WAS ALSO THE FIRST PERSON I KNEW WHO DID ONLINE DATING. WHEN WE GOT TOGETHER, YVONNE WOULD TELL ME HER DATING HORROR STORIES, WHILE I HALF-LISTENED, *DYING OF ENVY.*

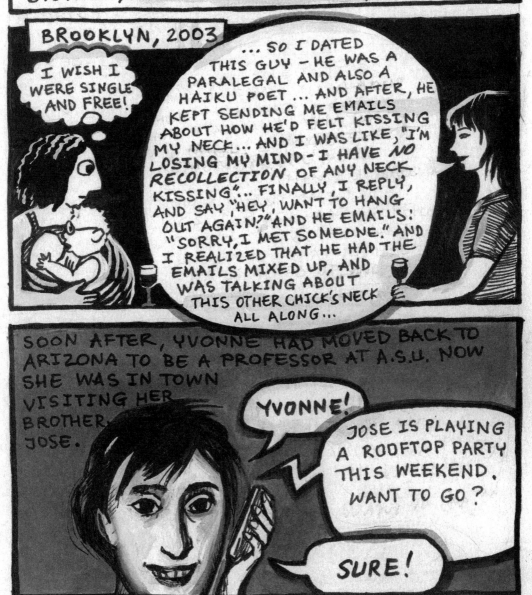

BROOKLYN, 2003

I WISH I WERE SINGLE AND FREE!

...SO I DATED THIS GUY — HE WAS A PARALEGAL AND ALSO A HAIKU POET... AND AFTER, HE KEPT SENDING ME EMAILS ABOUT HOW HE'D FELT KISSING MY NECK... AND I WAS LIKE, "I'M LOSING MY MIND — I HAVE *NO* RECOLLECTION OF ANY NECK KISSING"... FINALLY, I REPLY, AND SAY "HEY, WANT TO HANG OUT AGAIN?" AND HE EMAILS: "SORRY, I MET SOMEONE." AND I REALIZED THAT HE HAD THE EMAILS MIXED UP, AND WAS TALKING ABOUT THIS OTHER CHICK'S NECK ALL ALONG...

SOON AFTER, YVONNE HAD MOVED BACK TO ARIZONA TO BE A PROFESSOR AT A.S.U. NOW SHE WAS IN TOWN VISITING HER BROTHER, JOSE.

YVONNE!

JOSE IS PLAYING A ROOFTOP PARTY THIS WEEKEND. WANT TO GO?

SURE!

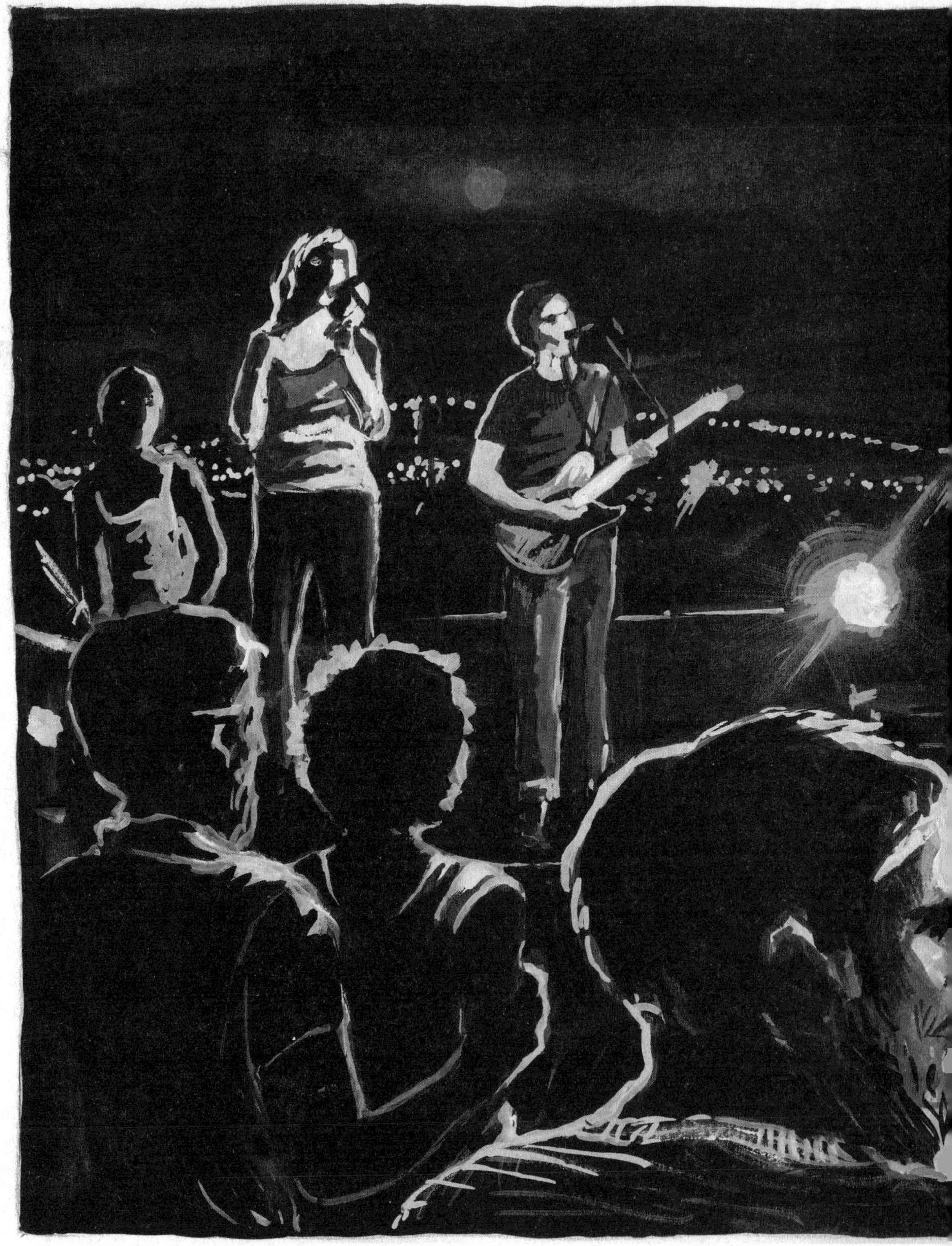

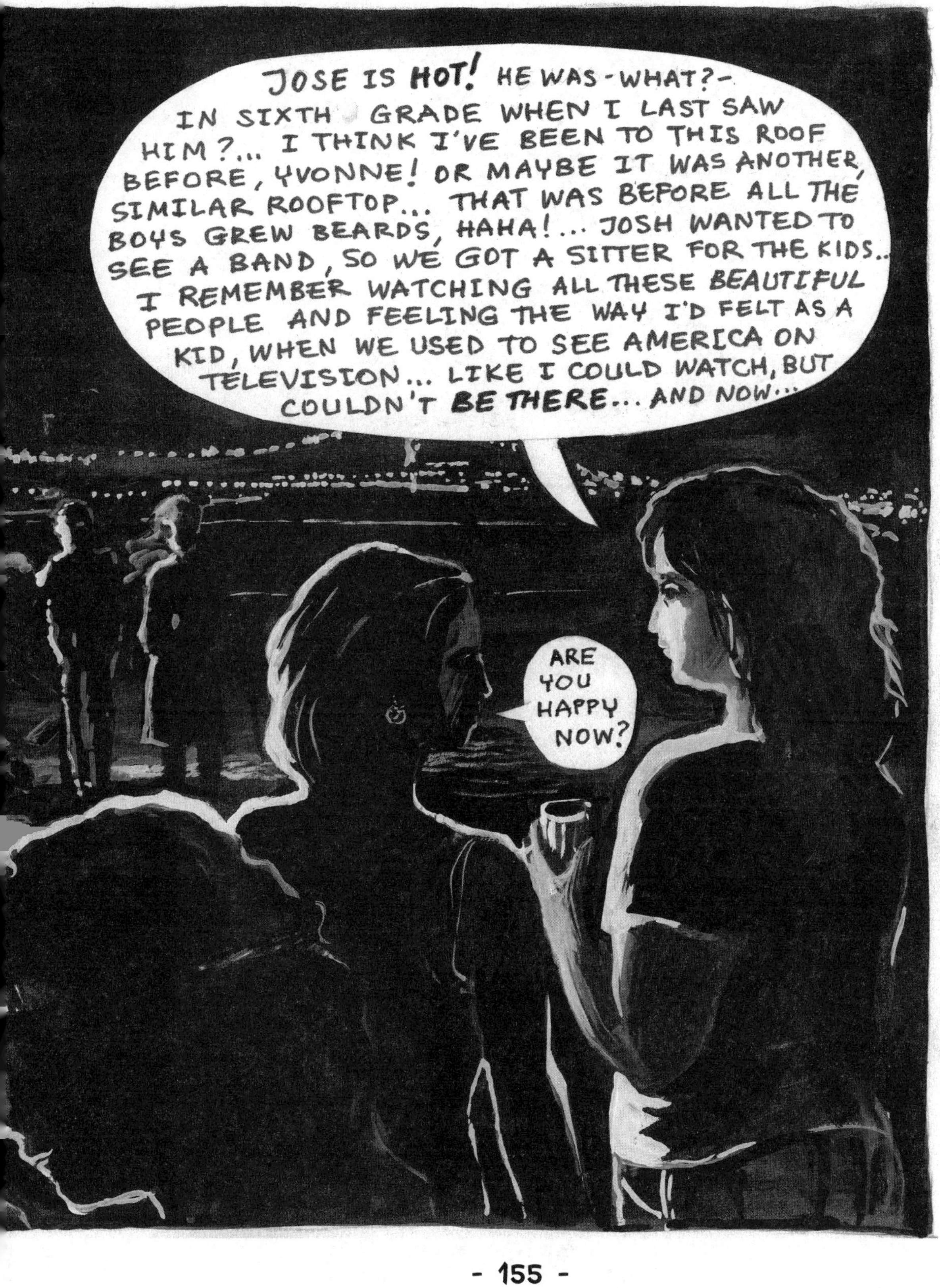
JOSE IS **HOT!** HE WAS-WHAT?- IN SIXTH GRADE WHEN I LAST SAW HIM?... I THINK I'VE BEEN TO THIS ROOF BEFORE, YVONNE! OR MAYBE IT WAS ANOTHER, SIMILAR ROOFTOP... THAT WAS BEFORE ALL THE BOYS GREW BEARDS, HAHA!... JOSH WANTED TO SEE A BAND, SO WE GOT A SITTER FOR THE KIDS... I REMEMBER WATCHING ALL THESE *BEAUTIFUL* PEOPLE AND FEELING THE WAY I'D FELT AS A KID, WHEN WE USED TO SEE AMERICA ON TELEVISION... LIKE I COULD WATCH, BUT COULDN'T **BE THERE**... AND NOW...
ARE YOU HAPPY NOW?

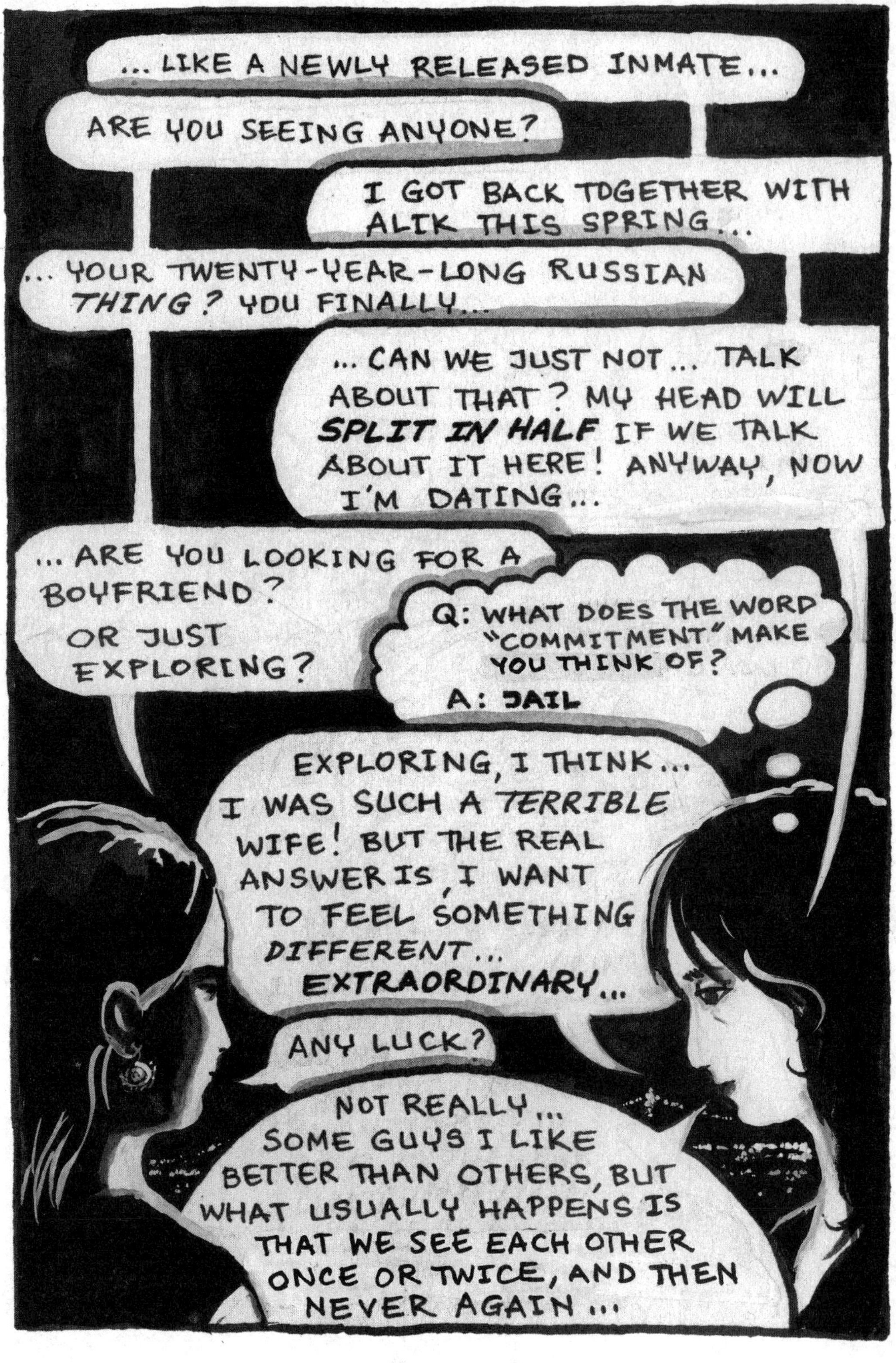
... LIKE A NEWLY RELEASED INMATE...
ARE YOU SEEING ANYONE?
I GOT BACK TOGETHER WITH ALIK THIS SPRING...
... YOUR TWENTY-YEAR-LONG RUSSIAN THING? YOU FINALLY...
... CAN WE JUST NOT... TALK ABOUT THAT? MY HEAD WILL SPLIT IN HALF IF WE TALK ABOUT IT HERE! ANYWAY, NOW I'M DATING...
... ARE YOU LOOKING FOR A BOYFRIEND? OR JUST EXPLORING?
Q: WHAT DOES THE WORD "COMMITMENT" MAKE YOU THINK OF? A: JAIL
EXPLORING, I THINK... I WAS SUCH A TERRIBLE WIFE! BUT THE REAL ANSWER IS, I WANT TO FEEL SOMETHING DIFFERENT... EXTRAORDINARY...
ANY LUCK?
NOT REALLY... SOME GUYS I LIKE BETTER THAN OTHERS, BUT WHAT USUALLY HAPPENS IS THAT WE SEE EACH OTHER ONCE OR TWICE, AND THEN NEVER AGAIN...

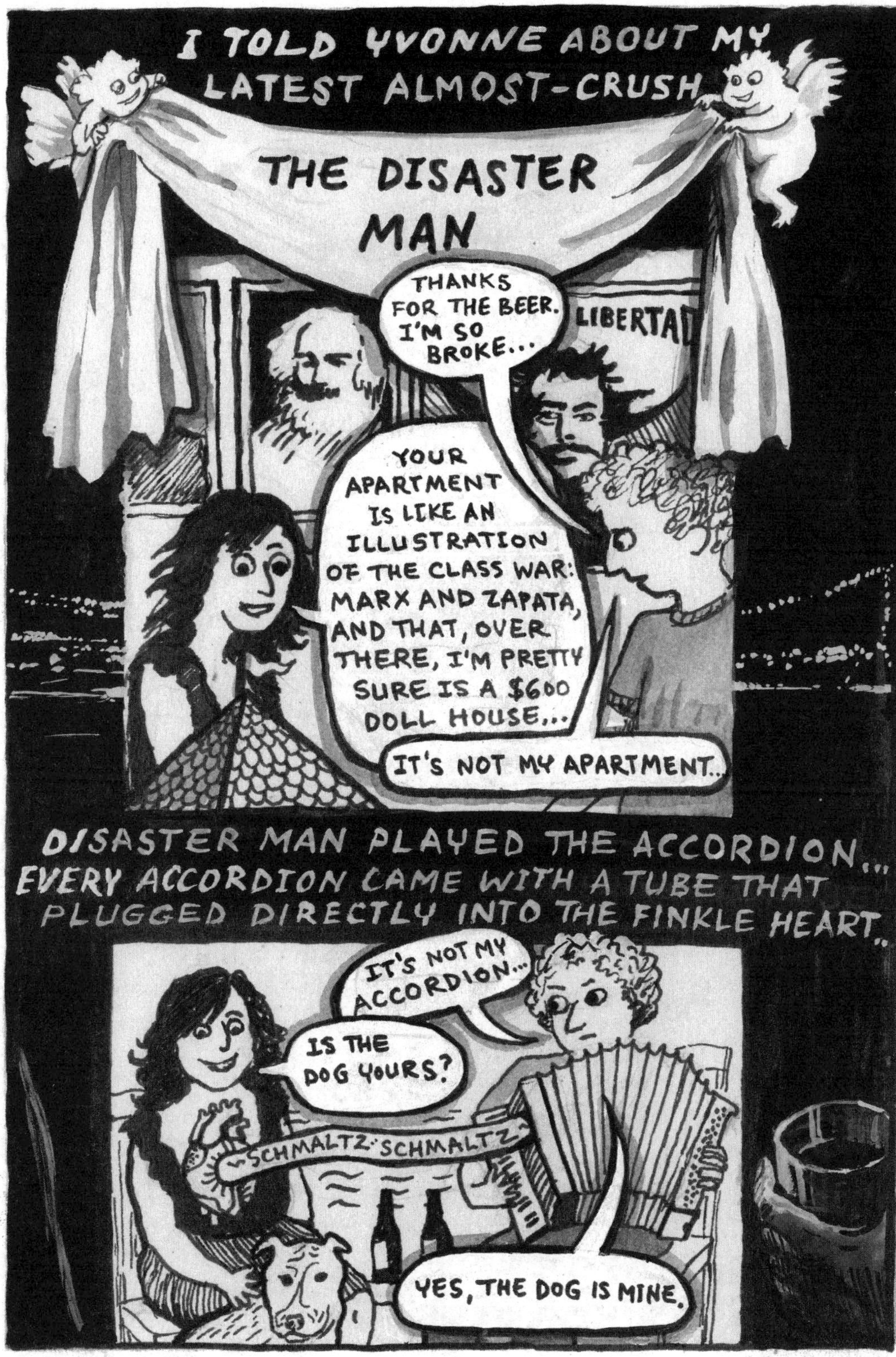
I TOLD YVONNE ABOUT MY LATEST ALMOST-CRUSH
THE DISASTER MAN
THANKS FOR THE BEER. I'M SO BROKE...
LIBERTAD
YOUR APARTMENT IS LIKE AN ILLUSTRATION OF THE CLASS WAR: MARX AND ZAPATA, AND THAT, OVER THERE, I'M PRETTY SURE IS A $600 DOLL HOUSE...
IT'S NOT MY APARTMENT...
DISASTER MAN PLAYED THE ACCORDION... EVERY ACCORDION CAME WITH A TUBE THAT PLUGGED DIRECTLY INTO THE FINKLE HEART...
IT'S NOT MY ACCORDION...
IS THE DOG YOURS?
SCHMALTZ SCHMALTZ
YES, THE DOG IS MINE.

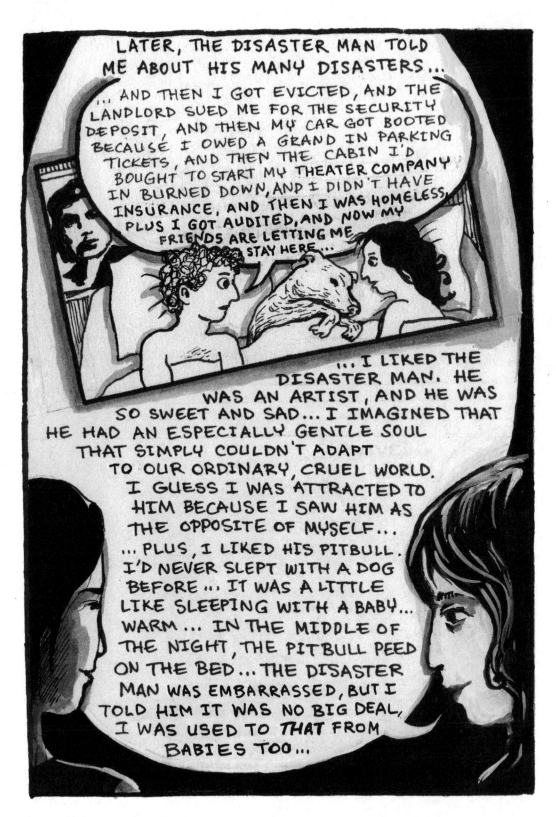

LATER, THE DISASTER MAN TOLD ME ABOUT HIS MANY DISASTERS...

... AND THEN I GOT EVICTED, AND THE LANDLORD SUED ME FOR THE SECURITY DEPOSIT, AND THEN MY CAR GOT BOOTED BECAUSE I OWED A GRAND IN PARKING TICKETS, AND THEN THE CABIN I'D BOUGHT TO START MY THEATER COMPANY IN BURNED DOWN, AND I DIDN'T HAVE INSURANCE, AND THEN I WAS HOMELESS, PLUS I GOT AUDITED, AND NOW MY FRIENDS ARE LETTING ME STAY HERE...

... I LIKED THE DISASTER MAN. HE WAS AN ARTIST, AND HE WAS SO SWEET AND SAD... I IMAGINED THAT HE HAD AN ESPECIALLY GENTLE SOUL THAT SIMPLY COULDN'T ADAPT TO OUR ORDINARY, CRUEL WORLD. I GUESS I WAS ATTRACTED TO HIM BECAUSE I SAW HIM AS THE OPPOSITE OF MYSELF...

... PLUS, I LIKED HIS PITBULL. I'D NEVER SLEPT WITH A DOG BEFORE ... IT WAS A LITTLE LIKE SLEEPING WITH A BABY... WARM ... IN THE MIDDLE OF THE NIGHT, THE PITBULL PEED ON THE BED... THE DISASTER MAN WAS EMBARRASSED, BUT I TOLD HIM IT WAS NO BIG DEAL, I WAS USED TO *THAT* FROM BABIES TOO...

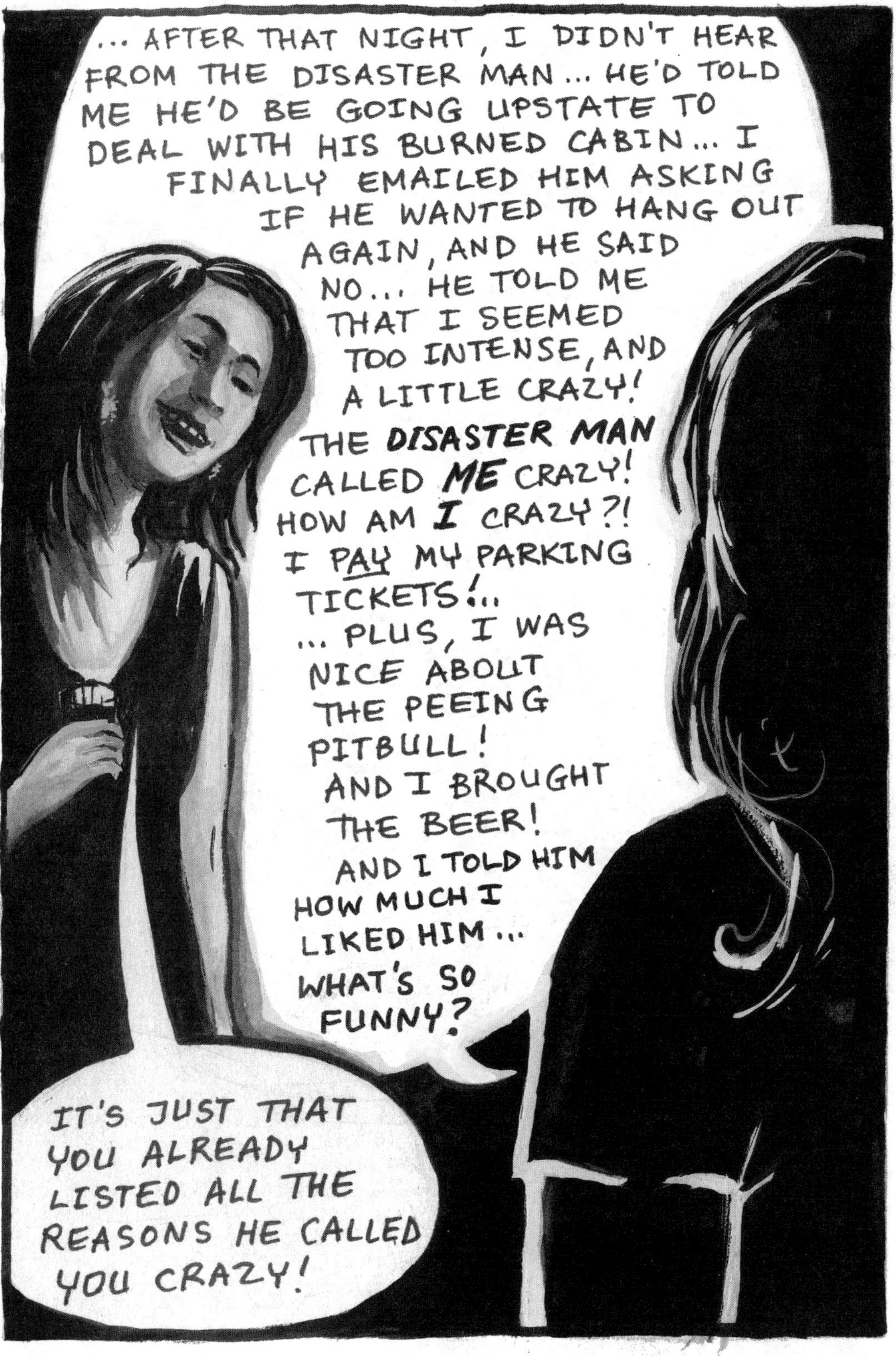
... AFTER THAT NIGHT, I DIDN'T HEAR FROM THE DISASTER MAN... HE'D TOLD ME HE'D BE GOING UPSTATE TO DEAL WITH HIS BURNED CABIN... I FINALLY EMAILED HIM ASKING IF HE WANTED TO HANG OUT AGAIN, AND HE SAID NO... HE TOLD ME THAT I SEEMED TOO INTENSE, AND A LITTLE CRAZY! THE DISASTER MAN CALLED ME CRAZY! HOW AM I CRAZY?! I PAY MY PARKING TICKETS!.. ... PLUS, I WAS NICE ABOUT THE PEEING PITBULL! AND I BROUGHT THE BEER! AND I TOLD HIM HOW MUCH I LIKED HIM... WHAT'S SO FUNNY?
IT'S JUST THAT YOU ALREADY LISTED ALL THE REASONS HE CALLED YOU CRAZY!

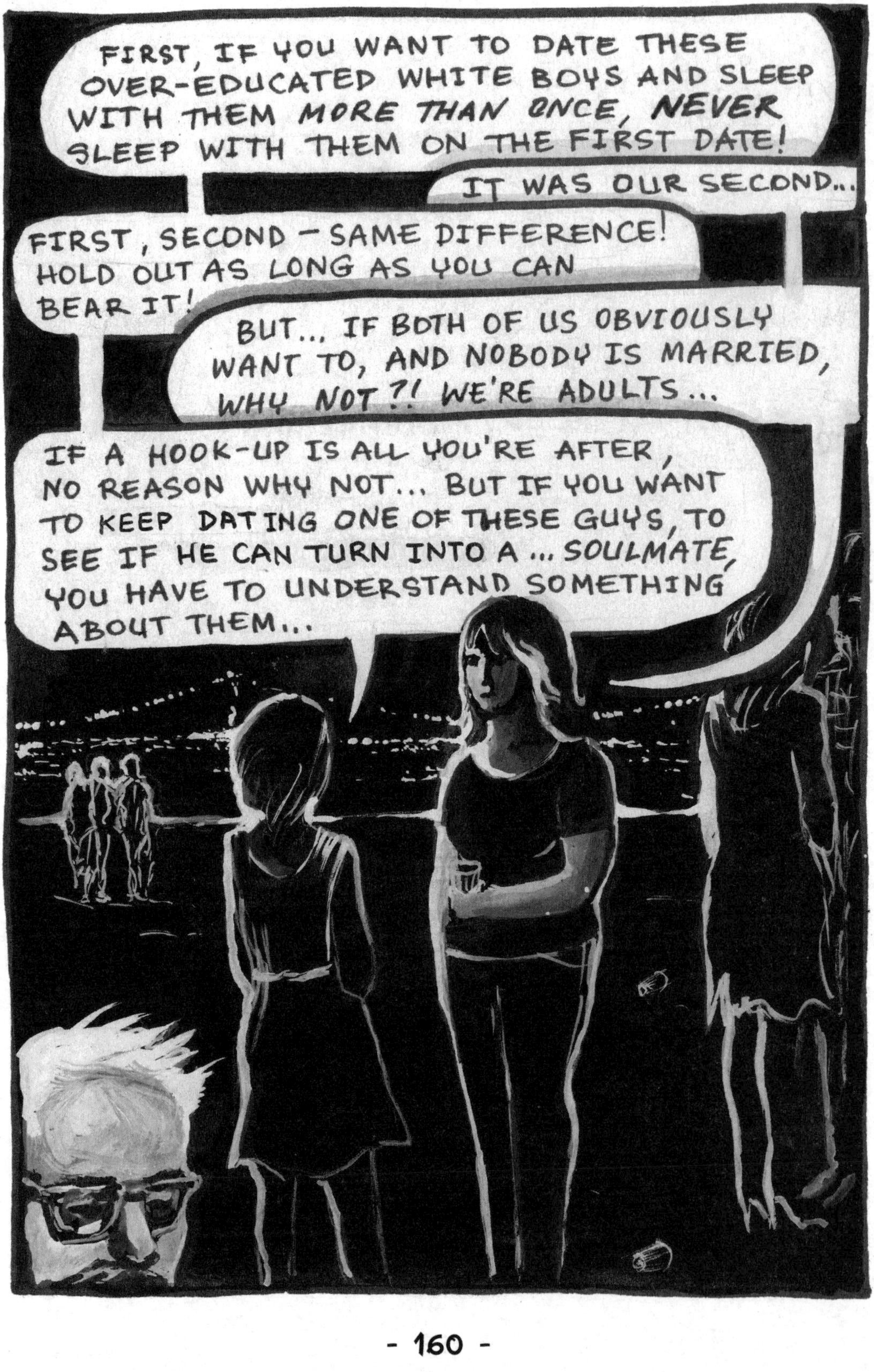
FIRST, IF YOU WANT TO DATE THESE OVER-EDUCATED WHITE BOYS AND SLEEP WITH THEM MORE THAN ONCE, NEVER SLEEP WITH THEM ON THE FIRST DATE!
IT WAS OUR SECOND...
FIRST, SECOND - SAME DIFFERENCE! HOLD OUT AS LONG AS YOU CAN BEAR IT!
BUT..., IF BOTH OF US OBVIOUSLY WANT TO, AND NOBODY IS MARRIED, WHY NOT?! WE'RE ADULTS...
IF A HOOK-UP IS ALL YOU'RE AFTER, NO REASON WHY NOT... BUT IF YOU WANT TO KEEP DATING ONE OF THESE GUYS, TO SEE IF HE CAN TURN INTO A ... SOULMATE, YOU HAVE TO UNDERSTAND SOMETHING ABOUT THEM...

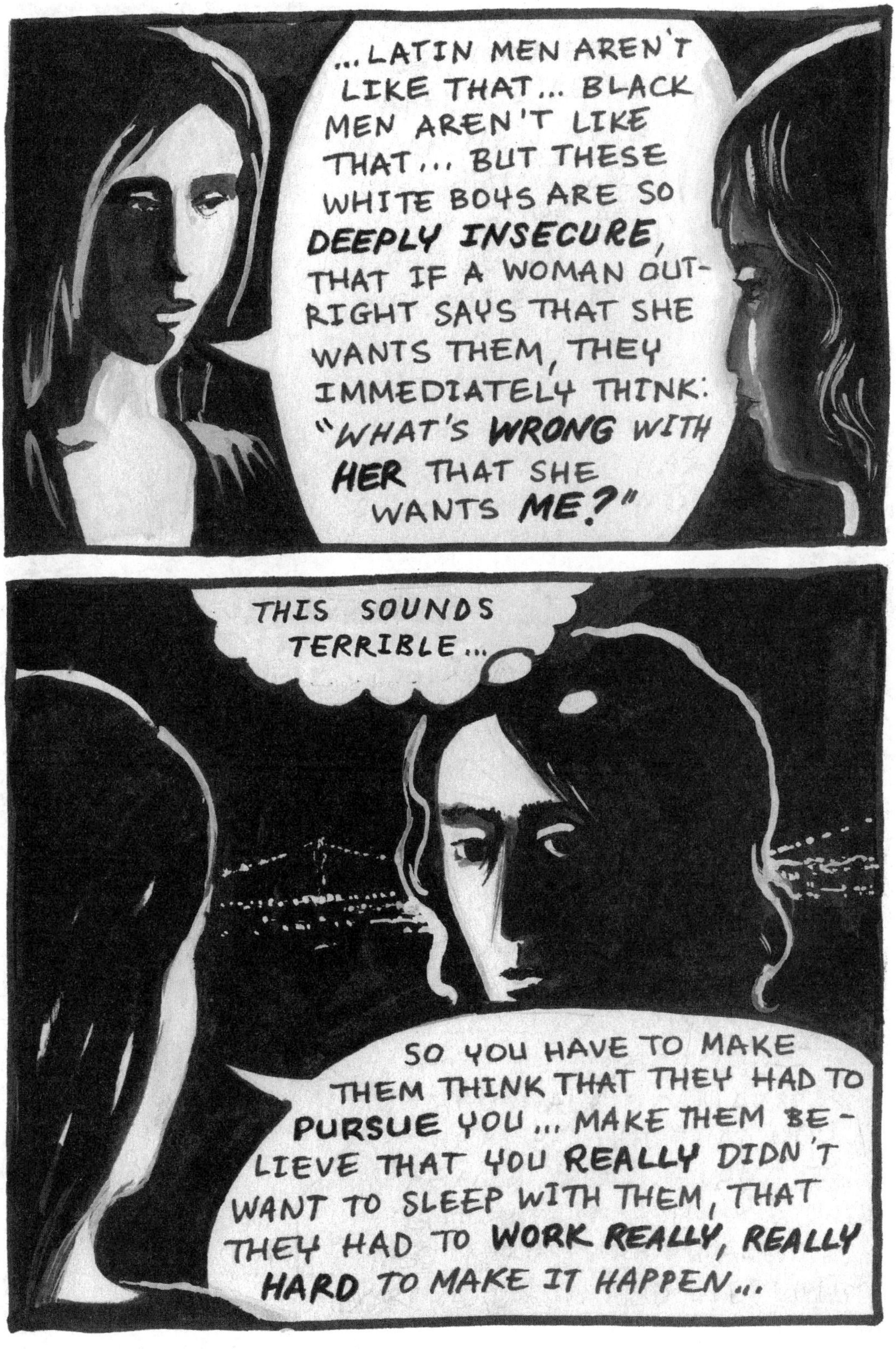
...LATIN MEN AREN'T LIKE THAT... BLACK MEN AREN'T LIKE THAT... BUT THESE WHITE BOYS ARE SO DEEPLY INSECURE, THAT IF A WOMAN OUT-RIGHT SAYS THAT SHE WANTS THEM, THEY IMMEDIATELY THINK: "WHAT'S WRONG WITH HER THAT SHE WANTS ME?"
THIS SOUNDS TERRIBLE...
SO YOU HAVE TO MAKE THEM THINK THAT THEY HAD TO PURSUE YOU... MAKE THEM BE-LIEVE THAT YOU REALLY DIDN'T WANT TO SLEEP WITH THEM, THAT THEY HAD TO WORK REALLY, REALLY HARD TO MAKE IT HAPPEN...

... SO, MISTAKE NUMBER ONE: BEING TOO EAGER. MISTAKE NUMBER TWO: BUYING A GUY BEER. NO MATTER HOW "BROKE" THEY ARE, THEY SHOULD BE PAYING FOR YOUR DRINKS...
... BUT I DON'T LIKE THAT... IT MAKES ME FEEL... YUCKY. OLD-FASHIONED. OBLIGATED... I PREFER TO PAY FOR MY OWN...
SURE! I'M JUST TELLING YOU WHAT YOU *SHOULD* DO... ... NUMBER THREE: WHEN A GUY'S PIT BULL PEES ON THE BED, GO: "*EWW!*"
... BUT **HONESTLY**, IT WASN'T A BIG DEAL...
I KNOW! SHIT, I GREW UP WITH DOGS... PIT BULLS, ACTUALLY. DAD HAD FIVE AT ONE POINT... STILL, PRACTICE: "*EWW!*"
OKAY! **EWW!**
THERE YOU GO!
OOH, LOOK AT **THAT** GUY! ISN'T HE CUTE?
... AND PRACTICE YOUR SMILE!
WHAT'S WRONG WITH MY SMILE?

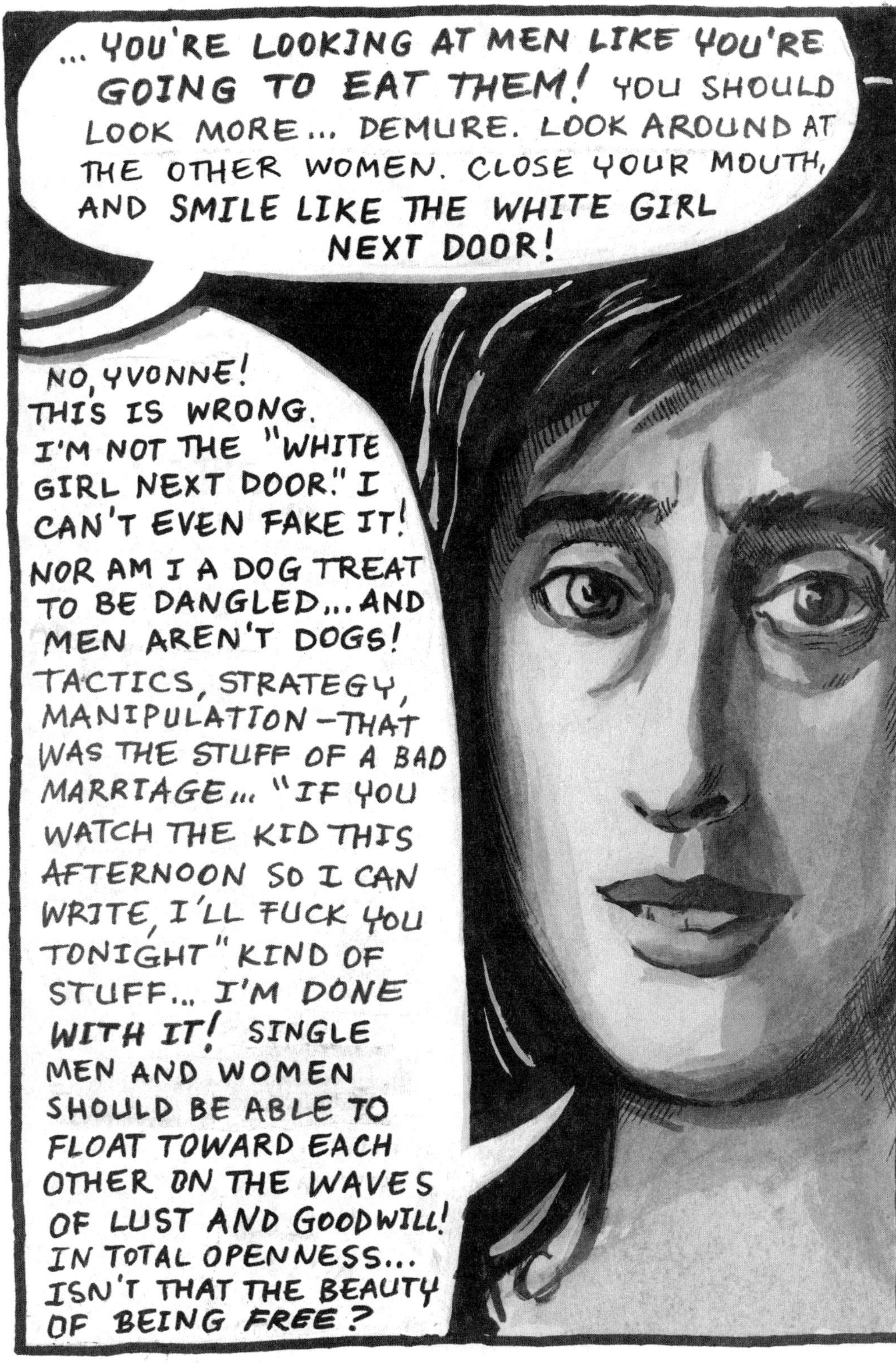
... YOU'RE LOOKING AT MEN LIKE YOU'RE GOING TO EAT THEM! YOU SHOULD LOOK MORE... DEMURE. LOOK AROUND AT THE OTHER WOMEN. CLOSE YOUR MOUTH, AND SMILE LIKE THE WHITE GIRL NEXT DOOR!
NO, YVONNE! THIS IS WRONG. I'M NOT THE "WHITE GIRL NEXT DOOR." I CAN'T EVEN FAKE IT! NOR AM I A DOG TREAT TO BE DANGLED... AND MEN AREN'T DOGS! TACTICS, STRATEGY, MANIPULATION—THAT WAS THE STUFF OF A BAD MARRIAGE... "IF YOU WATCH THE KID THIS AFTERNOON SO I CAN WRITE, I'LL FUCK YOU TONIGHT" KIND OF STUFF... I'M DONE WITH IT! SINGLE MEN AND WOMEN SHOULD BE ABLE TO FLOAT TOWARD EACH OTHER ON THE WAVES OF LUST AND GOODWILL! IN TOTAL OPENNESS... ISN'T THAT THE BEAUTY OF BEING FREE?

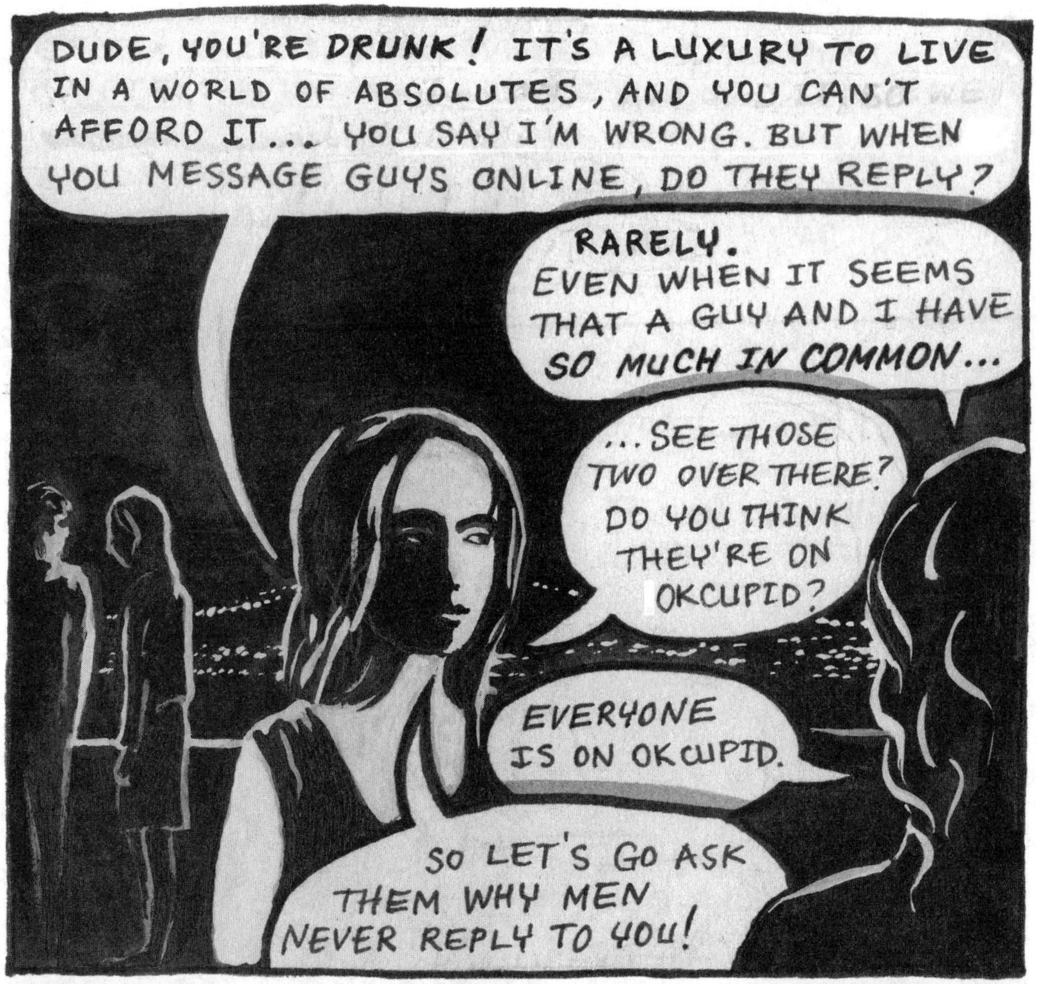
DUDE, YOU'RE DRUNK! IT'S A LUXURY TO LIVE IN A WORLD OF ABSOLUTES, AND YOU CAN'T AFFORD IT... YOU SAY I'M WRONG. BUT WHEN YOU MESSAGE GUYS ONLINE, DO THEY REPLY?
RARELY. EVEN WHEN IT SEEMS THAT A GUY AND I HAVE SO MUCH IN COMMON...
...SEE THOSE TWO OVER THERE? DO YOU THINK THEY'RE ON OKCUPID?
EVERYONE IS ON OKCUPID.
SO LET'S GO ASK THEM WHY MEN NEVER REPLY TO YOU!

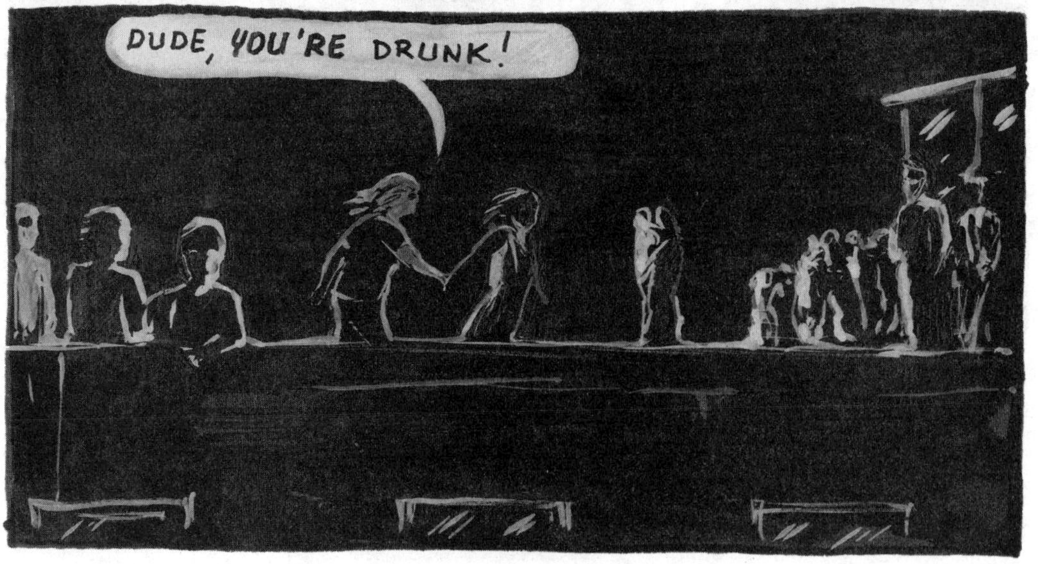
DUDE, YOU'RE DRUNK!

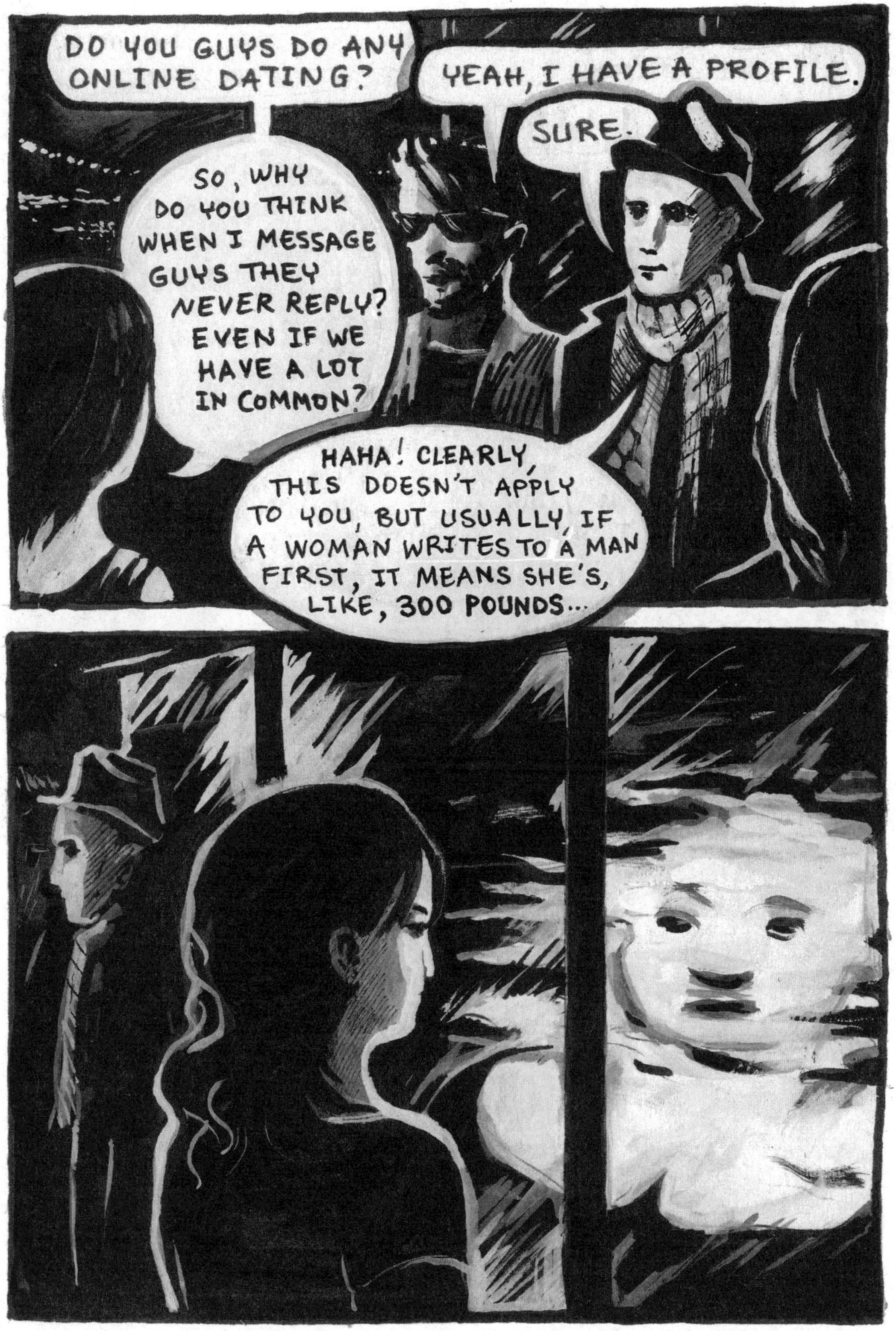
DO YOU GUYS DO ANY ONLINE DATING?
YEAH, I HAVE A PROFILE.
SURE.
SO, WHY DO YOU THINK WHEN I MESSAGE GUYS THEY NEVER REPLY? EVEN IF WE HAVE A LOT IN COMMON?
HAHA! CLEARLY, THIS DOESN'T APPLY TO YOU, BUT USUALLY, IF A WOMAN WRITES TO A MAN FIRST, IT MEANS SHE'S, LIKE, 300 POUNDS...

STILL THINK I'M WRONG? GO YOUR "OPENNESS" ROUTE, TELL THEM EXACTLY WHAT YOU WANT, AND YOU'LL BE CALLED "AGGRESSIVE," "DESPERATE," "CRAZY"... OR WORSE...
I'VE BEEN CALLED SOME OF THOSE THINGS... "FORWARD"- HAHA... JUST FOR SENDING A MESSAGE...
AND?
I DON'T WRITE TO THEM AGAIN. THOSE PEOPLE ARE RECRUITS IN THE GENDER WAR. I'M NOT ATTRACTED TO RECRUITS. "THE WHITE GIRL NEXT DOOR" CAN HAVE THEM...
WHO ARE YOU ATTRACTED TO?
HAHA... CONSCIENTIOUS OBJECTORS!
WHAT YOU'RE LOOKING FOR DOESN'T EXIST. THERE ARE NO OBJECTORS IN THE GENDER WAR. WE'RE ALL RECRUITS, BUT YOU DON'T HAVE TO OFFER YOURSELF UP AS CANNON FODDER!

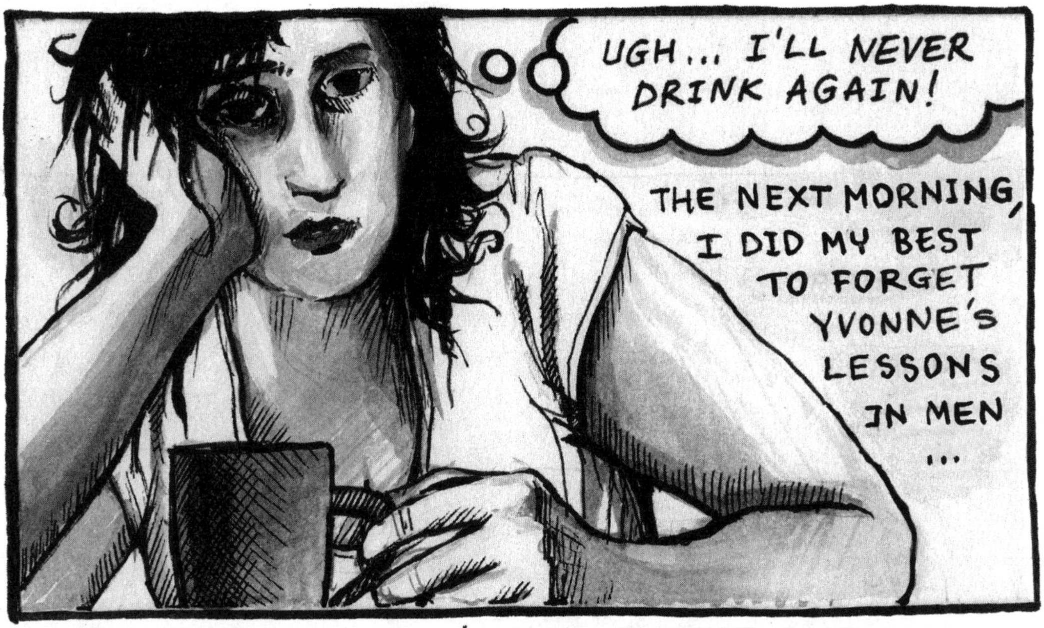
UGH... I'LL NEVER DRINK AGAIN!
THE NEXT MORNING, I DID MY BEST TO FORGET YVONNE'S LESSONS IN MEN ...

... BUT EVEN AFTER I'D HAD COFFEE AND SWALLOWED THREE ADVILS, I KEPT HAVING AN UNPLEASANT FEELING. IT WAS PART GUILT, PART ANXIETY, AND IT WASN'T CONNECTED TO MY HANGOVER, OR YVONNE'S WARNINGS...

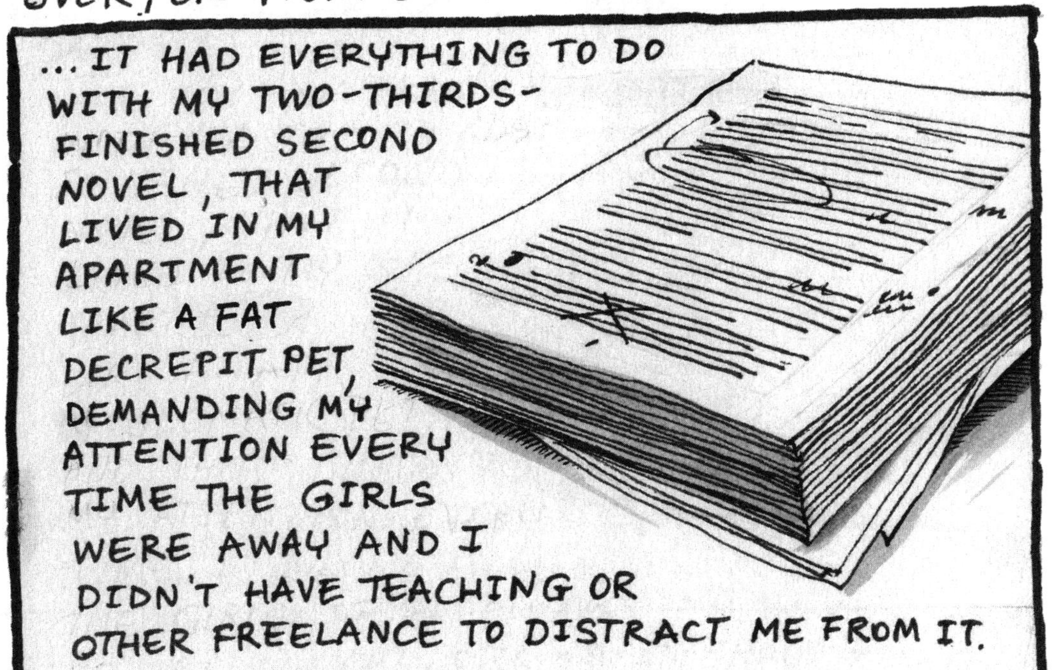
... IT HAD EVERYTHING TO DO WITH MY TWO-THIRDS-FINISHED SECOND NOVEL, THAT LIVED IN MY APARTMENT LIKE A FAT DECREPIT PET, DEMANDING MY ATTENTION EVERY TIME THE GIRLS WERE AWAY AND I DIDN'T HAVE TEACHING OR OTHER FREELANCE TO DISTRACT ME FROM IT.

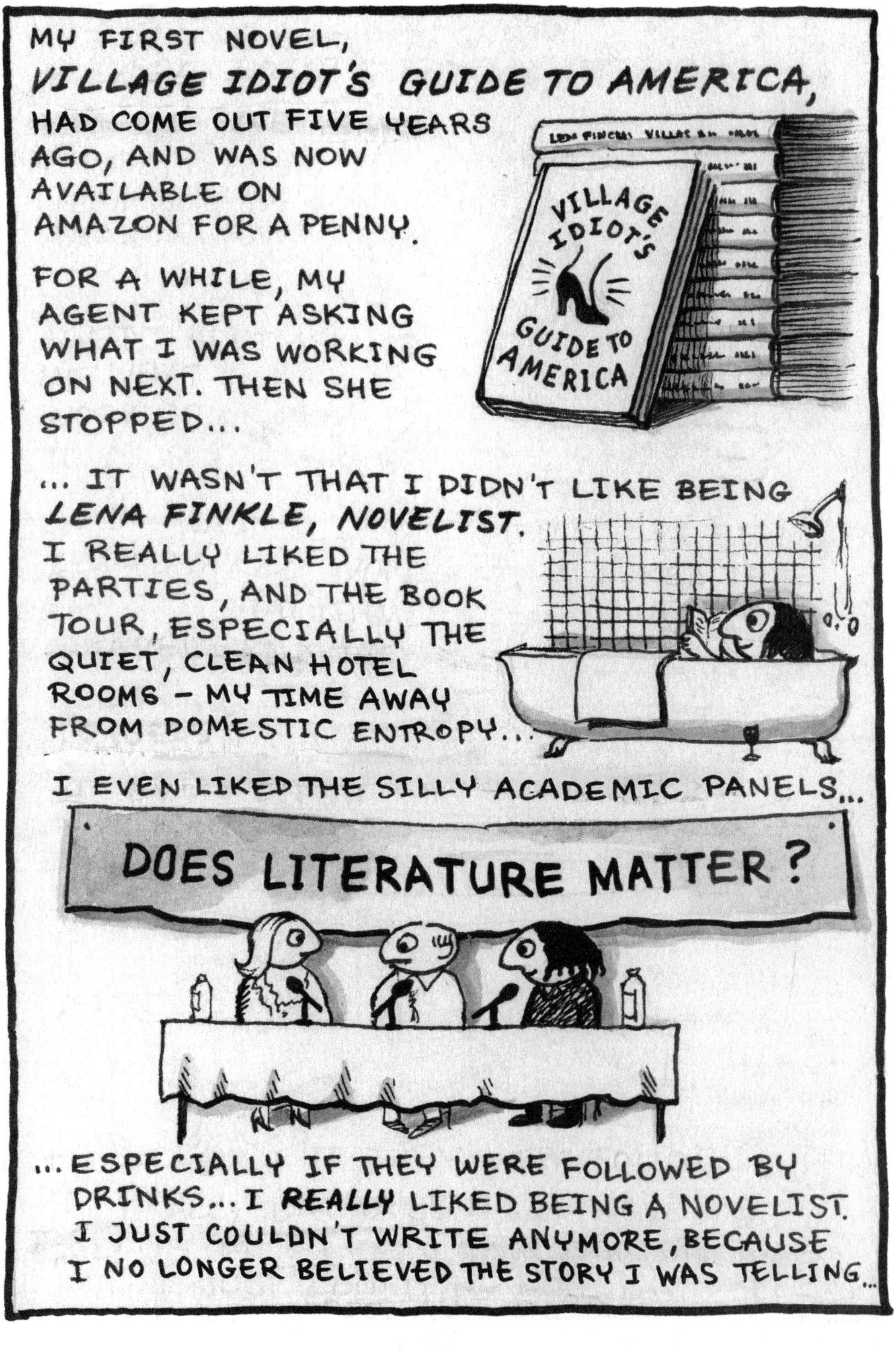
MY FIRST NOVEL,
VILLAGE IDIOT'S GUIDE TO AMERICA,
HAD COME OUT FIVE YEARS AGO, AND WAS NOW AVAILABLE ON AMAZON FOR A PENNY.
VILLAGE IDIOT'S GUIDE TO AMERICA
FOR A WHILE, MY AGENT KEPT ASKING WHAT I WAS WORKING ON NEXT. THEN SHE STOPPED...
... IT WASN'T THAT I DIDN'T LIKE BEING LENA FINKLE, NOVELIST.
I REALLY LIKED THE PARTIES, AND THE BOOK TOUR, ESPECIALLY THE QUIET, CLEAN HOTEL ROOMS – MY TIME AWAY FROM DOMESTIC ENTROPY...
I EVEN LIKED THE SILLY ACADEMIC PANELS...
DOES LITERATURE MATTER?
...ESPECIALLY IF THEY WERE FOLLOWED BY DRINKS... I REALLY LIKED BEING A NOVELIST. I JUST COULDN'T WRITE ANYMORE, BECAUSE I NO LONGER BELIEVED THE STORY I WAS TELLING...

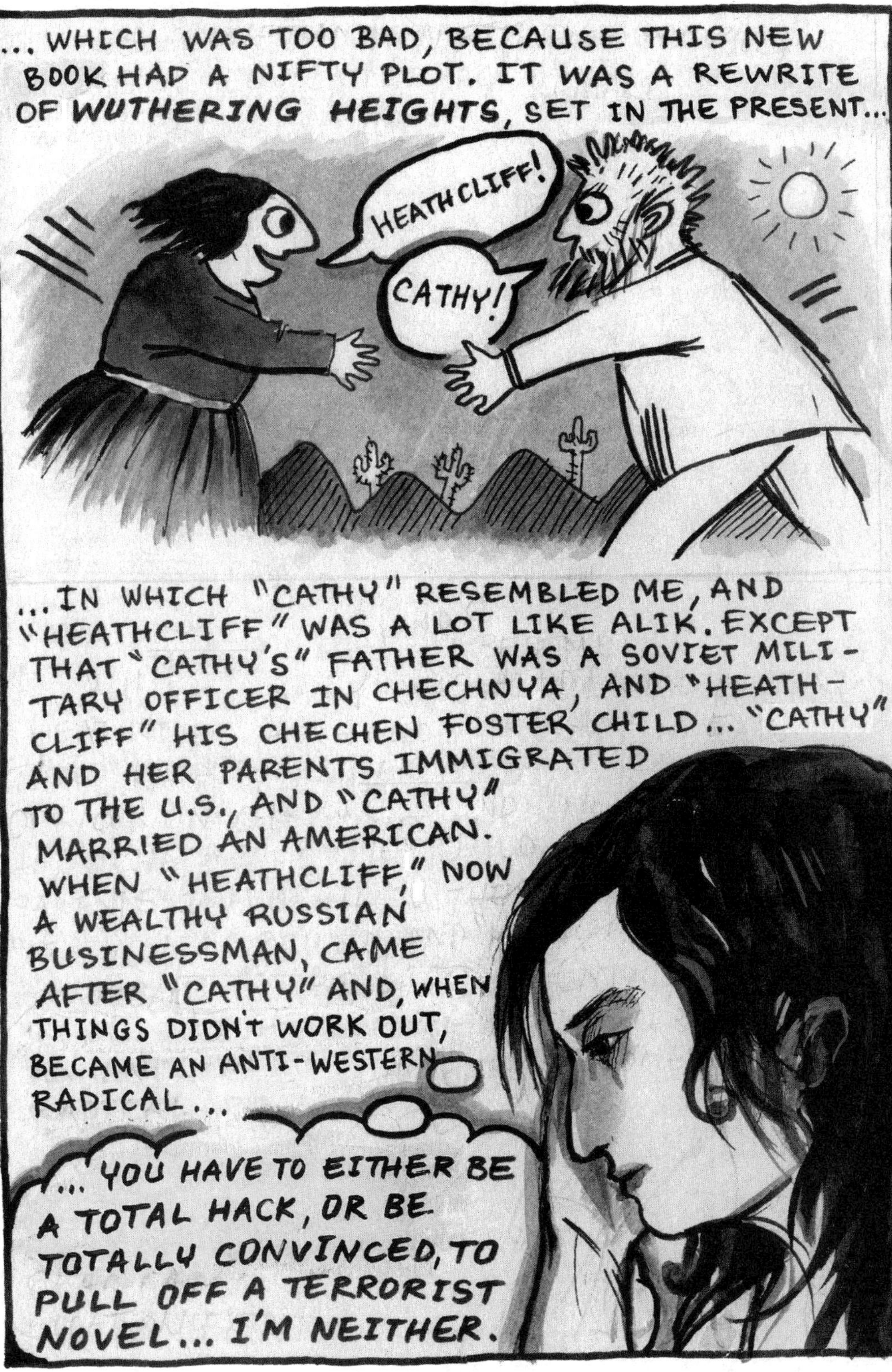
...WHICH WAS TOO BAD, BECAUSE THIS NEW BOOK HAD A NIFTY PLOT. IT WAS A REWRITE OF WUTHERING HEIGHTS, SET IN THE PRESENT...
HEATHCLIFF!
CATHY!
...IN WHICH "CATHY" RESEMBLED ME, AND "HEATHCLIFF" WAS A LOT LIKE ALIK. EXCEPT THAT "CATHY'S" FATHER WAS A SOVIET MILITARY OFFICER IN CHECHNYA, AND "HEATHCLIFF" HIS CHECHEN FOSTER CHILD... "CATHY" AND HER PARENTS IMMIGRATED TO THE U.S., AND "CATHY" MARRIED AN AMERICAN. WHEN "HEATHCLIFF," NOW A WEALTHY RUSSIAN BUSINESSMAN, CAME AFTER "CATHY" AND, WHEN THINGS DIDN'T WORK OUT, BECAME AN ANTI-WESTERN RADICAL...
...YOU HAVE TO EITHER BE A TOTAL HACK, OR BE TOTALLY CONVINCED, TO PULL OFF A TERRORIST NOVEL... I'M NEITHER.

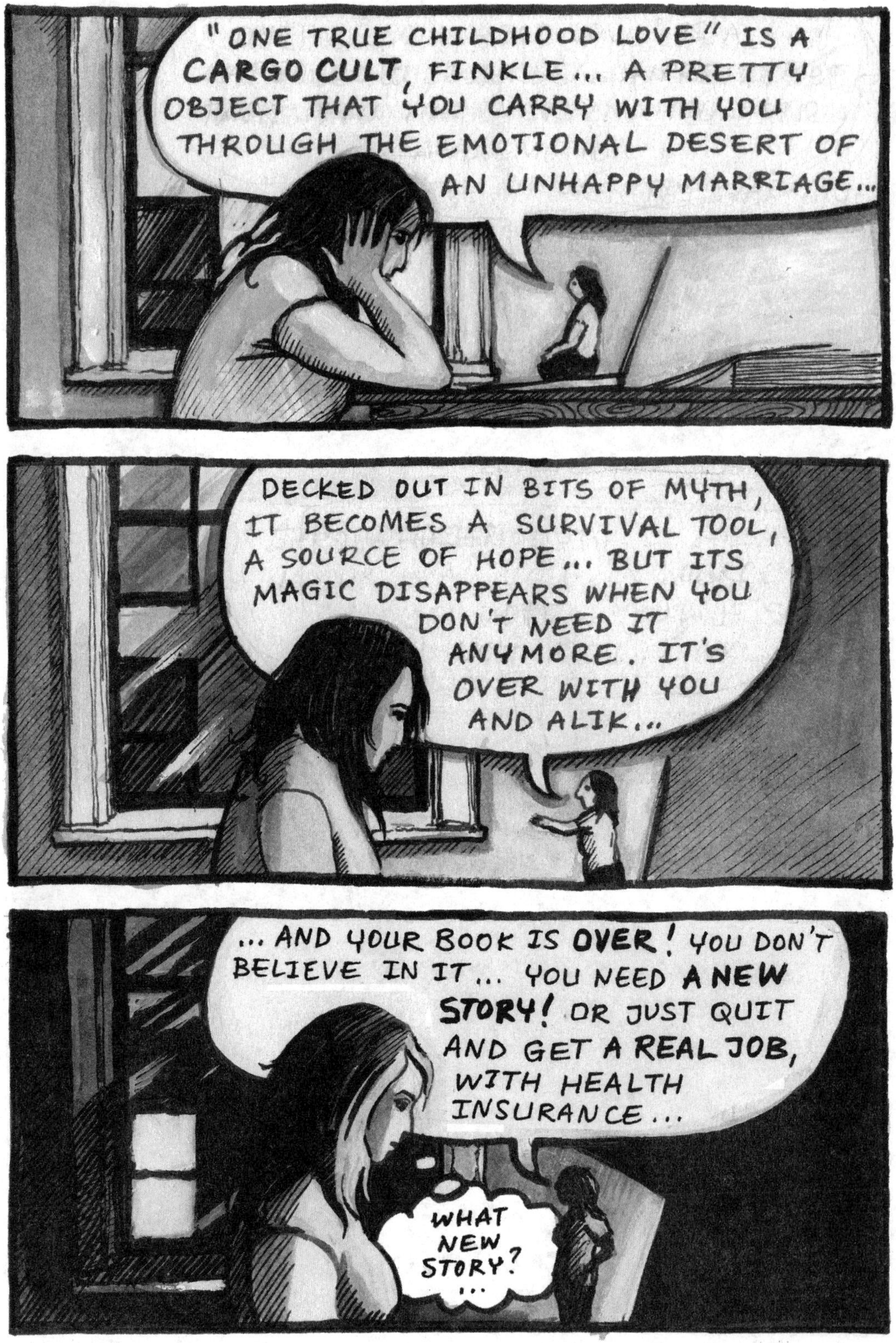
"ONE TRUE CHILDHOOD LOVE" IS A CARGO CULT, FINKLE... A PRETTY OBJECT THAT YOU CARRY WITH YOU THROUGH THE EMOTIONAL DESERT OF AN UNHAPPY MARRIAGE...
DECKED OUT IN BITS OF MYTH, IT BECOMES A SURVIVAL TOOL, A SOURCE OF HOPE... BUT ITS MAGIC DISAPPEARS WHEN YOU DON'T NEED IT ANYMORE. IT'S OVER WITH YOU AND ALIK...
... AND YOUR BOOK IS OVER! YOU DON'T BELIEVE IN IT... YOU NEED A NEW STORY! OR JUST QUIT AND GET A REAL JOB, WITH HEALTH INSURANCE...
WHAT NEW STORY? ...

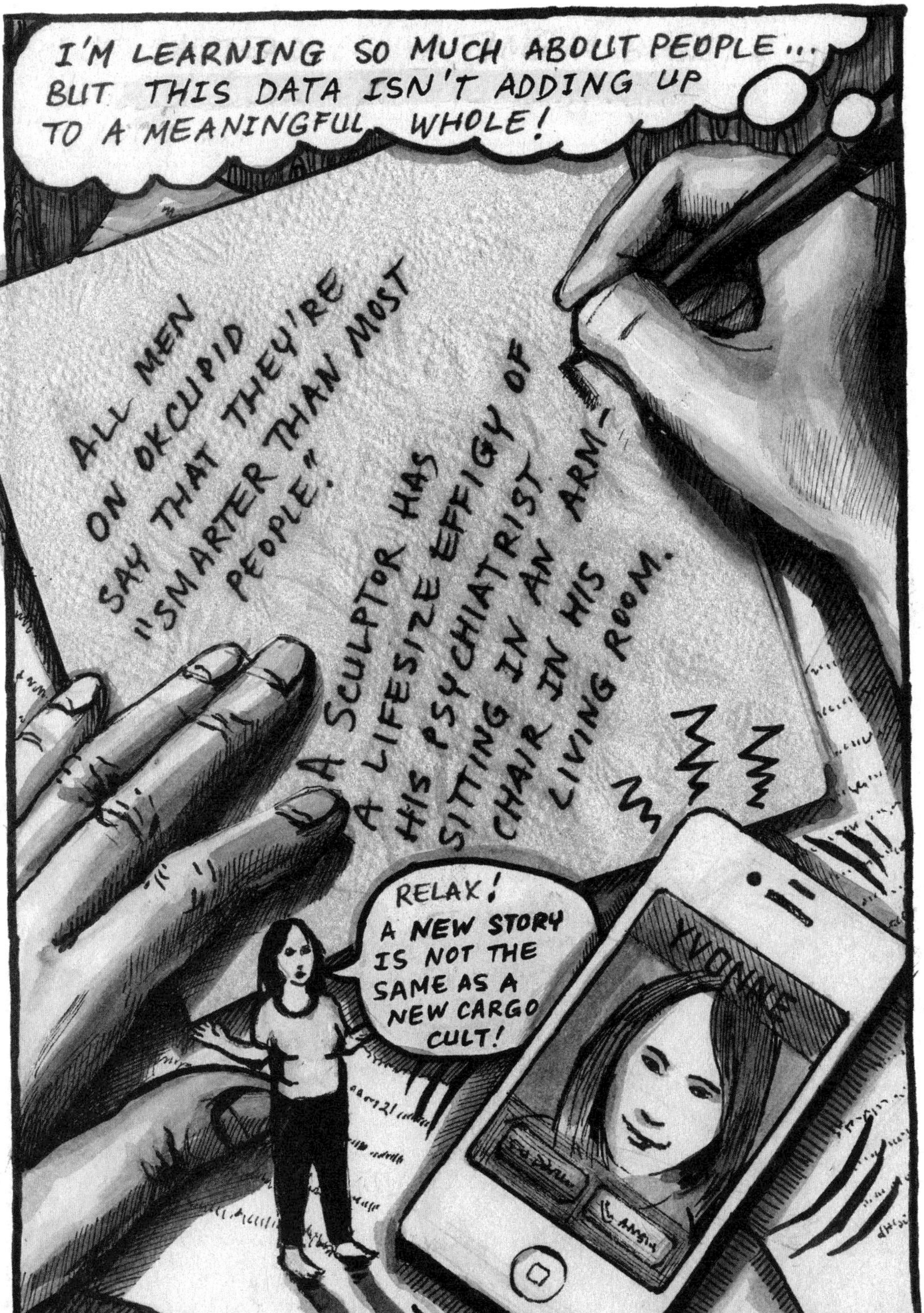
I'M LEARNING SO MUCH ABOUT PEOPLE... BUT THIS DATA ISN'T ADDING UP TO A MEANINGFUL WHOLE!
ALL MEN ON OKCUPID SAY THAT THEY'RE "SMARTER THAN MOST PEOPLE."
A SCULPTOR HAS A LIFESIZE EFFIGY OF HIS PSYCHIATRIST SITTING IN AN ARM-CHAIR IN HIS LIVING ROOM.
YVONNE
RELAX! A NEW STORY IS NOT THE SAME AS A NEW CARGO CULT!

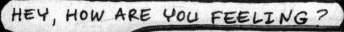

HEY, HOW ARE YOU FEELING?

OKAY... TRYING TO WRITE.

GOD, YOU'RE AMBITIOUS! I'M *STILL* HUNG OVER... LISTEN, ABOUT LAST NIGHT... I'M SORRY. I WAS PRETTY GRUMPY. JOSE IS SUCH A MESS! HE'S WITH THIS GIRL WHO KEEPS DUMPING AND REDUMPING HIM, AND THEY'RE DRINKING TOO MUCH... AND YOU'RE SO *GIDDY* WITH THIS FREEDOM OF YOURS, I HATE TO THINK OF YOU GETTING HURT...

WHAT CAN HURT ME, YVONNE? WHY IS EVERYONE WARNING ME TO BE CAREFUL?

YOU CAN END UP WITH SOMEONE WHO IS BAD FOR YOU... YOU CAN GET YOUR HEART BROKEN...

I DON'T THINK MY HEART CAN DO THAT, HAHA... HEY, CAN I CALL YOU BACK? THE KIDS JUST BUZZED FROM DOWNSTAIRS...

...I'M ABOUT TO GET ON A PLANE. LISTEN, YOU'RE RIGHT. HAVE FUN, ENJOY THE SEX... TALK SOON, OKAY?

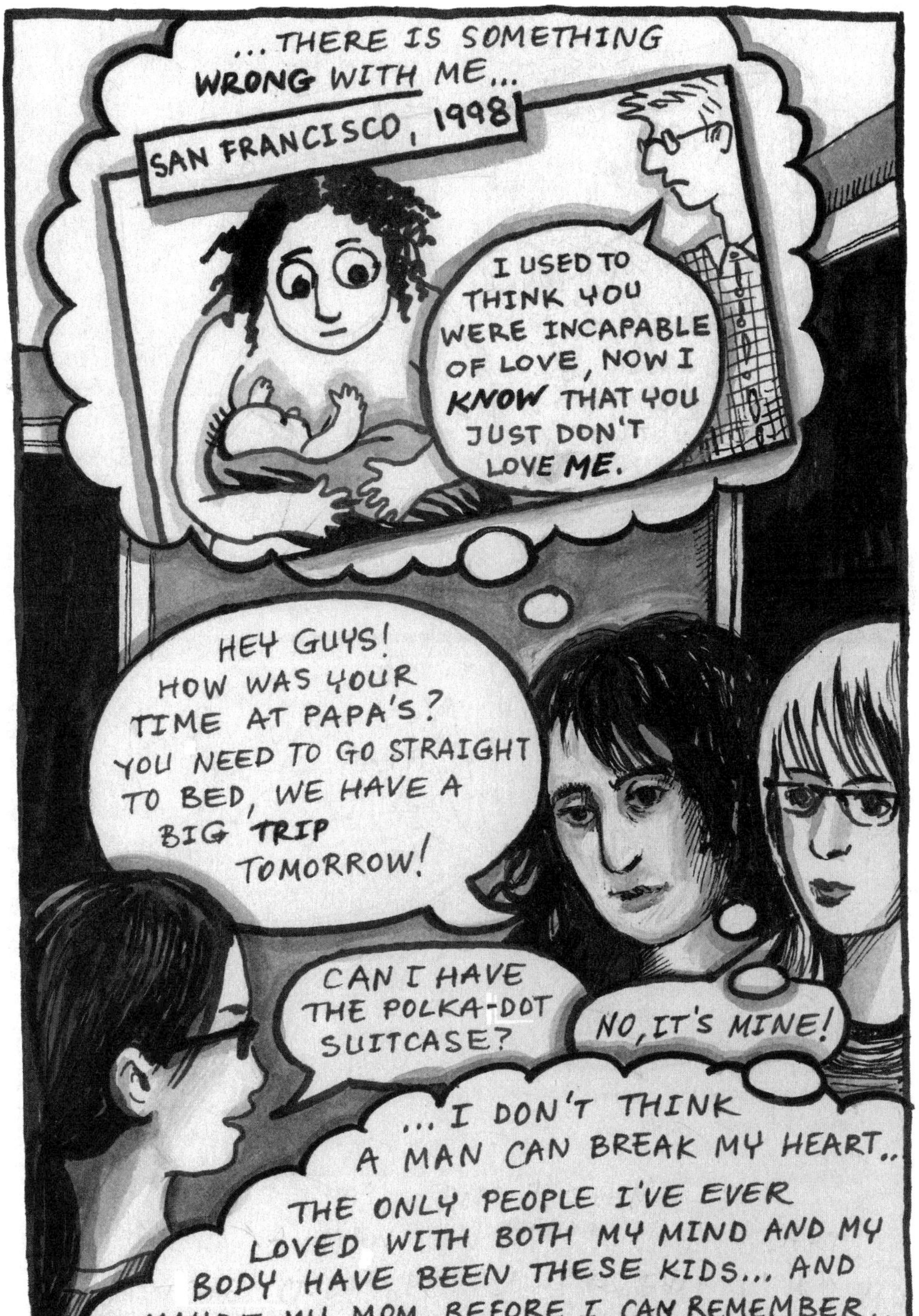
...THERE IS SOMETHING WRONG WITH ME...
SAN FRANCISCO, 1998
I USED TO THINK YOU WERE INCAPABLE OF LOVE, NOW I KNOW THAT YOU JUST DON'T LOVE ME.
HEY GUYS! HOW WAS YOUR TIME AT PAPA'S? YOU NEED TO GO STRAIGHT TO BED, WE HAVE A BIG TRIP TOMORROW!
CAN I HAVE THE POLKA-DOT SUITCASE?
NO, IT'S MINE!
...I DON'T THINK A MAN CAN BREAK MY HEART... THE ONLY PEOPLE I'VE EVER LOVED WITH BOTH MY MIND AND MY BODY HAVE BEEN THESE KIDS... AND MAYBE MY MOM, BEFORE I CAN REMEMBER...

AND SEX... ...WOW, I CAN'T BELIEVE I STILL HAVE THIS...

I READ IT RIGHT AFTER COLLEGE... JOSH AND I WERE WORKING AT A DOT-COM...

I RELATED TO CONNIE CHATTERLEY...

...BUT ONLY UP TO THE MIDDLE OF THE BOOK...

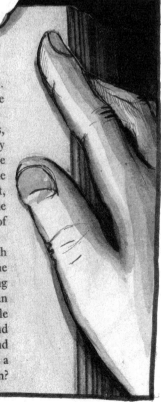

Lady Chatterley's Lover

fellows, free to do as they liked, and, above all, to say what they liked. It was the talk that mattered supremely: the impassioned interchange of talk. Love was only a minor accompaniment.

Both Hilda and Constance had had their tentative love affairs, by the time they were eighteen. The young men with whom they talked so passionately and sang so lustily and camped under the trees in such freedom wanted, of course, the love-connection. The girls were doubtful, but then the thing was so much talked about, it was supposed to be so important. And the men were so humble and craving. Why couldn't a girl be queenly, and give the gift of herself?

So they had given the gift of themselves each to the youth with whom she had the most intimate and subtle arguments. The arguments, the discussions were the great thing: the love-making and connection was only a sort of primitive reversion, and a bit of an anti-climax. One was less in love with the boy afterwards, and a little inclined to hate him, as if he had trespassed on one's privacy and inner freedom. For of course, being a girl, one's whole dignity and meaning in life consisted in the achievement of an absolute, a perfect, a pure and royal freedom. What else did a girl's life mean?

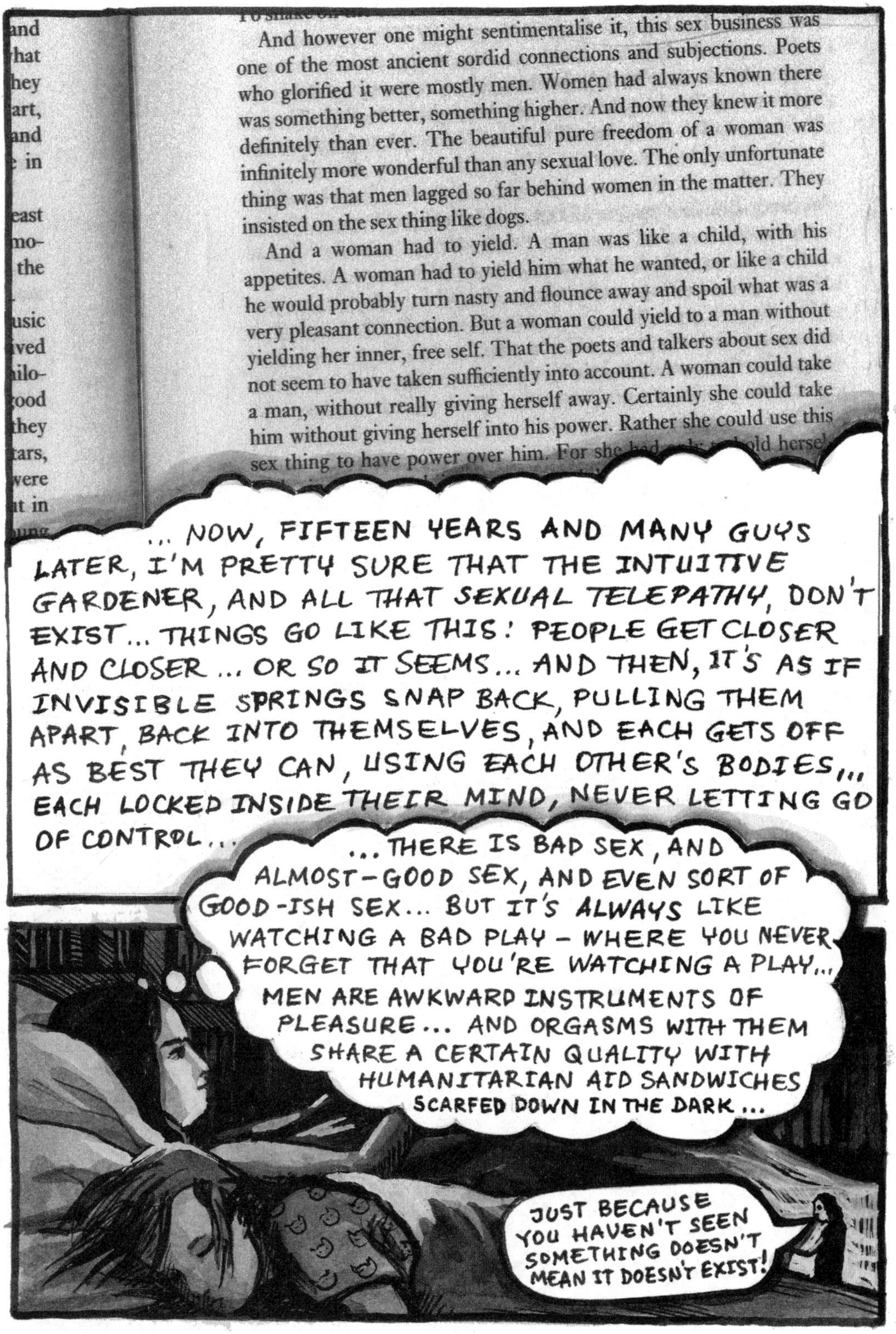
And however one might sentimentalise it, this sex business was one of the most ancient sordid connections and subjections. Poets who glorified it were mostly men. Women had always known there was something better, something higher. And now they knew it more definitely than ever. The beautiful pure freedom of a woman was infinitely more wonderful than any sexual love. The only unfortunate thing was that men lagged so far behind women in the matter. They insisted on the sex thing like dogs.
And a woman had to yield. A man was like a child, with his appetites. A woman had to yield him what he wanted, or like a child he would probably turn nasty and flounce away and spoil what was a very pleasant connection. But a woman could yield to a man without yielding her inner, free self. That the poets and talkers about sex did not seem to have taken sufficiently into account. A woman could take a man, without really giving herself away. Certainly she could take him without giving herself into his power. Rather she could use this sex thing to have power over him.
... NOW, FIFTEEN YEARS AND MANY GUYS LATER, I'M PRETTY SURE THAT THE INTUITIVE GARDENER, AND ALL THAT *SEXUAL TELEPATHY*, DON'T EXIST... THINGS GO LIKE THIS: PEOPLE GET CLOSER AND CLOSER ... OR SO IT SEEMS... AND THEN, IT'S AS IF INVISIBLE SPRINGS SNAP BACK, PULLING THEM APART, BACK INTO THEMSELVES, AND EACH GETS OFF AS BEST THEY CAN, USING EACH OTHER'S BODIES,,, EACH LOCKED INSIDE THEIR MIND, NEVER LETTING GO OF CONTROL...
... THERE IS BAD SEX, AND ALMOST-GOOD SEX, AND EVEN SORT OF GOOD-ISH SEX... BUT IT'S ALWAYS LIKE WATCHING A BAD PLAY - WHERE YOU NEVER FORGET THAT YOU'RE WATCHING A PLAY... MEN ARE AWKWARD INSTRUMENTS OF PLEASURE... AND ORGASMS WITH THEM SHARE A CERTAIN QUALITY WITH HUMANITARIAN AID SANDWICHES SCARFED DOWN IN THE DARK...
JUST BECAUSE YOU HAVEN'T SEEN SOMETHING DOESN'T MEAN IT DOESN'T EXIST!

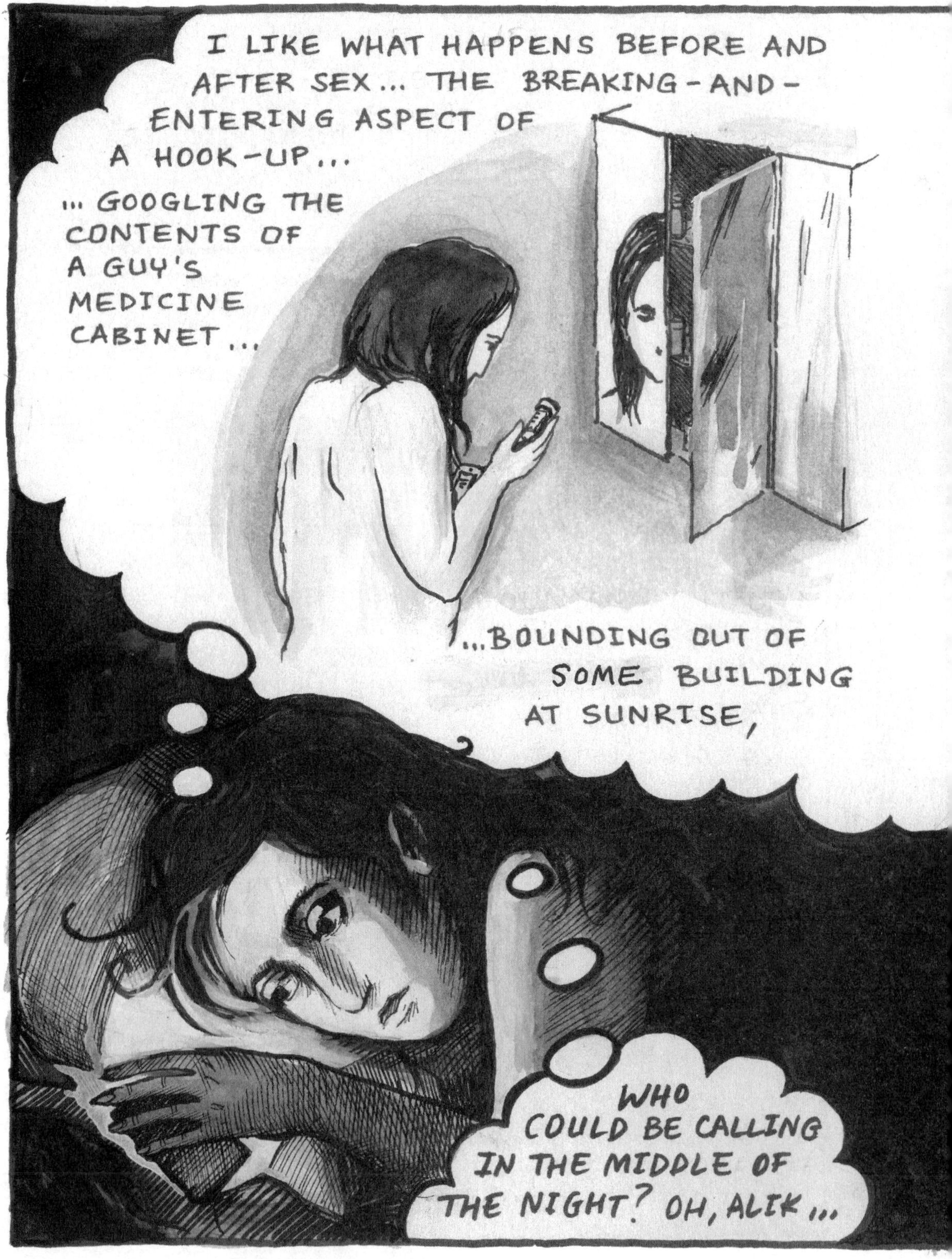
I LIKE WHAT HAPPENS BEFORE AND AFTER SEX... THE BREAKING-AND-ENTERING ASPECT OF A HOOK-UP...
...GOOGLING THE CONTENTS OF A GUY'S MEDICINE CABINET...
...BOUNDING OUT OF SOME BUILDING AT SUNRISE,
WHO COULD BE CALLING IN THE MIDDLE OF THE NIGHT? OH, ALIK...

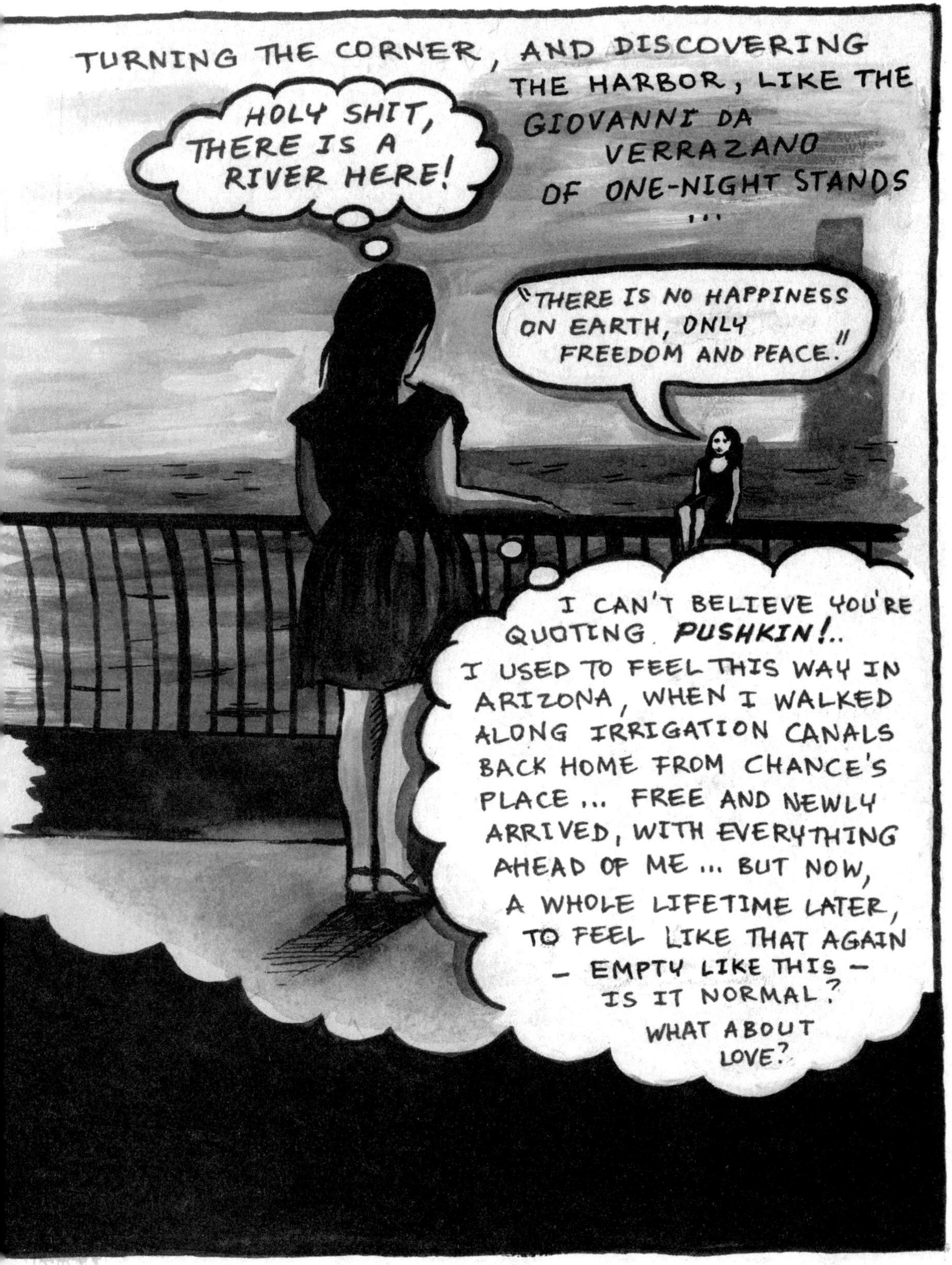

TURNING THE CORNER, AND DISCOVERING THE HARBOR, LIKE THE GIOVANNI DA VERRAZANO OF ONE-NIGHT STANDS ...
HOLY SHIT, THERE IS A RIVER HERE!
"THERE IS NO HAPPINESS ON EARTH, ONLY FREEDOM AND PEACE."
I CAN'T BELIEVE YOU'RE QUOTING PUSHKIN!.. I USED TO FEEL THIS WAY IN ARIZONA, WHEN I WALKED ALONG IRRIGATION CANALS BACK HOME FROM CHANCE'S PLACE ... FREE AND NEWLY ARRIVED, WITH EVERYTHING AHEAD OF ME ... BUT NOW, A WHOLE LIFETIME LATER, TO FEEL LIKE THAT AGAIN — EMPTY LIKE THIS — IS IT NORMAL? WHAT ABOUT LOVE?

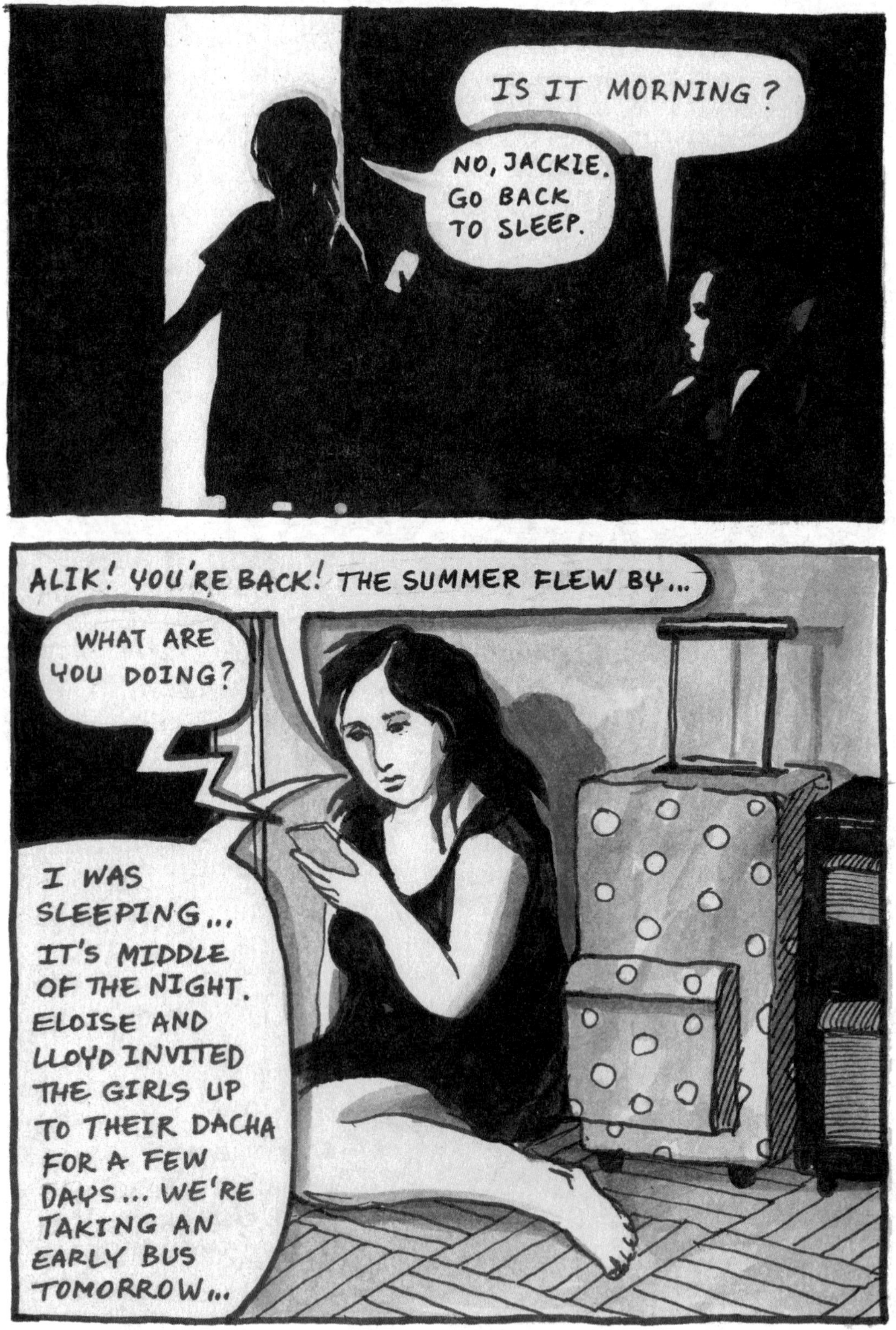
IS IT MORNING?
NO, JACKIE. GO BACK TO SLEEP.
ALIK! YOU'RE BACK! THE SUMMER FLEW BY...
WHAT ARE YOU DOING?
I WAS SLEEPING... IT'S MIDDLE OF THE NIGHT. ELOISE AND LLOYD INVITED THE GIRLS UP TO THEIR DACHA FOR A FEW DAYS... WE'RE TAKING AN EARLY BUS TOMORROW...

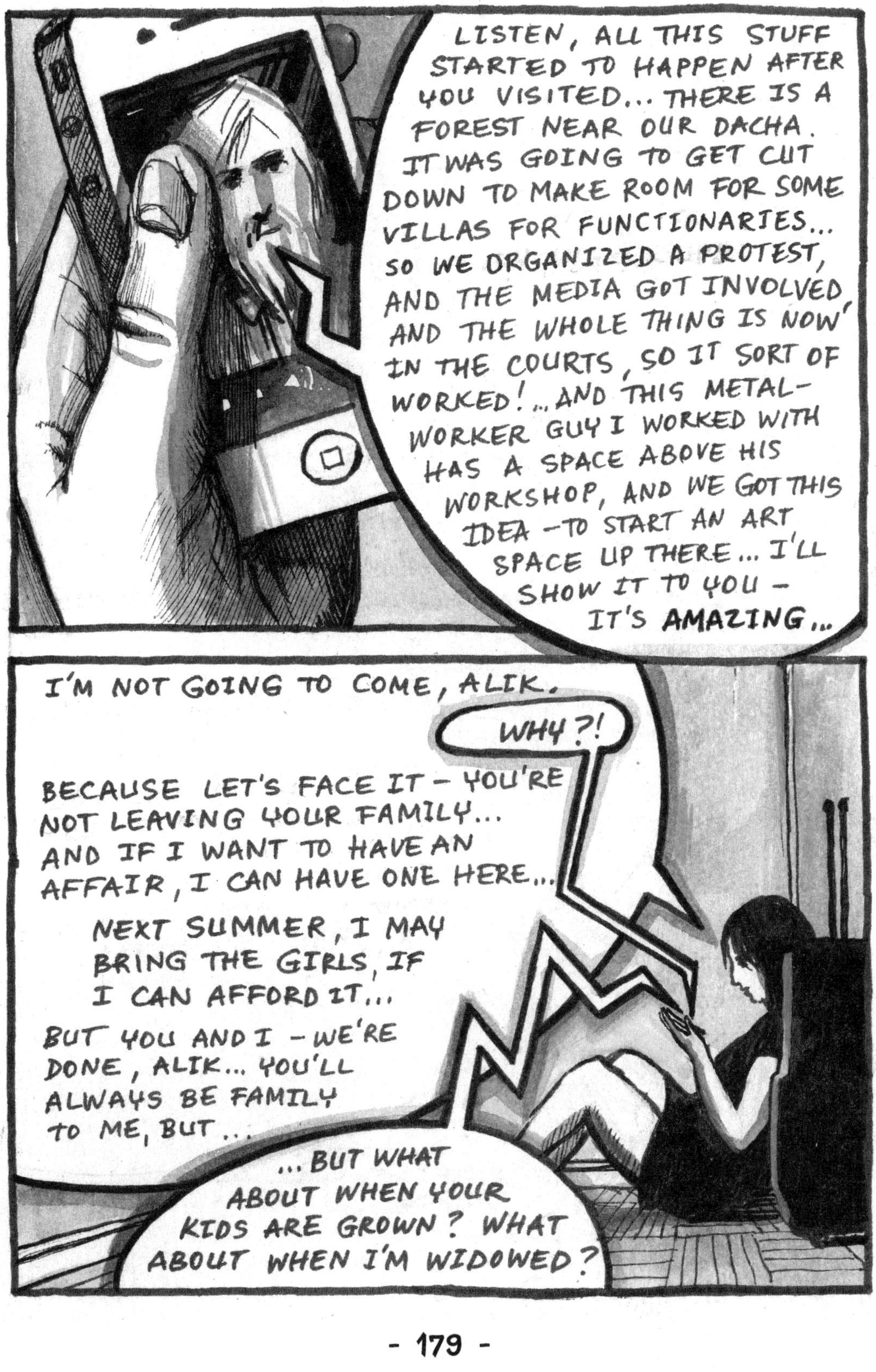
LISTEN, ALL THIS STUFF STARTED TO HAPPEN AFTER YOU VISITED... THERE IS A FOREST NEAR OUR DACHA. IT WAS GOING TO GET CUT DOWN TO MAKE ROOM FOR SOME VILLAS FOR FUNCTIONARIES... SO WE ORGANIZED A PROTEST, AND THE MEDIA GOT INVOLVED, AND THE WHOLE THING IS NOW IN THE COURTS, SO IT SORT OF WORKED!... AND THIS METAL-WORKER GUY I WORKED WITH HAS A SPACE ABOVE HIS WORKSHOP, AND WE GOT THIS IDEA - TO START AN ART SPACE UP THERE... I'LL SHOW IT TO YOU - IT'S AMAZING...
I'M NOT GOING TO COME, ALIK.
WHY?!
BECAUSE LET'S FACE IT - YOU'RE NOT LEAVING YOUR FAMILY... AND IF I WANT TO HAVE AN AFFAIR, I CAN HAVE ONE HERE...
NEXT SUMMER, I MAY BRING THE GIRLS, IF I CAN AFFORD IT...
BUT YOU AND I - WE'RE DONE, ALIK... YOU'LL ALWAYS BE FAMILY TO ME, BUT...
... BUT WHAT ABOUT WHEN YOUR KIDS ARE GROWN? WHAT ABOUT WHEN I'M WIDOWED?

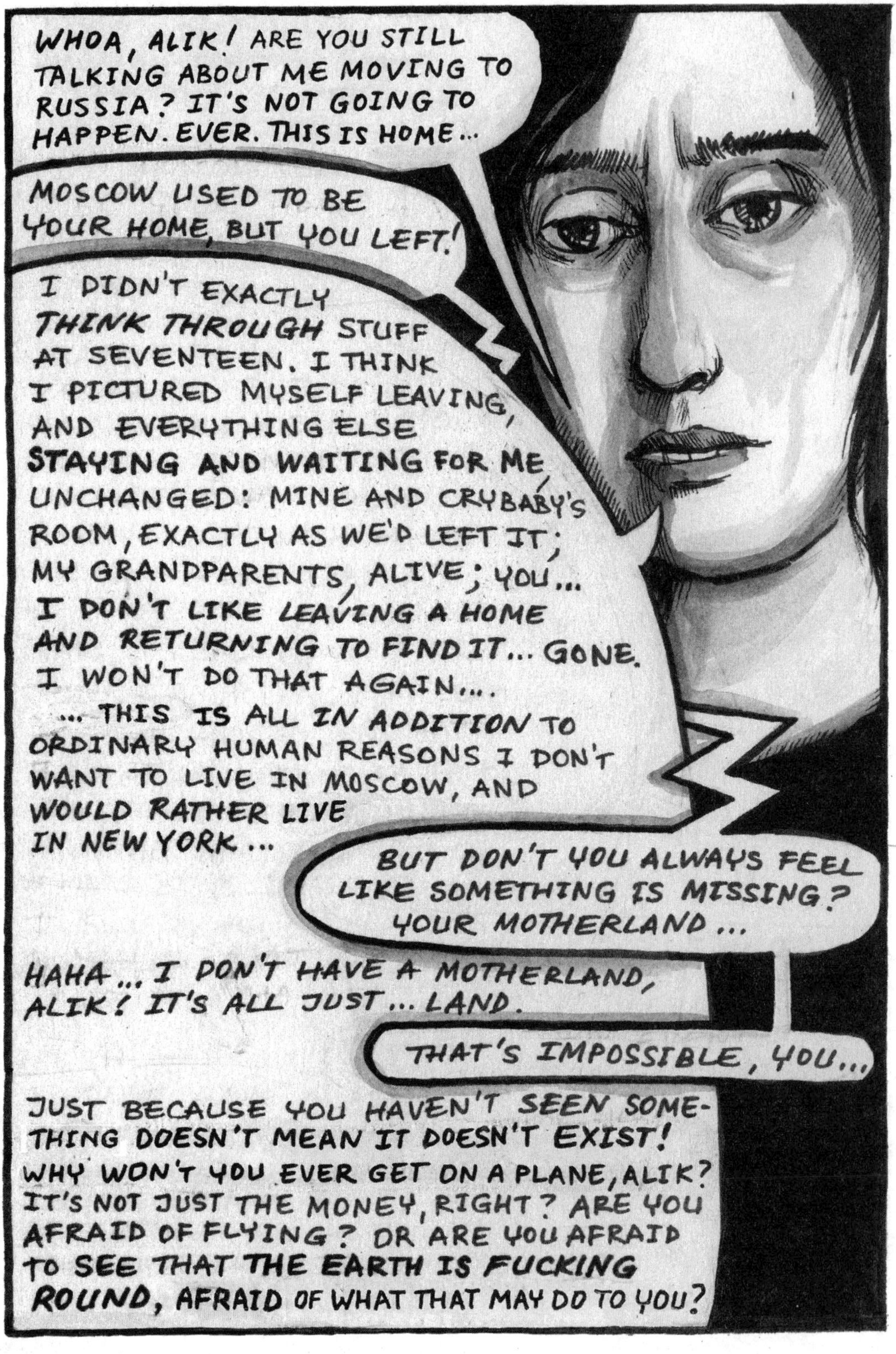
WHOA, ALIK! ARE YOU STILL TALKING ABOUT ME MOVING TO RUSSIA? IT'S NOT GOING TO HAPPEN. EVER. THIS IS HOME...
MOSCOW USED TO BE YOUR HOME, BUT YOU LEFT!
I DIDN'T EXACTLY THINK THROUGH STUFF AT SEVENTEEN. I THINK I PICTURED MYSELF LEAVING, AND EVERYTHING ELSE STAYING AND WAITING FOR ME, UNCHANGED: MINE AND CRYBABY'S ROOM, EXACTLY AS WE'D LEFT IT; MY GRANDPARENTS, ALIVE; YOU... I DON'T LIKE LEAVING A HOME AND RETURNING TO FIND IT... GONE. I WON'T DO THAT AGAIN....
... THIS IS ALL IN ADDITION TO ORDINARY HUMAN REASONS I DON'T WANT TO LIVE IN MOSCOW, AND WOULD RATHER LIVE IN NEW YORK...
BUT DON'T YOU ALWAYS FEEL LIKE SOMETHING IS MISSING? YOUR MOTHERLAND...
HAHA... I DON'T HAVE A MOTHERLAND, ALIK! IT'S ALL JUST... LAND.
THAT'S IMPOSSIBLE, YOU...
JUST BECAUSE YOU HAVEN'T SEEN SOMETHING DOESN'T MEAN IT DOESN'T EXIST! WHY WON'T YOU EVER GET ON A PLANE, ALIK? IT'S NOT JUST THE MONEY, RIGHT? ARE YOU AFRAID OF FLYING? OR ARE YOU AFRAID TO SEE THAT THE EARTH IS FUCKING ROUND, AFRAID OF WHAT THAT MAY DO TO YOU?

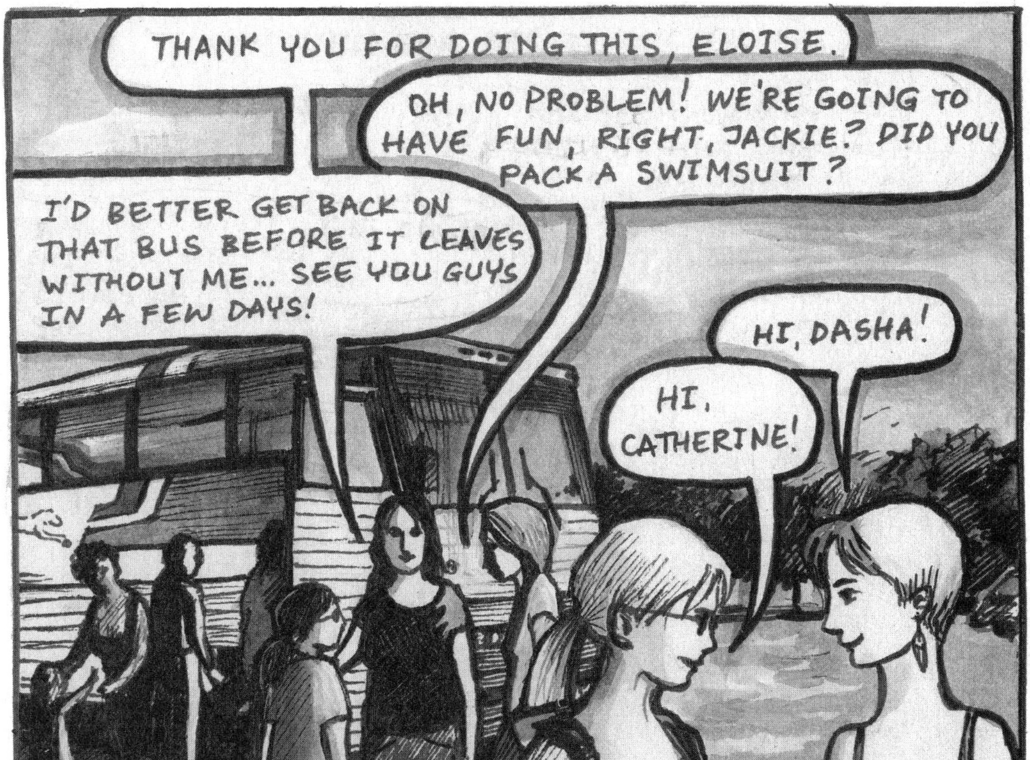
THANK YOU FOR DOING THIS, ELOISE.
OH, NO PROBLEM! WE'RE GOING TO HAVE FUN, RIGHT, JACKIE? DID YOU PACK A SWIMSUIT?
I'D BETTER GET BACK ON THAT BUS BEFORE IT LEAVES WITHOUT ME... SEE YOU GUYS IN A FEW DAYS!
HI, DASHA!
HI, CATHERINE!

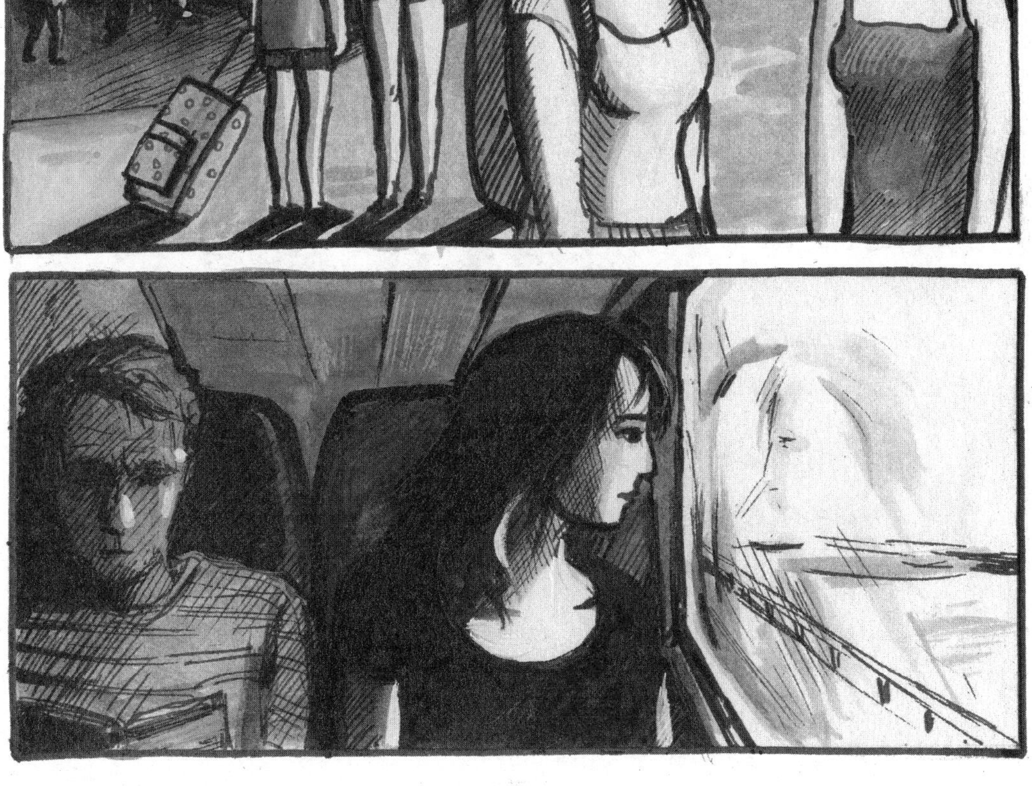

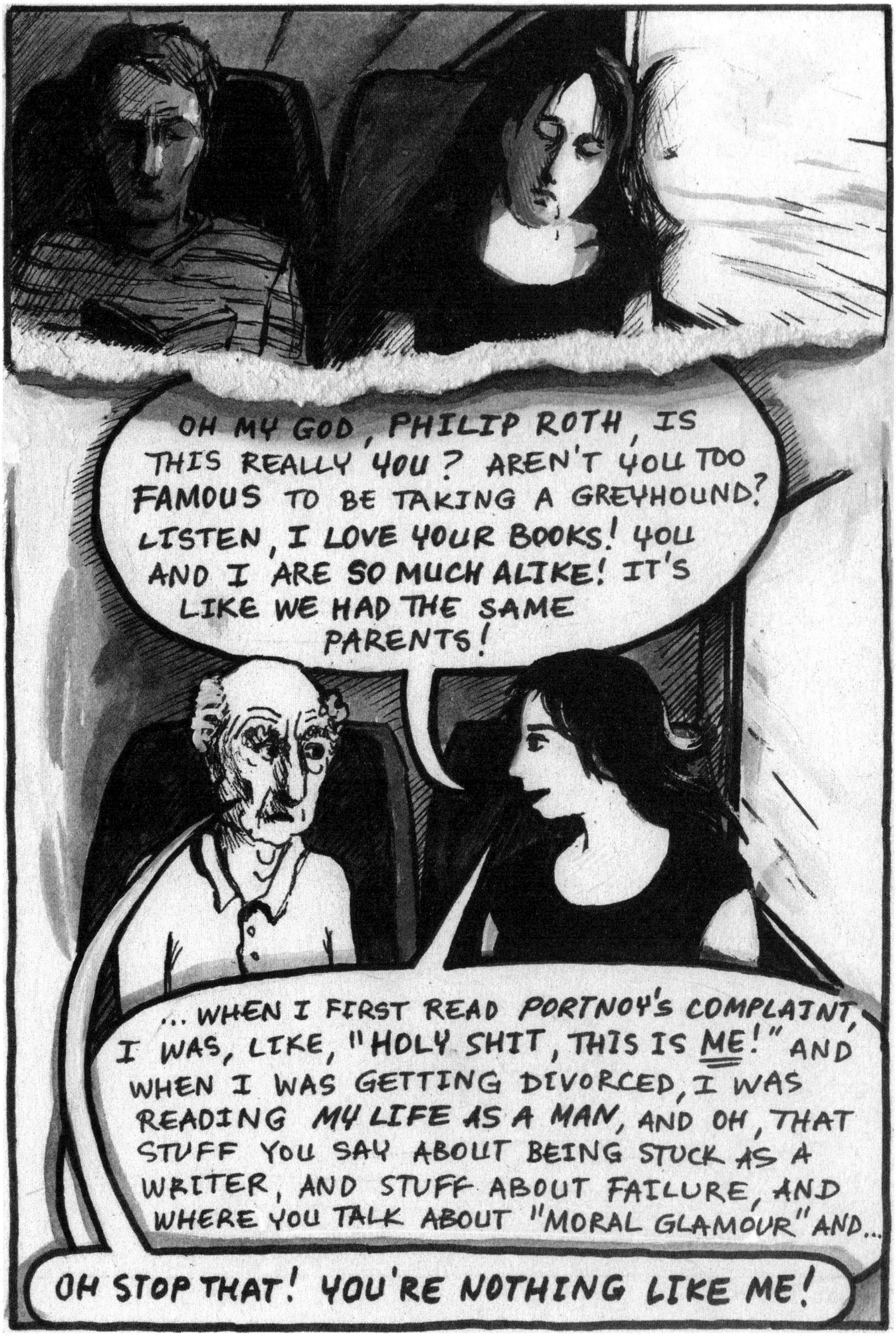

OH MY GOD, PHILIP ROTH, IS THIS REALLY YOU? AREN'T YOU TOO FAMOUS TO BE TAKING A GREYHOUND? LISTEN, I LOVE YOUR BOOKS! YOU AND I ARE SO MUCH ALIKE! IT'S LIKE WE HAD THE SAME PARENTS!
...WHEN I FIRST READ PORTNOY'S COMPLAINT, I WAS, LIKE, "HOLY SHIT, THIS IS ME!" AND WHEN I WAS GETTING DIVORCED, I WAS READING MY LIFE AS A MAN, AND OH, THAT STUFF YOU SAY ABOUT BEING STUCK AS A WRITER, AND STUFF ABOUT FAILURE, AND WHERE YOU TALK ABOUT "MORAL GLAMOUR" AND...
OH STOP THAT! YOU'RE NOTHING LIKE ME!

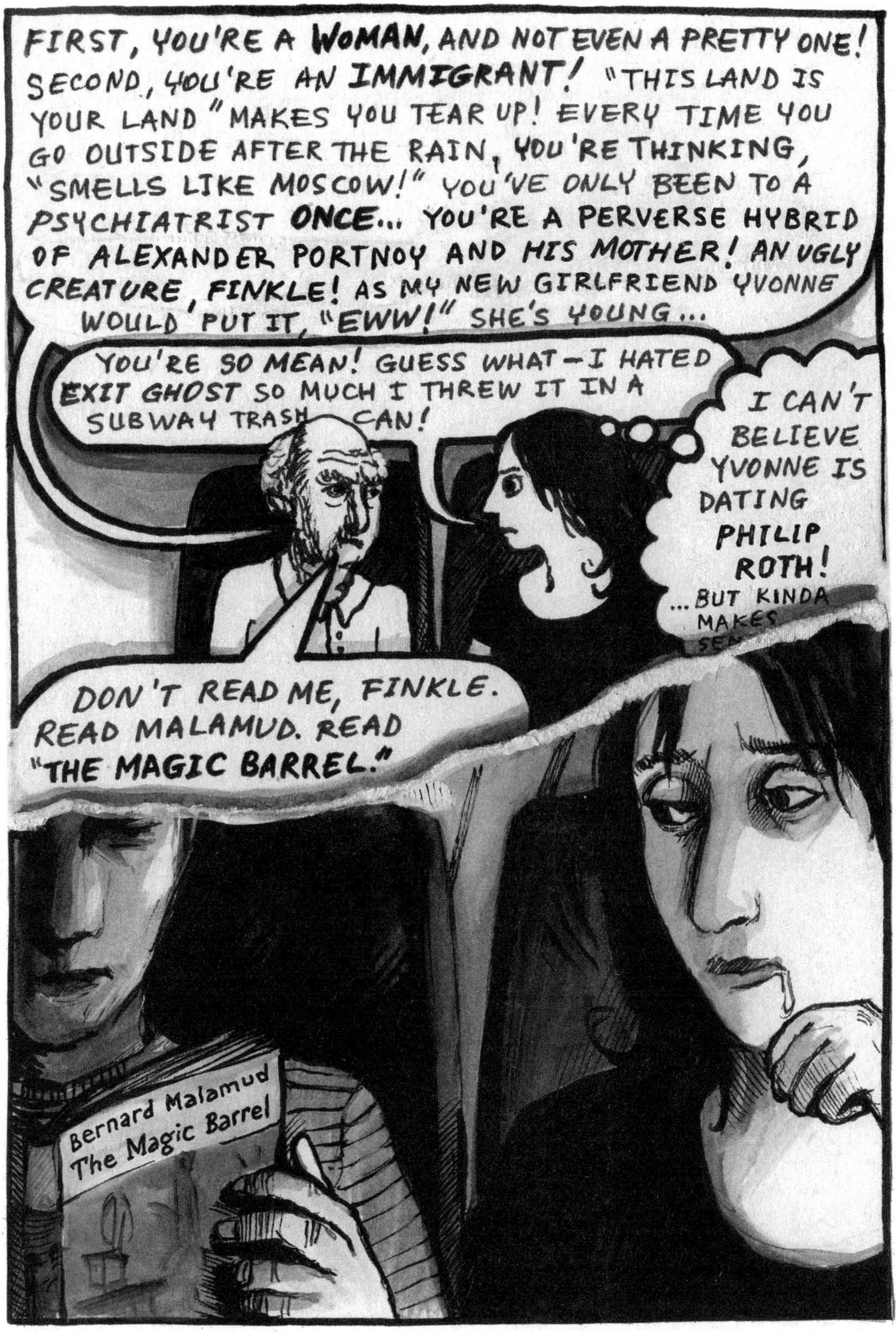

FIRST, YOU'RE A WOMAN, AND NOT EVEN A PRETTY ONE! SECOND, YOU'RE AN IMMIGRANT! "THIS LAND IS YOUR LAND" MAKES YOU TEAR UP! EVERY TIME YOU GO OUTSIDE AFTER THE RAIN, YOU'RE THINKING, "SMELLS LIKE MOSCOW!" YOU'VE ONLY BEEN TO A PSYCHIATRIST ONCE... YOU'RE A PERVERSE HYBRID OF ALEXANDER PORTNOY AND HIS MOTHER! AN UGLY CREATURE, FINKLE! AS MY NEW GIRLFRIEND YVONNE WOULD PUT IT, "EWW!" SHE'S YOUNG...
YOU'RE SO MEAN! GUESS WHAT—I HATED EXIT GHOST SO MUCH I THREW IT IN A SUBWAY TRASH CAN!
I CAN'T BELIEVE YVONNE IS DATING PHILIP ROTH!
...BUT KINDA MAKES SEN
DON'T READ ME, FINKLE. READ MALAMUD. READ "THE MAGIC BARREL."
Bernard Malamud
The Magic Barrel

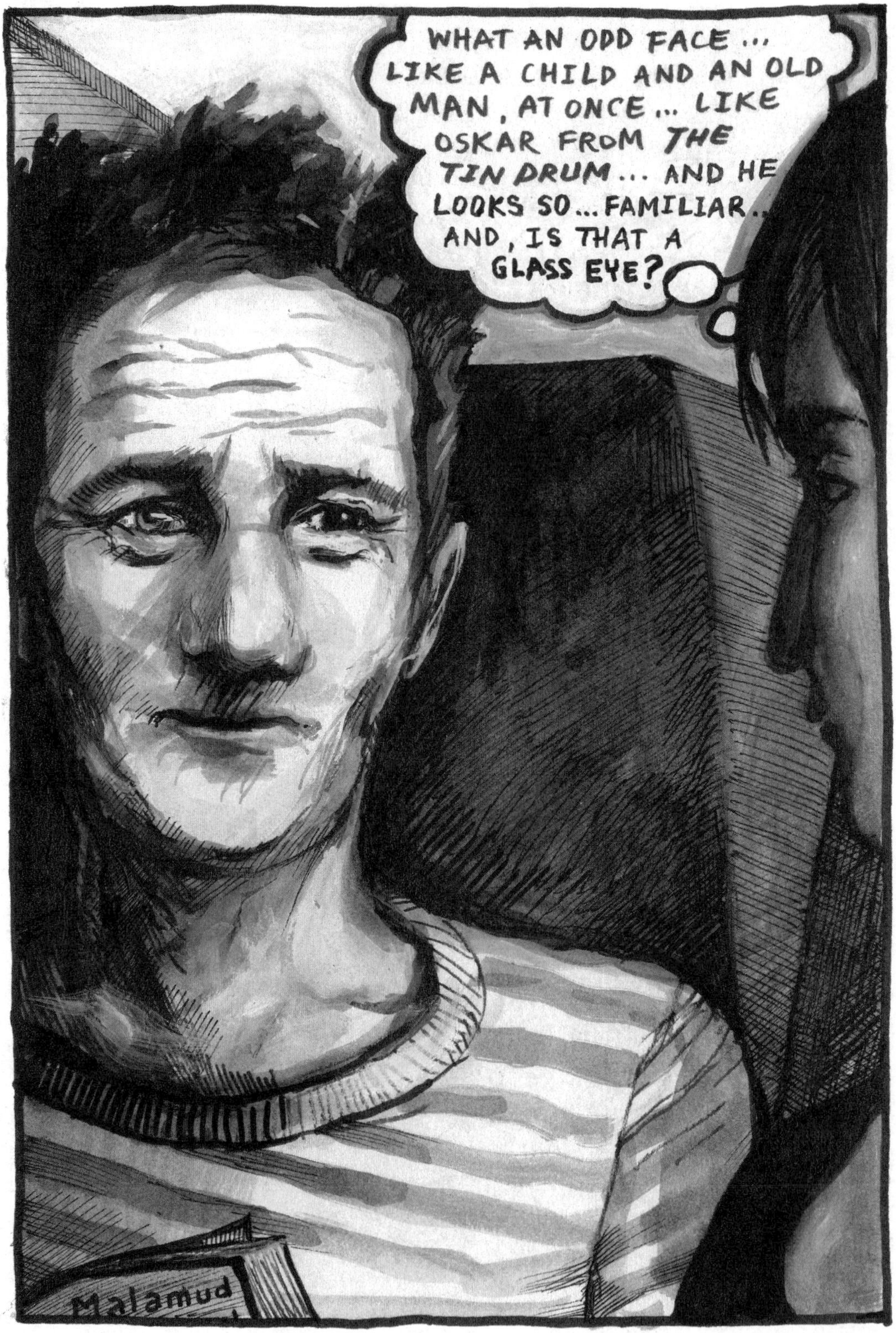
WHAT AN ODD FACE ... LIKE A CHILD AND AN OLD MAN, AT ONCE ... LIKE OSKAR FROM *THE TIN DRUM* ... AND HE LOOKS SO ... FAMILIAR ... AND, IS THAT A GLASS EYE?
Malamud

PART THREE

The Orphan

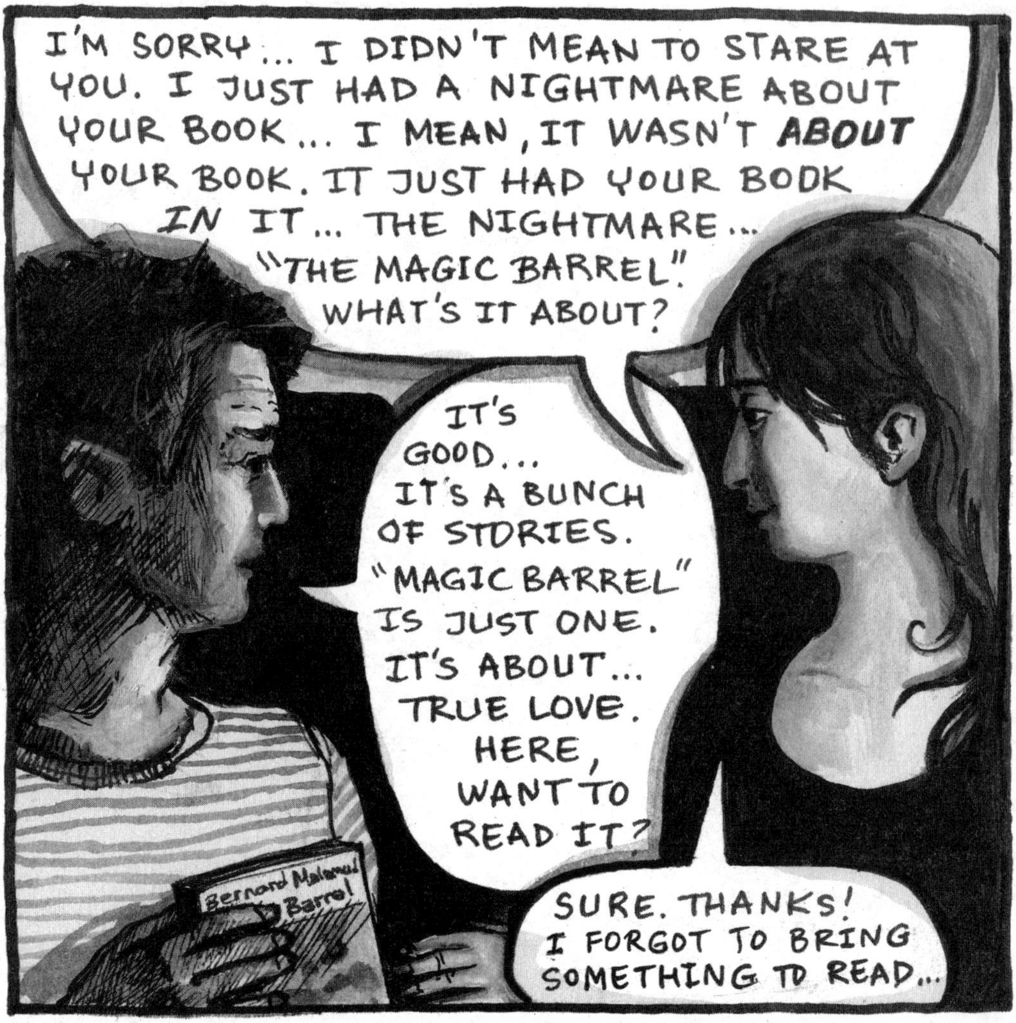
I'M SORRY... I DIDN'T MEAN TO STARE AT YOU. I JUST HAD A NIGHTMARE ABOUT YOUR BOOK... I MEAN, IT WASN'T ABOUT YOUR BOOK. IT JUST HAD YOUR BOOK IN IT... THE NIGHTMARE... "THE MAGIC BARREL." WHAT'S IT ABOUT?
IT'S GOOD... IT'S A BUNCH OF STORIES. "MAGIC BARREL" IS JUST ONE. IT'S ABOUT... TRUE LOVE. HERE, WANT TO READ IT?
SURE. THANKS! I FORGOT TO BRING SOMETHING TO READ...

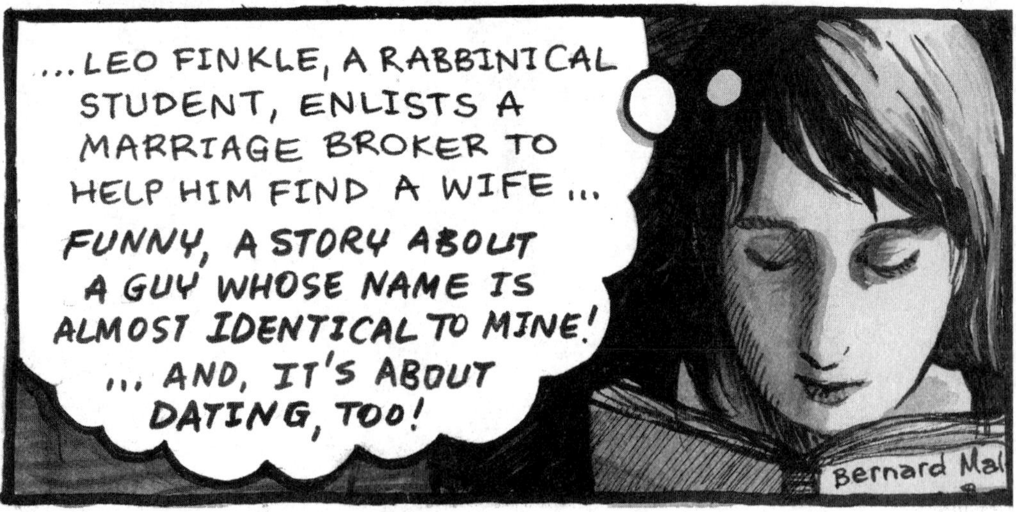
...LEO FINKLE, A RABBINICAL STUDENT, ENLISTS A MARRIAGE BROKER TO HELP HIM FIND A WIFE...
FUNNY, A STORY ABOUT A GUY WHOSE NAME IS ALMOST IDENTICAL TO MINE! ... AND, IT'S ABOUT DATING, TOO!
Bernard Mal

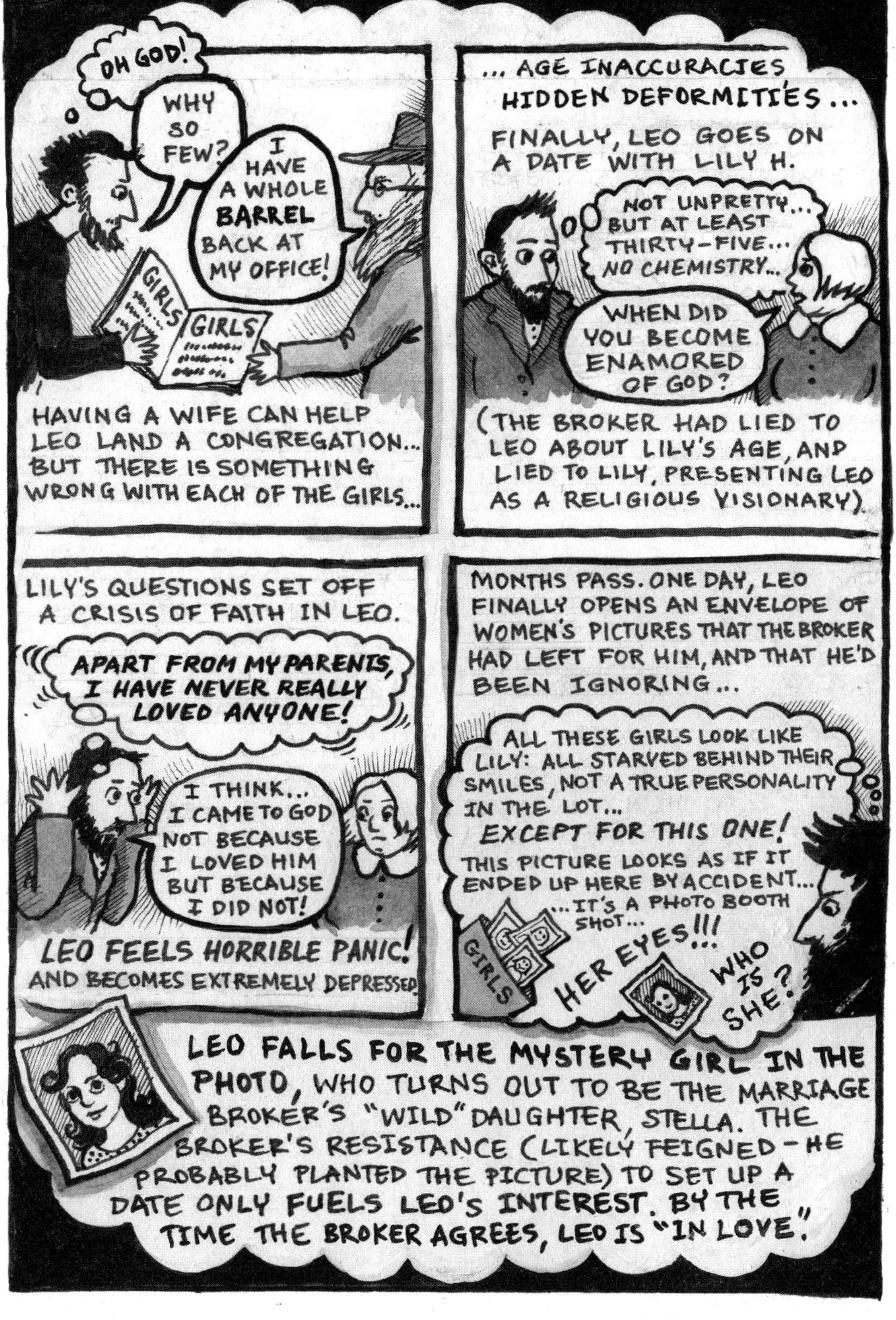
OH GOD!
WHY SO FEW?
I HAVE A WHOLE BARREL BACK AT MY OFFICE!
GIRLS
GIRLS
HAVING A WIFE CAN HELP LEO LAND A CONGREGATION... BUT THERE IS SOMETHING WRONG WITH EACH OF THE GIRLS...
... AGE INACCURACIES HIDDEN DEFORMITIES ...
FINALLY, LEO GOES ON A DATE WITH LILY H.
NOT UNPRETTY... BUT AT LEAST THIRTY-FIVE... NO CHEMISTRY...
WHEN DID YOU BECOME ENAMORED OF GOD?
(THE BROKER HAD LIED TO LEO ABOUT LILY'S AGE, AND LIED TO LILY, PRESENTING LEO AS A RELIGIOUS VISIONARY).
LILY'S QUESTIONS SET OFF A CRISIS OF FAITH IN LEO.
APART FROM MY PARENTS, I HAVE NEVER REALLY LOVED ANYONE!
I THINK... I CAME TO GOD NOT BECAUSE I LOVED HIM BUT BECAUSE I DID NOT!
LEO FEELS HORRIBLE PANIC! AND BECOMES EXTREMELY DEPRESSED.
MONTHS PASS. ONE DAY, LEO FINALLY OPENS AN ENVELOPE OF WOMEN'S PICTURES THAT THE BROKER HAD LEFT FOR HIM, AND THAT HE'D BEEN IGNORING...
ALL THESE GIRLS LOOK LIKE LILY: ALL STARVED BEHIND THEIR SMILES, NOT A TRUE PERSONALITY IN THE LOT... EXCEPT FOR THIS ONE! THIS PICTURE LOOKS AS IF IT ENDED UP HERE BY ACCIDENT... ...IT'S A PHOTO BOOTH SHOT...
GIRLS
HER EYES!!!
WHO IS SHE?
LEO FALLS FOR THE MYSTERY GIRL IN THE PHOTO, WHO TURNS OUT TO BE THE MARRIAGE BROKER'S "WILD" DAUGHTER, STELLA. THE BROKER'S RESISTANCE (LIKELY FEIGNED - HE PROBABLY PLANTED THE PICTURE) TO SET UP A DATE ONLY FUELS LEO'S INTEREST. BY THE TIME THE BROKER AGREES, LEO IS "IN LOVE".

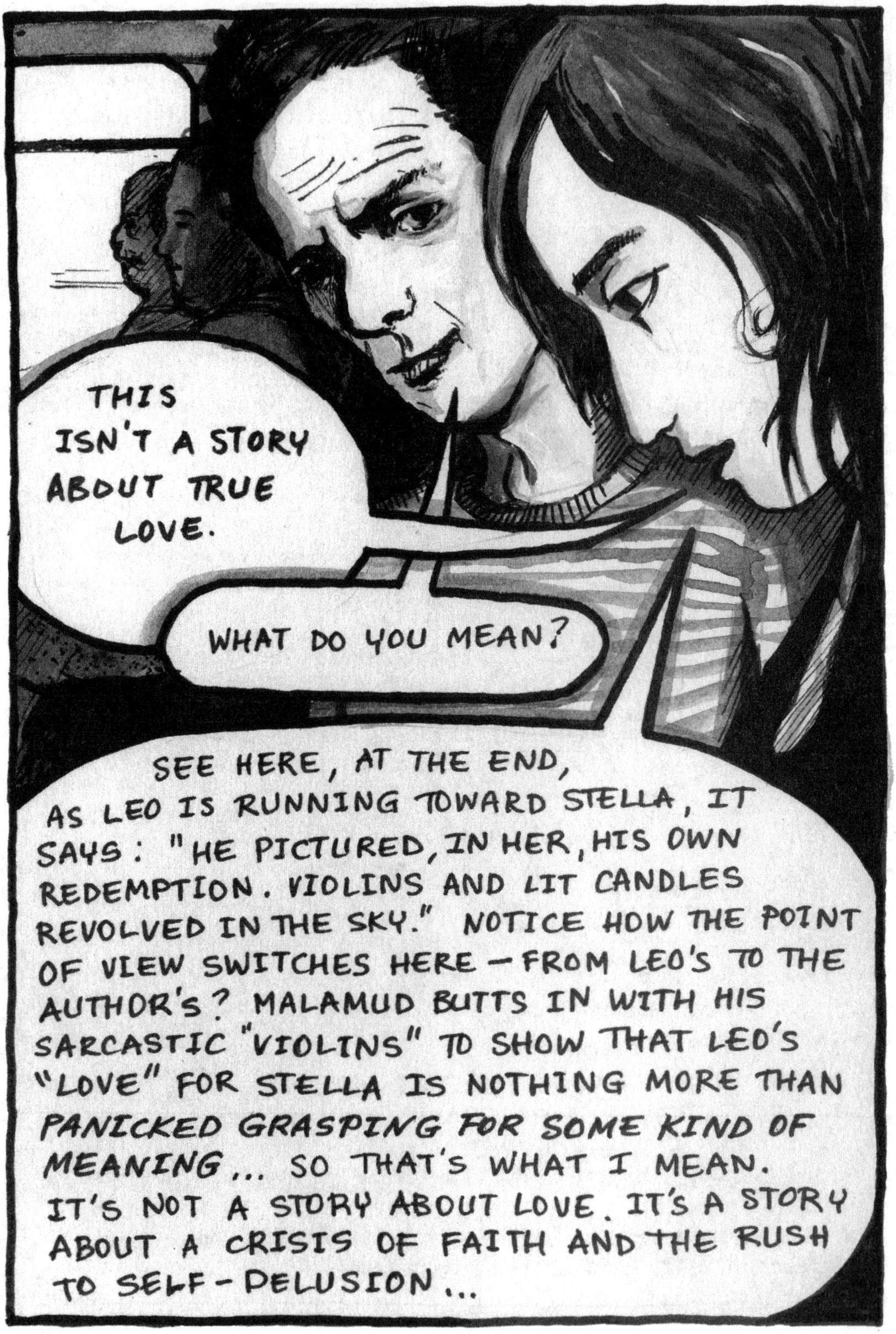
THIS ISN'T A STORY ABOUT TRUE LOVE.
WHAT DO YOU MEAN?
SEE HERE, AT THE END, AS LEO IS RUNNING TOWARD STELLA, IT SAYS: "HE PICTURED, IN HER, HIS OWN REDEMPTION. VIOLINS AND LIT CANDLES REVOLVED IN THE SKY." NOTICE HOW THE POINT OF VIEW SWITCHES HERE—FROM LEO'S TO THE AUTHOR'S? MALAMUD BUTTS IN WITH HIS SARCASTIC "VIOLINS" TO SHOW THAT LEO'S "LOVE" FOR STELLA IS NOTHING MORE THAN *PANICKED GRASPING FOR SOME KIND OF MEANING*... SO THAT'S WHAT I MEAN. IT'S NOT A STORY ABOUT LOVE. IT'S A STORY ABOUT A CRISIS OF FAITH AND THE RUSH TO SELF-DELUSION...

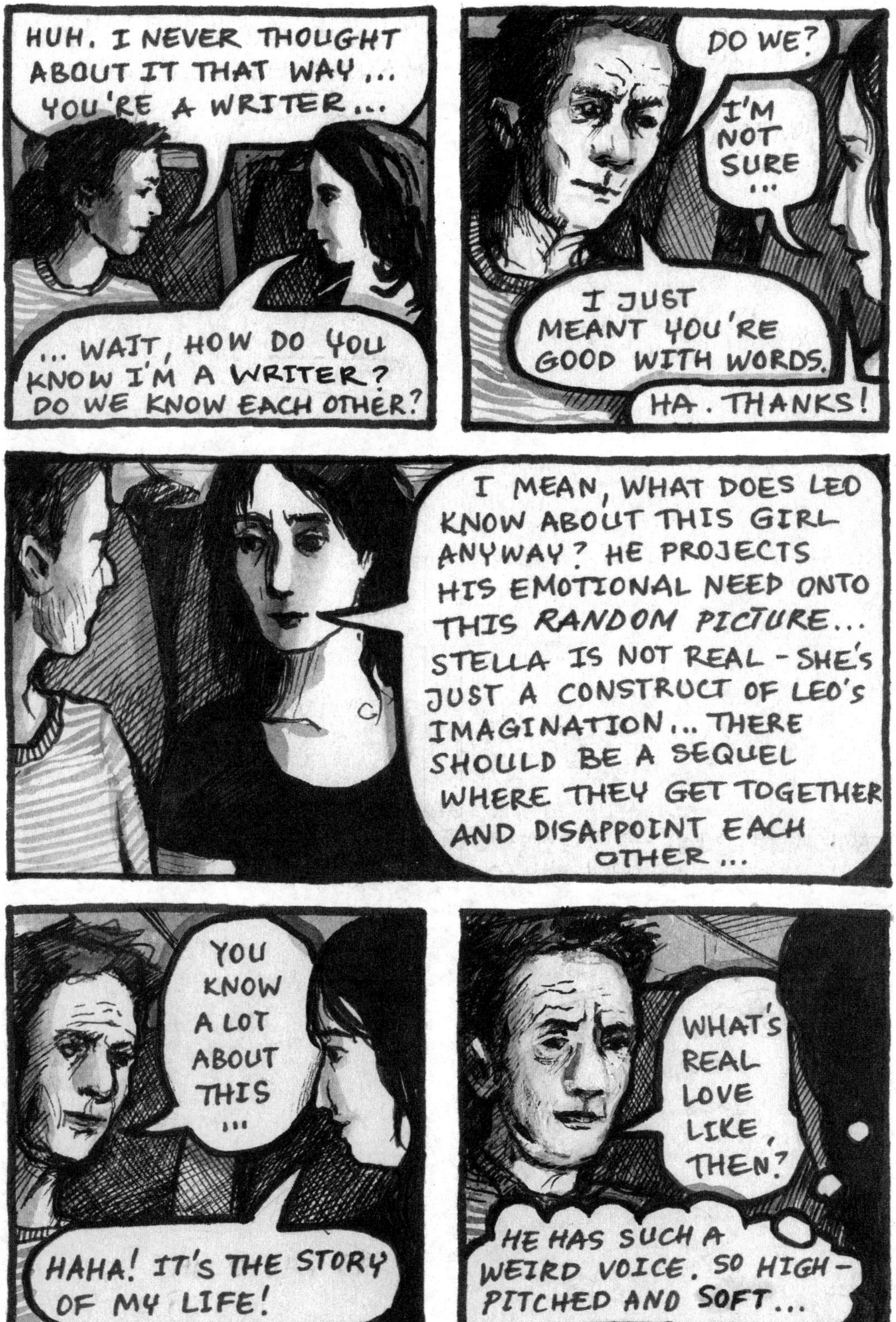
HUH. I NEVER THOUGHT ABOUT IT THAT WAY... YOU'RE A WRITER...
... WAIT, HOW DO YOU KNOW I'M A WRITER? DO WE KNOW EACH OTHER?
DO WE?
I'M NOT SURE ...
I JUST MEANT YOU'RE GOOD WITH WORDS.
HA. THANKS!
I MEAN, WHAT DOES LEO KNOW ABOUT THIS GIRL ANYWAY? HE PROJECTS HIS EMOTIONAL NEED ONTO THIS RANDOM PICTURE... STELLA IS NOT REAL - SHE'S JUST A CONSTRUCT OF LEO'S IMAGINATION... THERE SHOULD BE A SEQUEL WHERE THEY GET TOGETHER AND DISAPPOINT EACH OTHER...
YOU KNOW A LOT ABOUT THIS ...
HAHA! IT'S THE STORY OF MY LIFE!
WHAT'S REAL LOVE LIKE, THEN?
HE HAS SUCH A WEIRD VOICE. SO HIGH-PITCHED AND SOFT...

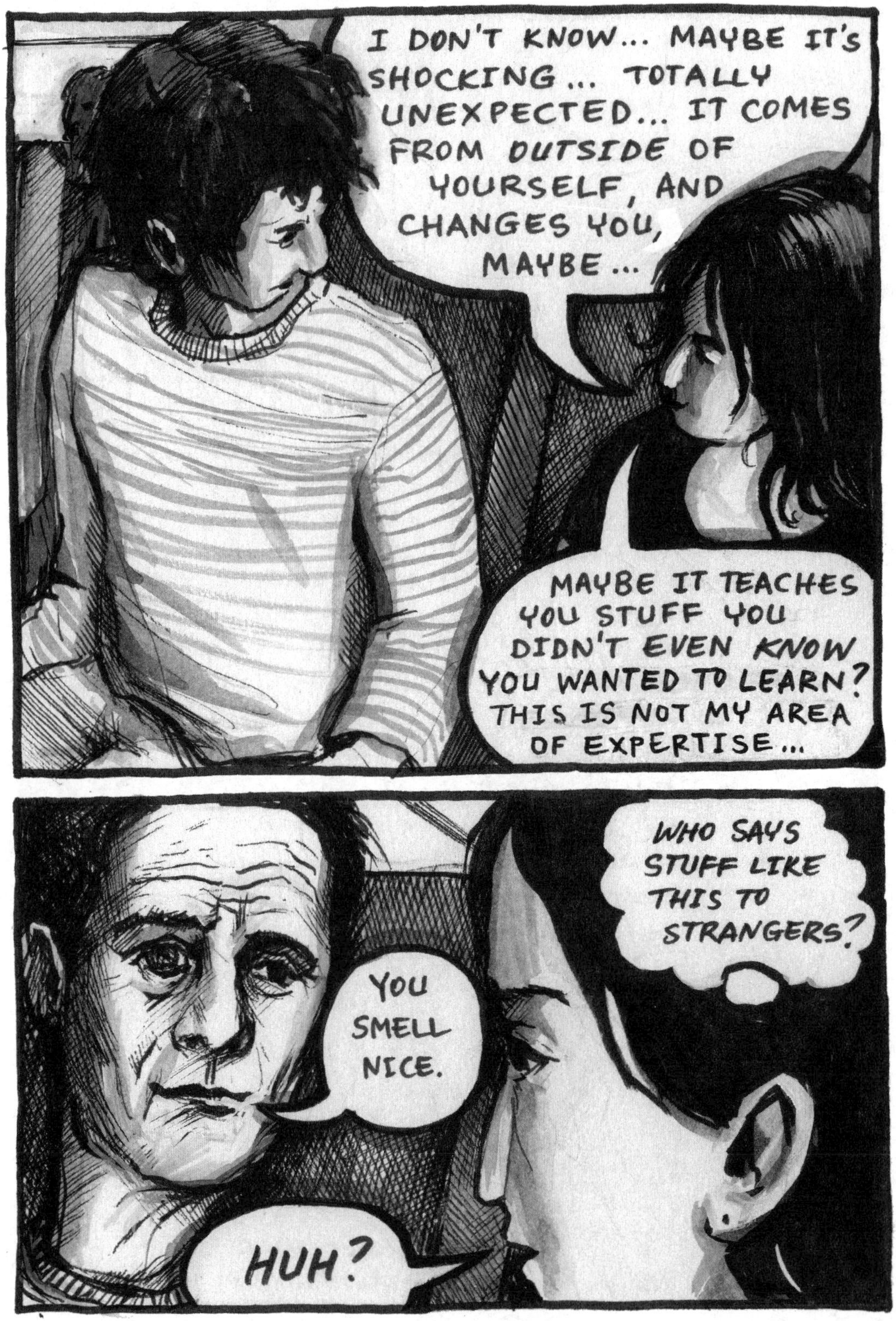
I DON'T KNOW... MAYBE IT'S SHOCKING... TOTALLY UNEXPECTED... IT COMES FROM *OUTSIDE* OF YOURSELF, AND CHANGES YOU, MAYBE...
MAYBE IT TEACHES YOU STUFF YOU DIDN'T EVEN *KNOW* YOU WANTED TO LEARN? THIS IS NOT MY AREA OF EXPERTISE...
WHO SAYS STUFF LIKE THIS TO STRANGERS?
YOU SMELL NICE.
HUH?

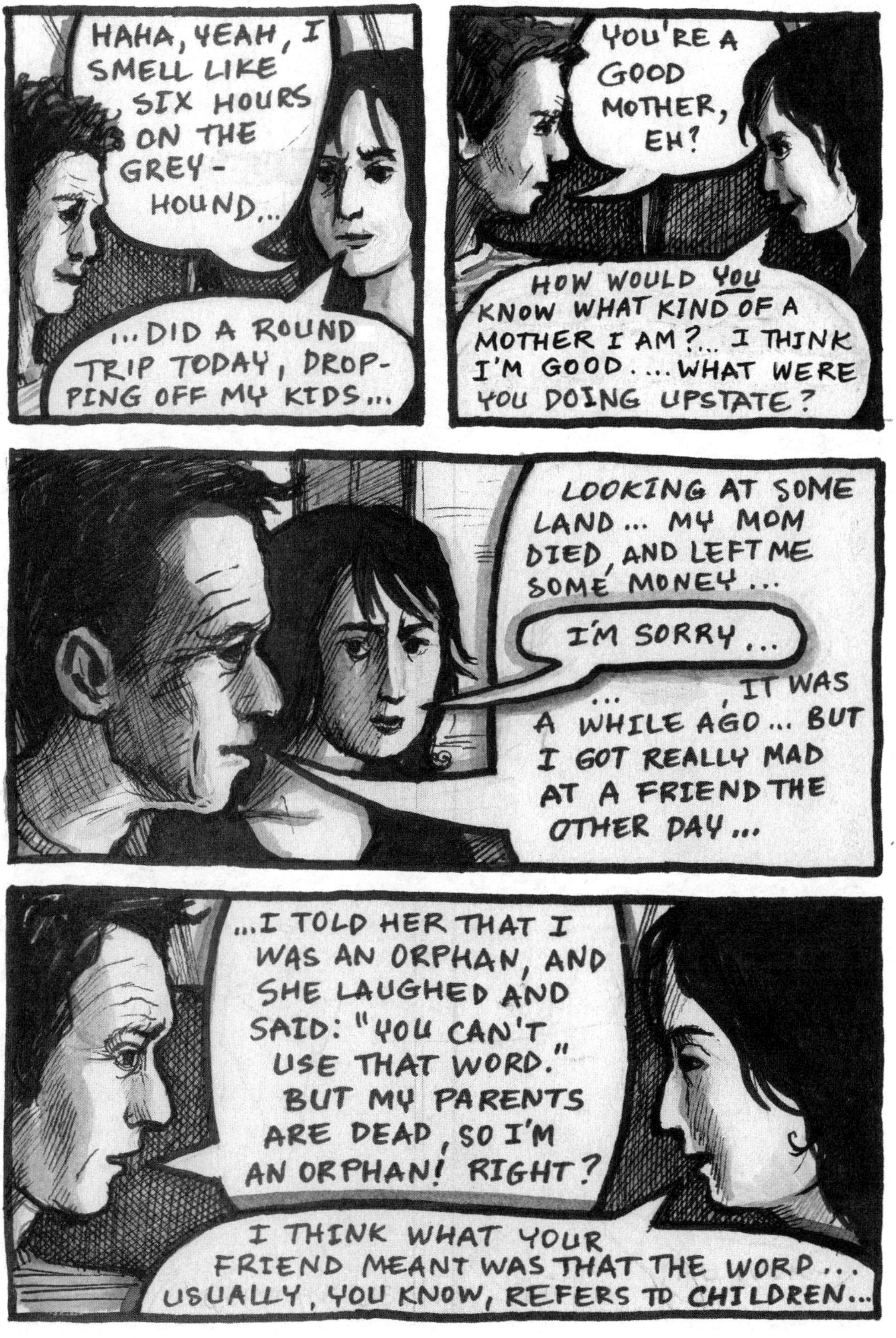
HAHA, YEAH, I SMELL LIKE SIX HOURS ON THE GREY-HOUND...
...DID A ROUND TRIP TODAY, DROP-PING OFF MY KIDS...
YOU'RE A GOOD MOTHER, EH?
HOW WOULD YOU KNOW WHAT KIND OF A MOTHER I AM?... I THINK I'M GOOD.... WHAT WERE YOU DOING UPSTATE?
LOOKING AT SOME LAND... MY MOM DIED, AND LEFT ME SOME MONEY...
I'M SORRY...
..., IT WAS A WHILE AGO... BUT I GOT REALLY MAD AT A FRIEND THE OTHER DAY...
...I TOLD HER THAT I WAS AN ORPHAN, AND SHE LAUGHED AND SAID: "YOU CAN'T USE THAT WORD." BUT MY PARENTS ARE DEAD, SO I'M AN ORPHAN! RIGHT?
I THINK WHAT YOUR FRIEND MEANT WAS THAT THE WORD... USUALLY, YOU KNOW, REFERS TO CHILDREN...

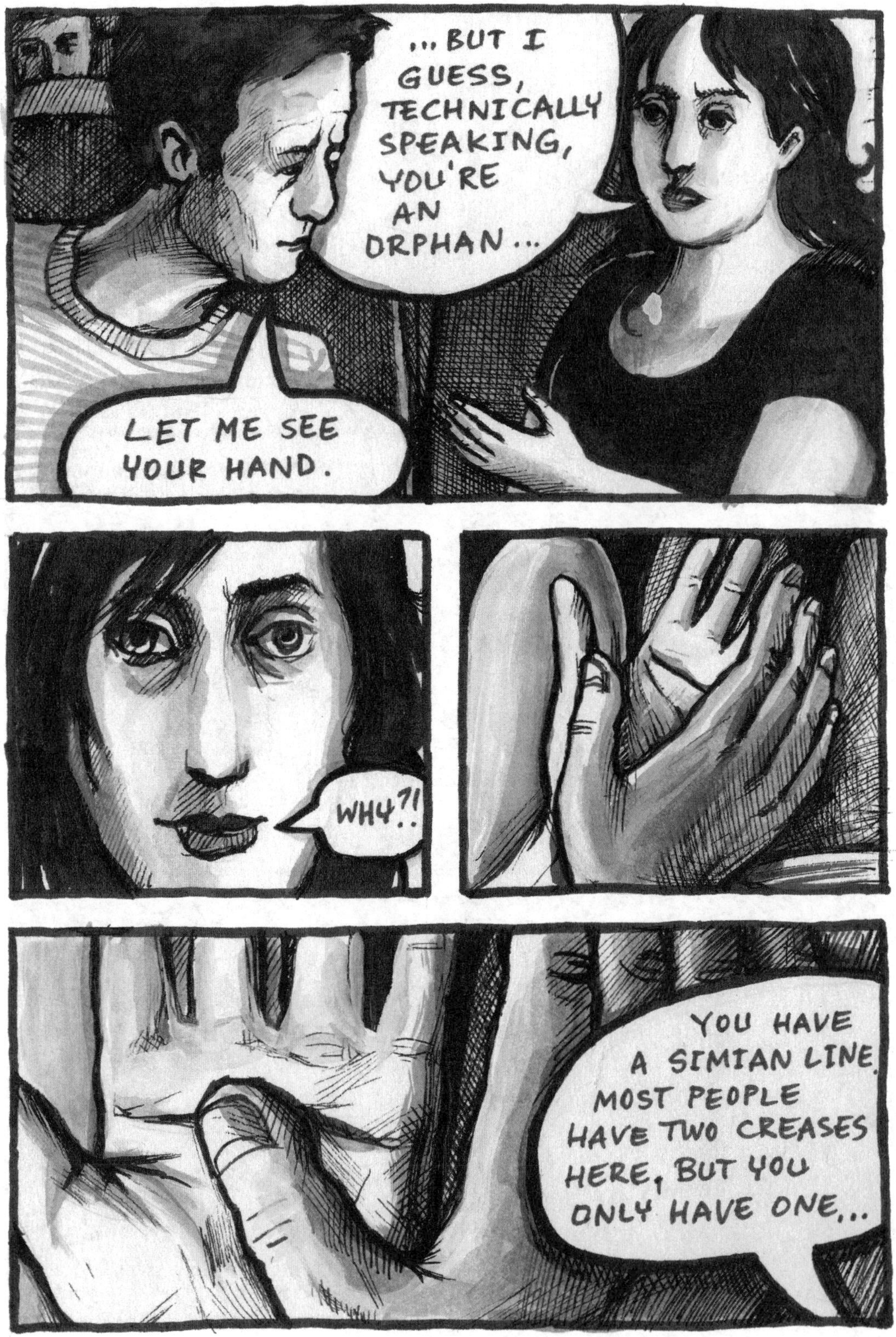
...BUT I GUESS, TECHNICALLY SPEAKING, YOU'RE AN ORPHAN...
LET ME SEE YOUR HAND.
WHY?!
YOU HAVE A SIMIAN LINE. MOST PEOPLE HAVE TWO CREASES HERE, BUT YOU ONLY HAVE ONE...

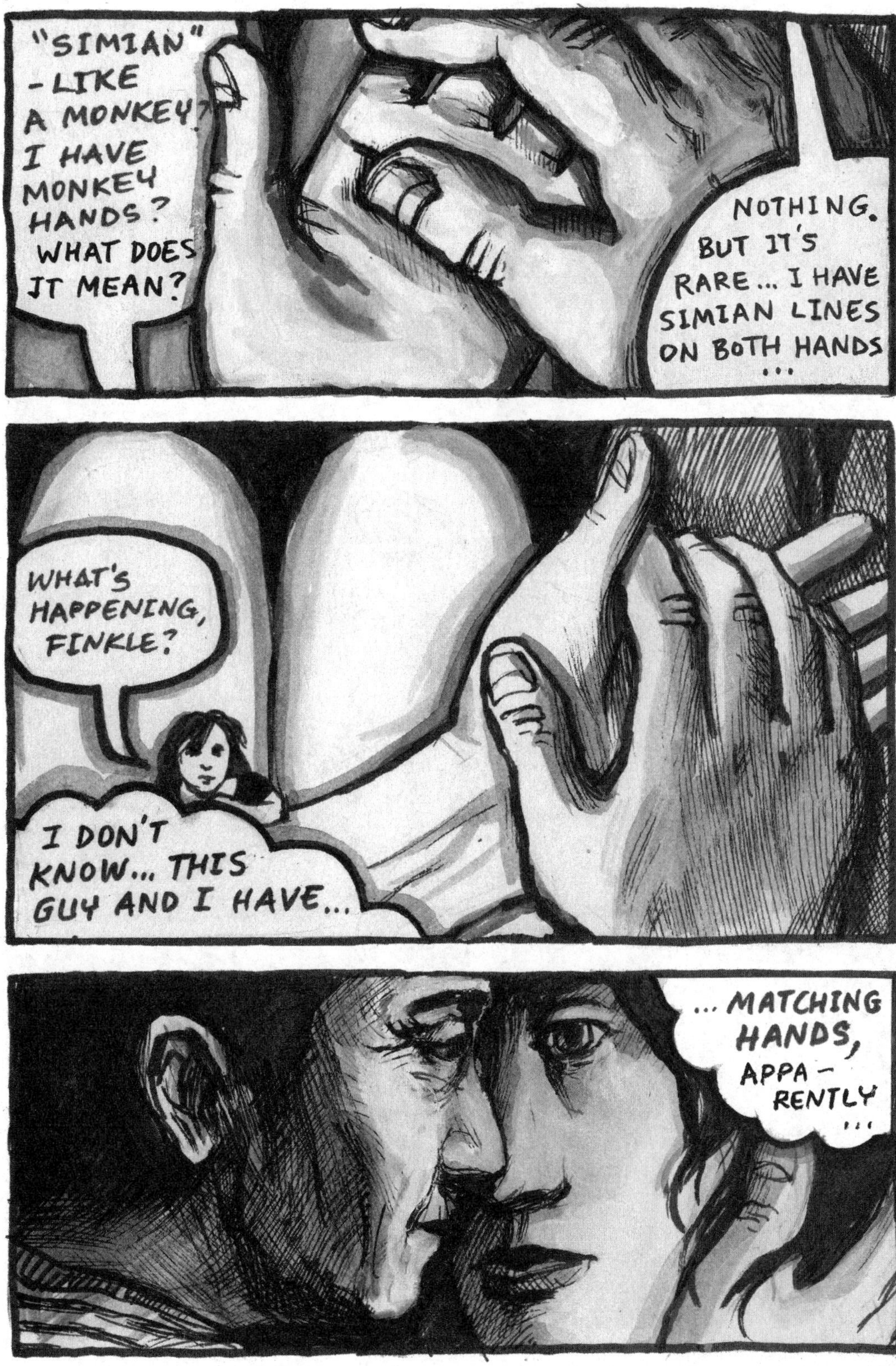
"SIMIAN" -LIKE A MONKEY? I HAVE MONKEY HANDS? WHAT DOES IT MEAN?
NOTHING. BUT IT'S RARE... I HAVE SIMIAN LINES ON BOTH HANDS...
WHAT'S HAPPENING, FINKLE?
I DON'T KNOW... THIS GUY AND I HAVE...
...MATCHING HANDS, APPA-RENTLY...

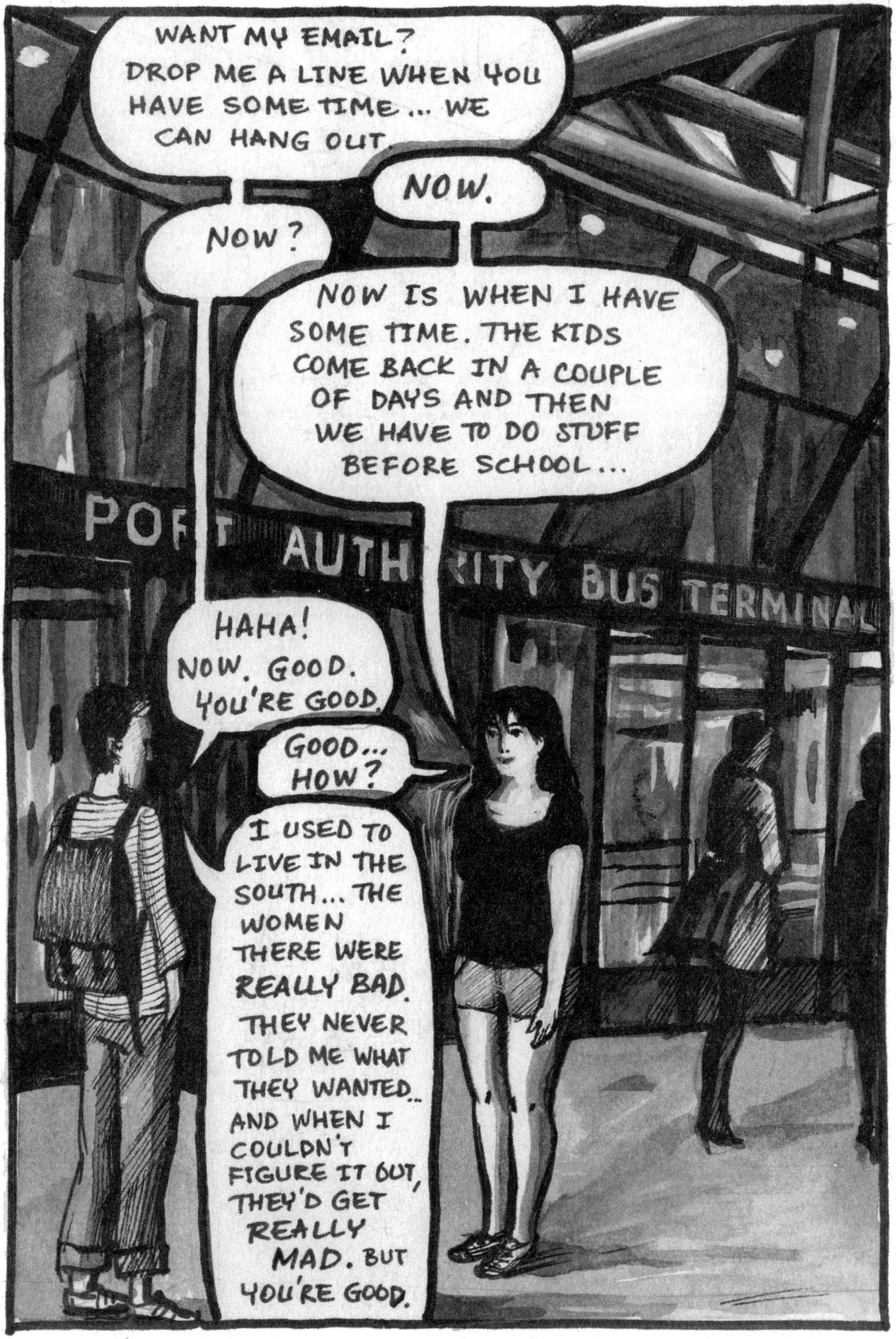
WANT MY EMAIL? DROP ME A LINE WHEN YOU HAVE SOME TIME ... WE CAN HANG OUT.
NOW?
NOW.
NOW IS WHEN I HAVE SOME TIME. THE KIDS COME BACK IN A COUPLE OF DAYS AND THEN WE HAVE TO DO STUFF BEFORE SCHOOL...
HAHA! NOW. GOOD. YOU'RE GOOD.
GOOD... HOW?
I USED TO LIVE IN THE SOUTH... THE WOMEN THERE WERE REALLY BAD. THEY NEVER TOLD ME WHAT THEY WANTED... AND WHEN I COULDN'T FIGURE IT OUT, THEY'D GET REALLY MAD. BUT YOU'RE GOOD.

...LATER, DURING MY YEAR OF UNREASONABLE GRIEF, I WOULD WONDER WHY I DID THIS. WAS IT JUST THE SCHEDULE? PROBABLY, A PART OF ME WAS *DYING* TO FLOUT YVONNE'S RULES.

MOSTLY, IT WAS THAT NOTHING ABOUT THE ORPHAN, INCLUDING MY OWN REACTIONS TO HIM, *ADDED UP.*

I FOUND HIS GAUNT, ASYMMETRIC FACE *FREAKISH* AND HARD TO LOOK AT. IT FLOODED MY BRAIN WITH MOVIE IMAGES OF TORTURED CHILDREN — **BUT I COULDN'T STOP LOOKING...**

(PERHAPS THIS WAS BECAUSE I COULDN'T TELL HOW OLD HE WAS — HE SEEMED TO HAVE SEVERAL FACES. SOME WERE TWENTY. SOME-FIFTY.)

BUT MAINLY, I WAS STARTLED BY THE DISCREPANCY BETWEEN HIS SOFT VOICE (LATER, JACKIE WOULD CALL IT "SQUEAKY") AND *HIS ASSERTIVE TOUCH.* I WANTED TO FEEL LIKE THAT AGAIN — STARTLED...

MOVED...

... AND THE WAY HE TALKS: "REALLY GOOD," "REALLY BAD," "REALLY MAD"... SO BLUNT... KIND OF FUNNY AND SWEET...

WANT TO KNOW SOMETHING? I'VE NEVER MET ANYONE IN REAL LIFE, I MEAN, NOT ON THE INTERNET, SINCE MY TWENTIES...

ME NEITHER!... WITH SOME EXCEPTIONS... *ARE YOU HUNGRY?*

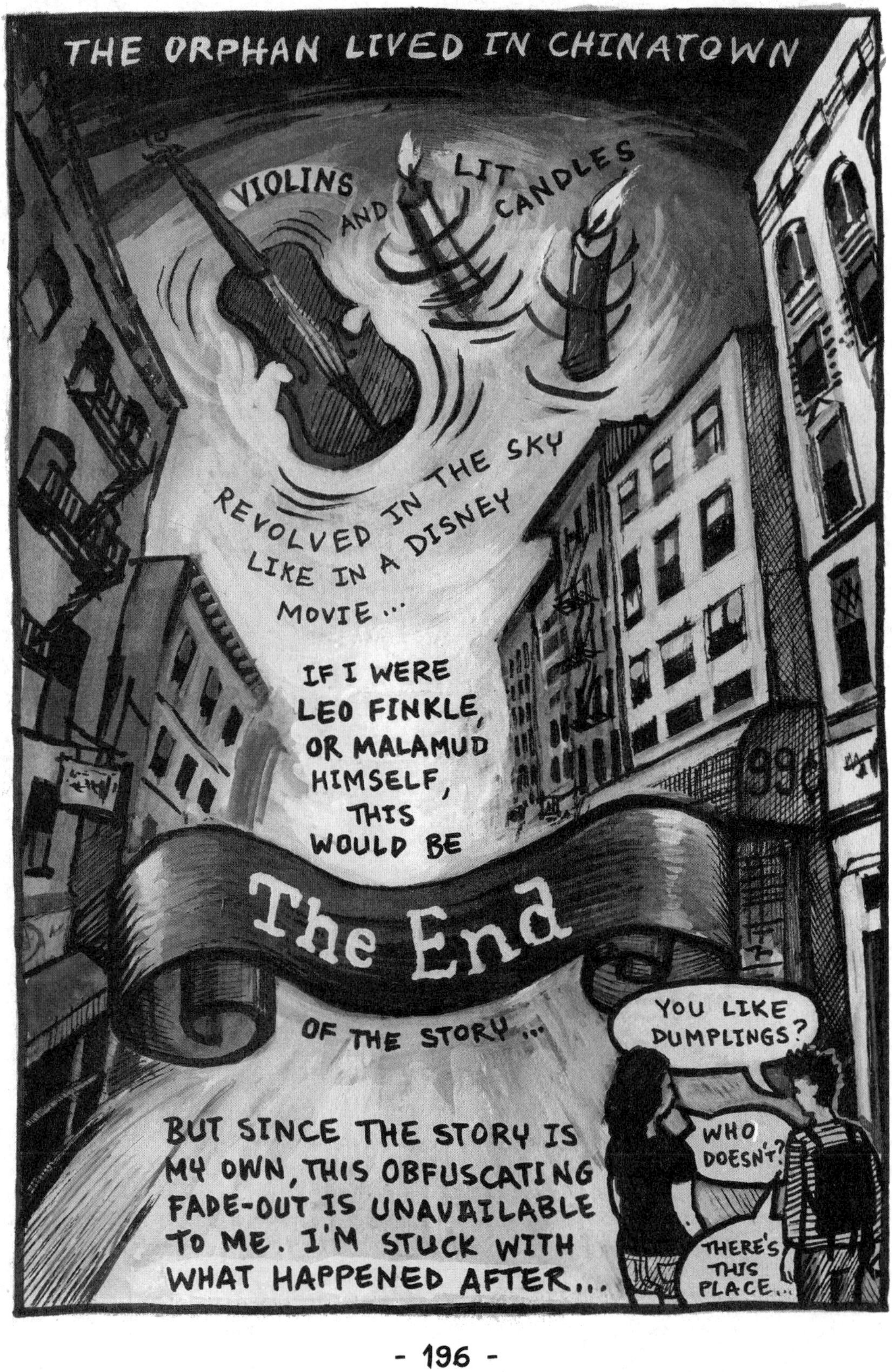
THE ORPHAN LIVED IN CHINATOWN
VIOLINS AND LIT CANDLES
REVOLVED IN THE SKY LIKE IN A DISNEY MOVIE...
IF I WERE LEO FINKLE, OR MALAMUD HIMSELF, THIS WOULD BE
The End
OF THE STORY...
YOU LIKE DUMPLINGS?
WHO DOESN'T?
THERE'S THIS PLACE...
BUT SINCE THE STORY IS MY OWN, THIS OBFUSCATING FADE-OUT IS UNAVAILABLE TO ME. I'M STUCK WITH WHAT HAPPENED AFTER...
99¢

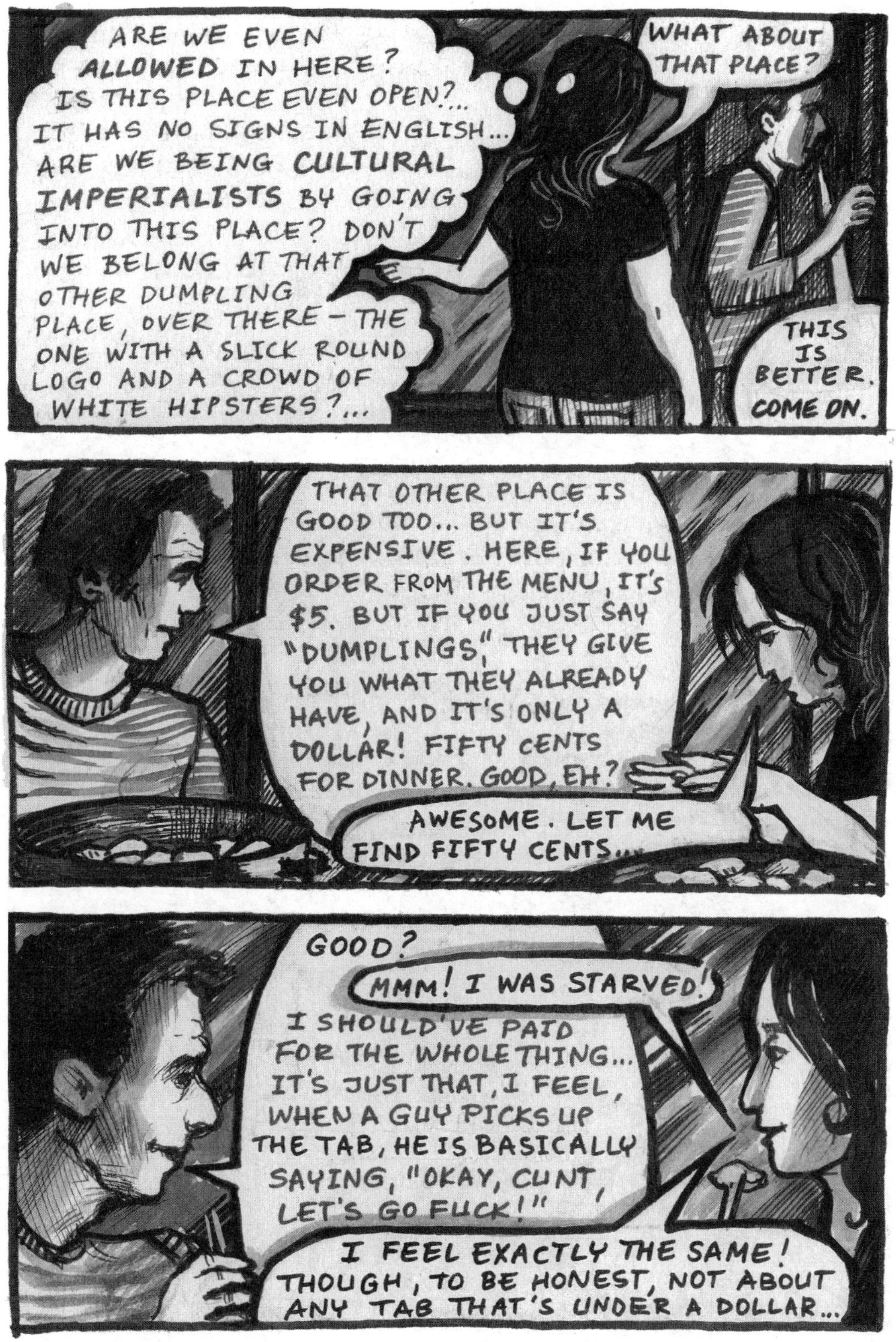

ARE WE EVEN ALLOWED IN HERE? IS THIS PLACE EVEN OPEN?... IT HAS NO SIGNS IN ENGLISH... ARE WE BEING CULTURAL IMPERIALISTS BY GOING INTO THIS PLACE? DON'T WE BELONG AT THAT OTHER DUMPLING PLACE, OVER THERE – THE ONE WITH A SLICK ROUND LOGO AND A CROWD OF WHITE HIPSTERS?...
WHAT ABOUT THAT PLACE?
THIS IS BETTER. COME ON.
THAT OTHER PLACE IS GOOD TOO... BUT IT'S EXPENSIVE. HERE, IF YOU ORDER FROM THE MENU, IT'S $5. BUT IF YOU JUST SAY "DUMPLINGS," THEY GIVE YOU WHAT THEY ALREADY HAVE, AND IT'S ONLY A DOLLAR! FIFTY CENTS FOR DINNER. GOOD, EH?
AWESOME. LET ME FIND FIFTY CENTS...
GOOD?
MMM! I WAS STARVED!
I SHOULD'VE PAID FOR THE WHOLE THING... IT'S JUST THAT, I FEEL, WHEN A GUY PICKS UP THE TAB, HE IS BASICALLY SAYING, "OKAY, CUNT, LET'S GO FUCK!"
I FEEL EXACTLY THE SAME! THOUGH, TO BE HONEST, NOT ABOUT ANY TAB THAT'S UNDER A DOLLAR...

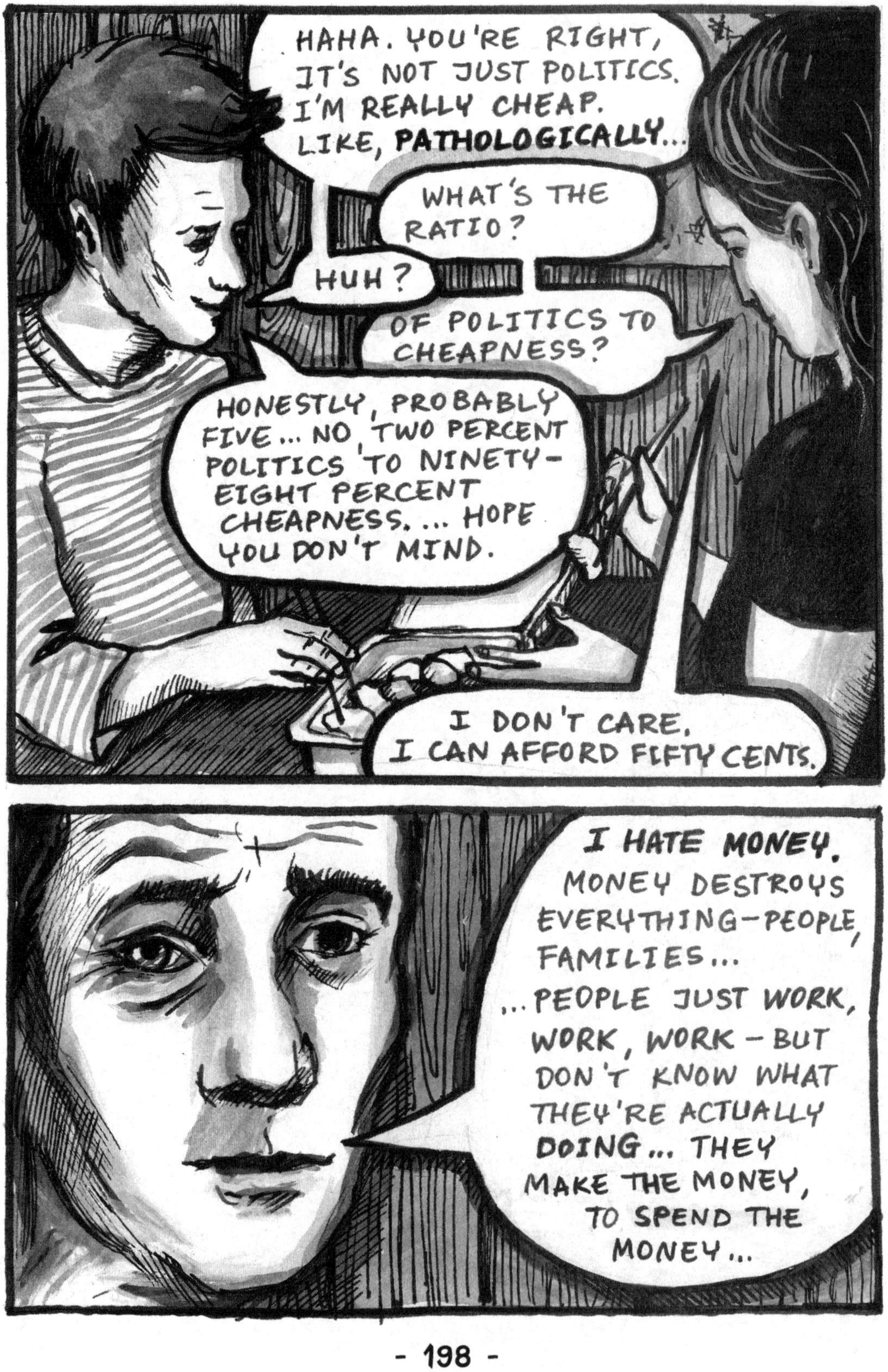
HAHA. YOU'RE RIGHT, IT'S NOT JUST POLITICS. I'M REALLY CHEAP. LIKE, **PATHOLOGICALLY**...
WHAT'S THE RATIO?
HUH?
OF POLITICS TO CHEAPNESS?
HONESTLY, PROBABLY FIVE... NO, TWO PERCENT POLITICS TO NINETY-EIGHT PERCENT CHEAPNESS. ... HOPE YOU DON'T MIND.
I DON'T CARE, I CAN AFFORD FIFTY CENTS.
I HATE MONEY. MONEY DESTROYS EVERYTHING—PEOPLE, FAMILIES... ...PEOPLE JUST **WORK**, WORK, WORK—BUT DON'T KNOW WHAT THEY'RE ACTUALLY **DOING**... THEY MAKE THE MONEY, TO SPEND THE MONEY...

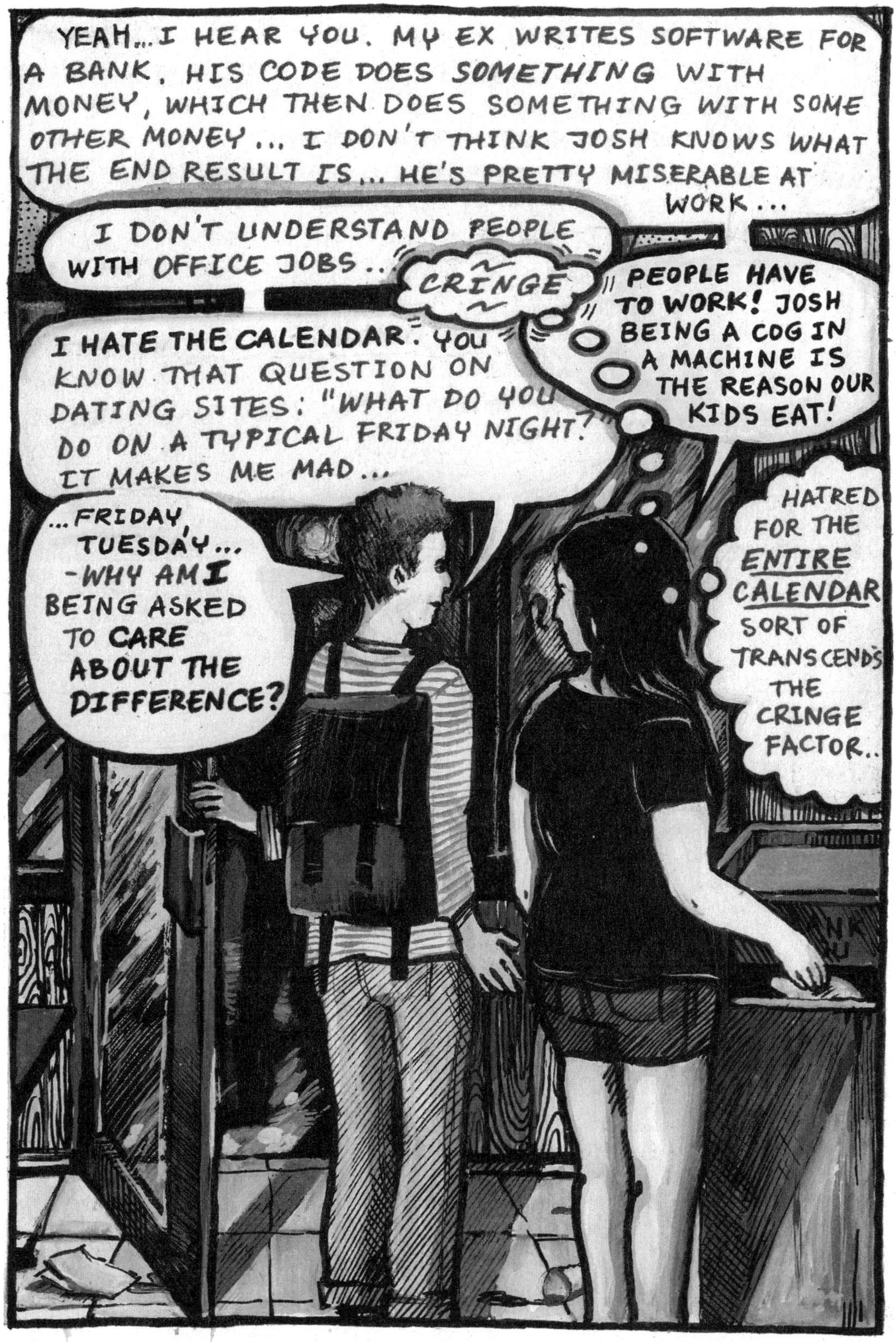
YEAH... I HEAR YOU. MY EX WRITES SOFTWARE FOR A BANK. HIS CODE DOES SOMETHING WITH MONEY, WHICH THEN DOES SOMETHING WITH SOME OTHER MONEY ... I DON'T THINK JOSH KNOWS WHAT THE END RESULT IS... HE'S PRETTY MISERABLE AT WORK...
I DON'T UNDERSTAND PEOPLE WITH OFFICE JOBS...
CRINGE
PEOPLE HAVE TO WORK! JOSH BEING A COG IN A MACHINE IS THE REASON OUR KIDS EAT!
I HATE THE CALENDAR. YOU KNOW THAT QUESTION ON DATING SITES: "WHAT DO YOU DO ON A TYPICAL FRIDAY NIGHT?" IT MAKES ME MAD...
...FRIDAY, TUESDAY... -WHY AM I BEING ASKED TO CARE ABOUT THE DIFFERENCE?
HATRED FOR THE ENTIRE CALENDAR SORT OF TRANSCENDS THE CRINGE FACTOR..

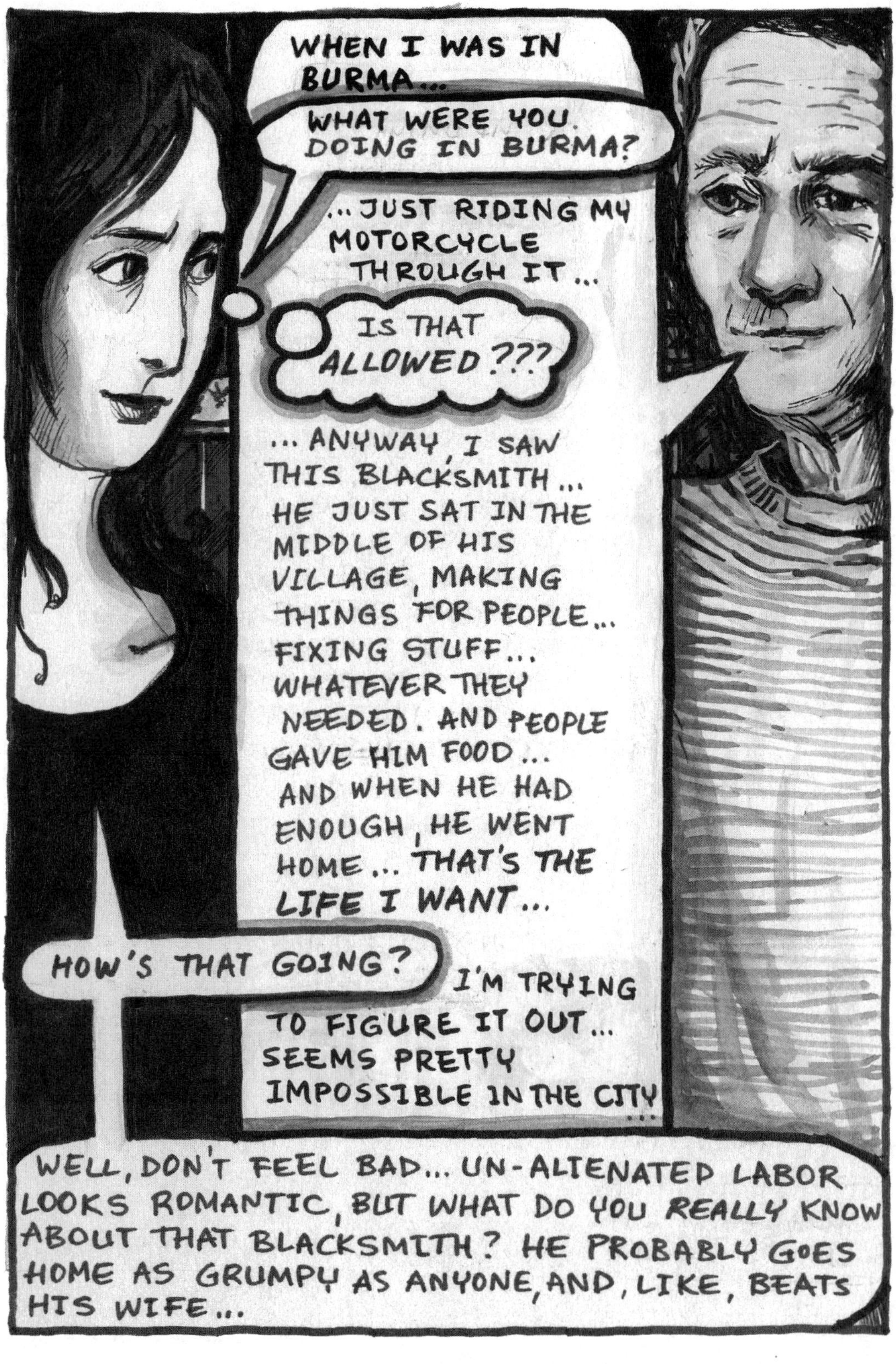
WHEN I WAS IN BURMA...
WHAT WERE YOU DOING IN BURMA?
...JUST RIDING MY MOTORCYCLE THROUGH IT...
IS THAT ALLOWED???
...ANYWAY, I SAW THIS BLACKSMITH... HE JUST SAT IN THE MIDDLE OF HIS VILLAGE, MAKING THINGS FOR PEOPLE... FIXING STUFF... WHATEVER THEY NEEDED. AND PEOPLE GAVE HIM FOOD... AND WHEN HE HAD ENOUGH, HE WENT HOME... THAT'S THE LIFE I WANT...
HOW'S THAT GOING?
I'M TRYING TO FIGURE IT OUT... SEEMS PRETTY IMPOSSIBLE IN THE CITY...
WELL, DON'T FEEL BAD... UN-ALIENATED LABOR LOOKS ROMANTIC, BUT WHAT DO YOU REALLY KNOW ABOUT THAT BLACKSMITH? HE PROBABLY GOES HOME AS GRUMPY AS ANYONE, AND, LIKE, BEATS HIS WIFE...

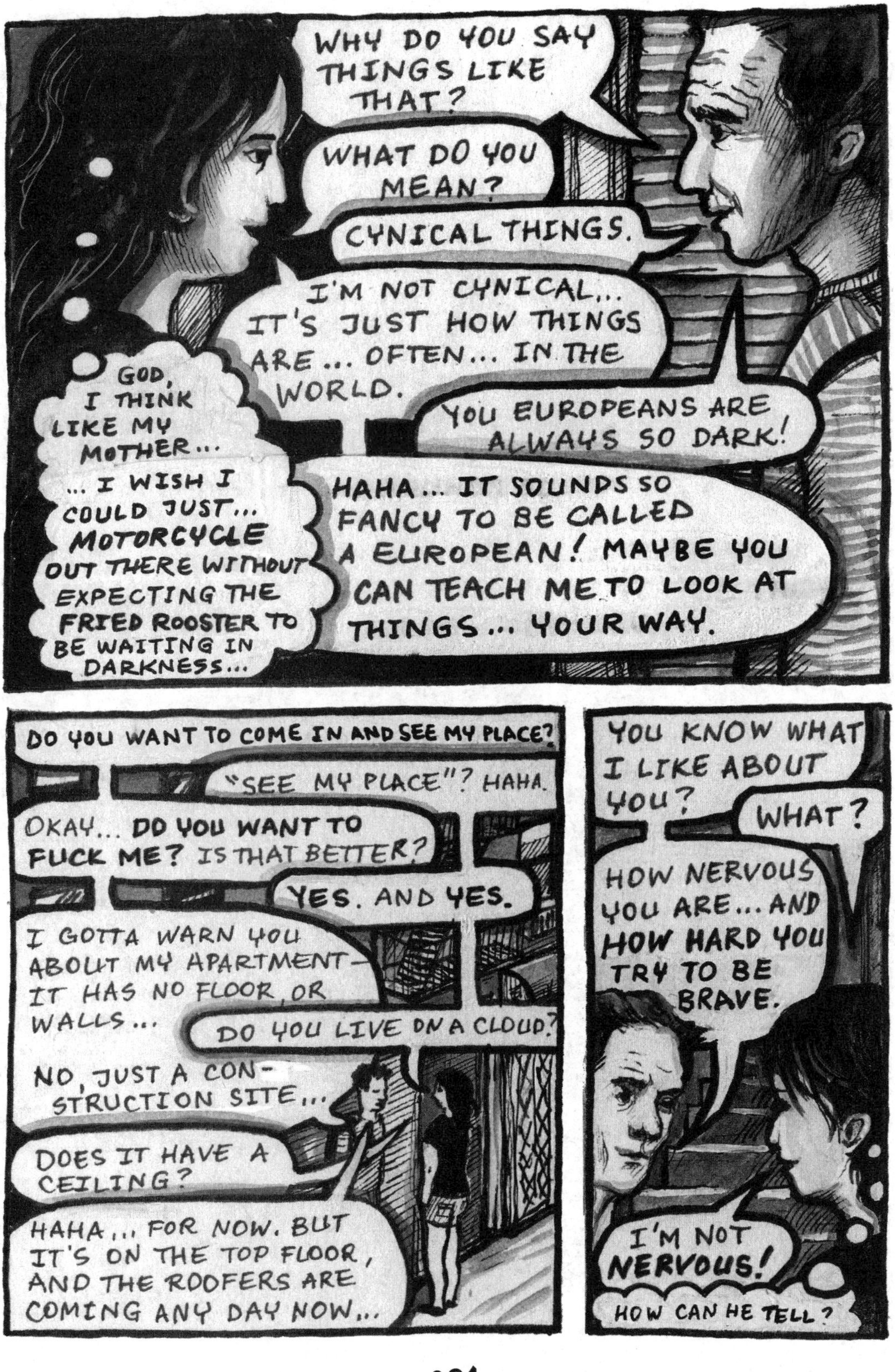
WHY DO YOU SAY THINGS LIKE THAT?
WHAT DO YOU MEAN?
CYNICAL THINGS.
I'M NOT CYNICAL... IT'S JUST HOW THINGS ARE... OFTEN... IN THE WORLD.
GOD, I THINK LIKE MY MOTHER...
YOU EUROPEANS ARE ALWAYS SO DARK!
... I WISH I COULD JUST... MOTORCYCLE OUT THERE WITHOUT EXPECTING THE FRIED ROOSTER TO BE WAITING IN DARKNESS...
HAHA... IT SOUNDS SO FANCY TO BE CALLED A EUROPEAN! MAYBE YOU CAN TEACH ME TO LOOK AT THINGS... YOUR WAY.
DO YOU WANT TO COME IN AND SEE MY PLACE?
"SEE MY PLACE"? HAHA.
OKAY... DO YOU WANT TO FUCK ME? IS THAT BETTER?
YES. AND YES.
I GOTTA WARN YOU ABOUT MY APARTMENT- IT HAS NO FLOOR, OR WALLS...
DO YOU LIVE ON A CLOUD?
NO, JUST A CON-STRUCTION SITE...
DOES IT HAVE A CEILING?
HAHA... FOR NOW. BUT IT'S ON THE TOP FLOOR, AND THE ROOFERS ARE COMING ANY DAY NOW...
YOU KNOW WHAT I LIKE ABOUT YOU?
WHAT?
HOW NERVOUS YOU ARE... AND HOW HARD YOU TRY TO BE BRAVE.
I'M NOT NERVOUS!
HOW CAN HE TELL?

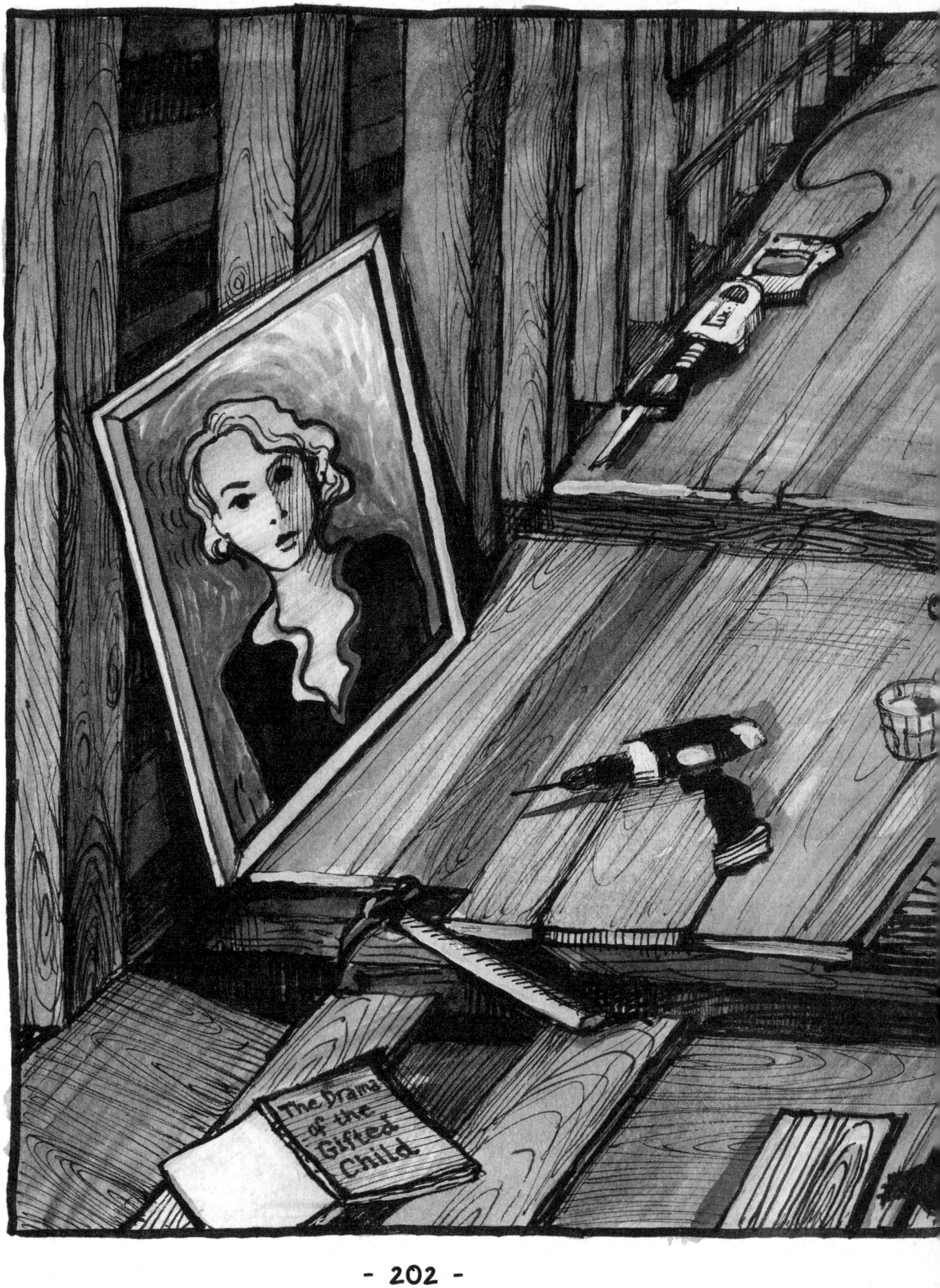
The Drama of the Gifted Child

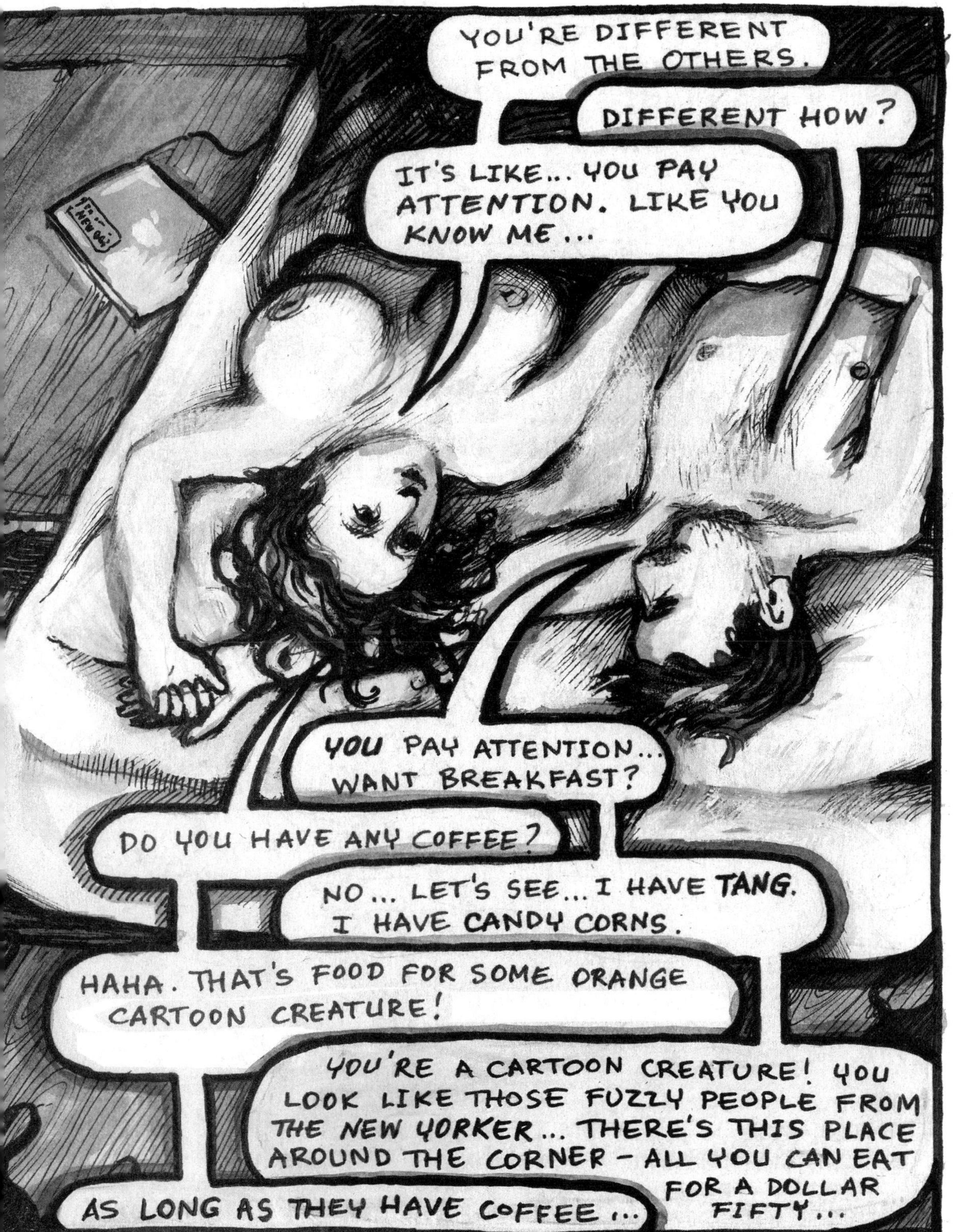
YOU'RE DIFFERENT FROM THE OTHERS.
DIFFERENT HOW?
IT'S LIKE... YOU PAY ATTENTION. LIKE YOU KNOW ME...
YOU PAY ATTENTION... WANT BREAKFAST?
DO YOU HAVE ANY COFFEE?
NO... LET'S SEE... I HAVE TANG. I HAVE CANDY CORNS.
HAHA. THAT'S FOOD FOR SOME ORANGE CARTOON CREATURE!
YOU'RE A CARTOON CREATURE! YOU LOOK LIKE THOSE FUZZY PEOPLE FROM THE NEW YORKER... THERE'S THIS PLACE AROUND THE CORNER - ALL YOU CAN EAT FOR A DOLLAR FIFTY...
AS LONG AS THEY HAVE COFFEE...

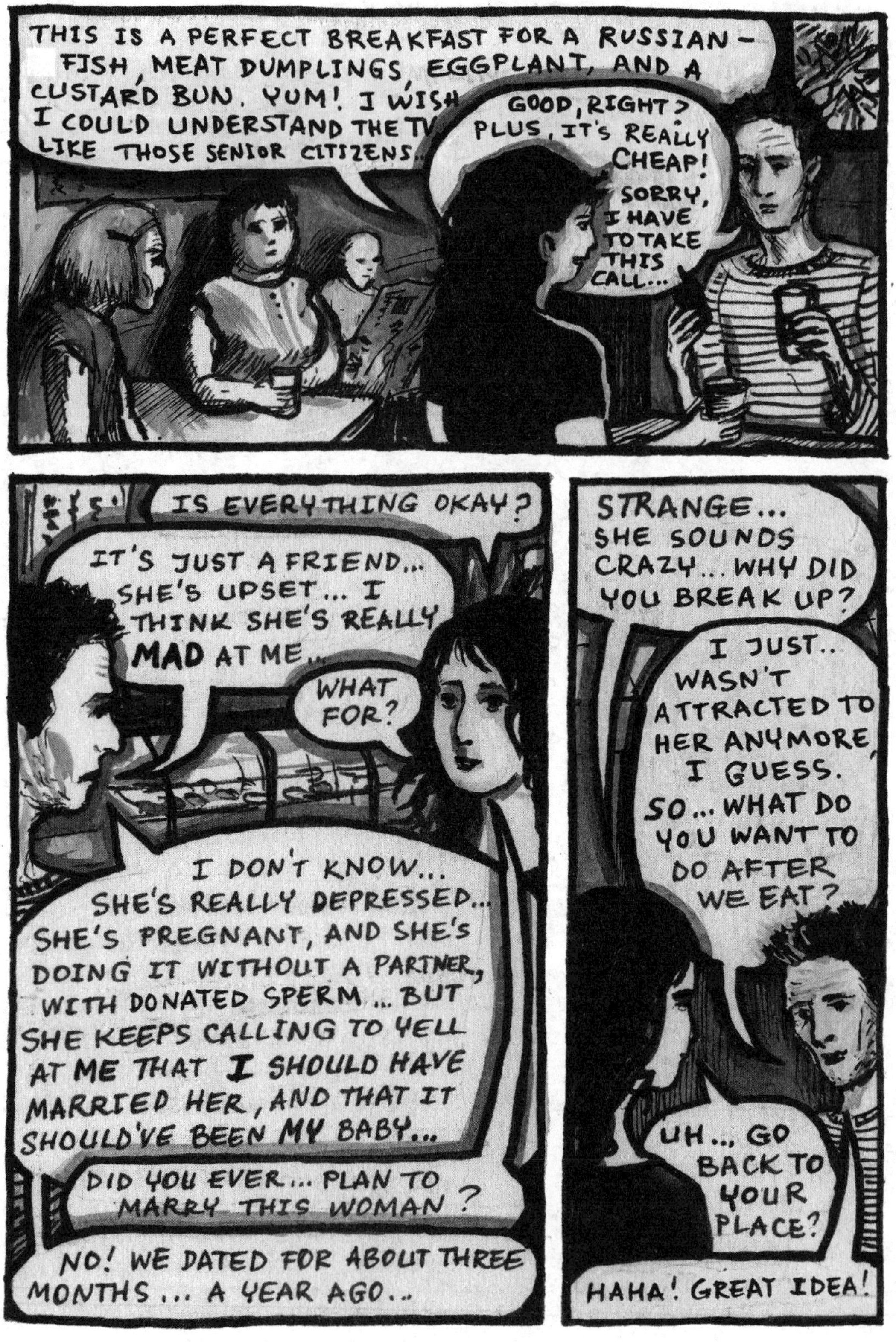

THIS IS A PERFECT BREAKFAST FOR A RUSSIAN - FISH, MEAT DUMPLINGS, EGGPLANT, AND A CUSTARD BUN. YUM! I WISH I COULD UNDERSTAND THE TV LIKE THOSE SENIOR CITIZENS...
GOOD, RIGHT? PLUS, IT'S REALLY CHEAP!
SORRY, I HAVE TO TAKE THIS CALL...
IS EVERYTHING OKAY?
IT'S JUST A FRIEND... SHE'S UPSET... I THINK SHE'S REALLY MAD AT ME...
WHAT FOR?
I DON'T KNOW... SHE'S REALLY DEPRESSED... SHE'S PREGNANT, AND SHE'S DOING IT WITHOUT A PARTNER, WITH DONATED SPERM... BUT SHE KEEPS CALLING TO YELL AT ME THAT I SHOULD HAVE MARRIED HER, AND THAT IT SHOULD'VE BEEN MY BABY...
DID YOU EVER... PLAN TO MARRY THIS WOMAN?
NO! WE DATED FOR ABOUT THREE MONTHS... A YEAR AGO...
STRANGE... SHE SOUNDS CRAZY... WHY DID YOU BREAK UP?
I JUST.. WASN'T ATTRACTED TO HER ANYMORE, I GUESS. SO... WHAT DO YOU WANT TO DO AFTER WE EAT?
UH..., GO BACK TO YOUR PLACE?
HAHA! GREAT IDEA!

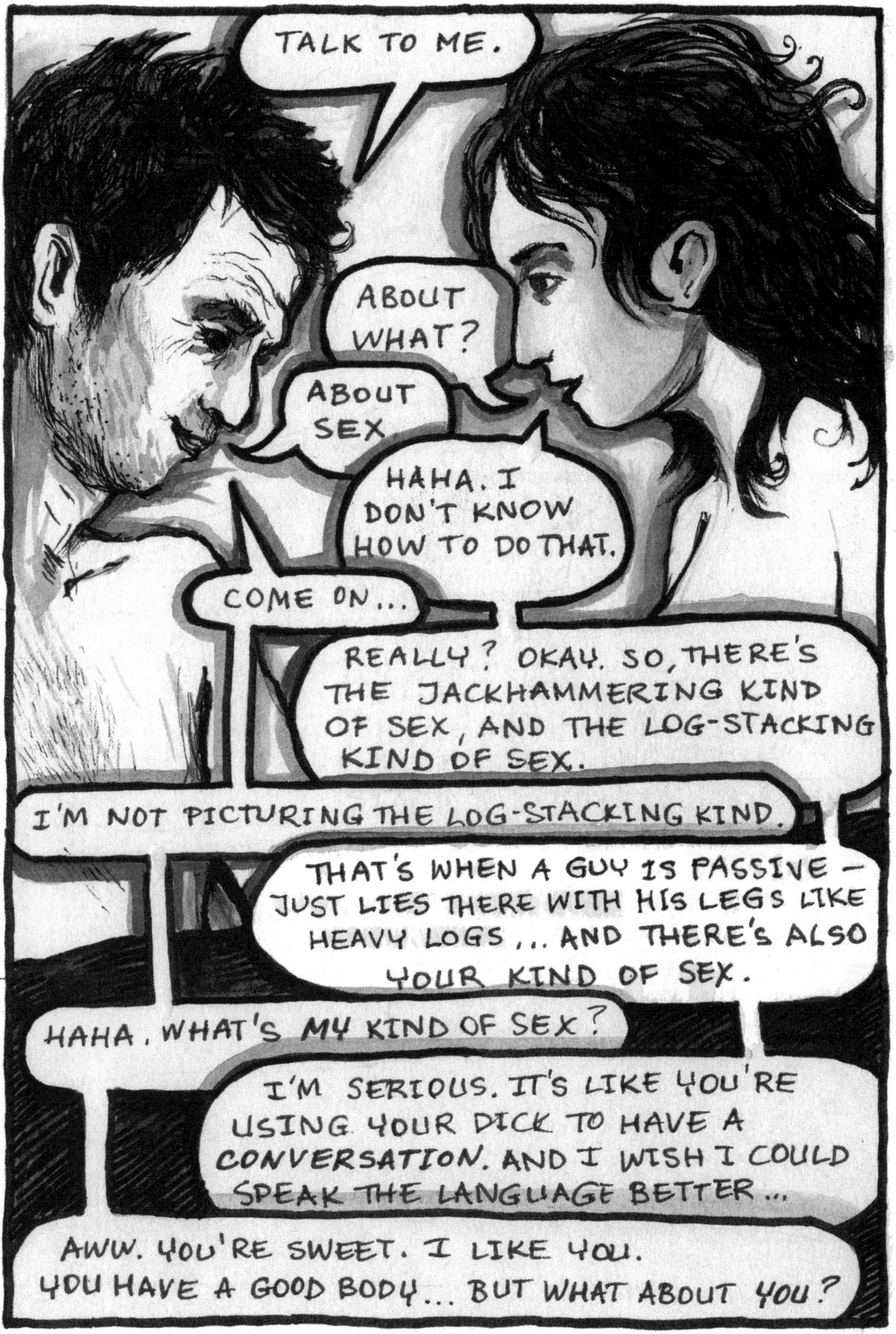
TALK TO ME.
ABOUT WHAT?
ABOUT SEX.
HAHA. I DON'T KNOW HOW TO DO THAT.
COME ON...
REALLY? OKAY. SO, THERE'S THE JACKHAMMERING KIND OF SEX, AND THE LOG-STACKING KIND OF SEX.
I'M NOT PICTURING THE LOG-STACKING KIND.
THAT'S WHEN A GUY IS PASSIVE – JUST LIES THERE WITH HIS LEGS LIKE HEAVY LOGS... AND THERE'S ALSO YOUR KIND OF SEX.
HAHA. WHAT'S MY KIND OF SEX?
I'M SERIOUS. IT'S LIKE YOU'RE USING YOUR DICK TO HAVE A CONVERSATION. AND I WISH I COULD SPEAK THE LANGUAGE BETTER...
AWW. YOU'RE SWEET. I LIKE YOU. YOU HAVE A GOOD BODY... BUT WHAT ABOUT YOU?

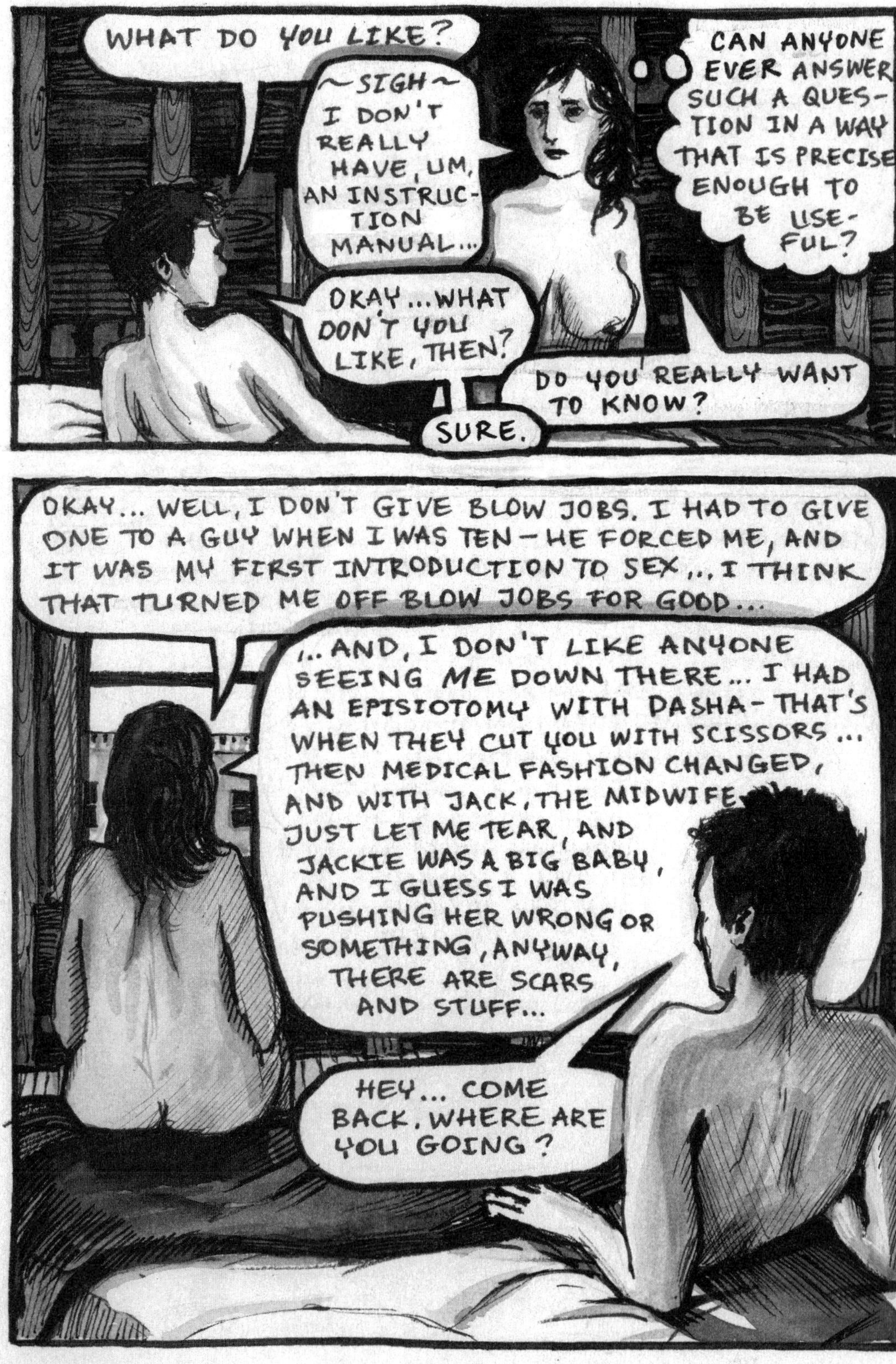
WHAT DO YOU LIKE?
~SIGH~ I DON'T REALLY HAVE, UM, AN INSTRUCTION MANUAL...
CAN ANYONE EVER ANSWER SUCH A QUESTION IN A WAY THAT IS PRECISE ENOUGH TO BE USEFUL?
OKAY... WHAT DON'T YOU LIKE, THEN?
DO YOU REALLY WANT TO KNOW?
SURE.
OKAY... WELL, I DON'T GIVE BLOW JOBS. I HAD TO GIVE ONE TO A GUY WHEN I WAS TEN—HE FORCED ME, AND IT WAS MY FIRST INTRODUCTION TO SEX... I THINK THAT TURNED ME OFF BLOW JOBS FOR GOOD...
...AND, I DON'T LIKE ANYONE SEEING ME DOWN THERE... I HAD AN EPISIOTOMY WITH DASHA—THAT'S WHEN THEY CUT YOU WITH SCISSORS... THEN MEDICAL FASHION CHANGED, AND WITH JACK, THE MIDWIFE JUST LET ME TEAR, AND JACKIE WAS A BIG BABY, AND I GUESS I WAS PUSHING HER WRONG OR SOMETHING, ANYWAY, THERE ARE SCARS AND STUFF...
HEY... COME BACK. WHERE ARE YOU GOING?

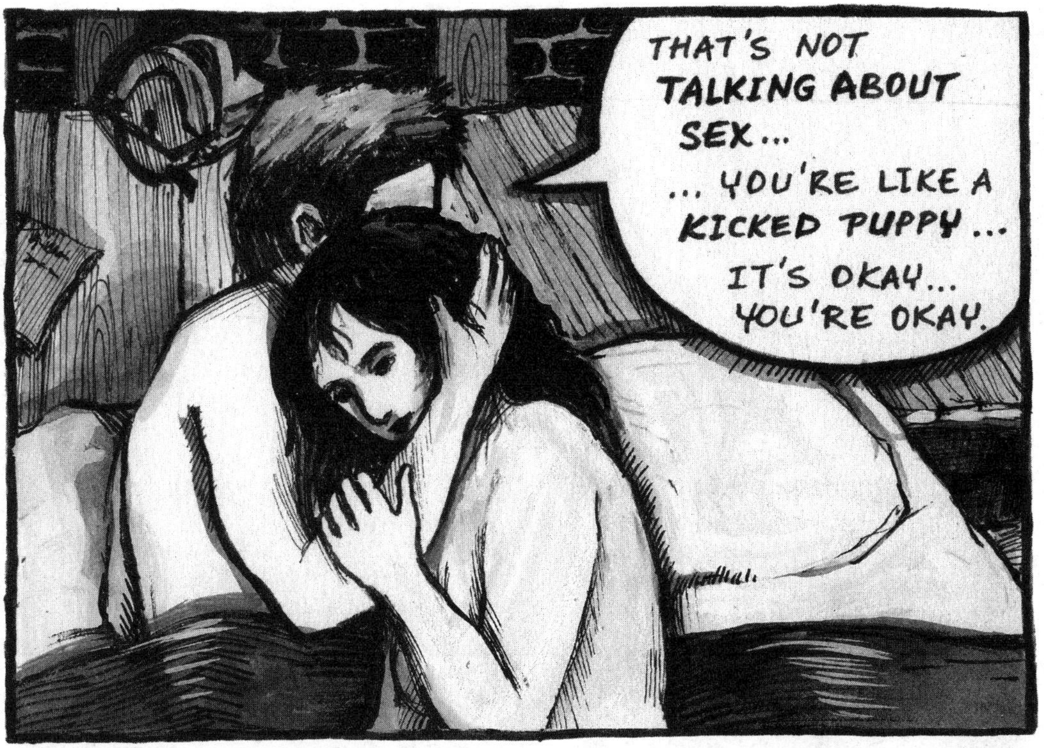
THAT'S NOT TALKING ABOUT SEX... ... YOU'RE LIKE A KICKED PUPPY... IT'S OKAY... YOU'RE OKAY.

I WANTED TO TELL THE ORPHAN THAT I WAS NOTHING LIKE A "KICKED PUPPY." (WHAT KIND OF A PHRASE WAS THAT, ANYWAY?) I WAS HAPPY, AND TOUGH, AND FINE. BUT THE SOUND OF THE ORPHAN'S VOICE, SO SOFT AND WHISPERY, FELT UNEXPECTEDLY GOOD. I COULD FEEL IT IN MY BODY, LIKE AN INJECTION OF A SUBSTANCE I DIDN'T KNOW I'D BEEN MISSING. MY EAST EUROPEAN BACK-BRAIN IMMEDIATELY FOUND THE WORD "PITY" TO DESCRIBE THIS THING, BUT THE SOCIALLY ACCEPTABLE WORD WAS PROBABLY "EMPATHY." APPARENTLY, THE "KICKED PUPPY" PART OF ME, SUCH AS IT WAS, HAD BEEN *DYING* TO BE DISCOVERED AND ACKNOWLEDGED.

I FELT HOT AND LIQUID ON THE INSIDE...

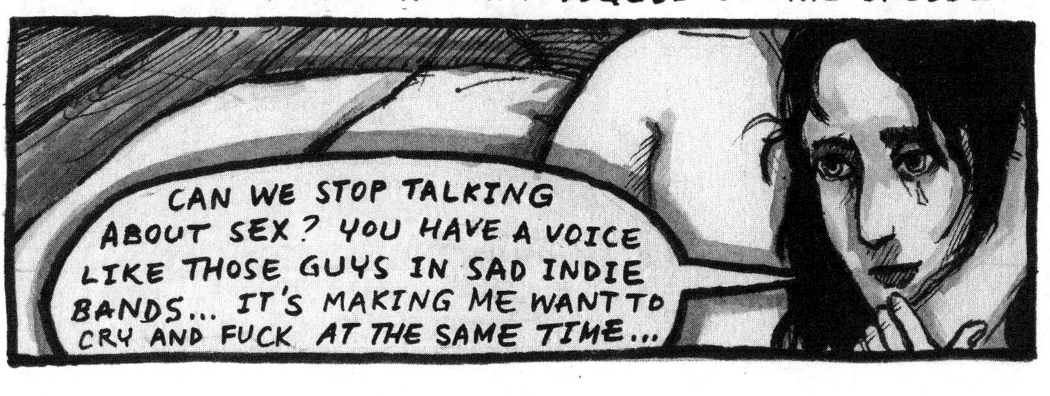
CAN WE STOP TALKING ABOUT SEX? YOU HAVE A VOICE LIKE THOSE GUYS IN SAD INDIE BANDS... IT'S MAKING ME WANT TO CRY AND FUCK AT THE SAME TIME...

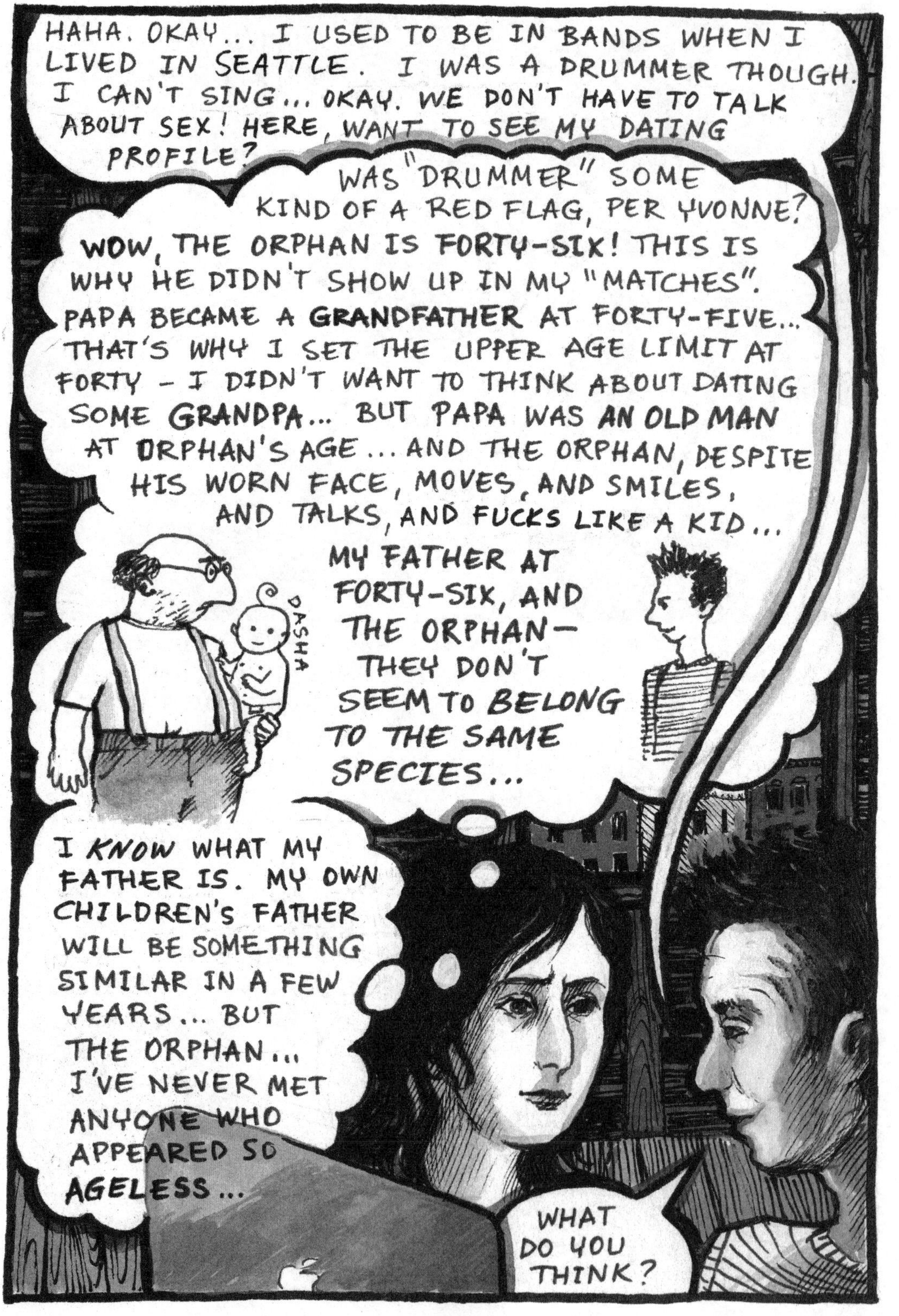
HAHA. OKAY... I USED TO BE IN BANDS WHEN I LIVED IN SEATTLE. I WAS A DRUMMER THOUGH. I CAN'T SING... OKAY. WE DON'T HAVE TO TALK ABOUT SEX! HERE, WANT TO SEE MY DATING PROFILE?
WAS "DRUMMER" SOME KIND OF A RED FLAG, PER YVONNE?
WOW, THE ORPHAN IS FORTY-SIX! THIS IS WHY HE DIDN'T SHOW UP IN MY "MATCHES". PAPA BECAME A GRANDFATHER AT FORTY-FIVE... THAT'S WHY I SET THE UPPER AGE LIMIT AT FORTY - I DIDN'T WANT TO THINK ABOUT DATING SOME GRANDPA... BUT PAPA WAS AN OLD MAN AT ORPHAN'S AGE... AND THE ORPHAN, DESPITE HIS WORN FACE, MOVES, AND SMILES, AND TALKS, AND FUCKS LIKE A KID...
DASHA
MY FATHER AT FORTY-SIX, AND THE ORPHAN— THEY DON'T SEEM TO BELONG TO THE SAME SPECIES...
I KNOW WHAT MY FATHER IS. MY OWN CHILDREN'S FATHER WILL BE SOMETHING SIMILAR IN A FEW YEARS... BUT THE ORPHAN... I'VE NEVER MET ANYONE WHO APPEARED SO AGELESS...
WHAT DO YOU THINK?

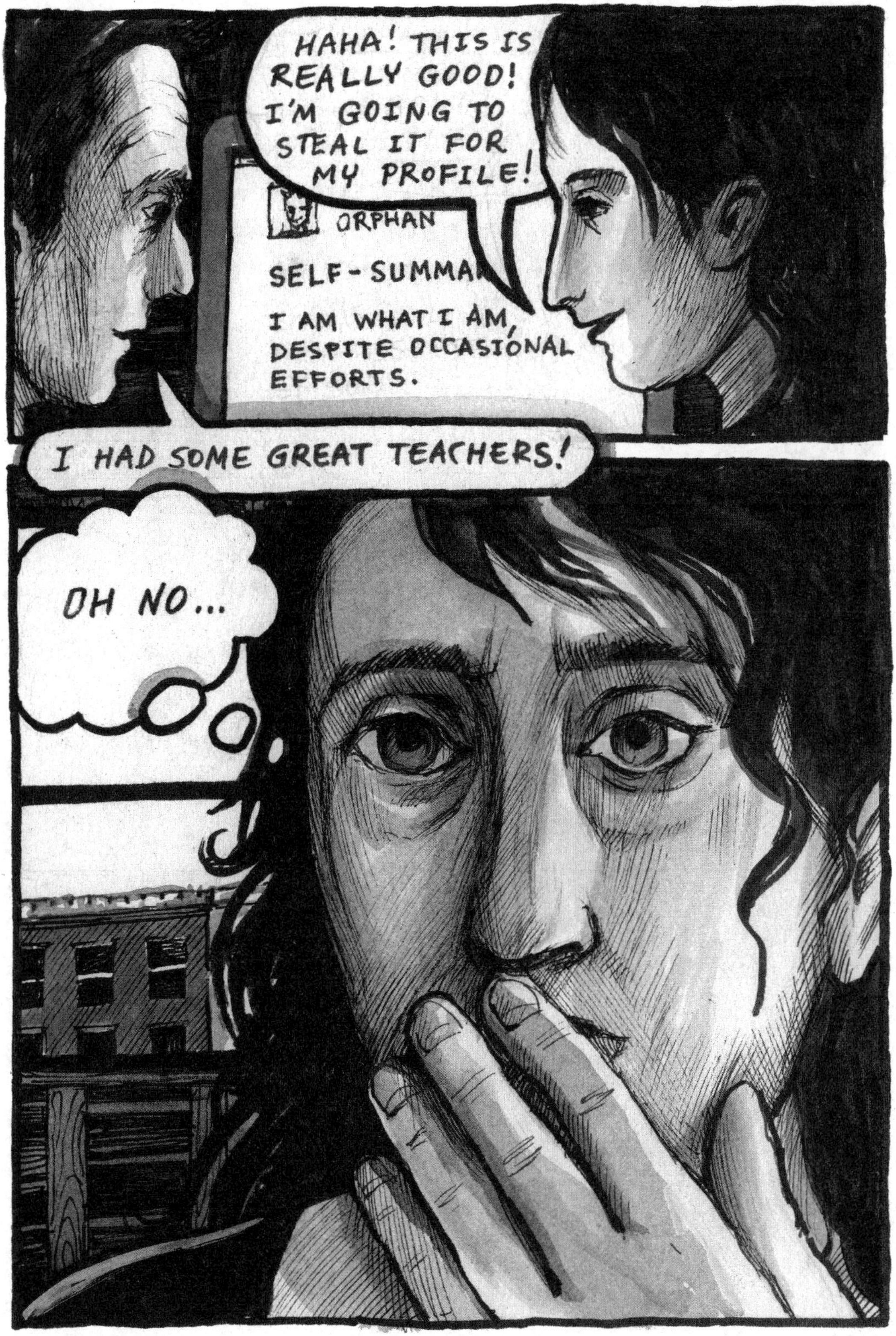
HAHA! THIS IS REALLY GOOD! I'M GOING TO STEAL IT FOR MY PROFILE!
ORPHAN
SELF-SUMMA
I AM WHAT I AM, DESPITE OCCASIONAL EFFORTS.
I HAD SOME GREAT TEACHERS!
OH NO...

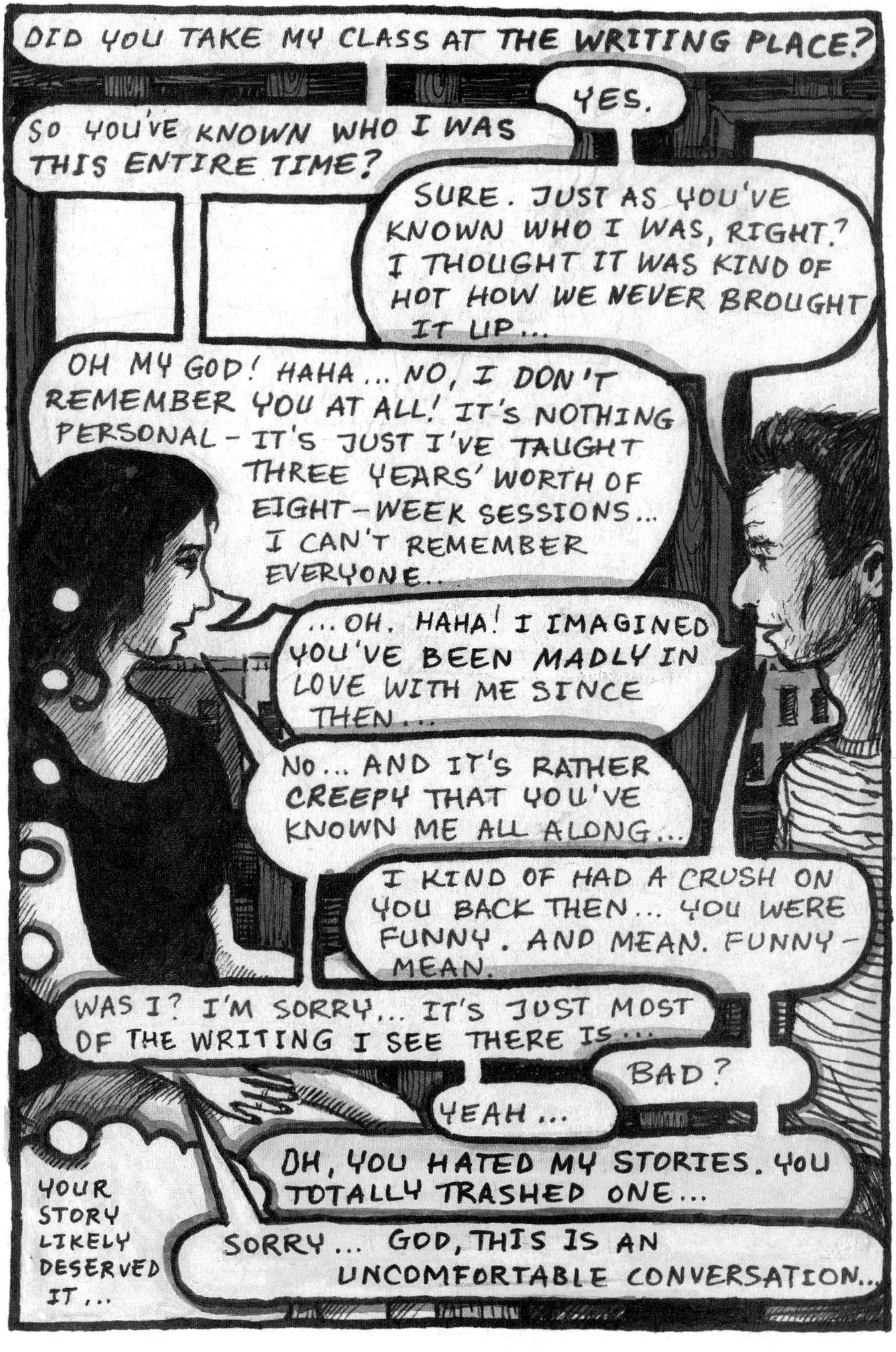
DID YOU TAKE MY CLASS AT THE WRITING PLACE?
YES.
SO YOU'VE KNOWN WHO I WAS THIS ENTIRE TIME?
SURE. JUST AS YOU'VE KNOWN WHO I WAS, RIGHT? I THOUGHT IT WAS KIND OF HOT HOW WE NEVER BROUGHT IT UP...
OH MY GOD! HAHA... NO, I DON'T REMEMBER YOU AT ALL! IT'S NOTHING PERSONAL - IT'S JUST I'VE TAUGHT THREE YEARS' WORTH OF EIGHT-WEEK SESSIONS... I CAN'T REMEMBER EVERYONE..
...OH. HAHA! I IMAGINED YOU'VE BEEN MADLY IN LOVE WITH ME SINCE THEN...
NO... AND IT'S RATHER CREEPY THAT YOU'VE KNOWN ME ALL ALONG...
I KIND OF HAD A CRUSH ON YOU BACK THEN... YOU WERE FUNNY. AND MEAN. FUNNY-MEAN.
WAS I? I'M SORRY... IT'S JUST MOST OF THE WRITING I SEE THERE IS...
BAD?
YEAH...
OH, YOU HATED MY STORIES. YOU TOTALLY TRASHED ONE...
YOUR STORY LIKELY DESERVED IT...
SORRY... GOD, THIS IS AN UNCOMFORTABLE CONVERSATION...

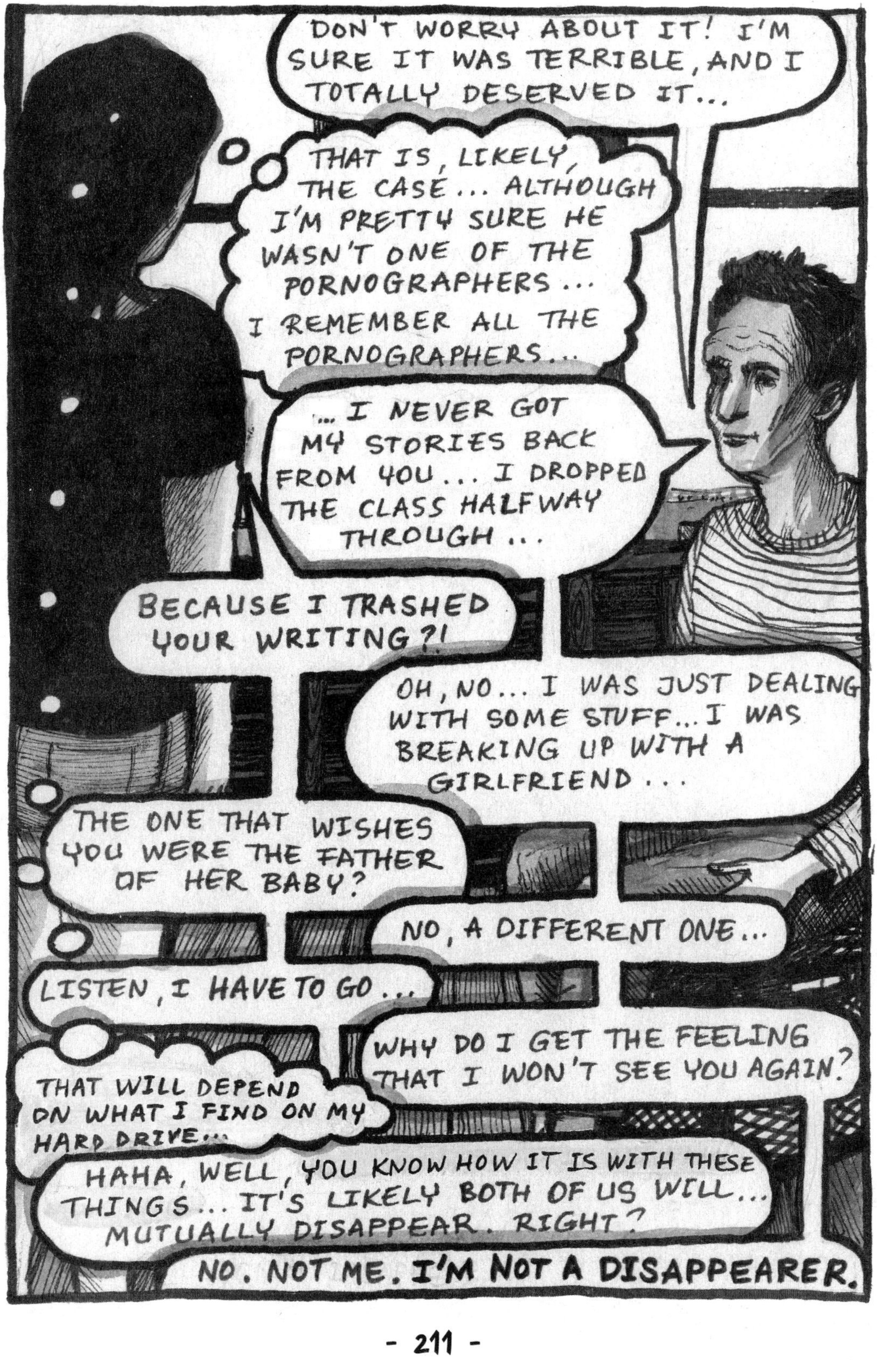
DON'T WORRY ABOUT IT! I'M SURE IT WAS TERRIBLE, AND I TOTALLY DESERVED IT...
THAT IS, LIKELY, THE CASE... ALTHOUGH I'M PRETTY SURE HE WASN'T ONE OF THE PORNOGRAPHERS... I REMEMBER ALL THE PORNOGRAPHERS...
...I NEVER GOT MY STORIES BACK FROM YOU... I DROPPED THE CLASS HALFWAY THROUGH...
BECAUSE I TRASHED YOUR WRITING?!
OH, NO... I WAS JUST DEALING WITH SOME STUFF... I WAS BREAKING UP WITH A GIRLFRIEND...
THE ONE THAT WISHES YOU WERE THE FATHER OF HER BABY?
NO, A DIFFERENT ONE...
LISTEN, I HAVE TO GO...
WHY DO I GET THE FEELING THAT I WON'T SEE YOU AGAIN?
THAT WILL DEPEND ON WHAT I FIND ON MY HARD DRIVE...
HAHA, WELL, YOU KNOW HOW IT IS WITH THESE THINGS... IT'S LIKELY BOTH OF US WILL... MUTUALLY DISAPPEAR. RIGHT?
NO. NOT ME. I'M NOT A DISAPPEARER.

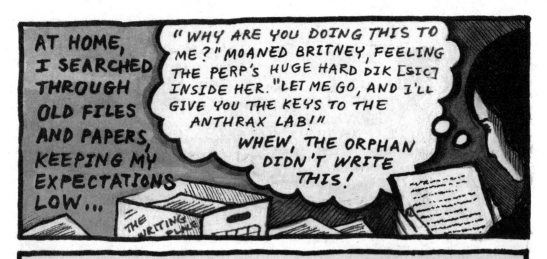

AT HOME, I SEARCHED THROUGH OLD FILES AND PAPERS, KEEPING MY EXPECTATIONS LOW...

THE WRITING PILE

"WHY ARE YOU DOING THIS TO ME?" MOANED BRITNEY, FEELING THE PERP'S HUGE HARD DIK [SIC] INSIDE HER. "LET ME GO, AND I'LL GIVE YOU THE KEYS TO THE ANTHRAX LAB!"

WHEW, THE ORPHAN DIDN'T WRITE THIS!

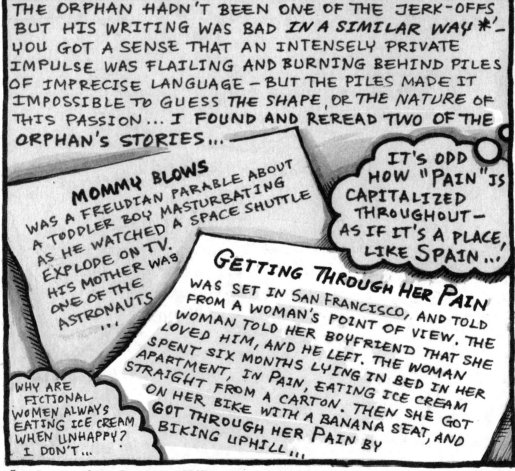

THE ORPHAN HADN'T BEEN ONE OF THE JERK-OFFS BUT HIS WRITING WAS BAD *IN A SIMILAR WAY* *‒ YOU GOT A SENSE THAT AN INTENSELY PRIVATE IMPULSE WAS FLAILING AND BURNING BEHIND PILES OF IMPRECISE LANGUAGE ‒ BUT THE PILES MADE IT IMPOSSIBLE TO GUESS THE SHAPE, OR THE NATURE OF THIS PASSION... I FOUND AND REREAD TWO OF THE ORPHAN'S STORIES...

MOMMY BLOWS WAS A FREUDIAN PARABLE ABOUT A TODDLER BOY MASTURBATING AS HE WATCHED A SPACE SHUTTLE EXPLODE ON TV. HIS MOTHER WAS ONE OF THE ASTRONAUTS...

IT'S ODD HOW "PAIN" IS CAPITALIZED THROUGHOUT‒ AS IF IT'S A PLACE, LIKE SPAIN...

GETTING THROUGH HER PAIN WAS SET IN SAN FRANCISCO, AND TOLD FROM A WOMAN'S POINT OF VIEW. THE WOMAN TOLD HER BOYFRIEND THAT SHE LOVED HIM, AND HE LEFT. THE WOMAN SPENT SIX MONTHS LYING IN BED IN HER APARTMENT, IN PAIN, EATING ICE CREAM STRAIGHT FROM A CARTON. THEN SHE GOT ON HER BIKE WITH A BANANA SEAT, AND GOT THROUGH HER PAIN BY BIKING UPHILL...

WHY ARE FICTIONAL WOMEN ALWAYS EATING ICE CREAM WHEN UNHAPPY? I DON'T...

* AS OPPOSED TO THE OTHER KIND OF BAD: THE LIFELESS YARNS OF GLAMOROUS DIAMOND HEISTS AND VAMPIRE ROMANCES, WRITTEN WITH HOPES OF PUBLICATION... THE JERK-OFFS, AND THE ORPHAN, APPEARED TO WRITE FOR THE DRAWER.

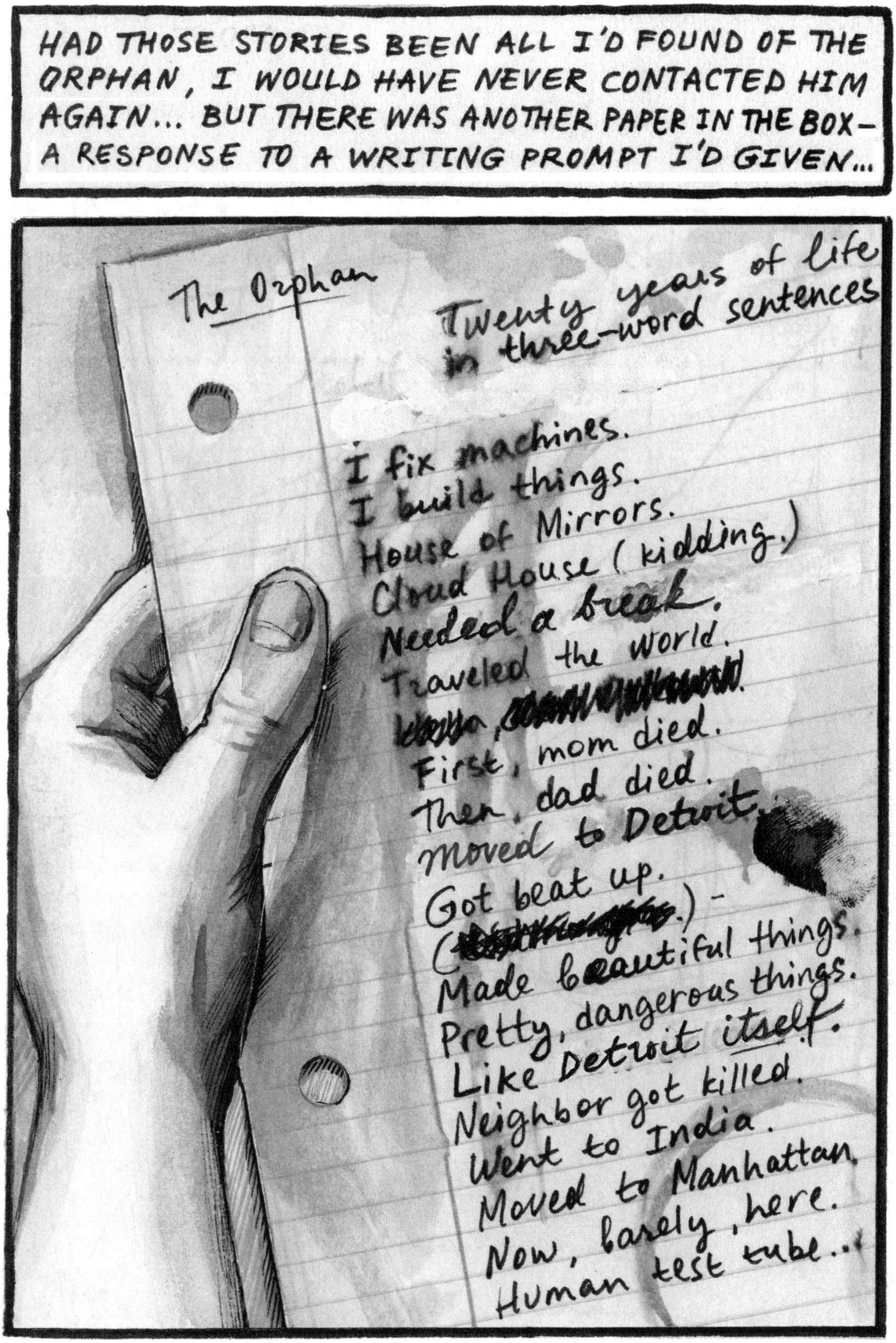
HAD THOSE STORIES BEEN ALL I'D FOUND OF THE ORPHAN, I WOULD HAVE NEVER CONTACTED HIM AGAIN... BUT THERE WAS ANOTHER PAPER IN THE BOX—A RESPONSE TO A WRITING PROMPT I'D GIVEN...
The Orphan
Twenty years of life in three-word sentences
I fix machines.
I build things.
House of Mirrors.
Cloud House (kidding.)
Needed a break.
Traveled the world.
First, mom died.
Then, dad died.
Moved to Detroit.
Got beat up.
Made beautiful things.
Pretty, dangerous things.
Like Detroit itself.
Neighbor got killed.
Went to India.
Moved to Manhattan.
Now, barely, here.
Human test tube...

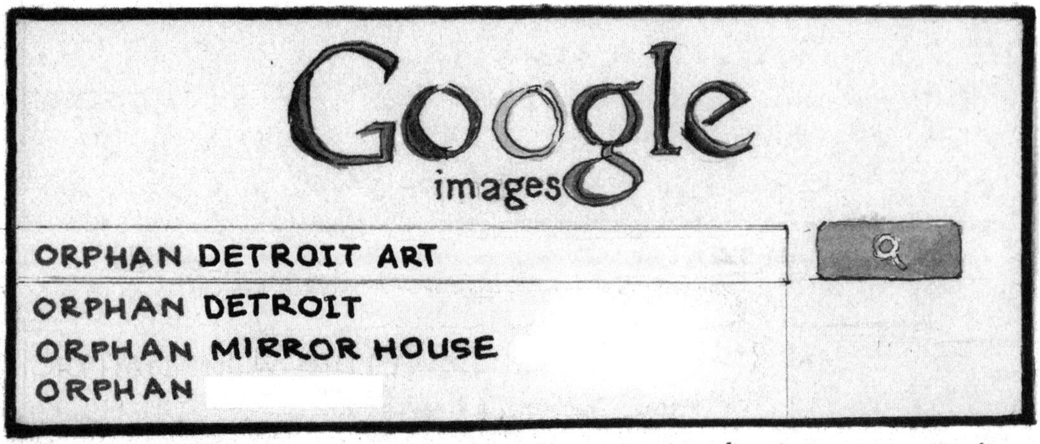
Google
images
ORPHAN DETROIT ART
ORPHAN DETROIT
ORPHAN MIRROR HOUSE
ORPHAN

I'D ALWAYS THOUGHT THAT I COULDN'T FALL FOR A BAD WRITER. BUT AS I SCROLLED THROUGH IMAGES OF THINGS THAT THE ORPHAN HAD BUILT—A HOUSE SHEATHED IN MIRRORS TO THE POINT OF DIS-APPEARING; LAMPS AND CLOCKS MADE OF URBAN DEBRIS, THAT DELIVERED A MILD ELECTRIC SHOCK WHEN TOUCHED—I REALIZED THAT THE ORPHAN'S WRITING WAS *BESIDE THE POINT*.

HE DIDN'T MAKE ART WITH LANGUAGE; HE MADE IT WITH HIS HANDS, AND HE WAS **GOOD**.

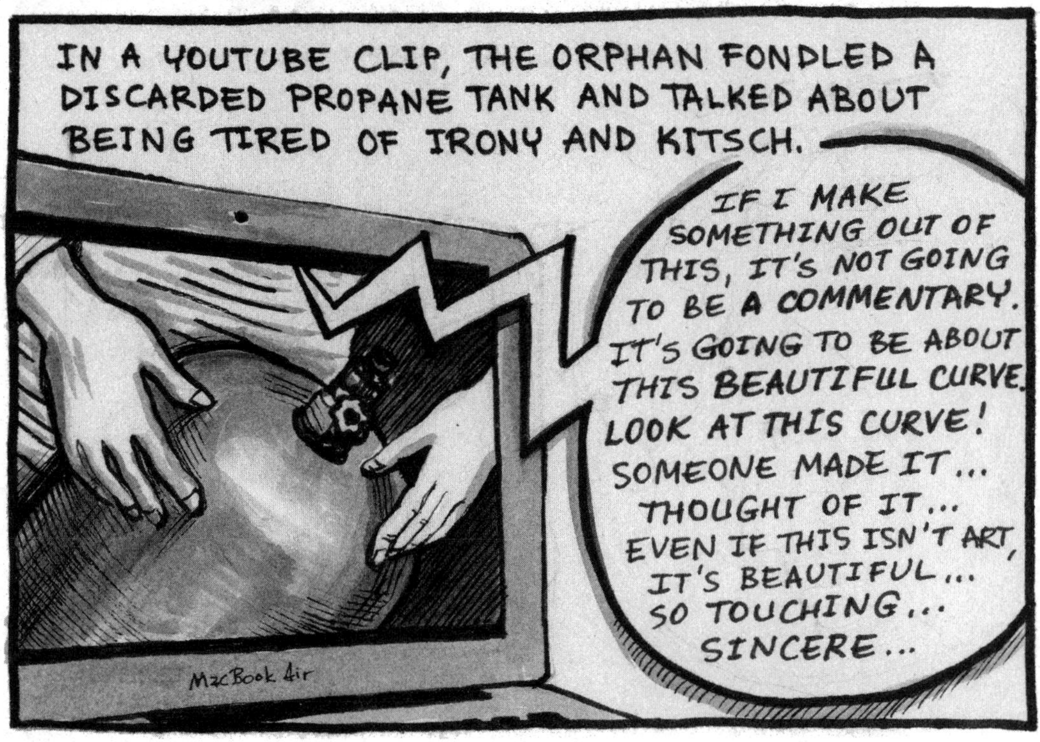
IN A YOUTUBE CLIP, THE ORPHAN FONDLED A DISCARDED PROPANE TANK AND TALKED ABOUT BEING TIRED OF IRONY AND KITSCH.
IF I MAKE SOMETHING OUT OF THIS, IT'S NOT GOING TO BE A COMMENTARY. IT'S GOING TO BE ABOUT THIS BEAUTIFUL CURVE. LOOK AT THIS CURVE! SOMEONE MADE IT... THOUGHT OF IT... EVEN IF THIS ISN'T ART, IT'S BEAUTIFUL... SO TOUCHING... SINCERE...
MacBook Air

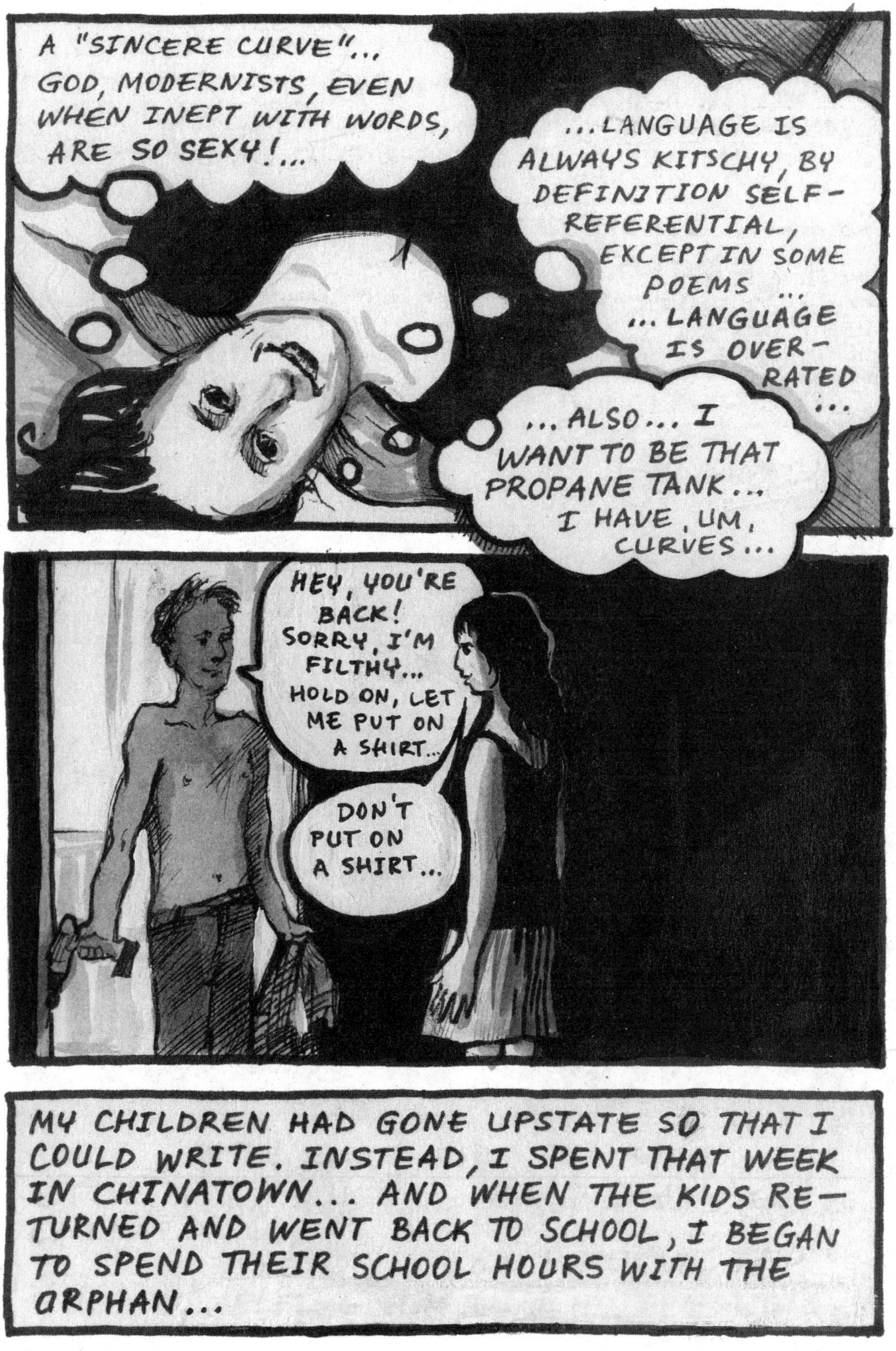
A "SINCERE CURVE"... GOD, MODERNISTS, EVEN WHEN INEPT WITH WORDS, ARE SO SEXY!...
...LANGUAGE IS ALWAYS KITSCHY, BY DEFINITION SELF-REFERENTIAL, EXCEPT IN SOME POEMS ... ...LANGUAGE IS OVER-RATED ...
...ALSO... I WANT TO BE THAT PROPANE TANK... I HAVE, UM, CURVES...
HEY, YOU'RE BACK! SORRY, I'M FILTHY... HOLD ON, LET ME PUT ON A SHIRT...
DON'T PUT ON A SHIRT...
MY CHILDREN HAD GONE UPSTATE SO THAT I COULD WRITE. INSTEAD, I SPENT THAT WEEK IN CHINATOWN... AND WHEN THE KIDS RE-TURNED AND WENT BACK TO SCHOOL, I BEGAN TO SPEND THEIR SCHOOL HOURS WITH THE ORPHAN...

WE STARTED EACH MORNING BY GOING BACK TO BED...

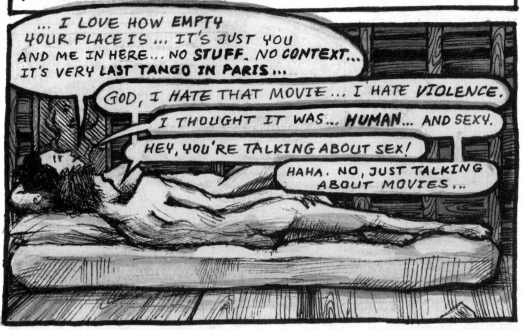

... I LOVE HOW EMPTY YOUR PLACE IS ... IT'S JUST YOU AND ME IN HERE... NO **STUFF**. NO **CONTEXT**... IT'S VERY **LAST TANGO IN PARIS**...

GOD, I HATE THAT MOVIE... I HATE **VIOLENCE**.

I THOUGHT IT WAS... **HUMAN**... AND SEXY.

HEY, YOU'RE TALKING ABOUT SEX!

HAHA. NO, JUST TALKING ABOUT MOVIES...

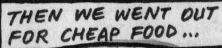

THEN WE WENT OUT FOR CHEAP FOOD...

...YOU LIKE THE WORST MOVIES! I LOOKED AT YOUR PROFILE ... YOU LIST ALL THESE CRUEL SATIRES — STORYTELLING! NEIL LABUTE'S FILMS! THE MEANEST STUFF!

I THINK THEY'RE **BRAVE**, NOT CRUEL! WHAT'S YOUR THRESHOLD FOR EMOTIONAL DISCOMFORT IN ART? THE **MUPPETS**?

HAHA! PRETTY MUCH! I'M A GENTLE SOUL...

... AND LATER, THE ORPHAN TAUGHT ME ABOUT CONSTRUCTION

WANT TO HELP ME INSTALL THE FLOOR?

SURE! WHAT DO I DO?

FIRST, HELP ME MOVE THESE BOARDS... MY AIR NAILER IS BACK THERE SOMEWHERE ...

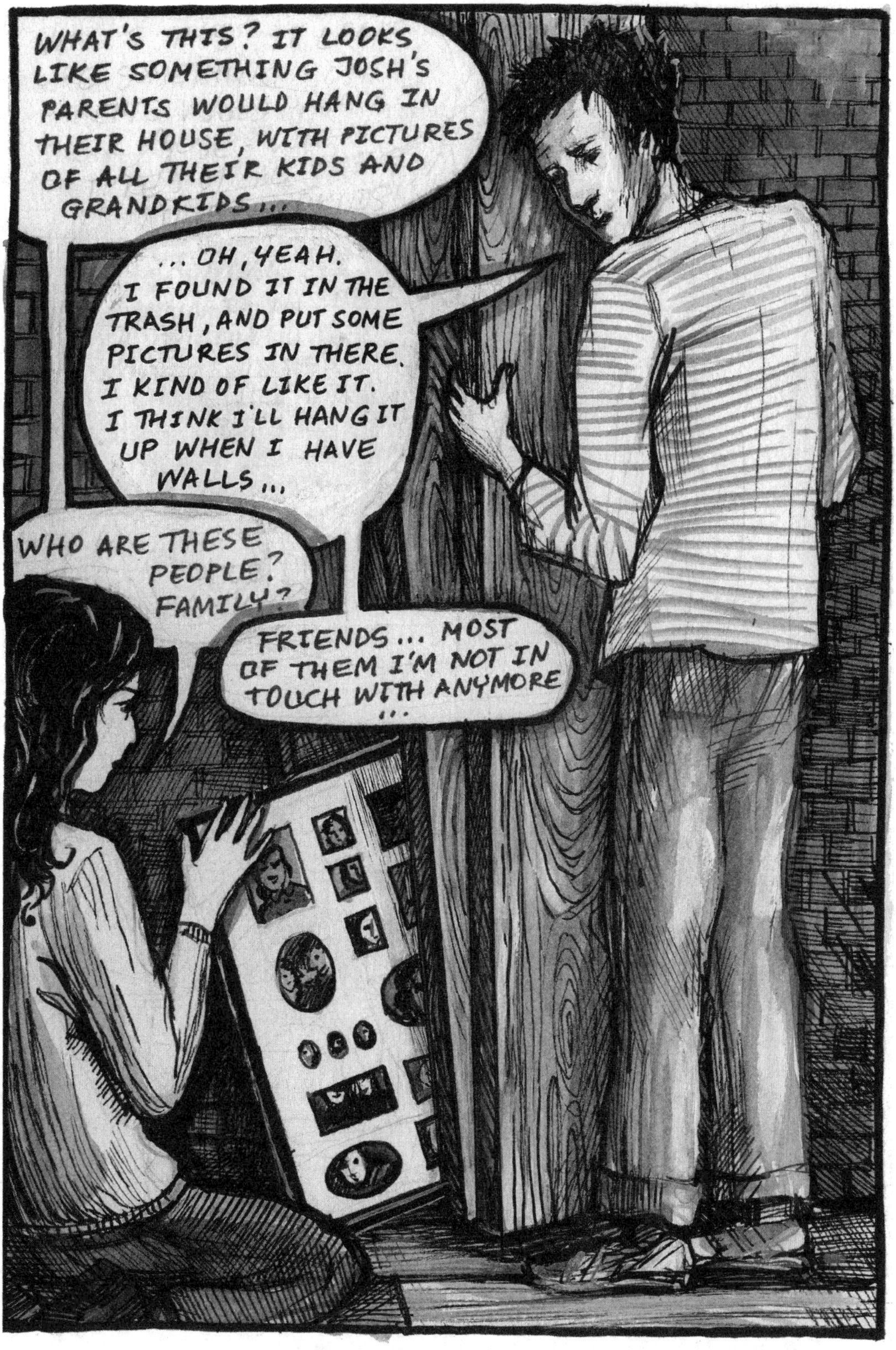
WHAT'S THIS? IT LOOKS LIKE SOMETHING JOSH'S PARENTS WOULD HANG IN THEIR HOUSE, WITH PICTURES OF ALL THEIR KIDS AND GRANDKIDS...
...OH, YEAH. I FOUND IT IN THE TRASH, AND PUT SOME PICTURES IN THERE. I KIND OF LIKE IT. I THINK I'LL HANG IT UP WHEN I HAVE WALLS...
WHO ARE THESE PEOPLE? FAMILY?
FRIENDS... MOST OF THEM I'M NOT IN TOUCH WITH ANYMORE ...

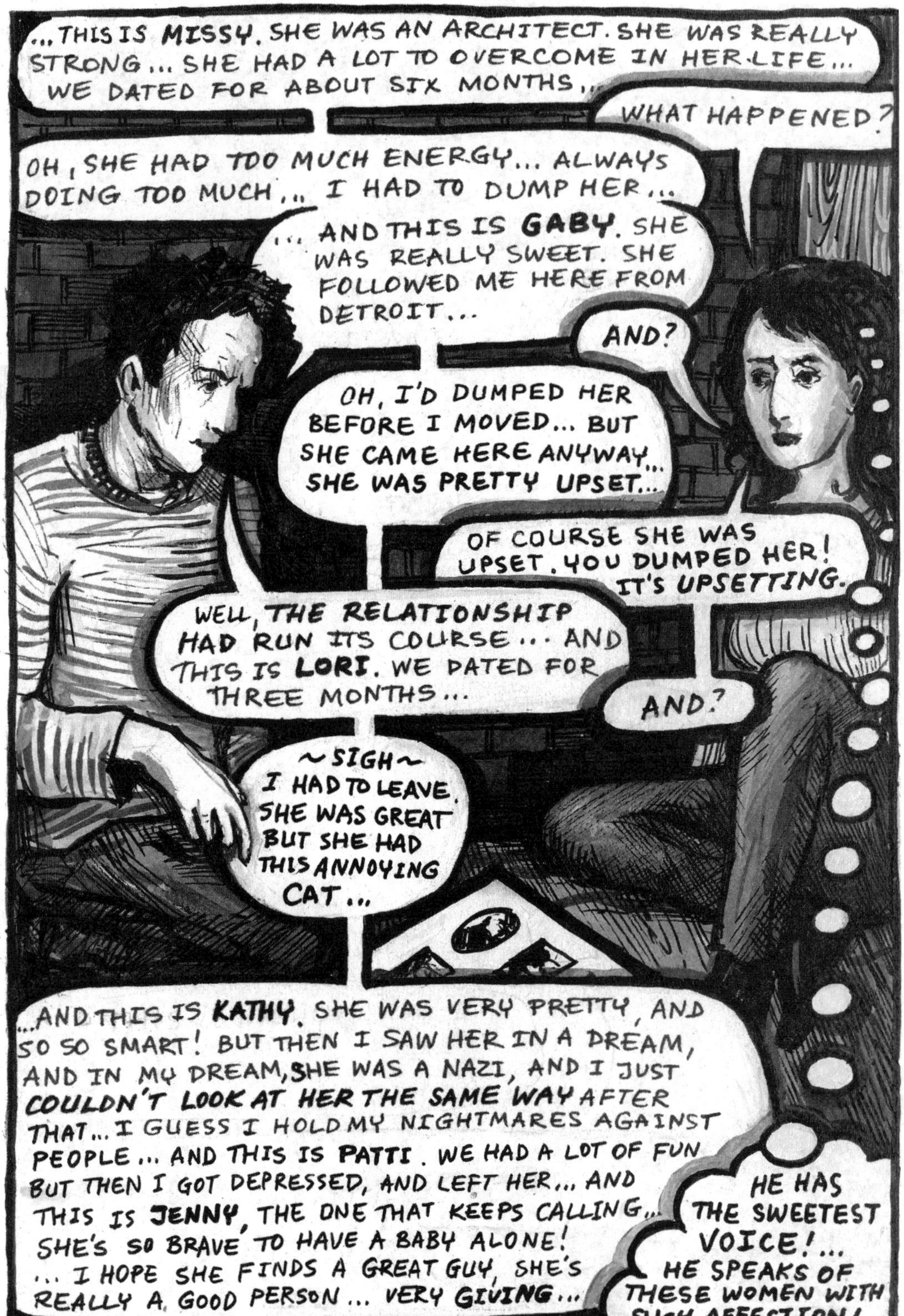
...THIS IS MISSY. SHE WAS AN ARCHITECT. SHE WAS REALLY STRONG... SHE HAD A LOT TO OVERCOME IN HER LIFE... WE DATED FOR ABOUT SIX MONTHS...
WHAT HAPPENED?
OH, SHE HAD TOO MUCH ENERGY... ALWAYS DOING TOO MUCH... I HAD TO DUMP HER...
...AND THIS IS GABY. SHE WAS REALLY SWEET. SHE FOLLOWED ME HERE FROM DETROIT...
AND?
OH, I'D DUMPED HER BEFORE I MOVED... BUT SHE CAME HERE ANYWAY... SHE WAS PRETTY UPSET...
OF COURSE SHE WAS UPSET. YOU DUMPED HER! IT'S UPSETTING.
WELL, THE RELATIONSHIP HAD RUN ITS COURSE... AND THIS IS LORI. WE DATED FOR THREE MONTHS...
AND?
~SIGH~ I HAD TO LEAVE. SHE WAS GREAT BUT SHE HAD THIS ANNOYING CAT...
...AND THIS IS KATHY. SHE WAS VERY PRETTY, AND SO SO SMART! BUT THEN I SAW HER IN A DREAM, AND IN MY DREAM, SHE WAS A NAZI, AND I JUST COULDN'T LOOK AT HER THE SAME WAY AFTER THAT... I GUESS I HOLD MY NIGHTMARES AGAINST PEOPLE... AND THIS IS PATTI. WE HAD A LOT OF FUN BUT THEN I GOT DEPRESSED, AND LEFT HER... AND THIS IS JENNY, THE ONE THAT KEEPS CALLING... SHE'S SO BRAVE TO HAVE A BABY ALONE! ...I HOPE SHE FINDS A GREAT GUY, SHE'S REALLY A GOOD PERSON... VERY GIVING...
HE HAS THE SWEETEST VOICE!... HE SPEAKS OF THESE WOMEN WITH SUCH AFFECTION!

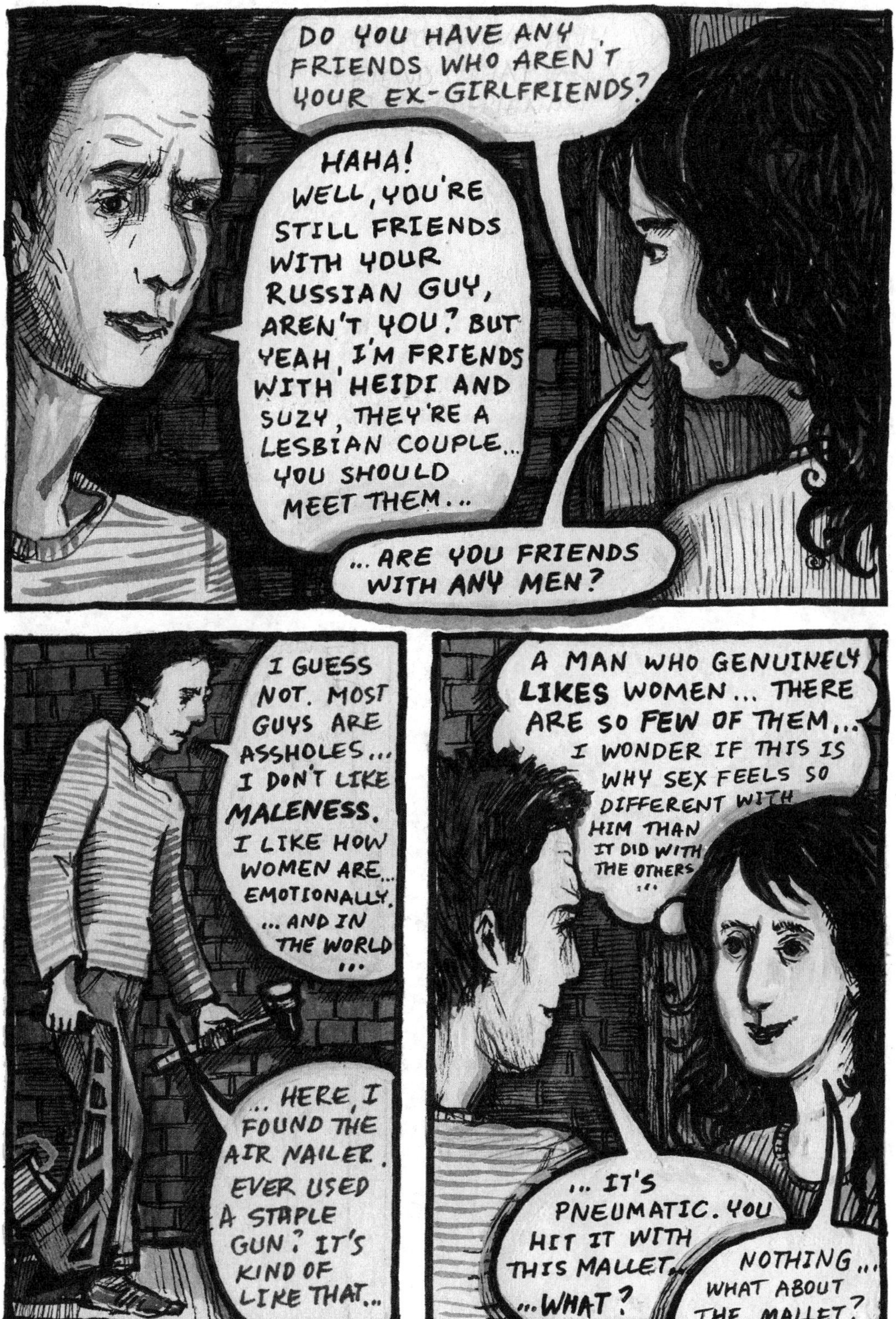

DO YOU HAVE ANY FRIENDS WHO AREN'T YOUR EX-GIRLFRIENDS?
HAHA! WELL, YOU'RE STILL FRIENDS WITH YOUR RUSSIAN GUY, AREN'T YOU? BUT YEAH, I'M FRIENDS WITH HEIDI AND SUZY, THEY'RE A LESBIAN COUPLE... YOU SHOULD MEET THEM...
...ARE YOU FRIENDS WITH ANY MEN?
I GUESS NOT. MOST GUYS ARE ASSHOLES... I DON'T LIKE MALENESS. I LIKE HOW WOMEN ARE... EMOTIONALLY. ...AND IN THE WORLD...
...HERE, I FOUND THE AIR NAILER. EVER USED A STAPLE GUN? IT'S KIND OF LIKE THAT...
A MAN WHO GENUINELY LIKES WOMEN... THERE ARE SO FEW OF THEM... I WONDER IF THIS IS WHY SEX FEELS SO DIFFERENT WITH HIM THAN IT DID WITH THE OTHERS...
... IT'S PNEUMATIC. YOU HIT IT WITH THIS MALLET... ...WHAT?
NOTHING... WHAT ABOUT THE MALLET?

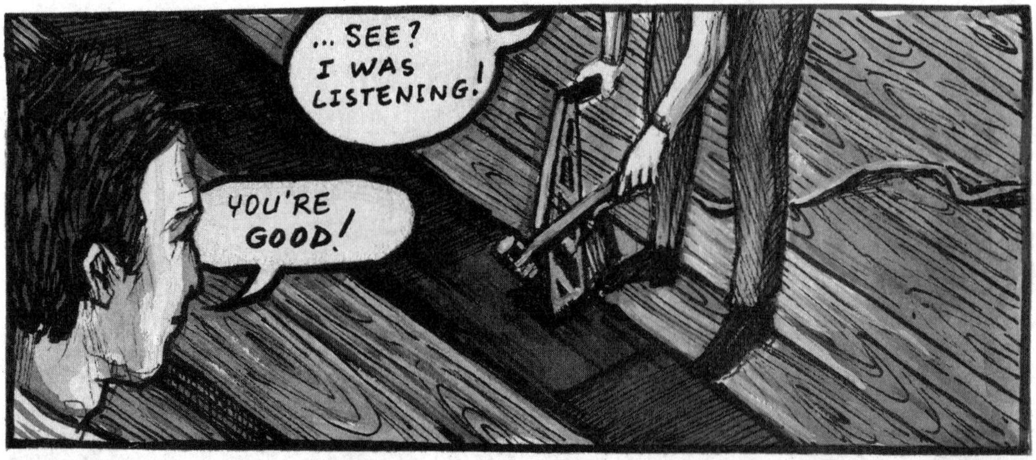
... SEE? I WAS LISTENING!
YOU'RE GOOD!

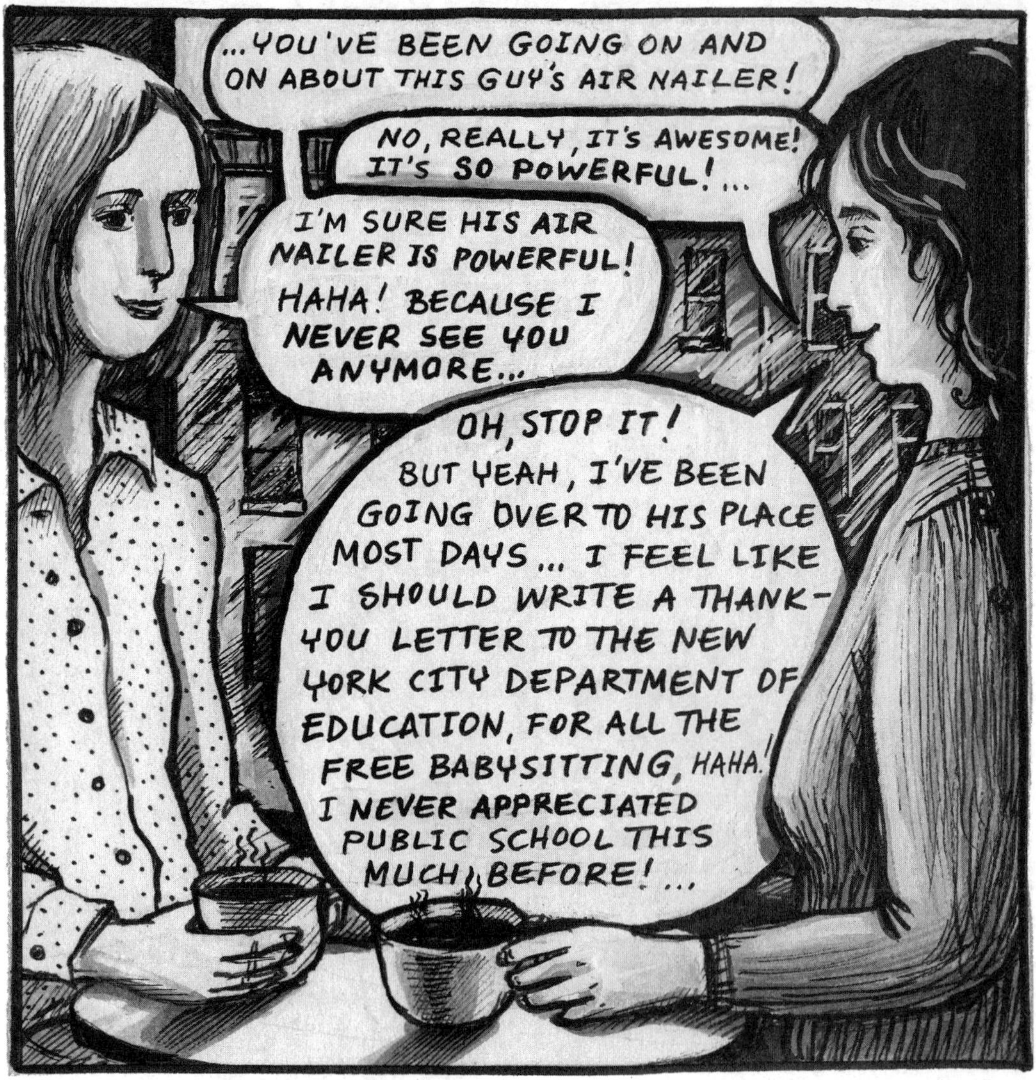
...YOU'VE BEEN GOING ON AND ON ABOUT THIS GUY'S AIR NAILER!
NO, REALLY, IT'S AWESOME! IT'S SO POWERFUL!...
I'M SURE HIS AIR NAILER IS POWERFUL! HAHA! BECAUSE I NEVER SEE YOU ANYMORE...
OH, STOP IT! BUT YEAH, I'VE BEEN GOING OVER TO HIS PLACE MOST DAYS... I FEEL LIKE I SHOULD WRITE A THANK-YOU LETTER TO THE NEW YORK CITY DEPARTMENT OF EDUCATION, FOR ALL THE FREE BABYSITTING, HAHA! I NEVER APPRECIATED PUBLIC SCHOOL THIS MUCH BEFORE!...

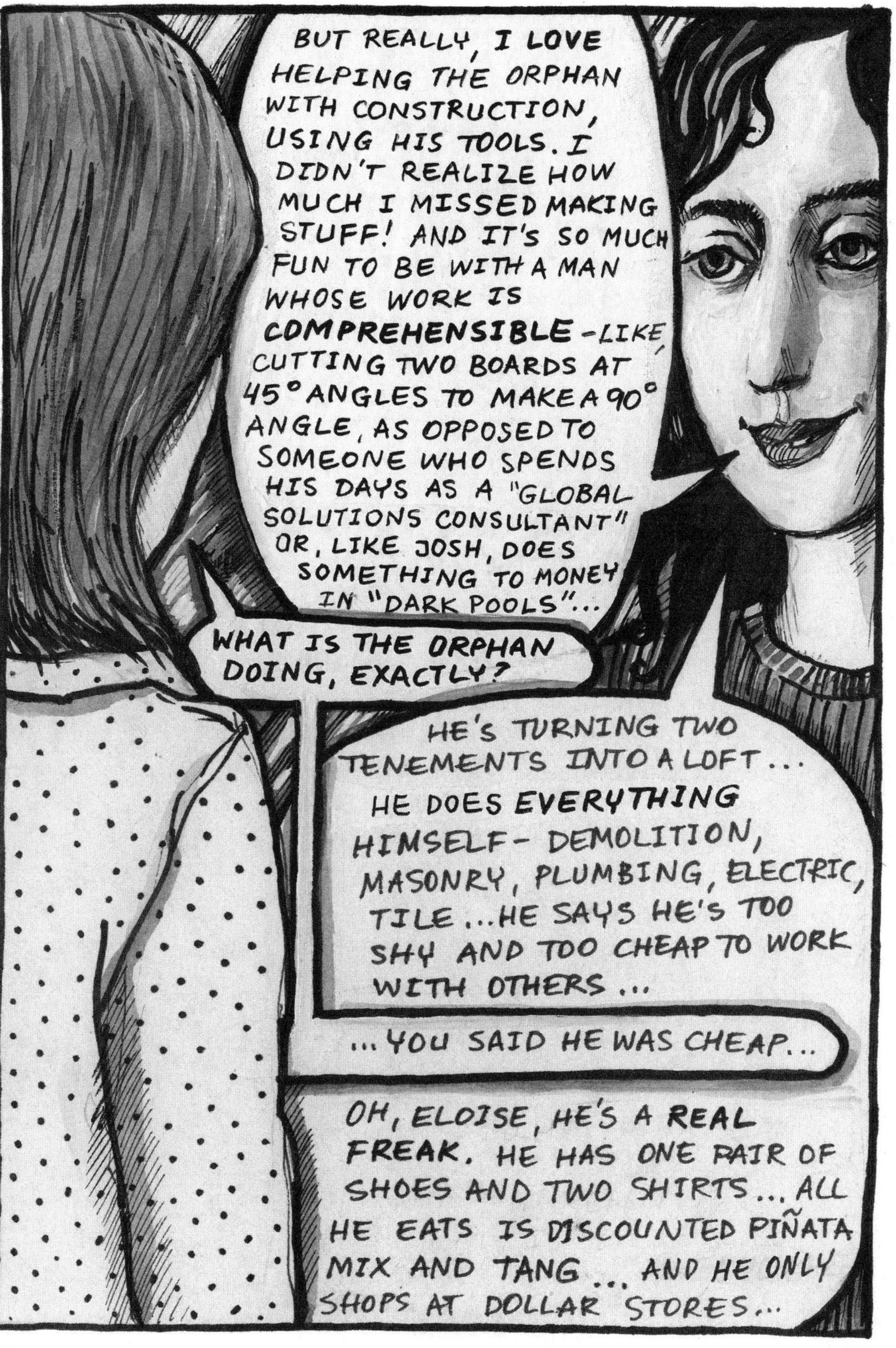

BUT REALLY, I LOVE HELPING THE ORPHAN WITH CONSTRUCTION, USING HIS TOOLS. I DIDN'T REALIZE HOW MUCH I MISSED MAKING STUFF! AND IT'S SO MUCH FUN TO BE WITH A MAN WHOSE WORK IS COMPREHENSIBLE -LIKE, CUTTING TWO BOARDS AT 45° ANGLES TO MAKE A 90° ANGLE, AS OPPOSED TO SOMEONE WHO SPENDS HIS DAYS AS A "GLOBAL SOLUTIONS CONSULTANT" OR, LIKE JOSH, DOES SOMETHING TO MONEY IN "DARK POOLS"...
WHAT IS THE ORPHAN DOING, EXACTLY?
HE'S TURNING TWO TENEMENTS INTO A LOFT... HE DOES EVERYTHING HIMSELF- DEMOLITION, MASONRY, PLUMBING, ELECTRIC, TILE...HE SAYS HE'S TOO SHY AND TOO CHEAP TO WORK WITH OTHERS...
...YOU SAID HE WAS CHEAP...
OH, ELOISE, HE'S A REAL FREAK. HE HAS ONE PAIR OF SHOES AND TWO SHIRTS... ALL HE EATS IS DISCOUNTED PIÑATA MIX AND TANG... AND HE ONLY SHOPS AT DOLLAR STORES...

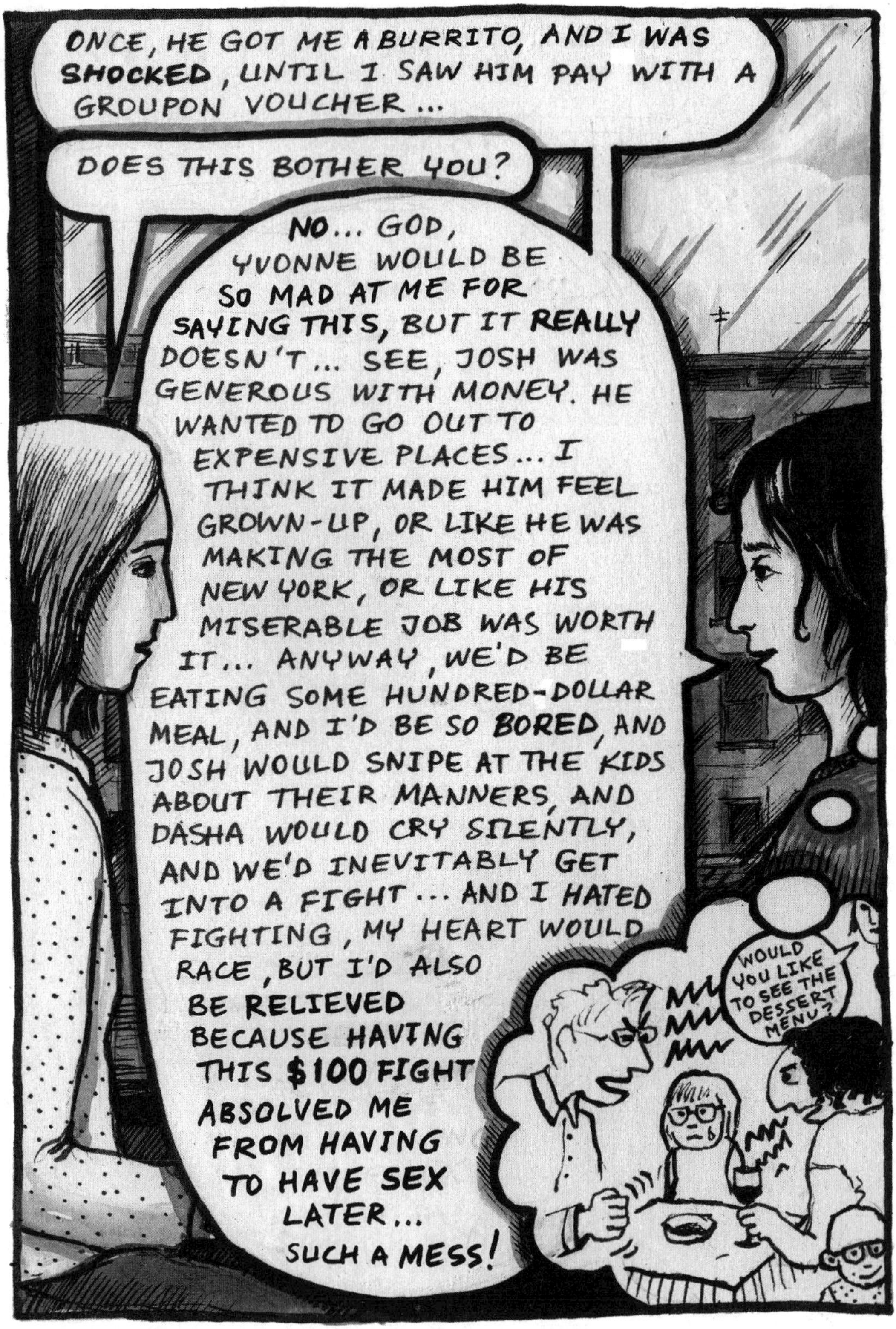
ONCE, HE GOT ME A BURRITO, AND I WAS SHOCKED, UNTIL I SAW HIM PAY WITH A GROUPON VOUCHER...
DOES THIS BOTHER YOU?
NO... GOD, YVONNE WOULD BE SO MAD AT ME FOR SAYING THIS, BUT IT REALLY DOESN'T... SEE, JOSH WAS GENEROUS WITH MONEY. HE WANTED TO GO OUT TO EXPENSIVE PLACES... I THINK IT MADE HIM FEEL GROWN-UP, OR LIKE HE WAS MAKING THE MOST OF NEW YORK, OR LIKE HIS MISERABLE JOB WAS WORTH IT... ANYWAY, WE'D BE EATING SOME HUNDRED-DOLLAR MEAL, AND I'D BE SO BORED, AND JOSH WOULD SNIPE AT THE KIDS ABOUT THEIR MANNERS, AND DASHA WOULD CRY SILENTLY, AND WE'D INEVITABLY GET INTO A FIGHT... AND I HATED FIGHTING, MY HEART WOULD RACE, BUT I'D ALSO BE RELIEVED BECAUSE HAVING THIS $100 FIGHT ABSOLVED ME FROM HAVING TO HAVE SEX LATER... SUCH A MESS!
WOULD YOU LIKE TO SEE THE DESSERT MENU?

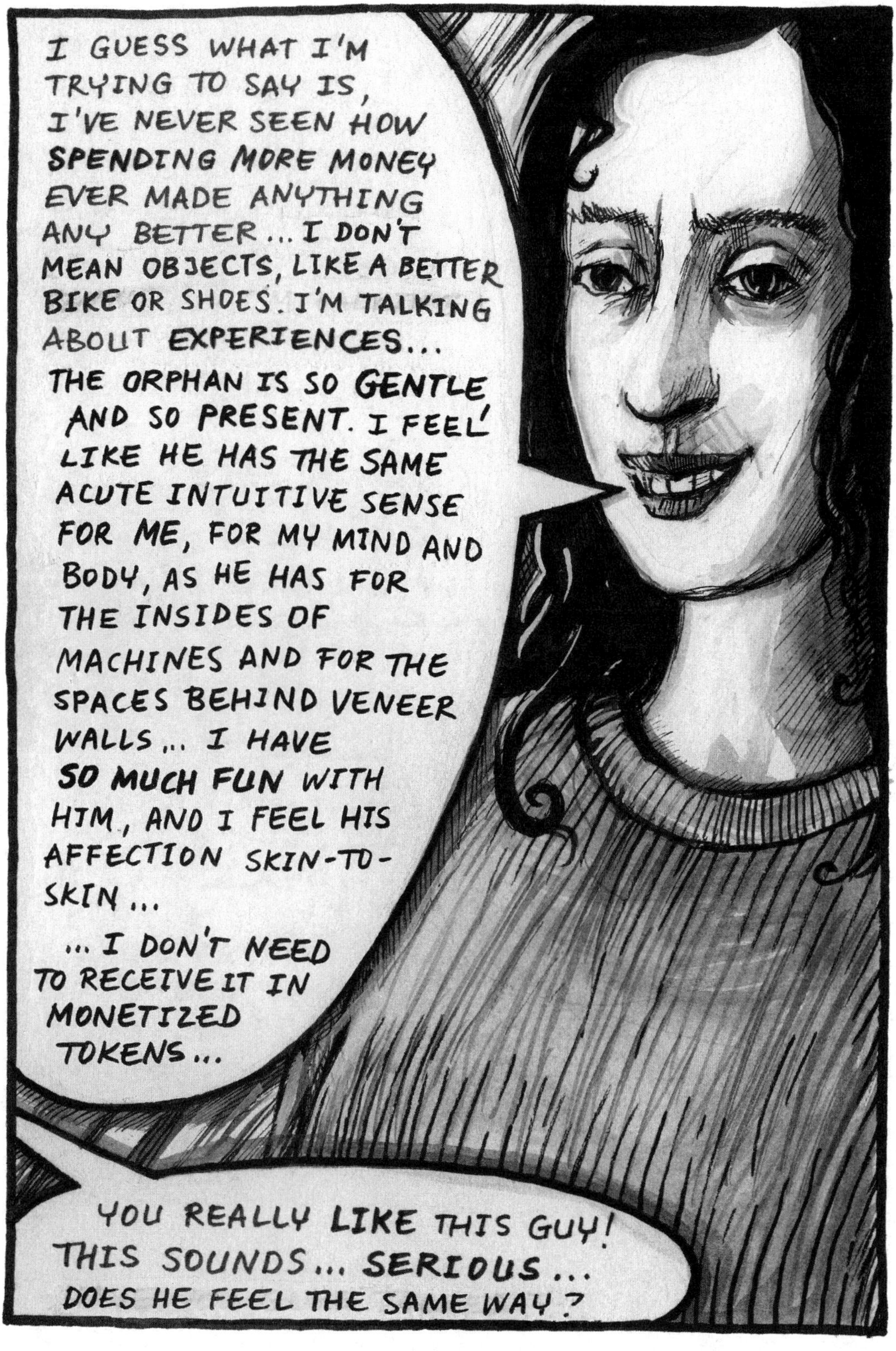
I GUESS WHAT I'M TRYING TO SAY IS, I'VE NEVER SEEN HOW SPENDING MORE MONEY EVER MADE ANYTHING ANY BETTER... I DON'T MEAN OBJECTS, LIKE A BETTER BIKE OR SHOES. I'M TALKING ABOUT EXPERIENCES...
THE ORPHAN IS SO GENTLE AND SO PRESENT. I FEEL LIKE HE HAS THE SAME ACUTE INTUITIVE SENSE FOR ME, FOR MY MIND AND BODY, AS HE HAS FOR THE INSIDES OF MACHINES AND FOR THE SPACES BEHIND VENEER WALLS... I HAVE SO MUCH FUN WITH HIM, AND I FEEL HIS AFFECTION SKIN-TO-SKIN...
... I DON'T NEED TO RECEIVE IT IN MONETIZED TOKENS...
YOU REALLY LIKE THIS GUY! THIS SOUNDS... SERIOUS... DOES HE FEEL THE SAME WAY?

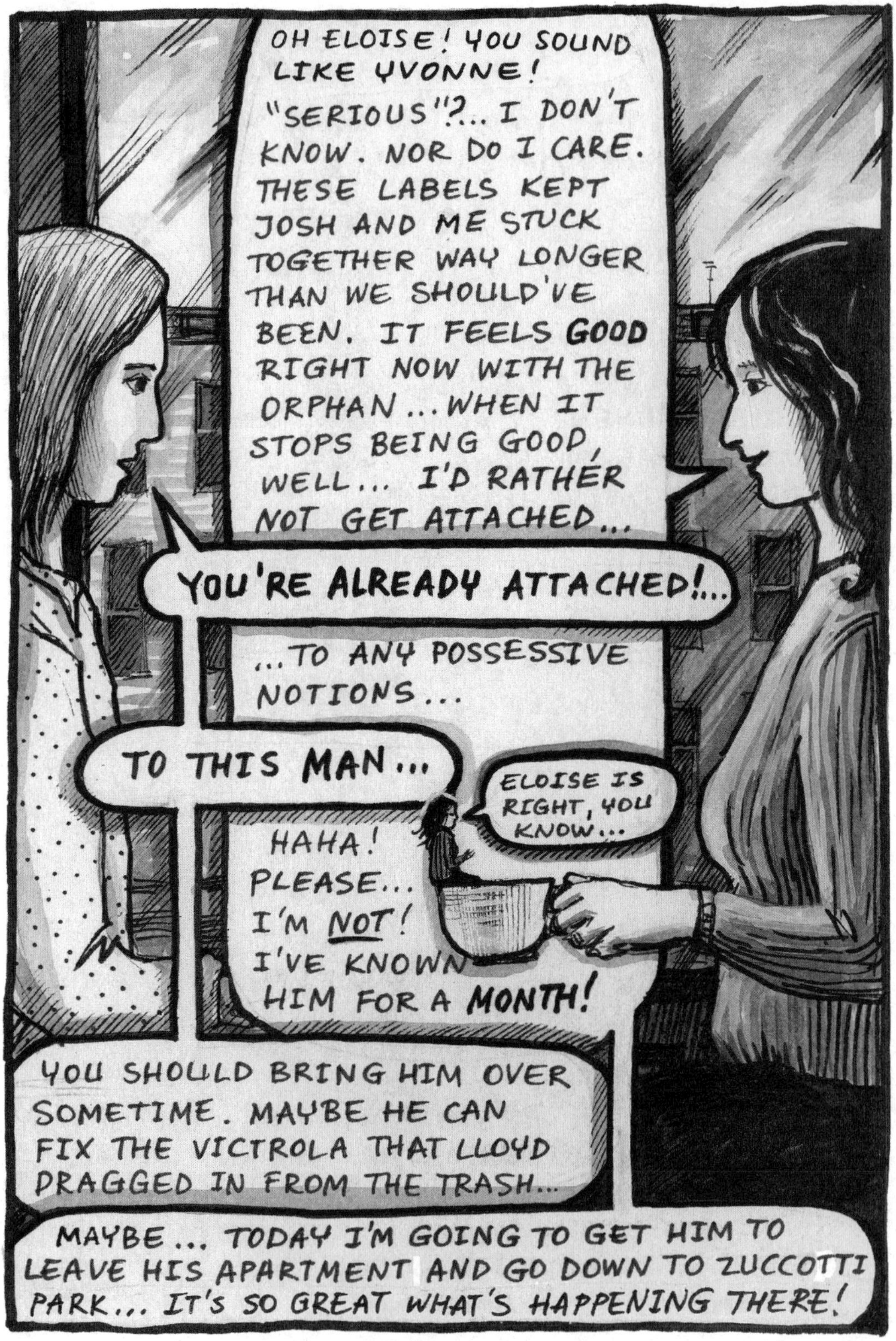
OH ELOISE! YOU SOUND LIKE YVONNE!
"SERIOUS"?... I DON'T KNOW. NOR DO I CARE. THESE LABELS KEPT JOSH AND ME STUCK TOGETHER WAY LONGER THAN WE SHOULD'VE BEEN. IT FEELS GOOD RIGHT NOW WITH THE ORPHAN... WHEN IT STOPS BEING GOOD, WELL... I'D RATHER NOT GET ATTACHED...
YOU'RE ALREADY ATTACHED!...
...TO ANY POSSESSIVE NOTIONS...
TO THIS MAN...
ELOISE IS RIGHT, YOU KNOW...
HAHA! PLEASE... I'M NOT! I'VE KNOWN HIM FOR A MONTH!
YOU SHOULD BRING HIM OVER SOMETIME. MAYBE HE CAN FIX THE VICTROLA THAT LLOYD DRAGGED IN FROM THE TRASH...
MAYBE... TODAY I'M GOING TO GET HIM TO LEAVE HIS APARTMENT AND GO DOWN TO ZUCCOTTI PARK... IT'S SO GREAT WHAT'S HAPPENING THERE!

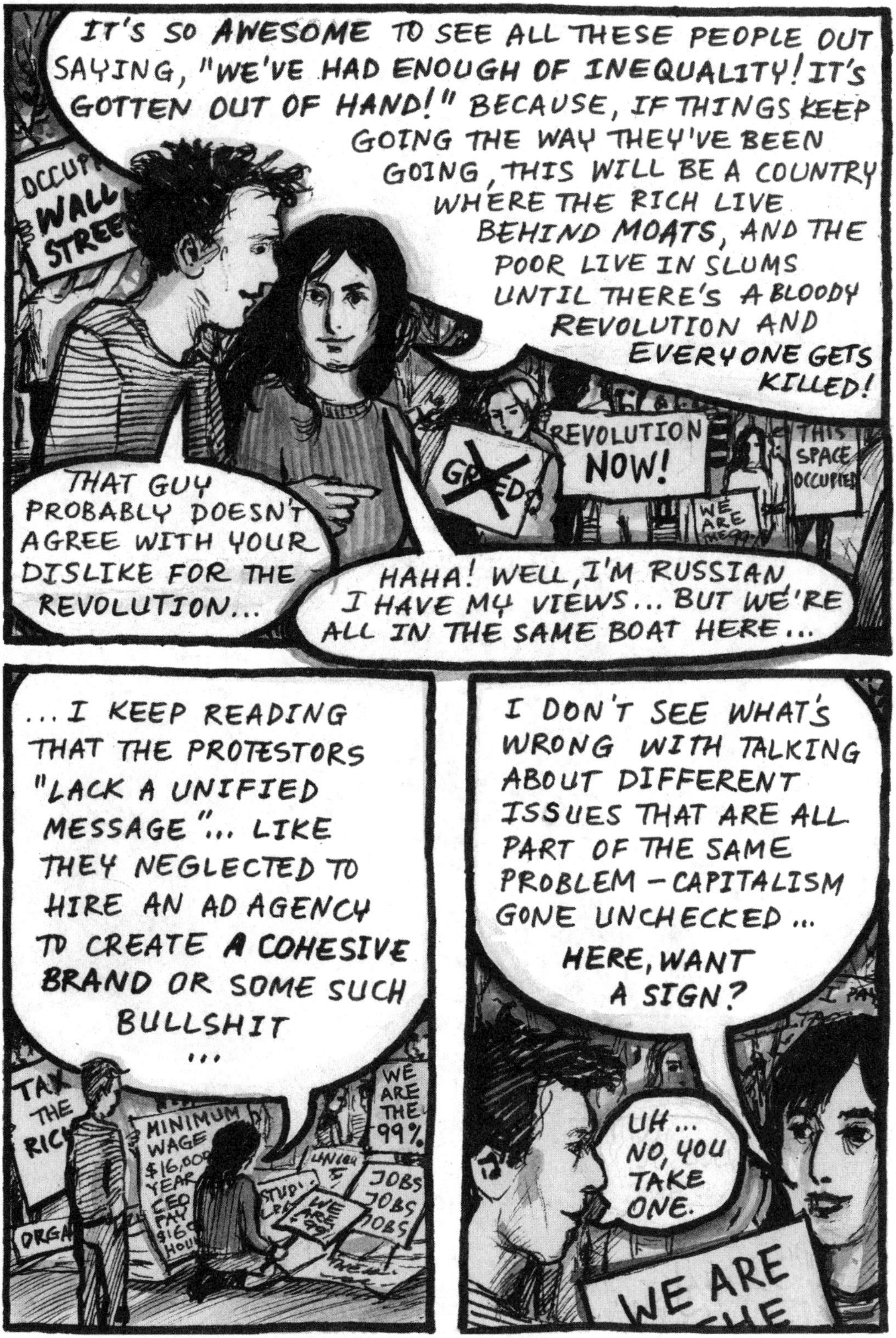
IT'S SO AWESOME TO SEE ALL THESE PEOPLE OUT SAYING, "WE'VE HAD ENOUGH OF INEQUALITY! IT'S GOTTEN OUT OF HAND!" BECAUSE, IF THINGS KEEP GOING THE WAY THEY'VE BEEN GOING, THIS WILL BE A COUNTRY WHERE THE RICH LIVE BEHIND MOATS, AND THE POOR LIVE IN SLUMS UNTIL THERE'S A BLOODY REVOLUTION AND EVERYONE GETS KILLED!
REVOLUTION NOW!
THIS SPACE OCCUPIED
THAT GUY PROBABLY DOESN'T AGREE WITH YOUR DISLIKE FOR THE REVOLUTION...
HAHA! WELL, I'M RUSSIAN I HAVE MY VIEWS... BUT WE'RE ALL IN THE SAME BOAT HERE...
...I KEEP READING THAT THE PROTESTORS "LACK A UNIFIED MESSAGE"... LIKE THEY NEGLECTED TO HIRE AN AD AGENCY TO CREATE A COHESIVE BRAND OR SOME SUCH BULLSHIT ...
WE ARE THE 99%.
MINIMUM WAGE
JOBS JOBS JOBS
I DON'T SEE WHAT'S WRONG WITH TALKING ABOUT DIFFERENT ISSUES THAT ARE ALL PART OF THE SAME PROBLEM – CAPITALISM GONE UNCHECKED... HERE, WANT A SIGN?
UH... NO, YOU TAKE ONE.
WE ARE

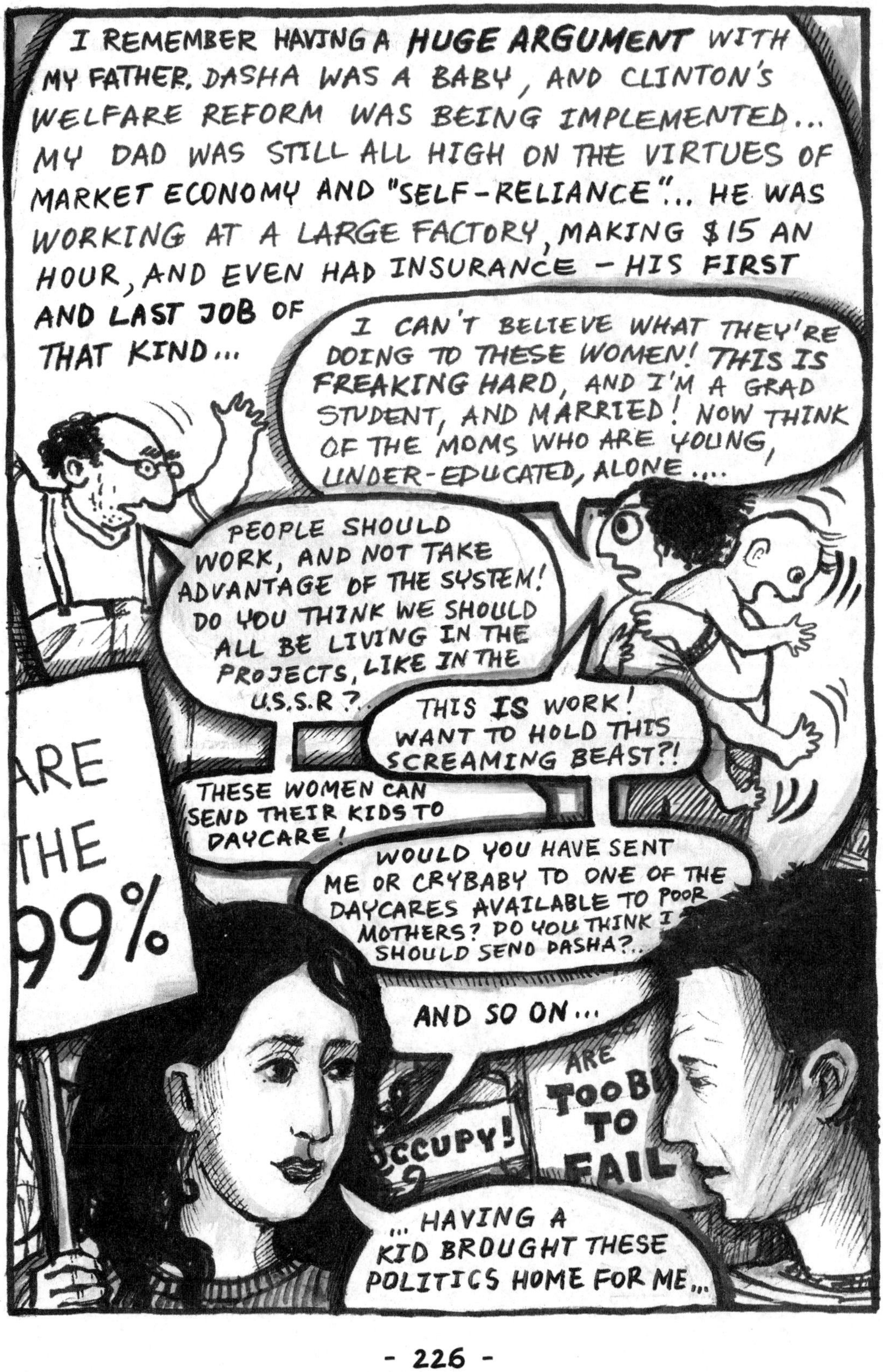
I REMEMBER HAVING A HUGE ARGUMENT WITH MY FATHER. DASHA WAS A BABY, AND CLINTON'S WELFARE REFORM WAS BEING IMPLEMENTED... MY DAD WAS STILL ALL HIGH ON THE VIRTUES OF MARKET ECONOMY AND "SELF-RELIANCE"... HE WAS WORKING AT A LARGE FACTORY, MAKING $15 AN HOUR, AND EVEN HAD INSURANCE - HIS FIRST AND LAST JOB OF THAT KIND...
I CAN'T BELIEVE WHAT THEY'RE DOING TO THESE WOMEN! THIS IS FREAKING HARD, AND I'M A GRAD STUDENT, AND MARRIED! NOW THINK OF THE MOMS WHO ARE YOUNG, UNDER-EDUCATED, ALONE...
PEOPLE SHOULD WORK, AND NOT TAKE ADVANTAGE OF THE SYSTEM! DO YOU THINK WE SHOULD ALL BE LIVING IN THE PROJECTS, LIKE IN THE U.S.S.R.?..
THIS IS WORK! WANT TO HOLD THIS SCREAMING BEAST?!
THESE WOMEN CAN SEND THEIR KIDS TO DAYCARE!
WOULD YOU HAVE SENT ME OR CRYBABY TO ONE OF THE DAYCARES AVAILABLE TO POOR MOTHERS? DO YOU THINK I SHOULD SEND DASHA?..
ARE THE 99%
AND SO ON...
ARE TOO B TO FAIL
OCCUPY!
... HAVING A KID BROUGHT THESE POLITICS HOME FOR ME...

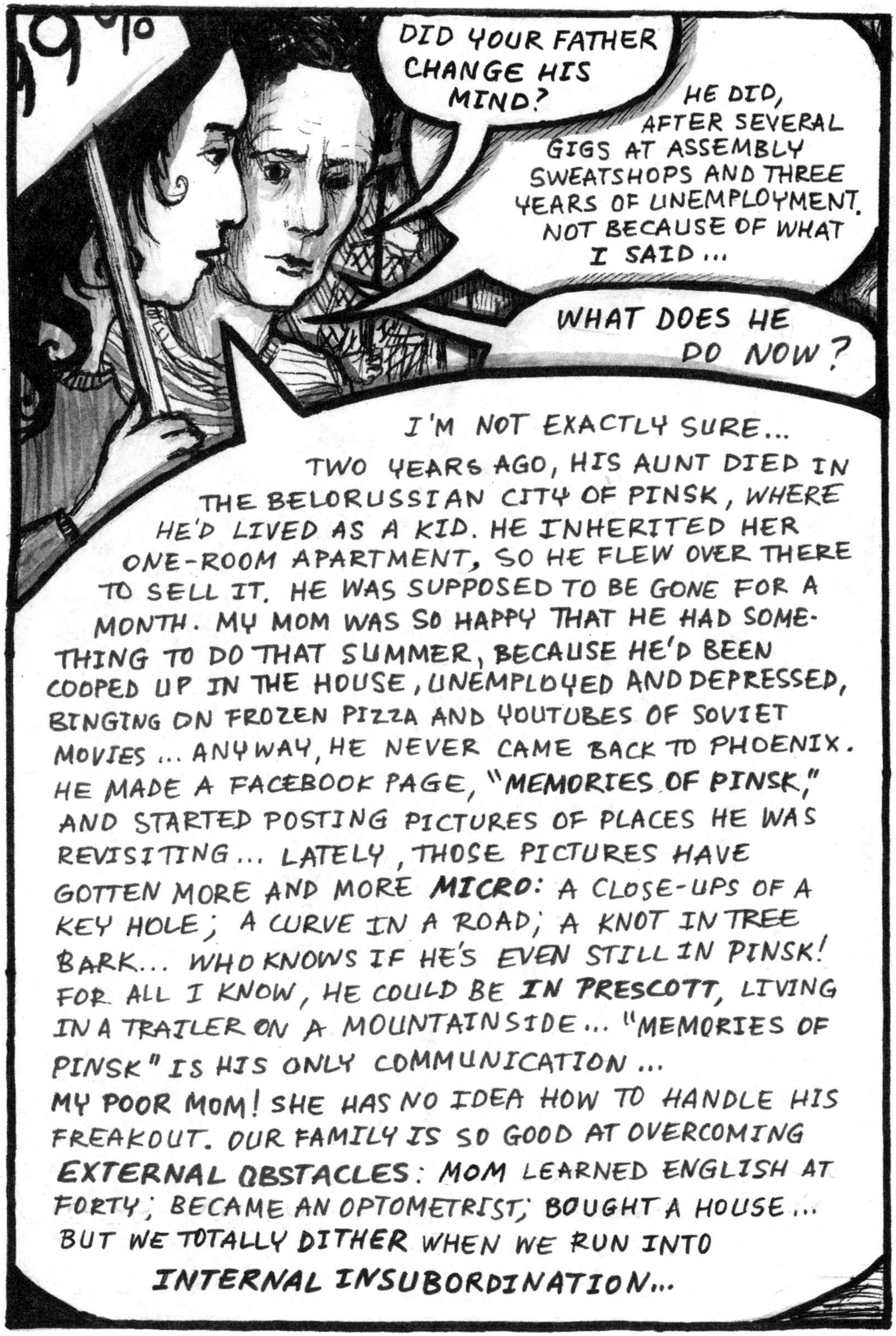
DID YOUR FATHER CHANGE HIS MIND?
HE DID, AFTER SEVERAL GIGS AT ASSEMBLY SWEATSHOPS AND THREE YEARS OF UNEMPLOYMENT. NOT BECAUSE OF WHAT I SAID...
WHAT DOES HE DO NOW?
I'M NOT EXACTLY SURE... TWO YEARS AGO, HIS AUNT DIED IN THE BELORUSSIAN CITY OF PINSK, WHERE HE'D LIVED AS A KID. HE INHERITED HER ONE-ROOM APARTMENT, SO HE FLEW OVER THERE TO SELL IT. HE WAS SUPPOSED TO BE GONE FOR A MONTH. MY MOM WAS SO HAPPY THAT HE HAD SOMETHING TO DO THAT SUMMER, BECAUSE HE'D BEEN COOPED UP IN THE HOUSE, UNEMPLOYED AND DEPRESSED, BINGING ON FROZEN PIZZA AND YOUTUBES OF SOVIET MOVIES... ANYWAY, HE NEVER CAME BACK TO PHOENIX. HE MADE A FACEBOOK PAGE, "MEMORIES OF PINSK," AND STARTED POSTING PICTURES OF PLACES HE WAS REVISITING... LATELY, THOSE PICTURES HAVE GOTTEN MORE AND MORE MICRO: A CLOSE-UPS OF A KEY HOLE; A CURVE IN A ROAD; A KNOT IN TREE BARK... WHO KNOWS IF HE'S EVEN STILL IN PINSK! FOR ALL I KNOW, HE COULD BE IN PRESCOTT, LIVING IN A TRAILER ON A MOUNTAINSIDE... "MEMORIES OF PINSK" IS HIS ONLY COMMUNICATION... MY POOR MOM! SHE HAS NO IDEA HOW TO HANDLE HIS FREAKOUT. OUR FAMILY IS SO GOOD AT OVERCOMING EXTERNAL OBSTACLES: MOM LEARNED ENGLISH AT FORTY; BECAME AN OPTOMETRIST; BOUGHT A HOUSE... BUT WE TOTALLY DITHER WHEN WE RUN INTO INTERNAL INSUBORDINATION...

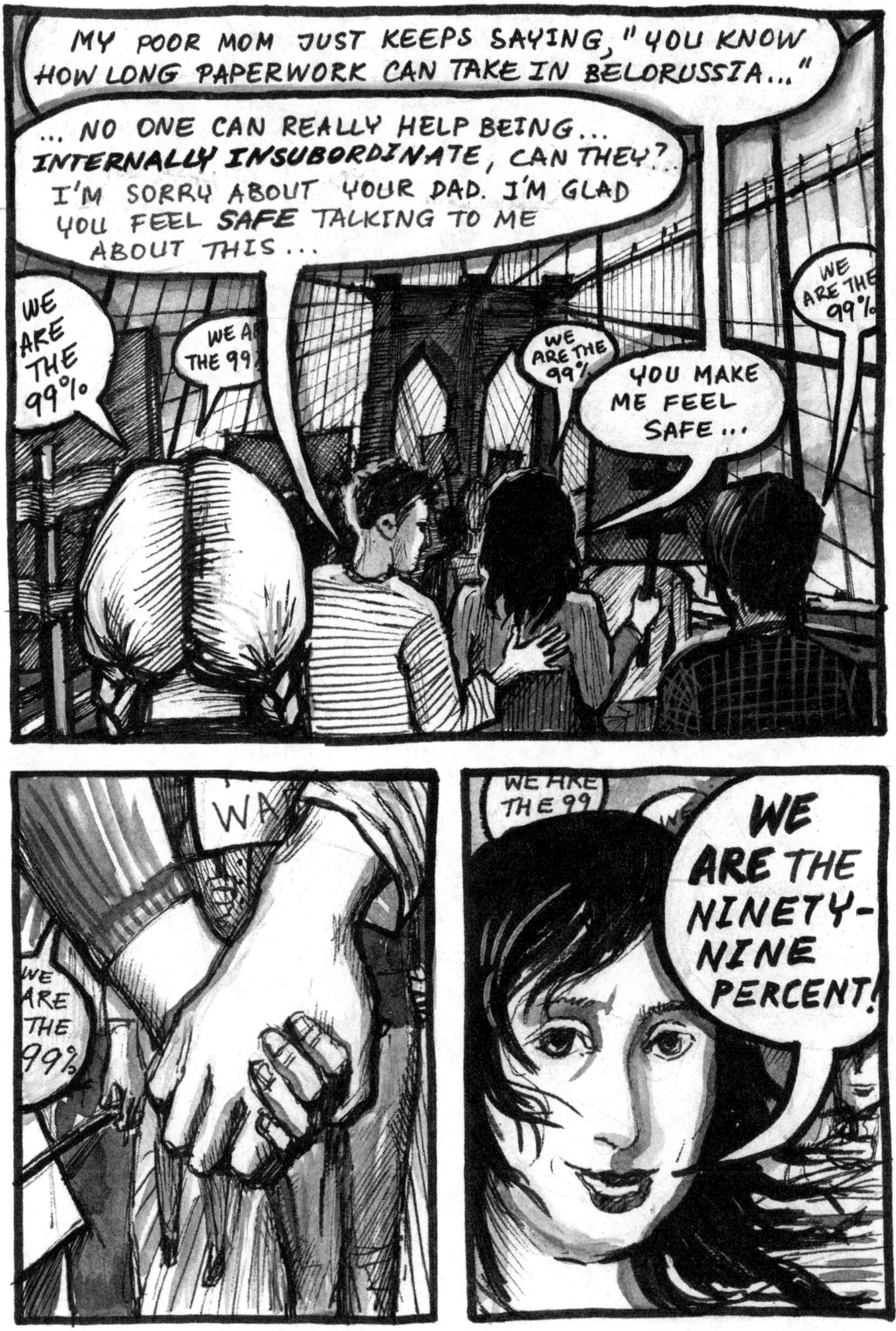
MY POOR MOM JUST KEEPS SAYING, "YOU KNOW HOW LONG PAPERWORK CAN TAKE IN BELORUSSIA..."
... NO ONE CAN REALLY HELP BEING... INTERNALLY INSUBORDINATE, CAN THEY?... I'M SORRY ABOUT YOUR DAD. I'M GLAD YOU FEEL SAFE TALKING TO ME ABOUT THIS...
WE ARE THE 99%
WE ARE THE 99%
YOU MAKE ME FEEL SAFE...
WE ARE THE 99%
WE ARE THE 99%
WE ARE THE 99%
WE ARE THE 99
WE ARE THE NINETY-NINE PERCENT!

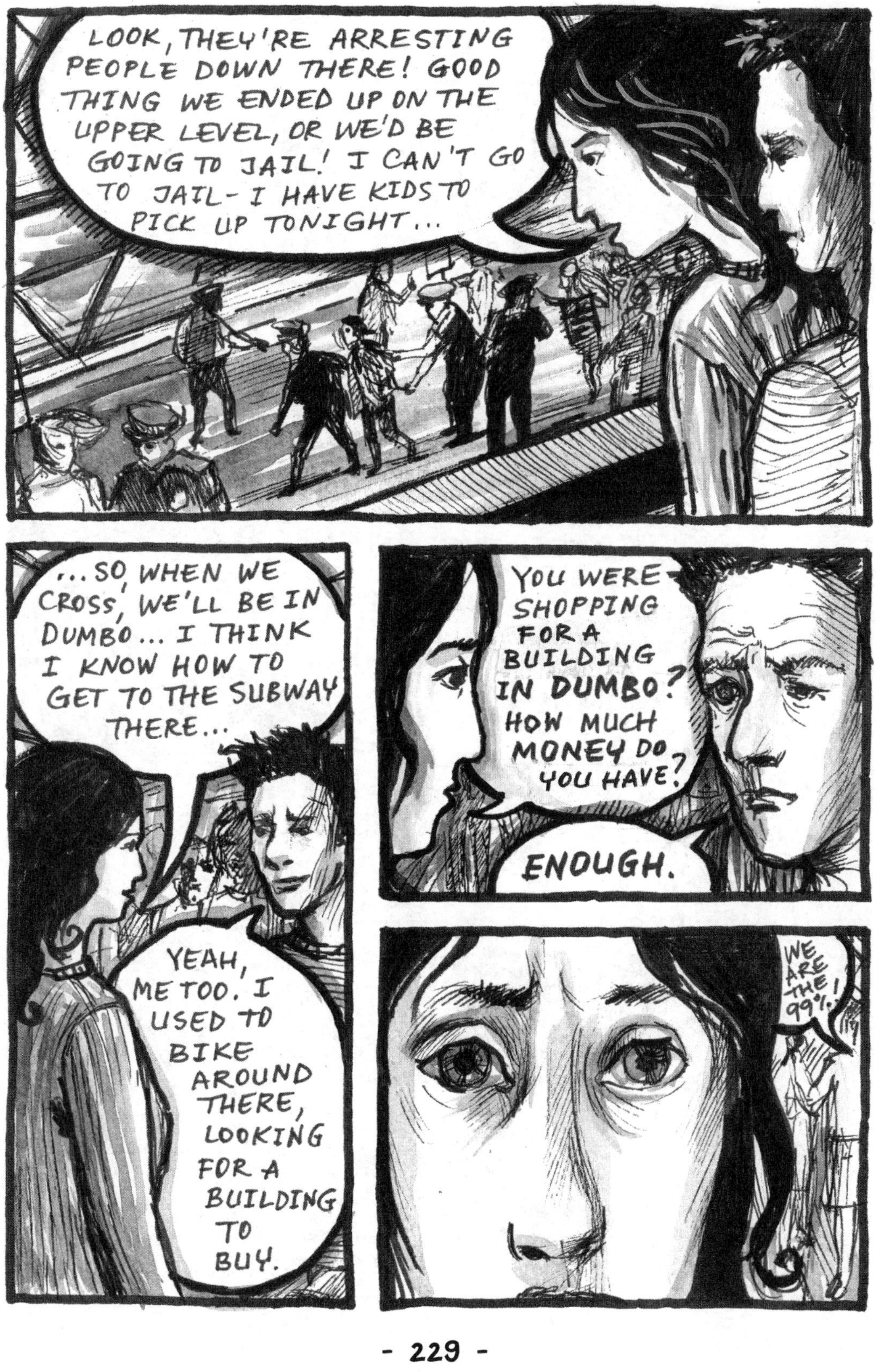
LOOK, THEY'RE ARRESTING PEOPLE DOWN THERE! GOOD THING WE ENDED UP ON THE UPPER LEVEL, OR WE'D BE GOING TO JAIL! I CAN'T GO TO JAIL- I HAVE KIDS TO PICK UP TONIGHT...
...SO, WHEN WE CROSS, WE'LL BE IN DUMBO... I THINK I KNOW HOW TO GET TO THE SUBWAY THERE...
YEAH, ME TOO. I USED TO BIKE AROUND THERE, LOOKING FOR A BUILDING TO BUY.
YOU WERE SHOPPING FOR A BUILDING IN DUMBO? HOW MUCH MONEY DO YOU HAVE?
ENOUGH.
WE ARE THE 99%!

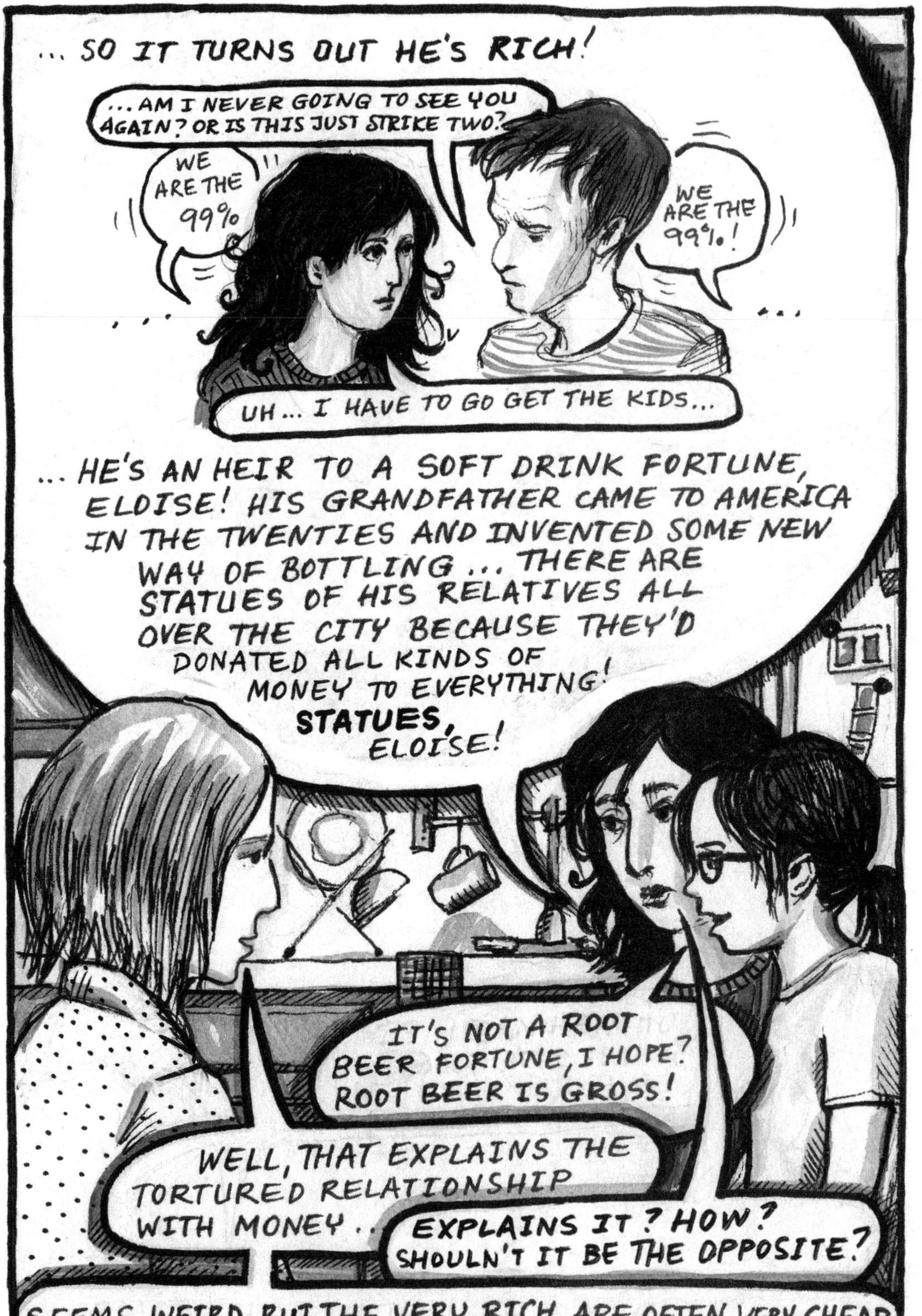
... SO IT TURNS OUT HE'S RICH!
...AM I NEVER GOING TO SEE YOU AGAIN? OR IS THIS JUST STRIKE TWO?
WE ARE THE 99%
WE ARE THE 99%!
UH ... I HAVE TO GO GET THE KIDS...
... HE'S AN HEIR TO A SOFT DRINK FORTUNE, ELOISE! HIS GRANDFATHER CAME TO AMERICA IN THE TWENTIES AND INVENTED SOME NEW WAY OF BOTTLING ... THERE ARE STATUES OF HIS RELATIVES ALL OVER THE CITY BECAUSE THEY'D DONATED ALL KINDS OF MONEY TO EVERYTHING! STATUES, ELOISE!
IT'S NOT A ROOT BEER FORTUNE, I HOPE? ROOT BEER IS GROSS!
WELL, THAT EXPLAINS THE TORTURED RELATIONSHIP WITH MONEY ..
EXPLAINS IT? HOW? SHOULN'T IT BE THE OPPOSITE?
SEEMS WEIRD, BUT THE VERY RICH ARE OFTEN VERY CHEAP.

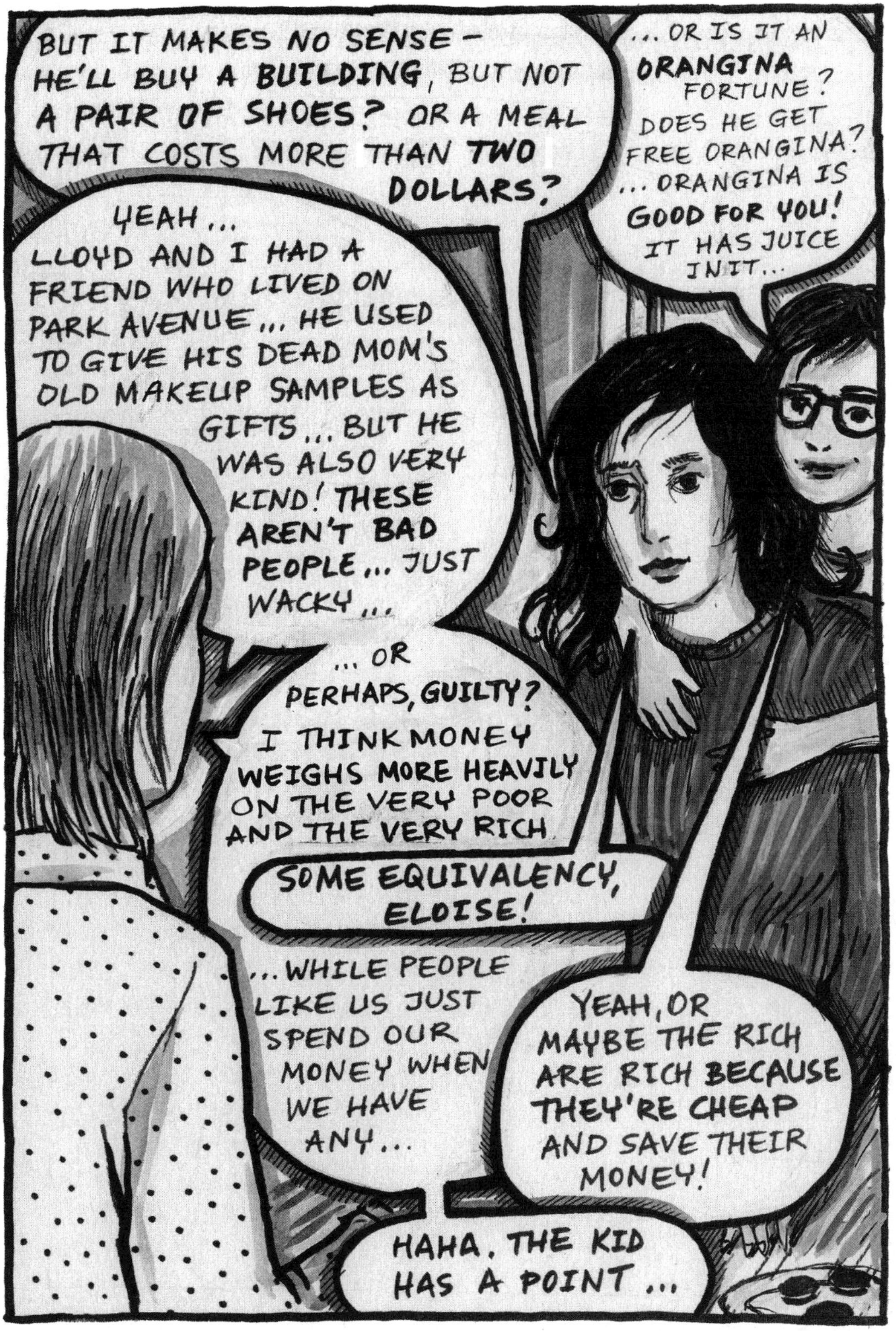
BUT IT MAKES NO SENSE — HE'LL BUY A BUILDING, BUT NOT A PAIR OF SHOES? OR A MEAL THAT COSTS MORE THAN TWO DOLLARS?
...OR IS IT AN ORANGINA FORTUNE? DOES HE GET FREE ORANGINA? ...ORANGINA IS GOOD FOR YOU! IT HAS JUICE IN IT...
YEAH... LLOYD AND I HAD A FRIEND WHO LIVED ON PARK AVENUE... HE USED TO GIVE HIS DEAD MOM'S OLD MAKEUP SAMPLES AS GIFTS... BUT HE WAS ALSO VERY KIND! THESE AREN'T BAD PEOPLE... JUST WACKY...
...OR PERHAPS, GUILTY? I THINK MONEY WEIGHS MORE HEAVILY ON THE VERY POOR AND THE VERY RICH.
SOME EQUIVALENCY, ELOISE!
...WHILE PEOPLE LIKE US JUST SPEND OUR MONEY WHEN WE HAVE ANY...
YEAH, OR MAYBE THE RICH ARE RICH BECAUSE THEY'RE CHEAP AND SAVE THEIR MONEY!
HAHA. THE KID HAS A POINT...

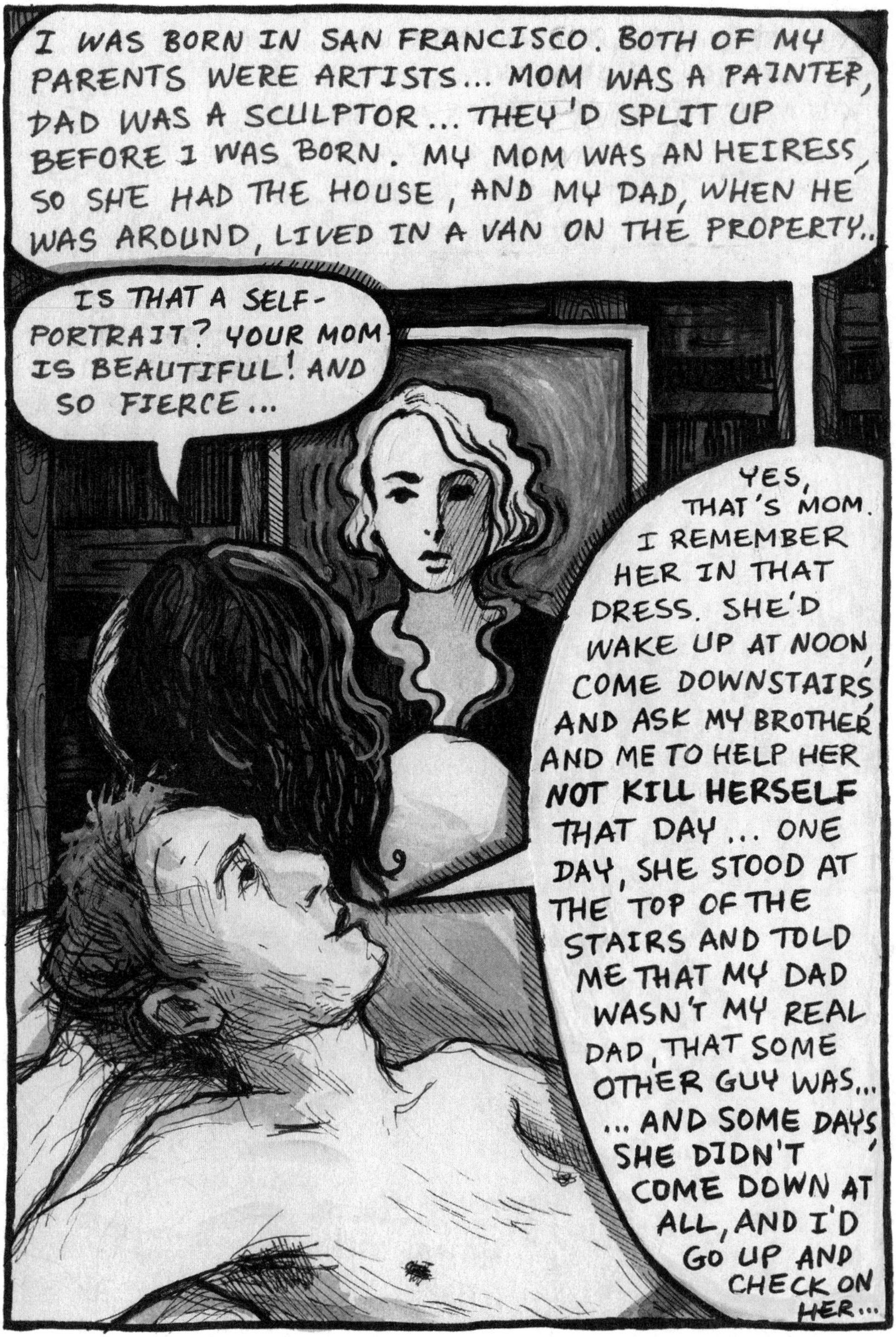
I WAS BORN IN SAN FRANCISCO. BOTH OF MY PARENTS WERE ARTISTS... MOM WAS A PAINTER, DAD WAS A SCULPTOR... THEY'D SPLIT UP BEFORE I WAS BORN. MY MOM WAS AN HEIRESS, SO SHE HAD THE HOUSE, AND MY DAD, WHEN HE WAS AROUND, LIVED IN A VAN ON THE PROPERTY...
IS THAT A SELF-PORTRAIT? YOUR MOM IS BEAUTIFUL! AND SO FIERCE...
YES, THAT'S MOM. I REMEMBER HER IN THAT DRESS. SHE'D WAKE UP AT NOON, COME DOWNSTAIRS, AND ASK MY BROTHER AND ME TO HELP HER **NOT KILL HERSELF** THAT DAY... ONE DAY, SHE STOOD AT THE TOP OF THE STAIRS AND TOLD ME THAT MY DAD WASN'T MY REAL DAD, THAT SOME OTHER GUY WAS... ...AND SOME DAYS, SHE DIDN'T COME DOWN AT ALL, AND I'D GO UP AND CHECK ON HER...

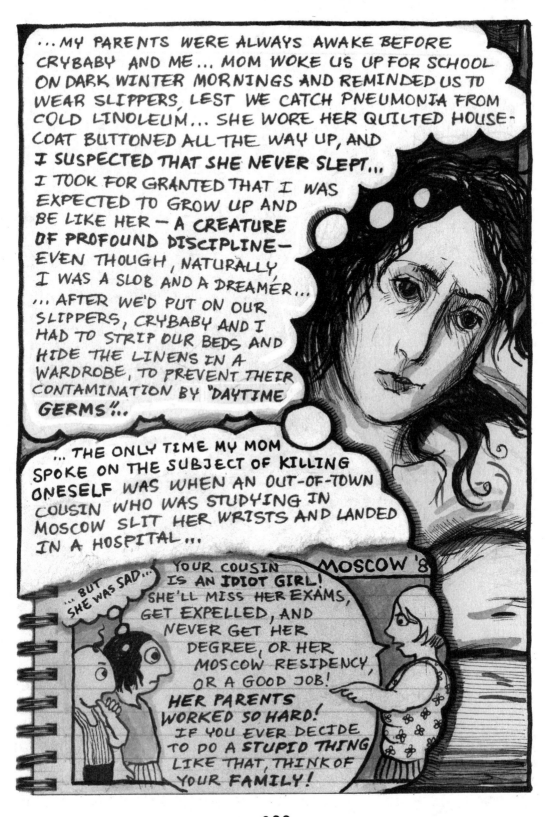

...MY PARENTS WERE ALWAYS AWAKE BEFORE CRYBABY AND ME... MOM WOKE US UP FOR SCHOOL ON DARK WINTER MORNINGS AND REMINDED US TO WEAR SLIPPERS, LEST WE CATCH PNEUMONIA FROM COLD LINOLEUM... SHE WORE HER QUILTED HOUSE-COAT BUTTONED ALL THE WAY UP, AND I SUSPECTED THAT SHE NEVER SLEPT... I TOOK FOR GRANTED THAT I WAS EXPECTED TO GROW UP AND BE LIKE HER — A CREATURE OF PROFOUND DISCIPLINE— EVEN THOUGH, NATURALLY, I WAS A SLOB AND A DREAMER... ...AFTER WE'D PUT ON OUR SLIPPERS, CRYBABY AND I HAD TO STRIP OUR BEDS AND HIDE THE LINENS IN A WARDROBE, TO PREVENT THEIR CONTAMINATION BY "DAYTIME GERMS"...

... THE ONLY TIME MY MOM SPOKE ON THE SUBJECT OF KILLING ONESELF WAS WHEN AN OUT-OF-TOWN COUSIN WHO WAS STUDYING IN MOSCOW SLIT HER WRISTS AND LANDED IN A HOSPITAL ...

MOSCOW '8

... BUT SHE WAS SAD...

YOUR COUSIN IS AN IDIOT GIRL! SHE'LL MISS HER EXAMS, GET EXPELLED, AND NEVER GET HER DEGREE, OR HER MOSCOW RESIDENCY, OR A GOOD JOB! HER PARENTS WORKED SO HARD! IF YOU EVER DECIDE TO DO A STUPID THING LIKE THAT, THINK OF YOUR FAMILY!

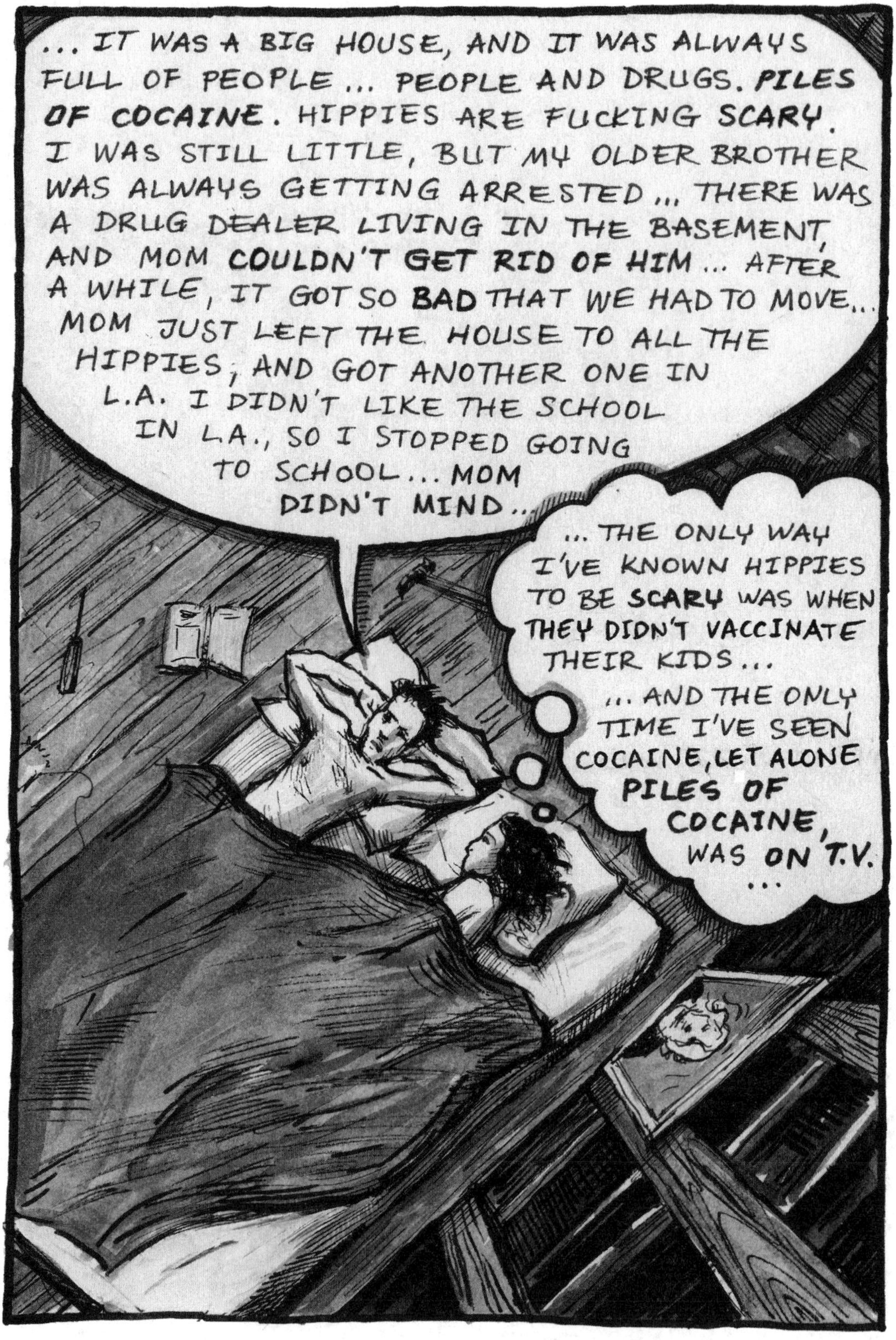
... IT WAS A BIG HOUSE, AND IT WAS ALWAYS FULL OF PEOPLE ... PEOPLE AND DRUGS. PILES OF COCAINE. HIPPIES ARE FUCKING SCARY. I WAS STILL LITTLE, BUT MY OLDER BROTHER WAS ALWAYS GETTING ARRESTED ... THERE WAS A DRUG DEALER LIVING IN THE BASEMENT, AND MOM COULDN'T GET RID OF HIM ... AFTER A WHILE, IT GOT SO BAD THAT WE HAD TO MOVE... MOM JUST LEFT THE HOUSE TO ALL THE HIPPIES, AND GOT ANOTHER ONE IN L.A. I DIDN'T LIKE THE SCHOOL IN L.A., SO I STOPPED GOING TO SCHOOL ... MOM DIDN'T MIND...
... THE ONLY WAY I'VE KNOWN HIPPIES TO BE SCARY WAS WHEN THEY DIDN'T VACCINATE THEIR KIDS ...
... AND THE ONLY TIME I'VE SEEN COCAINE, LET ALONE PILES OF COCAINE, WAS ON T.V. ...

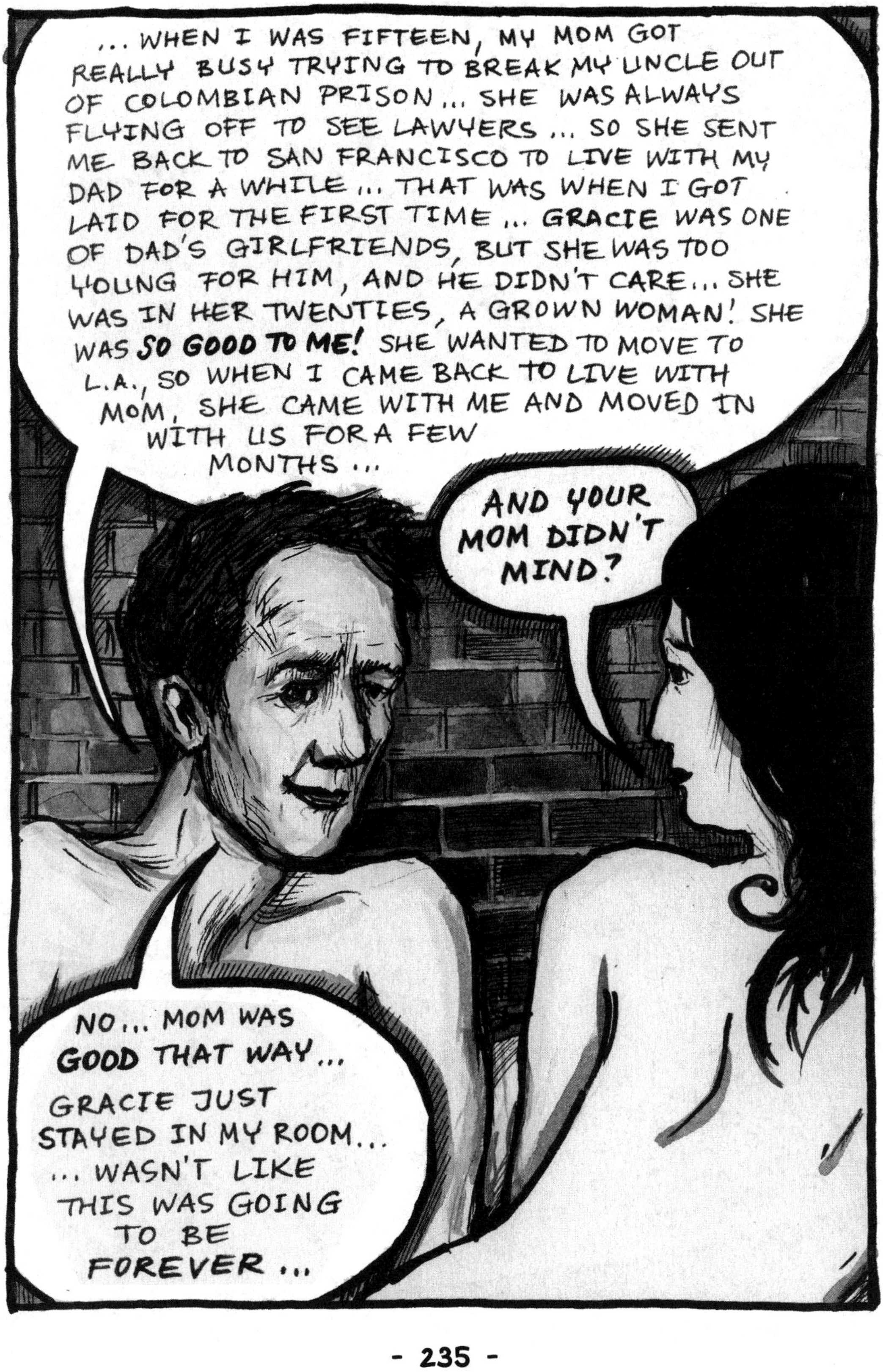
...WHEN I WAS FIFTEEN, MY MOM GOT REALLY BUSY TRYING TO BREAK MY UNCLE OUT OF COLOMBIAN PRISON... SHE WAS ALWAYS FLYING OFF TO SEE LAWYERS... SO SHE SENT ME BACK TO SAN FRANCISCO TO LIVE WITH MY DAD FOR A WHILE... THAT WAS WHEN I GOT LAID FOR THE FIRST TIME... GRACIE WAS ONE OF DAD'S GIRLFRIENDS, BUT SHE WAS TOO YOUNG FOR HIM, AND HE DIDN'T CARE... SHE WAS IN HER TWENTIES, A GROWN WOMAN! SHE WAS SO GOOD TO ME! SHE WANTED TO MOVE TO L.A., SO WHEN I CAME BACK TO LIVE WITH MOM, SHE CAME WITH ME AND MOVED IN WITH US FOR A FEW MONTHS...
AND YOUR MOM DIDN'T MIND?
NO... MOM WAS GOOD THAT WAY... GRACIE JUST STAYED IN MY ROOM... ...WASN'T LIKE THIS WAS GOING TO BE FOREVER...

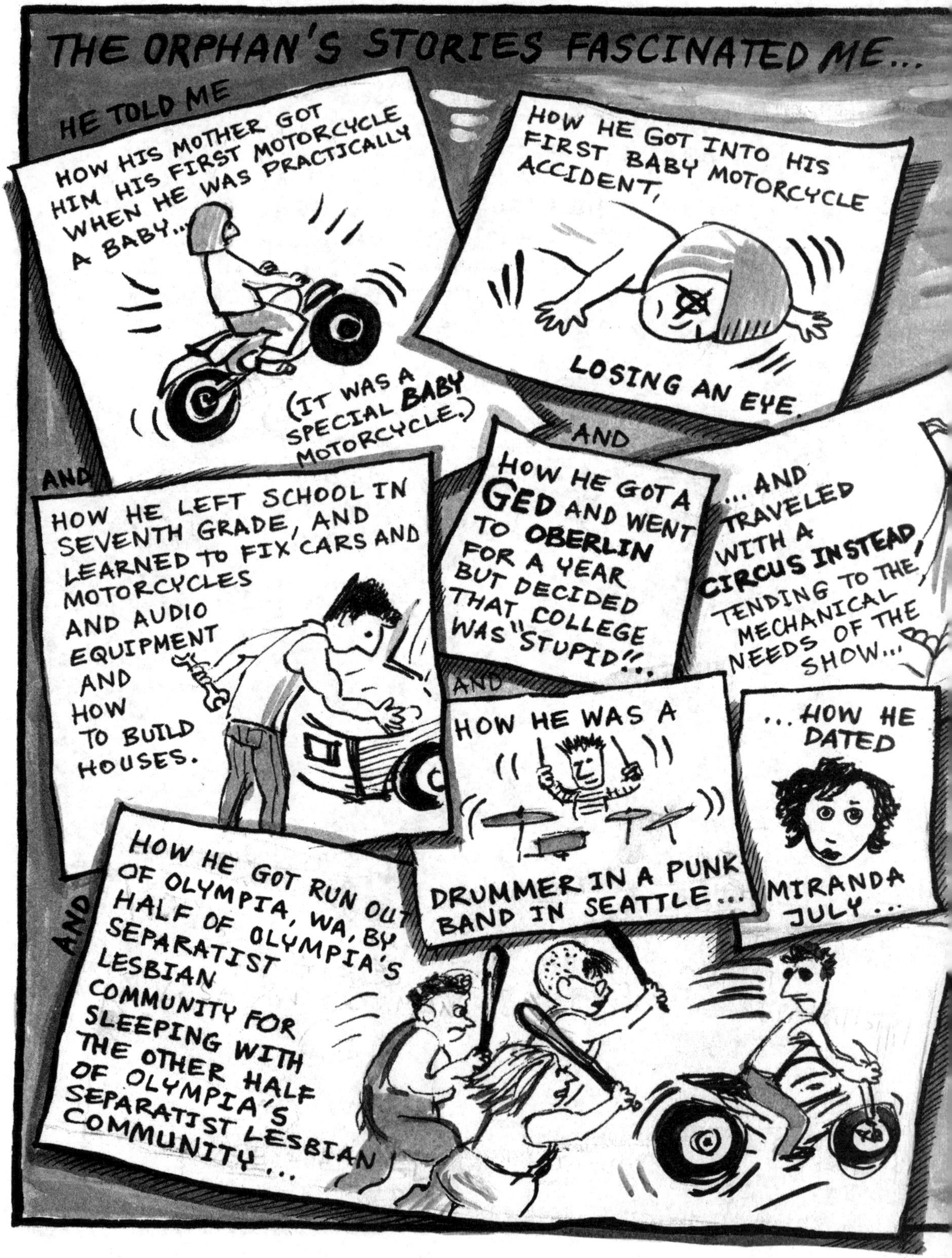
THE ORPHAN'S STORIES FASCINATED ME...
HE TOLD ME
HOW HIS MOTHER GOT HIM HIS FIRST MOTORCYCLE WHEN HE WAS PRACTICALLY A BABY...
(IT WAS A SPECIAL BABY MOTORCYCLE.)
HOW HE GOT INTO HIS FIRST BABY MOTORCYCLE ACCIDENT,
LOSING AN EYE.
AND
HOW HE LEFT SCHOOL IN SEVENTH GRADE, AND LEARNED TO FIX CARS AND MOTORCYCLES AND AUDIO EQUIPMENT AND HOW TO BUILD HOUSES.
AND
HOW HE GOT A GED AND WENT TO OBERLIN FOR A YEAR BUT DECIDED THAT COLLEGE WAS "STUPID!"...
...AND TRAVELED WITH A CIRCUS INSTEAD, TENDING TO THE MECHANICAL NEEDS OF THE SHOW...
AND
HOW HE WAS A
DRUMMER IN A PUNK BAND IN SEATTLE...
...HOW HE DATED
MIRANDA JULY...
AND
HOW HE GOT RUN OUT OF OLYMPIA, WA, BY HALF OF OLYMPIA'S SEPARATIST LESBIAN COMMUNITY FOR SLEEPING WITH THE OTHER HALF OF OLYMPIA'S SEPARATIST LESBIAN COMMUNITY...

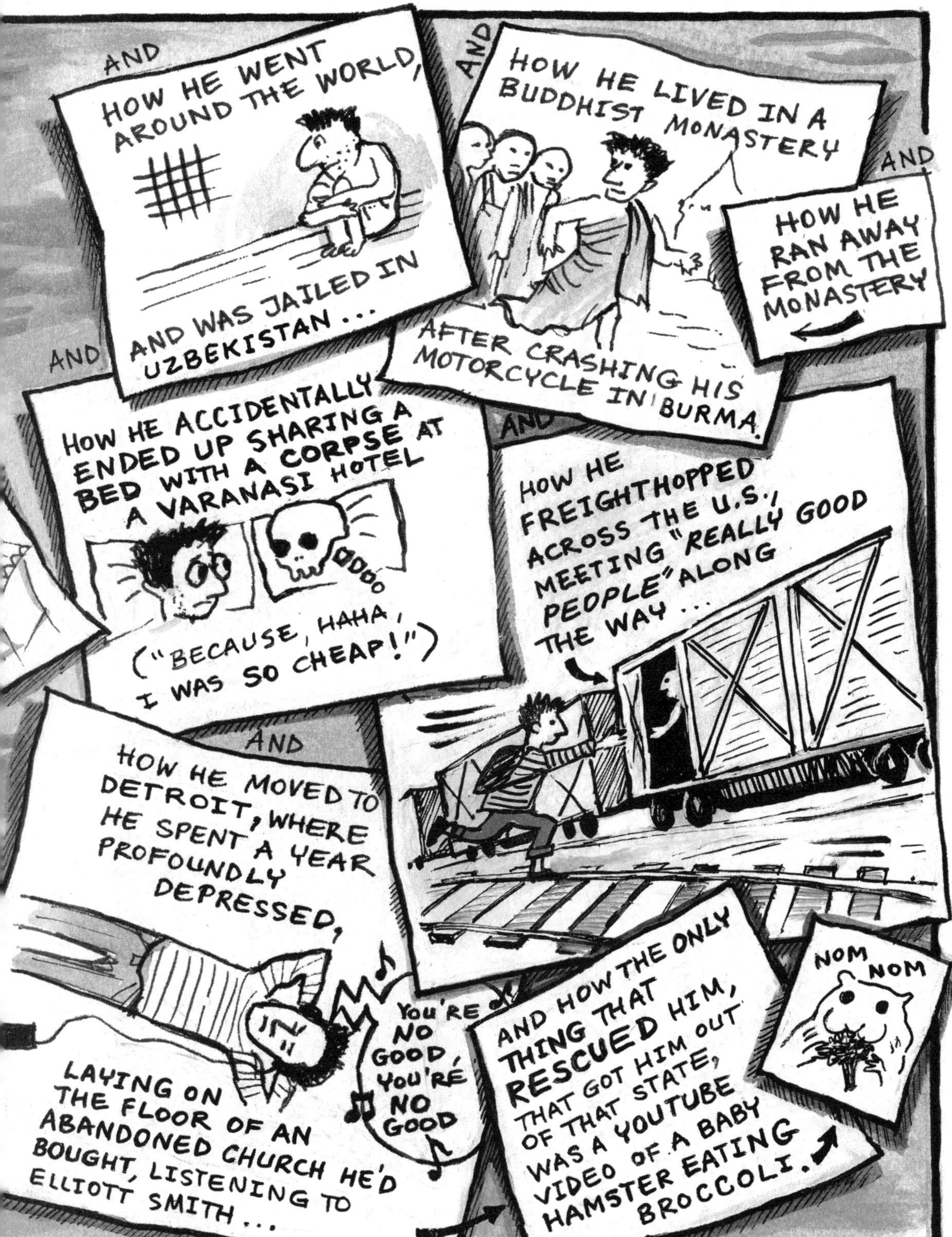
AND
HOW HE WENT AROUND THE WORLD,
AND WAS JAILED IN UZBEKISTAN...
AND
HOW HE LIVED IN A BUDDHIST MONASTERY
AFTER CRASHING HIS MOTORCYCLE IN BURMA.
AND
HOW HE RAN AWAY FROM THE MONASTERY
AND
HOW HE ACCIDENTALLY ENDED UP SHARING A BED WITH A CORPSE AT A VARANASI HOTEL
("BECAUSE, HAHA, I WAS SO CHEAP!")
AND
HOW HE FREIGHTHOPPED ACROSS THE U.S., MEETING "REALLY GOOD PEOPLE" ALONG THE WAY...
AND
HOW HE MOVED TO DETROIT, WHERE HE SPENT A YEAR PROFOUNDLY DEPRESSED,
LAYING ON THE FLOOR OF AN ABANDONED CHURCH HE'D BOUGHT, LISTENING TO ELLIOTT SMITH...
YOU'RE NO GOOD, YOU'RE NO GOOD
AND HOW THE ONLY THING THAT RESCUED HIM, THAT GOT HIM OUT OF THAT STATE, WAS A YOUTUBE VIDEO OF A BABY HAMSTER EATING BROCCOLI.
NOM NOM

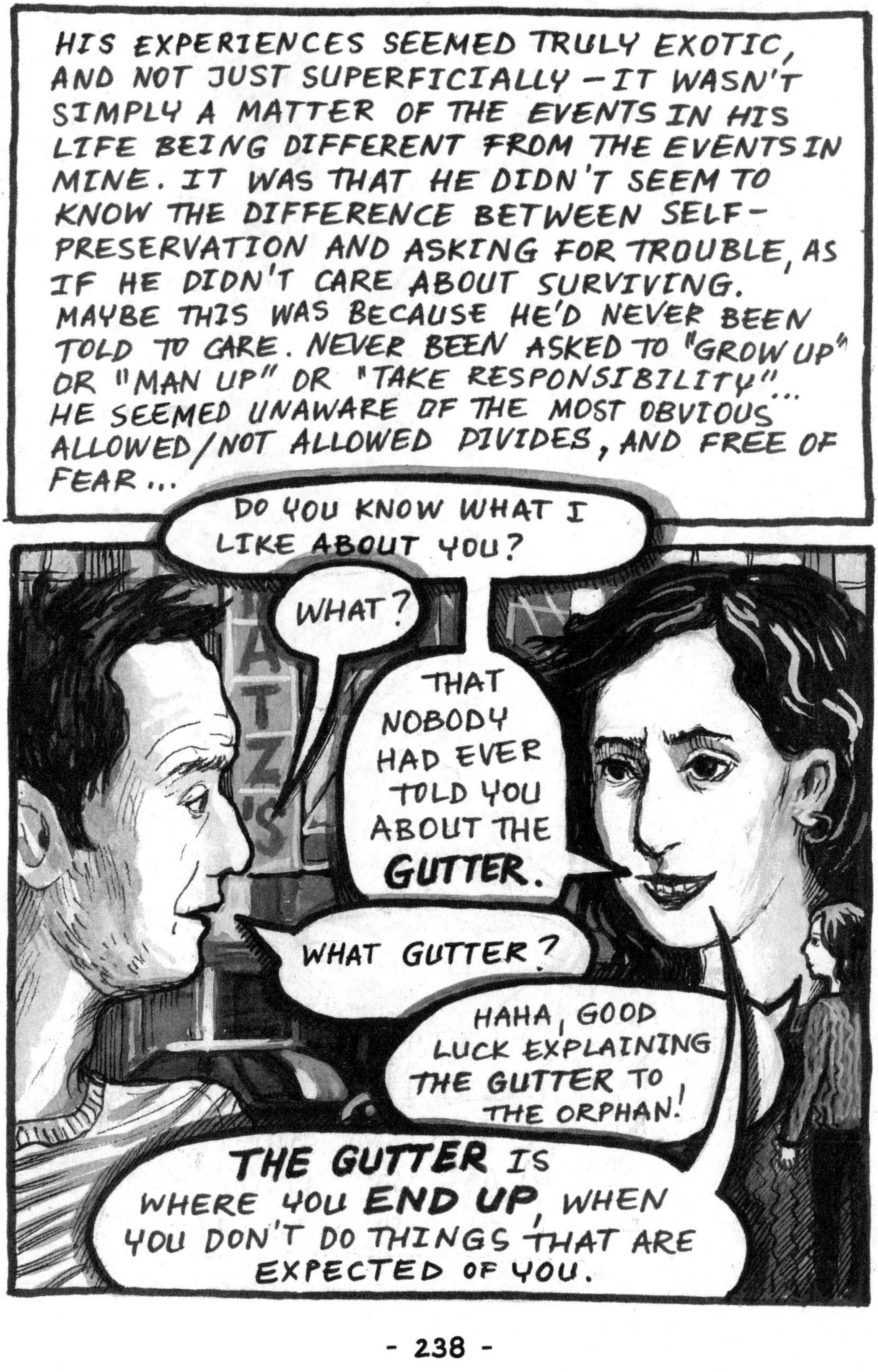
HIS EXPERIENCES SEEMED TRULY EXOTIC, AND NOT JUST SUPERFICIALLY — IT WASN'T SIMPLY A MATTER OF THE EVENTS IN HIS LIFE BEING DIFFERENT FROM THE EVENTS IN MINE. IT WAS THAT HE DIDN'T SEEM TO KNOW THE DIFFERENCE BETWEEN SELF-PRESERVATION AND ASKING FOR TROUBLE, AS IF HE DIDN'T CARE ABOUT SURVIVING. MAYBE THIS WAS BECAUSE HE'D NEVER BEEN TOLD TO CARE. NEVER BEEN ASKED TO "GROW UP" OR "MAN UP" OR "TAKE RESPONSIBILITY"... HE SEEMED UNAWARE OF THE MOST OBVIOUS ALLOWED/NOT ALLOWED DIVIDES, AND FREE OF FEAR...
DO YOU KNOW WHAT I LIKE ABOUT YOU?
WHAT?
THAT NOBODY HAD EVER TOLD YOU ABOUT THE **GUTTER**.
WHAT GUTTER?
HAHA, GOOD LUCK EXPLAINING THE GUTTER TO THE ORPHAN!
THE GUTTER IS WHERE YOU **END UP**, WHEN YOU DON'T DO THINGS THAT ARE EXPECTED OF YOU.

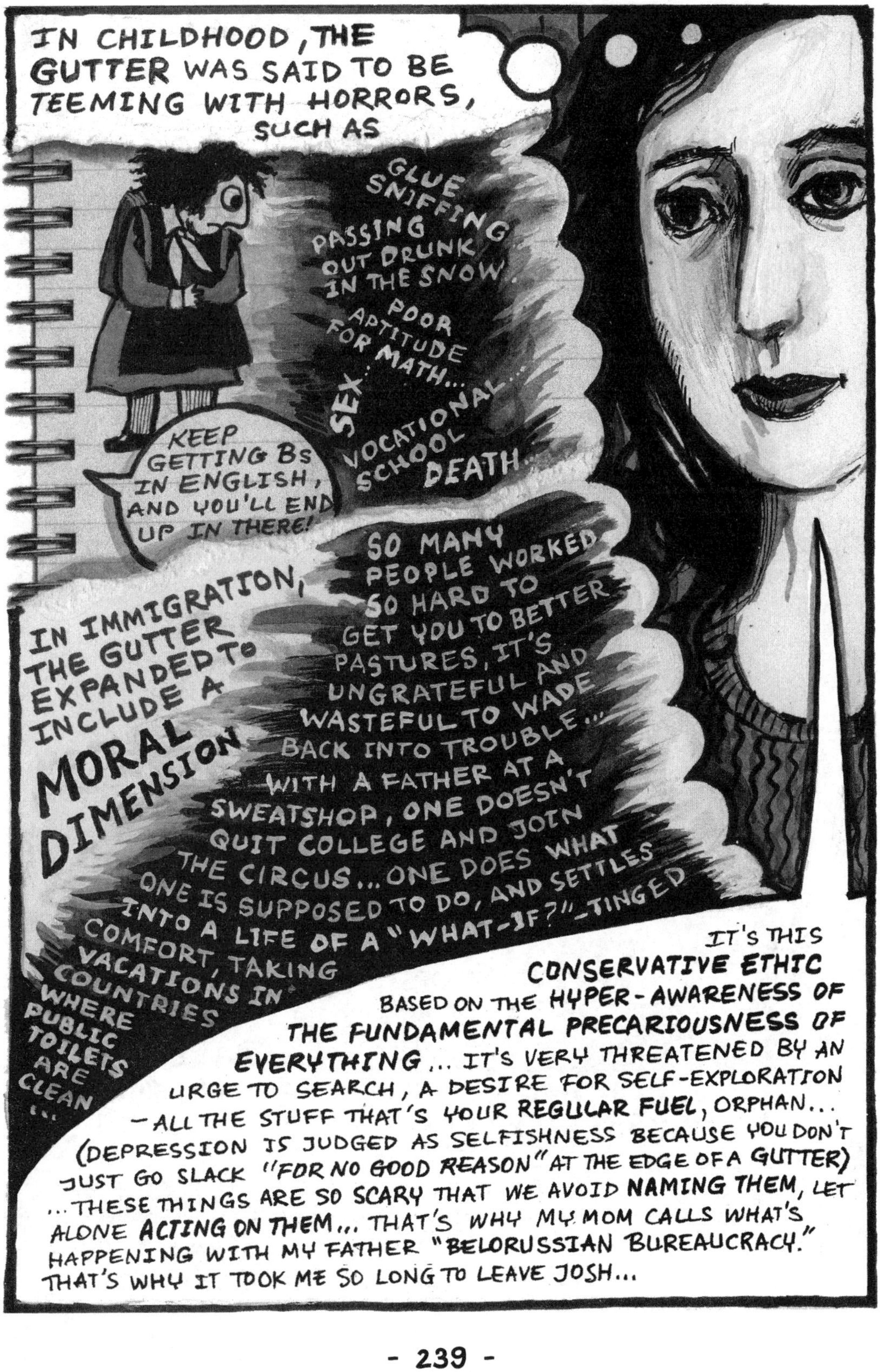
IN CHILDHOOD, THE GUTTER WAS SAID TO BE TEEMING WITH HORRORS, SUCH AS
GLUE SNIFFING
PASSING OUT DRUNK IN THE SNOW.
POOR APTITUDE FOR MATH...
SEX...
VOCATIONAL... SCHOOL
DEATH...
KEEP GETTING Bs IN ENGLISH, AND YOU'LL END UP IN THERE!
IN IMMIGRATION, THE GUTTER EXPANDED TO INCLUDE A MORAL DIMENSION
SO MANY PEOPLE WORKED SO HARD TO GET YOU TO BETTER PASTURES, IT'S UNGRATEFUL AND WASTEFUL TO WADE BACK INTO TROUBLE... WITH A FATHER AT A SWEATSHOP, ONE DOESN'T QUIT COLLEGE AND JOIN THE CIRCUS... ONE DOES WHAT ONE IS SUPPOSED TO DO, AND SETTLES INTO A LIFE OF A "WHAT-IF?"-TINGED COMFORT, TAKING VACATIONS IN COUNTRIES WHERE PUBLIC TOILETS ARE CLEAN...
IT'S THIS CONSERVATIVE ETHIC BASED ON THE HYPER-AWARENESS OF THE FUNDAMENTAL PRECARIOUSNESS OF EVERYTHING... IT'S VERY THREATENED BY AN URGE TO SEARCH, A DESIRE FOR SELF-EXPLORATION —ALL THE STUFF THAT'S YOUR REGULAR FUEL, ORPHAN... (DEPRESSION IS JUDGED AS SELFISHNESS BECAUSE YOU DON'T JUST GO SLACK "FOR NO GOOD REASON" AT THE EDGE OF A GUTTER) ...THESE THINGS ARE SO SCARY THAT WE AVOID NAMING THEM, LET ALONE ACTING ON THEM... THAT'S WHY MY MOM CALLS WHAT'S HAPPENING WITH MY FATHER "BELORUSSIAN BUREAUCRACY." THAT'S WHY IT TOOK ME SO LONG TO LEAVE JOSH...

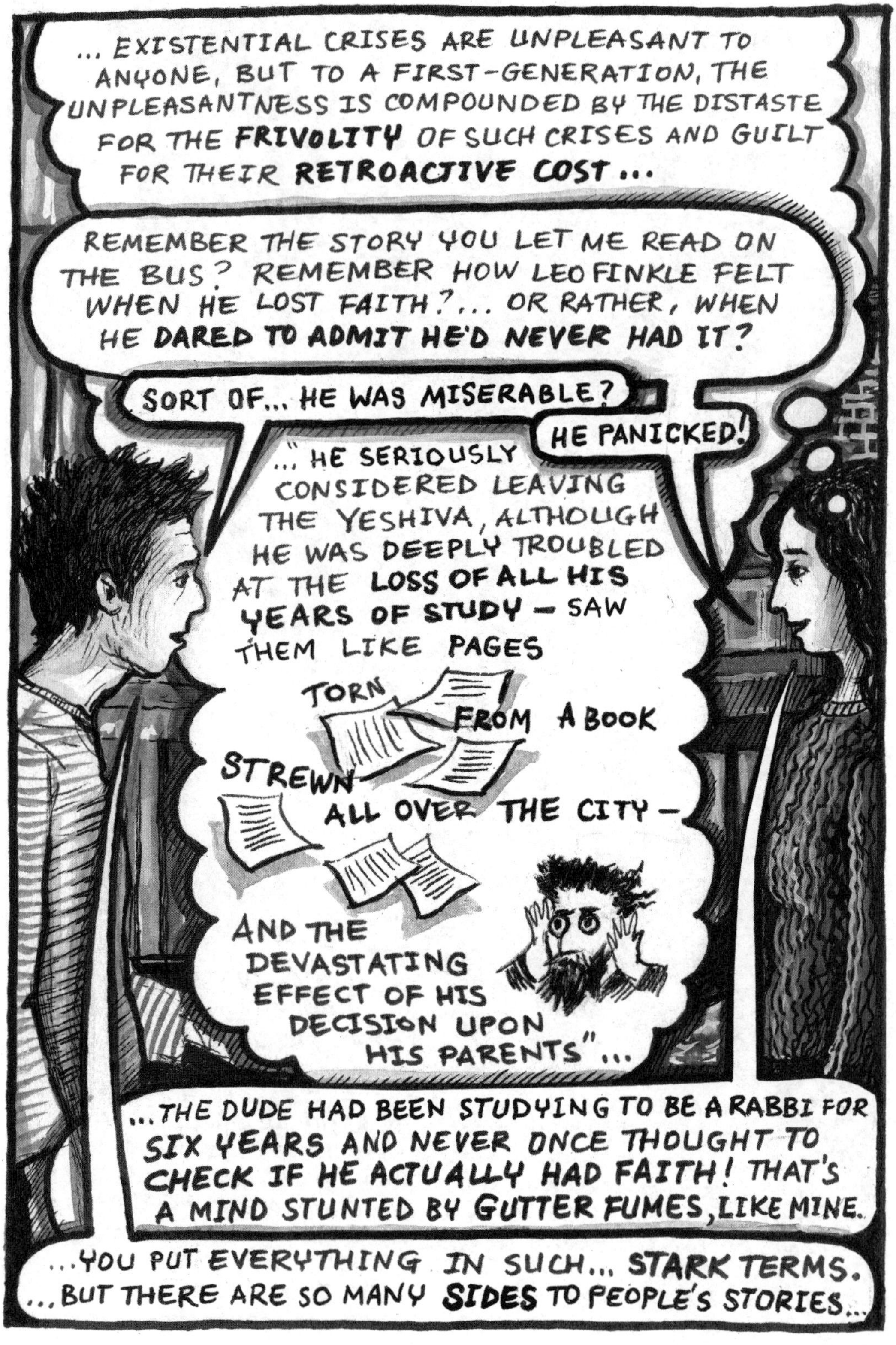
...EXISTENTIAL CRISES ARE UNPLEASANT TO ANYONE, BUT TO A FIRST-GENERATION, THE UNPLEASANTNESS IS COMPOUNDED BY THE DISTASTE FOR THE FRIVOLITY OF SUCH CRISES AND GUILT FOR THEIR RETROACTIVE COST...
REMEMBER THE STORY YOU LET ME READ ON THE BUS? REMEMBER HOW LEO FINKLE FELT WHEN HE LOST FAITH?... OR RATHER, WHEN HE DARED TO ADMIT HE'D NEVER HAD IT?
SORT OF... HE WAS MISERABLE?
HE PANICKED!
..."HE SERIOUSLY CONSIDERED LEAVING THE YESHIVA, ALTHOUGH HE WAS DEEPLY TROUBLED AT THE LOSS OF ALL HIS YEARS OF STUDY — SAW THEM LIKE PAGES TORN FROM A BOOK STREWN ALL OVER THE CITY — AND THE DEVASTATING EFFECT OF HIS DECISION UPON HIS PARENTS"...
...THE DUDE HAD BEEN STUDYING TO BE A RABBI FOR SIX YEARS AND NEVER ONCE THOUGHT TO CHECK IF HE ACTUALLY HAD FAITH! THAT'S A MIND STUNTED BY GUTTER FUMES, LIKE MINE.
...YOU PUT EVERYTHING IN SUCH... STARK TERMS. ...BUT THERE ARE SO MANY SIDES TO PEOPLE'S STORIES...

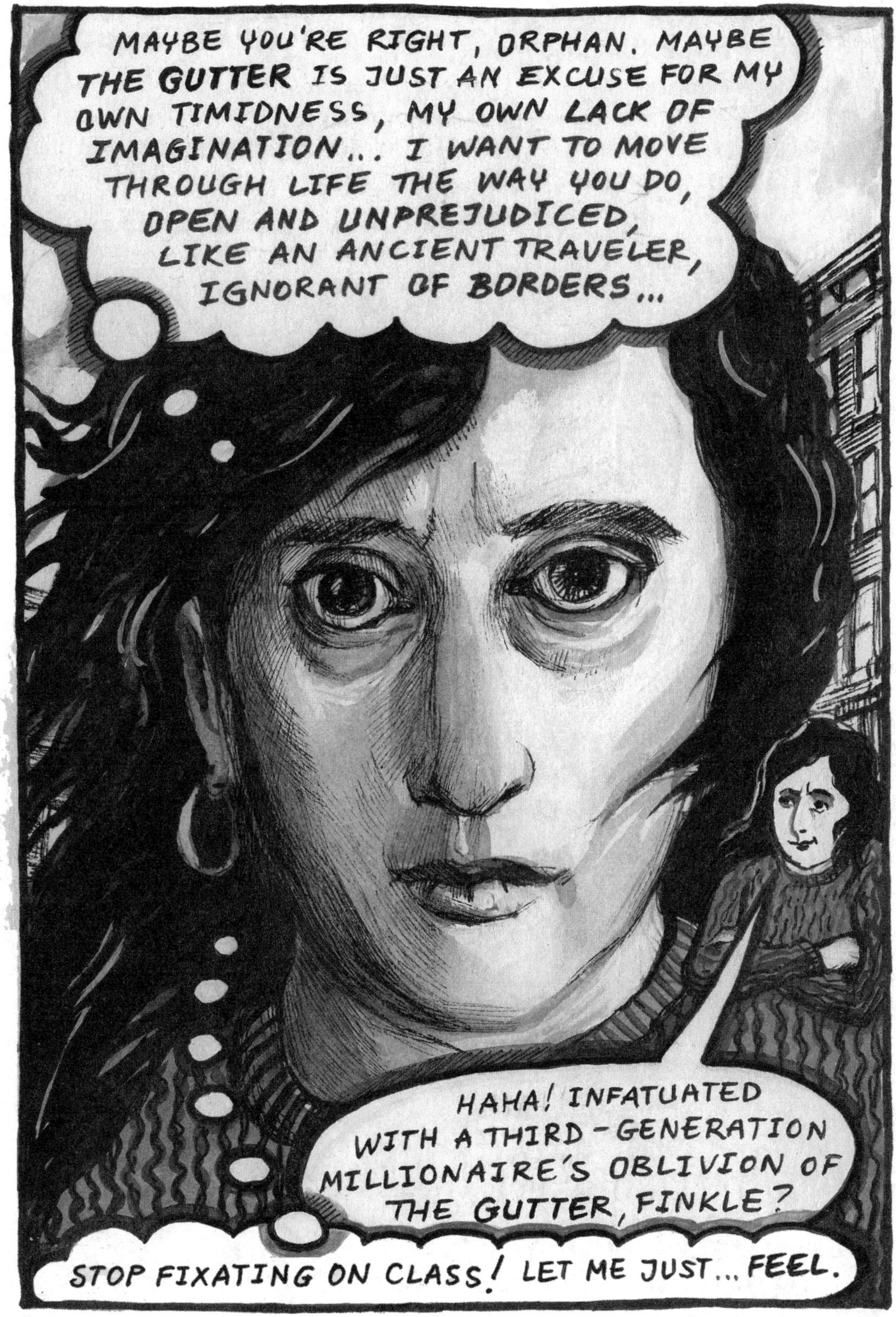
MAYBE YOU'RE RIGHT, ORPHAN. MAYBE THE GUTTER IS JUST AN EXCUSE FOR MY OWN TIMIDNESS, MY OWN LACK OF IMAGINATION... I WANT TO MOVE THROUGH LIFE THE WAY YOU DO, OPEN AND UNPREJUDICED, LIKE AN ANCIENT TRAVELER, IGNORANT OF BORDERS...
HAHA! INFATUATED WITH A THIRD-GENERATION MILLIONAIRE'S OBLIVION OF THE GUTTER, FINKLE?
STOP FIXATING ON CLASS! LET ME JUST... FEEL.

BUT CLASS WAS ON MY MIND AGAIN THE NIGHT THE ORPHAN AND I WENT TO SEE *THE CHERRY ORCHARD.* (I'D BOUGHT THE TICKETS, TELLING THE ORPHAN THAT I'D GOTTEN THEM FOR FREE. I KNEW HE COULDN'T SPEND $25 ON A TICKET, AND I DIDN'T WANT TO EMBARRASS HIM.)

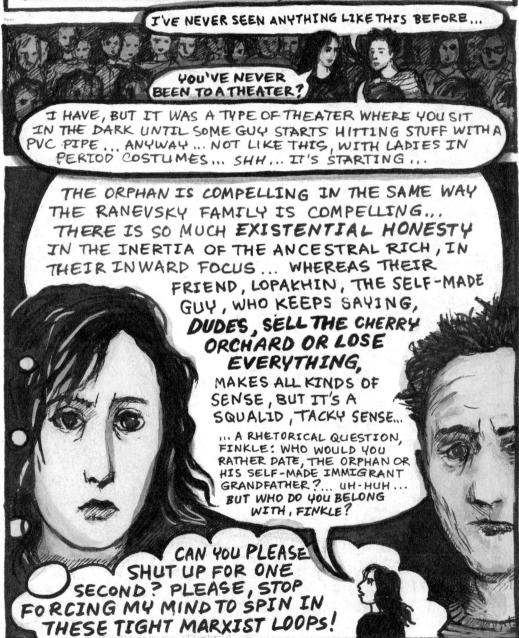

I'VE NEVER SEEN ANYTHING LIKE THIS BEFORE...

YOU'VE NEVER BEEN TO A THEATER?

I HAVE, BUT IT WAS A TYPE OF THEATER WHERE YOU SIT IN THE DARK UNTIL SOME GUY STARTS HITTING STUFF WITH A PVC PIPE... ANYWAY... NOT LIKE THIS, WITH LADIES IN PERIOD COSTUMES... SHH... IT'S STARTING...

THE ORPHAN IS COMPELLING IN THE SAME WAY THE RANEVSKY FAMILY IS COMPELLING... THERE IS SO MUCH *EXISTENTIAL HONESTY* IN THE INERTIA OF THE ANCESTRAL RICH, IN THEIR INWARD FOCUS... WHEREAS THEIR FRIEND, LOPAKHIN, THE SELF-MADE GUY, WHO KEEPS SAYING, **DUDES, SELL THE CHERRY ORCHARD OR LOSE EVERYTHING,** MAKES ALL KINDS OF SENSE, BUT IT'S A SQUALID, TACKY SENSE...

... A RHETORICAL QUESTION, FINKLE: WHO WOULD YOU RATHER DATE, THE ORPHAN OR HIS SELF-MADE IMMIGRANT GRANDFATHER?... UH-HUH... BUT WHO DO YOU BELONG WITH, FINKLE?

CAN YOU PLEASE SHUT UP FOR ONE SECOND? PLEASE, STOP FORCING MY MIND TO SPIN IN THESE TIGHT MARXIST LOOPS!

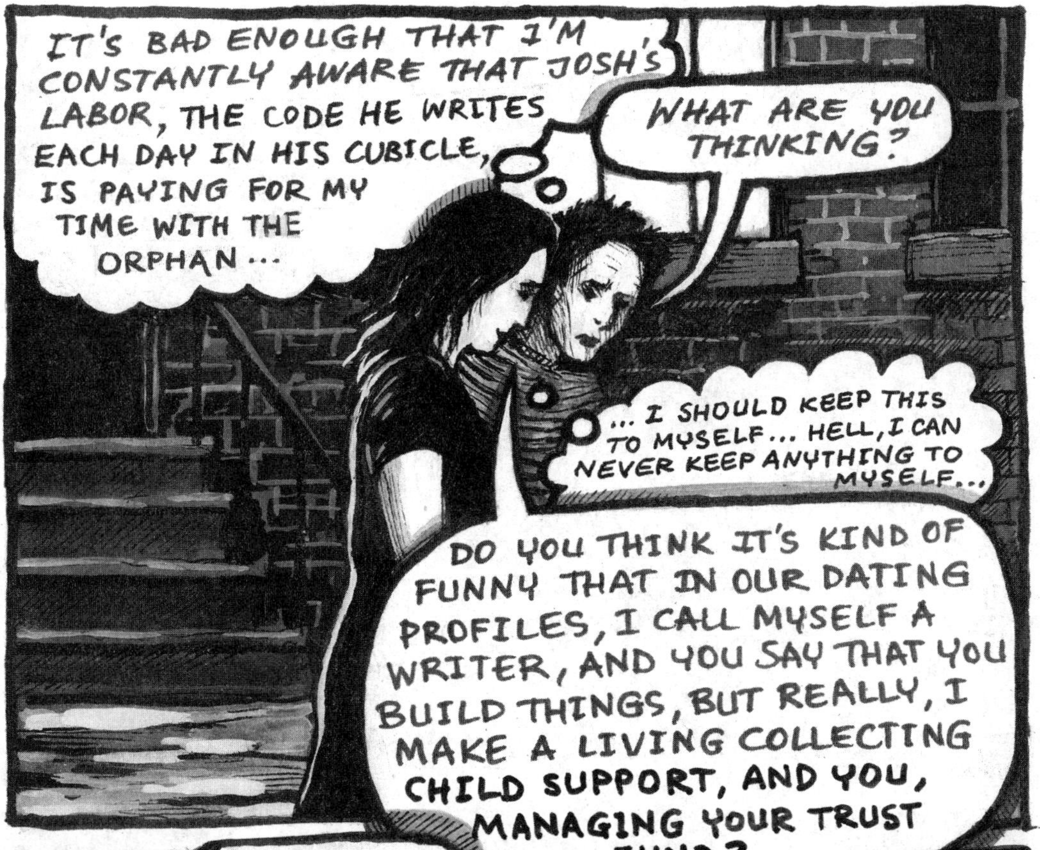
IT'S BAD ENOUGH THAT I'M CONSTANTLY AWARE THAT JOSH'S LABOR, THE CODE HE WRITES EACH DAY IN HIS CUBICLE, IS PAYING FOR MY TIME WITH THE ORPHAN...
WHAT ARE YOU THINKING?
... I SHOULD KEEP THIS TO MYSELF... HELL, I CAN NEVER KEEP ANYTHING TO MYSELF...
DO YOU THINK IT'S KIND OF FUNNY THAT IN OUR DATING PROFILES, I CALL MYSELF A WRITER, AND YOU SAY THAT YOU BUILD THINGS, BUT REALLY, I MAKE A LIVING COLLECTING CHILD SUPPORT, AND YOU, MANAGING YOUR TRUST FUND?

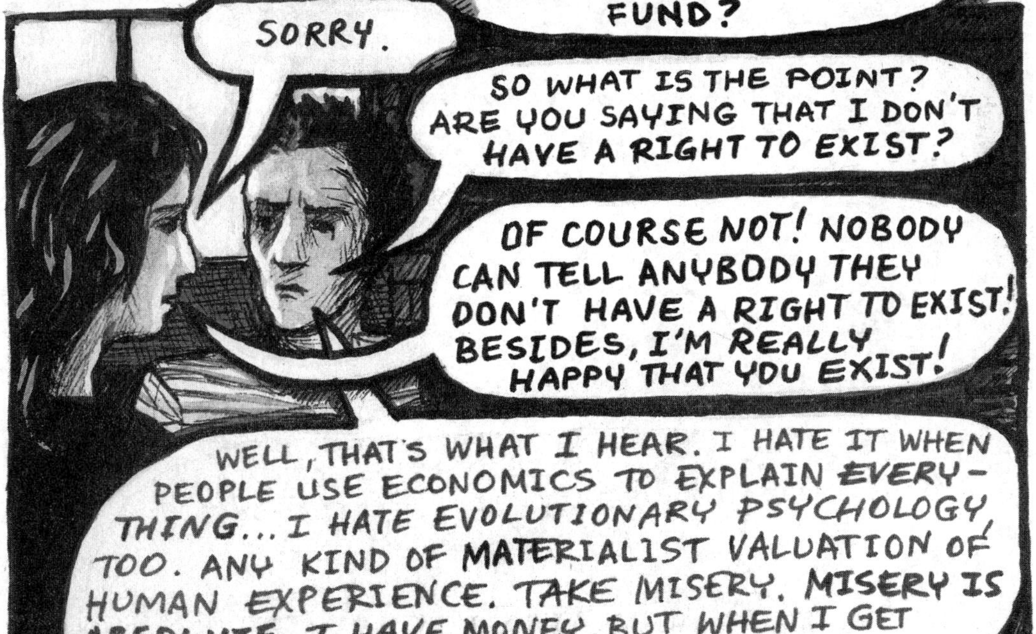
SORRY.
SO WHAT IS THE POINT? ARE YOU SAYING THAT I DON'T HAVE A RIGHT TO EXIST?
OF COURSE NOT! NOBODY CAN TELL ANYBODY THEY DON'T HAVE A RIGHT TO EXIST! BESIDES, I'M REALLY HAPPY THAT YOU EXIST!
WELL, THAT'S WHAT I HEAR. I HATE IT WHEN PEOPLE USE ECONOMICS TO EXPLAIN EVERYTHING... I HATE EVOLUTIONARY PSYCHOLOGY, TOO. ANY KIND OF MATERIALIST VALUATION OF HUMAN EXPERIENCE. TAKE MISERY. MISERY IS ABSOLUTE. I HAVE MONEY, BUT WHEN I GET DEPRESSED, IT'S HELL... NOT RELATIVE HELL.

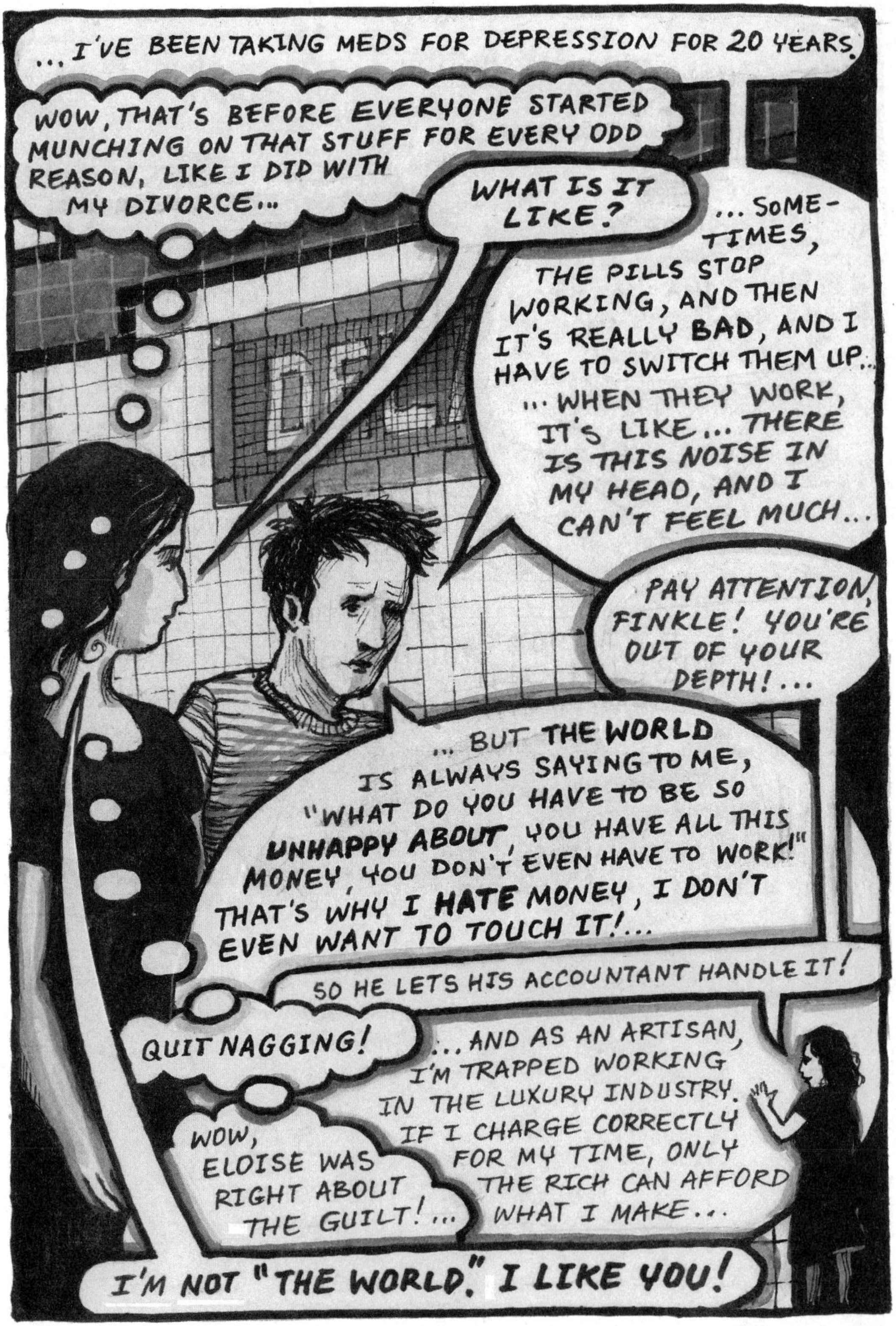

... I'VE BEEN TAKING MEDS FOR DEPRESSION FOR 20 YEARS.
WOW, THAT'S BEFORE EVERYONE STARTED MUNCHING ON THAT STUFF FOR EVERY ODD REASON, LIKE I DID WITH MY DIVORCE...
WHAT IS IT LIKE?
... SOMETIMES, THE PILLS STOP WORKING, AND THEN IT'S REALLY BAD, AND I HAVE TO SWITCH THEM UP... ... WHEN THEY WORK, IT'S LIKE... THERE IS THIS NOISE IN MY HEAD, AND I CAN'T FEEL MUCH...
PAY ATTENTION, FINKLE! YOU'RE OUT OF YOUR DEPTH!...
... BUT THE WORLD IS ALWAYS SAYING TO ME, "WHAT DO YOU HAVE TO BE SO UNHAPPY ABOUT, YOU HAVE ALL THIS MONEY, YOU DON'T EVEN HAVE TO WORK!" THAT'S WHY I HATE MONEY, I DON'T EVEN WANT TO TOUCH IT!...
SO HE LETS HIS ACCOUNTANT HANDLE IT!
QUIT NAGGING!
... AND AS AN ARTISAN, I'M TRAPPED WORKING IN THE LUXURY INDUSTRY. IF I CHARGE CORRECTLY FOR MY TIME, ONLY THE RICH CAN AFFORD WHAT I MAKE...
WOW, ELOISE WAS RIGHT ABOUT THE GUILT!...
I'M NOT "THE WORLD." I LIKE YOU!

WHAT I *REALLY* MEANT TO SAY TO THE ORPHAN WAS "I LOVE YOU," BUT I KNEW THAT THIS WAS NOT THE TIME TO MESS WITH THE CULTURAL PECULIARITIES OF AMERICAN COURTSHIP...

...WHEN I'D BEGUN MY LAST RELATIONSHIP, NEARLY TWO DECADES AGO, I'D BEEN UNAWARE OF THE RULE THAT NEW LOVERS MUST HOARD THE "L WORD" THE WAY ATOMIC NATIONS HOARD THEIR EXPLOSIVES, LIKE SOMETHING THAT, ***ONCE DETONATED, WOULD CHANGE THEIR WORLD FOREVER***...

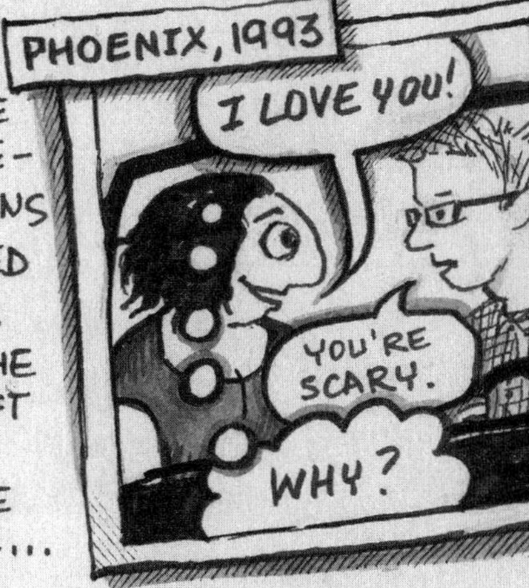
PHOENIX, 1993
I LOVE YOU!
YOU'RE SCARY.
WHY?

...I'D COME FROM A PLACE THAT WAS MUCH MORE FREE-WHEELING WITH DECLARATIONS OF AFFECTION, AND I BLURTED ***THE WORD*** TO JOSH TWO DAYS AFTER WE MET, THE MINUTE HE LEANED OVER THE GEAR SHIFT OF HIS PARENTS' SUBARU WAGON AND KISSED ME ON THE MOUTH FOR THE FIRST TIME...

...LATER, I'D COME TO APPRECIATE THE TABOO. IT BEGAN TO SEEM RATHER WISE, SINCE, AS SOON AS THE PHRASE ESCAPED MY LIPS, IT BEGAN TO FADE AND WEAR OUT AND SOON WEIGHED NO MORE THAN A FRIENDLY "HELLO" OR "DUDE, THANK YOU FOR REPLACING THAT INK CARTRIDGE..."

...BUT THE ORPHAN HAD GOTTEN TO ME THE WAY JOSH NEVER HAD, ENTERING ME LIKE HE SEEMED TO ENTER EVERY POINT OF HIS JOURNEY — GENTLY NUDGING ASIDE THE NOT ALLOWED ***AND*** FORBIDDEN ***AND*** STOP HERE! ***SIGNS, JUST BECAUSE HE WANTED TO, OR BECAUSE THE SIGNS WERE WRITTEN IN A LANGUAGE HE COULDN'T READ, SO HE JUST KEPT GOING.***

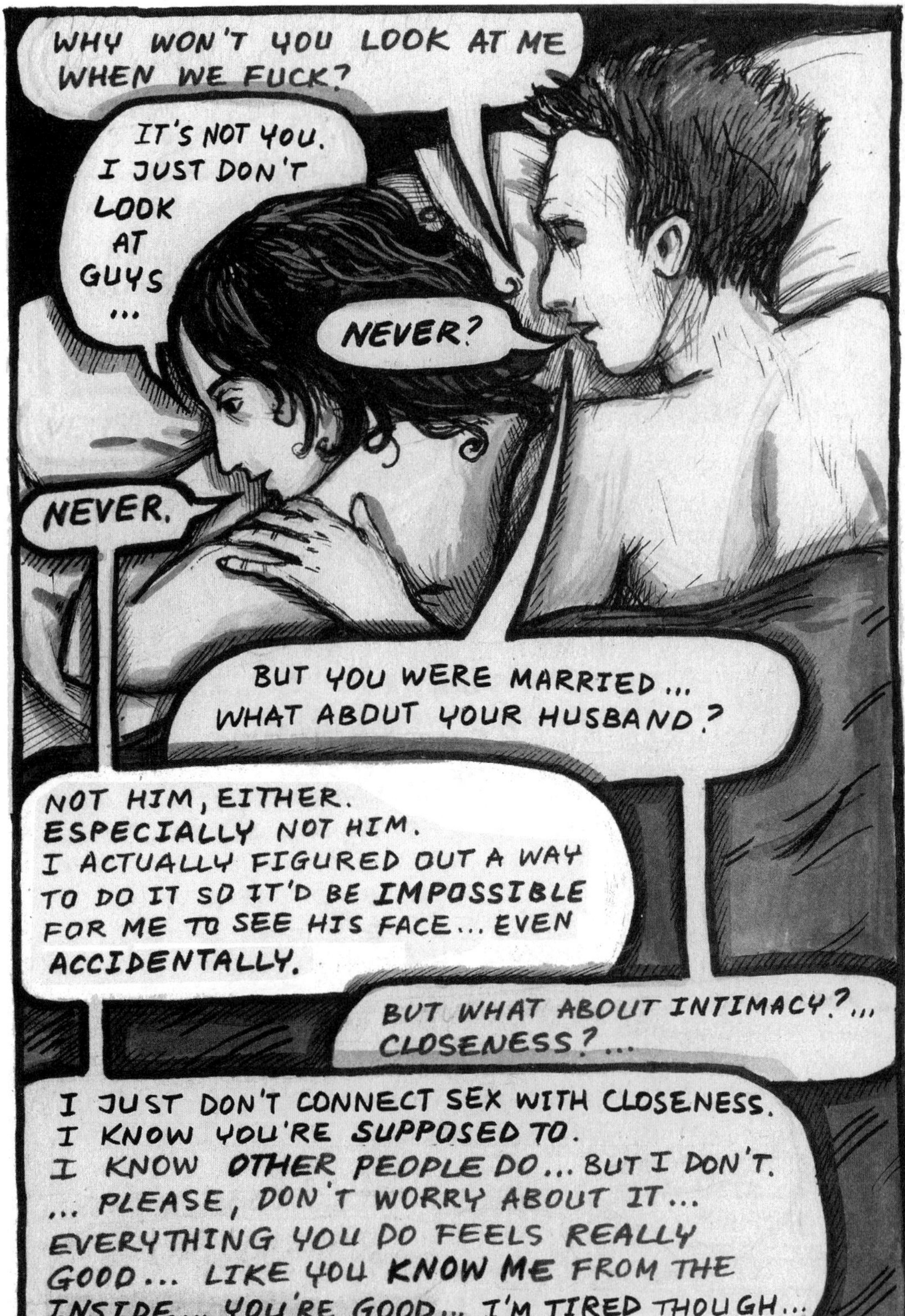
WHY WON'T YOU LOOK AT ME WHEN WE FUCK?
IT'S NOT YOU. I JUST DON'T LOOK AT GUYS ...
NEVER?
NEVER.
BUT YOU WERE MARRIED... WHAT ABOUT YOUR HUSBAND?
NOT HIM, EITHER. ESPECIALLY NOT HIM. I ACTUALLY FIGURED OUT A WAY TO DO IT SO IT'D BE IMPOSSIBLE FOR ME TO SEE HIS FACE... EVEN ACCIDENTALLY.
BUT WHAT ABOUT INTIMACY?... CLOSENESS?...
I JUST DON'T CONNECT SEX WITH CLOSENESS. I KNOW YOU'RE SUPPOSED TO. I KNOW OTHER PEOPLE DO... BUT I DON'T. ... PLEASE, DON'T WORRY ABOUT IT... EVERYTHING YOU DO FEELS REALLY GOOD... LIKE YOU KNOW ME FROM THE INSIDE... YOU'RE GOOD... I'M TIRED THOUGH...

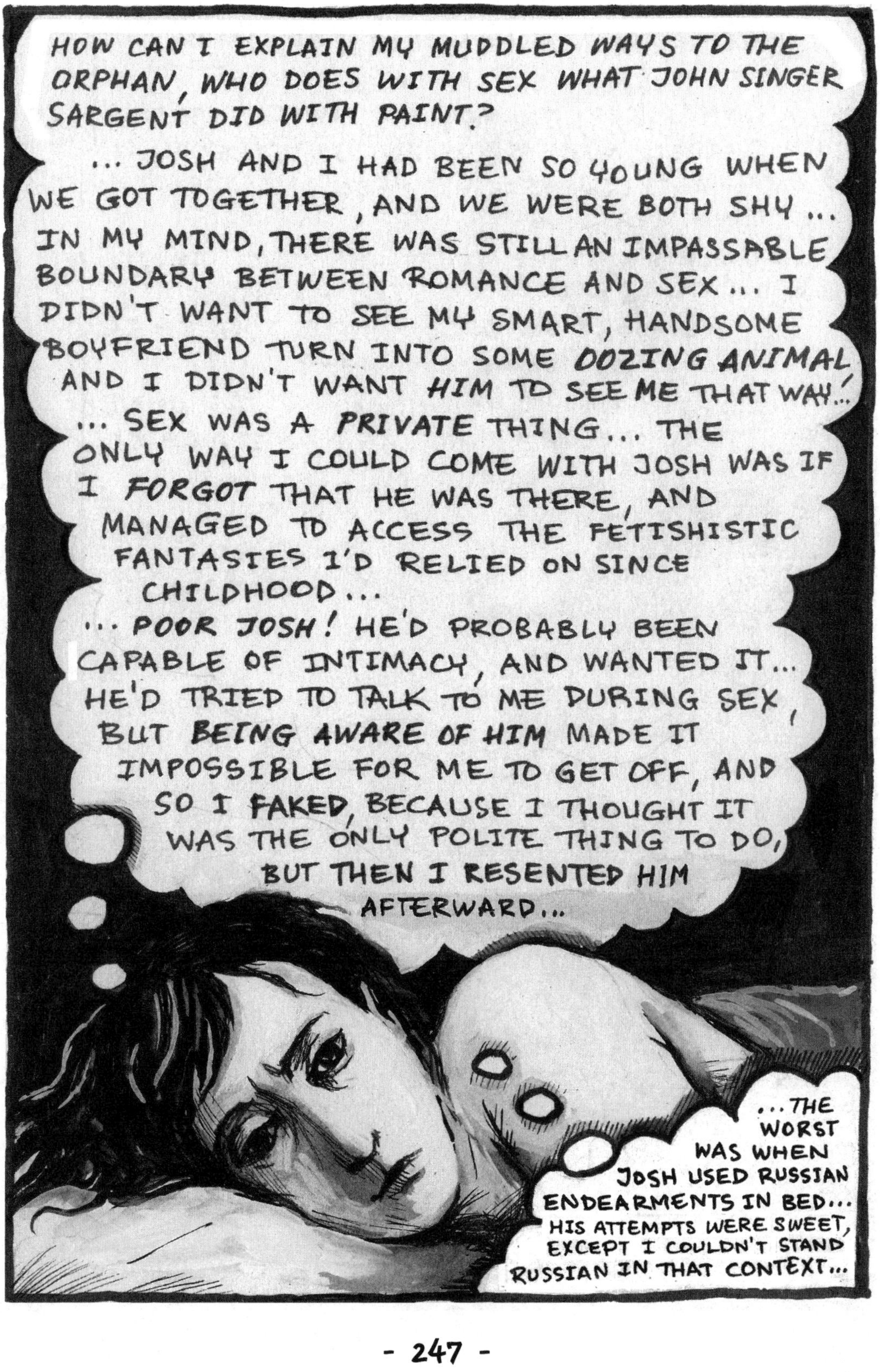
HOW CAN I EXPLAIN MY MUDDLED WAYS TO THE ORPHAN, WHO DOES WITH SEX WHAT JOHN SINGER SARGENT DID WITH PAINT?
... JOSH AND I HAD BEEN SO YOUNG WHEN WE GOT TOGETHER, AND WE WERE BOTH SHY... IN MY MIND, THERE WAS STILL AN IMPASSABLE BOUNDARY BETWEEN ROMANCE AND SEX... I DIDN'T WANT TO SEE MY SMART, HANDSOME BOYFRIEND TURN INTO SOME OOZING ANIMAL AND I DIDN'T WANT HIM TO SEE ME THAT WAY!...
... SEX WAS A PRIVATE THING... THE ONLY WAY I COULD COME WITH JOSH WAS IF I FORGOT THAT HE WAS THERE, AND MANAGED TO ACCESS THE FETISHISTIC FANTASIES I'D RELIED ON SINCE CHILDHOOD...
... POOR JOSH! HE'D PROBABLY BEEN CAPABLE OF INTIMACY, AND WANTED IT... HE'D TRIED TO TALK TO ME DURING SEX, BUT BEING AWARE OF HIM MADE IT IMPOSSIBLE FOR ME TO GET OFF, AND SO I FAKED, BECAUSE I THOUGHT IT WAS THE ONLY POLITE THING TO DO, BUT THEN I RESENTED HIM AFTERWARD...
... THE WORST WAS WHEN JOSH USED RUSSIAN ENDEARMENTS IN BED... HIS ATTEMPTS WERE SWEET, EXCEPT I COULDN'T STAND RUSSIAN IN THAT CONTEXT...

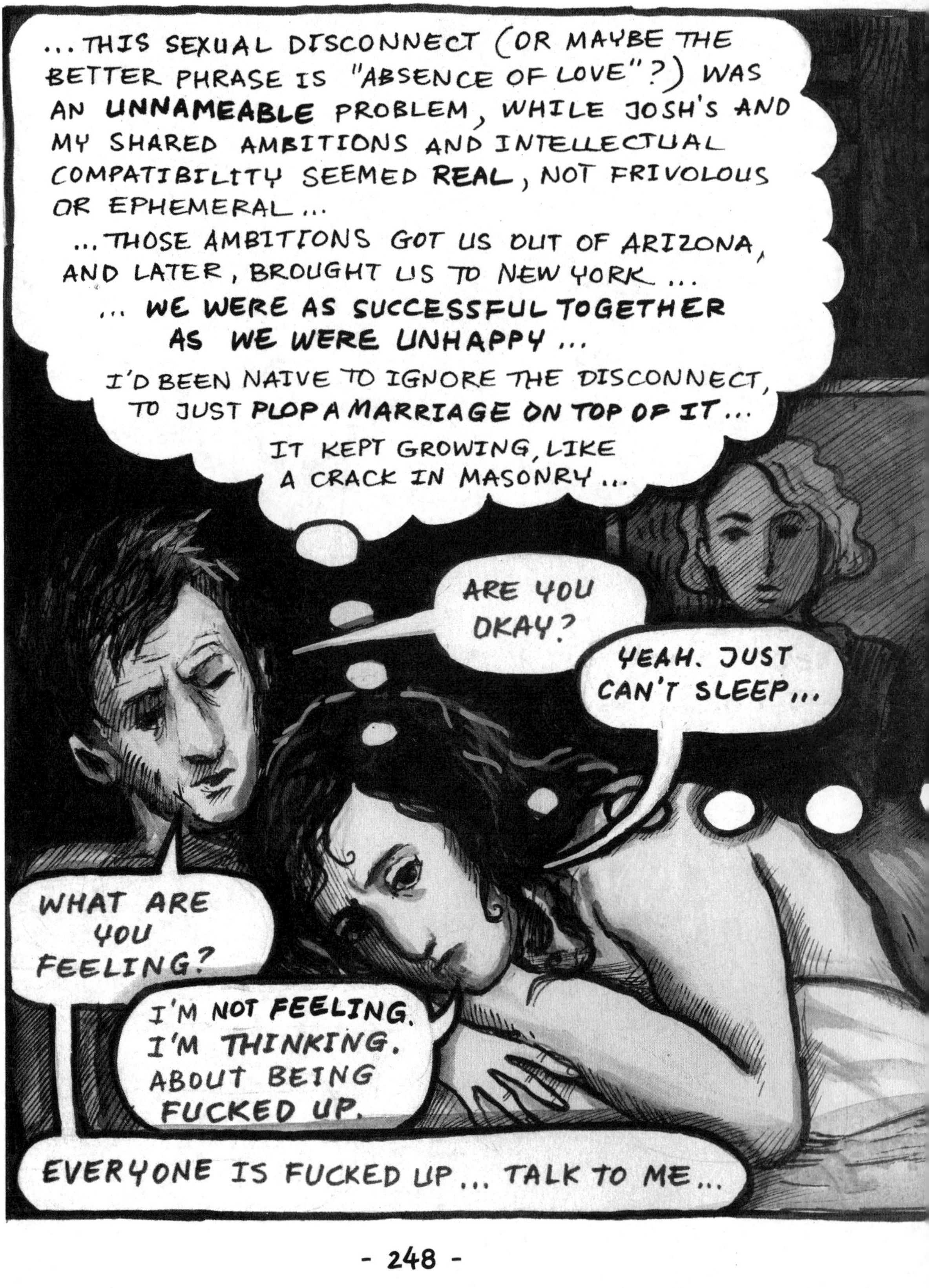
...THIS SEXUAL DISCONNECT (OR MAYBE THE BETTER PHRASE IS "ABSENCE OF LOVE"?) WAS AN UNNAMEABLE PROBLEM, WHILE JOSH'S AND MY SHARED AMBITIONS AND INTELLECTUAL COMPATIBILITY SEEMED REAL, NOT FRIVOLOUS OR EPHEMERAL...
...THOSE AMBITIONS GOT US OUT OF ARIZONA, AND LATER, BROUGHT US TO NEW YORK...
... WE WERE AS SUCCESSFUL TOGETHER AS WE WERE UNHAPPY...
I'D BEEN NAIVE TO IGNORE THE DISCONNECT, TO JUST PLOP A MARRIAGE ON TOP OF IT...
IT KEPT GROWING, LIKE A CRACK IN MASONRY...
ARE YOU OKAY?
YEAH. JUST CAN'T SLEEP...
WHAT ARE YOU FEELING?
I'M NOT FEELING. I'M THINKING. ABOUT BEING FUCKED UP.
EVERYONE IS FUCKED UP... TALK TO ME...

... BY THE TIME WE HAD KIDS, I COULD BARELY MAKE MYSELF SLEEP WITH JOSH. IT GOT MORE AWKWARD, NOT LESS, THE MORE **FAMILIAR** WE GOT, THE MORE TIME WE SPENT BICKERING IN THE FLUORESCENT BOWELS OF IKEA, OR DEBATING RELATIVE MERITS OF PRESCHOOLS...

... ALSO, I WAS HAUNTED BY THE TWO TIMES JOSH HAD SEEN THE BUSINESS END OF ME DURING **CHILDBIRTH**...

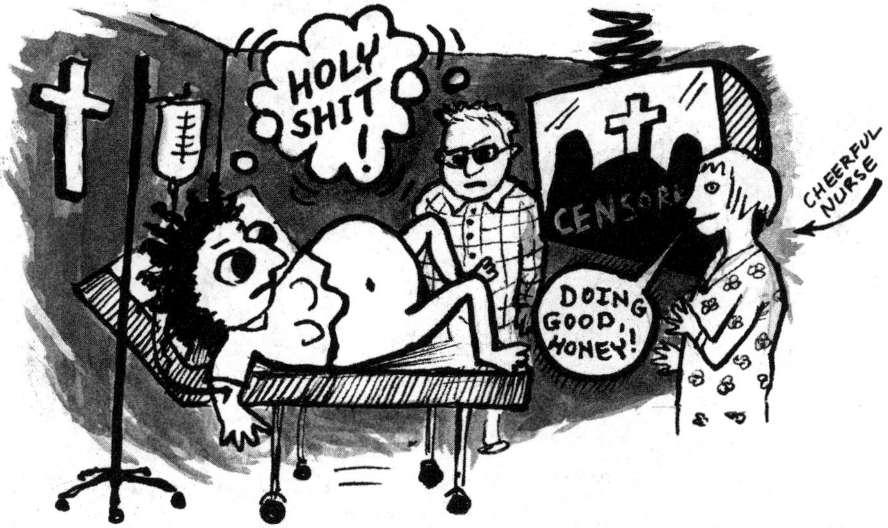
HOLY SHIT!
CENSOR
DOING GOOD, HONEY!
CHEERFUL NURSE

... BACK WHEN I HAD DASHA, HOSPITALS LIKED TO ARRANGE A MIRROR SO THAT A MOTHER COULD SEE HERSELF DOWN THERE... **I WONDER WHY? MAYBE IT WAS FOR MOTIVATION?** I WONDER IF THEY STILL DO THIS... NOBODY WARNED ME ABOUT THE STUPID MIRROR, AND WHEN A NURSE PULLED IT DOWN FROM THE CEILING, I WAS **SHOCKED** BY THE GORE BETWEEN MY LEGS, REFLECTED JUST BELOW THE CRUCIFIX THAT HUNG ABOVE MY BED...

... KNOWING **EXACTLY** WHAT JOSH HAD SEEN, I DIDN'T WANT HIM IN THE ROOM WHEN IT WAS TIME TO HAVE JACKIE, BUT I ALSO DIDN'T FEEL THAT I HAD ANY RIGHT TO KEEP HIM OUT...

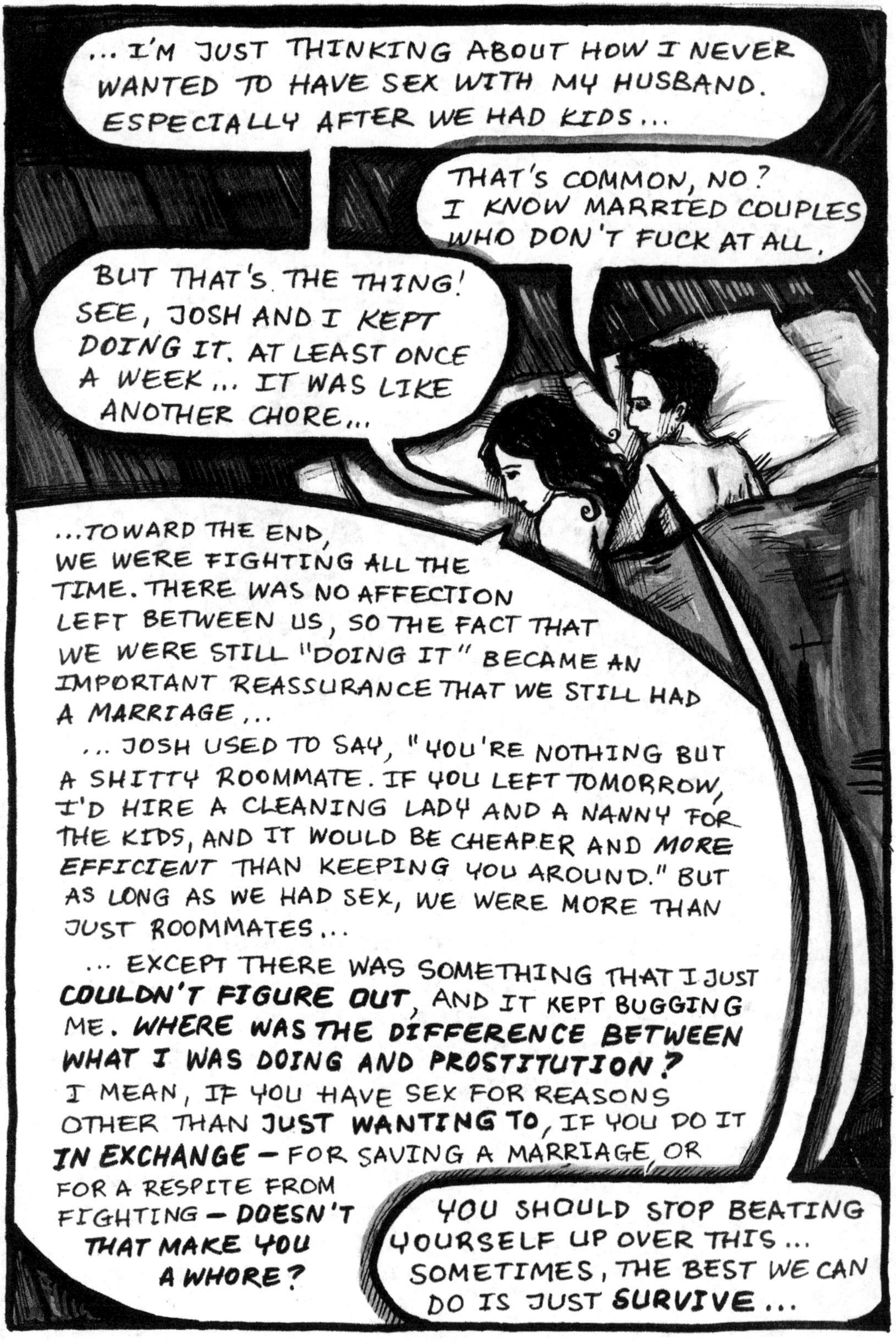
... I'M JUST THINKING ABOUT HOW I NEVER WANTED TO HAVE SEX WITH MY HUSBAND. ESPECIALLY AFTER WE HAD KIDS...
THAT'S COMMON, NO? I KNOW MARRIED COUPLES WHO DON'T FUCK AT ALL.
BUT THAT'S THE THING! SEE, JOSH AND I KEPT DOING IT. AT LEAST ONCE A WEEK... IT WAS LIKE ANOTHER CHORE...
...TOWARD THE END, WE WERE FIGHTING ALL THE TIME. THERE WAS NO AFFECTION LEFT BETWEEN US, SO THE FACT THAT WE WERE STILL "DOING IT" BECAME AN IMPORTANT REASSURANCE THAT WE STILL HAD A MARRIAGE...
... JOSH USED TO SAY, "YOU'RE NOTHING BUT A SHITTY ROOMMATE. IF YOU LEFT TOMORROW, I'D HIRE A CLEANING LADY AND A NANNY FOR THE KIDS, AND IT WOULD BE CHEAPER AND MORE EFFICIENT THAN KEEPING YOU AROUND." BUT AS LONG AS WE HAD SEX, WE WERE MORE THAN JUST ROOMMATES...
... EXCEPT THERE WAS SOMETHING THAT I JUST COULDN'T FIGURE OUT, AND IT KEPT BUGGING ME. WHERE WAS THE DIFFERENCE BETWEEN WHAT I WAS DOING AND PROSTITUTION? I MEAN, IF YOU HAVE SEX FOR REASONS OTHER THAN JUST WANTING TO, IF YOU DO IT IN EXCHANGE — FOR SAVING A MARRIAGE OR FOR A RESPITE FROM FIGHTING — DOESN'T THAT MAKE YOU A WHORE?
YOU SHOULD STOP BEATING YOURSELF UP OVER THIS... SOMETIMES, THE BEST WE CAN DO IS JUST SURVIVE...

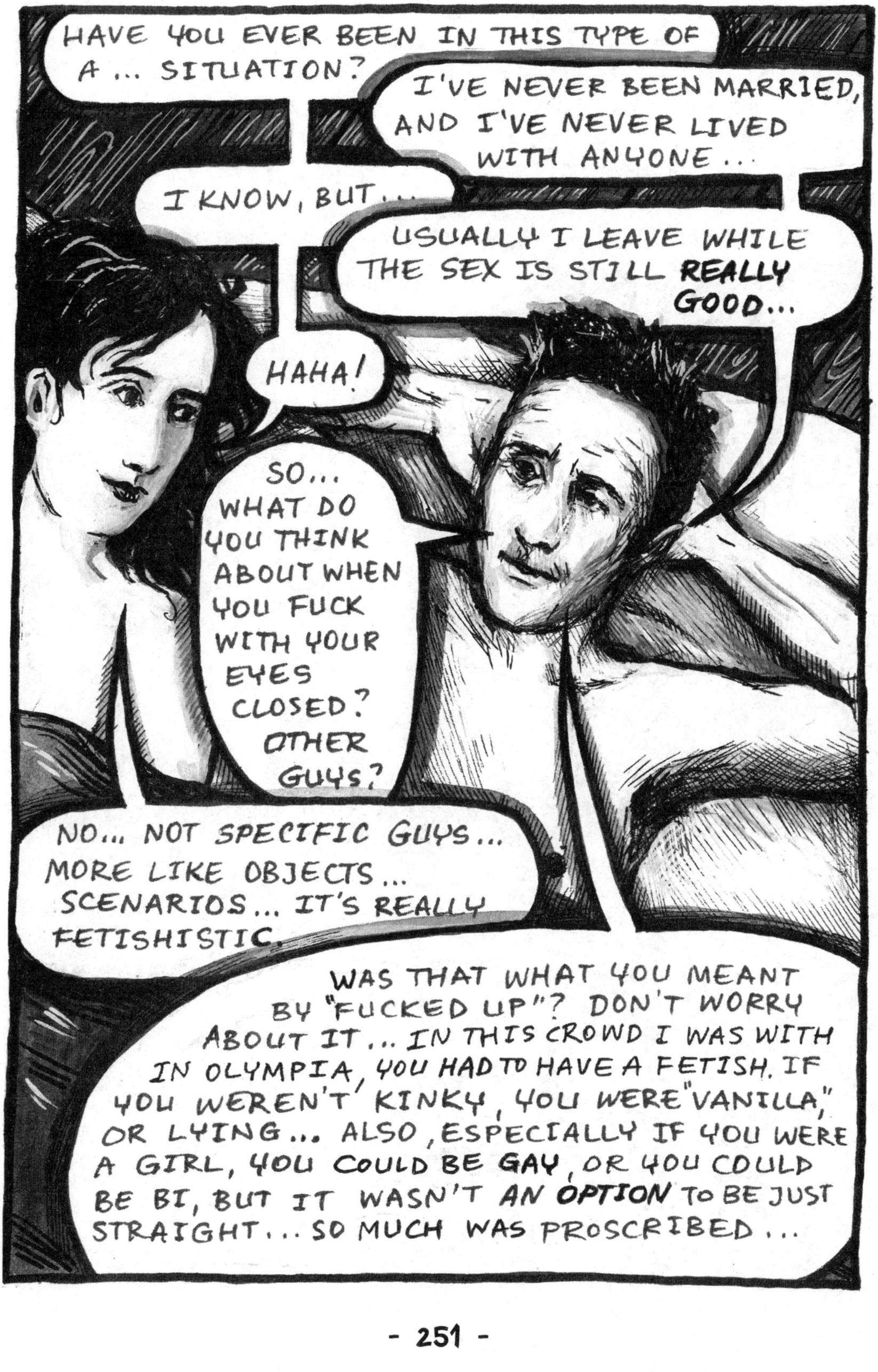
HAVE YOU EVER BEEN IN THIS TYPE OF A ... SITUATION?
I'VE NEVER BEEN MARRIED, AND I'VE NEVER LIVED WITH ANYONE...
I KNOW, BUT...
USUALLY I LEAVE WHILE THE SEX IS STILL **REALLY** GOOD...
HAHA!
SO... WHAT DO YOU THINK ABOUT WHEN YOU FUCK WITH YOUR EYES CLOSED? OTHER GUYS?
NO... NOT *SPECIFIC* GUYS... MORE LIKE OBJECTS... SCENARIOS... IT'S REALLY FETISHISTIC.
WAS THAT WHAT YOU MEANT BY "FUCKED UP"? DON'T WORRY ABOUT IT... IN THIS CROWD I WAS WITH IN OLYMPIA, YOU *HAD* TO HAVE A FETISH. IF YOU WEREN'T KINKY, YOU WERE "VANILLA," OR LYING... ALSO, ESPECIALLY IF YOU WERE A GIRL, YOU COULD BE **GAY**, OR YOU COULD BE BI, BUT IT WASN'T *AN* ***OPTION*** TO BE JUST STRAIGHT... SO MUCH WAS PROSCRIBED...

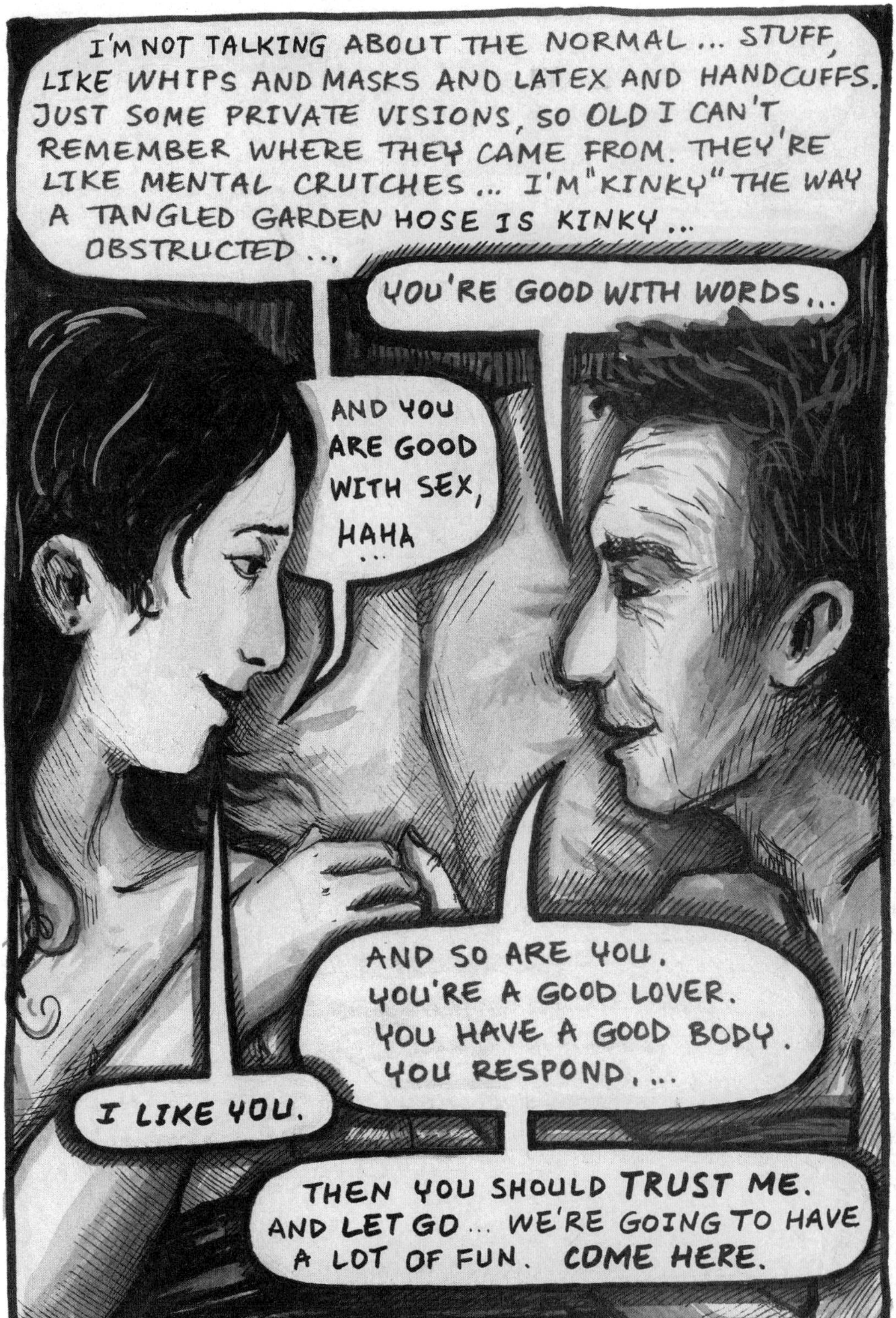
I'M NOT TALKING ABOUT THE NORMAL... STUFF, LIKE WHIPS AND MASKS AND LATEX AND HANDCUFFS. JUST SOME PRIVATE VISIONS, SO OLD I CAN'T REMEMBER WHERE THEY CAME FROM. THEY'RE LIKE MENTAL CRUTCHES... I'M "KINKY" THE WAY A TANGLED GARDEN HOSE IS KINKY... OBSTRUCTED...
YOU'RE GOOD WITH WORDS...
AND YOU ARE GOOD WITH SEX, HAHA...
AND SO ARE YOU. YOU'RE A GOOD LOVER. YOU HAVE A GOOD BODY. YOU RESPOND...
I LIKE YOU.
THEN YOU SHOULD TRUST ME. AND LET GO... WE'RE GOING TO HAVE A LOT OF FUN. COME HERE.

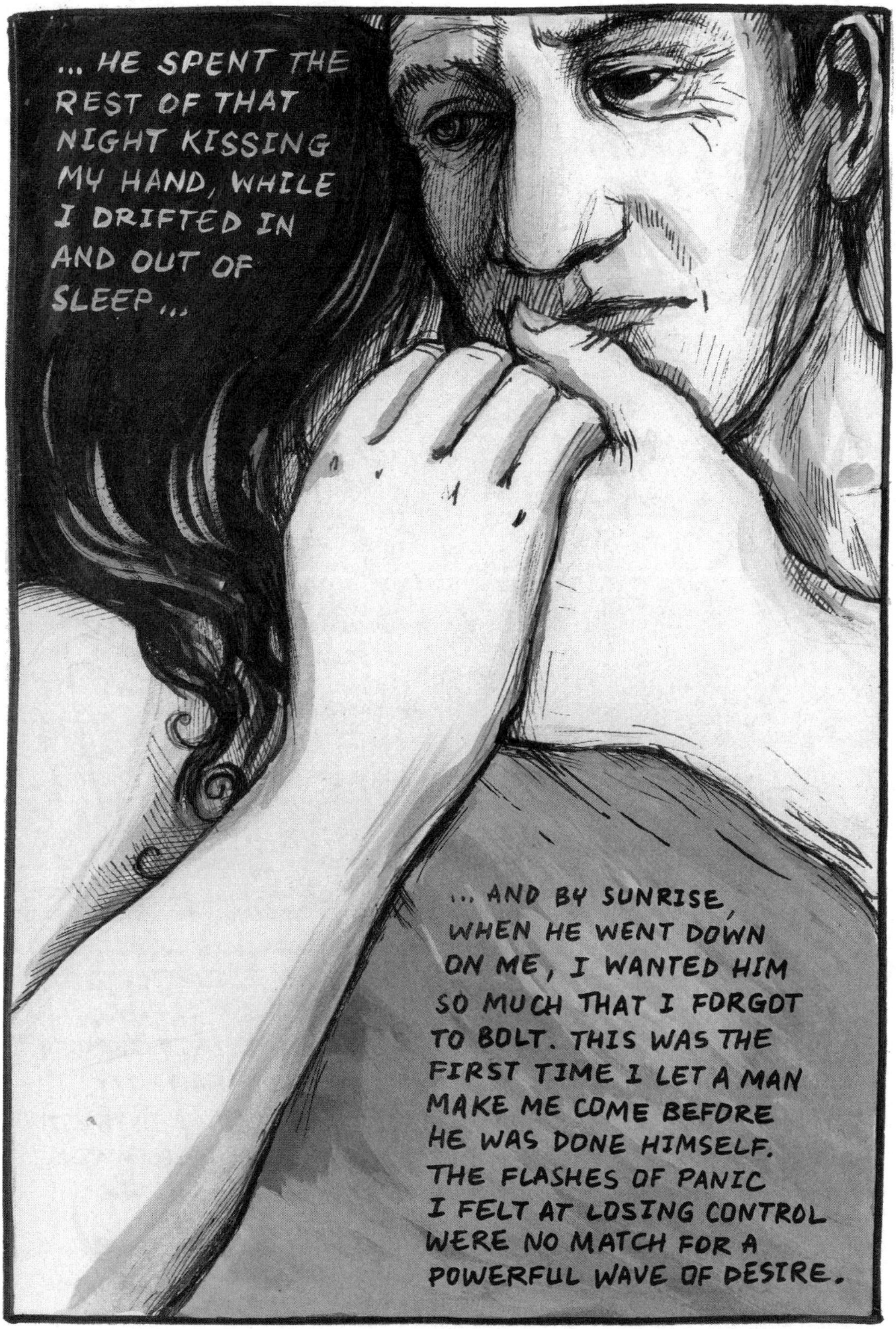
... HE SPENT THE REST OF THAT NIGHT KISSING MY HAND, WHILE I DRIFTED IN AND OUT OF SLEEP...
... AND BY SUNRISE, WHEN HE WENT DOWN ON ME, I WANTED HIM SO MUCH THAT I FORGOT TO BOLT. THIS WAS THE FIRST TIME I LET A MAN MAKE ME COME BEFORE HE WAS DONE HIMSELF. THE FLASHES OF PANIC I FELT AT LOSING CONTROL WERE NO MATCH FOR A POWERFUL WAVE OF DESIRE.

...SO I TRUSTED THE ORPHAN.

ONCE I LET HIM TAKE CHARGE, "LETTING GO" SEEMED INADVERTENT, LIKE SWIMMING... WITHIN A MONTH OF MY FIRST EXPERIENCE OF BEING TOGETHER IN SEX, I WAS READY TO DO ANYTHING WITH THE ORPHAN... MY INHIBITIONS AND LONG-ESTABLISHED BOUNDARIES FELL AWAY. I NO LONGER HAD ANY USE FOR MY MENTAL ESCAPE ROUTES ...

LOOK AT MY FACE. SAY MY NAME.

ORPHAN...

WILL YOU TATTOO MY NAME ON YOUR ASS?

TOTALLY! TODAY?

... AND THERE I WAS, SUDDENLY WITHOUT MY EXOSKELETON, BUT TOTALLY ALIVE.

MOST CERTAINLY, THE ORPHAN HAD NO IDEA THAT THIS WAS AS CLOSE AS I'D EVER COME TO A SPIRITUAL TRANSFORMATION. GETTING CLOSE LIKE THIS SEEMED TO BE A NORMAL MODE OF INTERACTION FOR HIM. BUT I FELL FOR THE ORPHAN WITH THE SAME INTENSITY I'D FALLEN FOR MAYBE SIX THINGS THAT HAD AWED ME IN THE PAST: FOUR RUSSIAN POEMS*AND THE BODIES OF TWO AMERICAN NEWBORNS.

* MAYBE NOT EVEN THE POEMS. HELL, JUST THE NEWBORNS!

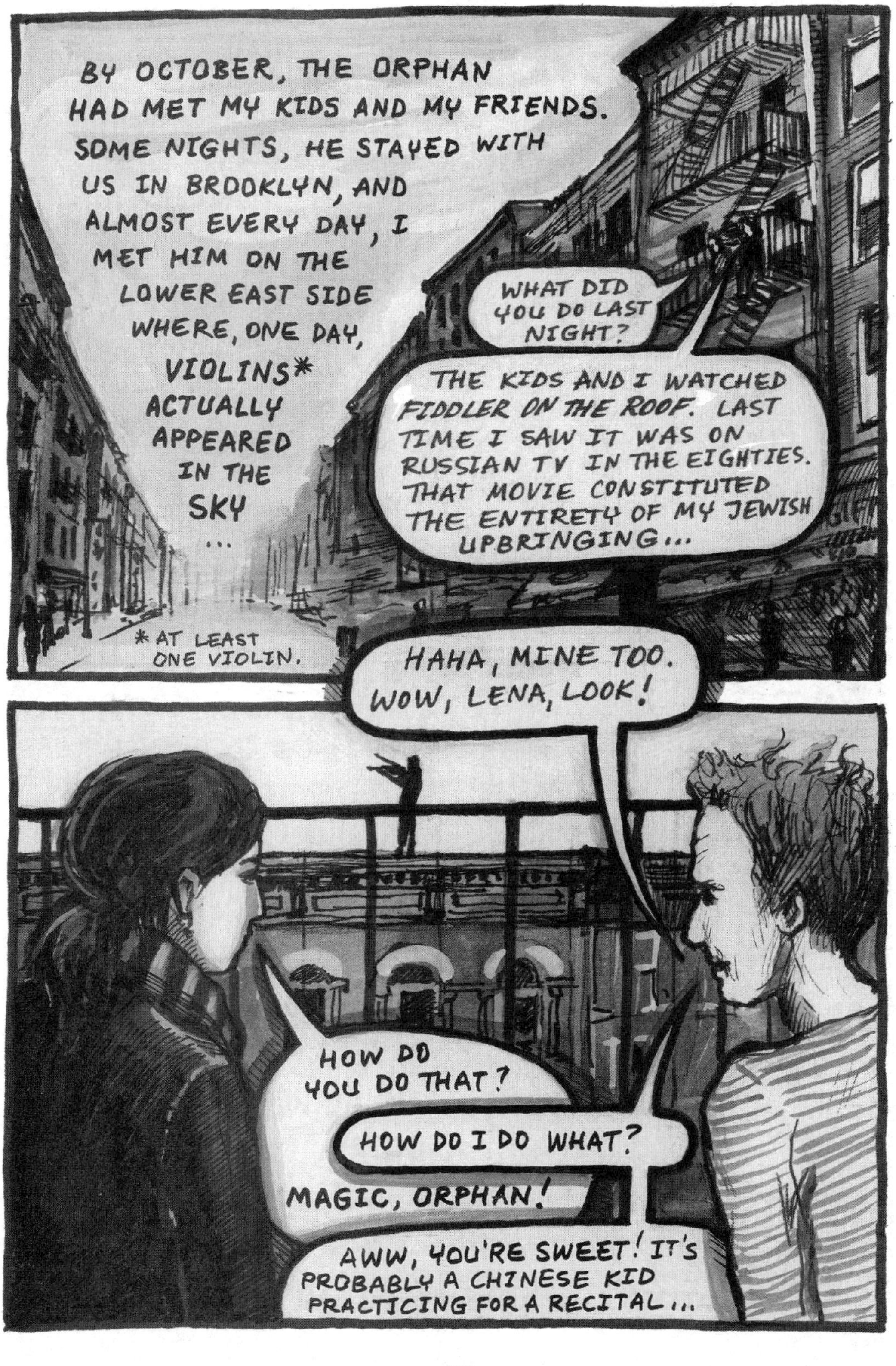

BY OCTOBER, THE ORPHAN HAD MET MY KIDS AND MY FRIENDS. SOME NIGHTS, HE STAYED WITH US IN BROOKLYN, AND ALMOST EVERY DAY, I MET HIM ON THE LOWER EAST SIDE WHERE, ONE DAY, VIOLINS* ACTUALLY APPEARED IN THE SKY ...
WHAT DID YOU DO LAST NIGHT?
THE KIDS AND I WATCHED FIDDLER ON THE ROOF. LAST TIME I SAW IT WAS ON RUSSIAN TV IN THE EIGHTIES. THAT MOVIE CONSTITUTED THE ENTIRETY OF MY JEWISH UPBRINGING...
* AT LEAST ONE VIOLIN.
HAHA, MINE TOO. WOW, LENA, LOOK!
HOW DO YOU DO THAT?
HOW DO I DO WHAT?
MAGIC, ORPHAN!
AWW, YOU'RE SWEET! IT'S PROBABLY A CHINESE KID PRACTICING FOR A RECITAL...

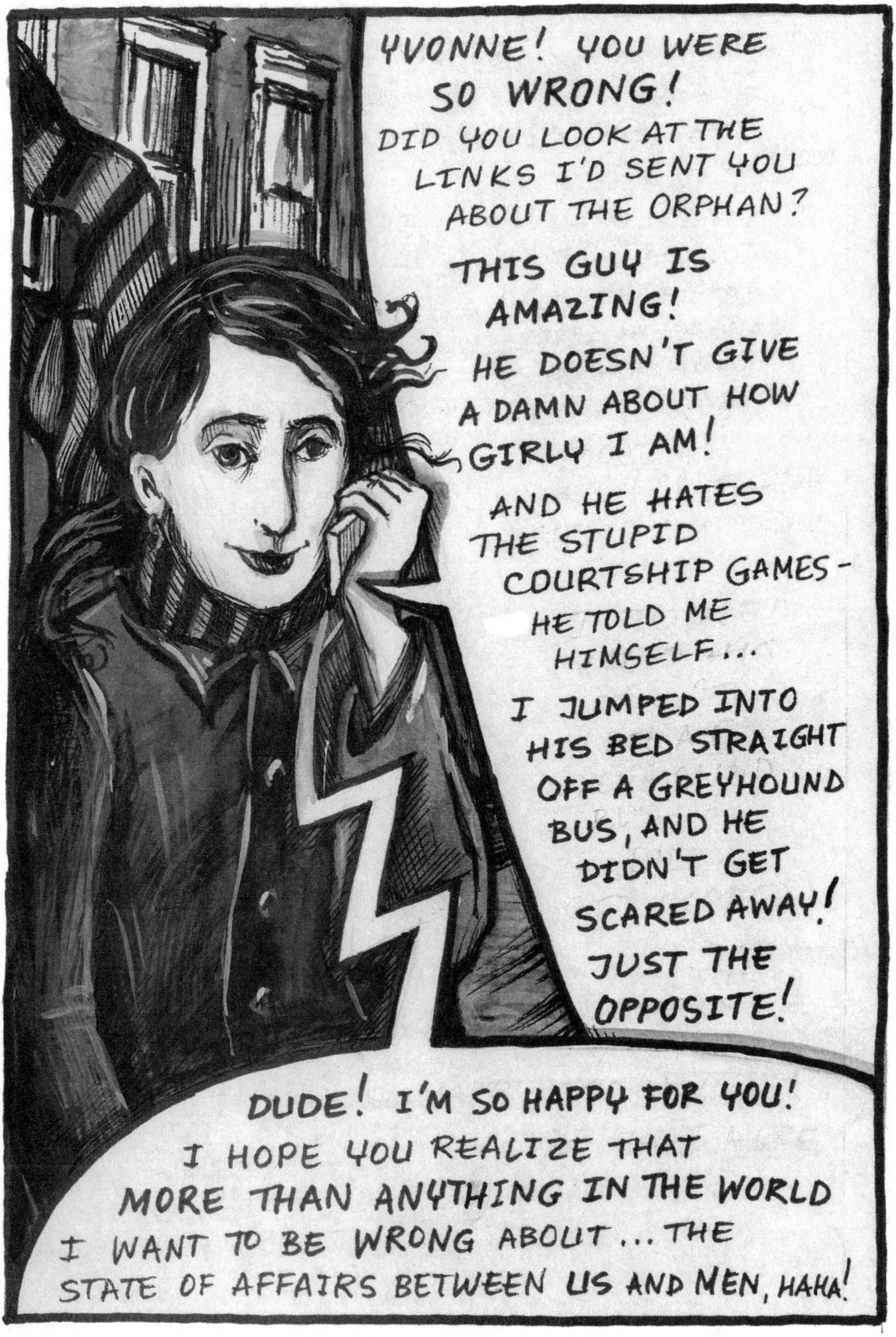
YVONNE! YOU WERE SO WRONG!
DID YOU LOOK AT THE LINKS I'D SENT YOU ABOUT THE ORPHAN?
THIS GUY IS AMAZING!
HE DOESN'T GIVE A DAMN ABOUT HOW GIRLY I AM!
AND HE HATES THE STUPID COURTSHIP GAMES- HE TOLD ME HIMSELF...
I JUMPED INTO HIS BED STRAIGHT OFF A GREYHOUND BUS, AND HE DIDN'T GET SCARED AWAY!
JUST THE OPPOSITE!
DUDE! I'M SO HAPPY FOR YOU!
I HOPE YOU REALIZE THAT MORE THAN ANYTHING IN THE WORLD I WANT TO BE WRONG ABOUT... THE STATE OF AFFAIRS BETWEEN US AND MEN, HAHA!

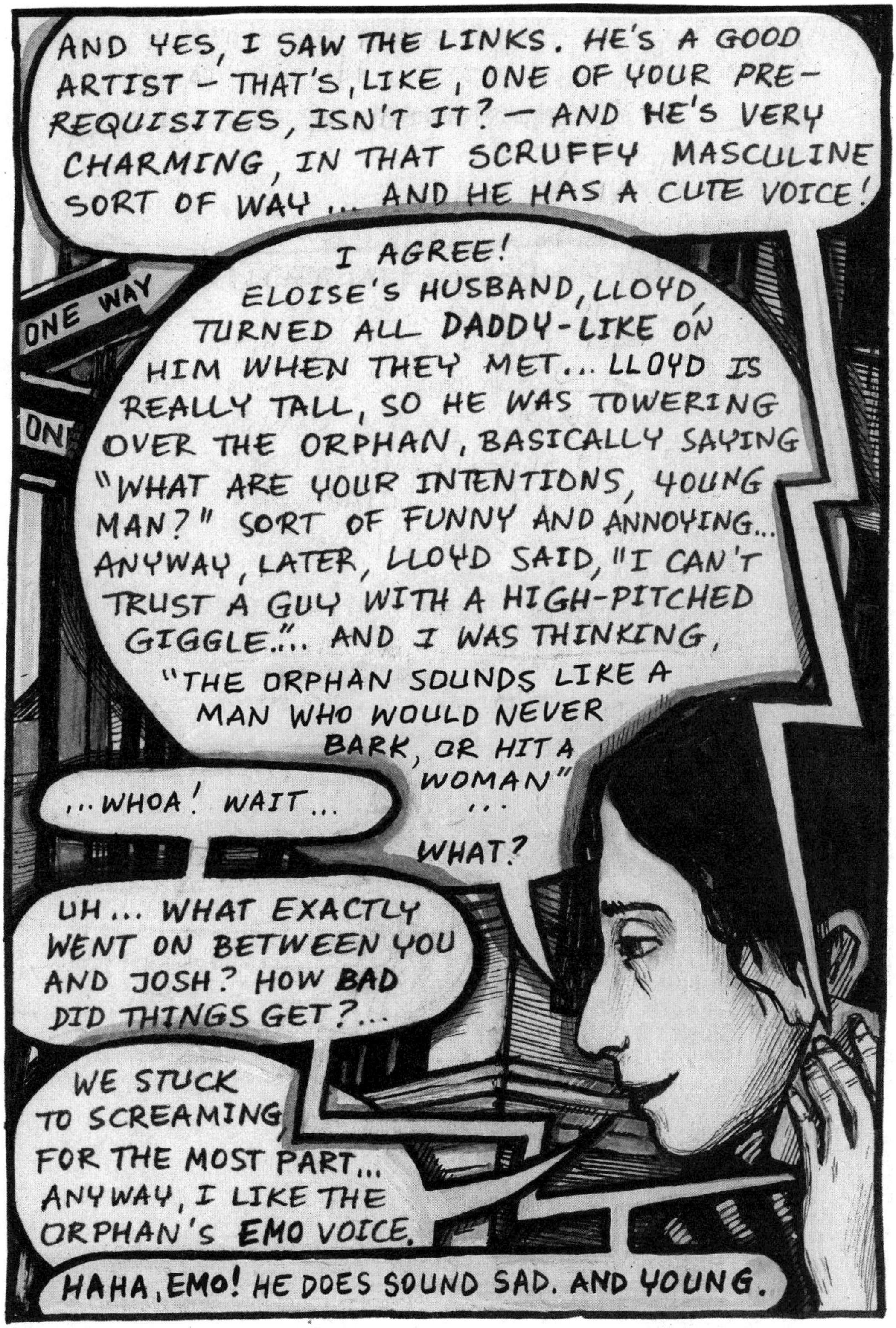
AND YES, I SAW THE LINKS. HE'S A GOOD ARTIST – THAT'S, LIKE, ONE OF YOUR PRE-REQUISITES, ISN'T IT? – AND HE'S VERY CHARMING, IN THAT SCRUFFY MASCULINE SORT OF WAY... AND HE HAS A CUTE VOICE!
ONE WAY
I AGREE! ELOISE'S HUSBAND, LLOYD, TURNED ALL DADDY-LIKE ON HIM WHEN THEY MET... LLOYD IS REALLY TALL, SO HE WAS TOWERING OVER THE ORPHAN, BASICALLY SAYING "WHAT ARE YOUR INTENTIONS, YOUNG MAN?" SORT OF FUNNY AND ANNOYING... ANYWAY, LATER, LLOYD SAID, "I CAN'T TRUST A GUY WITH A HIGH-PITCHED GIGGLE."... AND I WAS THINKING, "THE ORPHAN SOUNDS LIKE A MAN WHO WOULD NEVER BARK, OR HIT A WOMAN"
...WHOA! WAIT...
... WHAT?
UH... WHAT EXACTLY WENT ON BETWEEN YOU AND JOSH? HOW BAD DID THINGS GET?...
WE STUCK TO SCREAMING, FOR THE MOST PART... ANYWAY, I LIKE THE ORPHAN'S EMO VOICE.
HAHA, EMO! HE DOES SOUND SAD. AND YOUNG.

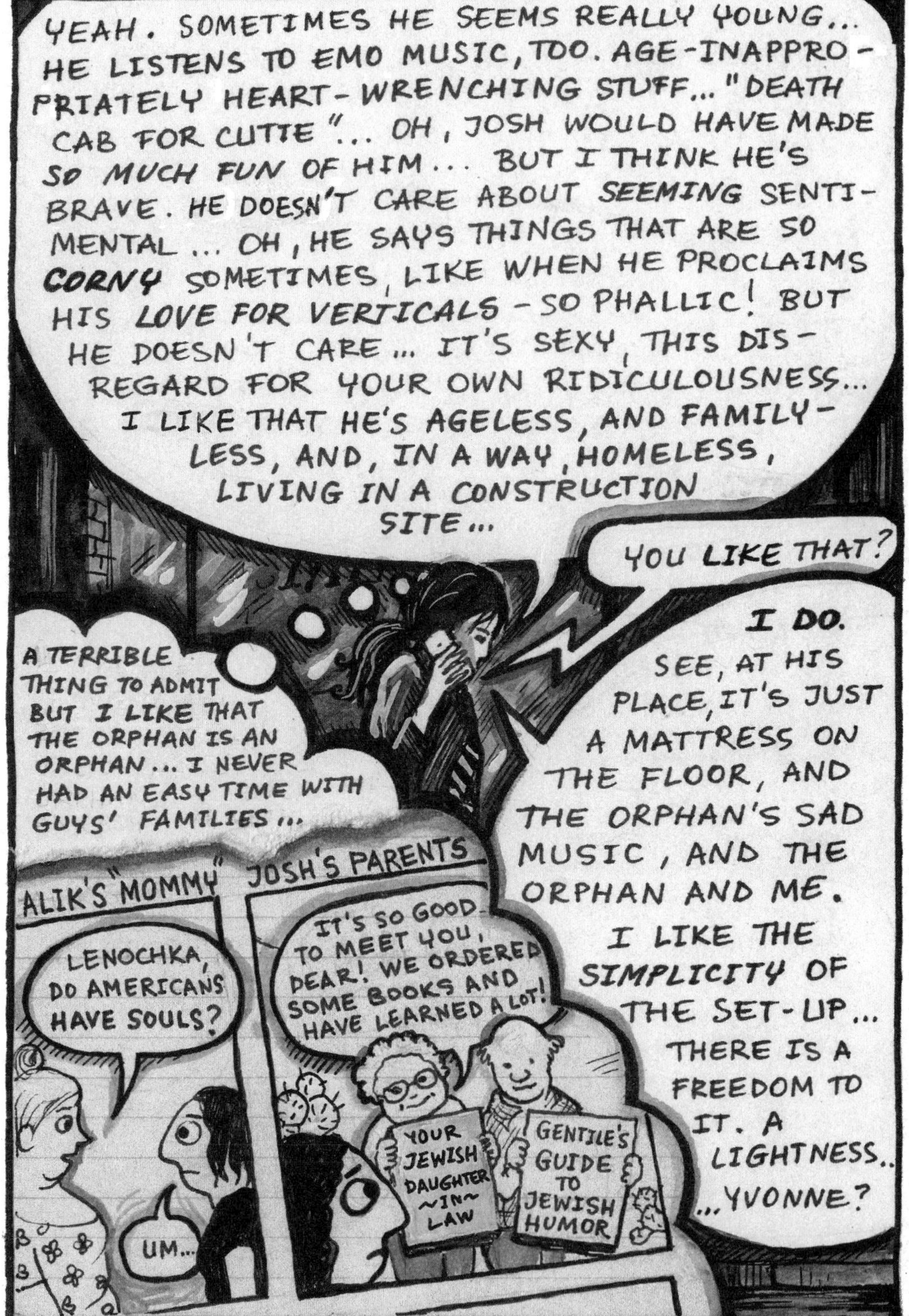

YEAH. SOMETIMES HE SEEMS REALLY YOUNG... HE LISTENS TO EMO MUSIC, TOO. AGE-INAPPROPRIATELY HEART-WRENCHING STUFF... "DEATH CAB FOR CUTIE"... OH, JOSH WOULD HAVE MADE SO MUCH FUN OF HIM... BUT I THINK HE'S BRAVE. HE DOESN'T CARE ABOUT SEEMING SENTIMENTAL... OH, HE SAYS THINGS THAT ARE SO CORNY SOMETIMES, LIKE WHEN HE PROCLAIMS HIS LOVE FOR VERTICALS - SO PHALLIC! BUT HE DOESN'T CARE... IT'S SEXY, THIS DISREGARD FOR YOUR OWN RIDICULOUSNESS... I LIKE THAT HE'S AGELESS, AND FAMILYLESS, AND, IN A WAY, HOMELESS, LIVING IN A CONSTRUCTION SITE...
YOU LIKE THAT?
I DO. SEE, AT HIS PLACE, IT'S JUST A MATTRESS ON THE FLOOR, AND THE ORPHAN'S SAD MUSIC, AND THE ORPHAN AND ME. I LIKE THE SIMPLICITY OF THE SET-UP... THERE IS A FREEDOM TO IT. A LIGHTNESS... ...YVONNE?
A TERRIBLE THING TO ADMIT BUT I LIKE THAT THE ORPHAN IS AN ORPHAN... I NEVER HAD AN EASY TIME WITH GUYS' FAMILIES...
ALIK'S "MOMMY"
LENOCHKA, DO AMERICANS HAVE SOULS?
UM...
JOSH'S PARENTS
IT'S SO GOOD TO MEET YOU, DEAR! WE ORDERED SOME BOOKS AND HAVE LEARNED A LOT!
YOUR JEWISH DAUGHTER ~IN~ LAW
GENTILE'S GUIDE TO JEWISH HUMOR

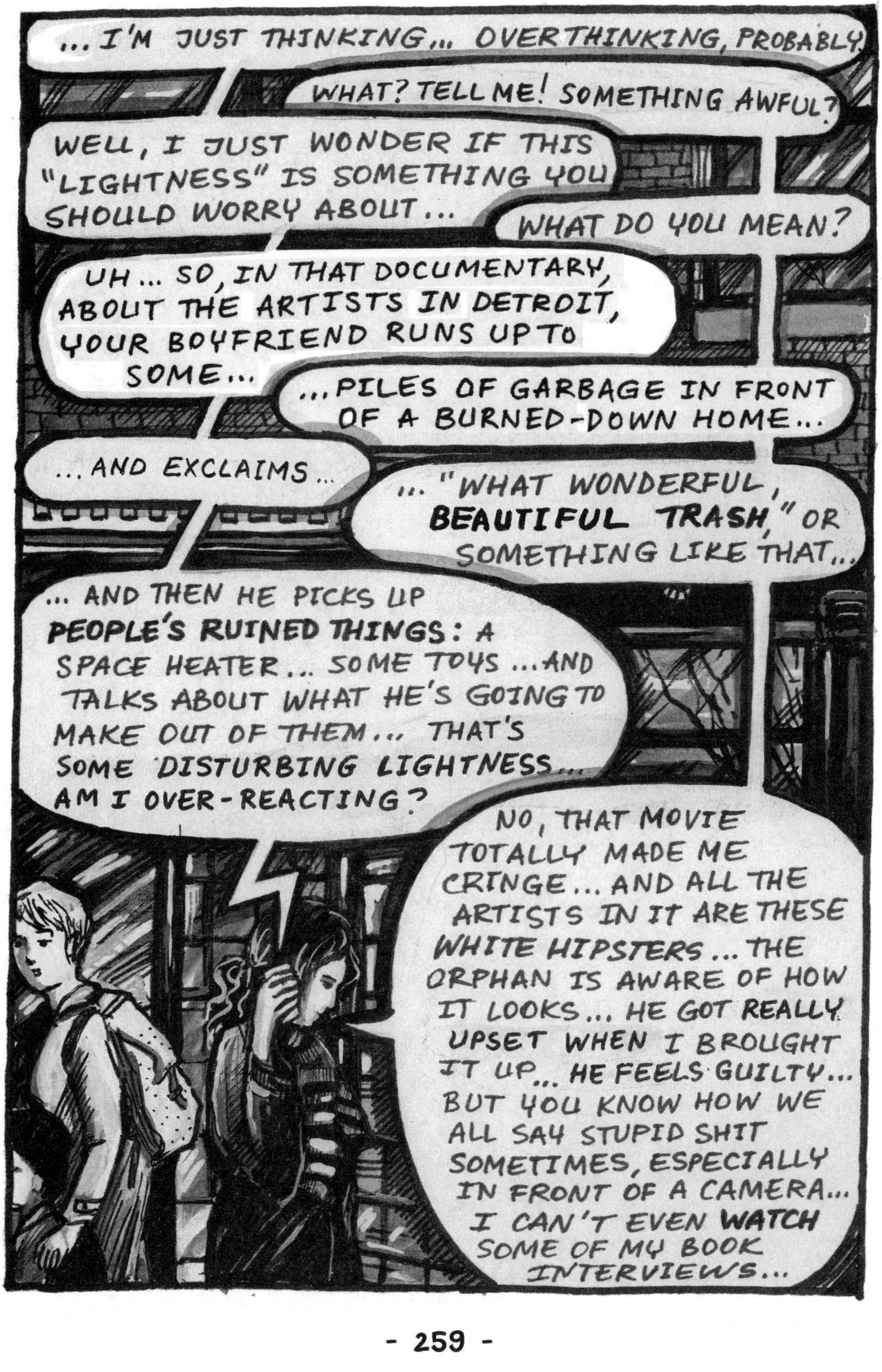
... I'M JUST THINKING... OVERTHINKING, PROBABLY.
WHAT? TELL ME! SOMETHING AWFUL?
WELL, I JUST WONDER IF THIS "LIGHTNESS" IS SOMETHING YOU SHOULD WORRY ABOUT...
WHAT DO YOU MEAN?
UH... SO, IN THAT DOCUMENTARY, ABOUT THE ARTISTS IN DETROIT, YOUR BOYFRIEND RUNS UP TO SOME...
...PILES OF GARBAGE IN FRONT OF A BURNED-DOWN HOME...
...AND EXCLAIMS...
... "WHAT WONDERFUL, BEAUTIFUL TRASH," OR SOMETHING LIKE THAT...
... AND THEN HE PICKS UP PEOPLE'S RUINED THINGS: A SPACE HEATER... SOME TOYS ...AND TALKS ABOUT WHAT HE'S GOING TO MAKE OUT OF THEM... THAT'S SOME DISTURBING LIGHTNESS... AM I OVER-REACTING?
NO, THAT MOVIE TOTALLY MADE ME CRINGE... AND ALL THE ARTISTS IN IT ARE THESE WHITE HIPSTERS... THE ORPHAN IS AWARE OF HOW IT LOOKS... HE GOT REALLY UPSET WHEN I BROUGHT IT UP... HE FEELS GUILTY... BUT YOU KNOW HOW WE ALL SAY STUPID SHIT SOMETIMES, ESPECIALLY IN FRONT OF A CAMERA... I CAN'T EVEN WATCH SOME OF MY BOOK INTERVIEWS...

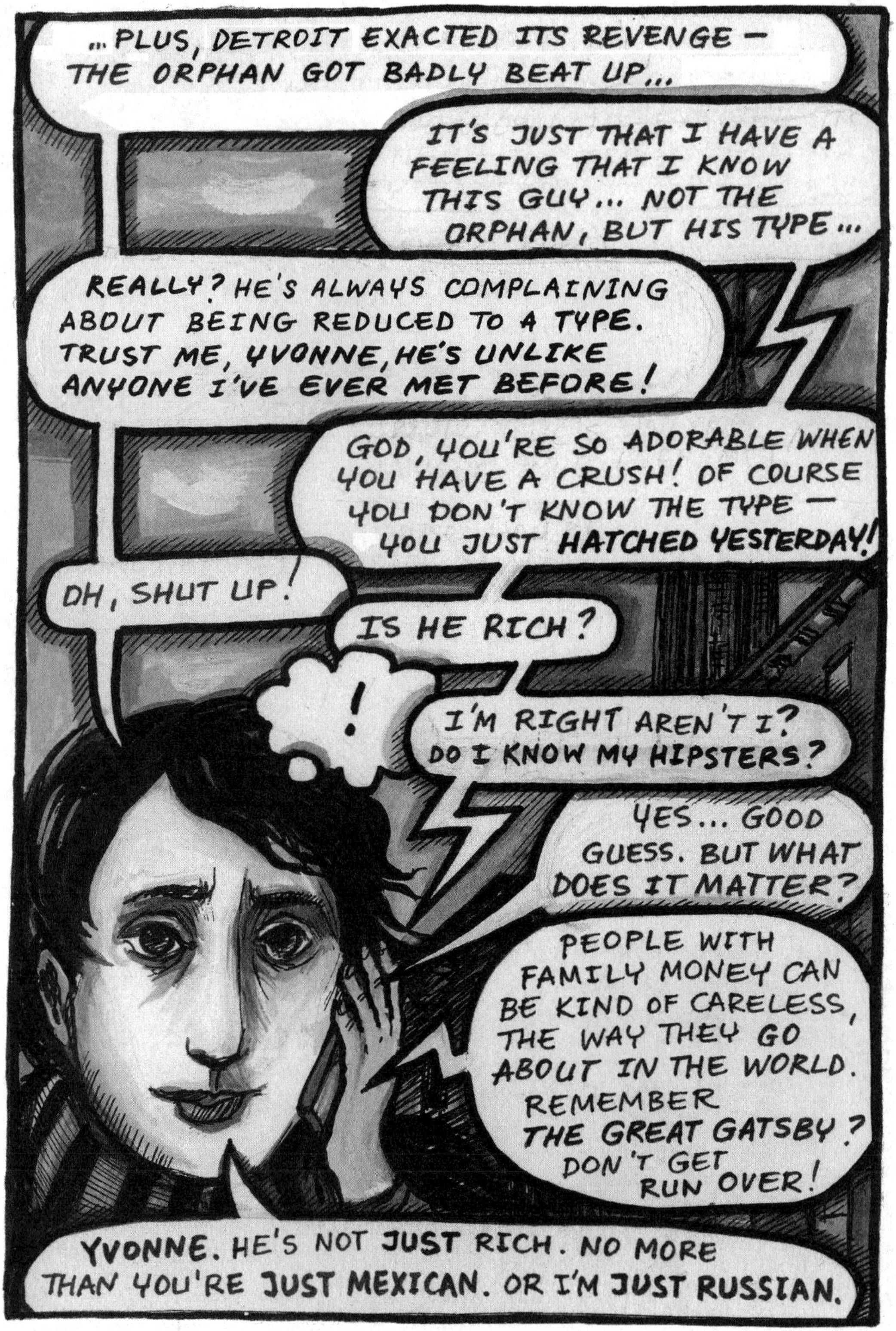
...PLUS, DETROIT EXACTED ITS REVENGE — THE ORPHAN GOT BADLY BEAT UP...
IT'S JUST THAT I HAVE A FEELING THAT I KNOW THIS GUY... NOT THE ORPHAN, BUT HIS TYPE...
REALLY? HE'S ALWAYS COMPLAINING ABOUT BEING REDUCED TO A TYPE. TRUST ME, YVONNE, HE'S UNLIKE ANYONE I'VE EVER MET BEFORE!
GOD, YOU'RE SO ADORABLE WHEN YOU HAVE A CRUSH! OF COURSE YOU DON'T KNOW THE TYPE — YOU JUST HATCHED YESTERDAY!
OH, SHUT UP!
IS HE RICH?
!
I'M RIGHT AREN'T I? DO I KNOW MY HIPSTERS?
YES... GOOD GUESS. BUT WHAT DOES IT MATTER?
PEOPLE WITH FAMILY MONEY CAN BE KIND OF CARELESS, THE WAY THEY GO ABOUT IN THE WORLD. REMEMBER THE GREAT GATSBY? DON'T GET RUN OVER!
YVONNE. HE'S NOT JUST RICH. NO MORE THAN YOU'RE JUST MEXICAN. OR I'M JUST RUSSIAN.

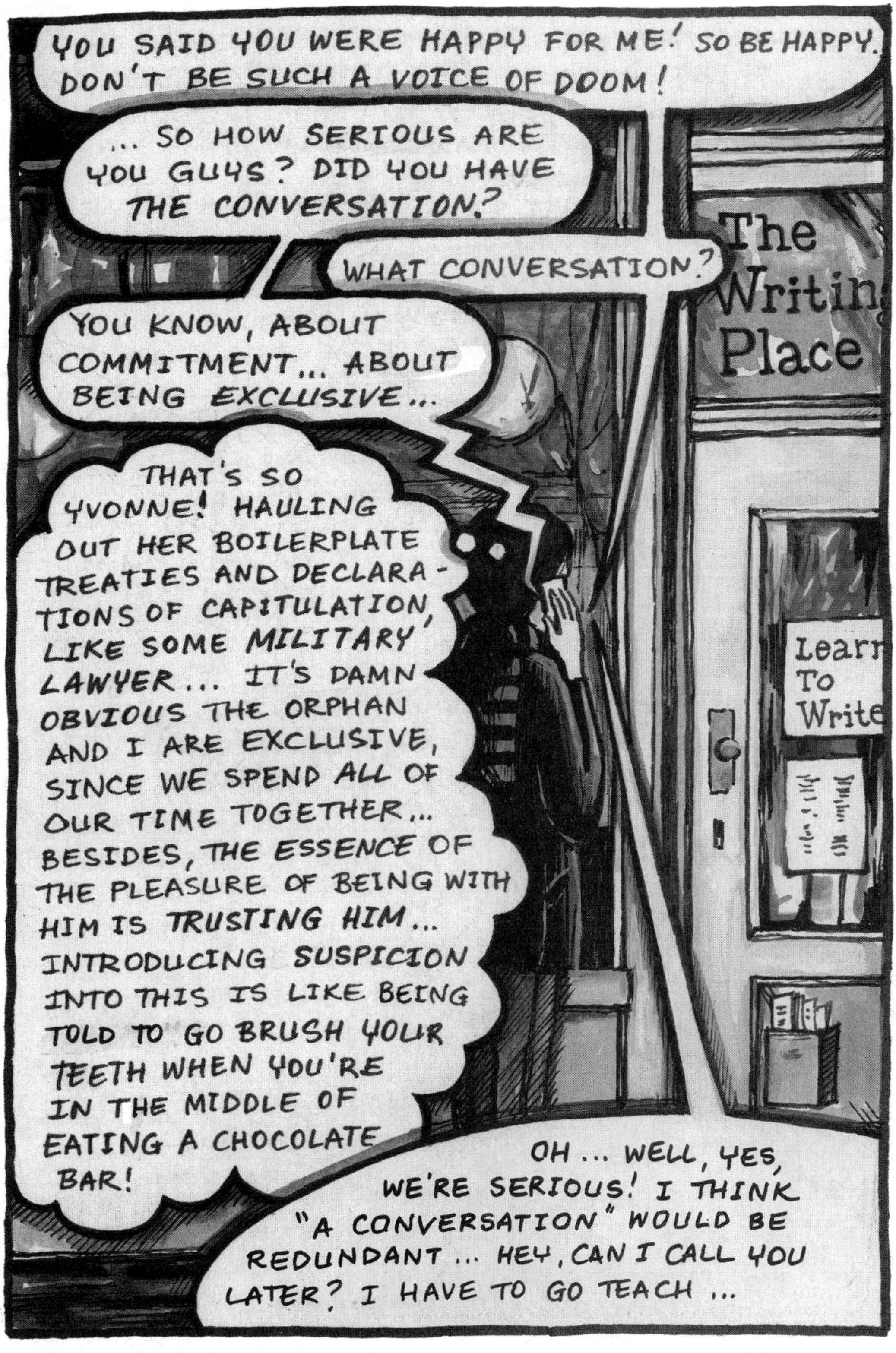
YOU SAID YOU WERE HAPPY FOR ME! SO BE HAPPY. DON'T BE SUCH A VOICE OF DOOM!
... SO HOW SERIOUS ARE YOU GUYS? DID YOU HAVE THE CONVERSATION?
WHAT CONVERSATION?
The Writing Place
YOU KNOW, ABOUT COMMITMENT... ABOUT BEING EXCLUSIVE...
THAT'S SO YVONNE! HAULING OUT HER BOILERPLATE TREATIES AND DECLARATIONS OF CAPITULATION, LIKE SOME MILITARY LAWYER... IT'S DAMN OBVIOUS THE ORPHAN AND I ARE EXCLUSIVE, SINCE WE SPEND ALL OF OUR TIME TOGETHER... BESIDES, THE ESSENCE OF THE PLEASURE OF BEING WITH HIM IS TRUSTING HIM... INTRODUCING SUSPICION INTO THIS IS LIKE BEING TOLD TO GO BRUSH YOUR TEETH WHEN YOU'RE IN THE MIDDLE OF EATING A CHOCOLATE BAR!
Learn To Write
OH... WELL, YES, WE'RE SERIOUS! I THINK "A CONVERSATION" WOULD BE REDUNDANT... HEY, CAN I CALL YOU LATER? I HAVE TO GO TEACH...

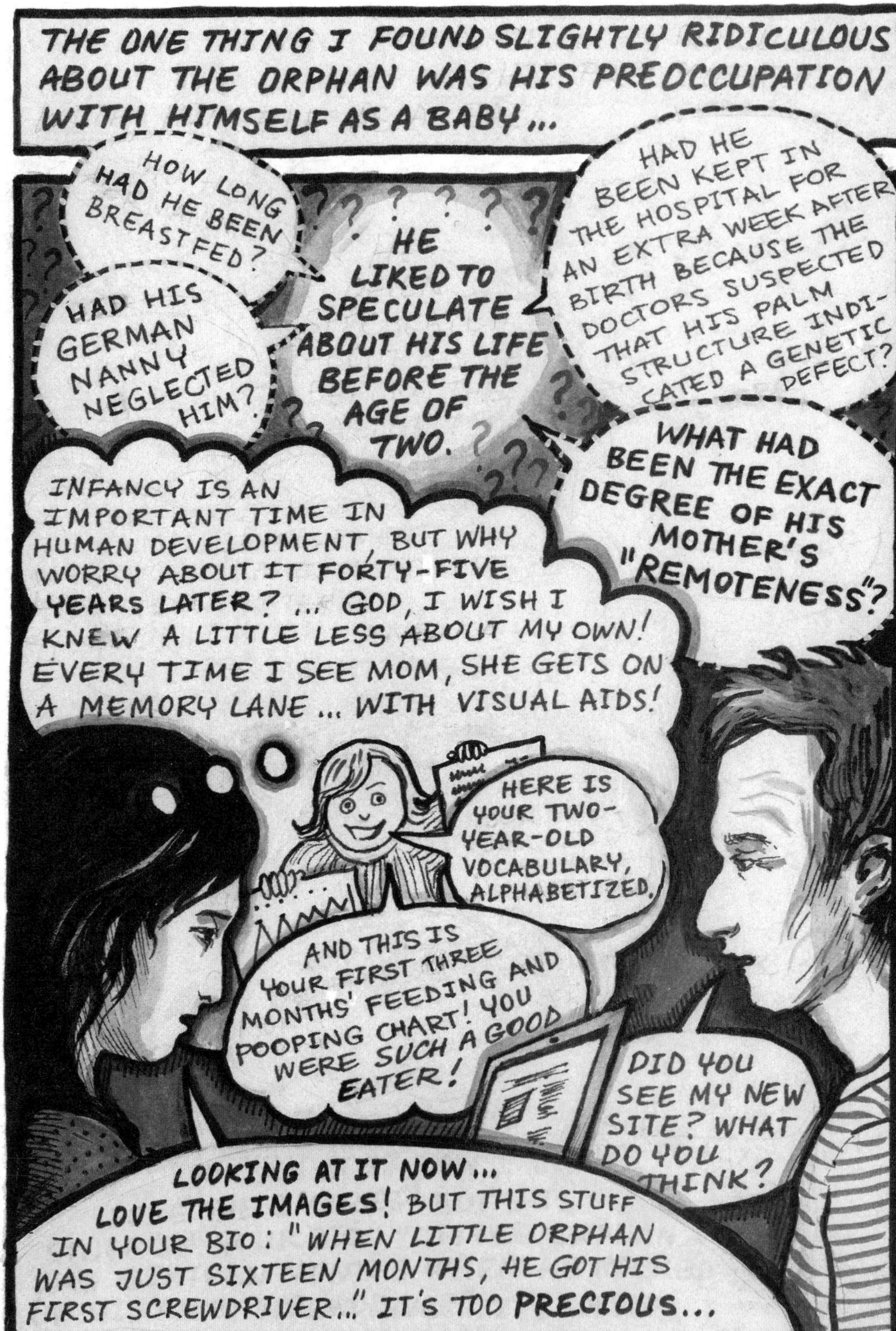
THE ONE THING I FOUND SLIGHTLY RIDICULOUS ABOUT THE ORPHAN WAS HIS PREOCCUPATION WITH HIMSELF AS A BABY...
HE LIKED TO SPECULATE ABOUT HIS LIFE BEFORE THE AGE OF TWO.
HOW LONG HAD HE BEEN BREASTFED?
HAD HIS GERMAN NANNY NEGLECTED HIM?
HAD HE BEEN KEPT IN THE HOSPITAL FOR AN EXTRA WEEK AFTER BIRTH BECAUSE THE DOCTORS SUSPECTED THAT HIS PALM STRUCTURE INDICATED A GENETIC DEFECT?
WHAT HAD BEEN THE EXACT DEGREE OF HIS MOTHER'S "REMOTENESS"?
INFANCY IS AN IMPORTANT TIME IN HUMAN DEVELOPMENT, BUT WHY WORRY ABOUT IT FORTY-FIVE YEARS LATER? ... GOD, I WISH I KNEW A LITTLE LESS ABOUT MY OWN! EVERY TIME I SEE MOM, SHE GETS ON A MEMORY LANE ... WITH VISUAL AIDS!
HERE IS YOUR TWO-YEAR-OLD VOCABULARY, ALPHABETIZED.
AND THIS IS YOUR FIRST THREE MONTHS' FEEDING AND POOPING CHART! YOU WERE SUCH A GOOD EATER!
DID YOU SEE MY NEW SITE? WHAT DO YOU THINK?
LOOKING AT IT NOW... LOVE THE IMAGES! BUT THIS STUFF IN YOUR BIO: "WHEN LITTLE ORPHAN WAS JUST SIXTEEN MONTHS, HE GOT HIS FIRST SCREWDRIVER..." IT'S TOO PRECIOUS...

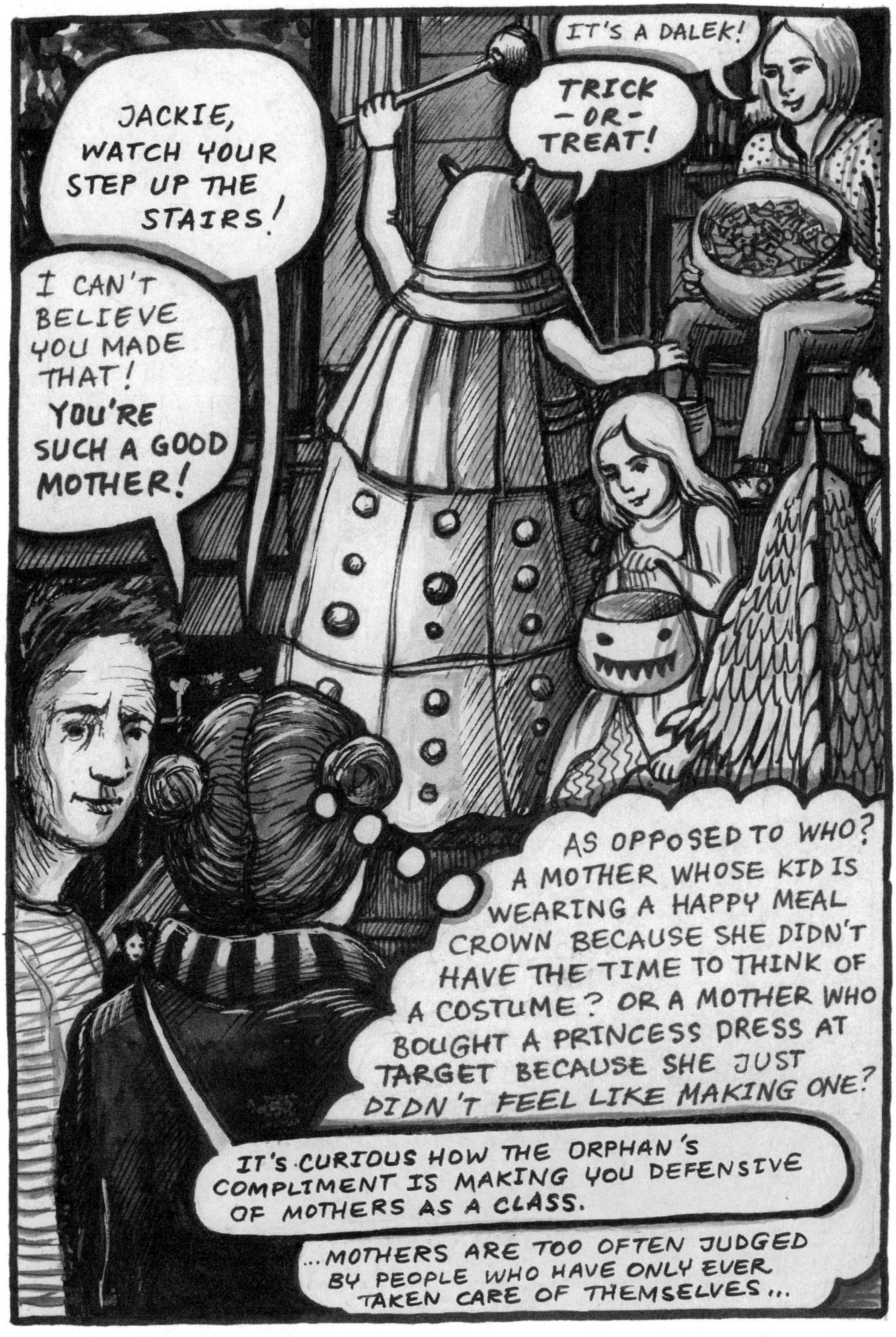
JACKIE, WATCH YOUR STEP UP THE STAIRS!
IT'S A DALEK!
TRICK -OR- TREAT!
I CAN'T BELIEVE YOU MADE THAT! YOU'RE SUCH A GOOD MOTHER!
AS OPPOSED TO WHO? A MOTHER WHOSE KID IS WEARING A HAPPY MEAL CROWN BECAUSE SHE DIDN'T HAVE THE TIME TO THINK OF A COSTUME? OR A MOTHER WHO BOUGHT A PRINCESS DRESS AT TARGET BECAUSE SHE JUST DIDN'T FEEL LIKE MAKING ONE?
IT'S CURIOUS HOW THE ORPHAN'S COMPLIMENT IS MAKING YOU DEFENSIVE OF MOTHERS AS A CLASS.
...MOTHERS ARE TOO OFTEN JUDGED BY PEOPLE WHO HAVE ONLY EVER TAKEN CARE OF THEMSELVES...

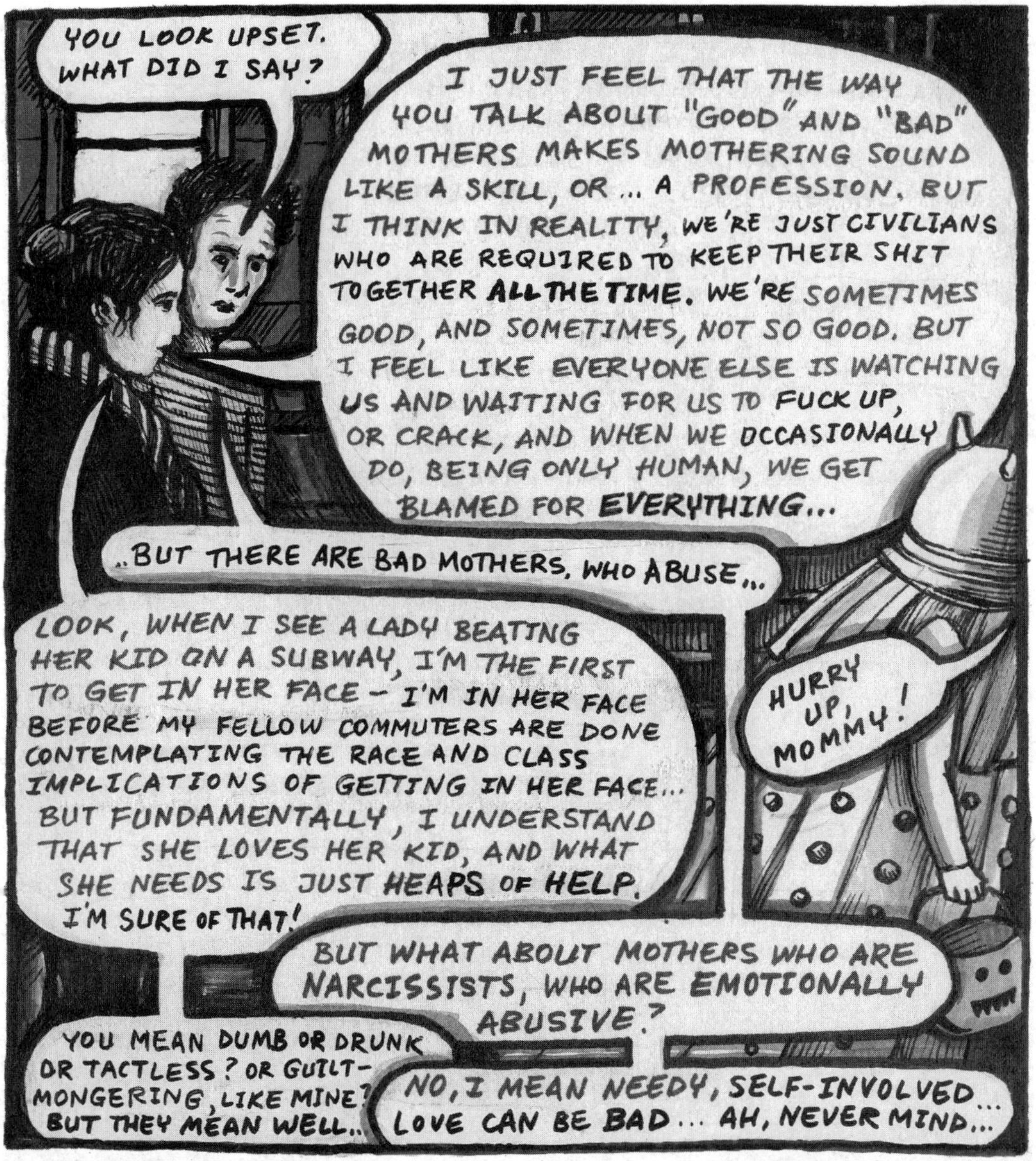
YOU LOOK UPSET. WHAT DID I SAY?
I JUST FEEL THAT THE WAY YOU TALK ABOUT "GOOD" AND "BAD" MOTHERS MAKES MOTHERING SOUND LIKE A SKILL, OR ... A PROFESSION. BUT I THINK IN REALITY, WE'RE JUST CIVILIANS WHO ARE REQUIRED TO KEEP THEIR SHIT TOGETHER **ALL THE TIME**. WE'RE SOMETIMES GOOD, AND SOMETIMES, NOT SO GOOD. BUT I FEEL LIKE EVERYONE ELSE IS WATCHING US AND WAITING FOR US TO FUCK UP, OR CRACK, AND WHEN WE OCCASIONALLY DO, BEING ONLY HUMAN, WE GET BLAMED FOR **EVERYTHING**...
..BUT THERE ARE BAD MOTHERS, WHO ABUSE...
LOOK, WHEN I SEE A LADY BEATING HER KID ON A SUBWAY, I'M THE FIRST TO GET IN HER FACE - I'M IN HER FACE BEFORE MY FELLOW COMMUTERS ARE DONE CONTEMPLATING THE RACE AND CLASS IMPLICATIONS OF GETTING IN HER FACE... BUT FUNDAMENTALLY, I UNDERSTAND THAT SHE LOVES HER KID, AND WHAT SHE NEEDS IS JUST **HEAPS** OF **HELP**. I'M SURE OF THAT!
HURRY UP, MOMMY!
BUT WHAT ABOUT MOTHERS WHO ARE NARCISSISTS, WHO ARE EMOTIONALLY ABUSIVE?
YOU MEAN DUMB OR DRUNK OR TACTLESS? OR GUILT-MONGERING, LIKE MINE? BUT THEY MEAN WELL...
NO, I MEAN NEEDY, SELF-INVOLVED... LOVE CAN BE **BAD**... AH, NEVER MIND...

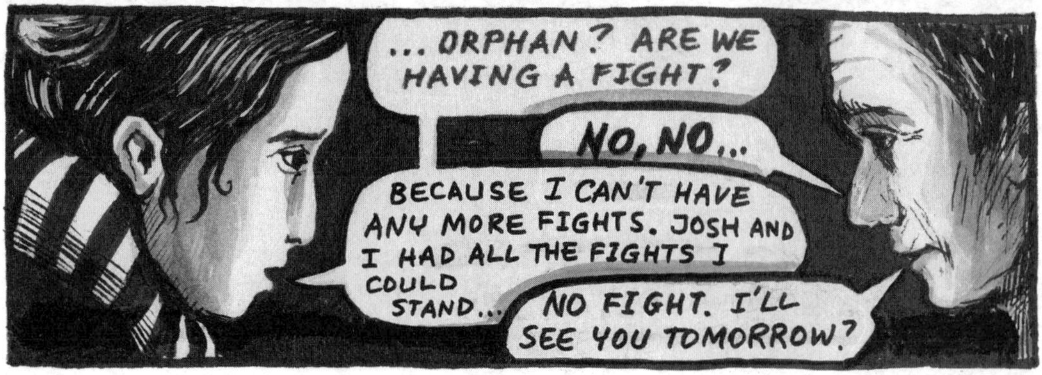
... ORPHAN? ARE WE HAVING A FIGHT?
NO, NO...
BECAUSE I CAN'T HAVE ANY MORE FIGHTS. JOSH AND I HAD ALL THE FIGHTS I COULD STAND...
NO FIGHT. I'LL SEE YOU TOMORROW?

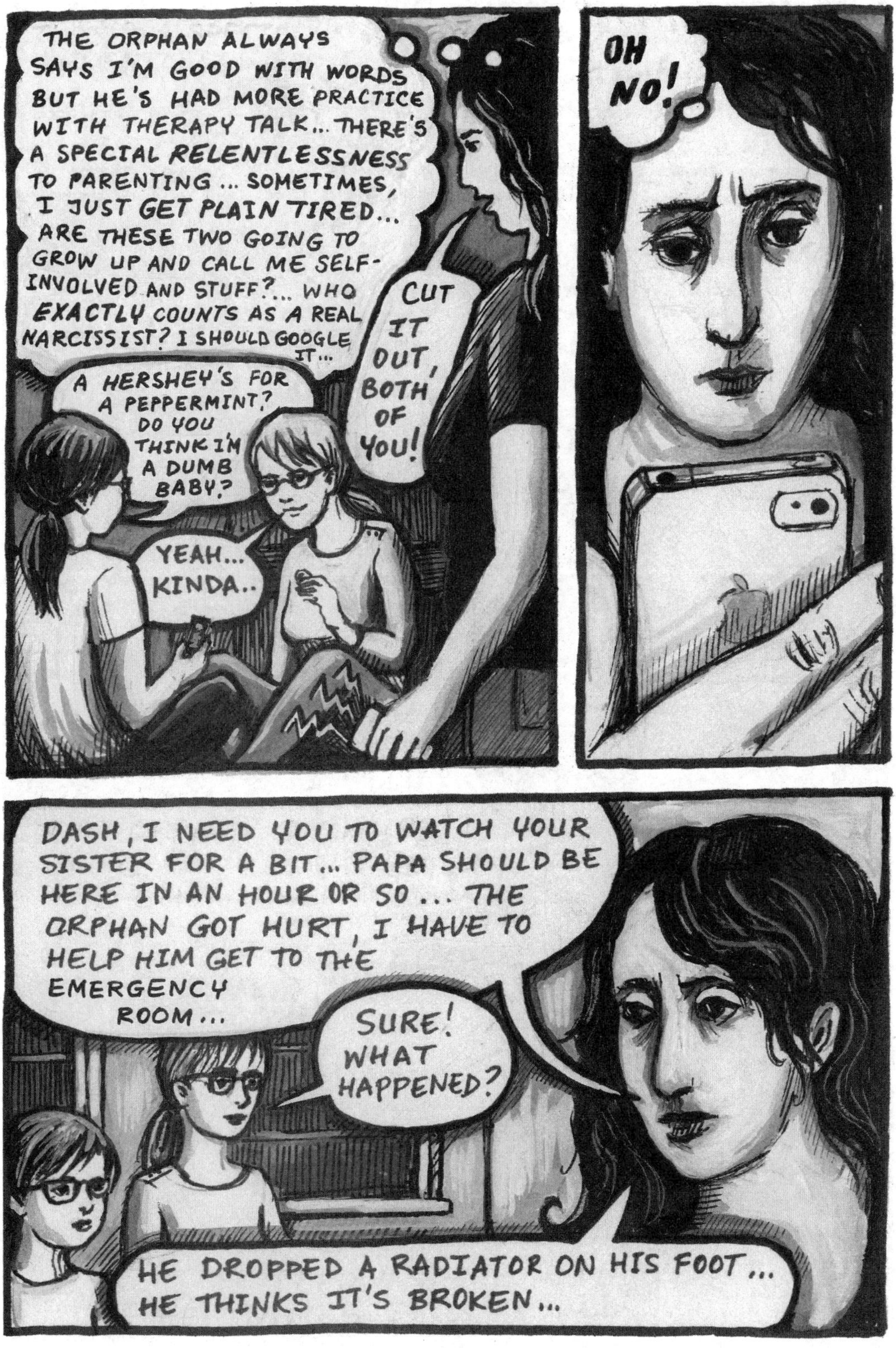
THE ORPHAN ALWAYS SAYS I'M GOOD WITH WORDS BUT HE'S HAD MORE PRACTICE WITH THERAPY TALK... THERE'S A SPECIAL RELENTLESSNESS TO PARENTING ... SOMETIMES, I JUST GET PLAIN TIRED... ARE THESE TWO GOING TO GROW UP AND CALL ME SELF-INVOLVED AND STUFF?... WHO EXACTLY COUNTS AS A REAL NARCISSIST? I SHOULD GOOGLE IT...
A HERSHEY'S FOR A PEPPERMINT? DO YOU THINK I'M A DUMB BABY?
YEAH... KINDA..
CUT IT OUT, BOTH OF YOU!
OH NO!
DASH, I NEED YOU TO WATCH YOUR SISTER FOR A BIT... PAPA SHOULD BE HERE IN AN HOUR OR SO ... THE ORPHAN GOT HURT, I HAVE TO HELP HIM GET TO THE EMERGENCY ROOM...
SURE! WHAT HAPPENED?
HE DROPPED A RADIATOR ON HIS FOOT... HE THINKS IT'S BROKEN...

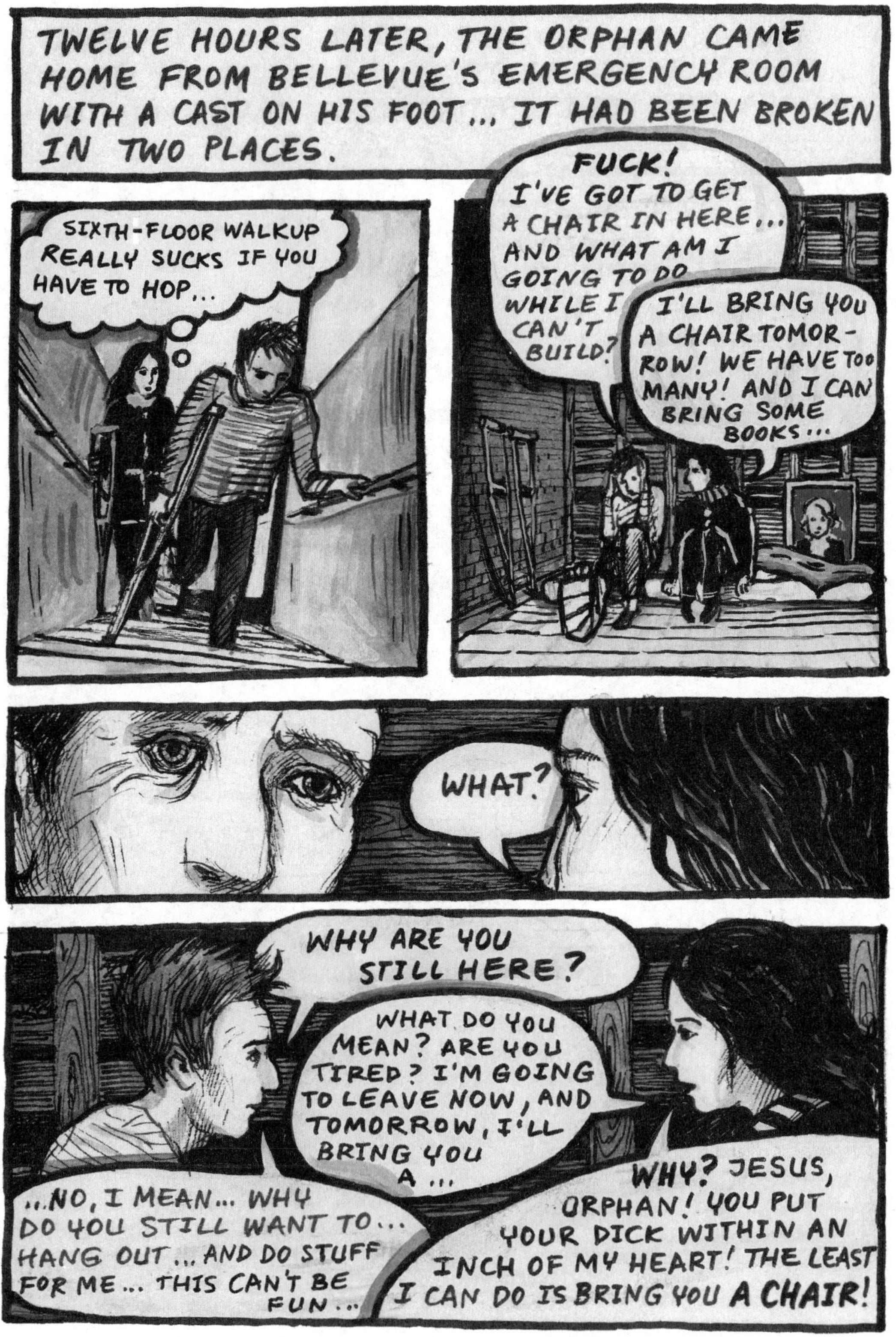
TWELVE HOURS LATER, THE ORPHAN CAME HOME FROM BELLEVUE'S EMERGENCY ROOM WITH A CAST ON HIS FOOT... IT HAD BEEN BROKEN IN TWO PLACES.
SIXTH-FLOOR WALKUP REALLY SUCKS IF YOU HAVE TO HOP...
FUCK! I'VE GOT TO GET A CHAIR IN HERE... AND WHAT AM I GOING TO DO WHILE I CAN'T BUILD?
I'LL BRING YOU A CHAIR TOMORROW! WE HAVE TOO MANY! AND I CAN BRING SOME BOOKS...
WHAT?
WHY ARE YOU STILL HERE?
WHAT DO YOU MEAN? ARE YOU TIRED? I'M GOING TO LEAVE NOW, AND TOMORROW, I'LL BRING YOU A...
...NO, I MEAN... WHY DO YOU STILL WANT TO... HANG OUT... AND DO STUFF FOR ME... THIS CAN'T BE FUN...
WHY? JESUS, ORPHAN! YOU PUT YOUR DICK WITHIN AN INCH OF MY HEART! THE LEAST I CAN DO IS BRING YOU A CHAIR!

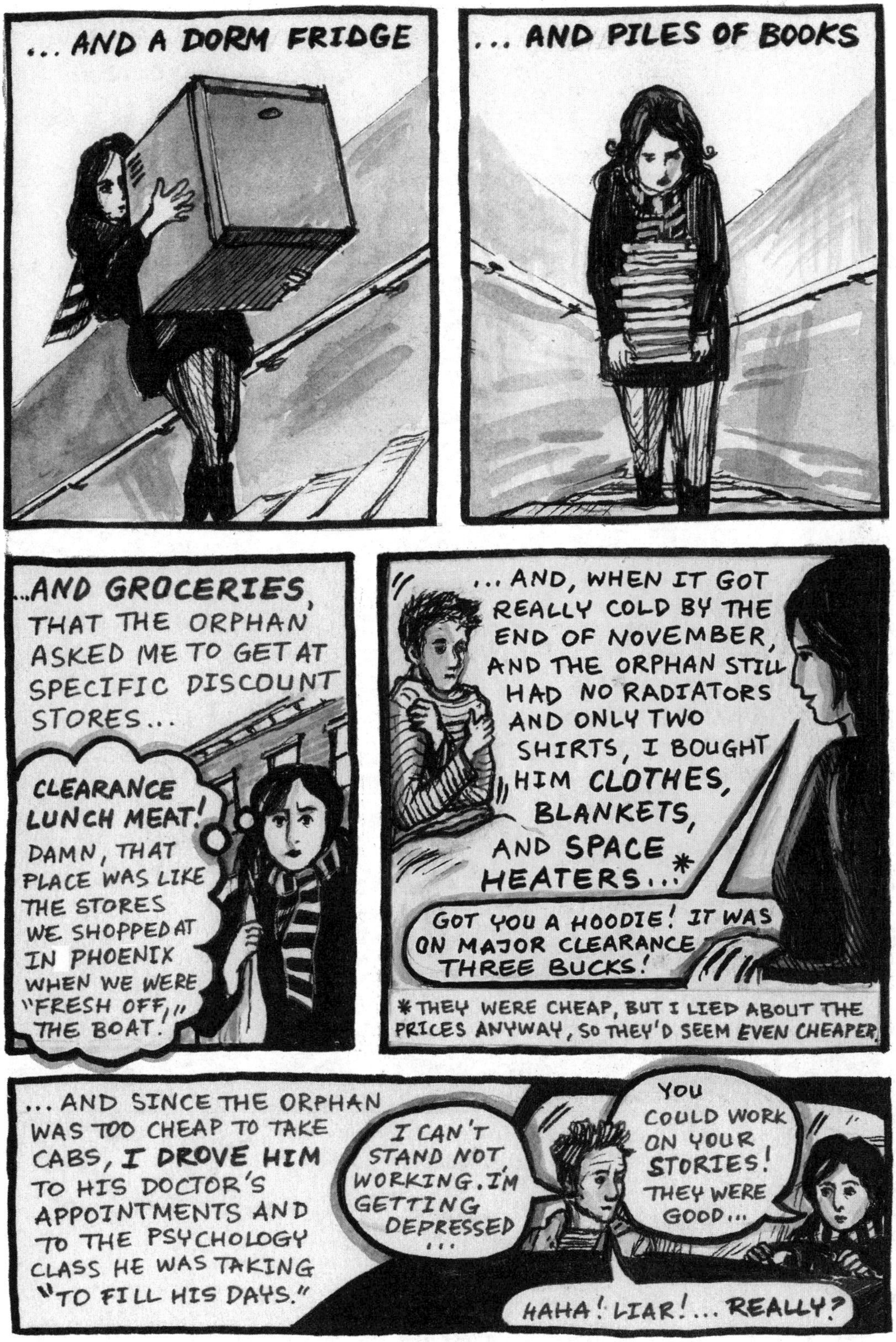
... AND A DORM FRIDGE
... AND PILES OF BOOKS
...AND GROCERIES, THAT THE ORPHAN ASKED ME TO GET AT SPECIFIC DISCOUNT STORES...
CLEARANCE LUNCH MEAT! DAMN, THAT PLACE WAS LIKE THE STORES WE SHOPPED AT IN PHOENIX WHEN WE WERE "FRESH OFF THE BOAT."
... AND, WHEN IT GOT REALLY COLD BY THE END OF NOVEMBER, AND THE ORPHAN STILL HAD NO RADIATORS AND ONLY TWO SHIRTS, I BOUGHT HIM CLOTHES, BLANKETS, AND SPACE HEATERS...*
GOT YOU A HOODIE! IT WAS ON MAJOR CLEARANCE - THREE BUCKS!
* THEY WERE CHEAP, BUT I LIED ABOUT THE PRICES ANYWAY, SO THEY'D SEEM EVEN CHEAPER.
... AND SINCE THE ORPHAN WAS TOO CHEAP TO TAKE CABS, I DROVE HIM TO HIS DOCTOR'S APPOINTMENTS AND TO THE PSYCHOLOGY CLASS HE WAS TAKING "TO FILL HIS DAYS."
I CAN'T STAND NOT WORKING. I'M GETTING DEPRESSED...
YOU COULD WORK ON YOUR STORIES! THEY WERE GOOD...
HAHA! LIAR! ... REALLY?

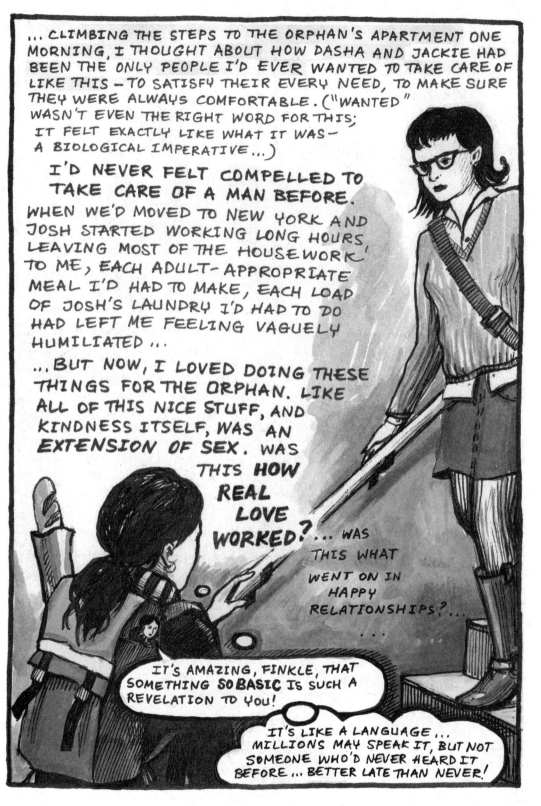

... CLIMBING THE STEPS TO THE ORPHAN'S APARTMENT ONE MORNING, I THOUGHT ABOUT HOW DASHA AND JACKIE HAD BEEN THE ONLY PEOPLE I'D EVER WANTED TO TAKE CARE OF LIKE THIS — TO SATISFY THEIR EVERY NEED, TO MAKE SURE THEY WERE ALWAYS COMFORTABLE. ("WANTED" WASN'T EVEN THE RIGHT WORD FOR THIS; IT FELT EXACTLY LIKE WHAT IT WAS — A BIOLOGICAL IMPERATIVE...)

I'D NEVER FELT COMPELLED TO TAKE CARE OF A MAN BEFORE. WHEN WE'D MOVED TO NEW YORK AND JOSH STARTED WORKING LONG HOURS, LEAVING MOST OF THE HOUSEWORK TO ME, EACH ADULT-APPROPRIATE MEAL I'D HAD TO MAKE, EACH LOAD OF JOSH'S LAUNDRY I'D HAD TO DO HAD LEFT ME FEELING VAGUELY HUMILIATED...

... BUT NOW, I LOVED DOING THESE THINGS FOR THE ORPHAN. LIKE ALL OF THIS NICE STUFF, AND KINDNESS ITSELF, WAS AN *EXTENSION OF SEX.* WAS THIS **HOW REAL LOVE WORKED?** ... WAS THIS WHAT WENT ON IN HAPPY RELATIONSHIPS? ...

IT'S AMAZING, FINKLE, THAT SOMETHING **SO BASIC** IS SUCH A REVELATION TO YOU!

IT'S LIKE A LANGUAGE ... MILLIONS MAY SPEAK IT, BUT NOT SOMEONE WHO'D NEVER HEARD IT BEFORE ... BETTER LATE THAN NEVER!

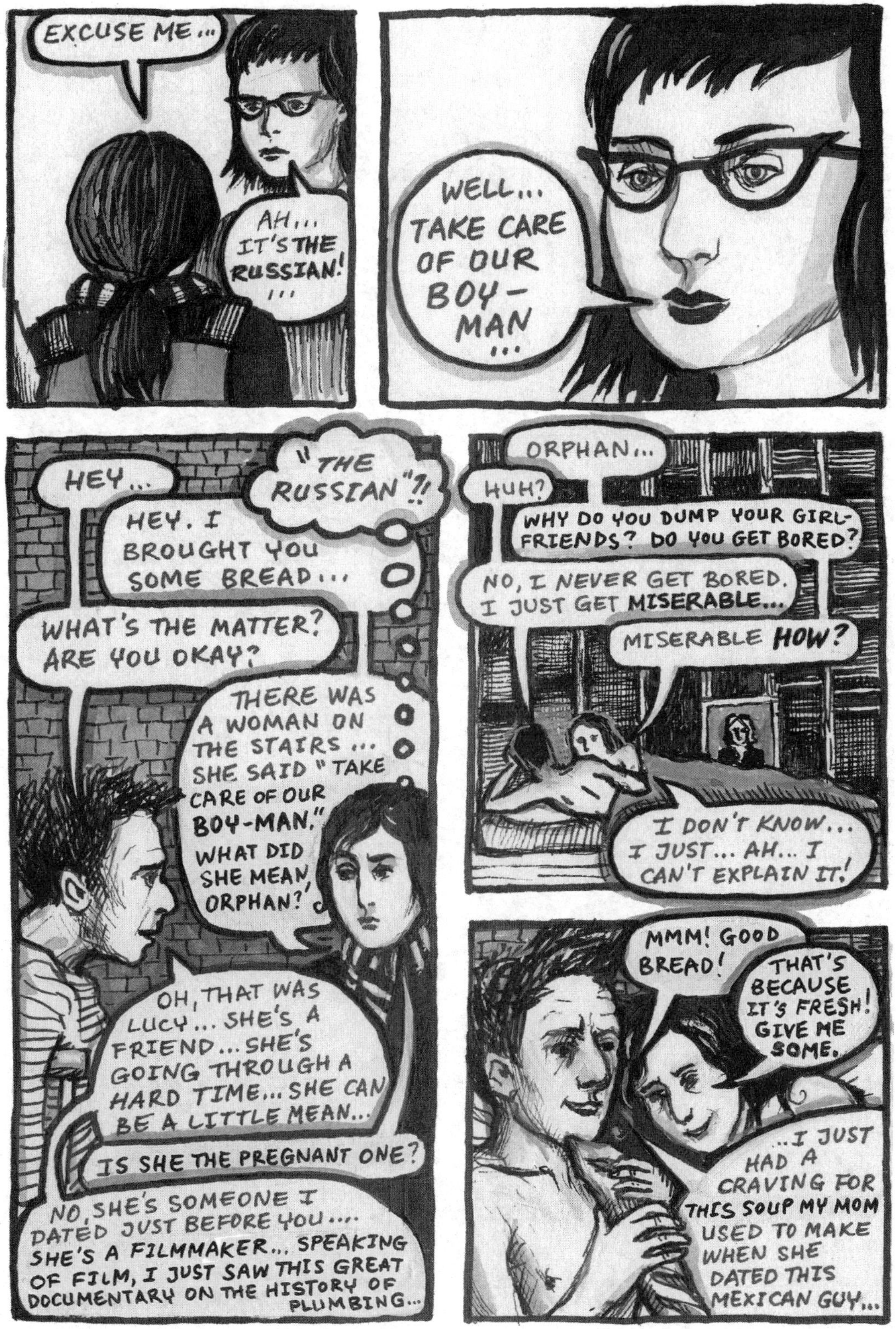
EXCUSE ME...
AH... IT'S THE RUSSIAN! ...
WELL... TAKE CARE OF OUR BOY-MAN ...
HEY...
"THE RUSSIAN"?!
HEY. I BROUGHT YOU SOME BREAD...
WHAT'S THE MATTER? ARE YOU OKAY?
THERE WAS A WOMAN ON THE STAIRS... SHE SAID "TAKE CARE OF OUR BOY-MAN." WHAT DID SHE MEAN, ORPHAN?
OH, THAT WAS LUCY... SHE'S A FRIEND... SHE'S GOING THROUGH A HARD TIME... SHE CAN BE A LITTLE MEAN...
IS SHE THE PREGNANT ONE?
NO, SHE'S SOMEONE I DATED JUST BEFORE YOU.... SHE'S A FILMMAKER... SPEAKING OF FILM, I JUST SAW THIS GREAT DOCUMENTARY ON THE HISTORY OF PLUMBING...
ORPHAN...
HUH?
WHY DO YOU DUMP YOUR GIRLFRIENDS? DO YOU GET BORED?
NO, I NEVER GET BORED. I JUST GET MISERABLE...
MISERABLE HOW?
I DON'T KNOW... I JUST... AH... I CAN'T EXPLAIN IT!
MMM! GOOD BREAD!
THAT'S BECAUSE IT'S FRESH! GIVE ME SOME.
...I JUST HAD A CRAVING FOR THIS SOUP MY MOM USED TO MAKE WHEN SHE DATED THIS MEXICAN GUY...

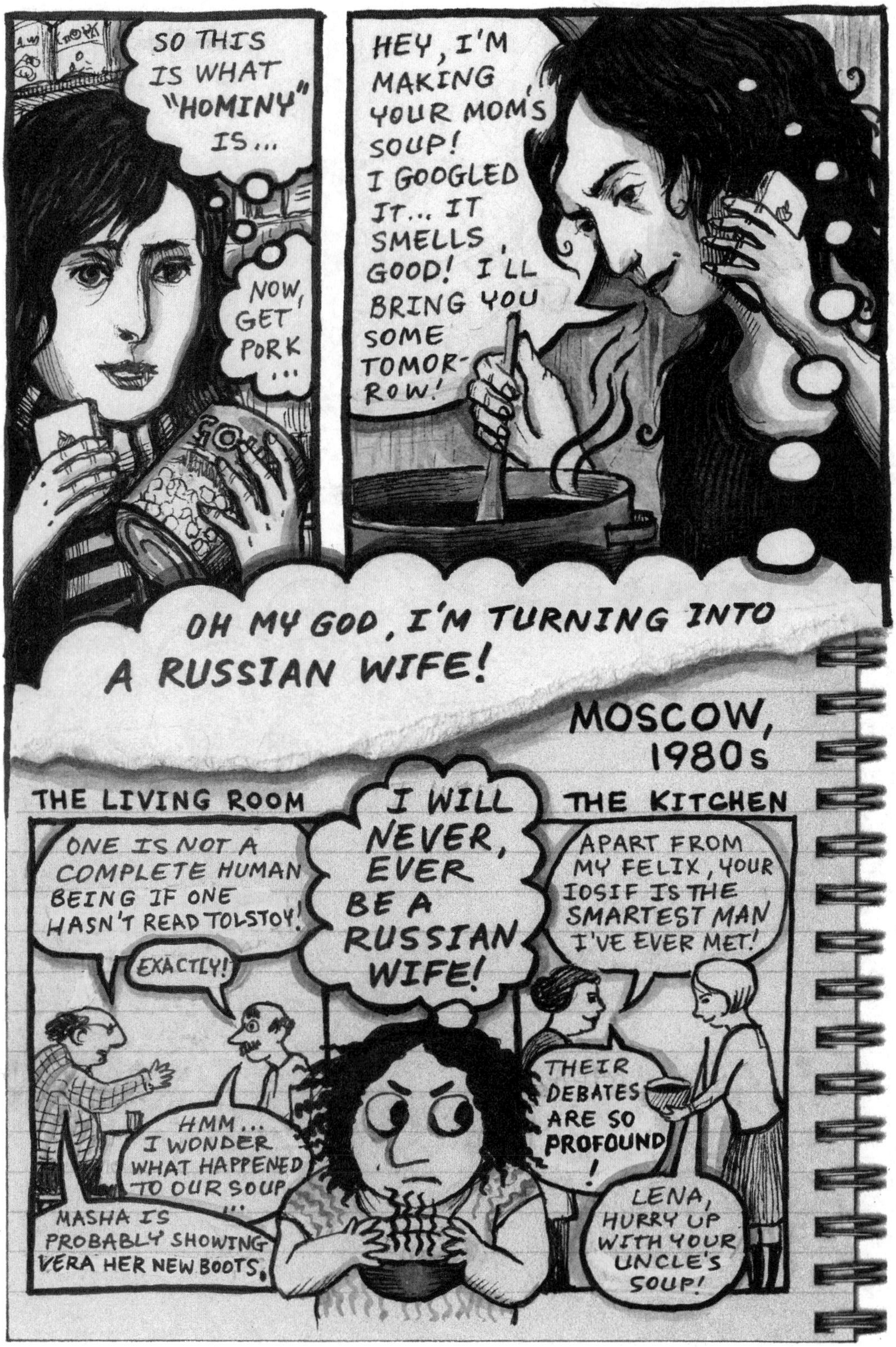
SO THIS IS WHAT "HOMINY" IS...
NOW, GET PORK...
HEY, I'M MAKING YOUR MOM'S SOUP! I GOOGLED IT... IT SMELLS GOOD! I'LL BRING YOU SOME TOMORROW!
OH MY GOD, I'M TURNING INTO A RUSSIAN WIFE!
MOSCOW, 1980s
THE LIVING ROOM
I WILL NEVER, EVER BE A RUSSIAN WIFE!
THE KITCHEN
ONE IS NOT A COMPLETE HUMAN BEING IF ONE HASN'T READ TOLSTOY!
EXACTLY!
HMM... I WONDER WHAT HAPPENED TO OUR SOUP...
MASHA IS PROBABLY SHOWING VERA HER NEW BOOTS.
APART FROM MY FELIX, YOUR IOSIF IS THE SMARTEST MAN I'VE EVER MET!
THEIR DEBATES ARE SO PROFOUND!
LENA, HURRY UP WITH YOUR UNCLE'S SOUP!

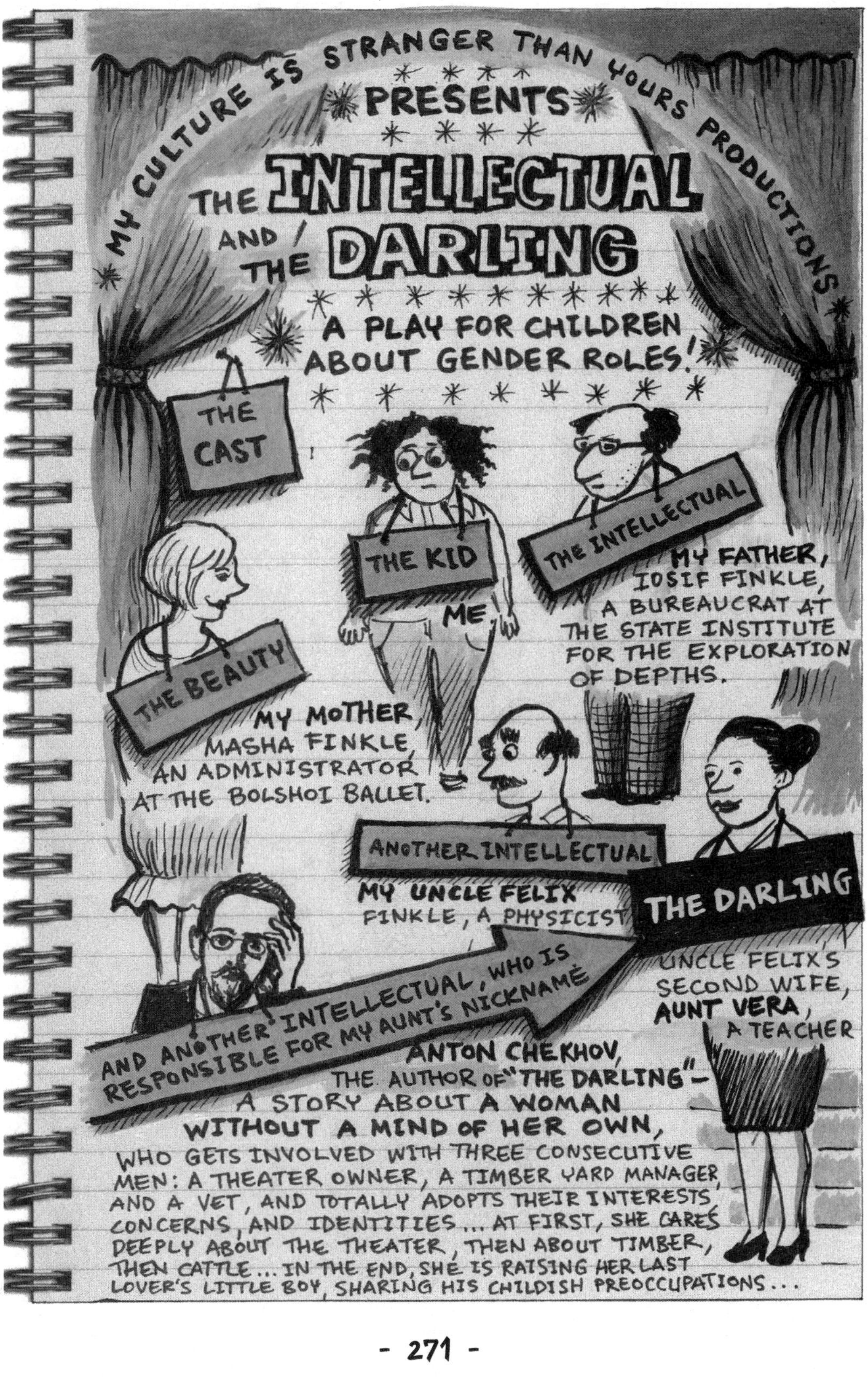

MY CULTURE IS STRANGER THAN YOURS PRODUCTIONS
PRESENTS
THE INTELLECTUAL AND THE DARLING
A PLAY FOR CHILDREN ABOUT GENDER ROLES!
THE CAST
THE KID
ME
THE INTELLECTUAL
MY FATHER, IOSIF FINKLE, A BUREAUCRAT AT THE STATE INSTITUTE FOR THE EXPLORATION OF DEPTHS.
THE BEAUTY
MY MOTHER, MASHA FINKLE, AN ADMINISTRATOR AT THE BOLSHOI BALLET.
ANOTHER INTELLECTUAL
MY UNCLE FELIX FINKLE, A PHYSICIST
THE DARLING
UNCLE FELIX'S SECOND WIFE, AUNT VERA, A TEACHER
AND ANOTHER INTELLECTUAL, WHO IS RESPONSIBLE FOR MY AUNT'S NICKNAME
ANTON CHEKHOV, THE AUTHOR OF "THE DARLING"— A STORY ABOUT A WOMAN WITHOUT A MIND OF HER OWN, WHO GETS INVOLVED WITH THREE CONSECUTIVE MEN: A THEATER OWNER, A TIMBER YARD MANAGER, AND A VET, AND TOTALLY ADOPTS THEIR INTERESTS, CONCERNS, AND IDENTITIES... AT FIRST, SHE CARES DEEPLY ABOUT THE THEATER, THEN ABOUT TIMBER, THEN CATTLE... IN THE END, SHE IS RAISING HER LAST LOVER'S LITTLE BOY, SHARING HIS CHILDISH PREOCCUPATIONS...

THE PLOT

WILL I BE A BEAUTY?

OR AN INTELLECTUAL?

THIS IS A CLASS DISTINCTION, AND, AS SUCH DISTINCTIONS ARE, UNBREACHABLE. **ONE CAN'T BE BOTH.**

BUT FOR AS LONG AS MY AGE OBSCURES THE IMPERATIVES OF MY GENDER, IT SEEMS THAT I HAVE A CHOICE... **AND IT'S A NO-BRAINER!**

MY MOTHER AND MY FATHER WENT TO THE SAME UNIVERSITY, WORK THE SAME HOURS, AND HAVE THE SAME LONG COMMUTE.

MOTHER MAKES 200 RUBLES A MONTH; FATHER MAKES 160.

BUT WHEN THEY COME HOME IN THE EVENING, FATHER SITS DOWN AND WAITS FOR DINNER; MOTHER REMAINS STANDING AND MAKES THE DINNER...

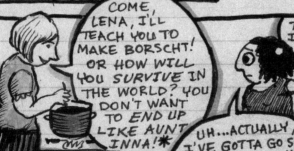

COME, LENA, I'LL TEACH YOU TO MAKE BORSCHT! OR HOW WILL YOU *SURVIVE* IN THE WORLD? YOU DON'T WANT TO *END UP* LIKE AUNT INNA!✱

THIS REGIME IS BOUND TO FAIL!

UH...ACTUALLY, I'VE GOTTA GO SEE WHAT'S UP WITH THE FAILING REGIME...

DON'T TEACH ME HOW TO MAKE BORSCHT, MOM! TEACH ME HOW TO RESIGN MY MEMBERSHIP IN THE "FAIR SEX"...

✱ AUNT INNA WAS MY UNCLE FELIX'S FIRST WIFE. AFTER YEARS AS A T.V. SOUND PERSON, AUNT INNA MADE FRIENDS WITH X., A FAMOUS DIRECTOR, AND ENDED UP WRITING A POPULAR SOVIET T.V. SERIES ABOUT SEXY EIGHTEENTH-CENTURY SAILORS... HOWEVER, AUNT INNA "ONLY CLEANED THE BATHROOM WHEN X. CAME OVER" AND UNCLE FELIX DIVORCED HER AND MARRIED AUNT VERA, *THE DARLING*...

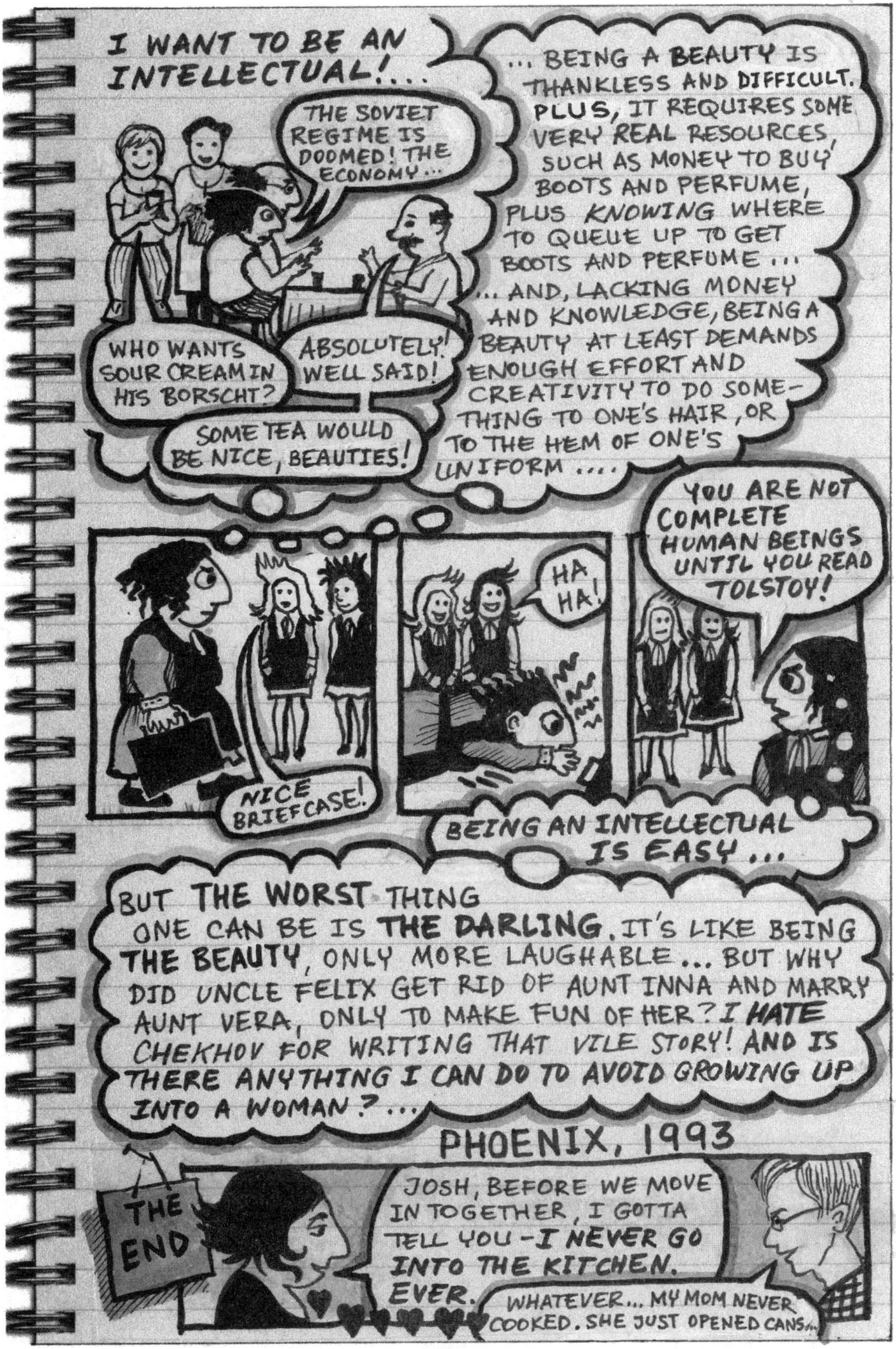
I WANT TO BE AN INTELLECTUAL!...
THE SOVIET REGIME IS DOOMED! THE ECONOMY...
WHO WANTS SOUR CREAM IN HIS BORSCHT?
ABSOLUTELY! WELL SAID!
SOME TEA WOULD BE NICE, BEAUTIES!
... BEING A BEAUTY IS THANKLESS AND DIFFICULT. PLUS, IT REQUIRES SOME VERY REAL RESOURCES, SUCH AS MONEY TO BUY BOOTS AND PERFUME, PLUS KNOWING WHERE TO QUEUE UP TO GET BOOTS AND PERFUME... ... AND, LACKING MONEY AND KNOWLEDGE, BEING A BEAUTY AT LEAST DEMANDS ENOUGH EFFORT AND CREATIVITY TO DO SOMETHING TO ONE'S HAIR, OR TO THE HEM OF ONE'S UNIFORM....
NICE BRIEFCASE!
HA HA!
YOU ARE NOT COMPLETE HUMAN BEINGS UNTIL YOU READ TOLSTOY!
BEING AN INTELLECTUAL IS EASY...
BUT THE WORST THING ONE CAN BE IS THE DARLING. IT'S LIKE BEING THE BEAUTY, ONLY MORE LAUGHABLE... BUT WHY DID UNCLE FELIX GET RID OF AUNT INNA AND MARRY AUNT VERA, ONLY TO MAKE FUN OF HER? I HATE CHEKHOV FOR WRITING THAT VILE STORY! AND IS THERE ANYTHING I CAN DO TO AVOID GROWING UP INTO A WOMAN?...
PHOENIX, 1993
THE END
JOSH, BEFORE WE MOVE IN TOGETHER, I GOTTA TELL YOU - I NEVER GO INTO THE KITCHEN. EVER.
WHATEVER... MY MOM NEVER COOKED. SHE JUST OPENED CANS...

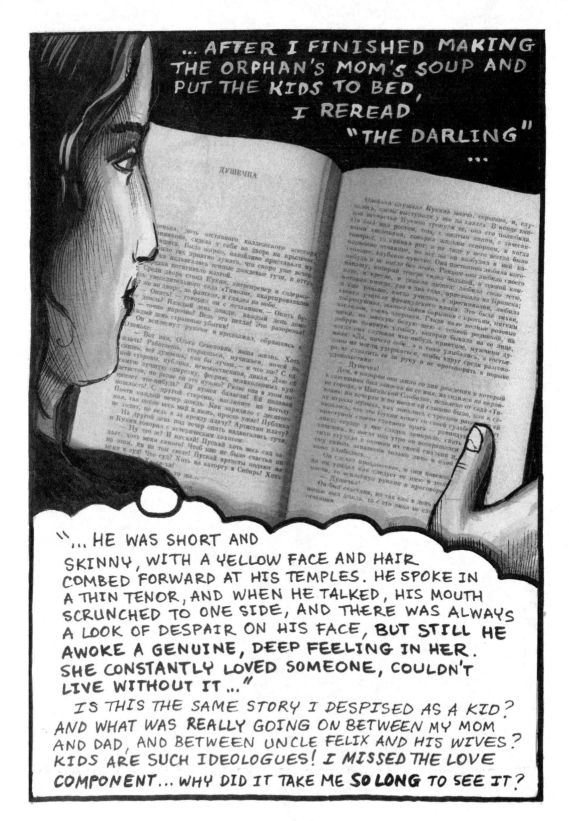

... AFTER I FINISHED MAKING THE ORPHAN'S MOM'S SOUP AND PUT THE KIDS TO BED, I REREAD "THE DARLING" ...

"... HE WAS SHORT AND SKINNY, WITH A YELLOW FACE AND HAIR COMBED FORWARD AT HIS TEMPLES. HE SPOKE IN A THIN TENOR, AND WHEN HE TALKED, HIS MOUTH SCRUNCHED TO ONE SIDE, AND THERE WAS ALWAYS A LOOK OF DESPAIR ON HIS FACE, BUT STILL HE AWOKE A GENUINE, DEEP FEELING IN HER. SHE CONSTANTLY LOVED SOMEONE, COULDN'T LIVE WITHOUT IT ..."

IS THIS THE SAME STORY I DESPISED AS A KID? AND WHAT WAS REALLY GOING ON BETWEEN MY MOM AND DAD, AND BETWEEN UNCLE FELIX AND HIS WIVES? KIDS ARE SUCH IDEOLOGUES! I MISSED THE LOVE COMPONENT... WHY DID IT TAKE ME SO LONG TO SEE IT?

...THE MORE I LOVED THE ORPHAN, THE MORE ENERGY I HAD TO BE GOOD AT ALL SORTS OF THINGS...

THE TRADITIONAL NARRATIVE OF SINGLE MOTHERHOOD HOLDS THAT WHEN A MOTHER MEETS A GUY, SHE STOPS PAYING ATTENTION TO THE CHILDREN... BUT, I BET, IN REALITY, THE MOST INSANE HANDMADE HALLOWEEN COSTUMES, THE MOST EXTRAVAGANT CHRISTMAS PRESENTS COME FROM MOTHERS IN LOVE!

SURE, WE CAN HAVE A JUST-BECAUSE CUPCAKE PARTY! AND YES, ALL OF YOUR FRIENDS CAN SLEEP OVER! WE'LL HAVE TO FIGURE OUT WHERE TO PUT THEM...

...SUDDENLY, I WAS EVEN MAKING REAL MONEY! AN EXHIBIT DESIGNER FRIEND HIRED ME TO DRAW HUGE HEADS OF THE FOUNDING FATHERS FOR A MUSEUM SHOW... THE FATHERS CAME WITH AMERICAN-DREAM-CALIBER PAY...

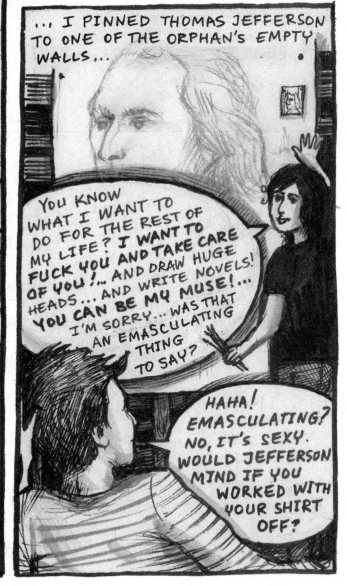

...I PINNED THOMAS JEFFERSON TO ONE OF THE ORPHAN'S EMPTY WALLS...

YOU KNOW WHAT I WANT TO DO FOR THE REST OF MY LIFE? I WANT TO FUCK YOU AND TAKE CARE OF YOU!... AND DRAW HUGE HEADS... AND WRITE NOVELS! YOU CAN BE MY MUSE!... I'M SORRY... WAS THAT AN EMASCULATING THING TO SAY?

HAHA! EMASCULATING? NO, IT'S SEXY. WOULD JEFFERSON MIND IF YOU WORKED WITH YOUR SHIRT OFF?

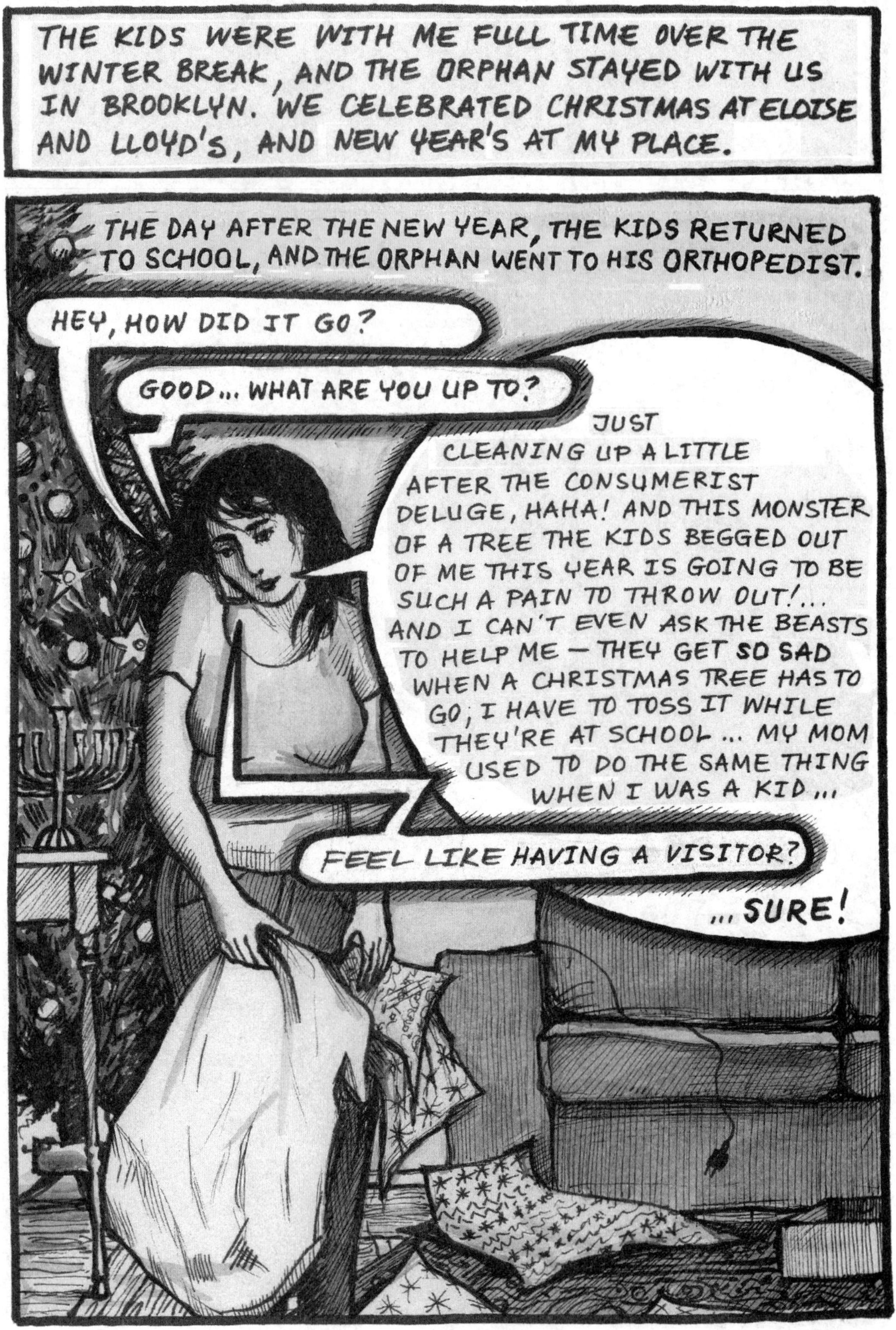
THE KIDS WERE WITH ME FULL TIME OVER THE WINTER BREAK, AND THE ORPHAN STAYED WITH US IN BROOKLYN. WE CELEBRATED CHRISTMAS AT ELOISE AND LLOYD'S, AND NEW YEAR'S AT MY PLACE.
THE DAY AFTER THE NEW YEAR, THE KIDS RETURNED TO SCHOOL, AND THE ORPHAN WENT TO HIS ORTHOPEDIST.
HEY, HOW DID IT GO?
GOOD... WHAT ARE YOU UP TO?
JUST CLEANING UP A LITTLE AFTER THE CONSUMERIST DELUGE, HAHA! AND THIS MONSTER OF A TREE THE KIDS BEGGED OUT OF ME THIS YEAR IS GOING TO BE SUCH A PAIN TO THROW OUT!... AND I CAN'T EVEN ASK THE BEASTS TO HELP ME — THEY GET SO SAD WHEN A CHRISTMAS TREE HAS TO GO, I HAVE TO TOSS IT WHILE THEY'RE AT SCHOOL... MY MOM USED TO DO THE SAME THING WHEN I WAS A KID...
FEEL LIKE HAVING A VISITOR?
...SURE!

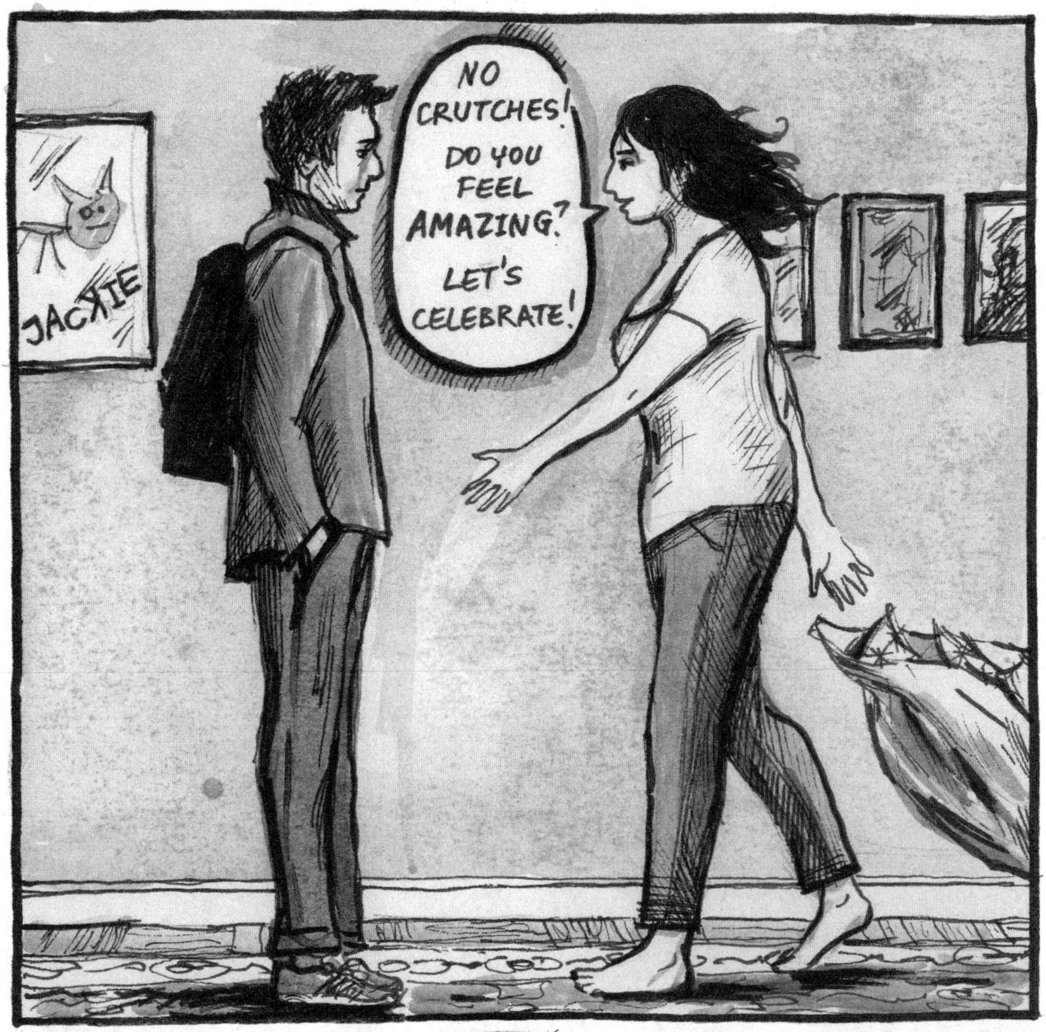

NO CRUTCHES! DO YOU FEEL AMAZING? LET'S CELEBRATE!
JACKIE

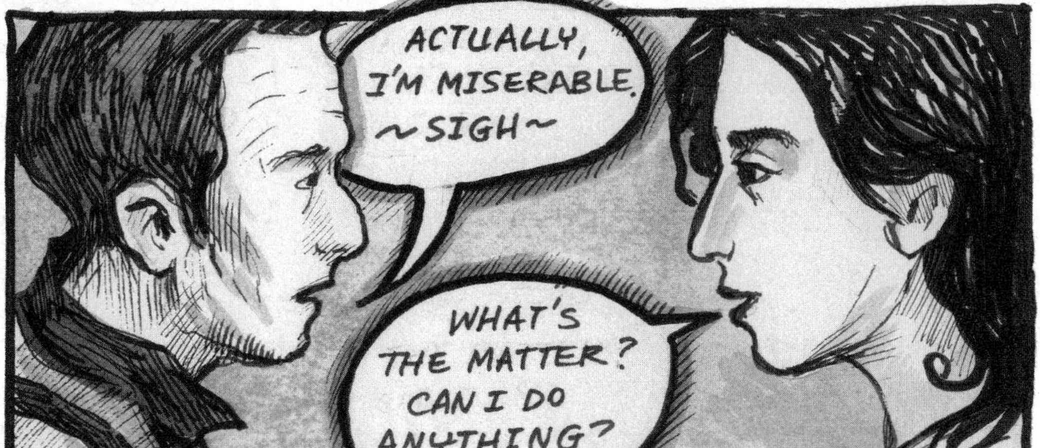

ACTUALLY, I'M MISERABLE. ~SIGH~
WHAT'S THE MATTER? CAN I DO ANYTHING?

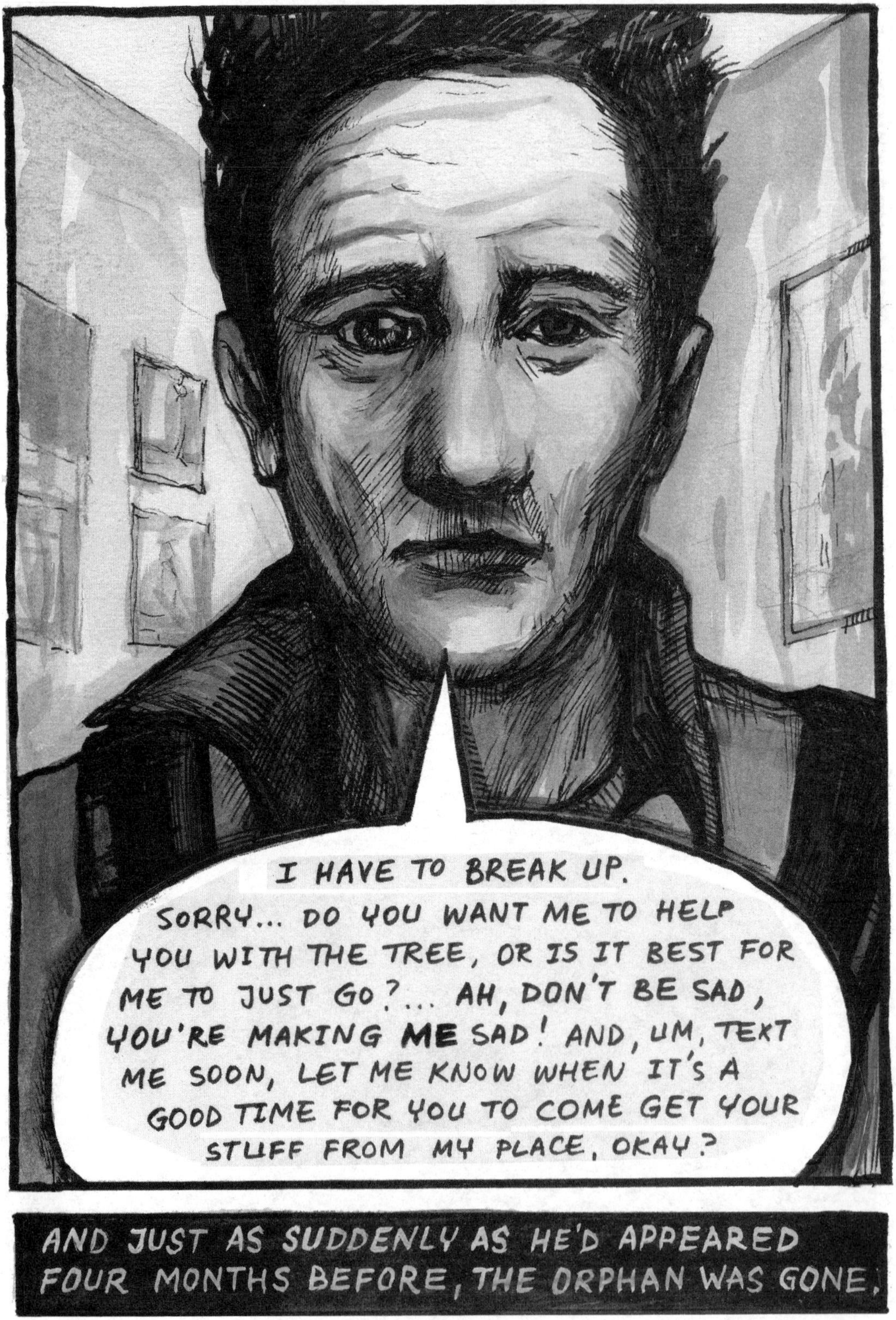
I HAVE TO BREAK UP.
SORRY... DO YOU WANT ME TO HELP YOU WITH THE TREE, OR IS IT BEST FOR ME TO JUST GO?... AH, DON'T BE SAD, YOU'RE MAKING **ME** SAD! AND, UM, TEXT ME SOON, LET ME KNOW WHEN IT'S A GOOD TIME FOR YOU TO COME GET YOUR STUFF FROM MY PLACE, OKAY?
AND JUST AS SUDDENLY AS HE'D APPEARED FOUR MONTHS BEFORE, THE ORPHAN WAS GONE.

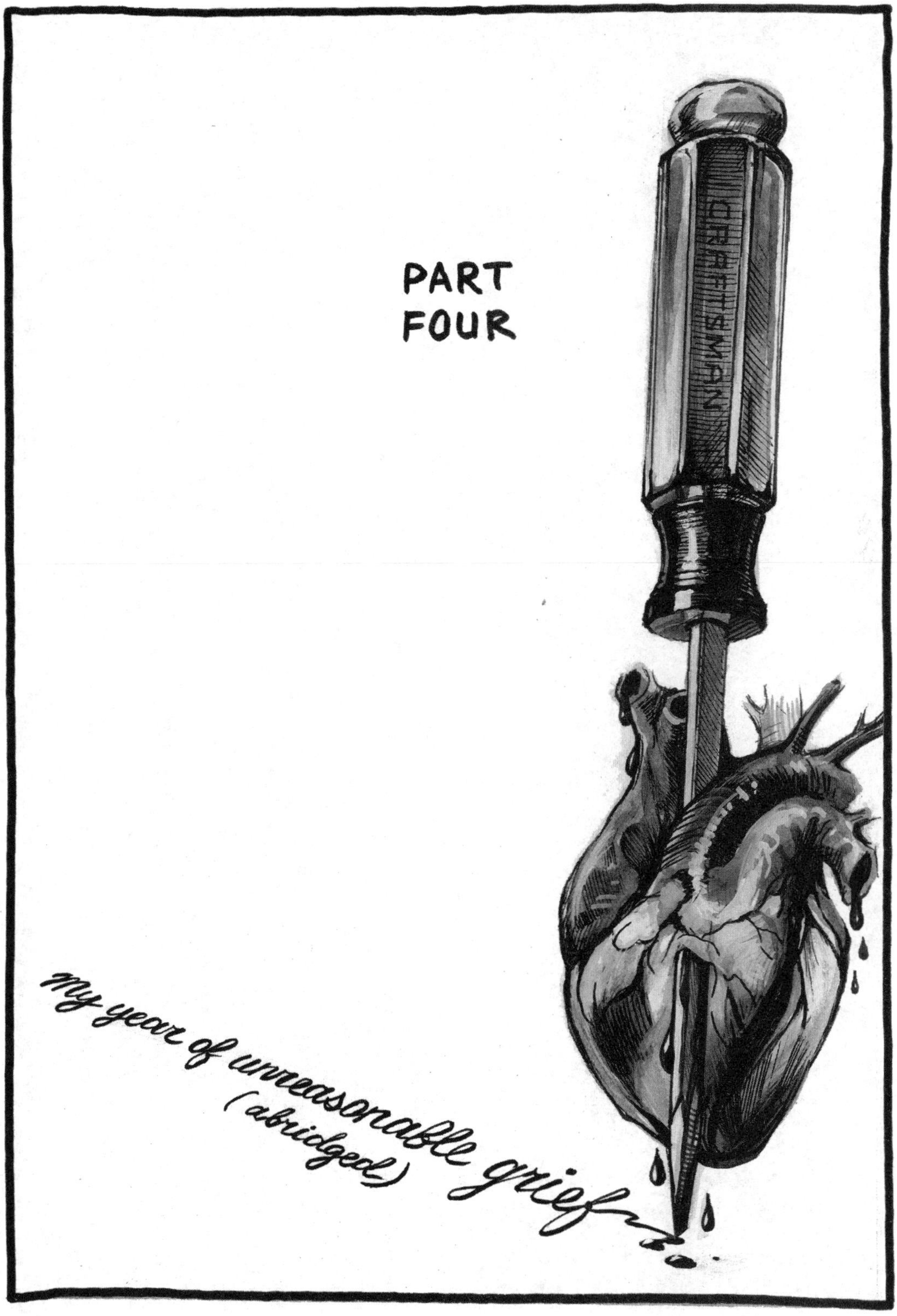
PART
FOUR
CRAFTSMAN
my year of unreasonable grief
(abridged)

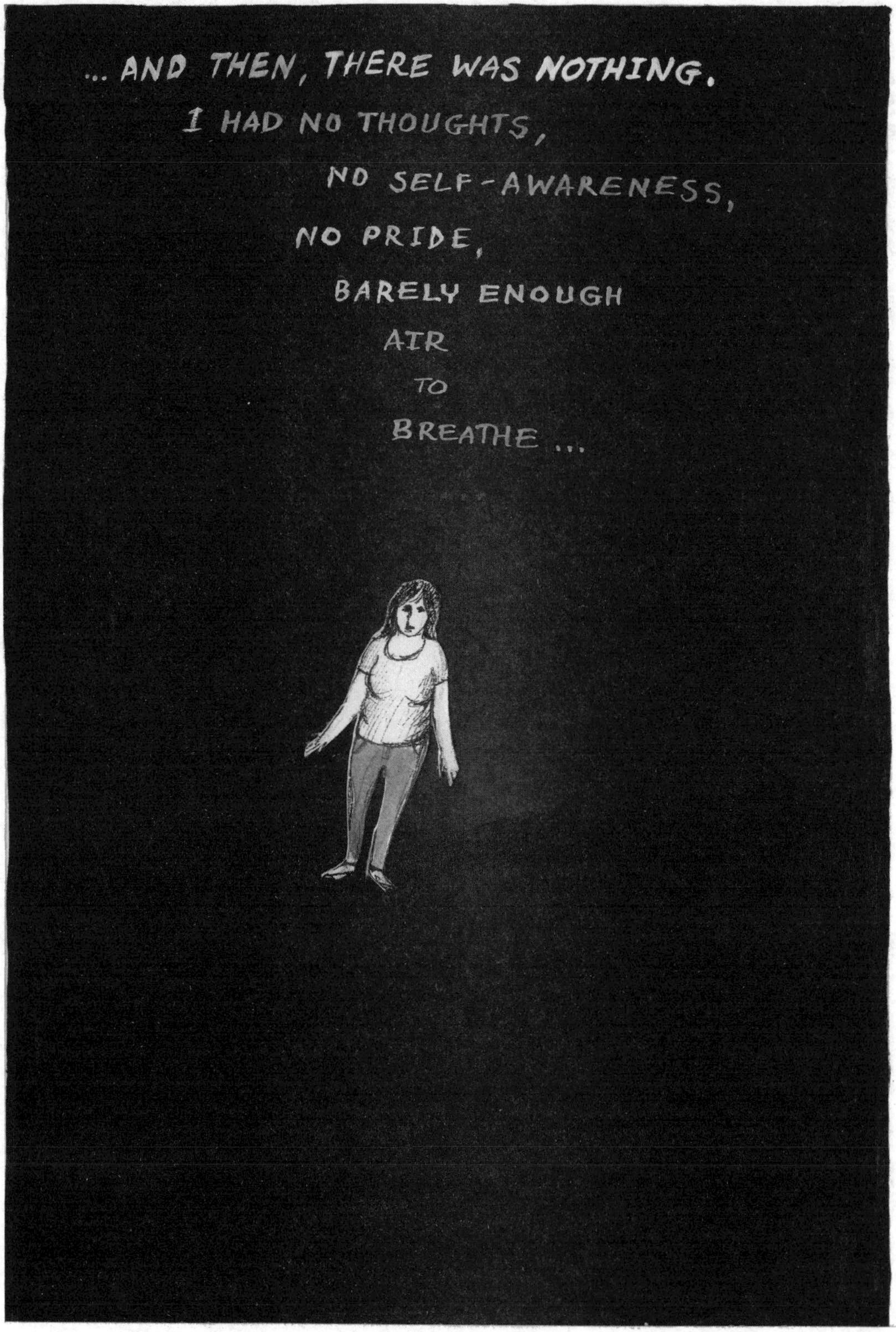
... AND THEN, THERE WAS NOTHING.
I HAD NO THOUGHTS,
NO SELF-AWARENESS,
NO PRIDE,
BARELY ENOUGH
AIR
TO
BREATHE ...

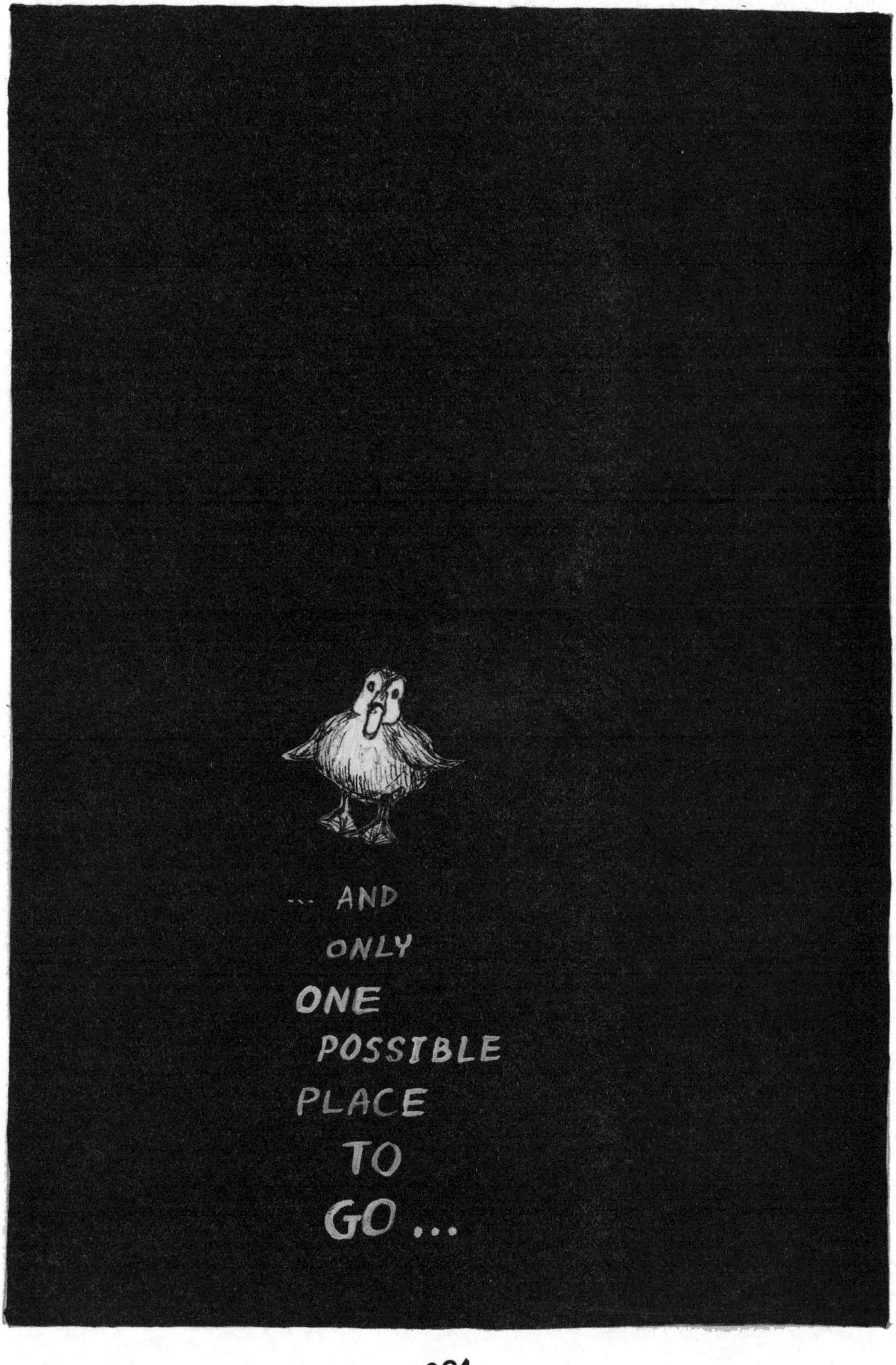
... AND ONLY ONE POSSIBLE PLACE TO GO ...

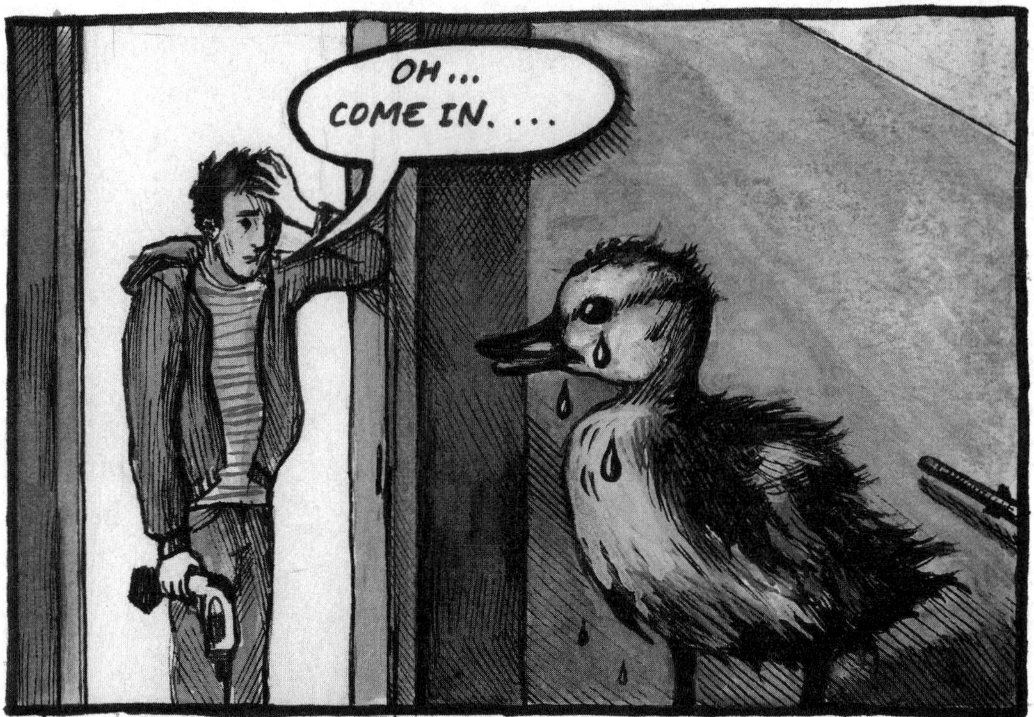
OH...
COME IN. ...

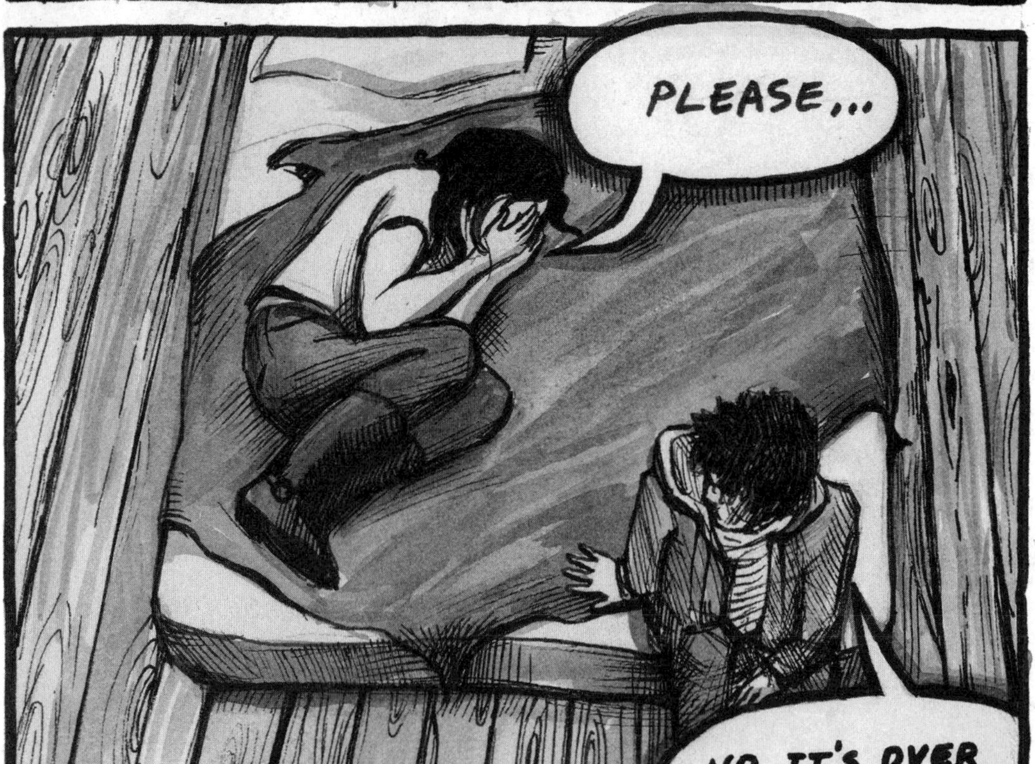
PLEASE...
NO. IT'S OVER.

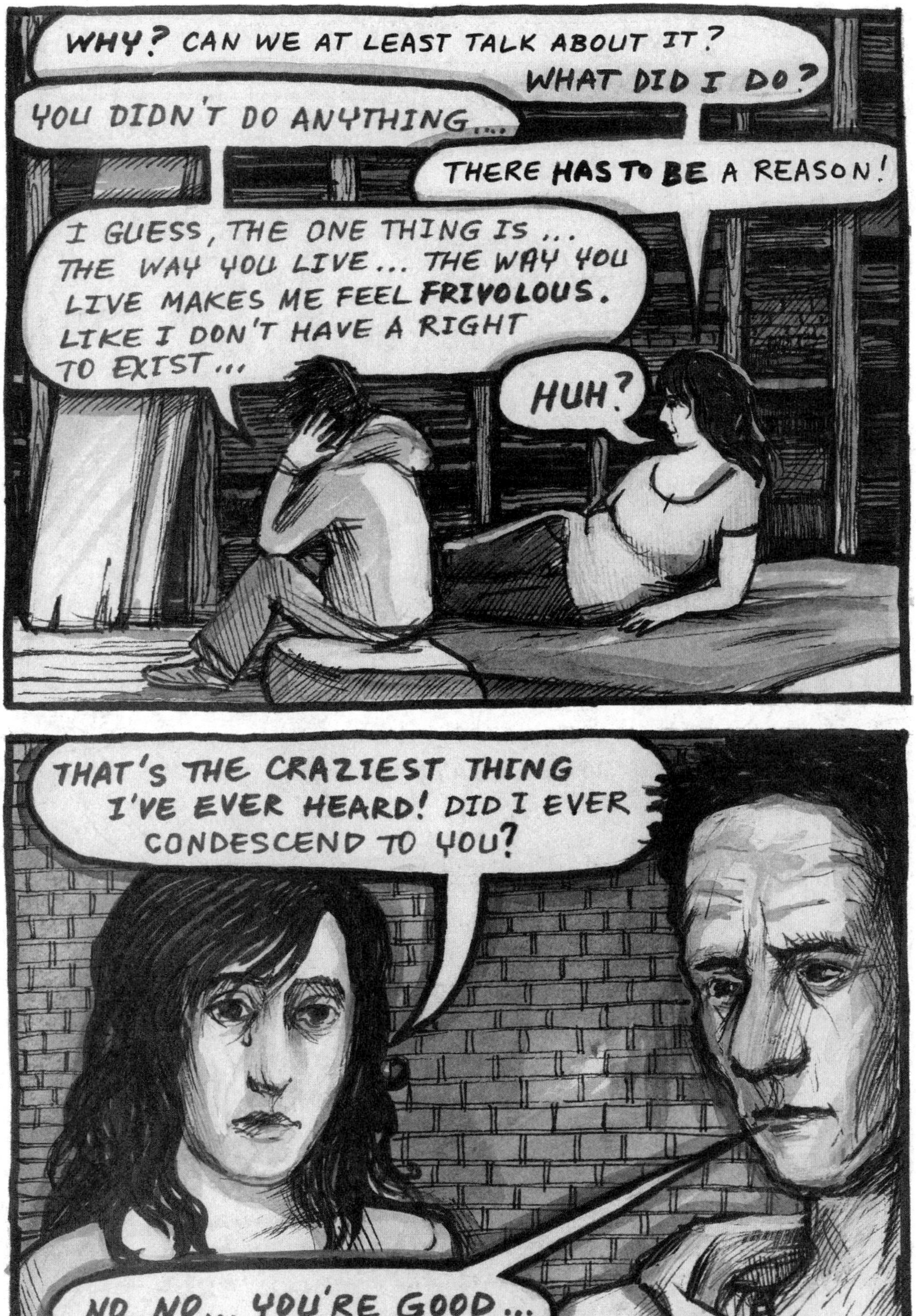
WHY? CAN WE AT LEAST TALK ABOUT IT? WHAT DID I DO?
YOU DIDN'T DO ANYTHING....
THERE HAS TO BE A REASON!
I GUESS, THE ONE THING IS ... THE WAY YOU LIVE... THE WAY YOU LIVE MAKES ME FEEL FRIVOLOUS. LIKE I DON'T HAVE A RIGHT TO EXIST...
HUH?
THAT'S THE CRAZIEST THING I'VE EVER HEARD! DID I EVER CONDESCEND TO YOU?
NO, NO... YOU'RE GOOD...

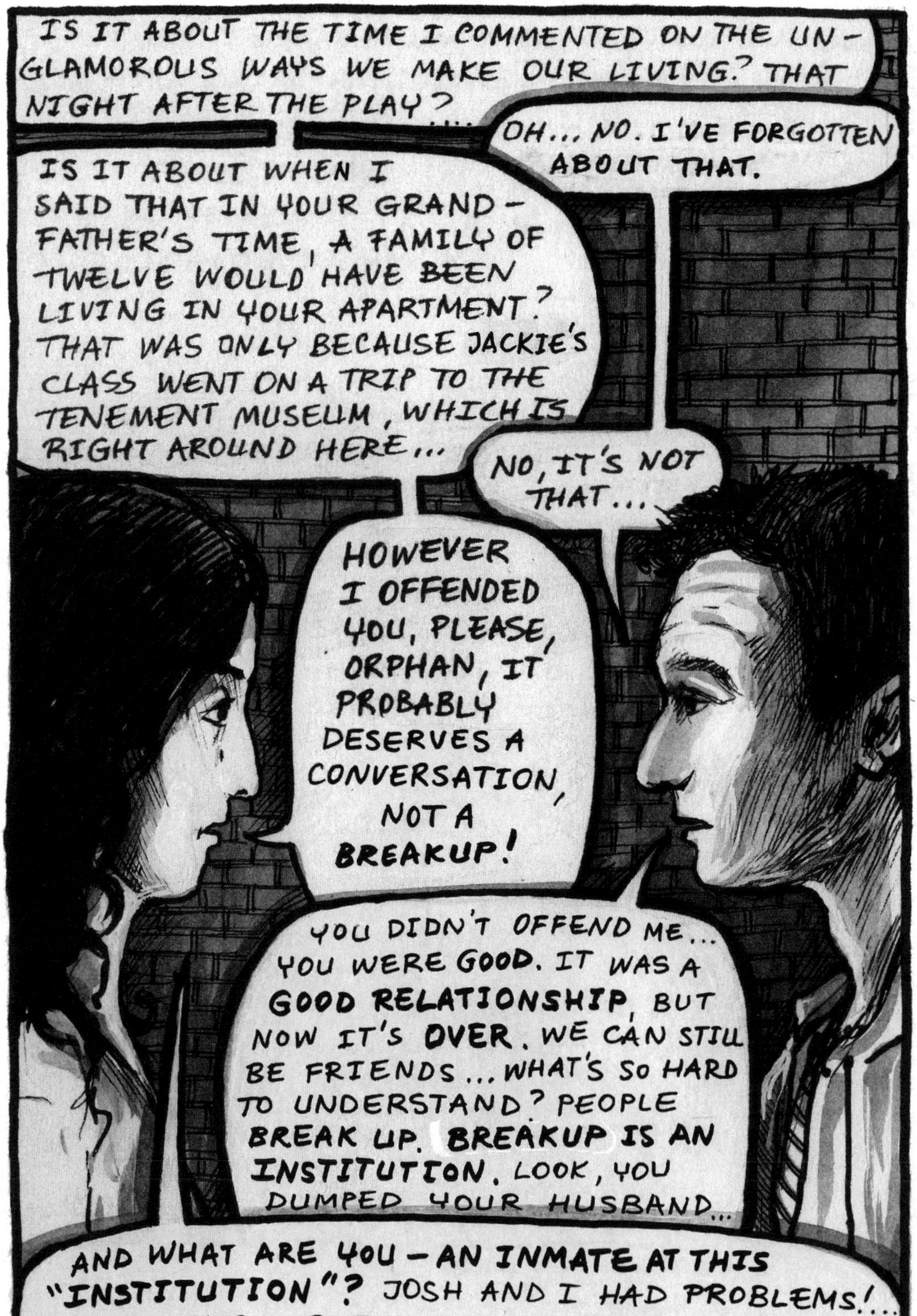
IS IT ABOUT THE TIME I COMMENTED ON THE UN-GLAMOROUS WAYS WE MAKE OUR LIVING? THAT NIGHT AFTER THE PLAY?
OH... NO. I'VE FORGOTTEN ABOUT THAT.
IS IT ABOUT WHEN I SAID THAT IN YOUR GRAND-FATHER'S TIME, A FAMILY OF TWELVE WOULD HAVE BEEN LIVING IN YOUR APARTMENT? THAT WAS ONLY BECAUSE JACKIE'S CLASS WENT ON A TRIP TO THE TENEMENT MUSEUM, WHICH IS RIGHT AROUND HERE...
NO, IT'S NOT THAT...
HOWEVER I OFFENDED YOU, PLEASE, ORPHAN, IT PROBABLY DESERVES A CONVERSATION, NOT A BREAKUP!
YOU DIDN'T OFFEND ME... YOU WERE GOOD. IT WAS A GOOD RELATIONSHIP, BUT NOW IT'S OVER. WE CAN STILL BE FRIENDS... WHAT'S SO HARD TO UNDERSTAND? PEOPLE BREAK UP. BREAKUP IS AN INSTITUTION. LOOK, YOU DUMPED YOUR HUSBAND...
AND WHAT ARE YOU — AN INMATE AT THIS "INSTITUTION"? JOSH AND I HAD PROBLEMS!... WE FOUGHT... BUT YOU AND I WERE ONLY HAPPY!...

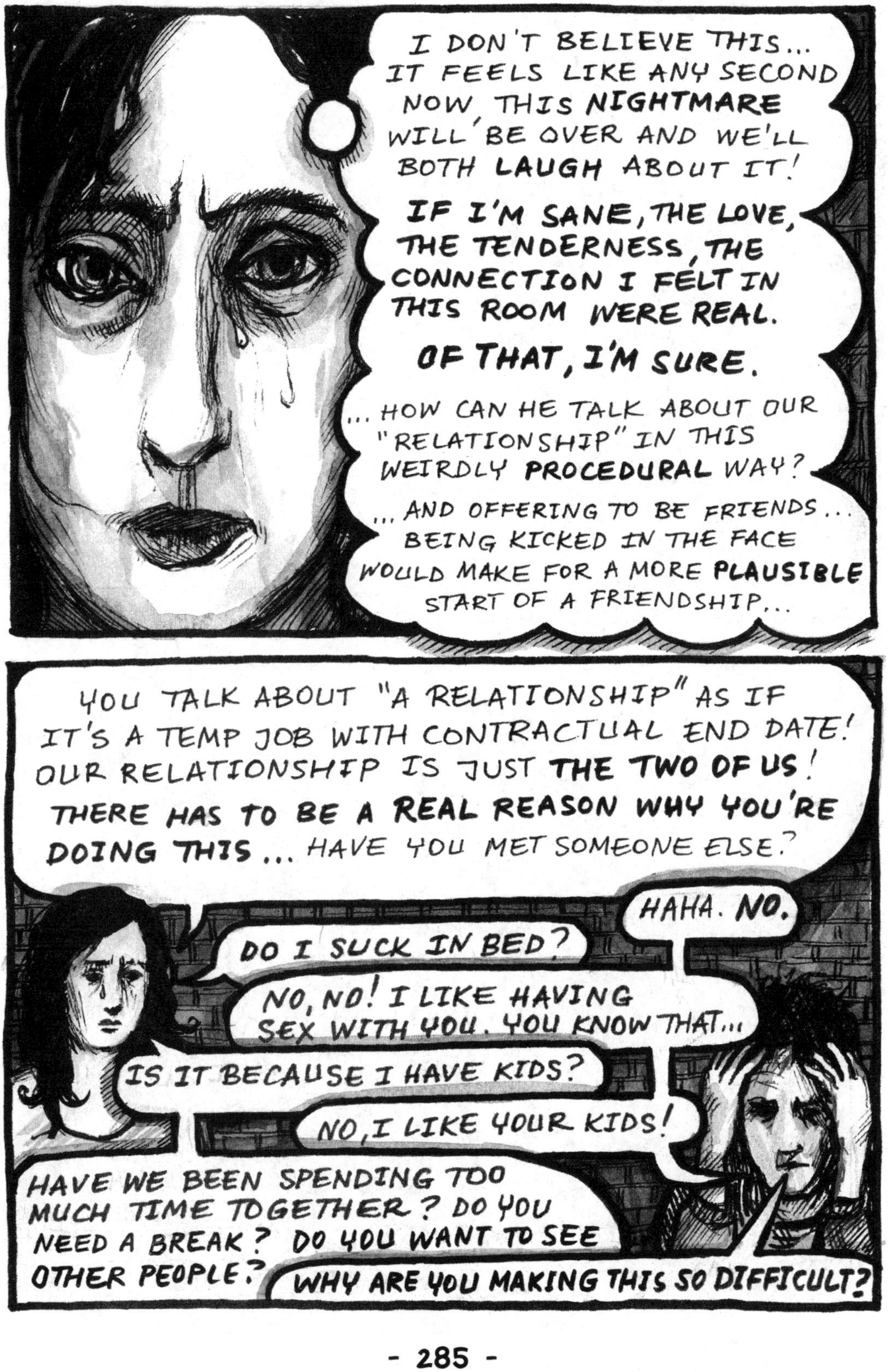
I DON'T BELIEVE THIS... IT FEELS LIKE ANY SECOND NOW, THIS NIGHTMARE WILL BE OVER AND WE'LL BOTH LAUGH ABOUT IT!
IF I'M SANE, THE LOVE, THE TENDERNESS, THE CONNECTION I FELT IN THIS ROOM WERE REAL.
OF THAT, I'M SURE.
...HOW CAN HE TALK ABOUT OUR "RELATIONSHIP" IN THIS WEIRDLY PROCEDURAL WAY?
...AND OFFERING TO BE FRIENDS... BEING KICKED IN THE FACE WOULD MAKE FOR A MORE PLAUSIBLE START OF A FRIENDSHIP...
YOU TALK ABOUT "A RELATIONSHIP" AS IF IT'S A TEMP JOB WITH CONTRACTUAL END DATE! OUR RELATIONSHIP IS JUST THE TWO OF US! THERE HAS TO BE A REAL REASON WHY YOU'RE DOING THIS... HAVE YOU MET SOMEONE ELSE?
HAHA. NO.
DO I SUCK IN BED?
NO, NO! I LIKE HAVING SEX WITH YOU. YOU KNOW THAT...
IS IT BECAUSE I HAVE KIDS?
NO, I LIKE YOUR KIDS!
HAVE WE BEEN SPENDING TOO MUCH TIME TOGETHER? DO YOU NEED A BREAK? DO YOU WANT TO SEE OTHER PEOPLE?
WHY ARE YOU MAKING THIS SO DIFFICULT?

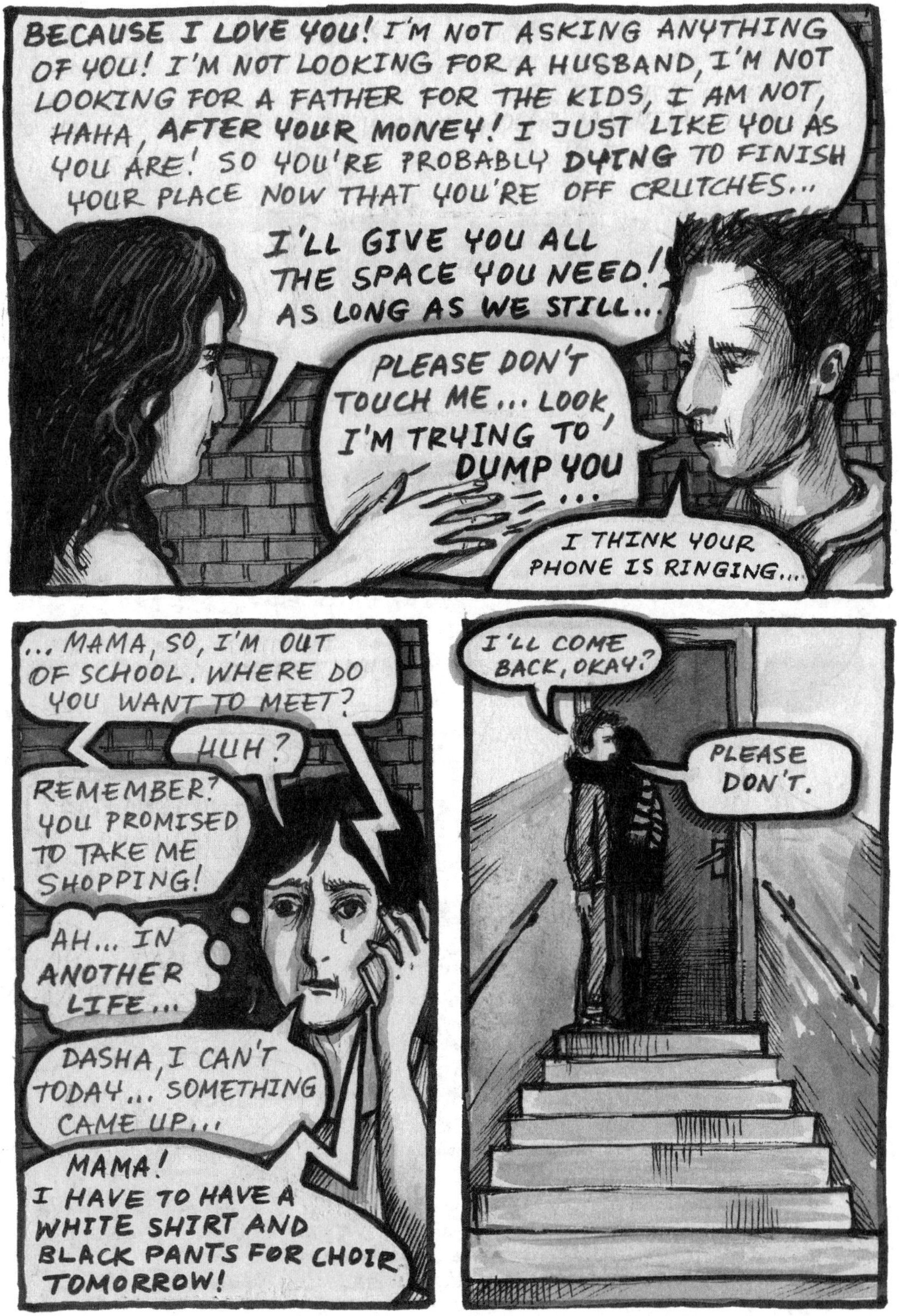
BECAUSE I LOVE YOU! I'M NOT ASKING ANYTHING OF YOU! I'M NOT LOOKING FOR A HUSBAND, I'M NOT LOOKING FOR A FATHER FOR THE KIDS, I AM NOT, HAHA, AFTER YOUR MONEY! I JUST LIKE YOU AS YOU ARE! SO YOU'RE PROBABLY DYING TO FINISH YOUR PLACE NOW THAT YOU'RE OFF CRUTCHES...
I'LL GIVE YOU ALL THE SPACE YOU NEED! AS LONG AS WE STILL...
PLEASE DON'T TOUCH ME... LOOK, I'M TRYING TO DUMP YOU ...
I THINK YOUR PHONE IS RINGING...
... MAMA, SO, I'M OUT OF SCHOOL. WHERE DO YOU WANT TO MEET?
HUH?
REMEMBER? YOU PROMISED TO TAKE ME SHOPPING!
AH... IN ANOTHER LIFE...
DASHA, I CAN'T TODAY... SOMETHING CAME UP...
MAMA! I HAVE TO HAVE A WHITE SHIRT AND BLACK PANTS FOR CHOIR TOMORROW!
I'LL COME BACK, OKAY?
PLEASE DON'T.

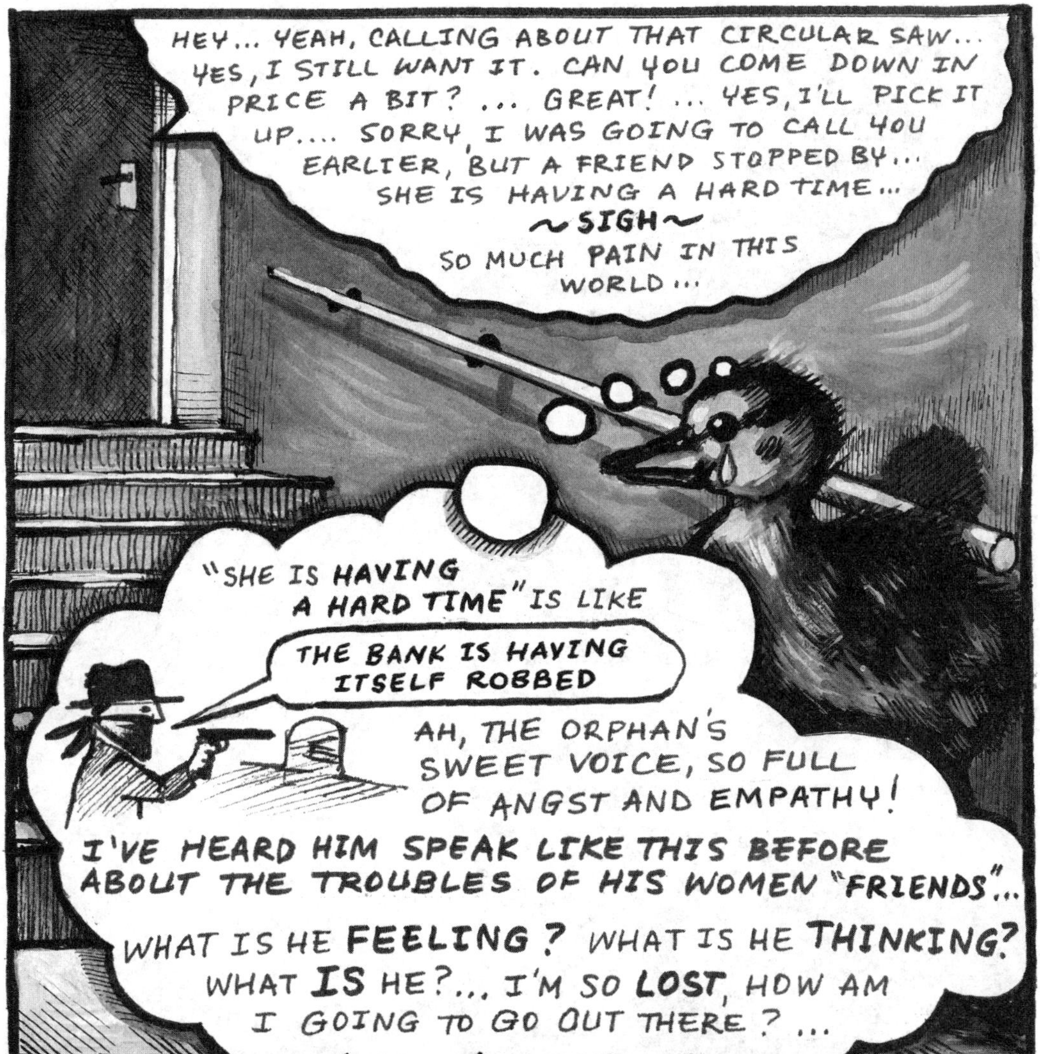
HEY... YEAH, CALLING ABOUT THAT CIRCULAR SAW... YES, I STILL WANT IT. CAN YOU COME DOWN IN PRICE A BIT? ... GREAT! ... YES, I'LL PICK IT UP.... SORRY, I WAS GOING TO CALL YOU EARLIER, BUT A FRIEND STOPPED BY... SHE IS HAVING A HARD TIME... ~SIGH~ SO MUCH PAIN IN THIS WORLD...
"SHE IS HAVING A HARD TIME" IS LIKE
THE BANK IS HAVING ITSELF ROBBED
AH, THE ORPHAN'S SWEET VOICE, SO FULL OF ANGST AND EMPATHY!
I'VE HEARD HIM SPEAK LIKE THIS BEFORE ABOUT THE TROUBLES OF HIS WOMEN "FRIENDS"...
WHAT IS HE FEELING? WHAT IS HE THINKING? WHAT IS HE?... I'M SO LOST, HOW AM I GOING TO GO OUT THERE?...

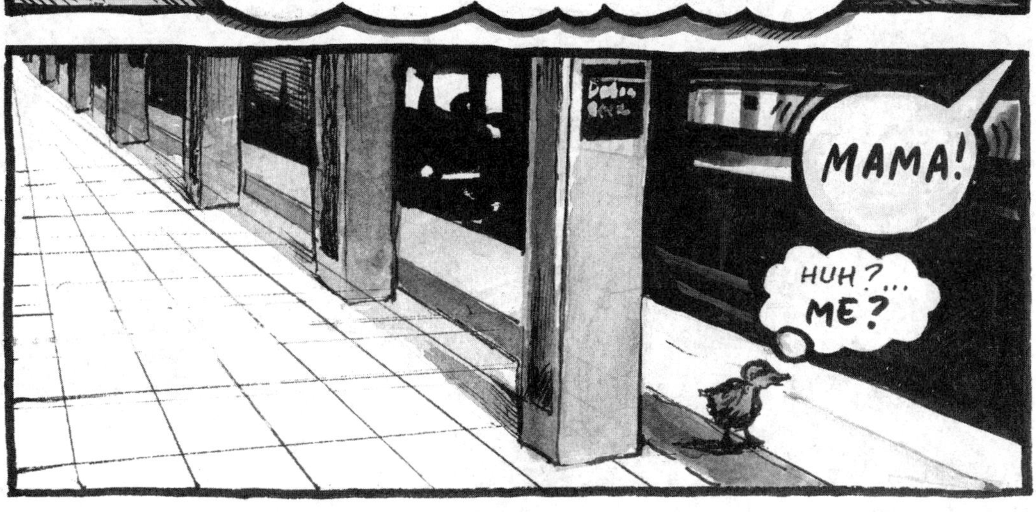
MAMA!
HUH?... ME?

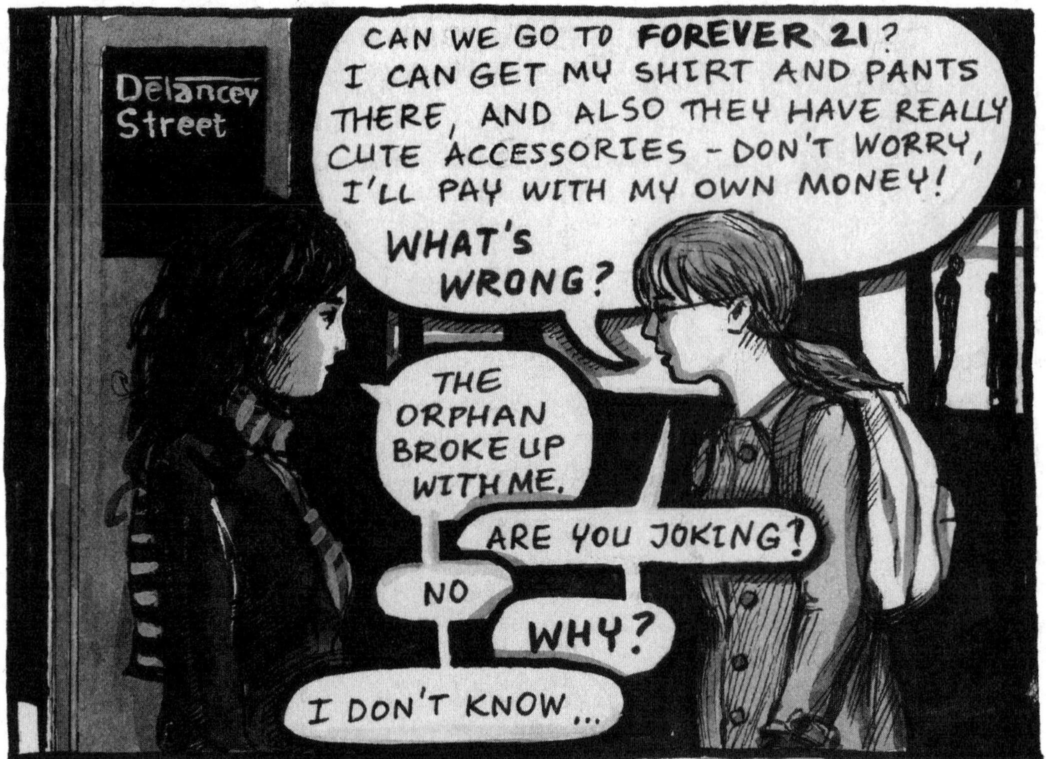
Delancey Street
CAN WE GO TO FOREVER 21? I CAN GET MY SHIRT AND PANTS THERE, AND ALSO THEY HAVE REALLY CUTE ACCESSORIES - DON'T WORRY, I'LL PAY WITH MY OWN MONEY!
WHAT'S WRONG?
THE ORPHAN BROKE UP WITH ME.
ARE YOU JOKING?
NO
WHY?
I DON'T KNOW...

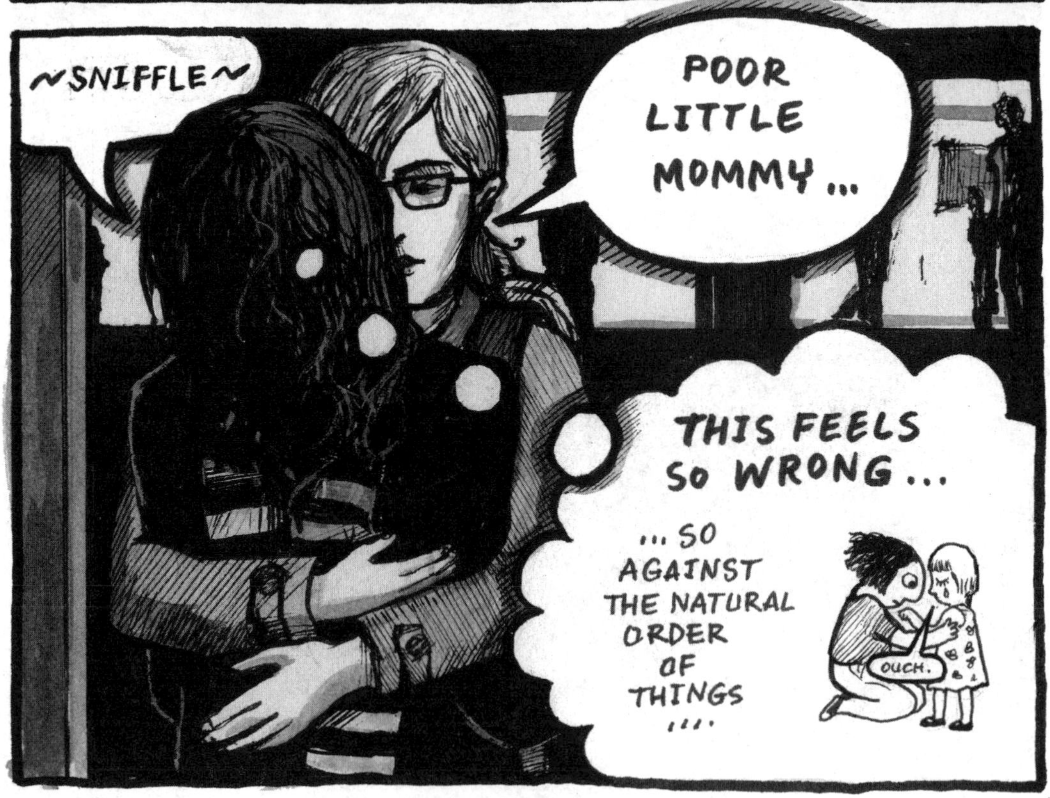
~SNIFFLE~
POOR LITTLE MOMMY...
THIS FEELS SO WRONG...
...SO AGAINST THE NATURAL ORDER OF THINGS...
OUCH.

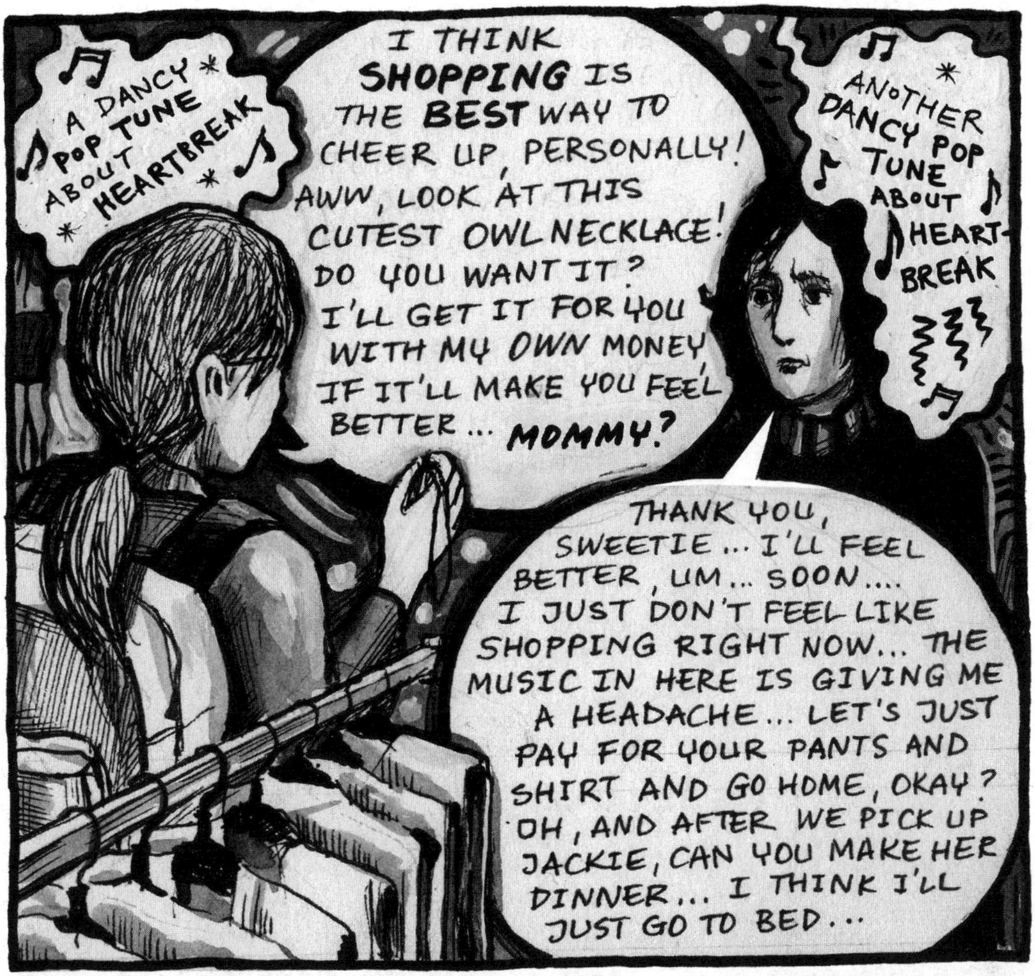
A DANCY POP TUNE ABOUT HEARTBREAK
I THINK SHOPPING IS THE BEST WAY TO CHEER UP, PERSONALLY! AWW, LOOK AT THIS CUTEST OWL NECKLACE! DO YOU WANT IT? I'LL GET IT FOR YOU WITH MY OWN MONEY IF IT'LL MAKE YOU FEEL BETTER... MOMMY?
ANOTHER DANCY POP TUNE ABOUT HEART-BREAK
THANK YOU, SWEETIE... I'LL FEEL BETTER, UM... SOON.... I JUST DON'T FEEL LIKE SHOPPING RIGHT NOW... THE MUSIC IN HERE IS GIVING ME A HEADACHE... LET'S JUST PAY FOR YOUR PANTS AND SHIRT AND GO HOME, OKAY? OH, AND AFTER WE PICK UP JACKIE, CAN YOU MAKE HER DINNER... I THINK I'LL JUST GO TO BED...

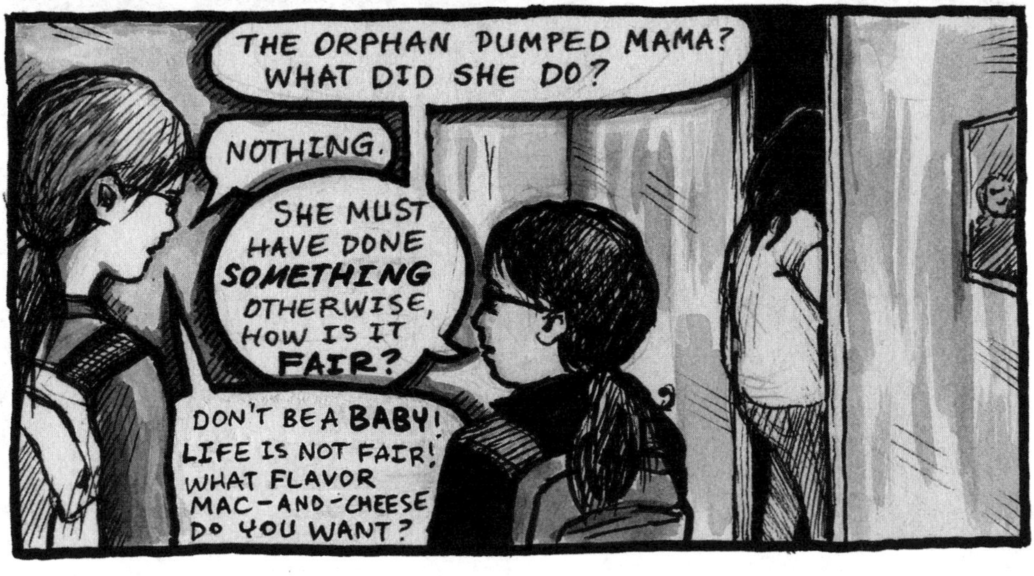
THE ORPHAN DUMPED MAMA? WHAT DID SHE DO?
NOTHING.
SHE MUST HAVE DONE SOMETHING OTHERWISE, HOW IS IT FAIR?
DON'T BE A BABY! LIFE IS NOT FAIR! WHAT FLAVOR MAC-AND-CHEESE DO YOU WANT?

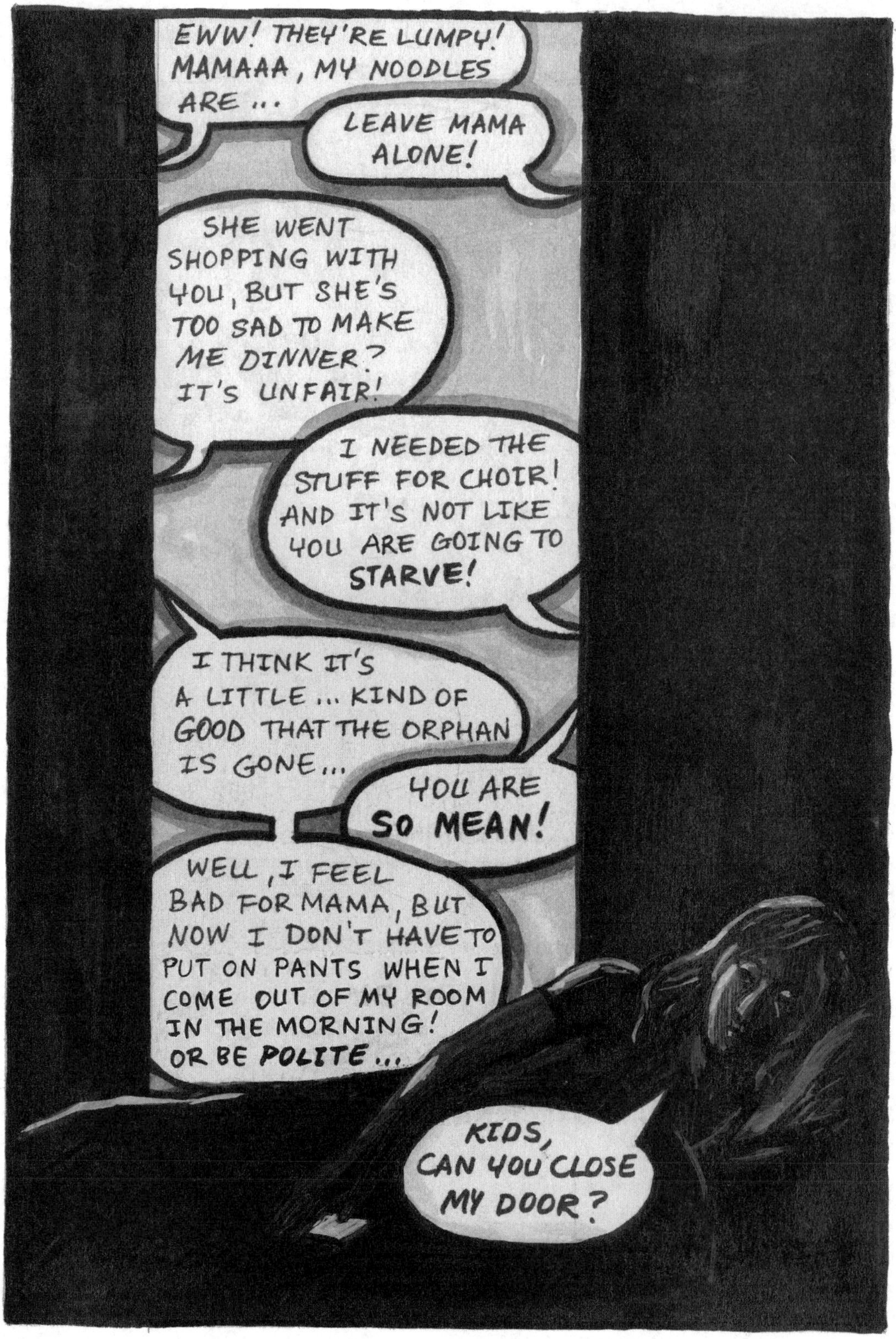
EWW! THEY'RE LUMPY! MAMAAA, MY NOODLES ARE ...
LEAVE MAMA ALONE!
SHE WENT SHOPPING WITH YOU, BUT SHE'S TOO SAD TO MAKE ME DINNER? IT'S UNFAIR!
I NEEDED THE STUFF FOR CHOIR! AND IT'S NOT LIKE YOU ARE GOING TO STARVE!
I THINK IT'S A LITTLE ... KIND OF GOOD THAT THE ORPHAN IS GONE...
YOU ARE SO MEAN!
WELL, I FEEL BAD FOR MAMA, BUT NOW I DON'T HAVE TO PUT ON PANTS WHEN I COME OUT OF MY ROOM IN THE MORNING! OR BE POLITE ...
KIDS, CAN YOU CLOSE MY DOOR?

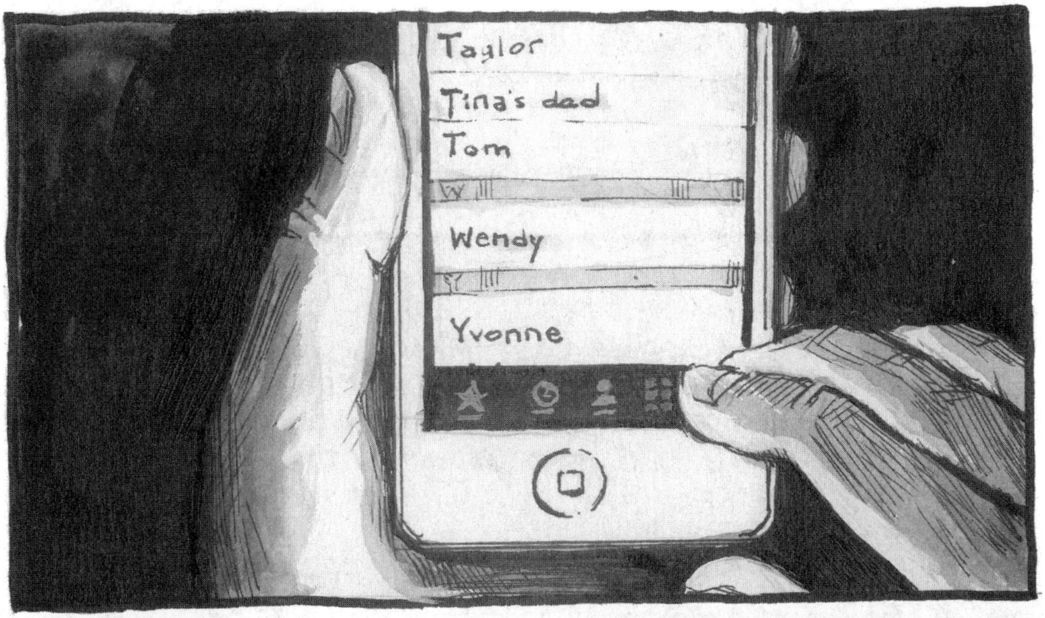
Taylor
Tina's dad
Tom
Wendy
Yvonne

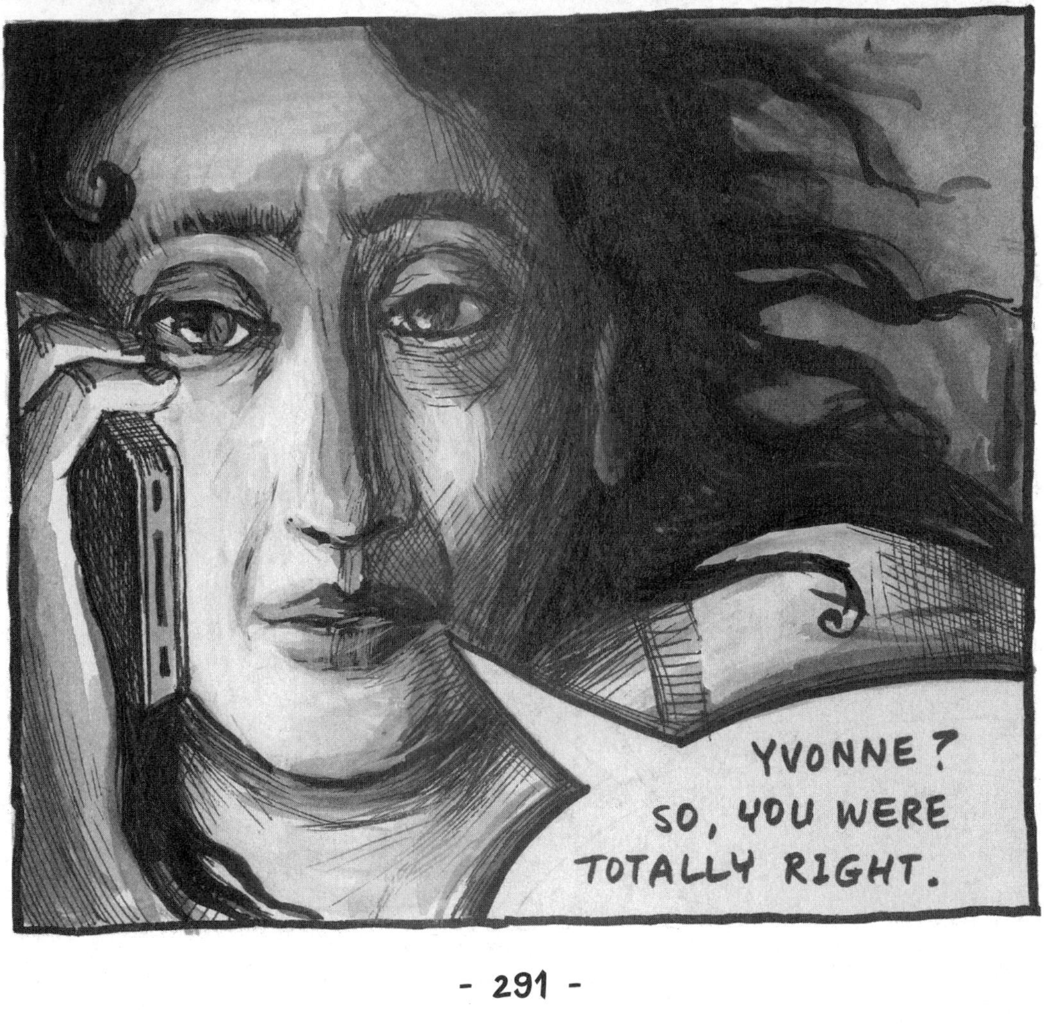
YVONNE?
SO, YOU WERE
TOTALLY RIGHT.

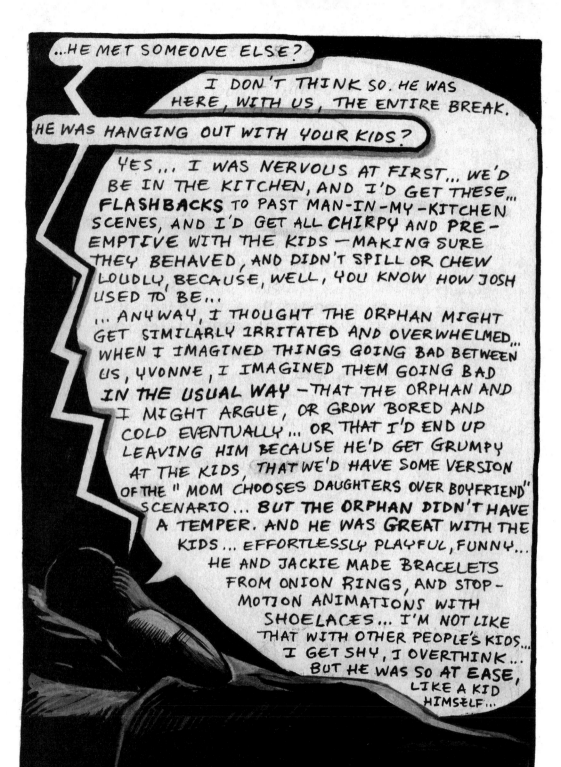

...HE MET SOMEONE ELSE?

I DON'T THINK SO. HE WAS HERE, WITH US, THE ENTIRE BREAK.

HE WAS HANGING OUT WITH YOUR KIDS?

YES... I WAS NERVOUS AT FIRST... WE'D BE IN THE KITCHEN, AND I'D GET THESE... **FLASHBACKS** TO PAST MAN-IN-MY-KITCHEN SCENES, AND I'D GET ALL **CHIRPY** AND **PRE-EMPTIVE** WITH THE KIDS — MAKING SURE THEY BEHAVED, AND DIDN'T SPILL OR CHEW LOUDLY, BECAUSE, WELL, YOU KNOW HOW JOSH USED TO BE...

... ANYWAY, I THOUGHT THE ORPHAN MIGHT GET SIMILARLY IRRITATED AND OVERWHELMED... WHEN I IMAGINED THINGS GOING BAD BETWEEN US, YVONNE, I IMAGINED THEM GOING BAD **IN THE USUAL WAY** — THAT THE ORPHAN AND I MIGHT ARGUE, OR GROW BORED AND COLD EVENTUALLY... OR THAT I'D END UP LEAVING HIM BECAUSE HE'D GET GRUMPY AT THE KIDS, THAT WE'D HAVE SOME VERSION OF THE " MOM CHOOSES DAUGHTERS OVER BOYFRIEND" SCENARIO... BUT THE ORPHAN DIDN'T HAVE A TEMPER. AND HE WAS **GREAT** WITH THE KIDS... EFFORTLESSLY PLAYFUL, FUNNY... HE AND JACKIE MADE BRACELETS FROM ONION RINGS, AND STOP-MOTION ANIMATIONS WITH SHOELACES... I'M NOT LIKE THAT WITH OTHER PEOPLE'S KIDS... I GET SHY, I OVERTHINK... BUT HE WAS SO AT EASE, LIKE A KID HIMSELF...

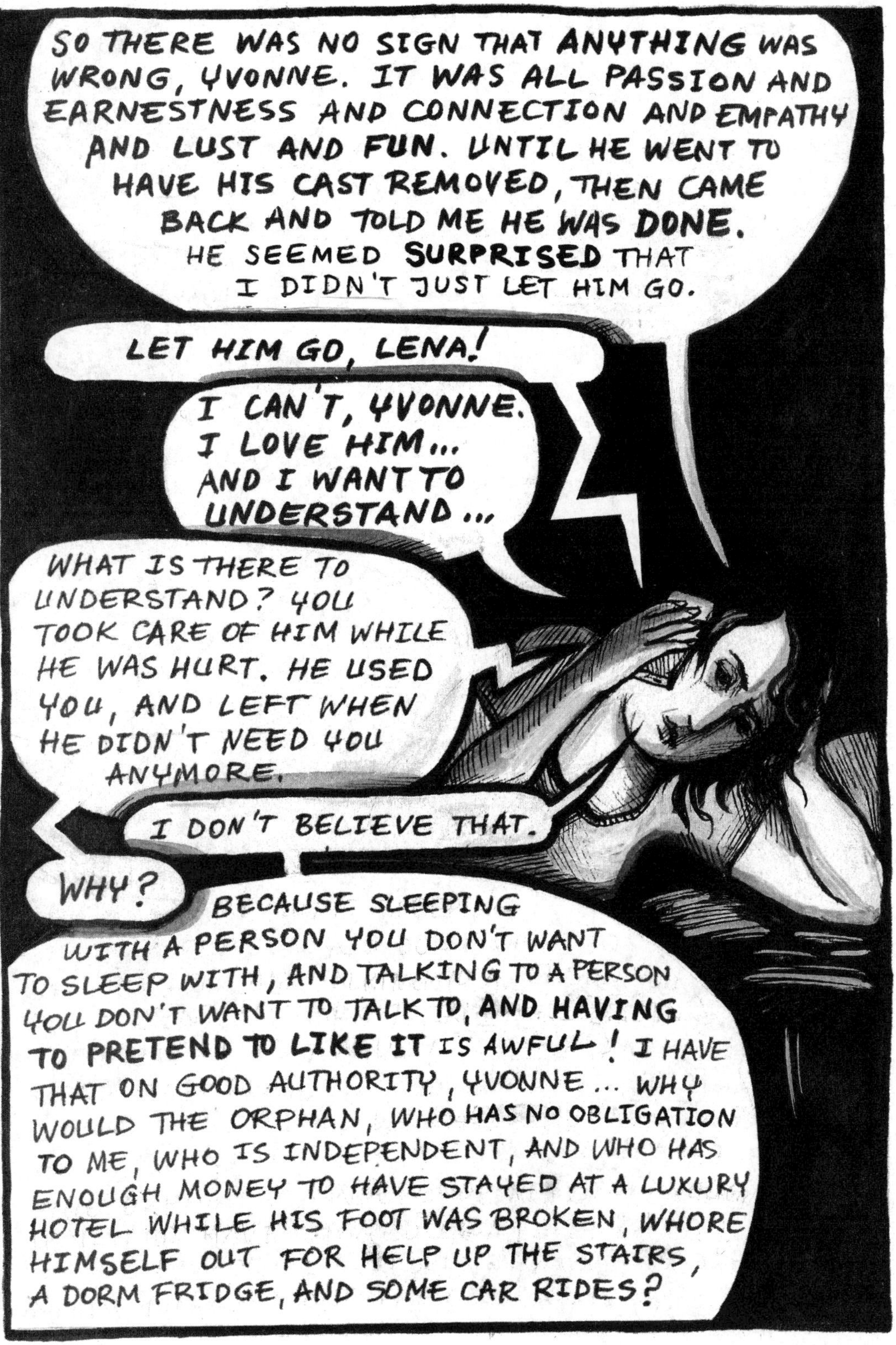
SO THERE WAS NO SIGN THAT ANYTHING WAS WRONG, YVONNE. IT WAS ALL PASSION AND EARNESTNESS AND CONNECTION AND EMPATHY AND LUST AND FUN. UNTIL HE WENT TO HAVE HIS CAST REMOVED, THEN CAME BACK AND TOLD ME HE WAS DONE. HE SEEMED SURPRISED THAT I DIDN'T JUST LET HIM GO.
LET HIM GO, LENA!
I CAN'T, YVONNE. I LOVE HIM... AND I WANT TO UNDERSTAND...
WHAT IS THERE TO UNDERSTAND? YOU TOOK CARE OF HIM WHILE HE WAS HURT. HE USED YOU, AND LEFT WHEN HE DIDN'T NEED YOU ANYMORE.
I DON'T BELIEVE THAT.
WHY?
BECAUSE SLEEPING WITH A PERSON YOU DON'T WANT TO SLEEP WITH, AND TALKING TO A PERSON YOU DON'T WANT TO TALK TO, AND HAVING TO PRETEND TO LIKE IT IS AWFUL! I HAVE THAT ON GOOD AUTHORITY, YVONNE... WHY WOULD THE ORPHAN, WHO HAS NO OBLIGATION TO ME, WHO IS INDEPENDENT, AND WHO HAS ENOUGH MONEY TO HAVE STAYED AT A LUXURY HOTEL WHILE HIS FOOT WAS BROKEN, WHORE HIMSELF OUT FOR HELP UP THE STAIRS, A DORM FRIDGE, AND SOME CAR RIDES?

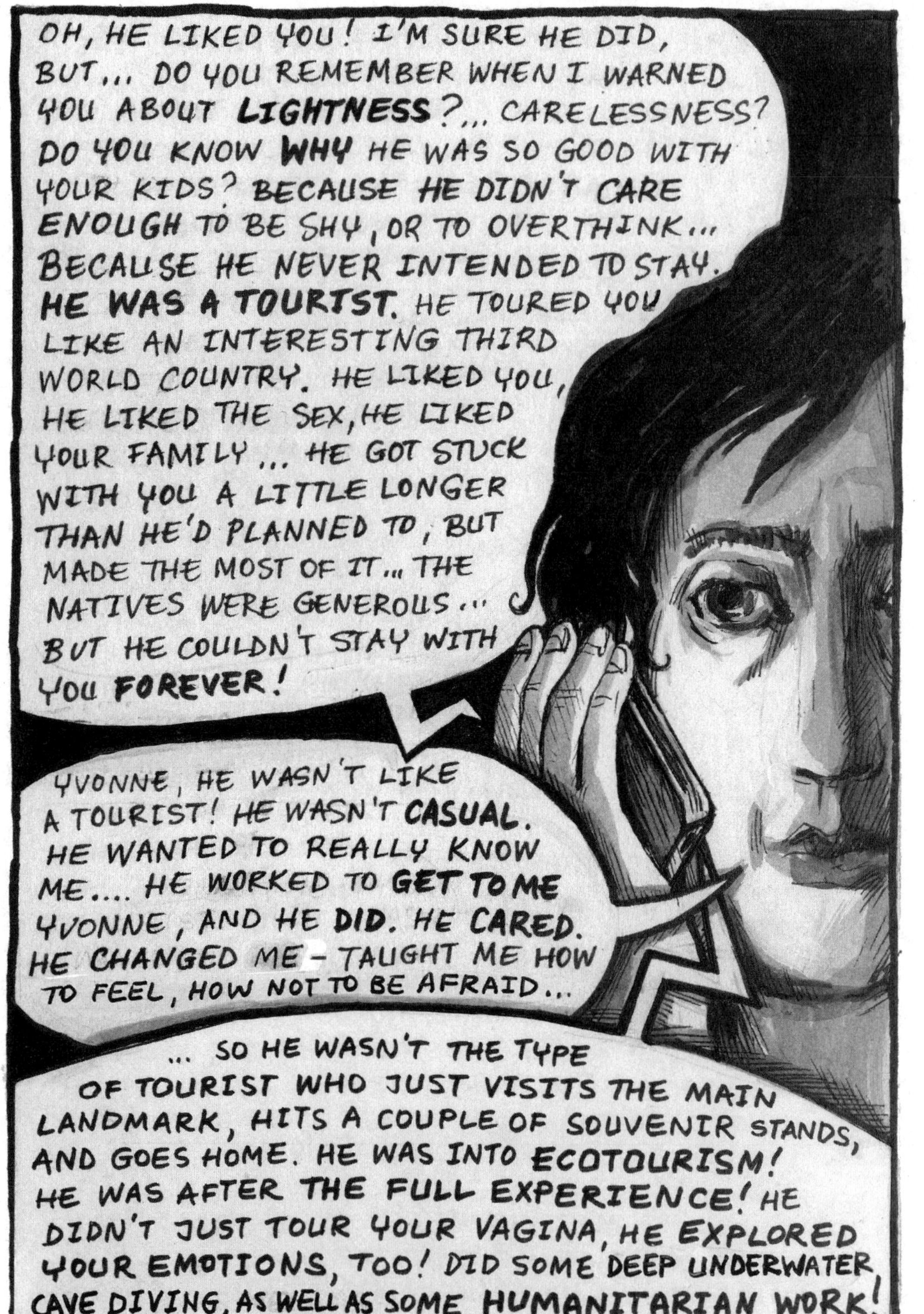
OH, HE LIKED YOU! I'M SURE HE DID, BUT... DO YOU REMEMBER WHEN I WARNED YOU ABOUT LIGHTNESS?... CARELESSNESS? DO YOU KNOW WHY HE WAS SO GOOD WITH YOUR KIDS? BECAUSE HE DIDN'T CARE ENOUGH TO BE SHY, OR TO OVERTHINK... BECAUSE HE NEVER INTENDED TO STAY. HE WAS A TOURIST. HE TOURED YOU LIKE AN INTERESTING THIRD WORLD COUNTRY. HE LIKED YOU, HE LIKED THE SEX, HE LIKED YOUR FAMILY... HE GOT STUCK WITH YOU A LITTLE LONGER THAN HE'D PLANNED TO, BUT MADE THE MOST OF IT... THE NATIVES WERE GENEROUS... BUT HE COULDN'T STAY WITH YOU FOREVER!
YVONNE, HE WASN'T LIKE A TOURIST! HE WASN'T CASUAL. HE WANTED TO REALLY KNOW ME.... HE WORKED TO GET TO ME YVONNE, AND HE DID. HE CARED. HE CHANGED ME – TAUGHT ME HOW TO FEEL, HOW NOT TO BE AFRAID...
... SO HE WASN'T THE TYPE OF TOURIST WHO JUST VISITS THE MAIN LANDMARK, HITS A COUPLE OF SOUVENIR STANDS, AND GOES HOME. HE WAS INTO ECOTOURISM! HE WAS AFTER THE FULL EXPERIENCE! HE DIDN'T JUST TOUR YOUR VAGINA, HE EXPLORED YOUR EMOTIONS, TOO! DID SOME DEEP UNDERWATER CAVE DIVING, AS WELL AS SOME HUMANITARIAN WORK!

... BUT EVENTUALLY, HE HAD TO GO... HE HAS A LOFT TO FINISH, BEFORE HIS NEXT ADVENTURE. HIS EAMES CHAIR HAD BEEN IN STORAGE TOO LONG...
WHAT'S AN EAMES CHAIR?
GOOGLE IT...
~SNIFFLE~
YVONNE?
WHAT?
AM I A SHITTY THIRD WORLD COUNTRY? MEAGER AND SQUALID, JEALOUS OF THE WEST, FILLED WITH CHEAP JUNK, IGNORANT, LOUD, OBNOXIOUS, REPRESSED AND OPPRESSIVE?
NO! ARE YOU KIDDING? YOU'RE AN INDUSTRIALIZED NATION, FINKLE! LOOK AT YOUR UPWARD MOBILITY RATE! AND YOUR NON-EXISTENT INFANT MORTALITY! YOU'RE FUCKING SWEDEN!
... AND YOU'RE NOT FAT, EITHER - IF THAT WAS GOING TO BE YOUR NEXT QUESTION...
HAHA! ~SNIFFLE~ OH YVONNE, I FEEL LIKE SHIT! MY WHOLE BODY HURTS - I MISS HIM SO MUCH!

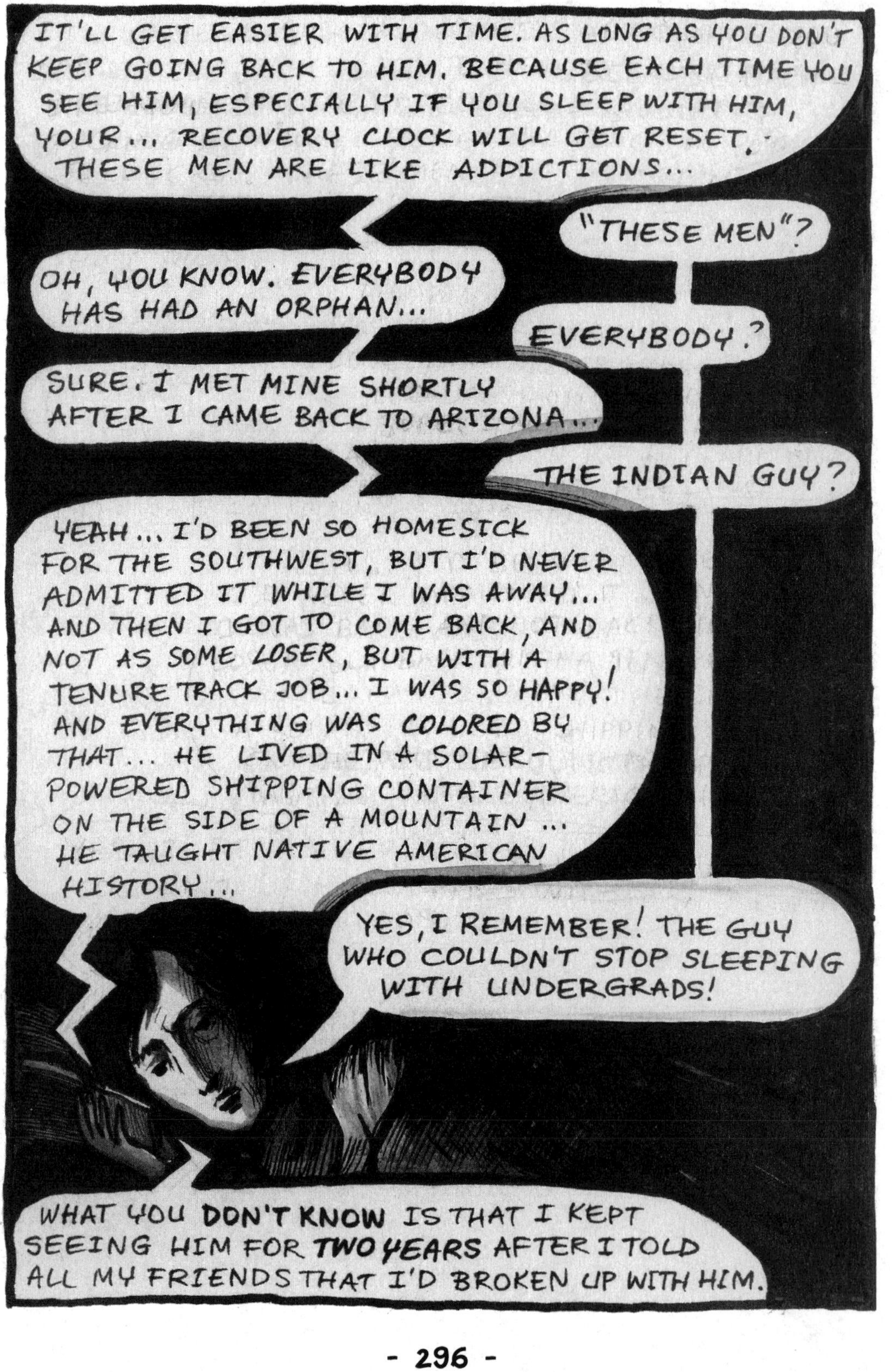
IT'LL GET EASIER WITH TIME. AS LONG AS YOU DON'T KEEP GOING BACK TO HIM. BECAUSE EACH TIME YOU SEE HIM, ESPECIALLY IF YOU SLEEP WITH HIM, YOUR... RECOVERY CLOCK WILL GET RESET. THESE MEN ARE LIKE ADDICTIONS...
"THESE MEN"?
OH, YOU KNOW. EVERYBODY HAS HAD AN ORPHAN...
EVERYBODY?
SURE. I MET MINE SHORTLY AFTER I CAME BACK TO ARIZONA...
THE INDIAN GUY?
YEAH... I'D BEEN SO HOMESICK FOR THE SOUTHWEST, BUT I'D NEVER ADMITTED IT WHILE I WAS AWAY... AND THEN I GOT TO COME BACK, AND NOT AS SOME *LOSER*, BUT WITH A TENURE TRACK JOB... I WAS SO HAPPY! AND EVERYTHING WAS *COLORED* BY THAT... HE LIVED IN A SOLAR-POWERED SHIPPING CONTAINER ON THE SIDE OF A MOUNTAIN... HE TAUGHT NATIVE AMERICAN HISTORY...
YES, I REMEMBER! THE GUY WHO COULDN'T STOP SLEEPING WITH UNDERGRADS!
WHAT YOU **DON'T KNOW** IS THAT I KEPT SEEING HIM FOR ***TWO YEARS*** AFTER I TOLD ALL MY FRIENDS THAT I'D BROKEN UP WITH HIM.

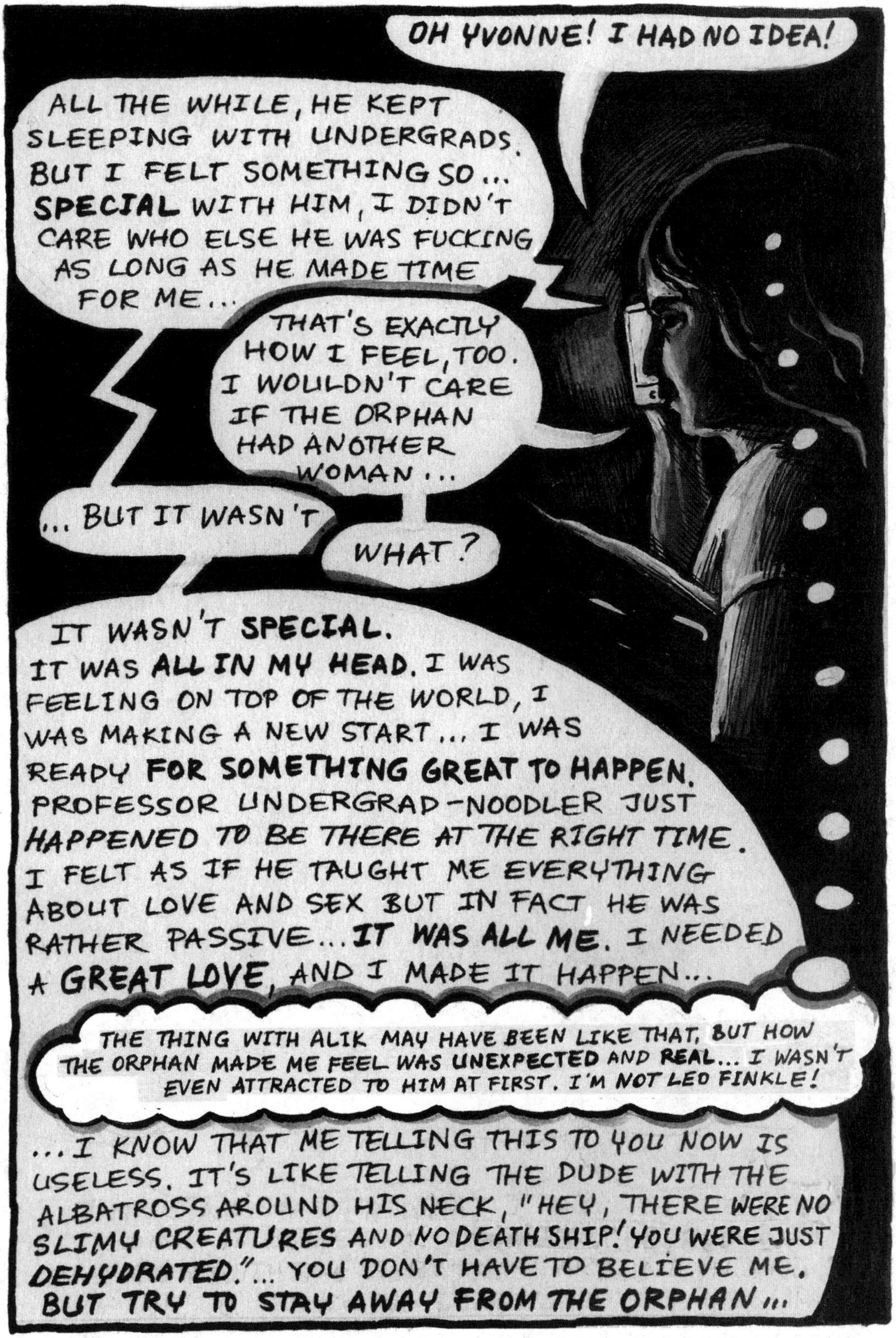
OH YVONNE! I HAD NO IDEA!
ALL THE WHILE, HE KEPT SLEEPING WITH UNDERGRADS. BUT I FELT SOMETHING SO... SPECIAL WITH HIM, I DIDN'T CARE WHO ELSE HE WAS FUCKING AS LONG AS HE MADE TIME FOR ME...
THAT'S EXACTLY HOW I FEEL, TOO. I WOULDN'T CARE IF THE ORPHAN HAD ANOTHER WOMAN...
... BUT IT WASN'T
WHAT?
IT WASN'T SPECIAL. IT WAS ALL IN MY HEAD. I WAS FEELING ON TOP OF THE WORLD, I WAS MAKING A NEW START... I WAS READY FOR SOMETHING GREAT TO HAPPEN. PROFESSOR UNDERGRAD-NOODLER JUST HAPPENED TO BE THERE AT THE RIGHT TIME. I FELT AS IF HE TAUGHT ME EVERYTHING ABOUT LOVE AND SEX BUT IN FACT HE WAS RATHER PASSIVE... IT WAS ALL ME. I NEEDED A GREAT LOVE, AND I MADE IT HAPPEN...
THE THING WITH ALIK MAY HAVE BEEN LIKE THAT, BUT HOW THE ORPHAN MADE ME FEEL WAS UNEXPECTED AND REAL... I WASN'T EVEN ATTRACTED TO HIM AT FIRST. I'M NOT LEO FINKLE!
... I KNOW THAT ME TELLING THIS TO YOU NOW IS USELESS. IT'S LIKE TELLING THE DUDE WITH THE ALBATROSS AROUND HIS NECK, "HEY, THERE WERE NO SLIMY CREATURES AND NO DEATH SHIP! YOU WERE JUST DEHYDRATED."... YOU DON'T HAVE TO BELIEVE ME. BUT TRY TO STAY AWAY FROM THE ORPHAN...

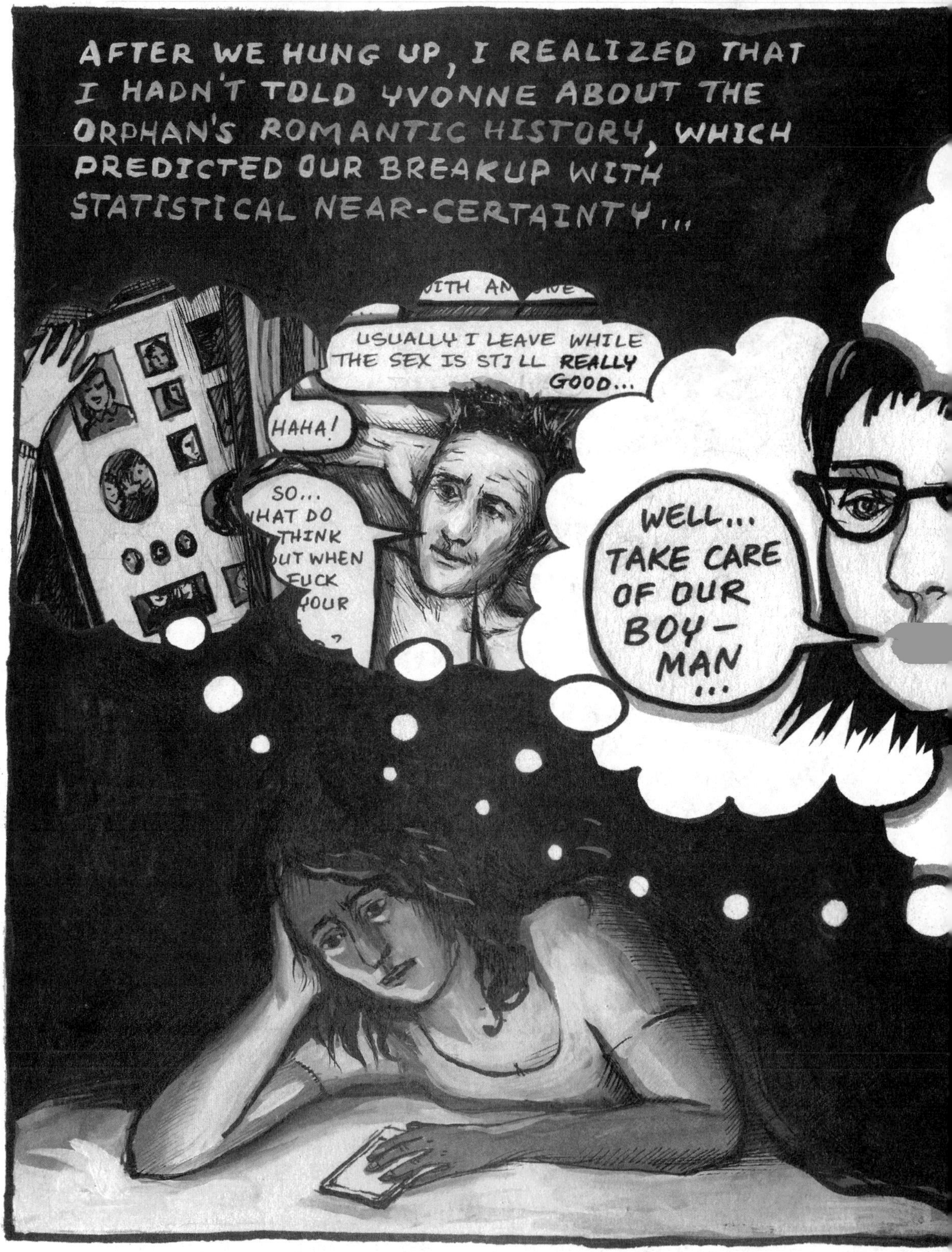
AFTER WE HUNG UP, I REALIZED THAT I HADN'T TOLD YVONNE ABOUT THE ORPHAN'S ROMANTIC HISTORY, WHICH PREDICTED OUR BREAKUP WITH STATISTICAL NEAR-CERTAINTY...
USUALLY I LEAVE WHILE THE SEX IS STILL REALLY GOOD...
HAHA!
WELL... TAKE CARE OF OUR BOY-MAN ...

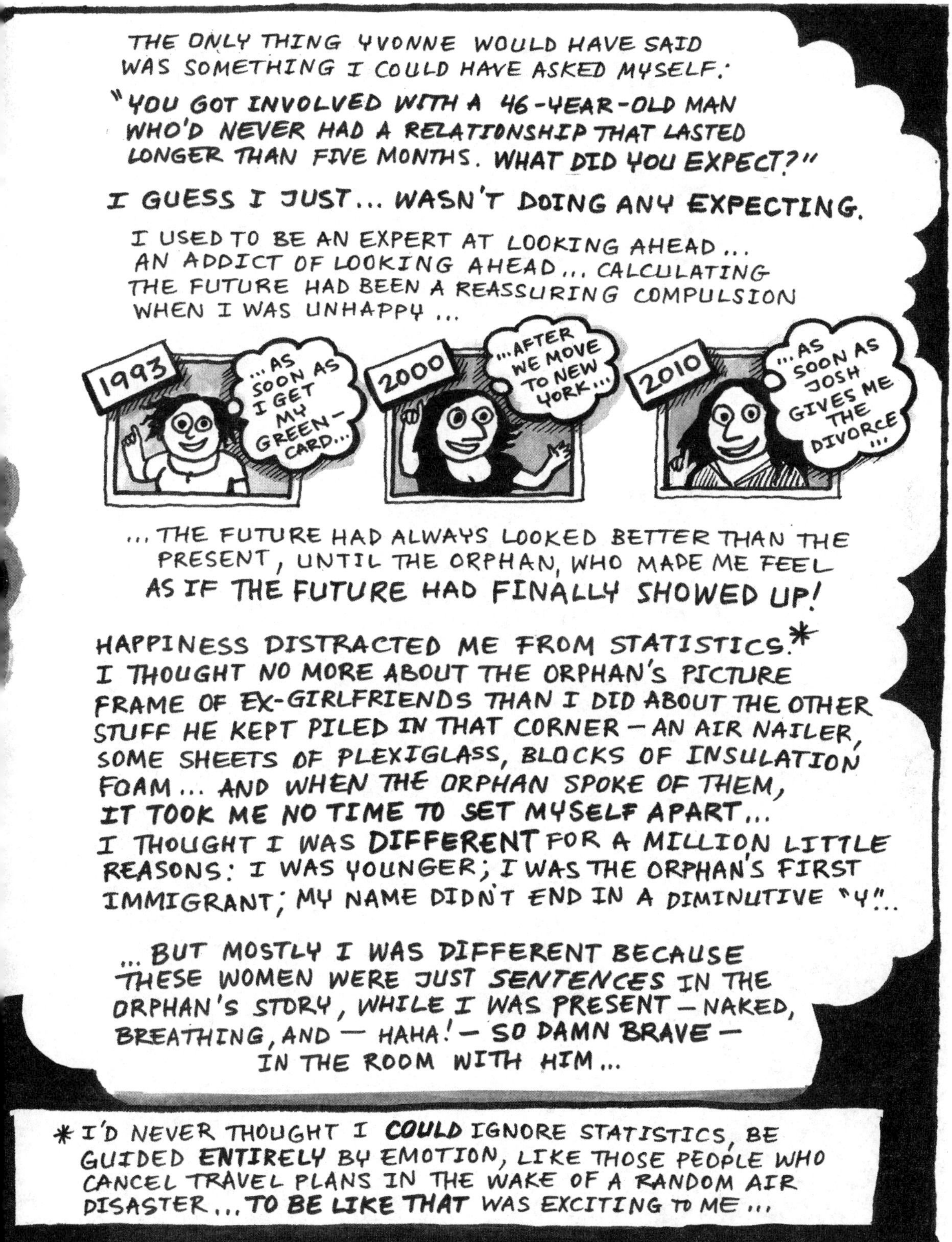
THE ONLY THING YVONNE WOULD HAVE SAID WAS SOMETHING I COULD HAVE ASKED MYSELF:
"YOU GOT INVOLVED WITH A 46-YEAR-OLD MAN WHO'D NEVER HAD A RELATIONSHIP THAT LASTED LONGER THAN FIVE MONTHS. WHAT DID YOU EXPECT?"
I GUESS I JUST... WASN'T DOING ANY EXPECTING.
I USED TO BE AN EXPERT AT LOOKING AHEAD... AN ADDICT OF LOOKING AHEAD... CALCULATING THE FUTURE HAD BEEN A REASSURING COMPULSION WHEN I WAS UNHAPPY...
1993
...AS SOON AS I GET MY GREEN-CARD...
2000
...AFTER WE MOVE TO NEW YORK...
2010
...AS SOON AS JOSH GIVES ME THE DIVORCE...
...THE FUTURE HAD ALWAYS LOOKED BETTER THAN THE PRESENT, UNTIL THE ORPHAN, WHO MADE ME FEEL AS IF THE FUTURE HAD FINALLY SHOWED UP!
HAPPINESS DISTRACTED ME FROM STATISTICS.* I THOUGHT NO MORE ABOUT THE ORPHAN'S PICTURE FRAME OF EX-GIRLFRIENDS THAN I DID ABOUT THE OTHER STUFF HE KEPT PILED IN THAT CORNER — AN AIR NAILER, SOME SHEETS OF PLEXIGLASS, BLOCKS OF INSULATION FOAM... AND WHEN THE ORPHAN SPOKE OF THEM, IT TOOK ME NO TIME TO SET MYSELF APART...
I THOUGHT I WAS DIFFERENT FOR A MILLION LITTLE REASONS: I WAS YOUNGER; I WAS THE ORPHAN'S FIRST IMMIGRANT; MY NAME DIDN'T END IN A DIMINUTIVE "Y"...
...BUT MOSTLY I WAS DIFFERENT BECAUSE THESE WOMEN WERE JUST SENTENCES IN THE ORPHAN'S STORY, WHILE I WAS PRESENT — NAKED, BREATHING, AND — HAHA! — SO DAMN BRAVE — IN THE ROOM WITH HIM...
* I'D NEVER THOUGHT I COULD IGNORE STATISTICS, BE GUIDED ENTIRELY BY EMOTION, LIKE THOSE PEOPLE WHO CANCEL TRAVEL PLANS IN THE WAKE OF A RANDOM AIR DISASTER... TO BE LIKE THAT WAS EXCITING TO ME...

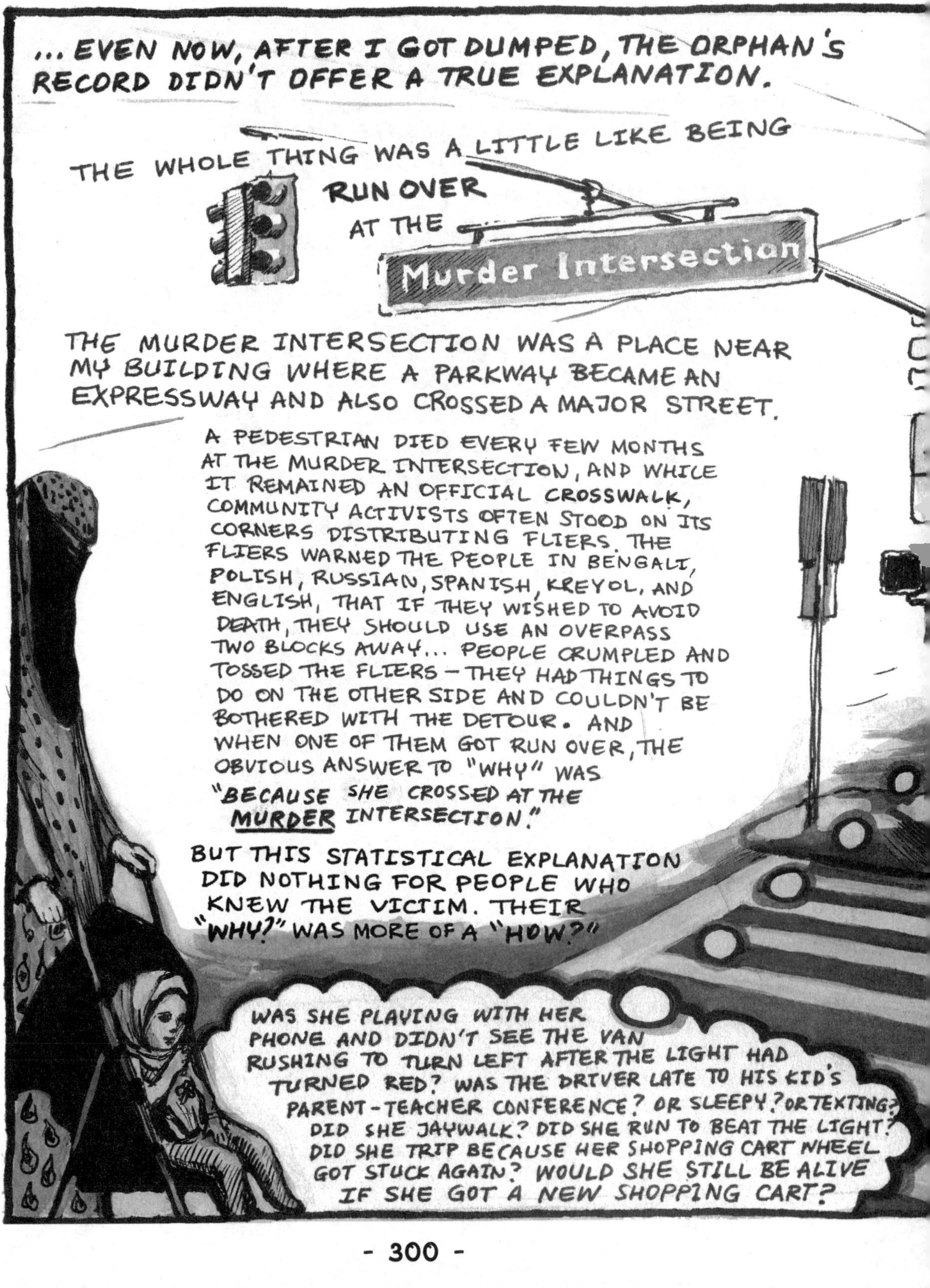

... EVEN NOW, AFTER I GOT DUMPED, THE ORPHAN'S RECORD DIDN'T OFFER A TRUE EXPLANATION.

THE WHOLE THING WAS A LITTLE LIKE BEING

 RUN OVER AT THE 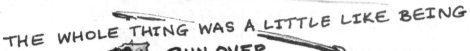 Murder Intersection

THE MURDER INTERSECTION WAS A PLACE NEAR MY BUILDING WHERE A PARKWAY BECAME AN EXPRESSWAY AND ALSO CROSSED A MAJOR STREET.

A PEDESTRIAN DIED EVERY FEW MONTHS AT THE MURDER INTERSECTION, AND WHILE IT REMAINED AN OFFICIAL CROSSWALK, COMMUNITY ACTIVISTS OFTEN STOOD ON ITS CORNERS DISTRIBUTING FLIERS. THE FLIERS WARNED THE PEOPLE IN BENGALI, POLISH, RUSSIAN, SPANISH, KREYOL, AND ENGLISH, THAT IF THEY WISHED TO AVOID DEATH, THEY SHOULD USE AN OVERPASS TWO BLOCKS AWAY... PEOPLE CRUMPLED AND TOSSED THE FLIERS — THEY HAD THINGS TO DO ON THE OTHER SIDE AND COULDN'T BE BOTHERED WITH THE DETOUR. AND WHEN ONE OF THEM GOT RUN OVER, THE OBVIOUS ANSWER TO "WHY" WAS "BECAUSE SHE CROSSED AT THE MURDER INTERSECTION."

BUT THIS STATISTICAL EXPLANATION DID NOTHING FOR PEOPLE WHO KNEW THE VICTIM. THEIR "WHY?" WAS MORE OF A "HOW?"

WAS SHE PLAYING WITH HER PHONE AND DIDN'T SEE THE VAN RUSHING TO TURN LEFT AFTER THE LIGHT HAD TURNED RED? WAS THE DRIVER LATE TO HIS KID'S PARENT-TEACHER CONFERENCE? OR SLEEPY? OR TEXTING? DID SHE JAYWALK? DID SHE RUN TO BEAT THE LIGHT? DID SHE TRIP BECAUSE HER SHOPPING CART WHEEL GOT STUCK AGAIN? WOULD SHE STILL BE ALIVE IF SHE GOT A NEW SHOPPING CART?

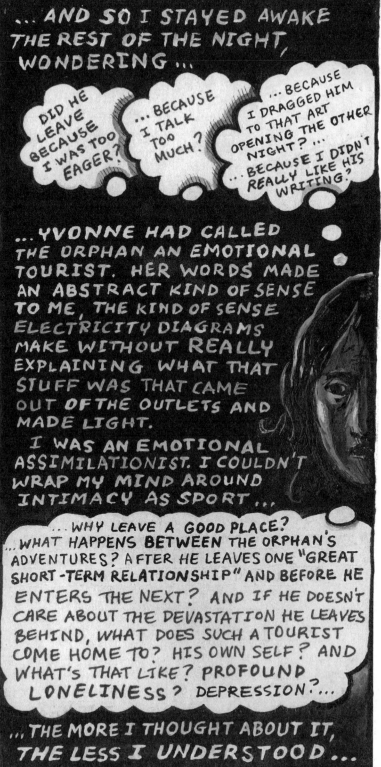

...AND SO I STAYED AWAKE THE REST OF THE NIGHT, WONDERING...

DID HE LEAVE BECAUSE I WAS TOO EAGER?

...BECAUSE I TALK TOO MUCH?

...BECAUSE I DRAGGED HIM TO THAT ART OPENING THE OTHER NIGHT?...

...BECAUSE I DIDN'T REALLY LIKE HIS WRITING?

...YVONNE HAD CALLED THE ORPHAN AN EMOTIONAL TOURIST. HER WORDS MADE AN ABSTRACT KIND OF SENSE TO ME, THE KIND OF SENSE ELECTRICITY DIAGRAMS MAKE WITHOUT REALLY EXPLAINING WHAT THAT STUFF WAS THAT CAME OUT OF THE OUTLETS AND MADE LIGHT.

I WAS AN EMOTIONAL ASSIMILATIONIST. I COULDN'T WRAP MY MIND AROUND INTIMACY AS SPORT...

...WHY LEAVE A GOOD PLACE? ...WHAT HAPPENS BETWEEN THE ORPHAN'S ADVENTURES? AFTER HE LEAVES ONE "GREAT SHORT-TERM RELATIONSHIP" AND BEFORE HE ENTERS THE NEXT? AND IF HE DOESN'T CARE ABOUT THE DEVASTATION HE LEAVES BEHIND, WHAT DOES SUCH A TOURIST COME HOME TO? HIS OWN SELF? AND WHAT'S THAT LIKE? PROFOUND LONELINESS? DEPRESSION?...

...THE MORE I THOUGHT ABOUT IT, THE LESS I UNDERSTOOD...

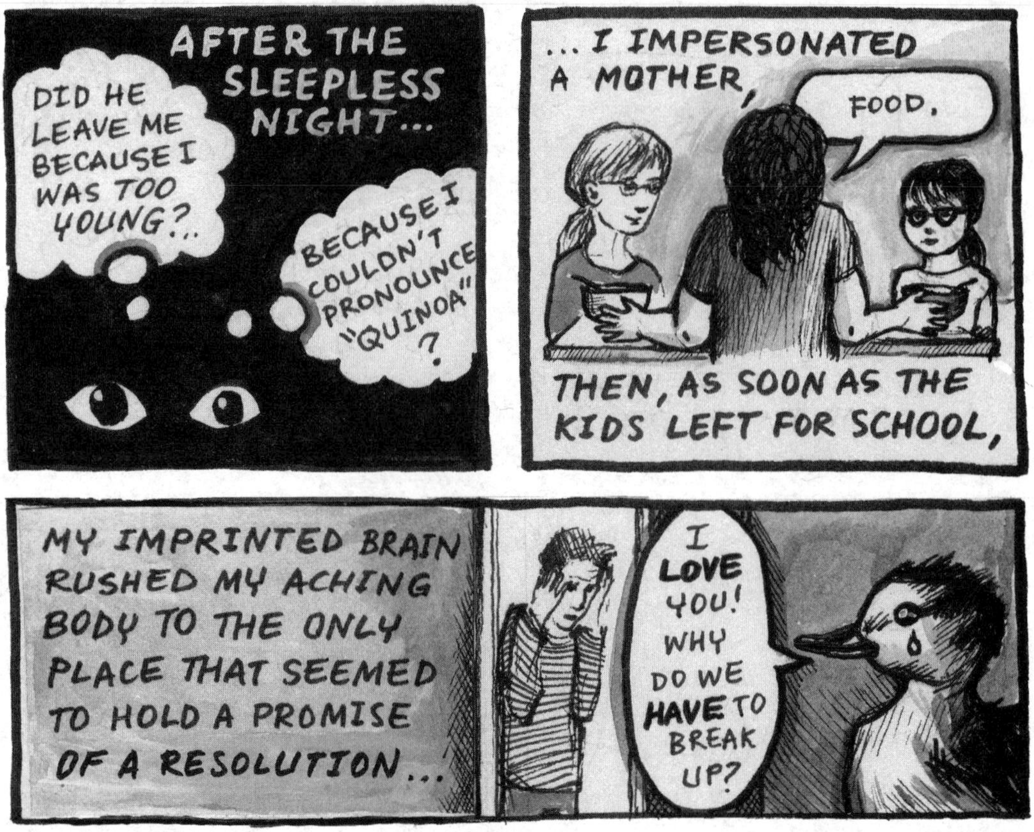
AFTER THE SLEEPLESS NIGHT...
DID HE LEAVE ME BECAUSE I WAS TOO YOUNG?...
BECAUSE I COULDN'T PRONOUNCE "QUINOA"?
... I IMPERSONATED A MOTHER,
FOOD.
THEN, AS SOON AS THE KIDS LEFT FOR SCHOOL,
MY IMPRINTED BRAIN RUSHED MY ACHING BODY TO THE ONLY PLACE THAT SEEMED TO HOLD A PROMISE OF A RESOLUTION...
I LOVE YOU! WHY DO WE HAVE TO BREAK UP?

(YVONNE HAD TOLD ME TO STAY AWAY FROM THE ORPHAN, BUT STAYING AWAY FROM THE ORPHAN WOULD HAVE REQUIRED PHYSICAL RESTRAINT, AND YVONNE WASN'T AROUND TO CHAIN ME TO A RADIATOR.)

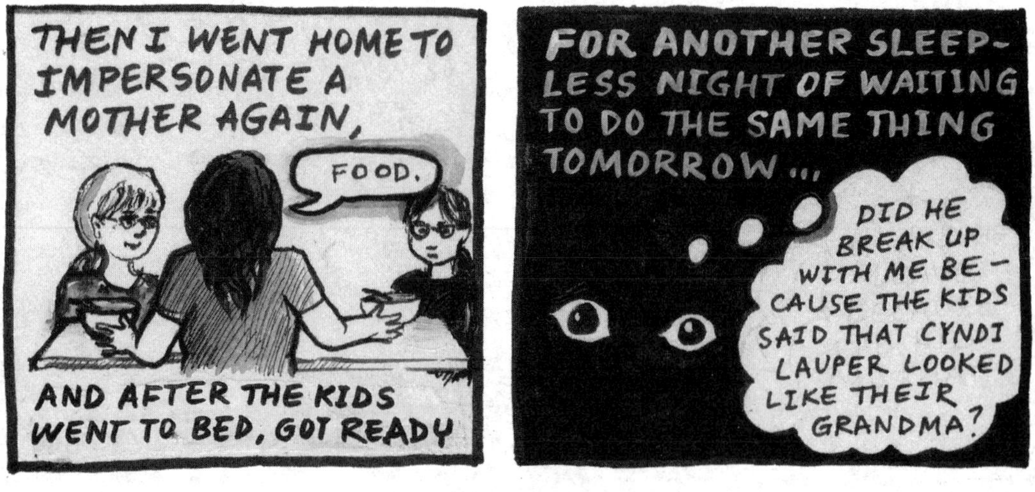
THEN I WENT HOME TO IMPERSONATE A MOTHER AGAIN,
FOOD.
AND AFTER THE KIDS WENT TO BED, GOT READY
FOR ANOTHER SLEEP-LESS NIGHT OF WAITING TO DO THE SAME THING TOMORROW...
DID HE BREAK UP WITH ME BE-CAUSE THE KIDS SAID THAT CYNDI LAUPER LOOKED LIKE THEIR GRANDMA?

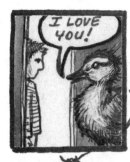

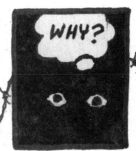

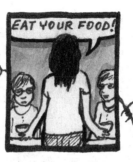

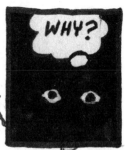

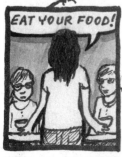

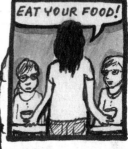

I LOVE YOU!
WHY?
EAT YOUR FOOD!
WHY?
EAT YOUR FOOD!
AND THAT WAS, BASICALLY, WHAT I DID WITH MY LIFE FOR THE REST OF THAT **WINTER** AND WELL INTO **SPRING**....
EAT YOUR FOOD!
WHY?
I LOVE YOU!
I LOVE YOU!
WHY?
... IT WASN'T WHAT I'D NORMALLY CALL "LIVING." RATHER, IT WAS A KIND OF WAITING.
EAT YOUR FOOD!
WHY?
I LOVE YOU!
EAT YOUR FOOD!

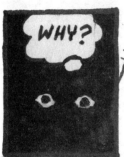

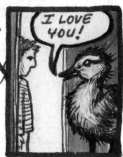

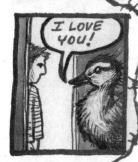

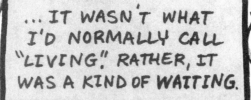

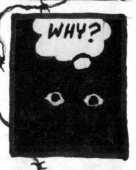

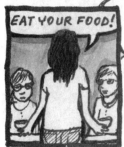

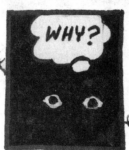

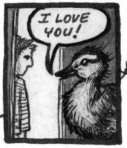

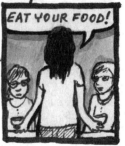

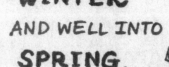

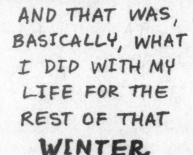

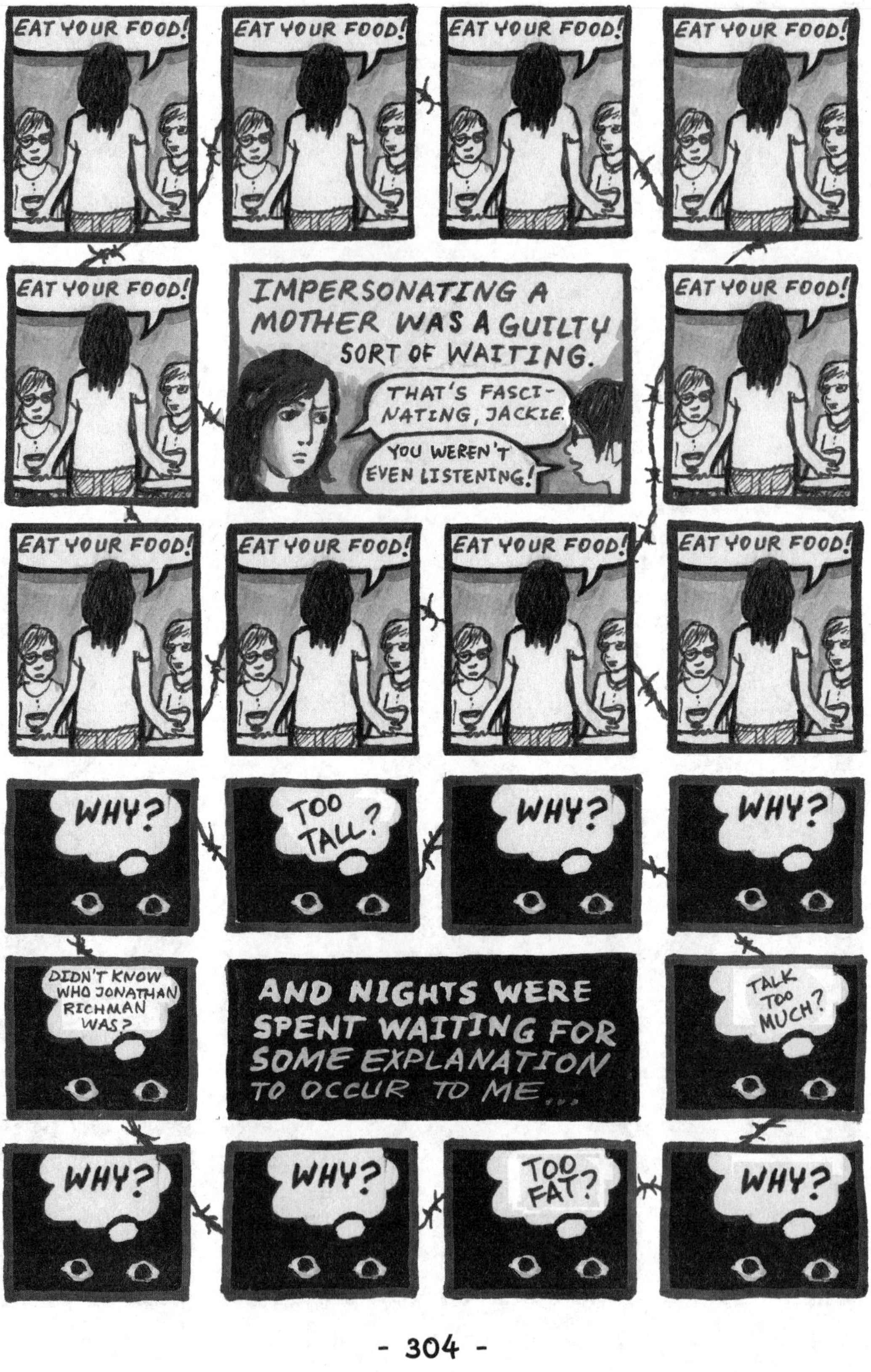
EAT YOUR FOOD!
EAT YOUR FOOD!
EAT YOUR FOOD!
EAT YOUR FOOD!
EAT YOUR FOOD!
IMPERSONATING A MOTHER WAS A GUILTY SORT OF WAITING.
THAT'S FASCINATING, JACKIE.
YOU WEREN'T EVEN LISTENING!
EAT YOUR FOOD!
EAT YOUR FOOD!
EAT YOUR FOOD!
EAT YOUR FOOD!
EAT YOUR FOOD!
WHY?
TOO TALL?
WHY?
WHY?
DIDN'T KNOW WHO JONATHAN RICHMAN WAS?
AND NIGHTS WERE SPENT WAITING FOR SOME EXPLANATION TO OCCUR TO ME...
TALK TOO MUCH?
WHY?
WHY?
TOO FAT?
WHY?

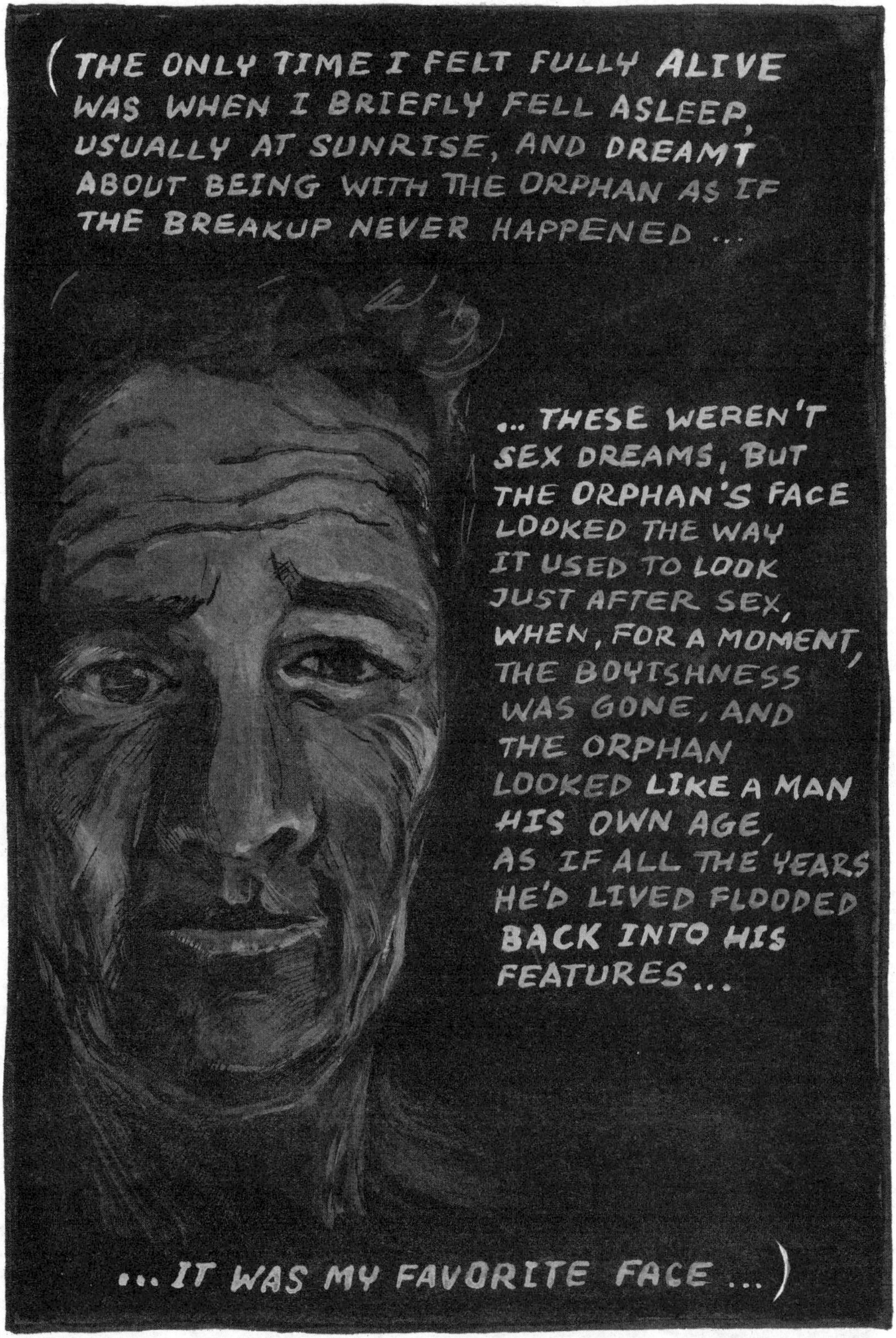
(THE ONLY TIME I FELT FULLY ALIVE WAS WHEN I BRIEFLY FELL ASLEEP, USUALLY AT SUNRISE, AND DREAMT ABOUT BEING WITH THE ORPHAN AS IF THE BREAKUP NEVER HAPPENED ...
... THESE WEREN'T SEX DREAMS, BUT THE ORPHAN'S FACE LOOKED THE WAY IT USED TO LOOK JUST AFTER SEX, WHEN, FOR A MOMENT, THE BOYISHNESS WAS GONE, AND THE ORPHAN LOOKED LIKE A MAN HIS OWN AGE, AS IF ALL THE YEARS HE'D LIVED FLOODED BACK INTO HIS FEATURES ...
... IT WAS MY FAVORITE FACE ...)

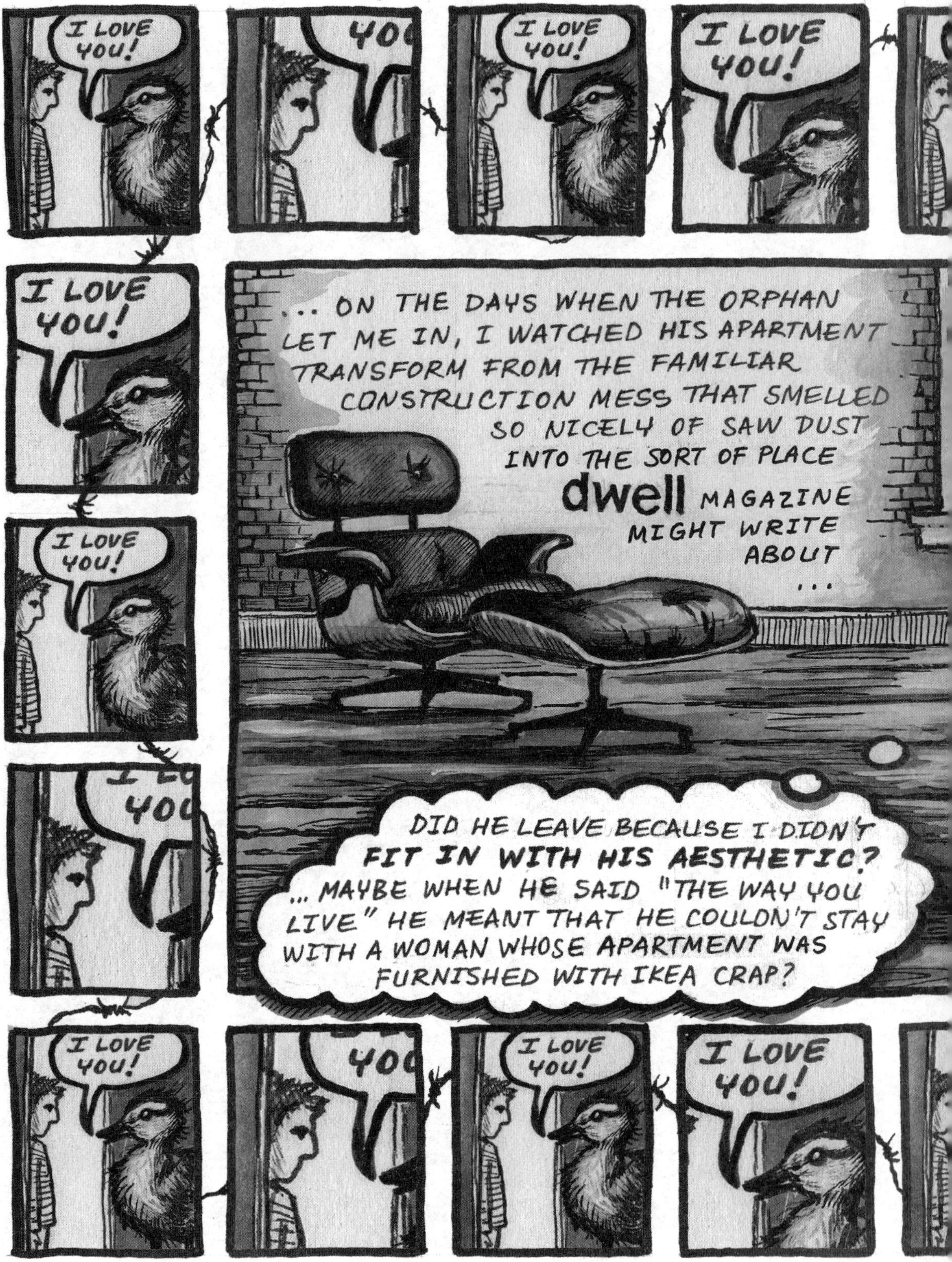
I LOVE YOU!
I LOVE YOU!
I LOVE YOU!
I LOVE YOU!
I LOVE YOU!
... ON THE DAYS WHEN THE ORPHAN LET ME IN, I WATCHED HIS APARTMENT TRANSFORM FROM THE FAMILIAR CONSTRUCTION MESS THAT SMELLED SO NICELY OF SAW DUST INTO THE SORT OF PLACE dwell MAGAZINE MIGHT WRITE ABOUT ...
DID HE LEAVE BECAUSE I DIDN'T FIT IN WITH HIS AESTHETIC? ... MAYBE WHEN HE SAID "THE WAY YOU LIVE" HE MEANT THAT HE COULDN'T STAY WITH A WOMAN WHOSE APARTMENT WAS FURNISHED WITH IKEA CRAP?
I LOVE YOU!
I LOVE YOU!
I LOVE YOU!

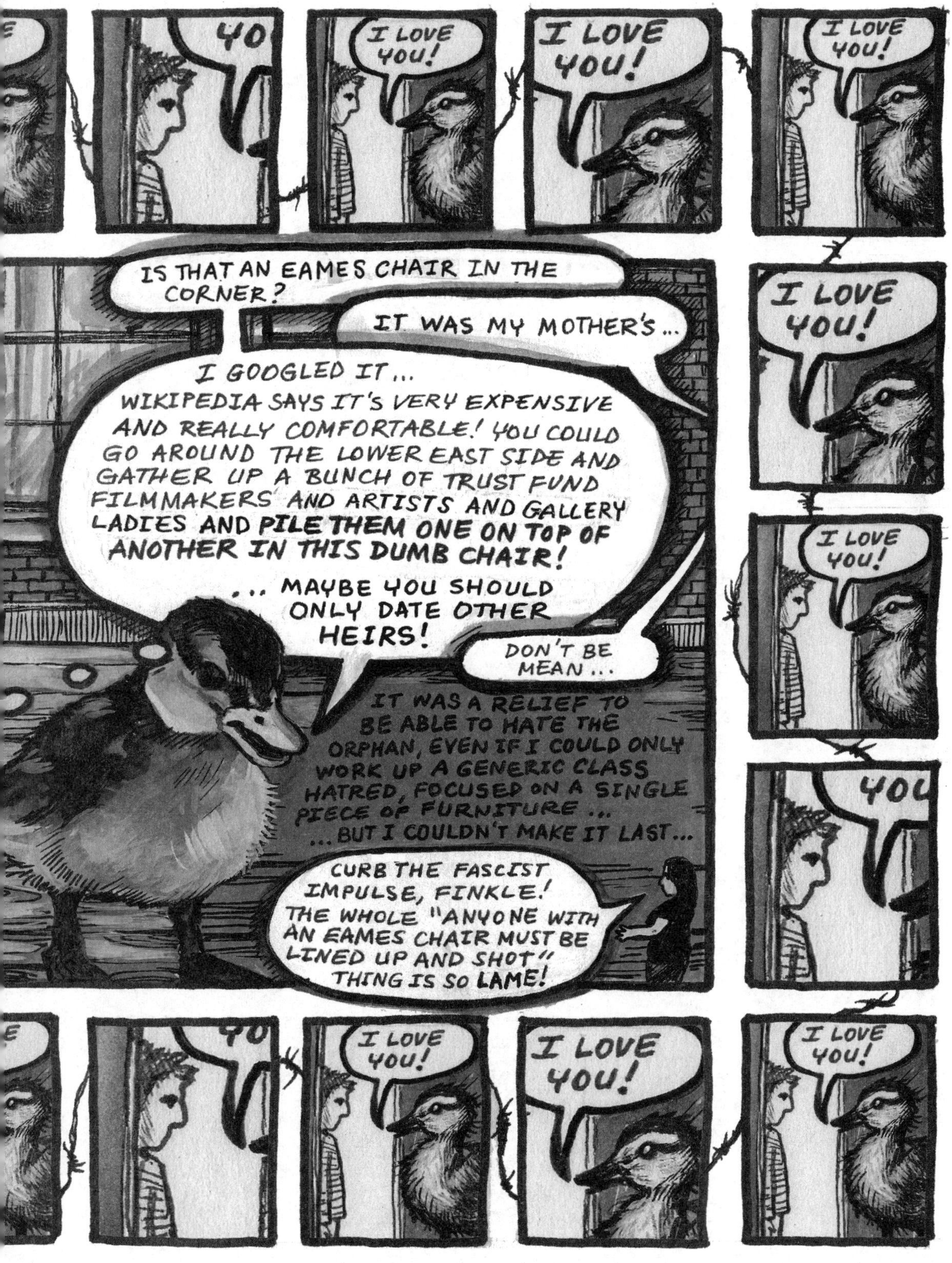

YO
I LOVE YOU!
I LOVE YOU!
I LOVE YOU!
IS THAT AN EAMES CHAIR IN THE CORNER?
IT WAS MY MOTHER'S...
I GOOGLED IT... WIKIPEDIA SAYS IT'S VERY EXPENSIVE AND REALLY COMFORTABLE! YOU COULD GO AROUND THE LOWER EAST SIDE AND GATHER UP A BUNCH OF TRUST FUND FILMMAKERS AND ARTISTS AND GALLERY LADIES AND PILE THEM ONE ON TOP OF ANOTHER IN THIS DUMB CHAIR!
... MAYBE YOU SHOULD ONLY DATE OTHER HEIRS!
DON'T BE MEAN...
IT WAS A RELIEF TO BE ABLE TO HATE THE ORPHAN, EVEN IF I COULD ONLY WORK UP A GENERIC CLASS HATRED, FOCUSED ON A SINGLE PIECE OF FURNITURE...
...BUT I COULDN'T MAKE IT LAST...
CURB THE FASCIST IMPULSE, FINKLE! THE WHOLE "ANYONE WITH AN EAMES CHAIR MUST BE LINED UP AND SHOT" THING IS SO LAME!
I LOVE YOU!
I LOVE YOU!
I LOVE YOU!
YOU
YO
I LOVE YOU!
I LOVE YOU!
I LOVE YOU!

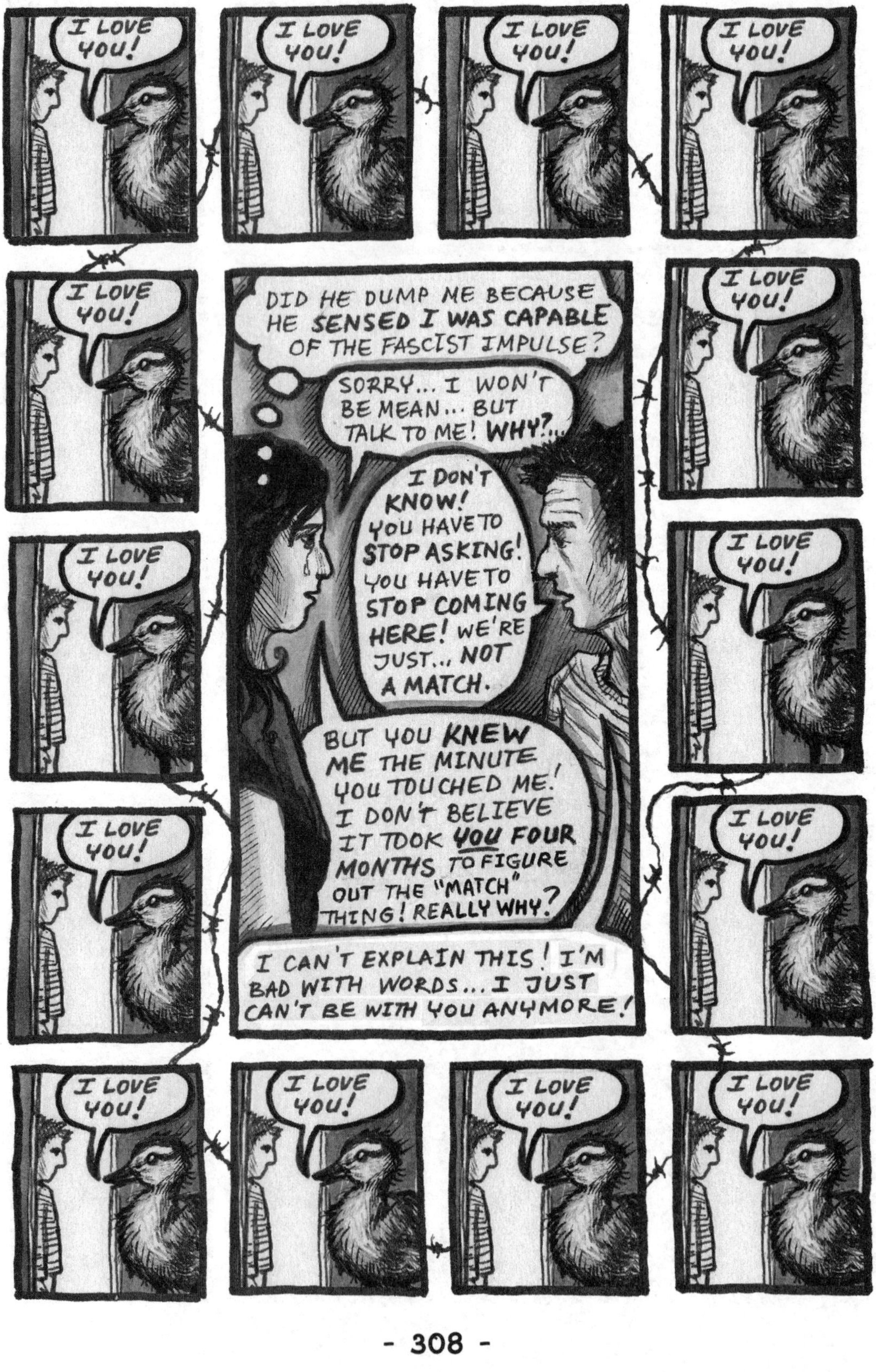
I LOVE YOU!
I LOVE YOU!
I LOVE YOU!
I LOVE YOU!
I LOVE YOU!
DID HE DUMP ME BECAUSE HE SENSED I WAS CAPABLE OF THE FASCIST IMPULSE?
SORRY... I WON'T BE MEAN... BUT TALK TO ME! WHY?...
I DON'T KNOW! YOU HAVE TO STOP ASKING! YOU HAVE TO STOP COMING HERE! WE'RE JUST... NOT A MATCH.
BUT YOU KNEW ME THE MINUTE YOU TOUCHED ME! I DON'T BELIEVE IT TOOK YOU FOUR MONTHS TO FIGURE OUT THE "MATCH" THING! REALLY WHY?
I CAN'T EXPLAIN THIS! I'M BAD WITH WORDS... I JUST CAN'T BE WITH YOU ANYMORE!
I LOVE YOU!
I LOVE YOU!
I LOVE YOU!
I LOVE YOU!
I LOVE YOU!
I LOVE YOU!
I LOVE YOU!
I LOVE YOU!
I LOVE YOU!

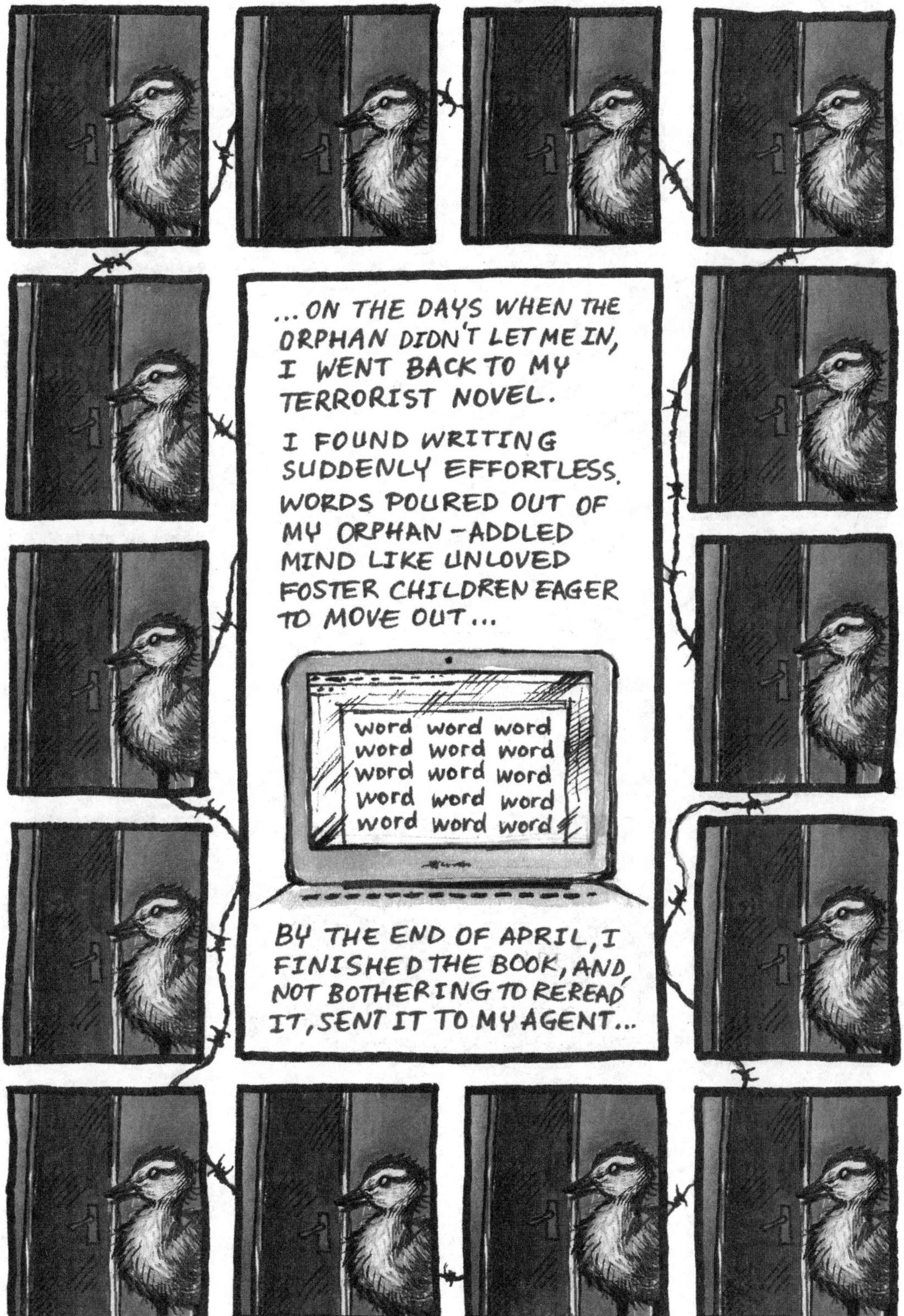
...ON THE DAYS WHEN THE ORPHAN DIDN'T LET ME IN, I WENT BACK TO MY TERRORIST NOVEL.
I FOUND WRITING SUDDENLY EFFORTLESS. WORDS POURED OUT OF MY ORPHAN-ADDLED MIND LIKE UNLOVED FOSTER CHILDREN EAGER TO MOVE OUT...
word word word word word word word word word word word word word word word
BY THE END OF APRIL, I FINISHED THE BOOK, AND, NOT BOTHERING TO REREAD IT, SENT IT TO MY AGENT...

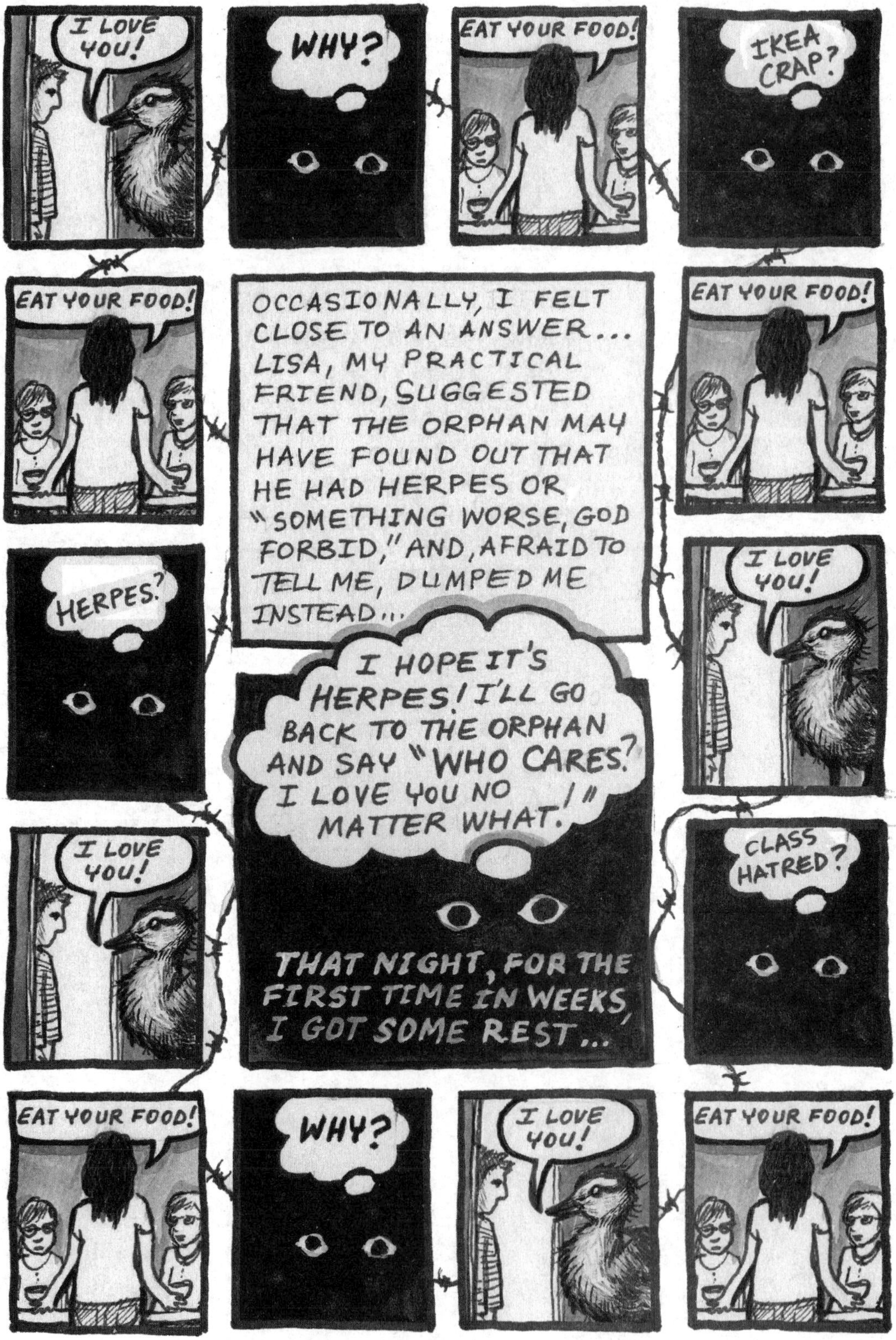
I LOVE YOU!
WHY?
EAT YOUR FOOD!
IKEA CRAP?
EAT YOUR FOOD!
OCCASIONALLY, I FELT CLOSE TO AN ANSWER... LISA, MY PRACTICAL FRIEND, SUGGESTED THAT THE ORPHAN MAY HAVE FOUND OUT THAT HE HAD HERPES OR "SOMETHING WORSE, GOD FORBID," AND, AFRAID TO TELL ME, DUMPED ME INSTEAD...
EAT YOUR FOOD!
HERPES?
I LOVE YOU!
I HOPE IT'S HERPES! I'LL GO BACK TO THE ORPHAN AND SAY "WHO CARES? I LOVE YOU NO MATTER WHAT!"
THAT NIGHT, FOR THE FIRST TIME IN WEEKS, I GOT SOME REST...
I LOVE YOU!
CLASS HATRED?
EAT YOUR FOOD!
WHY?
I LOVE YOU!
EAT YOUR FOOD!

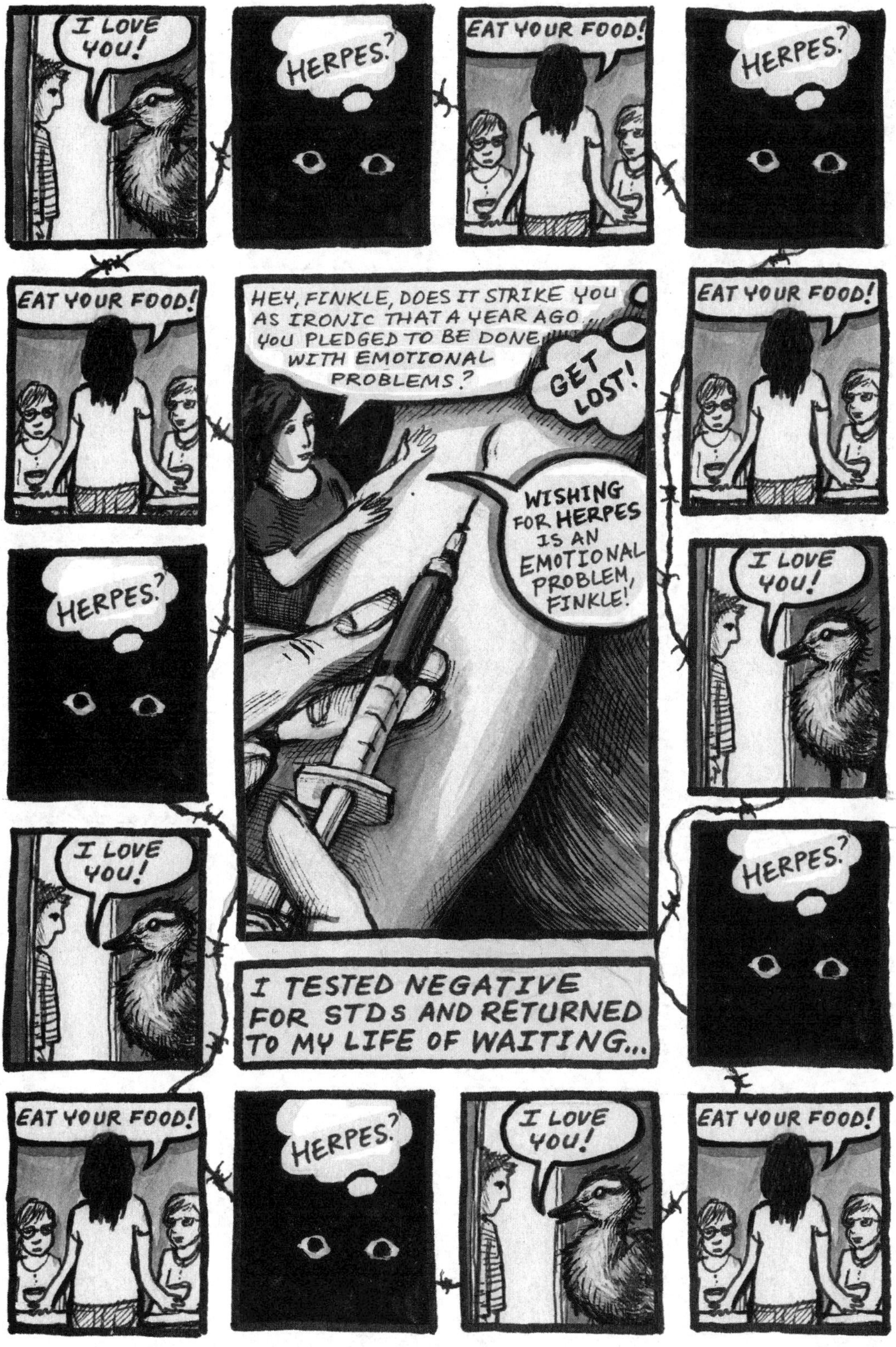
I LOVE YOU!
HERPES?
EAT YOUR FOOD!
HERPES?
EAT YOUR FOOD!
HEY, FINKLE, DOES IT STRIKE YOU AS IRONIC THAT A YEAR AGO YOU PLEDGED TO BE DONE WITH EMOTIONAL PROBLEMS?
GET LOST!
WISHING FOR HERPES IS AN EMOTIONAL PROBLEM, FINKLE!
EAT YOUR FOOD!
HERPES?
I LOVE YOU!
I LOVE YOU!
HERPES?
I TESTED NEGATIVE FOR STDS AND RETURNED TO MY LIFE OF WAITING...
EAT YOUR FOOD!
HERPES?
I LOVE YOU!
EAT YOUR FOOD!

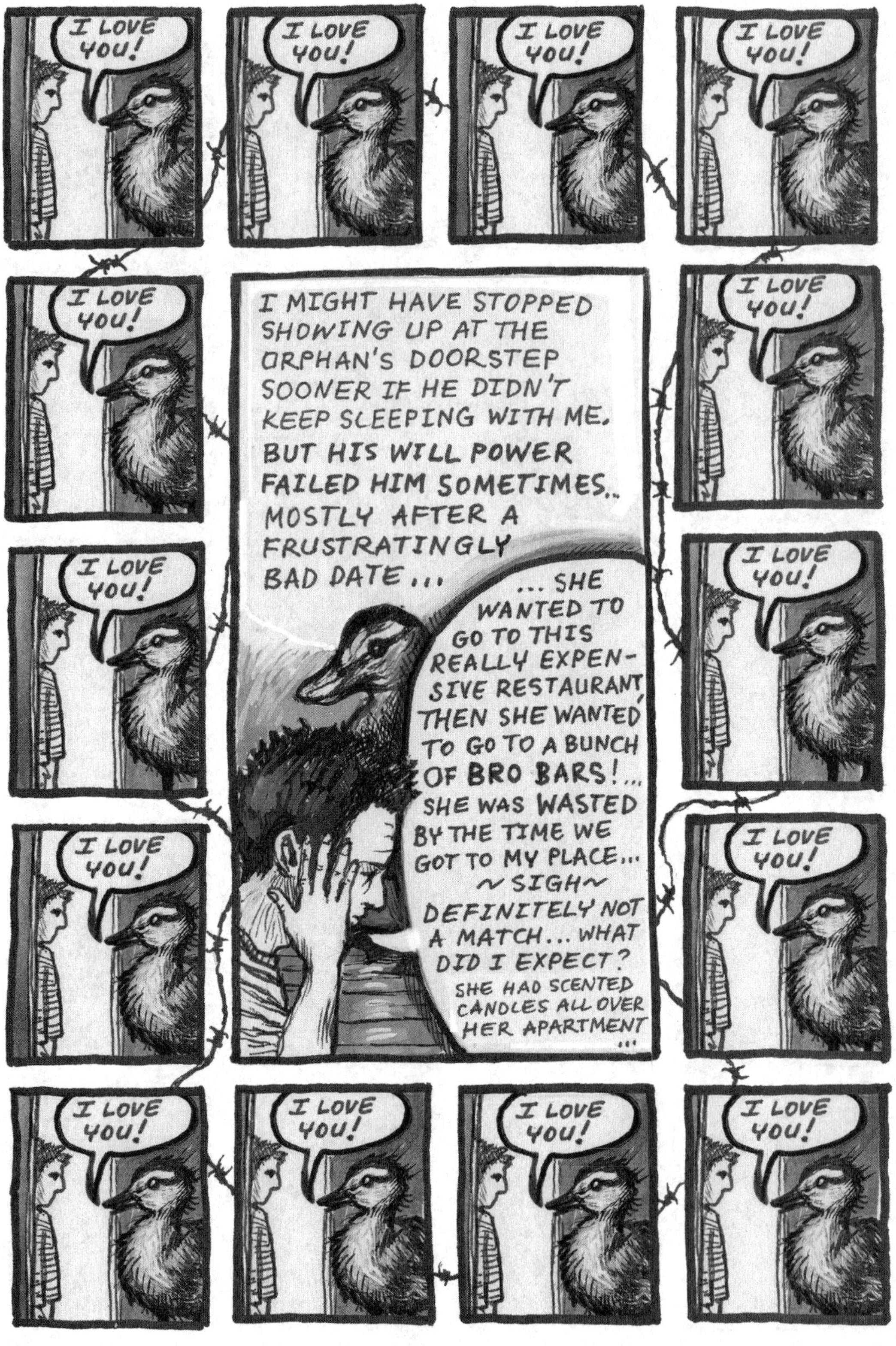
I LOVE YOU!
I LOVE YOU!
I LOVE YOU!
I LOVE YOU!
I LOVE YOU!
I MIGHT HAVE STOPPED SHOWING UP AT THE ORPHAN'S DOORSTEP SOONER IF HE DIDN'T KEEP SLEEPING WITH ME.
BUT HIS WILL POWER FAILED HIM SOMETIMES.. MOSTLY AFTER A FRUSTRATINGLY BAD DATE...
... SHE WANTED TO GO TO THIS REALLY EXPENSIVE RESTAURANT, THEN SHE WANTED TO GO TO A BUNCH OF BRO BARS!... SHE WAS WASTED BY THE TIME WE GOT TO MY PLACE... ~SIGH~ DEFINITELY NOT A MATCH... WHAT DID I EXPECT? SHE HAD SCENTED CANDLES ALL OVER HER APARTMENT...
I LOVE YOU!
I LOVE YOU!
I LOVE YOU!
I LOVE YOU!
I LOVE YOU!
I LOVE YOU!
I LOVE YOU!
I LOVE YOU!
I LOVE YOU!

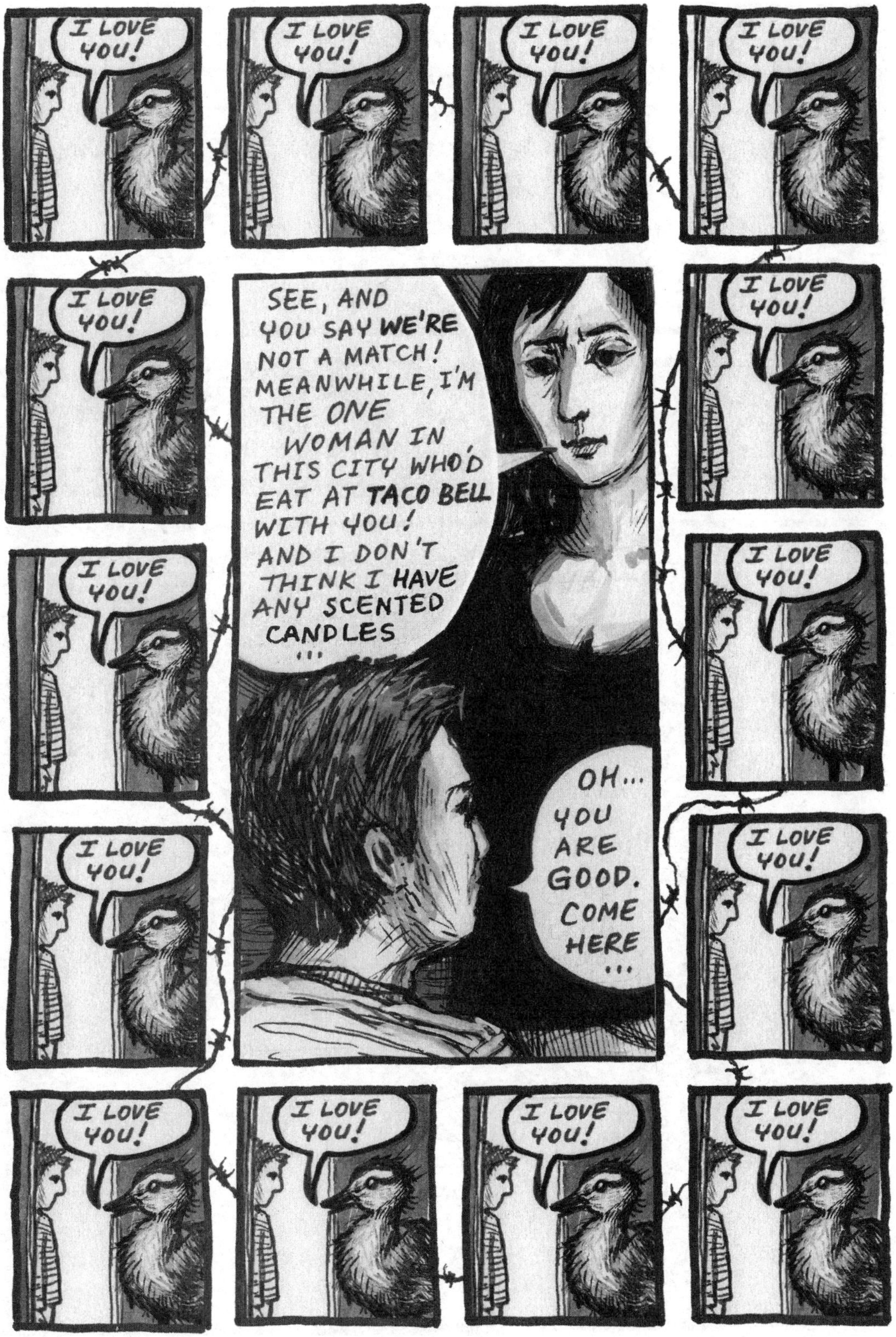
I LOVE YOU!
I LOVE YOU!
I LOVE YOU!
I LOVE YOU!
I LOVE YOU!
I LOVE YOU!
SEE, AND YOU SAY WE'RE NOT A MATCH! MEANWHILE, I'M THE ONE WOMAN IN THIS CITY WHO'D EAT AT TACO BELL WITH YOU! AND I DON'T THINK I HAVE ANY SCENTED CANDLES ...
I LOVE YOU!
I LOVE YOU!
OH... YOU ARE GOOD. COME HERE ...
I LOVE YOU!
I LOVE YOU!
I LOVE YOU!
I LOVE YOU!
I LOVE YOU!
I LOVE YOU!
I LOVE YOU!

THE FIRST TIME THIS HAPPENED, I EXPECTED THAT SEX WOULD BE DIFFERENT NOW THAT WE WERE BROKEN UP. I ALMOST **WANTED** THE ORPHAN TO HAVE CHANGED. HE COULD **TELL** ME TO GO AWAY A MILLION TIMES, AND IT WOULD MEAN NOTHING... BUT THE SLIGHTEST SHADE OF ALOOFNESS OR HOSTILITY WHILE WE WERE FUCKING WOULD HAVE MADE ME FINALLY ACCEPT THE BREAKUP ...

... I ACTUALLY WANTED HIM TO BE AN IDIOT, TO BE AN AGGRESSOR, A JERK. BUT THE ORPHAN DIDN'T KNOW FROM BAD SEX ...

LOOK AT ME... TALK TO ME ...

NOTHING CHANGED... WHAT WEIGHT CAN BREAKUP **TALK** HAVE, RELATIVE TO **THIS?**

REMEMBER YOUR BIG DRAWINGS? WE SHOULD COVER THIS WHOLE APARTMENT WITH HUGE SHEETS OF PAPER, AND YOU CAN STAY HERE ALL DAY AND DRAW...

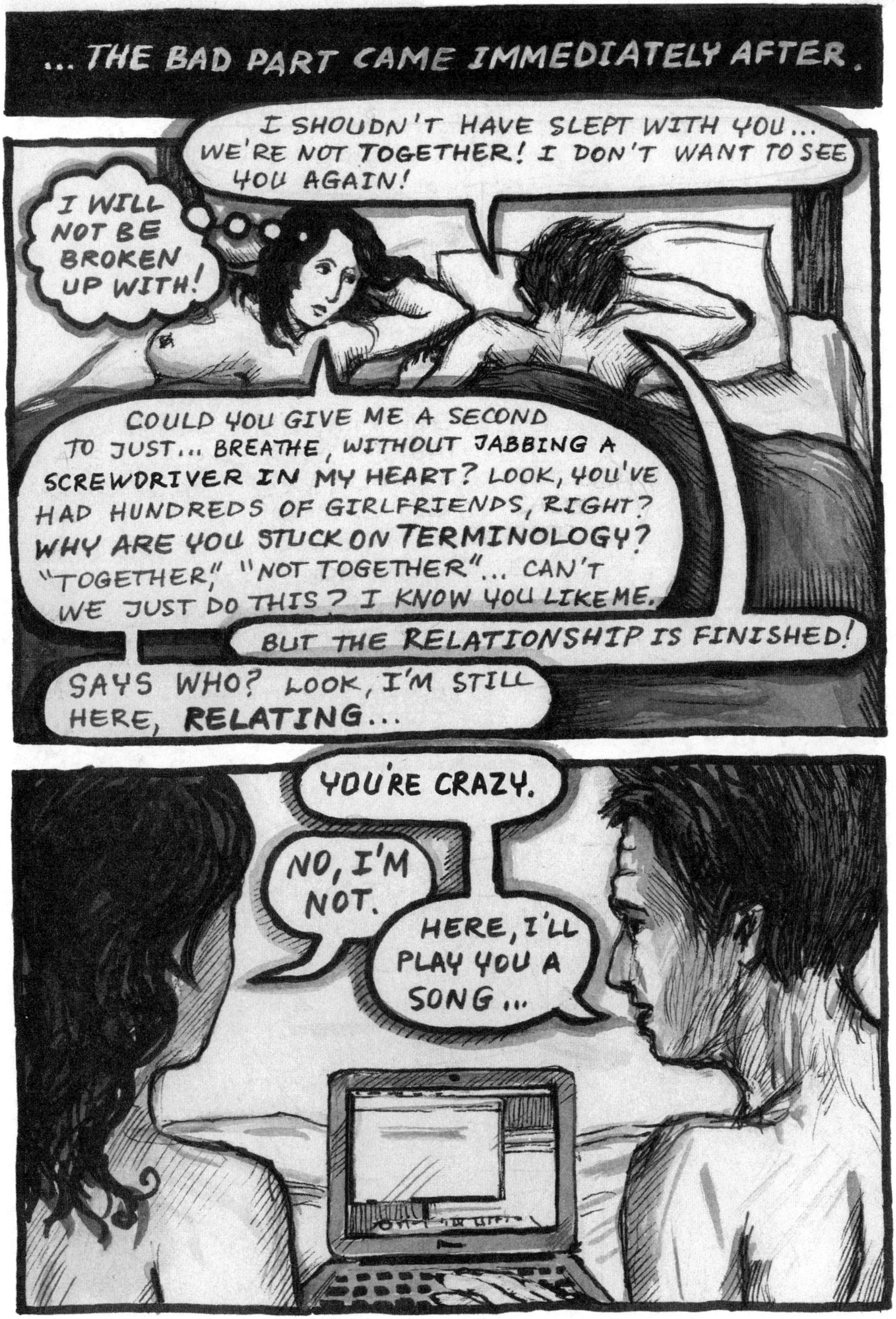
...THE BAD PART CAME IMMEDIATELY AFTER.
I SHOUDN'T HAVE SLEPT WITH YOU... WE'RE NOT TOGETHER! I DON'T WANT TO SEE YOU AGAIN!
I WILL NOT BE BROKEN UP WITH!
COULD YOU GIVE ME A SECOND TO JUST... BREATHE, WITHOUT JABBING A SCREWDRIVER IN MY HEART? LOOK, YOU'VE HAD HUNDREDS OF GIRLFRIENDS, RIGHT? WHY ARE YOU STUCK ON TERMINOLOGY? "TOGETHER," "NOT TOGETHER"... CAN'T WE JUST DO THIS? I KNOW YOU LIKE ME.
BUT THE RELATIONSHIP IS FINISHED!
SAYS WHO? LOOK, I'M STILL HERE, RELATING...
YOU'RE CRAZY.
NO, I'M NOT.
HERE, I'LL PLAY YOU A SONG...

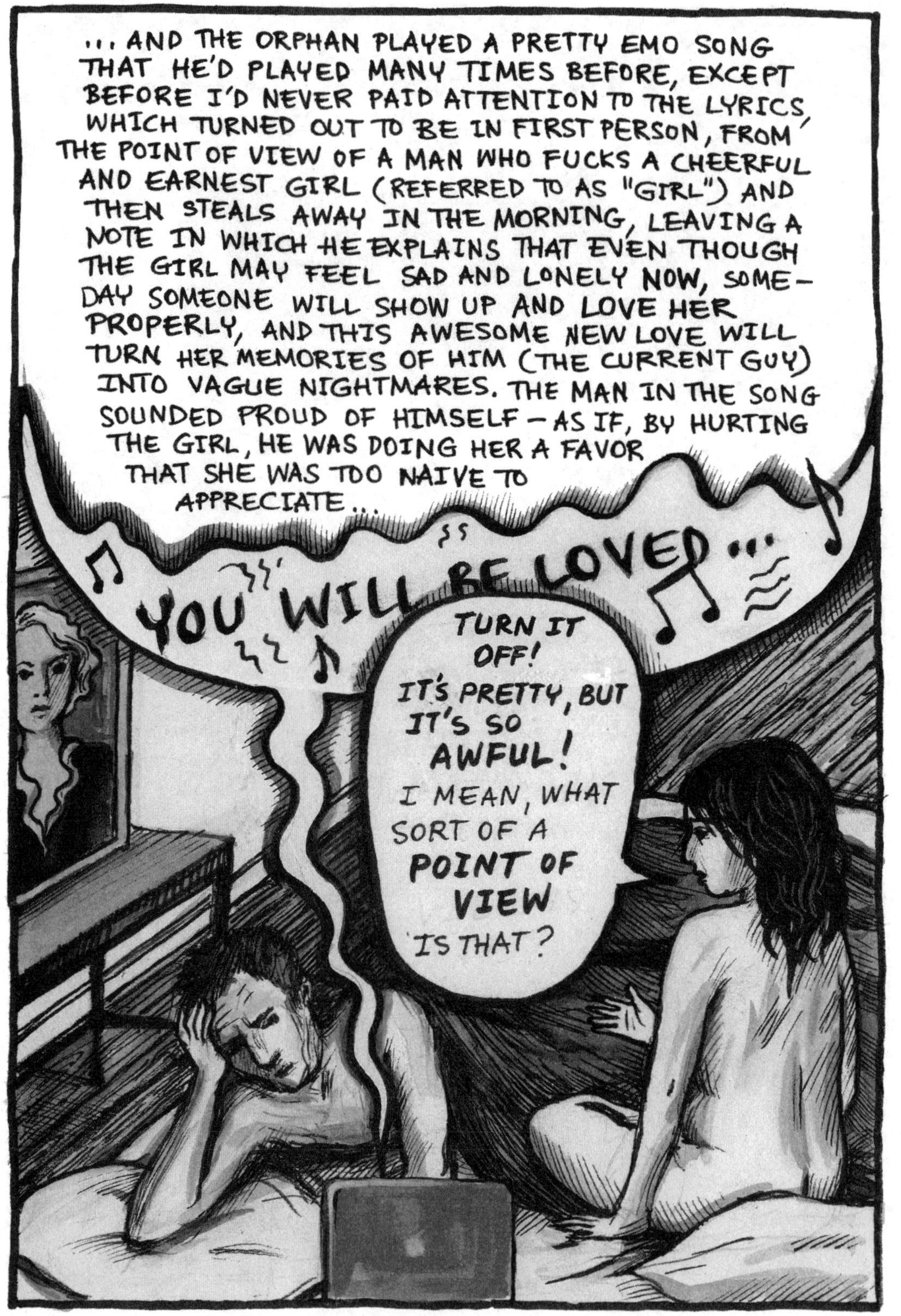
...AND THE ORPHAN PLAYED A PRETTY EMO SONG THAT HE'D PLAYED MANY TIMES BEFORE, EXCEPT BEFORE I'D NEVER PAID ATTENTION TO THE LYRICS, WHICH TURNED OUT TO BE IN FIRST PERSON, FROM THE POINT OF VIEW OF A MAN WHO FUCKS A CHEERFUL AND EARNEST GIRL (REFERRED TO AS "GIRL") AND THEN STEALS AWAY IN THE MORNING, LEAVING A NOTE IN WHICH HE EXPLAINS THAT EVEN THOUGH THE GIRL MAY FEEL SAD AND LONELY NOW, SOMEDAY SOMEONE WILL SHOW UP AND LOVE HER PROPERLY, AND THIS AWESOME NEW LOVE WILL TURN HER MEMORIES OF HIM (THE CURRENT GUY) INTO VAGUE NIGHTMARES. THE MAN IN THE SONG SOUNDED PROUD OF HIMSELF — AS IF, BY HURTING THE GIRL, HE WAS DOING HER A FAVOR THAT SHE WAS TOO NAIVE TO APPRECIATE...
YOU WILL BE LOVED...
TURN IT OFF! IT'S PRETTY, BUT IT'S SO AWFUL! I MEAN, WHAT SORT OF A POINT OF VIEW IS THAT?

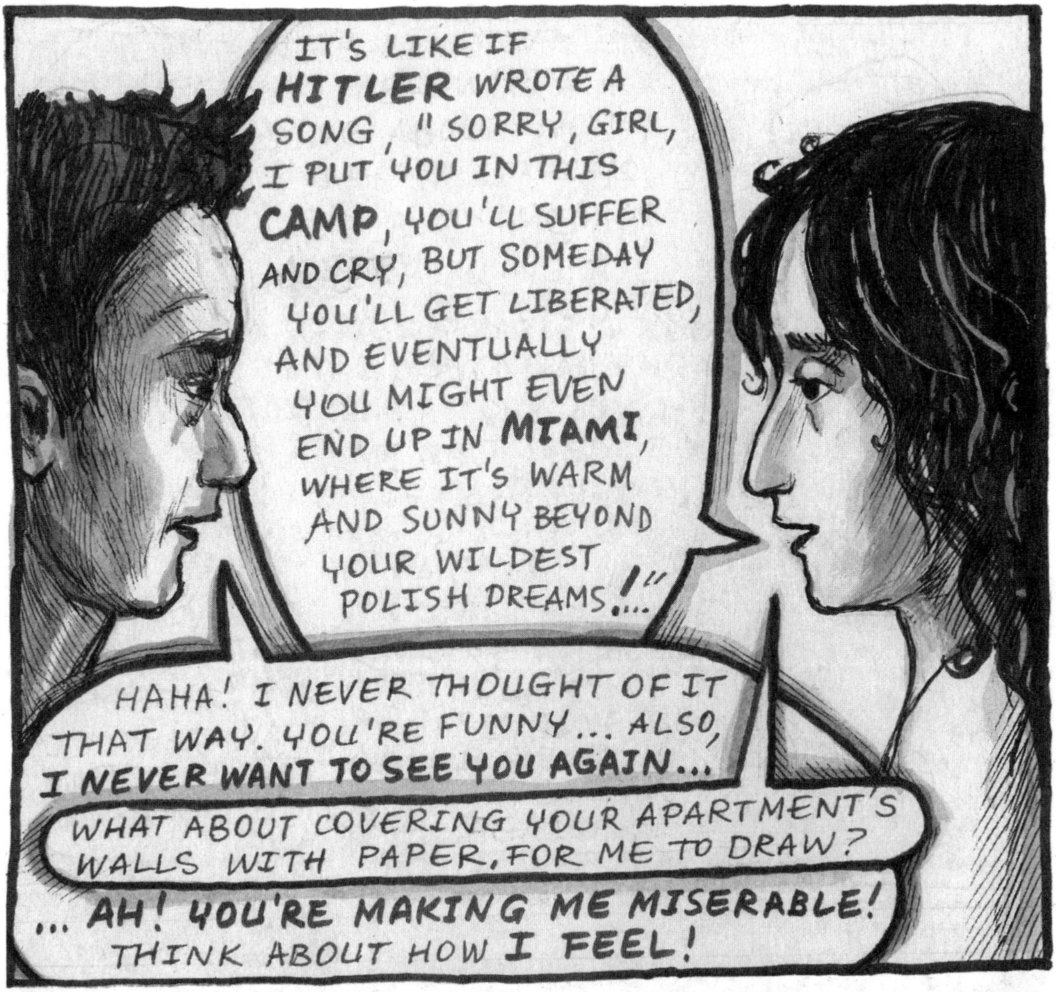
IT'S LIKE IF HITLER WROTE A SONG, "SORRY, GIRL, I PUT YOU IN THIS CAMP, YOU'LL SUFFER AND CRY, BUT SOMEDAY YOU'LL GET LIBERATED, AND EVENTUALLY YOU MIGHT EVEN END UP IN MIAMI, WHERE IT'S WARM AND SUNNY BEYOND YOUR WILDEST POLISH DREAMS!"...
HAHA! I NEVER THOUGHT OF IT THAT WAY. YOU'RE FUNNY... ALSO, I NEVER WANT TO SEE YOU AGAIN...
WHAT ABOUT COVERING YOUR APARTMENT'S WALLS WITH PAPER, FOR ME TO DRAW?
... AH! YOU'RE MAKING ME MISERABLE! THINK ABOUT HOW I FEEL!

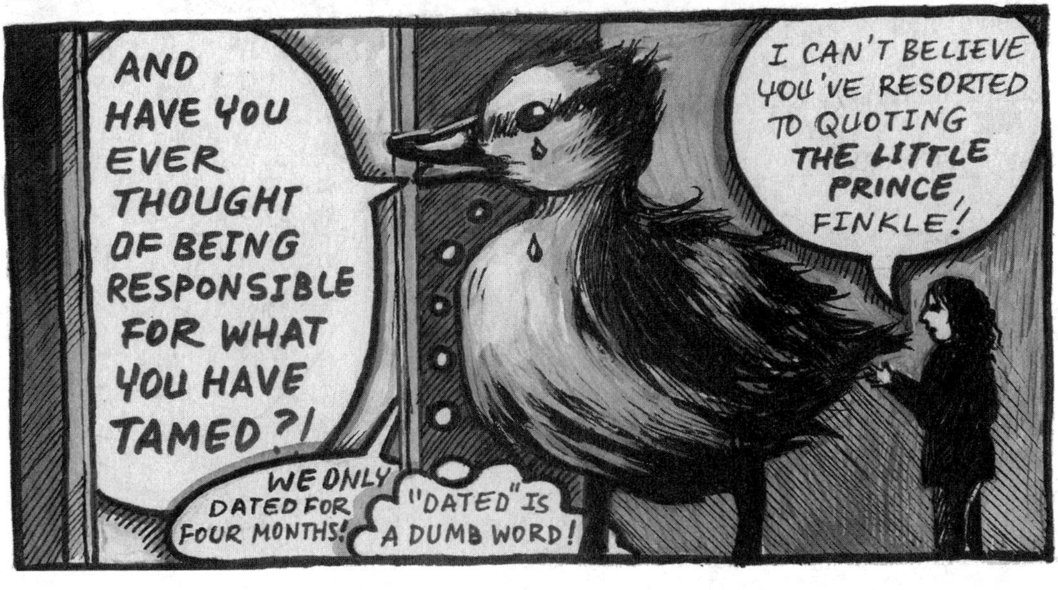
AND HAVE YOU EVER THOUGHT OF BEING RESPONSIBLE FOR WHAT YOU HAVE TAMED?!
I CAN'T BELIEVE YOU'VE RESORTED TO QUOTING THE LITTLE PRINCE, FINKLE!
WE ONLY DATED FOR FOUR MONTHS!
"DATED" IS A DUMB WORD!

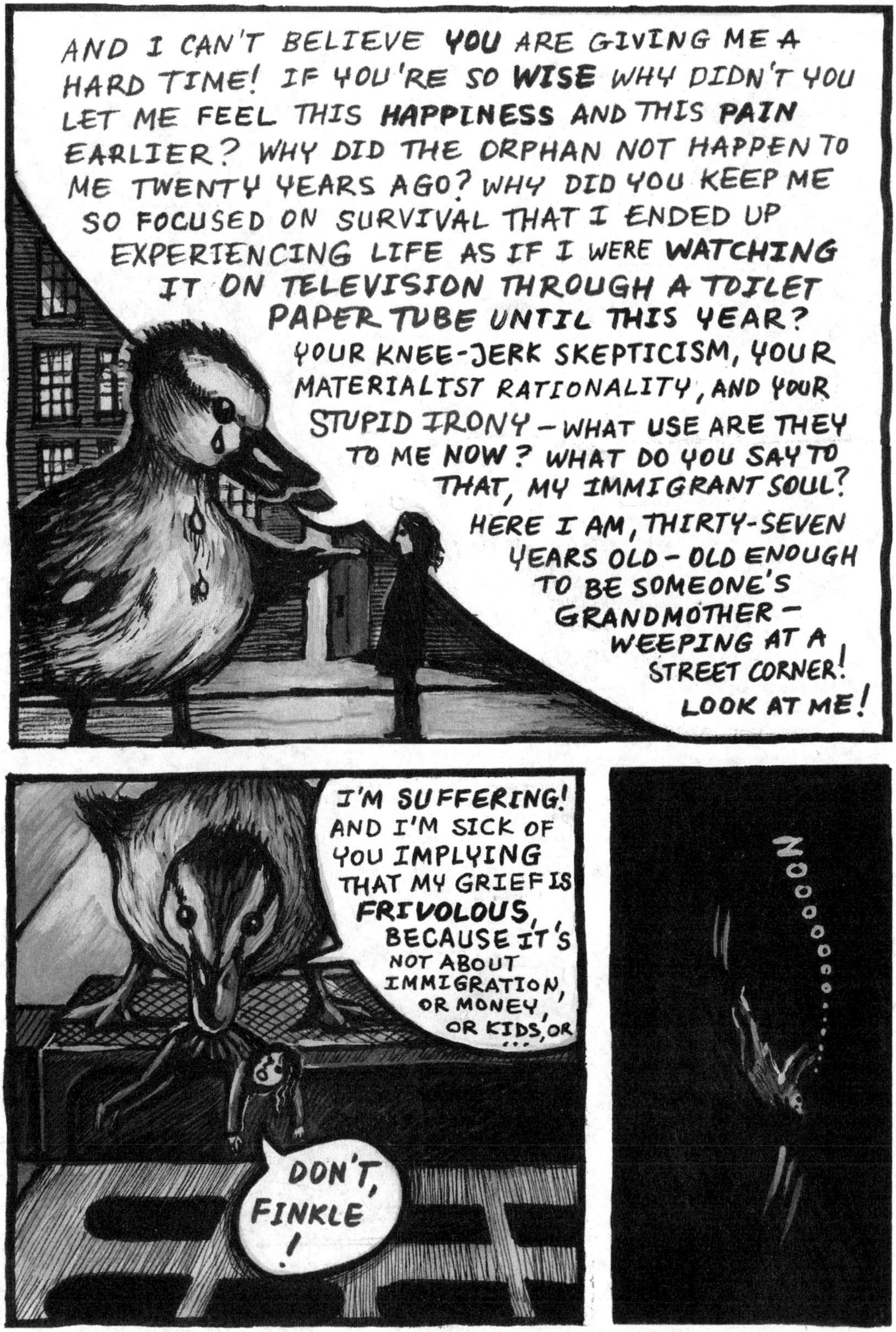
AND I CAN'T BELIEVE **YOU** ARE GIVING ME A HARD TIME! IF YOU'RE SO **WISE** WHY DIDN'T YOU LET ME FEEL THIS **HAPPINESS** AND THIS **PAIN** EARLIER? WHY DID THE ORPHAN NOT HAPPEN TO ME TWENTY YEARS AGO? WHY DID YOU KEEP ME SO FOCUSED ON SURVIVAL THAT I ENDED UP EXPERIENCING LIFE AS IF I WERE **WATCHING IT ON TELEVISION THROUGH A TOILET PAPER TUBE** UNTIL THIS YEAR?
YOUR KNEE-JERK SKEPTICISM, YOUR MATERIALIST RATIONALITY, AND YOUR STUPID IRONY – WHAT USE ARE THEY TO ME **NOW**? WHAT DO YOU SAY TO THAT, MY IMMIGRANT SOUL?
HERE I AM, THIRTY-SEVEN YEARS OLD – OLD ENOUGH TO BE SOMEONE'S GRANDMOTHER – WEEPING AT A STREET CORNER!
LOOK AT ME!
I'M **SUFFERING**! AND I'M SICK OF YOU **IMPLYING** THAT MY GRIEF IS **FRIVOLOUS**, BECAUSE IT'S NOT ABOUT IMMIGRATION, OR MONEY, OR KIDS, OR ...
DON'T, FINKLE!
NOOOOOOOOO......

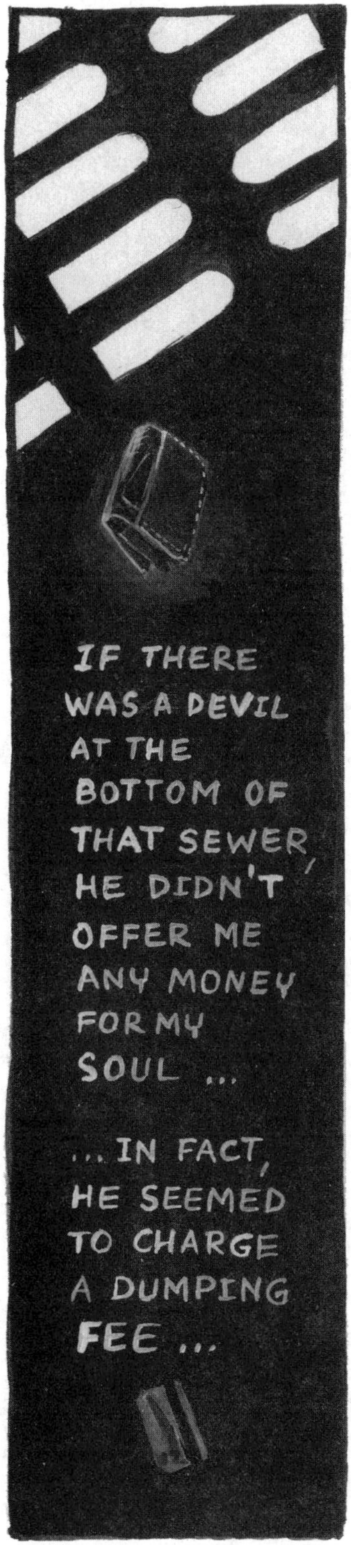
IF THERE WAS A DEVIL AT THE BOTTOM OF THAT SEWER, HE DIDN'T OFFER ME ANY MONEY FOR MY SOUL ...
... IN FACT, HE SEEMED TO CHARGE A DUMPING FEE ...

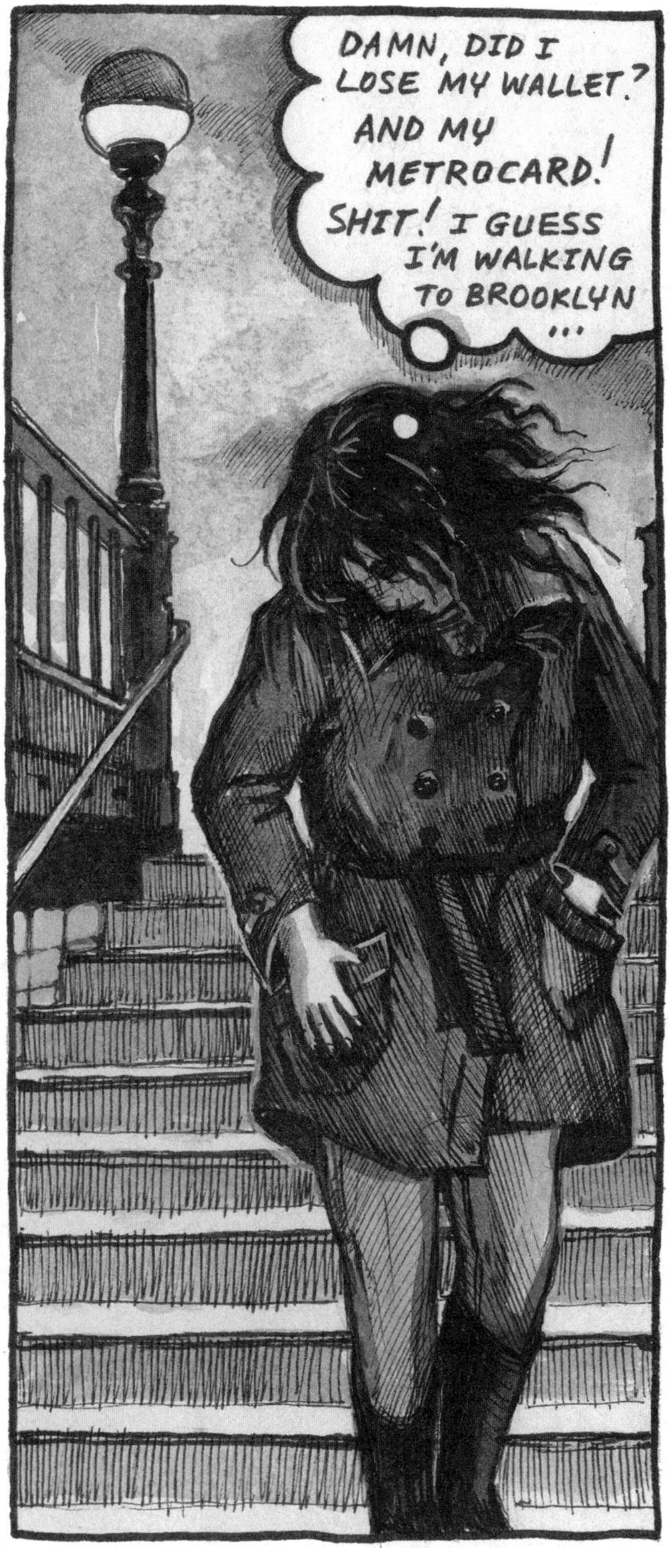
DAMN, DID I LOSE MY WALLET? AND MY METROCARD! SHIT! I GUESS I'M WALKING TO BROOKLYN ...

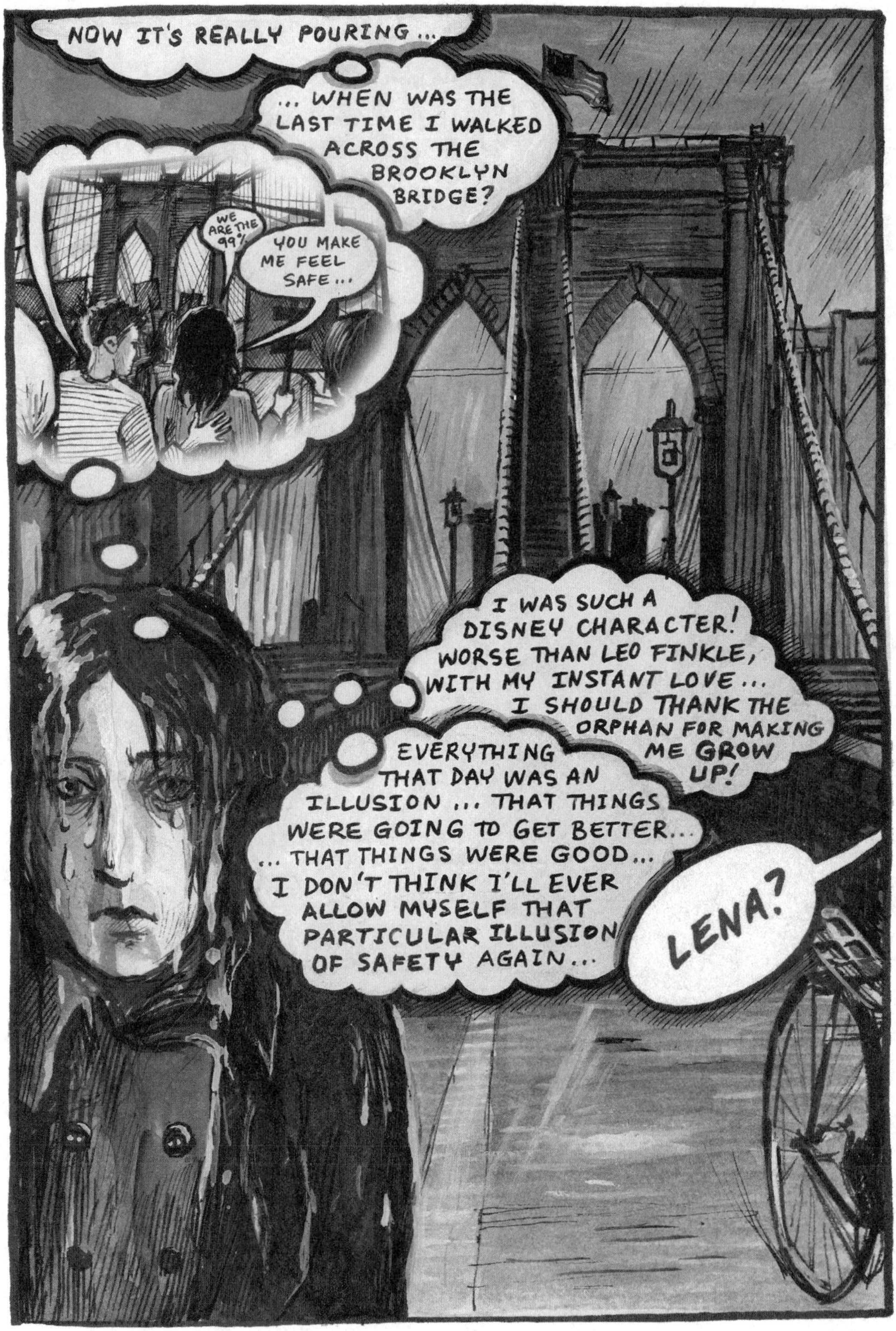
NOW IT'S REALLY POURING...
... WHEN WAS THE LAST TIME I WALKED ACROSS THE BROOKLYN BRIDGE?
WE ARE THE 99%
YOU MAKE ME FEEL SAFE...
I WAS SUCH A DISNEY CHARACTER! WORSE THAN LEO FINKLE, WITH MY INSTANT LOVE... I SHOULD THANK THE ORPHAN FOR MAKING ME GROW UP!
EVERYTHING THAT DAY WAS AN ILLUSION ... THAT THINGS WERE GOING TO GET BETTER... ... THAT THINGS WERE GOOD... I DON'T THINK I'LL EVER ALLOW MYSELF THAT PARTICULAR ILLUSION OF SAFETY AGAIN...
LENA?

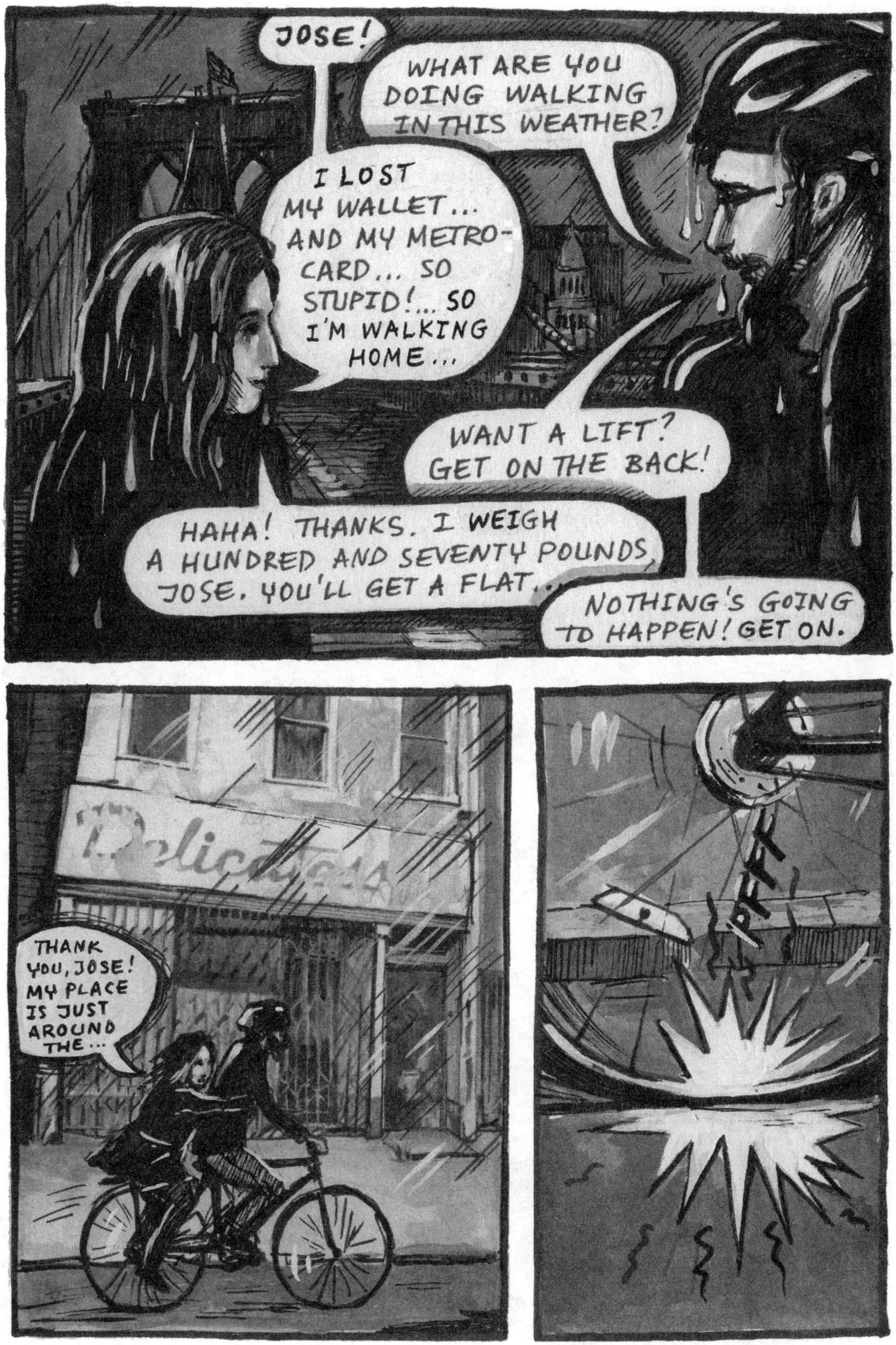
JOSE!
WHAT ARE YOU DOING WALKING IN THIS WEATHER?
I LOST MY WALLET... AND MY METRO-CARD... SO STUPID!... SO I'M WALKING HOME...
WANT A LIFT? GET ON THE BACK!
HAHA! THANKS. I WEIGH A HUNDRED AND SEVENTY POUNDS, JOSE. YOU'LL GET A FLAT...
NOTHING'S GOING TO HAPPEN! GET ON.
THANK YOU, JOSE! MY PLACE IS JUST AROUND THE...
PFFT

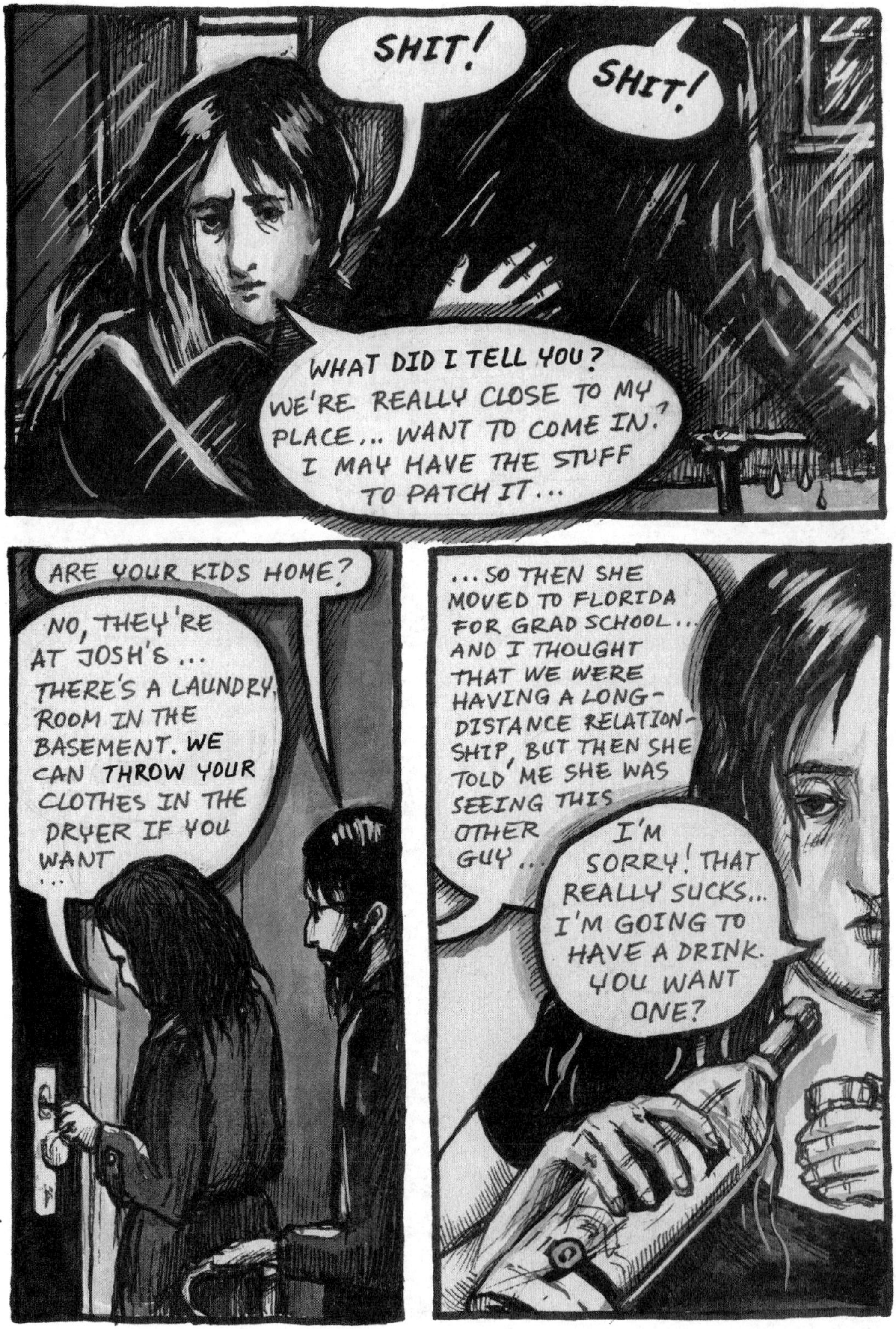
SHIT!
SHIT!
WHAT DID I TELL YOU? WE'RE REALLY CLOSE TO MY PLACE... WANT TO COME IN? I MAY HAVE THE STUFF TO PATCH IT...
ARE YOUR KIDS HOME?
NO, THEY'RE AT JOSH'S... THERE'S A LAUNDRY ROOM IN THE BASEMENT. WE CAN THROW YOUR CLOTHES IN THE DRYER IF YOU WANT...
...SO THEN SHE MOVED TO FLORIDA FOR GRAD SCHOOL... AND I THOUGHT THAT WE WERE HAVING A LONG-DISTANCE RELATIONSHIP, BUT THEN SHE TOLD ME SHE WAS SEEING THIS OTHER GUY...
I'M SORRY! THAT REALLY SUCKS... I'M GOING TO HAVE A DRINK. YOU WANT ONE?

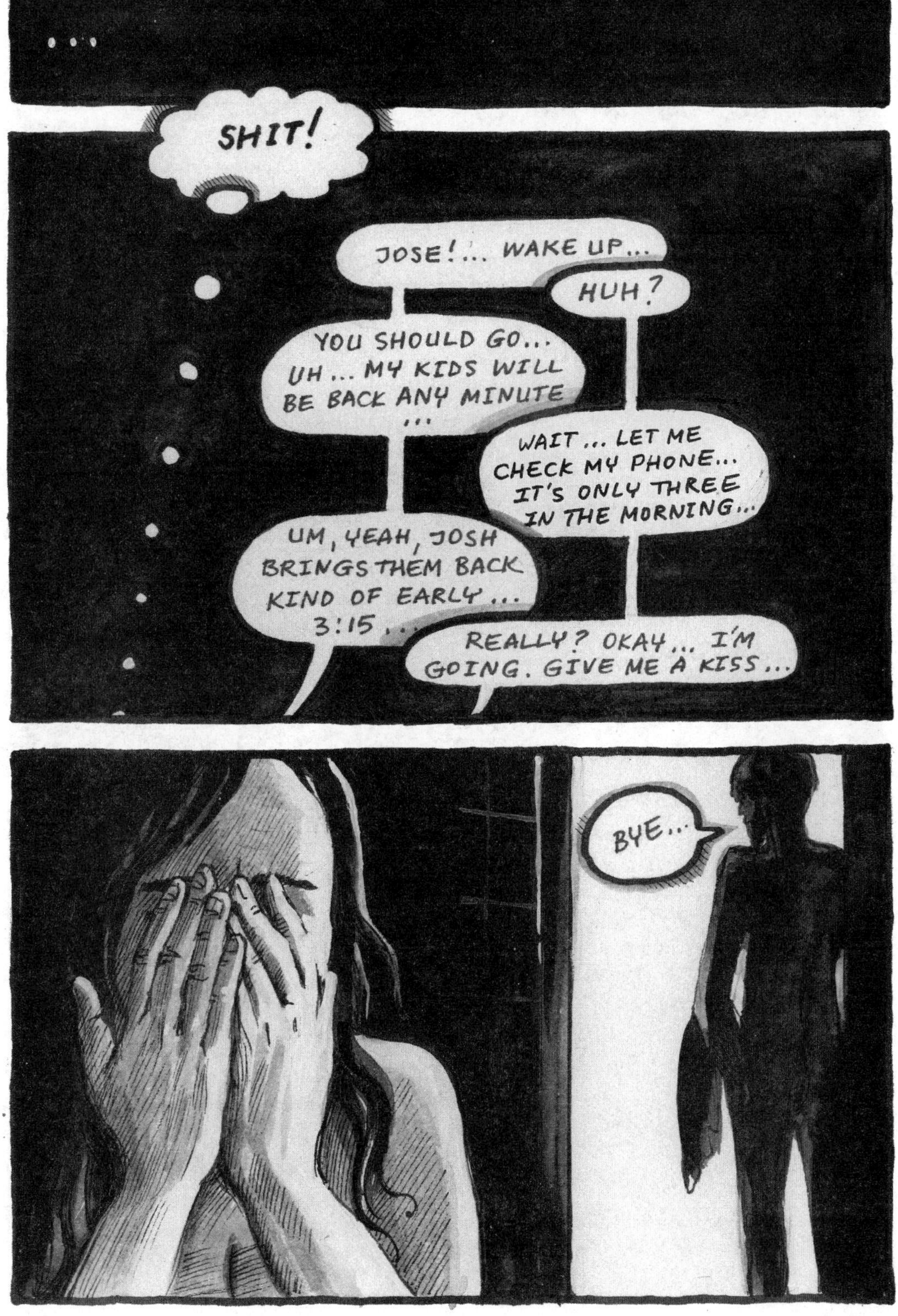
...
SHIT!
JOSE!... WAKE UP...
HUH?
YOU SHOULD GO... UH... MY KIDS WILL BE BACK ANY MINUTE ...
WAIT... LET ME CHECK MY PHONE... IT'S ONLY THREE IN THE MORNING...
UM, YEAH, JOSH BRINGS THEM BACK KIND OF EARLY... 3:15...
REALLY? OKAY... I'M GOING. GIVE ME A KISS...
BYE...

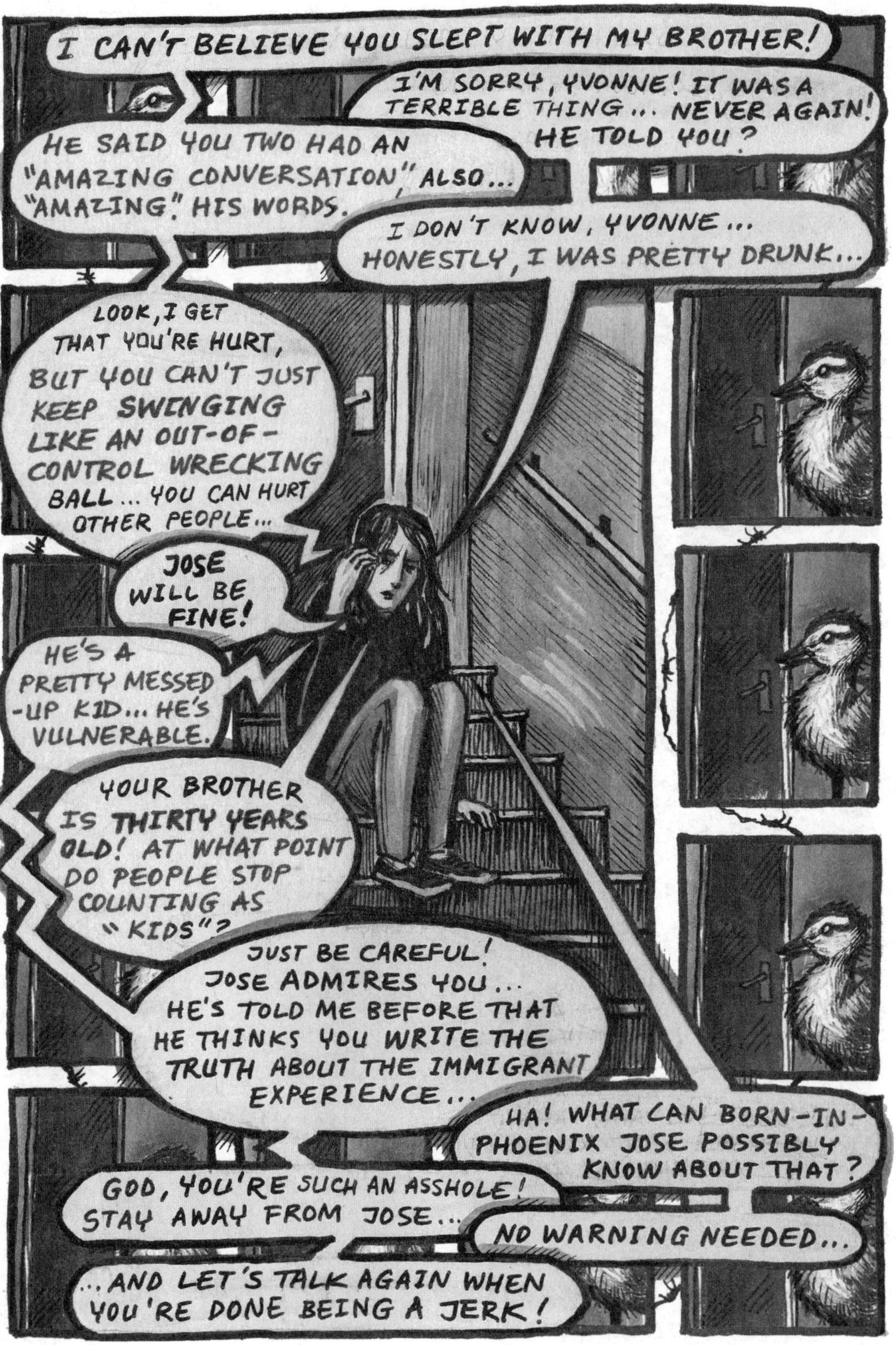
I CAN'T BELIEVE YOU SLEPT WITH MY BROTHER!
I'M SORRY, YVONNE! IT WAS A TERRIBLE THING... NEVER AGAIN! HE TOLD YOU?
HE SAID YOU TWO HAD AN "AMAZING CONVERSATION," ALSO... "AMAZING." HIS WORDS.
I DON'T KNOW, YVONNE... HONESTLY, I WAS PRETTY DRUNK...
LOOK, I GET THAT YOU'RE HURT, BUT YOU CAN'T JUST KEEP SWINGING LIKE AN OUT-OF-CONTROL WRECKING BALL... YOU CAN HURT OTHER PEOPLE...
JOSE WILL BE FINE!
HE'S A PRETTY MESSED-UP KID... HE'S VULNERABLE.
YOUR BROTHER IS THIRTY YEARS OLD! AT WHAT POINT DO PEOPLE STOP COUNTING AS "KIDS"?
JUST BE CAREFUL! JOSE ADMIRES YOU... HE'S TOLD ME BEFORE THAT HE THINKS YOU WRITE THE TRUTH ABOUT THE IMMIGRANT EXPERIENCE...
HA! WHAT CAN BORN-IN-PHOENIX JOSE POSSIBLY KNOW ABOUT THAT?
GOD, YOU'RE SUCH AN ASSHOLE! STAY AWAY FROM JOSE...
NO WARNING NEEDED...
...AND LET'S TALK AGAIN WHEN YOU'RE DONE BEING A JERK!

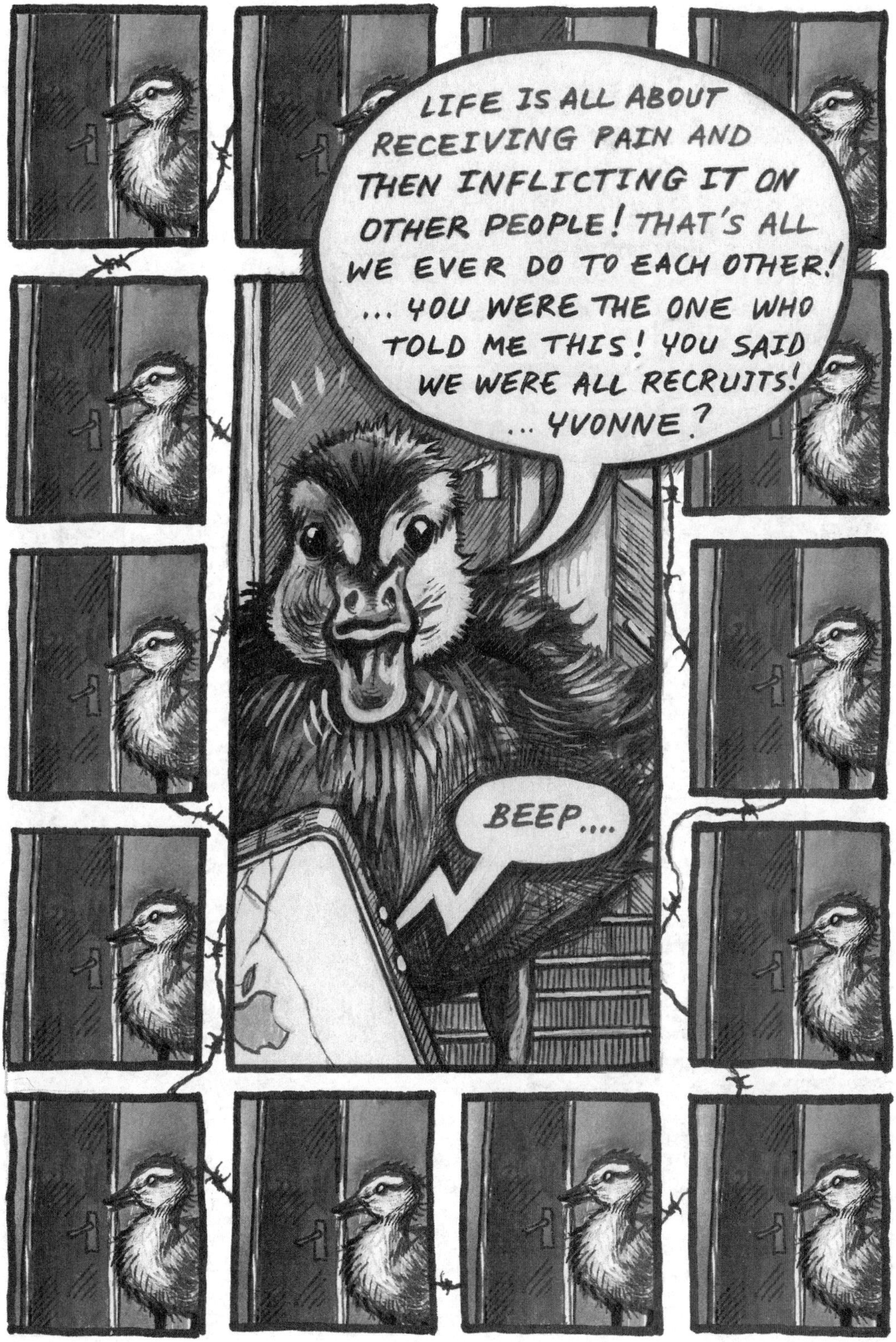
LIFE IS ALL ABOUT RECEIVING PAIN AND THEN INFLICTING IT ON OTHER PEOPLE! THAT'S ALL WE EVER DO TO EACH OTHER! ... YOU WERE THE ONE WHO TOLD ME THIS! YOU SAID WE WERE ALL RECRUITS! ... YVONNE?
BEEP....

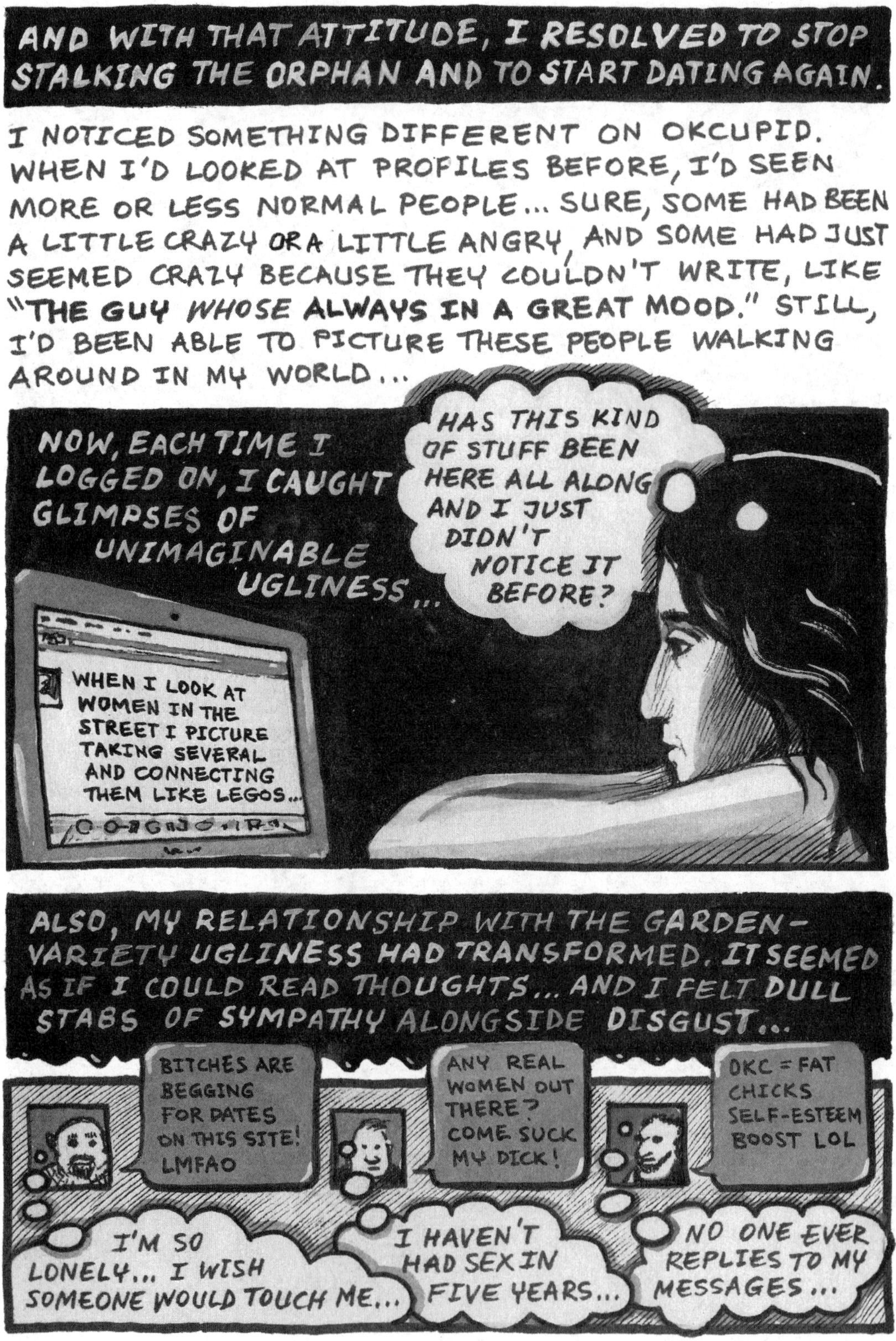
AND WITH THAT ATTITUDE, I RESOLVED TO STOP STALKING THE ORPHAN AND TO START DATING AGAIN.
I NOTICED SOMETHING DIFFERENT ON OKCUPID. WHEN I'D LOOKED AT PROFILES BEFORE, I'D SEEN MORE OR LESS NORMAL PEOPLE... SURE, SOME HAD BEEN A LITTLE CRAZY OR A LITTLE ANGRY, AND SOME HAD JUST SEEMED CRAZY BECAUSE THEY COULDN'T WRITE, LIKE "THE GUY *WHOSE* ALWAYS IN A GREAT MOOD." STILL, I'D BEEN ABLE TO PICTURE THESE PEOPLE WALKING AROUND IN MY WORLD...
NOW, EACH TIME I LOGGED ON, I CAUGHT GLIMPSES OF UNIMAGINABLE UGLINESS...
HAS THIS KIND OF STUFF BEEN HERE ALL ALONG AND I JUST DIDN'T NOTICE IT BEFORE?
WHEN I LOOK AT WOMEN IN THE STREET I PICTURE TAKING SEVERAL AND CONNECTING THEM LIKE LEGOS...
ALSO, MY RELATIONSHIP WITH THE GARDEN-VARIETY UGLINESS HAD TRANSFORMED. IT SEEMED AS IF I COULD READ THOUGHTS... AND I FELT DULL STABS OF SYMPATHY ALONGSIDE DISGUST...
BITCHES ARE BEGGING FOR DATES ON THIS SITE! LMFAO
ANY REAL WOMEN OUT THERE? COME SUCK MY DICK!
OKC = FAT CHICKS SELF-ESTEEM BOOST LOL
I'M SO LONELY... I WISH SOMEONE WOULD TOUCH ME...
I HAVEN'T HAD SEX IN FIVE YEARS...
NO ONE EVER REPLIES TO MY MESSAGES...

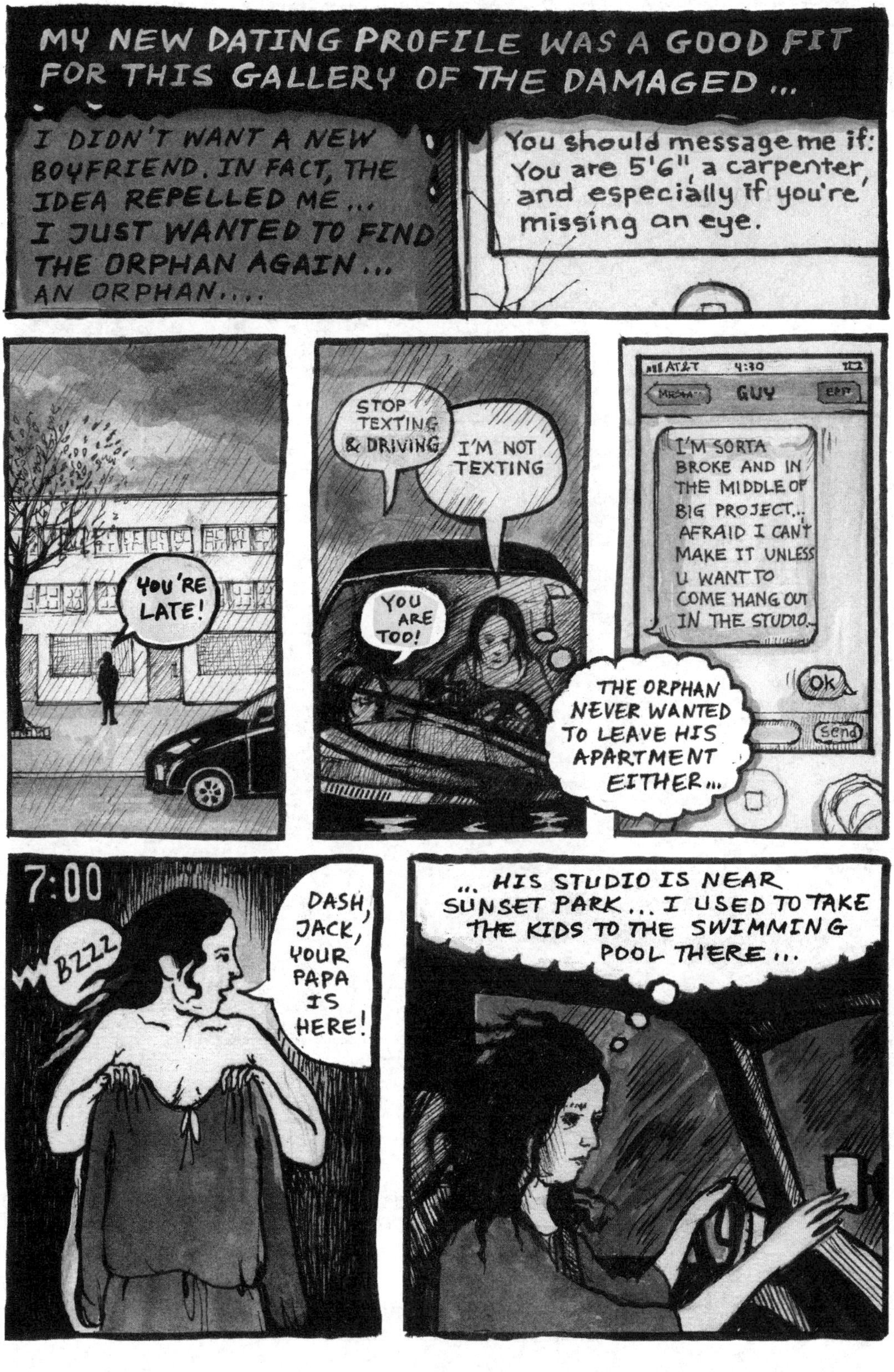
MY NEW DATING PROFILE WAS A GOOD FIT FOR THIS GALLERY OF THE DAMAGED...
I DIDN'T WANT A NEW BOYFRIEND. IN FACT, THE IDEA REPELLED ME... I JUST WANTED TO FIND THE ORPHAN AGAIN... AN ORPHAN....
You should message me if: You are 5'6", a carpenter, and especially if you're missing an eye.
YOU'RE LATE!
STOP TEXTING & DRIVING
I'M NOT TEXTING
YOU ARE TOO!
AT&T 4:30
GUY
I'M SORTA BROKE AND IN THE MIDDLE OF BIG PROJECT... AFRAID I CAN'T MAKE IT UNLESS U WANT TO COME HANG OUT IN THE STUDIO...
Ok
Send
THE ORPHAN NEVER WANTED TO LEAVE HIS APARTMENT EITHER...
7:00
BZZZ
DASH, JACK, YOUR PAPA IS HERE!
... HIS STUDIO IS NEAR SUNSET PARK... I USED TO TAKE THE KIDS TO THE SWIMMING POOL THERE...

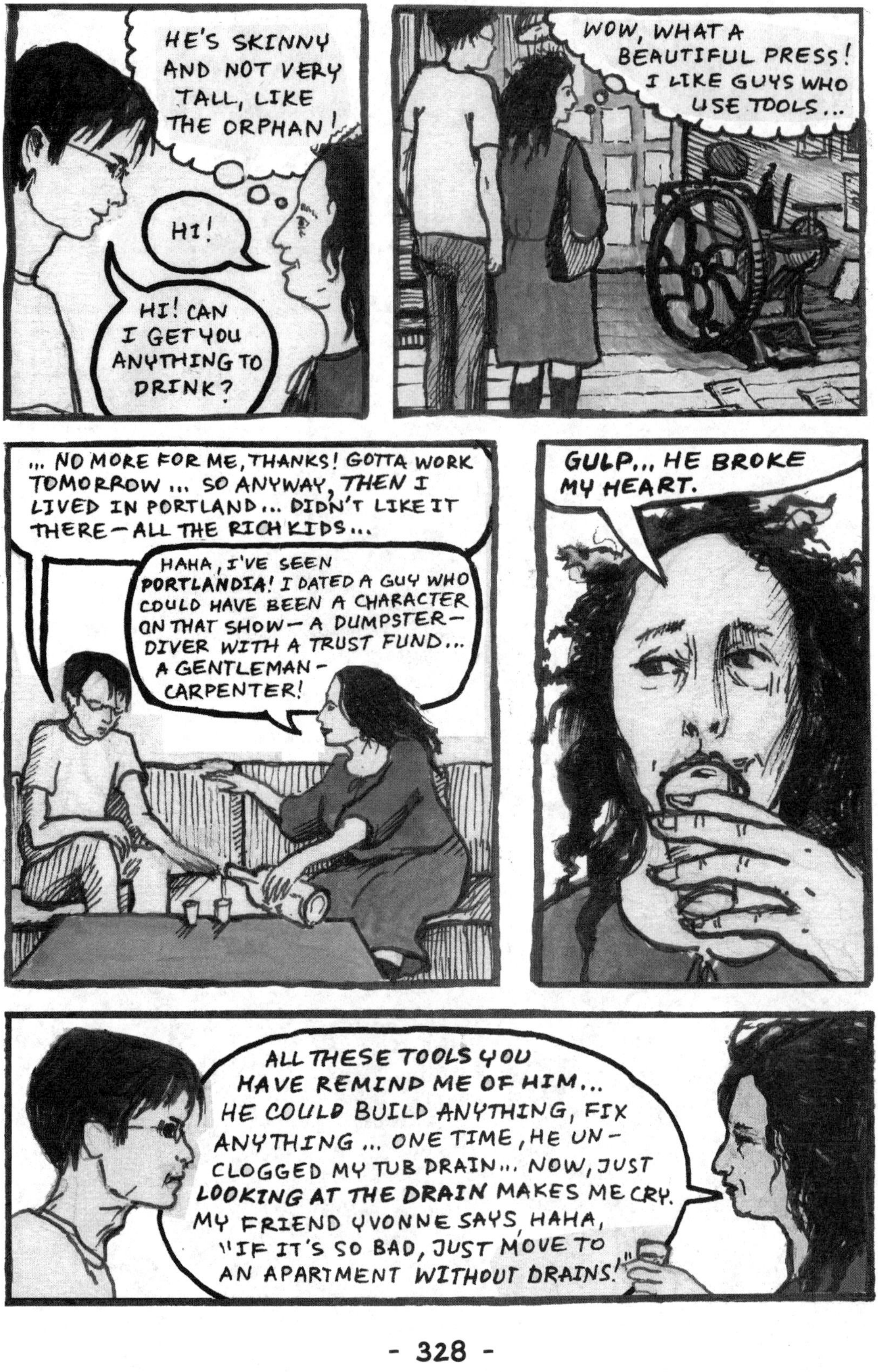

HE'S SKINNY AND NOT VERY TALL, LIKE THE ORPHAN!
HI!
HI! CAN I GET YOU ANYTHING TO DRINK?
WOW, WHAT A BEAUTIFUL PRESS! I LIKE GUYS WHO USE TOOLS...
... NO MORE FOR ME, THANKS! GOTTA WORK TOMORROW... SO ANYWAY, THEN I LIVED IN PORTLAND... DIDN'T LIKE IT THERE—ALL THE RICH KIDS...
HAHA, I'VE SEEN PORTLANDIA! I DATED A GUY WHO COULD HAVE BEEN A CHARACTER ON THAT SHOW—A DUMPSTER-DIVER WITH A TRUST FUND... A GENTLEMAN-CARPENTER!
GULP... HE BROKE MY HEART.
ALL THESE TOOLS YOU HAVE REMIND ME OF HIM... HE COULD BUILD ANYTHING, FIX ANYTHING... ONE TIME, HE UN-CLOGGED MY TUB DRAIN... NOW, JUST LOOKING AT THE DRAIN MAKES ME CRY. MY FRIEND YVONNE SAYS, HAHA, "IF IT'S SO BAD, JUST MOVE TO AN APARTMENT WITHOUT DRAINS!"

I'M TRYING TO GET OVER HIM... ALL MY FRIENDS...

WHY IS HE DOING THIS WEIRD THING WITH HIS TONGUE?

...YVONNE ALSO SAYS THAT I SHOULD NEVER HAVE SEX ON THE FIRST DATE, ESPECIALLY WITH AN OVER-EDUCATED WHITE GUY BECAUSE...

HAHA, I TOLD YOU, I DROPPED OUT...

HAHA...

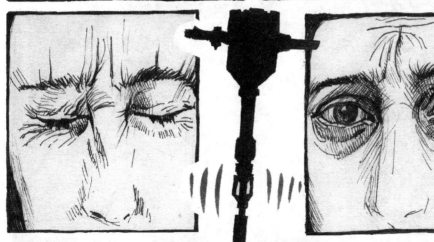

BYE

DAMN, IT'S LATE... IS THERE A WORD FOR A SORT-OF-CONSENSUAL SEX THAT FEELS LIKE RAPE? SEMI-RAPE?... ...WHERE DID I PARK?...

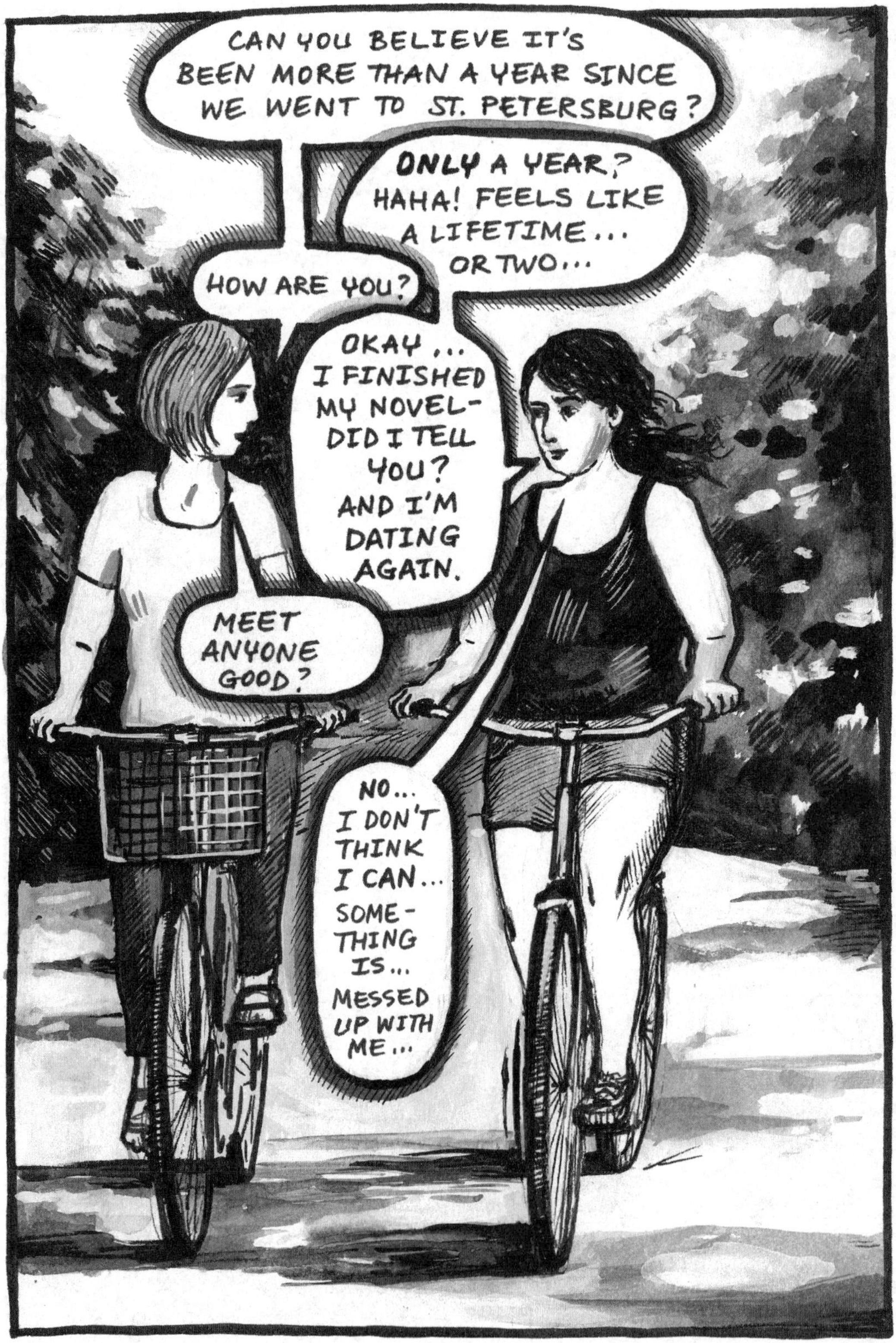
CAN YOU BELIEVE IT'S BEEN MORE THAN A YEAR SINCE WE WENT TO ST. PETERSBURG?
HOW ARE YOU?
ONLY A YEAR? HAHA! FEELS LIKE A LIFETIME... OR TWO...
OKAY... I FINISHED MY NOVEL- DID I TELL YOU? AND I'M DATING AGAIN.
MEET ANYONE GOOD?
NO... I DON'T THINK I CAN... SOME-THING IS... MESSED UP WITH ME...

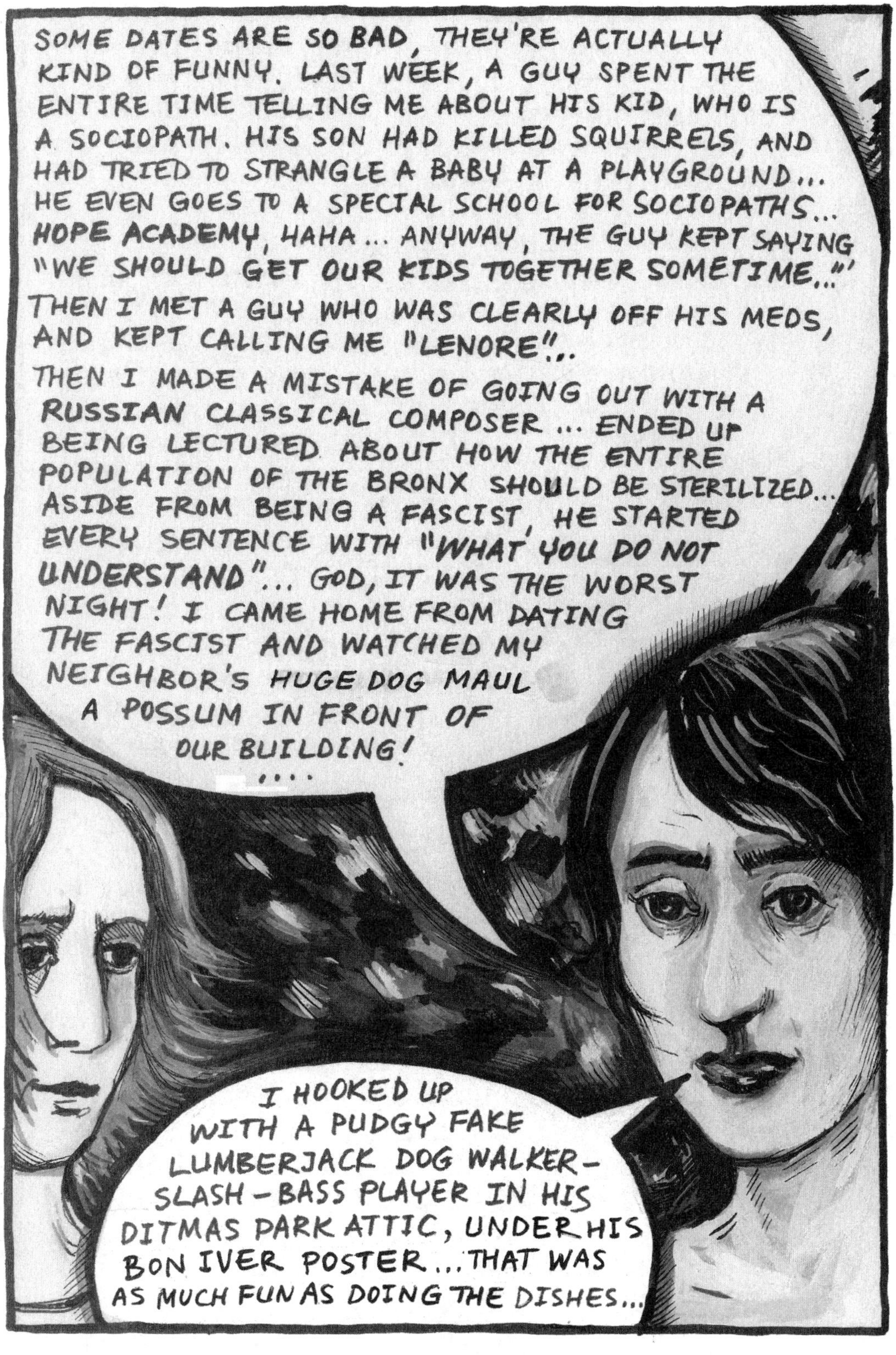
SOME DATES ARE SO BAD, THEY'RE ACTUALLY KIND OF FUNNY. LAST WEEK, A GUY SPENT THE ENTIRE TIME TELLING ME ABOUT HIS KID, WHO IS A SOCIOPATH. HIS SON HAD KILLED SQUIRRELS, AND HAD TRIED TO STRANGLE A BABY AT A PLAYGROUND... HE EVEN GOES TO A SPECIAL SCHOOL FOR SOCIOPATHS... HOPE ACADEMY, HAHA... ANYWAY, THE GUY KEPT SAYING "WE SHOULD GET OUR KIDS TOGETHER SOMETIME..." THEN I MET A GUY WHO WAS CLEARLY OFF HIS MEDS, AND KEPT CALLING ME "LENORE"... THEN I MADE A MISTAKE OF GOING OUT WITH A RUSSIAN CLASSICAL COMPOSER... ENDED UP BEING LECTURED ABOUT HOW THE ENTIRE POPULATION OF THE BRONX SHOULD BE STERILIZED... ASIDE FROM BEING A FASCIST, HE STARTED EVERY SENTENCE WITH "WHAT YOU DO NOT UNDERSTAND"... GOD, IT WAS THE WORST NIGHT! I CAME HOME FROM DATING THE FASCIST AND WATCHED MY NEIGHBOR'S HUGE DOG MAUL A POSSUM IN FRONT OF OUR BUILDING! ....
I HOOKED UP WITH A PUDGY FAKE LUMBERJACK DOG WALKER-SLASH-BASS PLAYER IN HIS DITMAS PARK ATTIC, UNDER HIS BON IVER POSTER... THAT WAS AS MUCH FUN AS DOING THE DISHES...

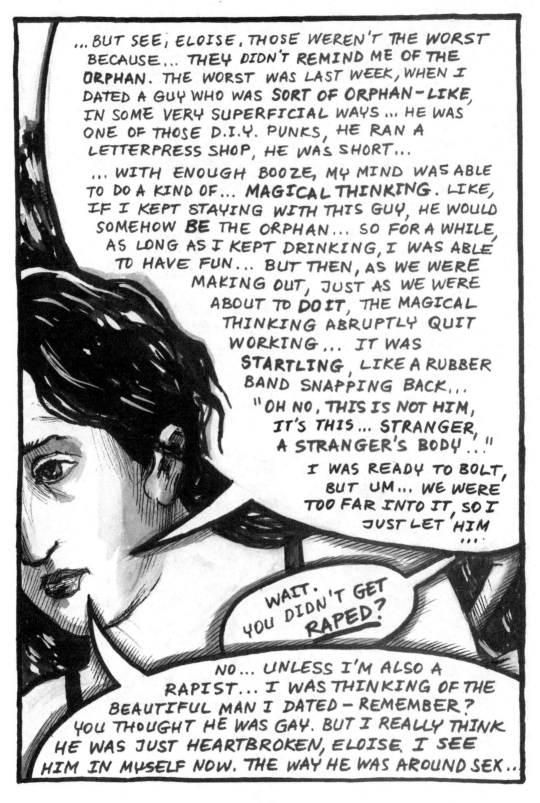

...BUT SEE, ELOISE, THOSE WEREN'T THE WORST BECAUSE... THEY DIDN'T REMIND ME OF THE ORPHAN. THE WORST WAS LAST WEEK, WHEN I DATED A GUY WHO WAS SORT OF ORPHAN-LIKE, IN SOME VERY SUPERFICIAL WAYS... HE WAS ONE OF THOSE D.I.Y. PUNKS, HE RAN A LETTERPRESS SHOP, HE WAS SHORT...

...WITH ENOUGH BOOZE, MY MIND WAS ABLE TO DO A KIND OF... MAGICAL THINKING. LIKE, IF I KEPT STAYING WITH THIS GUY, HE WOULD SOMEHOW BE THE ORPHAN... SO FOR A WHILE, AS LONG AS I KEPT DRINKING, I WAS ABLE TO HAVE FUN... BUT THEN, AS WE WERE MAKING OUT, JUST AS WE WERE ABOUT TO DO IT, THE MAGICAL THINKING ABRUPTLY QUIT WORKING... IT WAS STARTLING, LIKE A RUBBER BAND SNAPPING BACK...

"OH NO, THIS IS NOT HIM, IT'S THIS... STRANGER, A STRANGER'S BODY..."

I WAS READY TO BOLT, BUT UM... WE WERE TOO FAR INTO IT, SO I JUST LET HIM
...

WAIT. YOU DIDN'T GET RAPED?

NO... UNLESS I'M ALSO A RAPIST... I WAS THINKING OF THE BEAUTIFUL MAN I DATED — REMEMBER? YOU THOUGHT HE WAS GAY. BUT I REALLY THINK HE WAS JUST HEARTBROKEN, ELOISE. I SEE HIM IN MYSELF NOW. THE WAY HE WAS AROUND SEX...

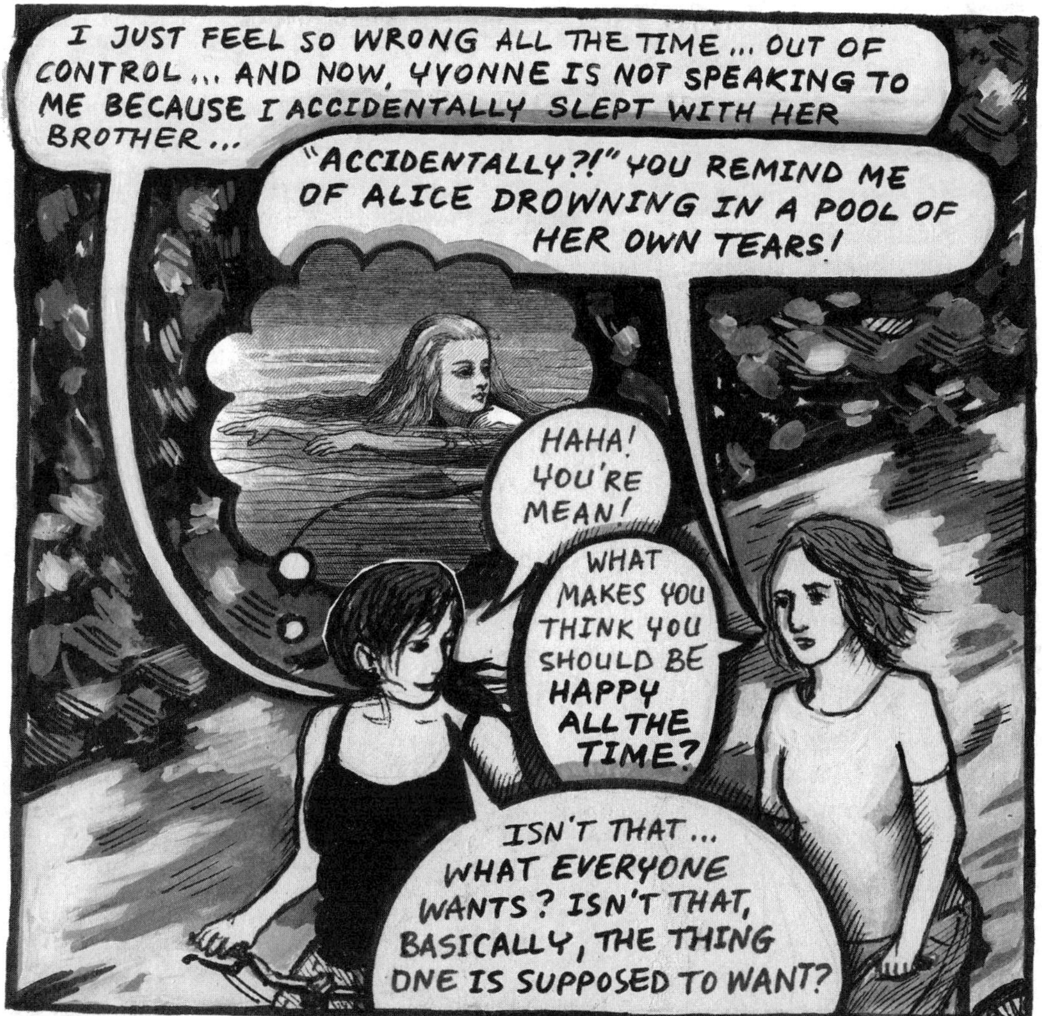
I JUST FEEL SO WRONG ALL THE TIME... OUT OF CONTROL... AND NOW, YVONNE IS NOT SPEAKING TO ME BECAUSE I ACCIDENTALLY SLEPT WITH HER BROTHER...
"ACCIDENTALLY?!" YOU REMIND ME OF ALICE DROWNING IN A POOL OF HER OWN TEARS!
HAHA! YOU'RE MEAN!
WHAT MAKES YOU THINK YOU SHOULD BE HAPPY ALL THE TIME?
ISN'T THAT... WHAT EVERYONE WANTS? ISN'T THAT, BASICALLY, THE THING ONE IS SUPPOSED TO WANT?
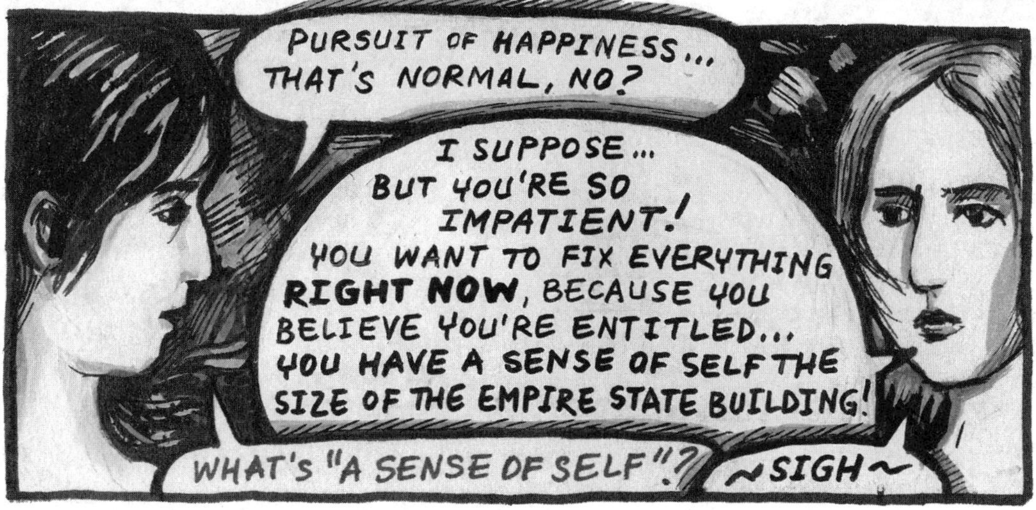
PURSUIT OF HAPPINESS... THAT'S NORMAL, NO?
I SUPPOSE... BUT YOU'RE SO IMPATIENT! YOU WANT TO FIX EVERYTHING RIGHT NOW, BECAUSE YOU BELIEVE YOU'RE ENTITLED... YOU HAVE A SENSE OF SELF THE SIZE OF THE EMPIRE STATE BUILDING!
WHAT'S "A SENSE OF SELF"?
~SIGH~

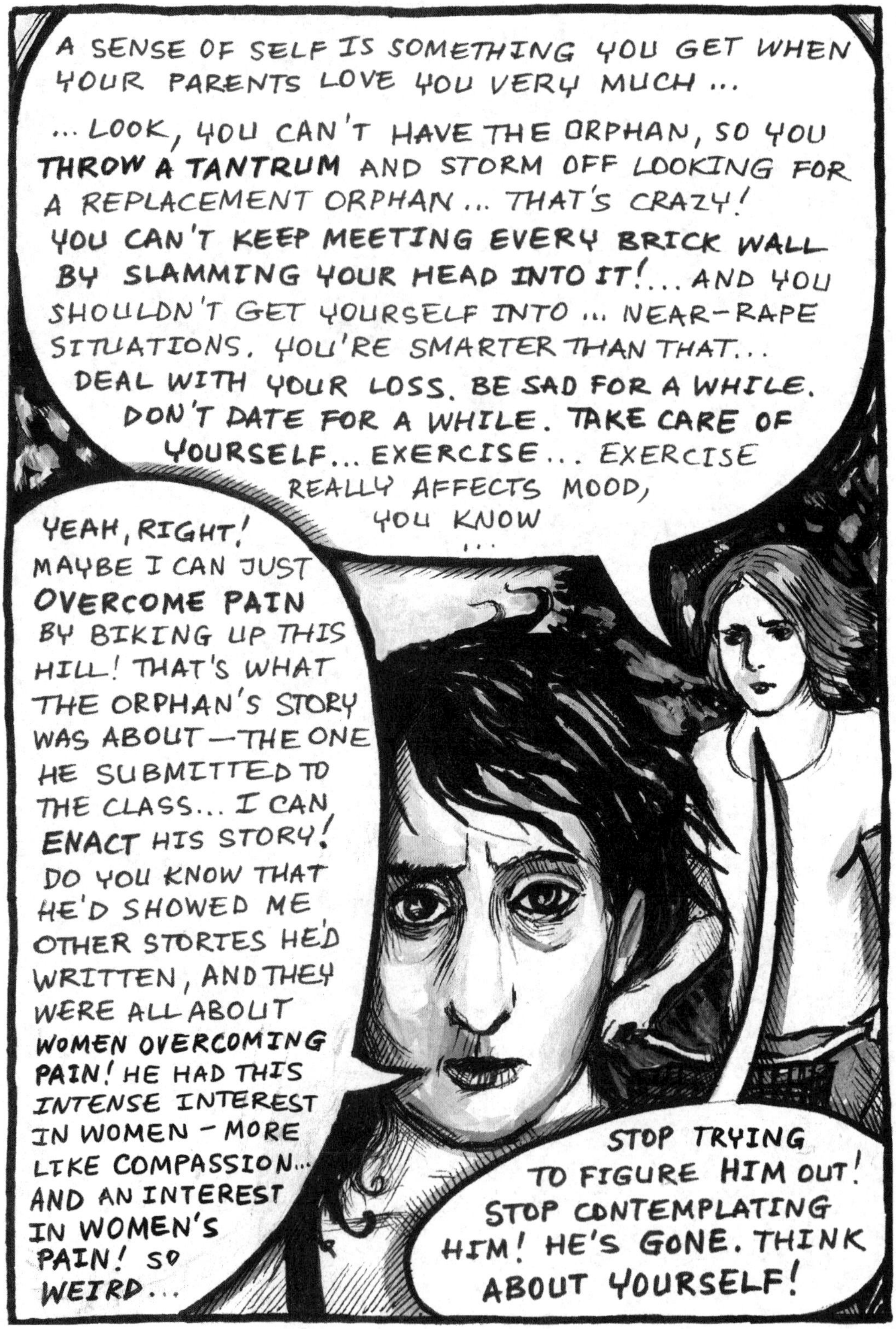
A SENSE OF SELF IS SOMETHING YOU GET WHEN YOUR PARENTS LOVE YOU VERY MUCH ...
... LOOK, YOU CAN'T HAVE THE ORPHAN, SO YOU THROW A TANTRUM AND STORM OFF LOOKING FOR A REPLACEMENT ORPHAN ... THAT'S CRAZY! YOU CAN'T KEEP MEETING EVERY BRICK WALL BY SLAMMING YOUR HEAD INTO IT! ... AND YOU SHOULDN'T GET YOURSELF INTO ... NEAR-RAPE SITUATIONS. YOU'RE SMARTER THAN THAT... DEAL WITH YOUR LOSS. BE SAD FOR A WHILE. DON'T DATE FOR A WHILE. TAKE CARE OF YOURSELF... EXERCISE... EXERCISE REALLY AFFECTS MOOD, YOU KNOW ...
YEAH, RIGHT! MAYBE I CAN JUST OVERCOME PAIN BY BIKING UP THIS HILL! THAT'S WHAT THE ORPHAN'S STORY WAS ABOUT — THE ONE HE SUBMITTED TO THE CLASS... I CAN ENACT HIS STORY! DO YOU KNOW THAT HE'D SHOWED ME OTHER STORIES HE'D WRITTEN, AND THEY WERE ALL ABOUT WOMEN OVERCOMING PAIN! HE HAD THIS INTENSE INTEREST IN WOMEN - MORE LIKE COMPASSION... AND AN INTEREST IN WOMEN'S PAIN! SO WEIRD...
STOP TRYING TO FIGURE HIM OUT! STOP CONTEMPLATING HIM! HE'S GONE. THINK ABOUT YOURSELF!

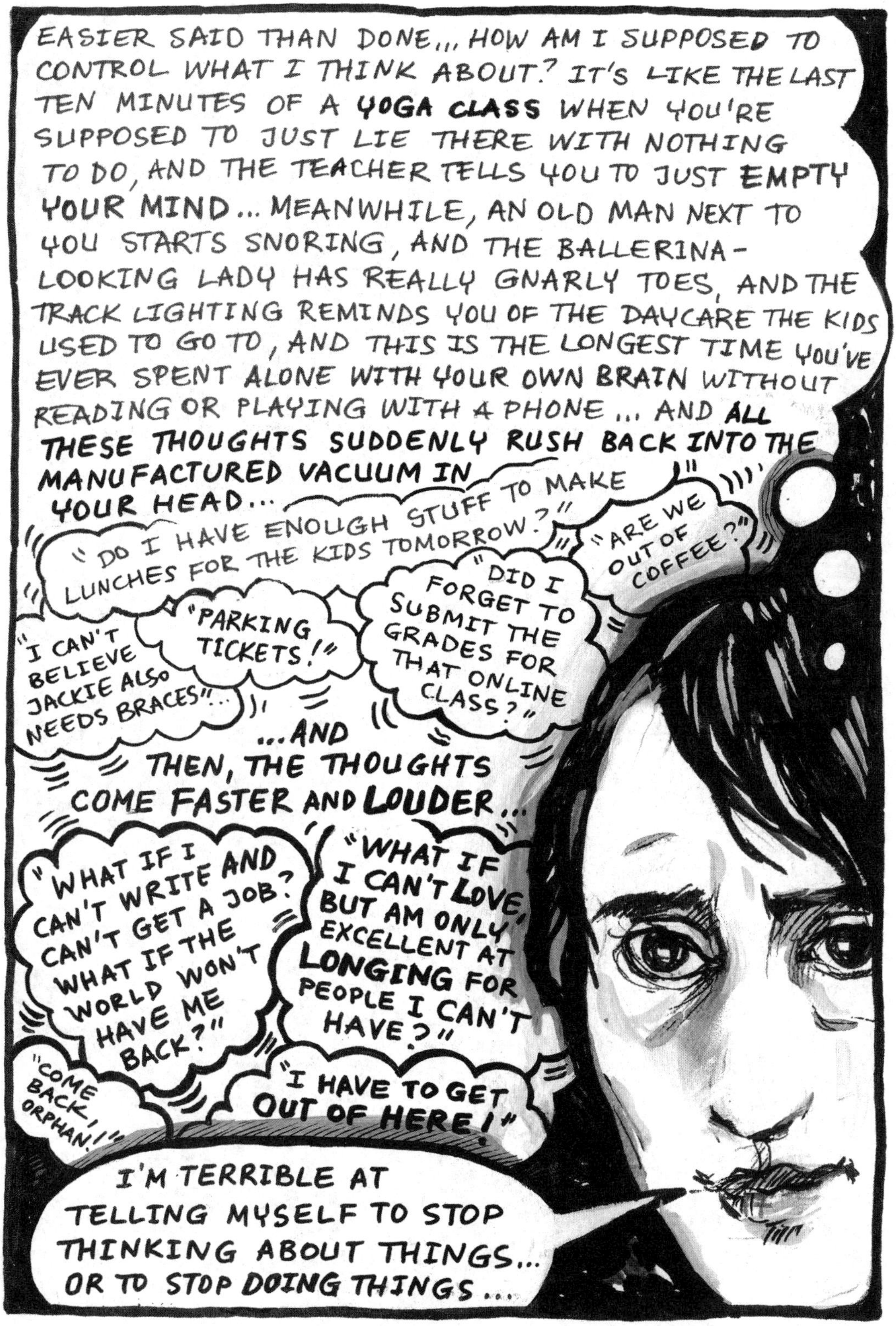
EASIER SAID THAN DONE... HOW AM I SUPPOSED TO CONTROL WHAT I THINK ABOUT? IT'S LIKE THE LAST TEN MINUTES OF A YOGA CLASS WHEN YOU'RE SUPPOSED TO JUST LIE THERE WITH NOTHING TO DO, AND THE TEACHER TELLS YOU TO JUST EMPTY YOUR MIND... MEANWHILE, AN OLD MAN NEXT TO YOU STARTS SNORING, AND THE BALLERINA-LOOKING LADY HAS REALLY GNARLY TOES, AND THE TRACK LIGHTING REMINDS YOU OF THE DAYCARE THE KIDS USED TO GO TO, AND THIS IS THE LONGEST TIME YOU'VE EVER SPENT ALONE WITH YOUR OWN BRAIN WITHOUT READING OR PLAYING WITH A PHONE... AND ALL THESE THOUGHTS SUDDENLY RUSH BACK INTO THE MANUFACTURED VACUUM IN YOUR HEAD...
"DO I HAVE ENOUGH STUFF TO MAKE LUNCHES FOR THE KIDS TOMORROW?"
"ARE WE OUT OF COFFEE?"
"DID I FORGET TO SUBMIT THE GRADES FOR THAT ONLINE CLASS?"
"PARKING TICKETS!"
"I CAN'T BELIEVE JACKIE ALSO NEEDS BRACES"...
...AND THEN, THE THOUGHTS COME FASTER AND LOUDER...
"WHAT IF I CAN'T WRITE AND CAN'T GET A JOB? WHAT IF THE WORLD WON'T HAVE ME BACK?"
"WHAT IF I CAN'T LOVE, BUT AM ONLY EXCELLENT AT LONGING FOR PEOPLE I CAN'T HAVE?"
"COME BACK, ORPHAN!"
"I HAVE TO GET OUT OF HERE!"
I'M TERRIBLE AT TELLING MYSELF TO STOP THINKING ABOUT THINGS... OR TO STOP DOING THINGS...

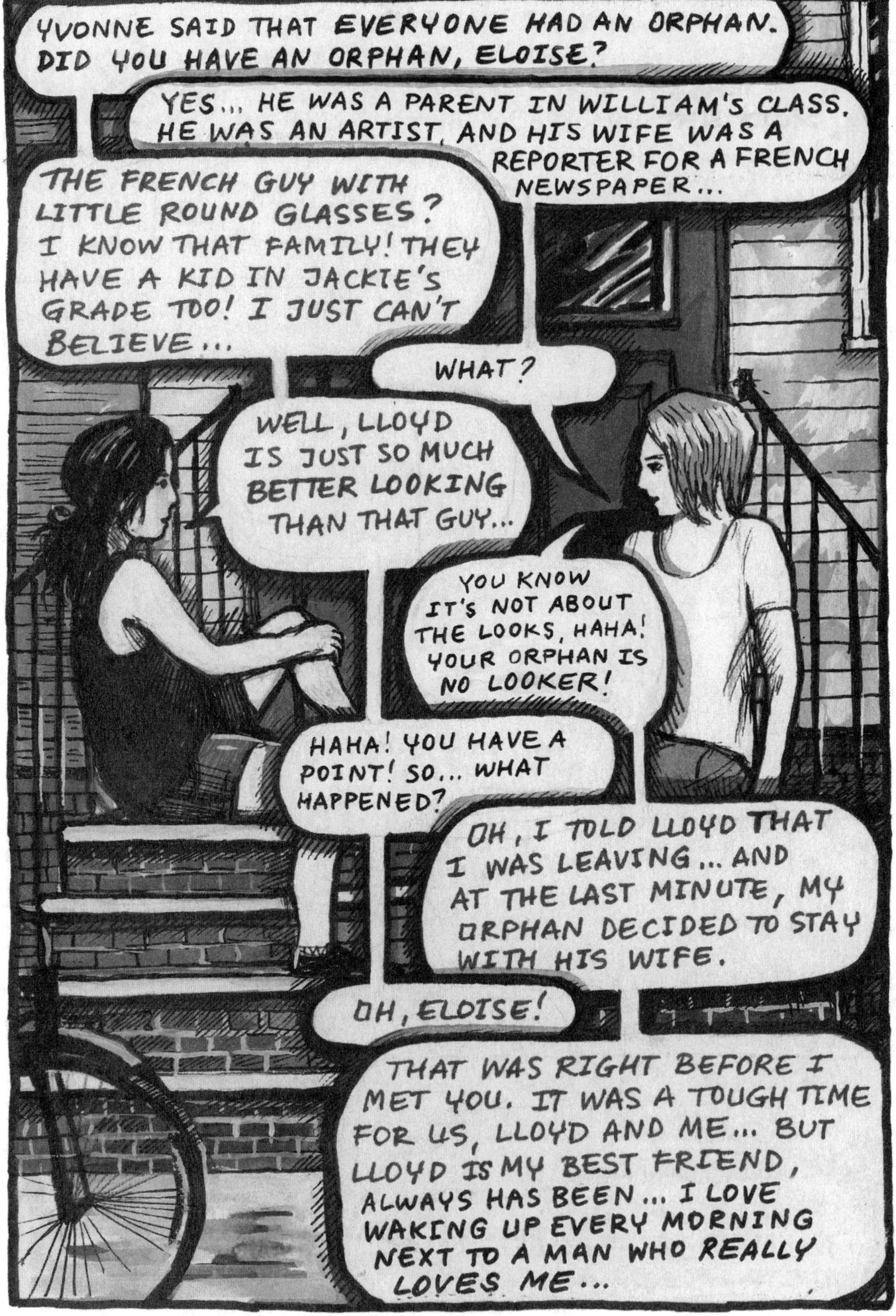
YVONNE SAID THAT EVERYONE HAD AN ORPHAN. DID YOU HAVE AN ORPHAN, ELOISE?
YES... HE WAS A PARENT IN WILLIAM'S CLASS. HE WAS AN ARTIST, AND HIS WIFE WAS A REPORTER FOR A FRENCH NEWSPAPER...
THE FRENCH GUY WITH LITTLE ROUND GLASSES? I KNOW THAT FAMILY! THEY HAVE A KID IN JACKIE'S GRADE TOO! I JUST CAN'T BELIEVE...
WHAT?
WELL, LLOYD IS JUST SO MUCH BETTER LOOKING THAN THAT GUY...
YOU KNOW IT'S NOT ABOUT THE LOOKS, HAHA! YOUR ORPHAN IS NO LOOKER!
HAHA! YOU HAVE A POINT! SO... WHAT HAPPENED?
OH, I TOLD LLOYD THAT I WAS LEAVING... AND AT THE LAST MINUTE, MY ORPHAN DECIDED TO STAY WITH HIS WIFE.
OH, ELOISE!
THAT WAS RIGHT BEFORE I MET YOU. IT WAS A TOUGH TIME FOR US, LLOYD AND ME... BUT LLOYD IS MY BEST FRIEND, ALWAYS HAS BEEN... I LOVE WAKING UP EVERY MORNING NEXT TO A MAN WHO REALLY LOVES ME...

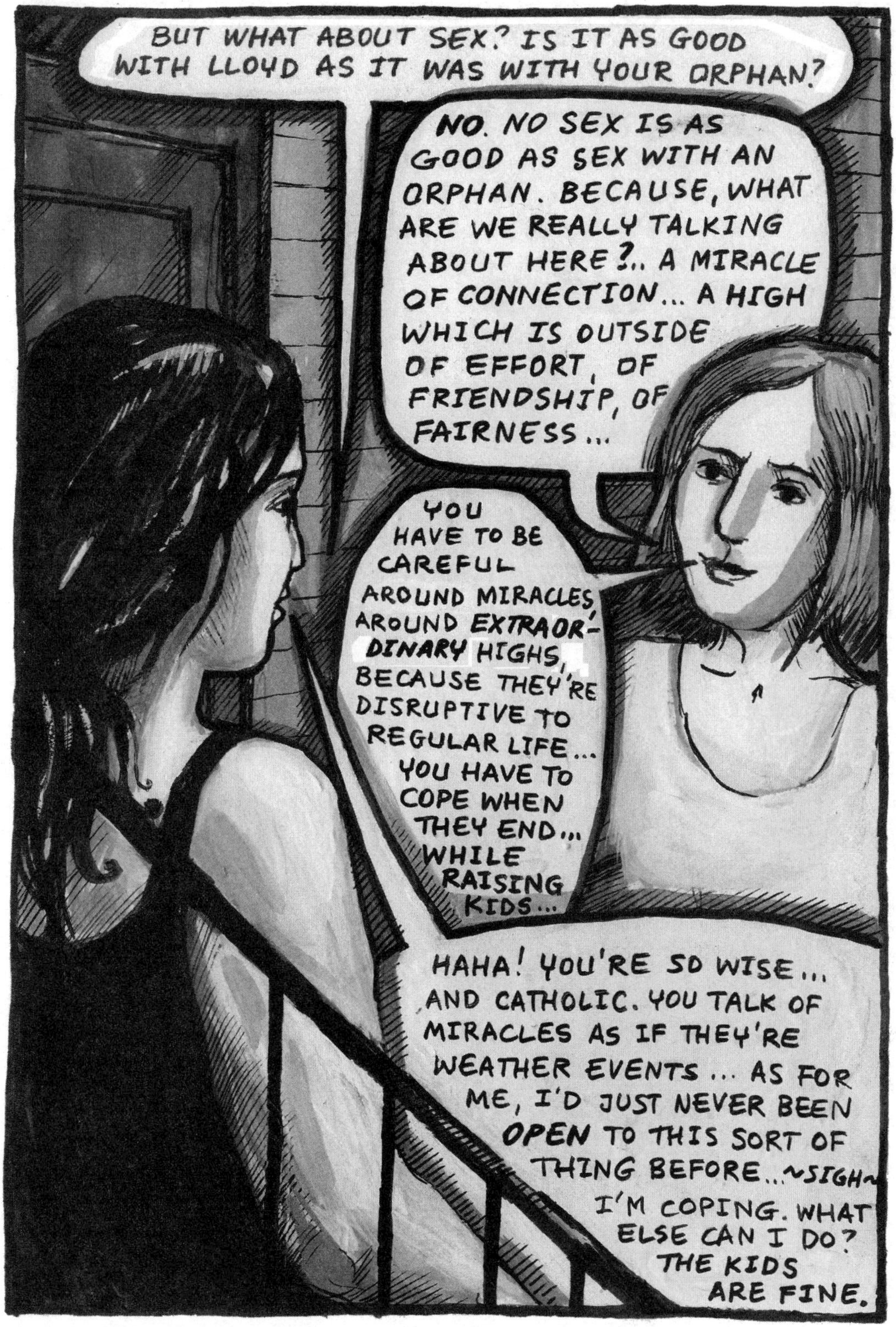
BUT WHAT ABOUT SEX? IS IT AS GOOD WITH LLOYD AS IT WAS WITH YOUR ORPHAN?
NO. NO SEX IS AS GOOD AS SEX WITH AN ORPHAN. BECAUSE, WHAT ARE WE REALLY TALKING ABOUT HERE?.. A MIRACLE OF CONNECTION... A HIGH WHICH IS OUTSIDE OF EFFORT, OF FRIENDSHIP, OF FAIRNESS...
YOU HAVE TO BE CAREFUL AROUND MIRACLES, AROUND EXTRAORDINARY HIGHS, BECAUSE THEY'RE DISRUPTIVE TO REGULAR LIFE... YOU HAVE TO COPE WHEN THEY END... WHILE RAISING KIDS...
HAHA! YOU'RE SO WISE... AND CATHOLIC. YOU TALK OF MIRACLES AS IF THEY'RE WEATHER EVENTS... AS FOR ME, I'D JUST NEVER BEEN OPEN TO THIS SORT OF THING BEFORE... ~SIGH~ I'M COPING. WHAT ELSE CAN I DO? THE KIDS ARE FINE.

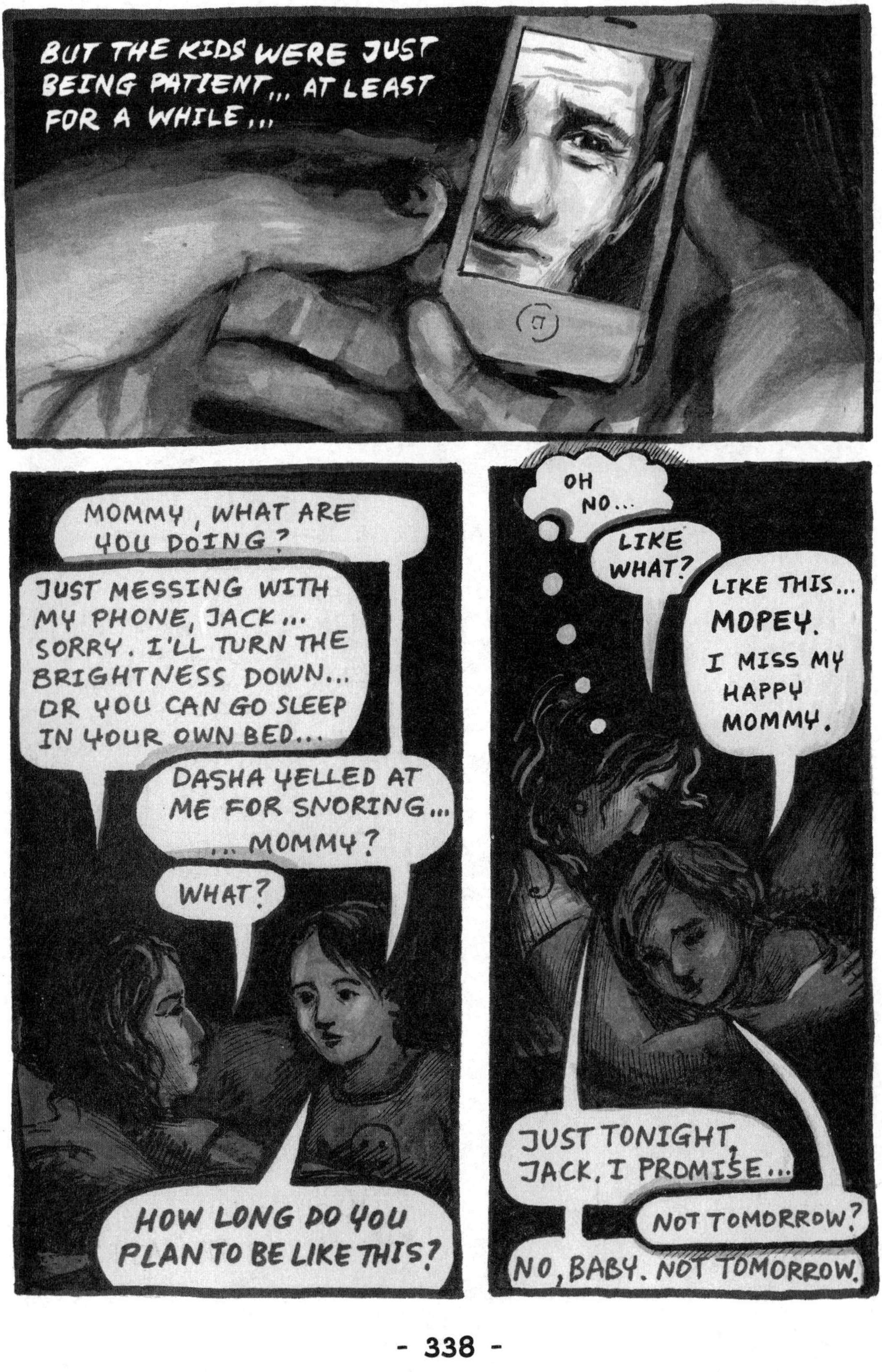
BUT THE KIDS WERE JUST BEING PATIENT... AT LEAST FOR A WHILE...
MOMMY, WHAT ARE YOU DOING?
JUST MESSING WITH MY PHONE, JACK... SORRY. I'LL TURN THE BRIGHTNESS DOWN... OR YOU CAN GO SLEEP IN YOUR OWN BED...
DASHA YELLED AT ME FOR SNORING... ...MOMMY?
WHAT?
HOW LONG DO YOU PLAN TO BE LIKE THIS?
OH NO...
LIKE WHAT?
LIKE THIS... MOPEY. I MISS MY HAPPY MOMMY.
JUST TONIGHT, JACK, I PROMISE...
NOT TOMORROW?
NO, BABY. NOT TOMORROW.

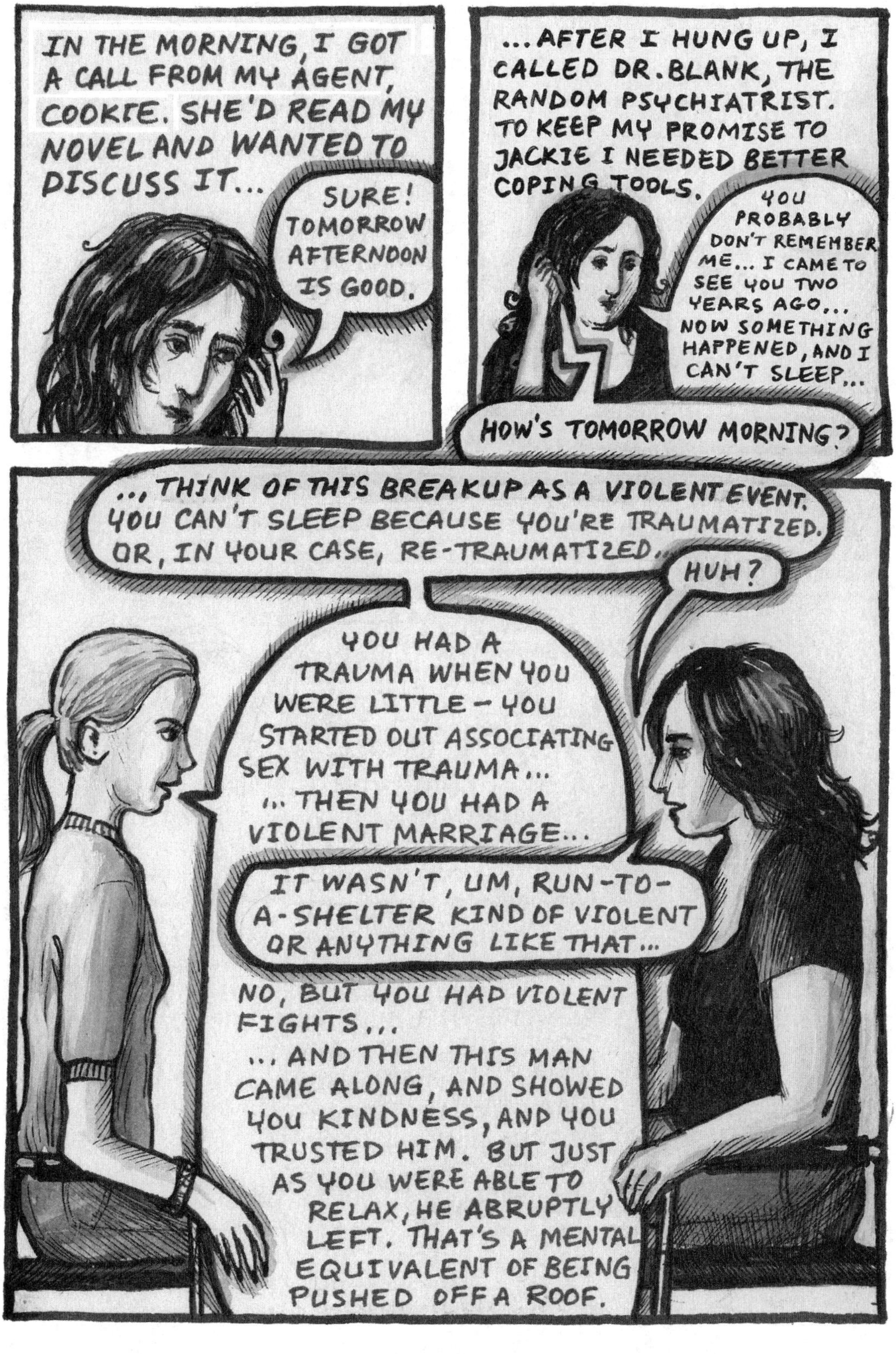
IN THE MORNING, I GOT A CALL FROM MY AGENT, COOKIE. SHE'D READ MY NOVEL AND WANTED TO DISCUSS IT...
SURE! TOMORROW AFTERNOON IS GOOD.
...AFTER I HUNG UP, I CALLED DR. BLANK, THE RANDOM PSYCHIATRIST. TO KEEP MY PROMISE TO JACKIE I NEEDED BETTER COPING TOOLS.
YOU PROBABLY DON'T REMEMBER ME... I CAME TO SEE YOU TWO YEARS AGO... NOW SOMETHING HAPPENED, AND I CAN'T SLEEP...
HOW'S TOMORROW MORNING?
..., THINK OF THIS BREAKUP AS A VIOLENT EVENT. YOU CAN'T SLEEP BECAUSE YOU'RE TRAUMATIZED. OR, IN YOUR CASE, RE-TRAUMATIZED...
HUH?
YOU HAD A TRAUMA WHEN YOU WERE LITTLE – YOU STARTED OUT ASSOCIATING SEX WITH TRAUMA... ...THEN YOU HAD A VIOLENT MARRIAGE...
IT WASN'T, UM, RUN-TO-A-SHELTER KIND OF VIOLENT OR ANYTHING LIKE THAT...
NO, BUT YOU HAD VIOLENT FIGHTS... ...AND THEN THIS MAN CAME ALONG, AND SHOWED YOU KINDNESS, AND YOU TRUSTED HIM. BUT JUST AS YOU WERE ABLE TO RELAX, HE ABRUPTLY LEFT. THAT'S A MENTAL EQUIVALENT OF BEING PUSHED OFF A ROOF.

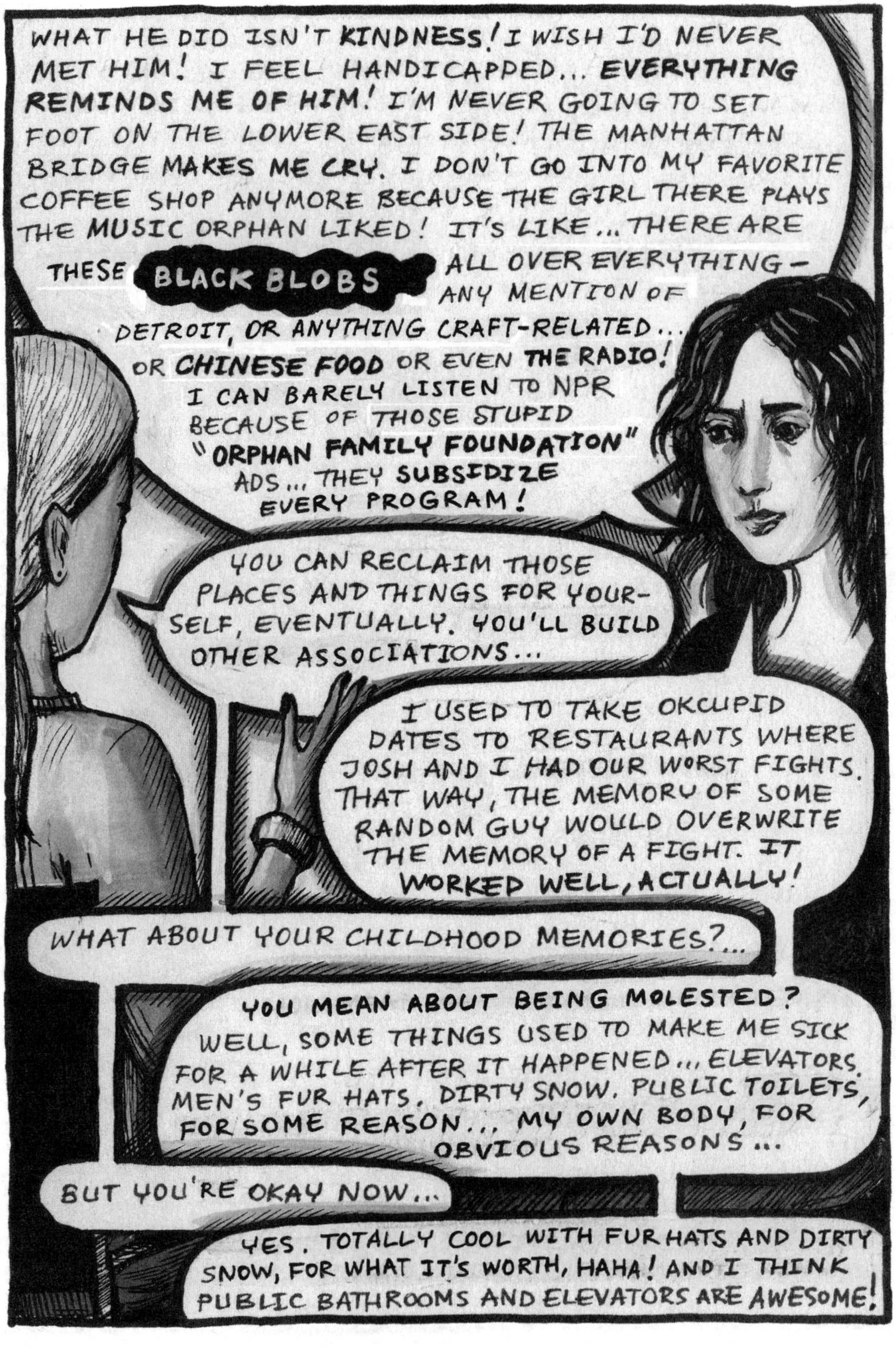
WHAT HE DID ISN'T KINDNESS! I WISH I'D NEVER MET HIM! I FEEL HANDICAPPED... EVERYTHING REMINDS ME OF HIM! I'M NEVER GOING TO SET FOOT ON THE LOWER EAST SIDE! THE MANHATTAN BRIDGE MAKES ME CRY. I DON'T GO INTO MY FAVORITE COFFEE SHOP ANYMORE BECAUSE THE GIRL THERE PLAYS THE MUSIC ORPHAN LIKED! IT'S LIKE... THERE ARE THESE BLACK BLOBS ALL OVER EVERYTHING - ANY MENTION OF DETROIT, OR ANYTHING CRAFT-RELATED... OR CHINESE FOOD OR EVEN THE RADIO! I CAN BARELY LISTEN TO NPR BECAUSE OF THOSE STUPID "ORPHAN FAMILY FOUNDATION" ADS... THEY SUBSIDIZE EVERY PROGRAM!
YOU CAN RECLAIM THOSE PLACES AND THINGS FOR YOURSELF, EVENTUALLY. YOU'LL BUILD OTHER ASSOCIATIONS...
I USED TO TAKE OKCUPID DATES TO RESTAURANTS WHERE JOSH AND I HAD OUR WORST FIGHTS. THAT WAY, THE MEMORY OF SOME RANDOM GUY WOULD OVERWRITE THE MEMORY OF A FIGHT. IT WORKED WELL, ACTUALLY!
WHAT ABOUT YOUR CHILDHOOD MEMORIES?...
YOU MEAN ABOUT BEING MOLESTED? WELL, SOME THINGS USED TO MAKE ME SICK FOR A WHILE AFTER IT HAPPENED... ELEVATORS. MEN'S FUR HATS. DIRTY SNOW. PUBLIC TOILETS, FOR SOME REASON... MY OWN BODY, FOR OBVIOUS REASONS...
BUT YOU'RE OKAY NOW...
YES. TOTALLY COOL WITH FUR HATS AND DIRTY SNOW, FOR WHAT IT'S WORTH, HAHA! AND I THINK PUBLIC BATHROOMS AND ELEVATORS ARE AWESOME!

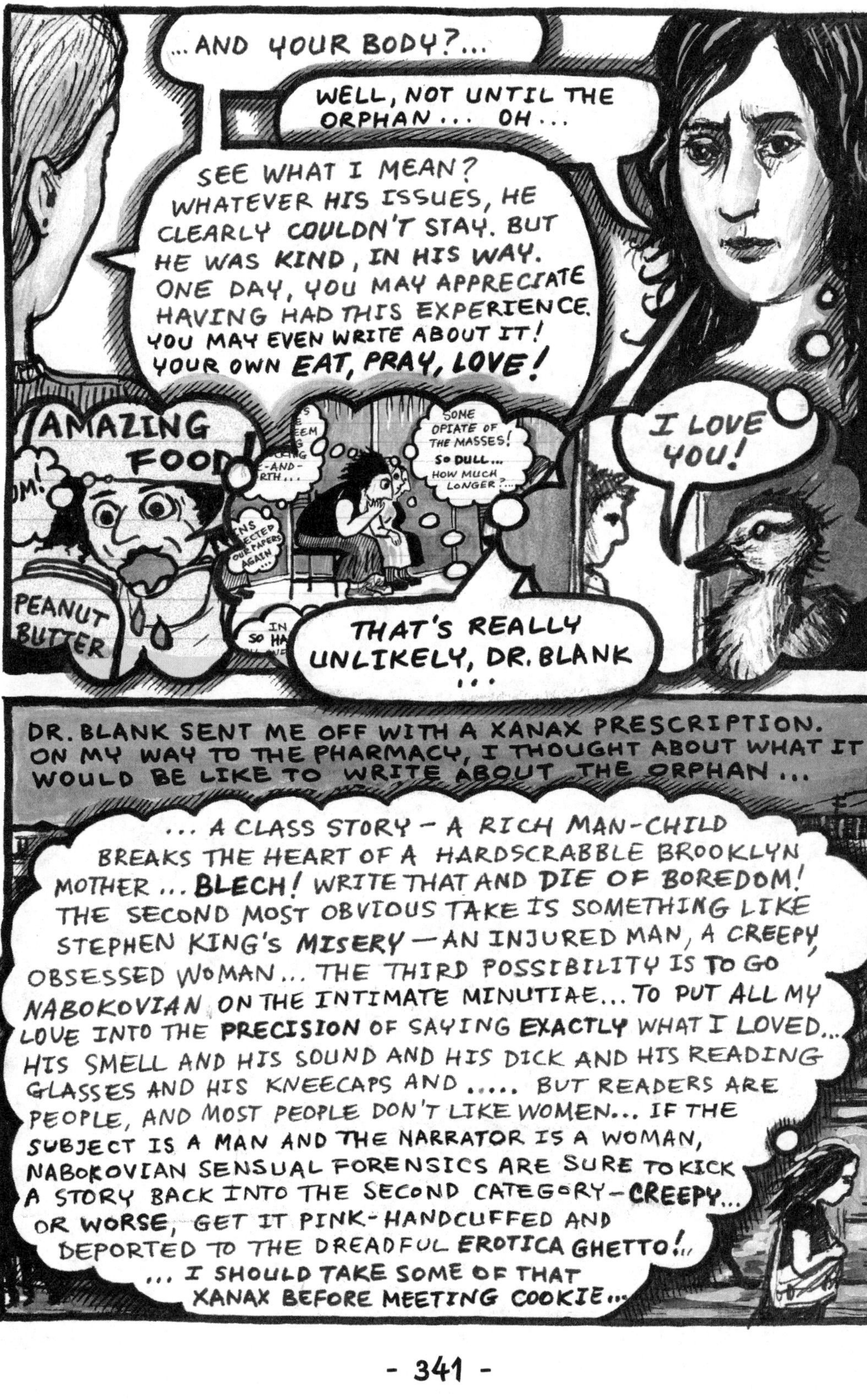
... AND YOUR BODY? ...
WELL, NOT UNTIL THE ORPHAN ... OH ...
SEE WHAT I MEAN? WHATEVER HIS ISSUES, HE CLEARLY COULDN'T STAY. BUT HE WAS KIND, IN HIS WAY. ONE DAY, YOU MAY APPRECIATE HAVING HAD THIS EXPERIENCE. YOU MAY EVEN WRITE ABOUT IT! YOUR OWN EAT, PRAY, LOVE!
AMAZING FOOD!
PEANUT BUTTER
SOME OPIATE OF THE MASSES! SO DULL... HOW MUCH LONGER?...
I LOVE YOU!
THAT'S REALLY UNLIKELY, DR. BLANK ...
DR. BLANK SENT ME OFF WITH A XANAX PRESCRIPTION. ON MY WAY TO THE PHARMACY, I THOUGHT ABOUT WHAT IT WOULD BE LIKE TO WRITE ABOUT THE ORPHAN ...
... A CLASS STORY - A RICH MAN-CHILD BREAKS THE HEART OF A HARDSCRABBLE BROOKLYN MOTHER ... BLECH! WRITE THAT AND DIE OF BOREDOM! THE SECOND MOST OBVIOUS TAKE IS SOMETHING LIKE STEPHEN KING'S MISERY — AN INJURED MAN, A CREEPY, OBSESSED WOMAN ... THE THIRD POSSIBILITY IS TO GO NABOKOVIAN ON THE INTIMATE MINUTIAE ... TO PUT ALL MY LOVE INTO THE PRECISION OF SAYING EXACTLY WHAT I LOVED... HIS SMELL AND HIS SOUND AND HIS DICK AND HIS READING GLASSES AND HIS KNEECAPS AND ..... BUT READERS ARE PEOPLE, AND MOST PEOPLE DON'T LIKE WOMEN ... IF THE SUBJECT IS A MAN AND THE NARRATOR IS A WOMAN, NABOKOVIAN SENSUAL FORENSICS ARE SURE TO KICK A STORY BACK INTO THE SECOND CATEGORY — CREEPY... OR WORSE, GET IT PINK-HANDCUFFED AND DEPORTED TO THE DREADFUL EROTICA GHETTO!... ... I SHOULD TAKE SOME OF THAT XANAX BEFORE MEETING COOKIE...

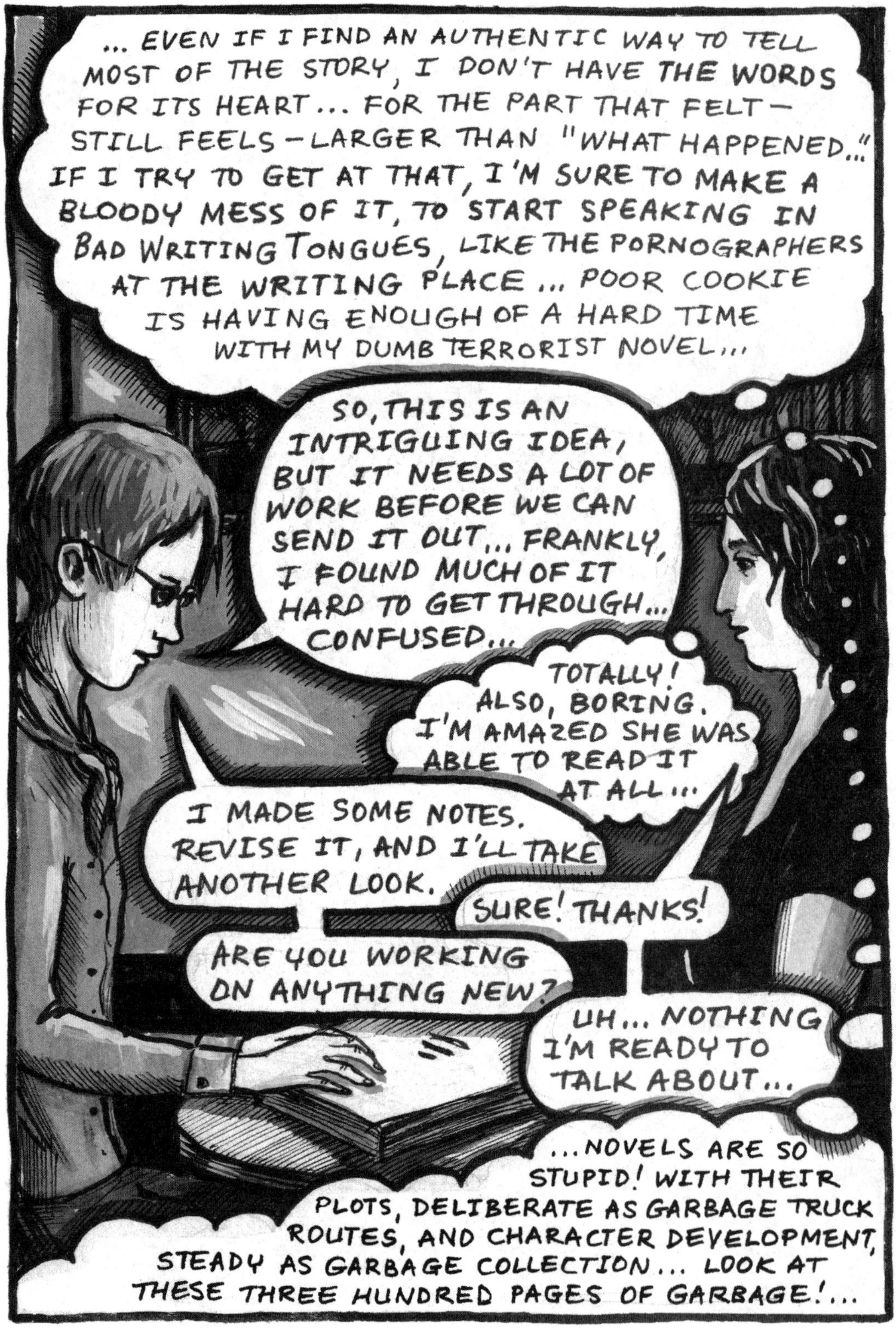
... EVEN IF I FIND AN AUTHENTIC WAY TO TELL MOST OF THE STORY, I DON'T HAVE THE WORDS FOR ITS HEART... FOR THE PART THAT FELT— STILL FEELS—LARGER THAN "WHAT HAPPENED..." IF I TRY TO GET AT THAT, I'M SURE TO MAKE A BLOODY MESS OF IT, TO START SPEAKING IN BAD WRITING TONGUES, LIKE THE PORNOGRAPHERS AT THE WRITING PLACE... POOR COOKIE IS HAVING ENOUGH OF A HARD TIME WITH MY DUMB TERRORIST NOVEL...
SO, THIS IS AN INTRIGUING IDEA, BUT IT NEEDS A LOT OF WORK BEFORE WE CAN SEND IT OUT... FRANKLY, I FOUND MUCH OF IT HARD TO GET THROUGH... CONFUSED...
TOTALLY! ALSO, BORING. I'M AMAZED SHE WAS ABLE TO READ IT AT ALL...
I MADE SOME NOTES. REVISE IT, AND I'LL TAKE ANOTHER LOOK.
SURE! THANKS!
ARE YOU WORKING ON ANYTHING NEW?
UH... NOTHING I'M READY TO TALK ABOUT...
...NOVELS ARE SO STUPID! WITH THEIR PLOTS, DELIBERATE AS GARBAGE TRUCK ROUTES, AND CHARACTER DEVELOPMENT, STEADY AS GARBAGE COLLECTION... LOOK AT THESE THREE HUNDRED PAGES OF GARBAGE!...

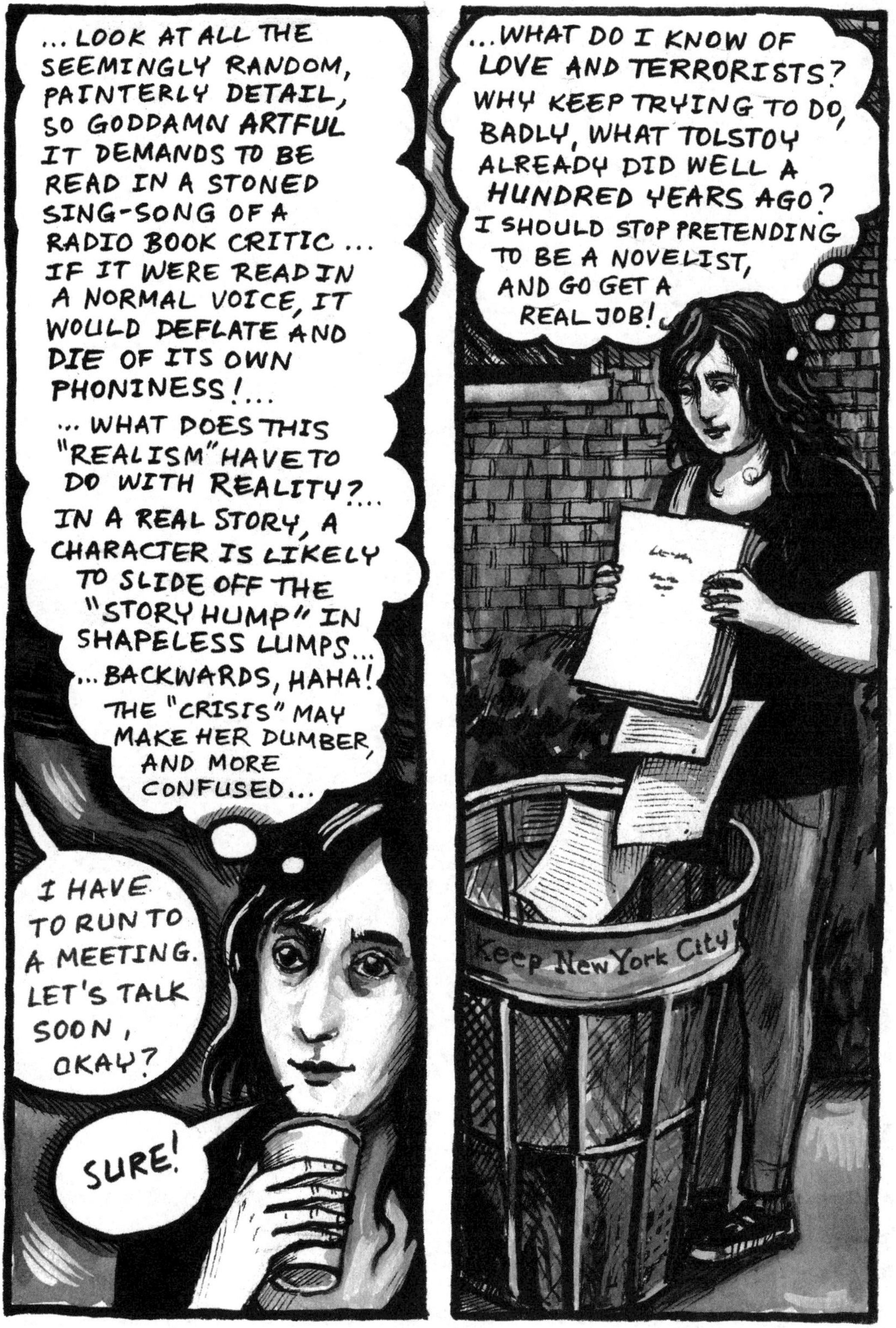
...LOOK AT ALL THE SEEMINGLY RANDOM, PAINTERLY DETAIL, SO GODDAMN ARTFUL IT DEMANDS TO BE READ IN A STONED SING-SONG OF A RADIO BOOK CRITIC... IF IT WERE READ IN A NORMAL VOICE, IT WOULD DEFLATE AND DIE OF ITS OWN PHONINESS!...
...WHAT DOES THIS "REALISM" HAVE TO DO WITH REALITY?... IN A REAL STORY, A CHARACTER IS LIKELY TO SLIDE OFF THE "STORY HUMP" IN SHAPELESS LUMPS... ...BACKWARDS, HAHA! THE "CRISIS" MAY MAKE HER DUMBER, AND MORE CONFUSED...
I HAVE TO RUN TO A MEETING. LET'S TALK SOON, OKAY?
SURE!
...WHAT DO I KNOW OF LOVE AND TERRORISTS? WHY KEEP TRYING TO DO, BADLY, WHAT TOLSTOY ALREADY DID WELL A HUNDRED YEARS AGO? I SHOULD STOP PRETENDING TO BE A NOVELIST, AND GO GET A REAL JOB!
Keep New York City

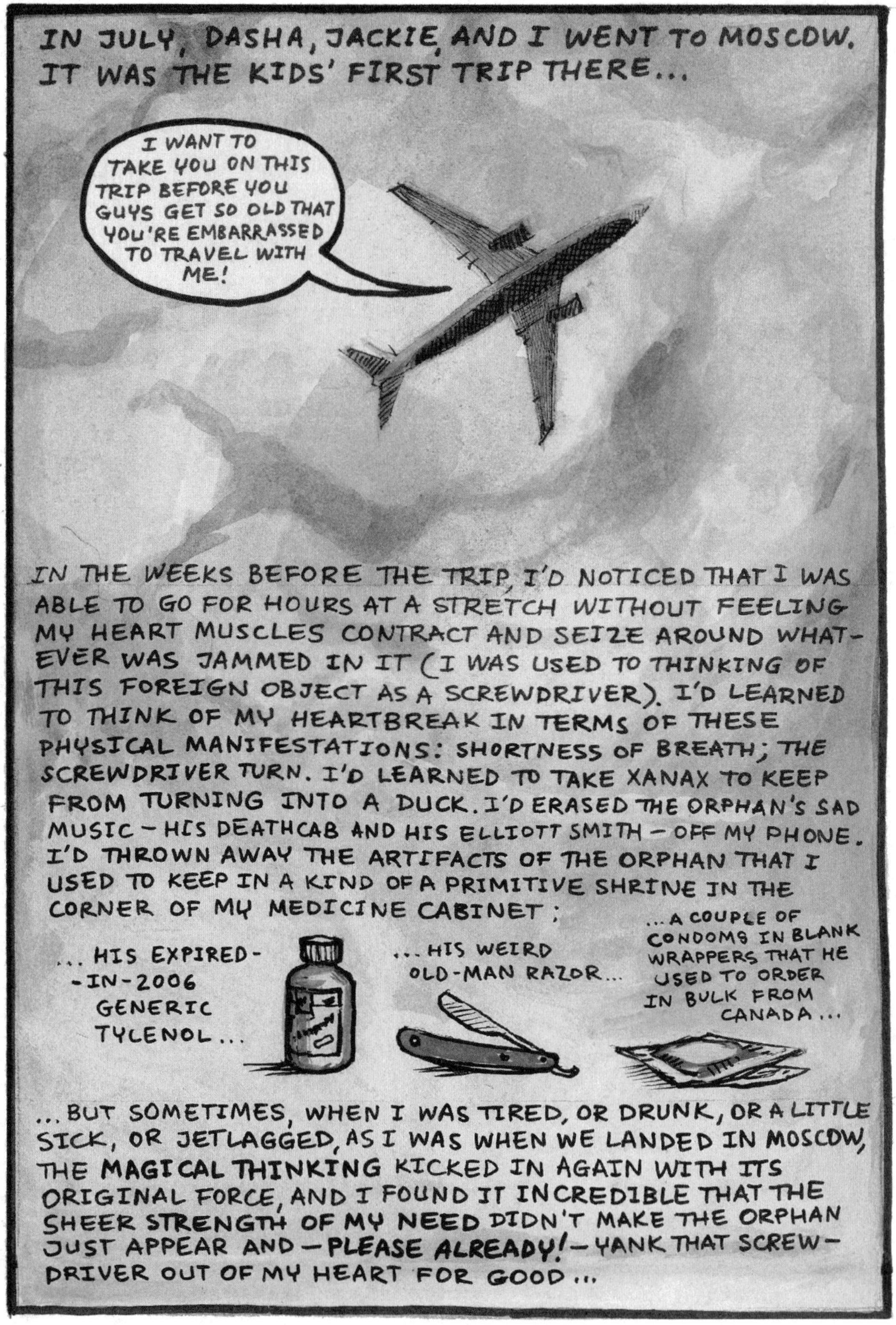
IN JULY, DASHA, JACKIE, AND I WENT TO MOSCOW. IT WAS THE KIDS' FIRST TRIP THERE...
I WANT TO TAKE YOU ON THIS TRIP BEFORE YOU GUYS GET SO OLD THAT YOU'RE EMBARRASSED TO TRAVEL WITH ME!
IN THE WEEKS BEFORE THE TRIP, I'D NOTICED THAT I WAS ABLE TO GO FOR HOURS AT A STRETCH WITHOUT FEELING MY HEART MUSCLES CONTRACT AND SEIZE AROUND WHATEVER WAS JAMMED IN IT (I WAS USED TO THINKING OF THIS FOREIGN OBJECT AS A SCREWDRIVER). I'D LEARNED TO THINK OF MY HEARTBREAK IN TERMS OF THESE PHYSICAL MANIFESTATIONS: SHORTNESS OF BREATH; THE SCREWDRIVER TURN. I'D LEARNED TO TAKE XANAX TO KEEP FROM TURNING INTO A DUCK. I'D ERASED THE ORPHAN'S SAD MUSIC – HIS DEATHCAB AND HIS ELLIOTT SMITH – OFF MY PHONE. I'D THROWN AWAY THE ARTIFACTS OF THE ORPHAN THAT I USED TO KEEP IN A KIND OF A PRIMITIVE SHRINE IN THE CORNER OF MY MEDICINE CABINET;
... HIS EXPIRED-IN-2006 GENERIC TYLENOL...
... HIS WEIRD OLD-MAN RAZOR...
... A COUPLE OF CONDOMS IN BLANK WRAPPERS THAT HE USED TO ORDER IN BULK FROM CANADA...
... BUT SOMETIMES, WHEN I WAS TIRED, OR DRUNK, OR A LITTLE SICK, OR JETLAGGED, AS I WAS WHEN WE LANDED IN MOSCOW, THE MAGICAL THINKING KICKED IN AGAIN WITH ITS ORIGINAL FORCE, AND I FOUND IT INCREDIBLE THAT THE SHEER STRENGTH OF MY NEED DIDN'T MAKE THE ORPHAN JUST APPEAR AND – PLEASE ALREADY! – YANK THAT SCREWDRIVER OUT OF MY HEART FOR GOOD...

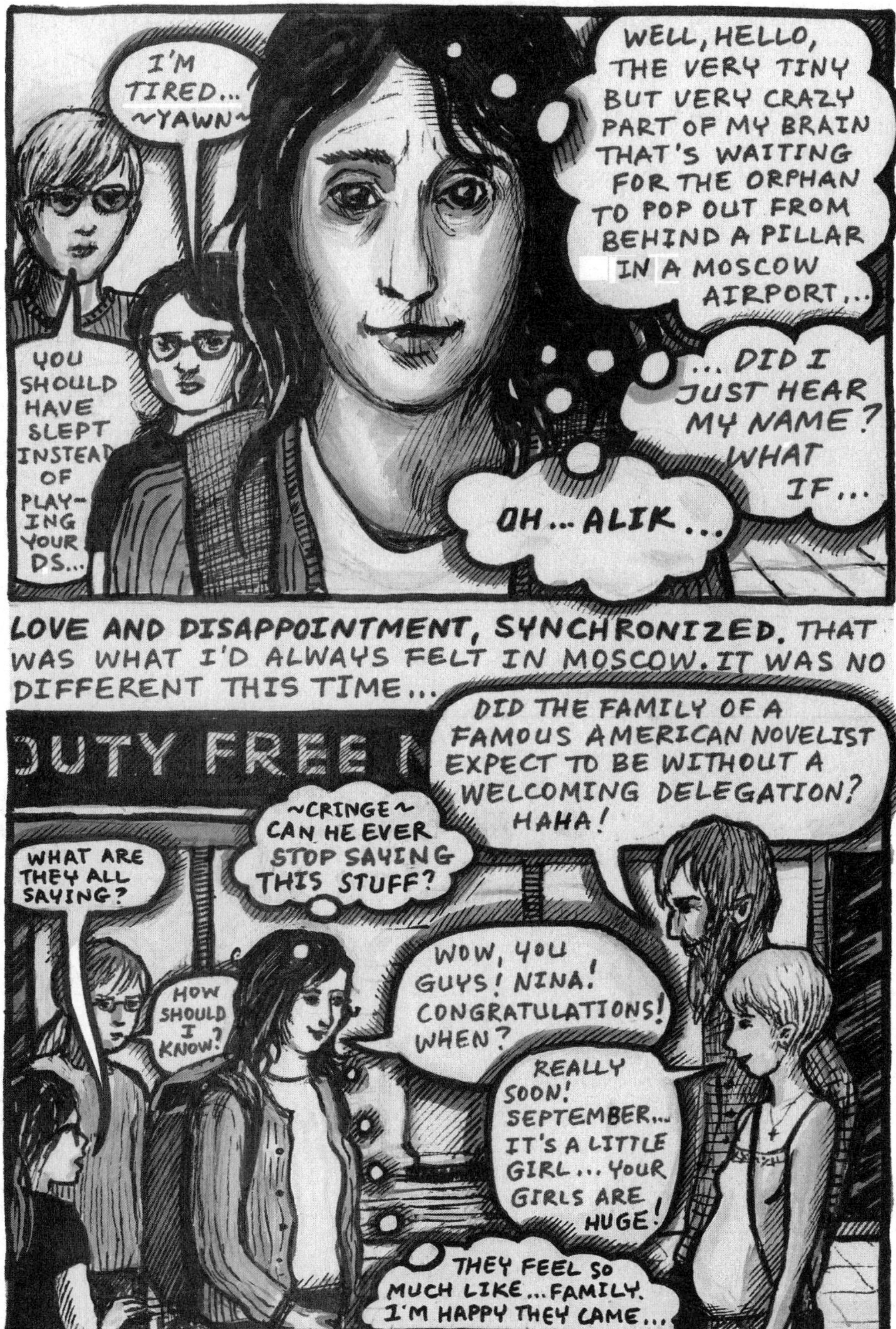
I'M TIRED... ~YAWN~
YOU SHOULD HAVE SLEPT INSTEAD OF PLAYING YOUR DS...
WELL, HELLO, THE VERY TINY BUT VERY CRAZY PART OF MY BRAIN THAT'S WAITING FOR THE ORPHAN TO POP OUT FROM BEHIND A PILLAR IN A MOSCOW AIRPORT...
...DID I JUST HEAR MY NAME? WHAT IF...
OH... ALIK...
LOVE AND DISAPPOINTMENT, SYNCHRONIZED. THAT WAS WHAT I'D ALWAYS FELT IN MOSCOW. IT WAS NO DIFFERENT THIS TIME...
DUTY FREE
DID THE FAMILY OF A FAMOUS AMERICAN NOVELIST EXPECT TO BE WITHOUT A WELCOMING DELEGATION? HAHA!
~CRINGE~ CAN HE EVER STOP SAYING THIS STUFF?
WHAT ARE THEY ALL SAYING?
HOW SHOULD I KNOW?
WOW, YOU GUYS! NINA! CONGRATULATIONS! WHEN?
REALLY SOON! SEPTEMBER... IT'S A LITTLE GIRL... YOUR GIRLS ARE HUGE!
THEY FEEL SO MUCH LIKE... FAMILY. I'M HAPPY THEY CAME...

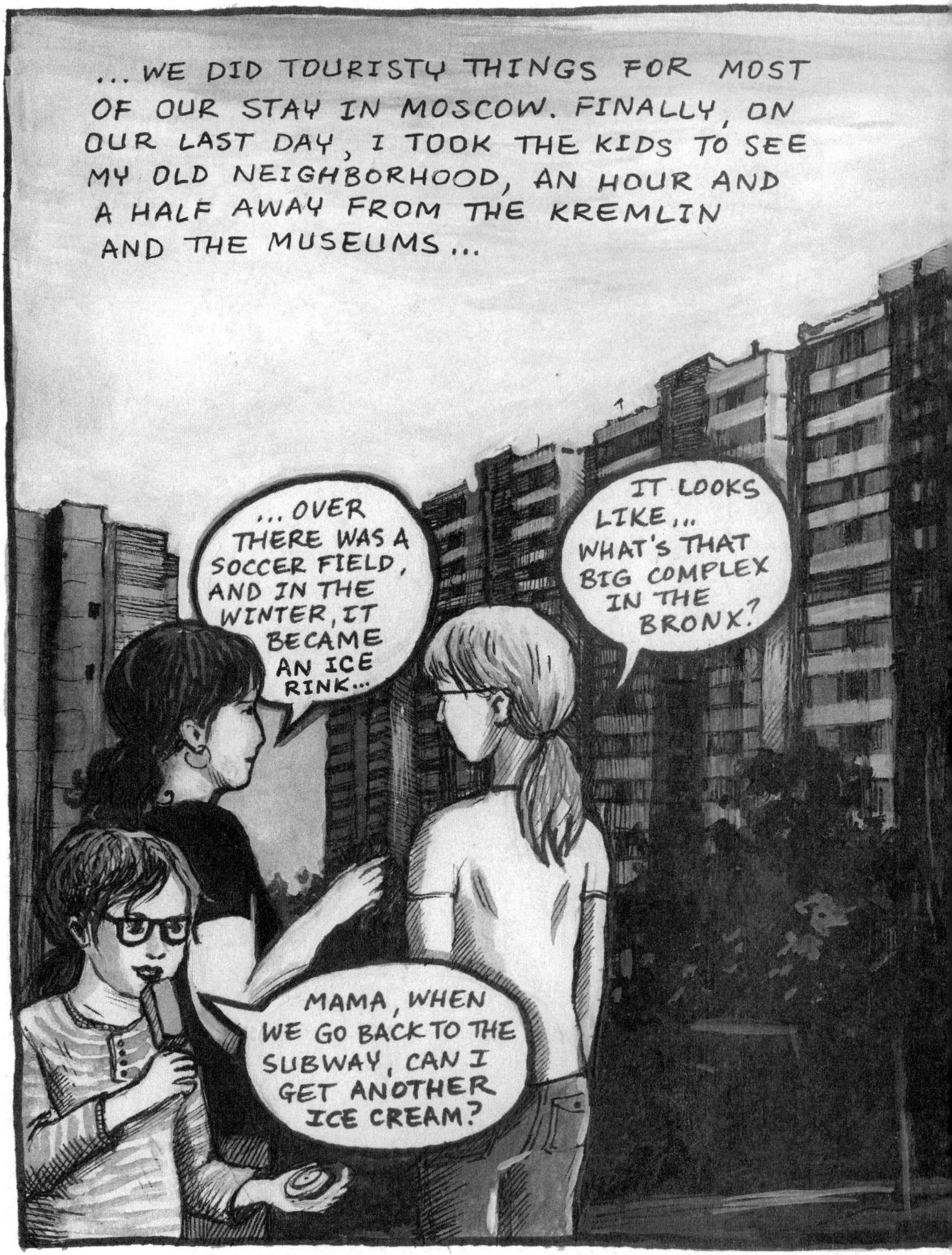
...WE DID TOURISTY THINGS FOR MOST OF OUR STAY IN MOSCOW. FINALLY, ON OUR LAST DAY, I TOOK THE KIDS TO SEE MY OLD NEIGHBORHOOD, AN HOUR AND A HALF AWAY FROM THE KREMLIN AND THE MUSEUMS...
...OVER THERE WAS A SOCCER FIELD, AND IN THE WINTER, IT BECAME AN ICE RINK...
IT LOOKS LIKE... WHAT'S THAT BIG COMPLEX IN THE BRONX?
MAMA, WHEN WE GO BACK TO THE SUBWAY, CAN I GET ANOTHER ICE CREAM?

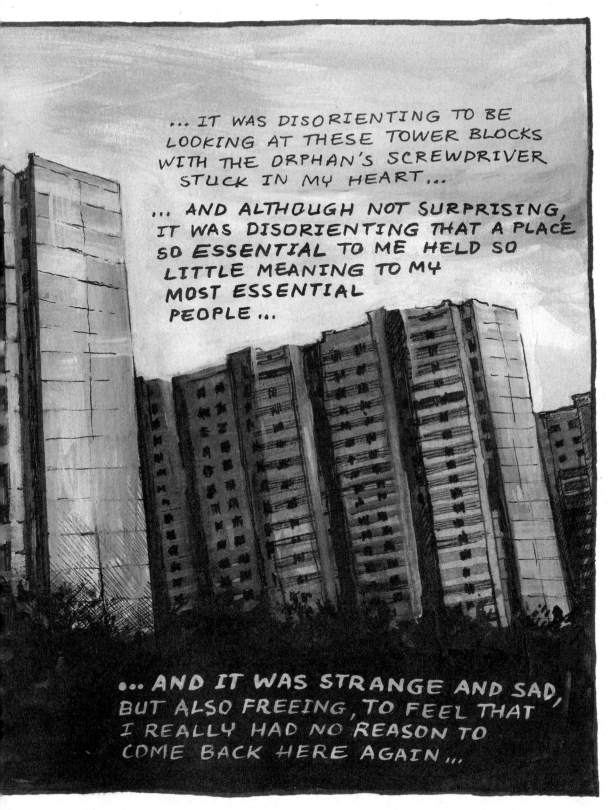

... IT WAS DISORIENTING TO BE LOOKING AT THESE TOWER BLOCKS WITH THE ORPHAN'S SCREWDRIVER STUCK IN MY HEART...

... AND ALTHOUGH NOT SURPRISING, IT WAS DISORIENTING THAT A PLACE SO ESSENTIAL TO ME HELD SO LITTLE MEANING TO MY MOST ESSENTIAL PEOPLE...

... AND IT WAS STRANGE AND SAD, BUT ALSO FREEING, TO FEEL THAT I REALLY HAD NO REASON TO COME BACK HERE AGAIN...

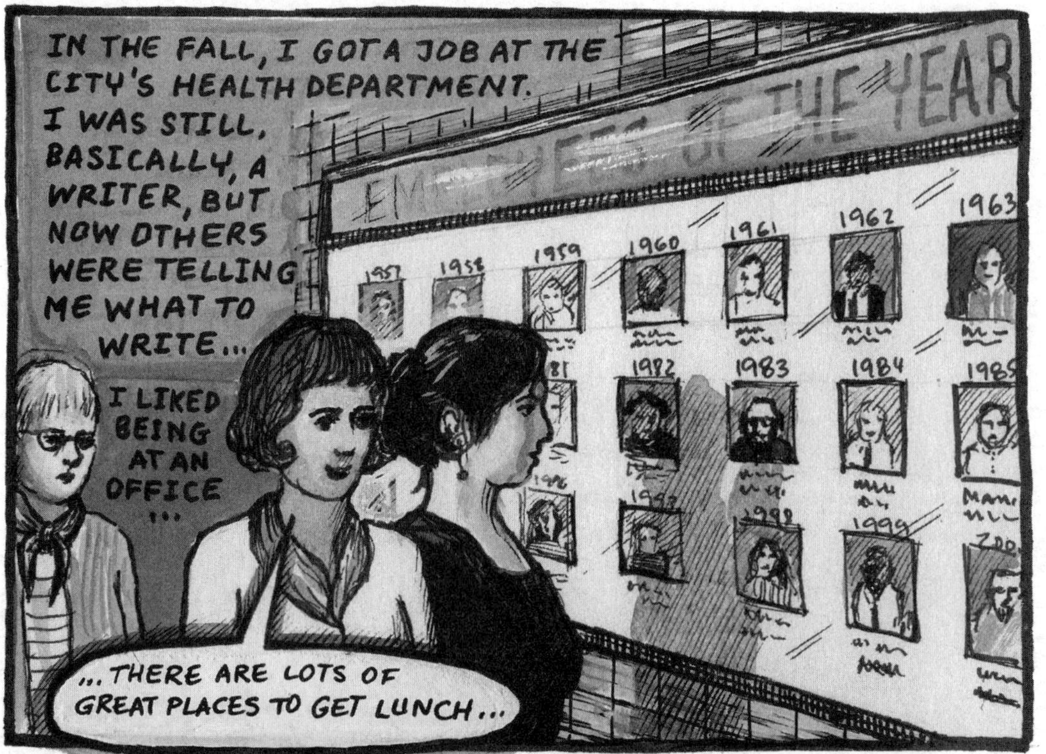
IN THE FALL, I GOT A JOB AT THE CITY'S HEALTH DEPARTMENT. I WAS STILL, BASICALLY, A WRITER, BUT NOW OTHERS WERE TELLING ME WHAT TO WRITE...
I LIKED BEING AT AN OFFICE...
...THERE ARE LOTS OF GREAT PLACES TO GET LUNCH...
1957
1958
1959
1960
1961
1962
1963
1982
1983
1984

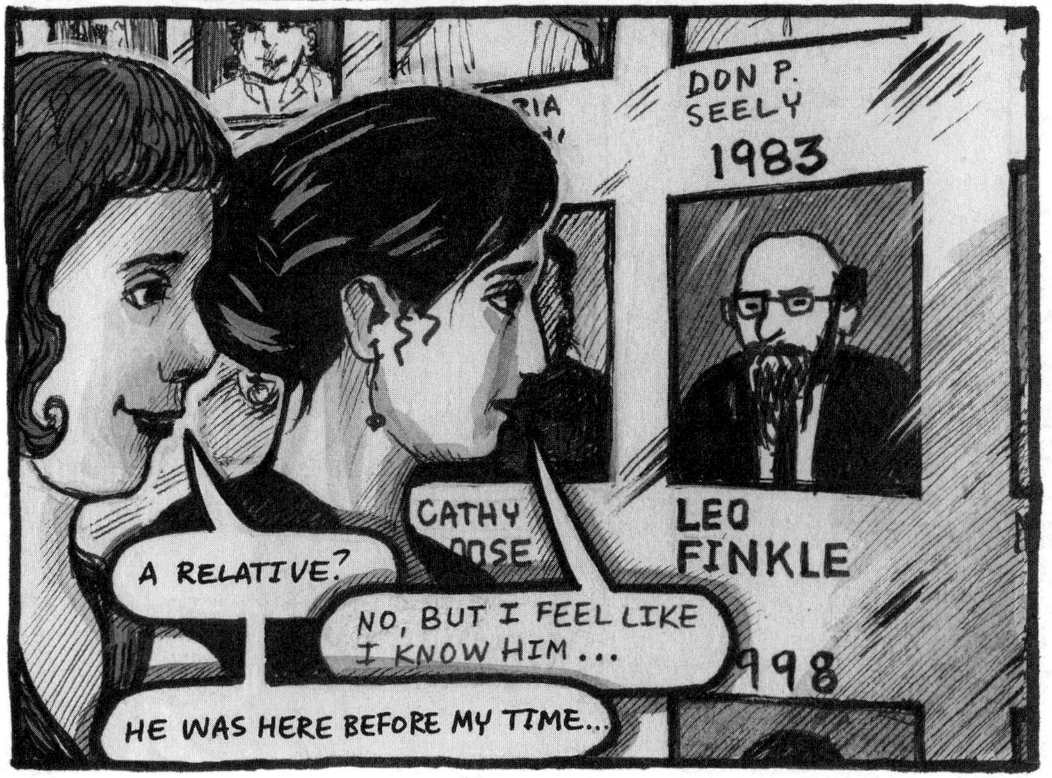
DON P. SEELY
1983
LEO FINKLE
CATHY
A RELATIVE?
NO, BUT I FEEL LIKE I KNOW HIM...
HE WAS HERE BEFORE MY TIME...

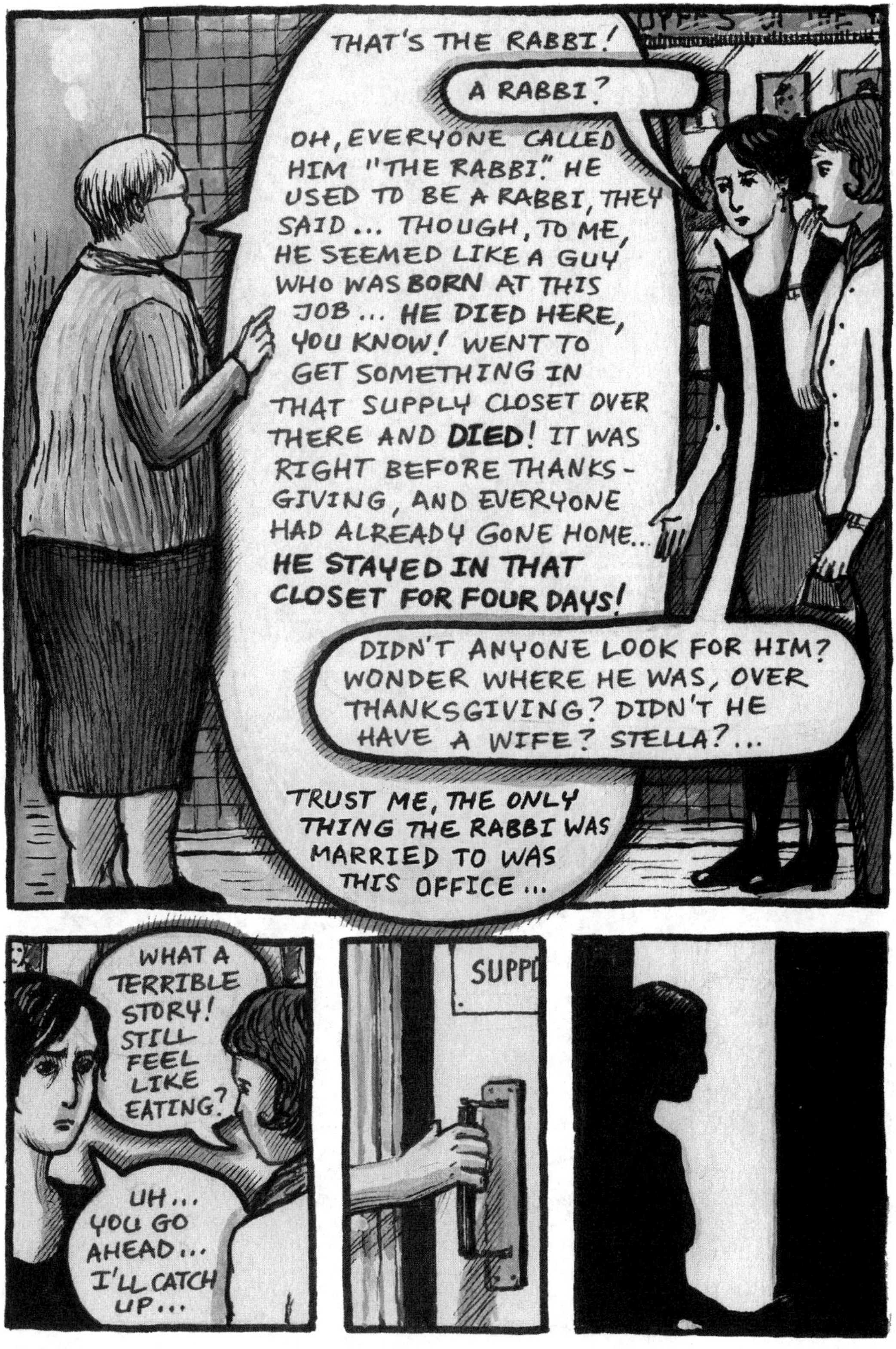
THAT'S THE RABBI!
A RABBI?
OH, EVERYONE CALLED HIM "THE RABBI." HE USED TO BE A RABBI, THEY SAID... THOUGH, TO ME, HE SEEMED LIKE A GUY WHO WAS BORN AT THIS JOB... HE DIED HERE, YOU KNOW! WENT TO GET SOMETHING IN THAT SUPPLY CLOSET OVER THERE AND DIED! IT WAS RIGHT BEFORE THANKS-GIVING, AND EVERYONE HAD ALREADY GONE HOME... HE STAYED IN THAT CLOSET FOR FOUR DAYS!
DIDN'T ANYONE LOOK FOR HIM? WONDER WHERE HE WAS, OVER THANKSGIVING? DIDN'T HE HAVE A WIFE? STELLA?...
TRUST ME, THE ONLY THING THE RABBI WAS MARRIED TO WAS THIS OFFICE...
WHAT A TERRIBLE STORY! STILL FEEL LIKE EATING?
UH... YOU GO AHEAD... I'LL CATCH UP...
SUPPL

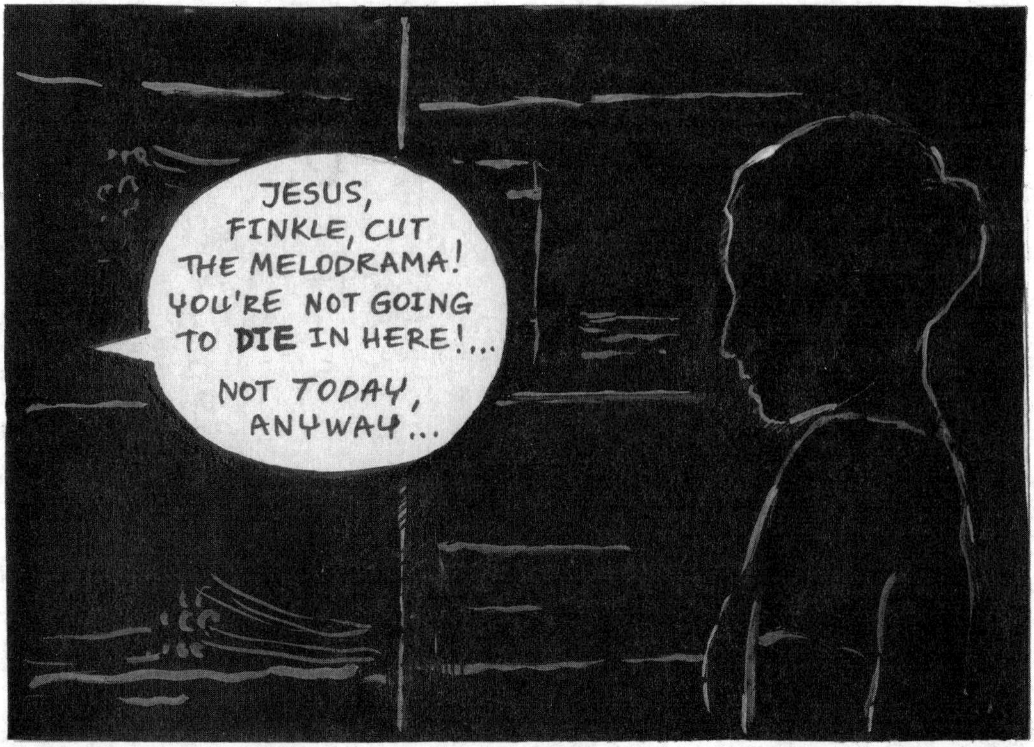
JESUS, FINKLE, CUT THE MELODRAMA! YOU'RE NOT GOING TO **DIE** IN HERE!...
NOT TODAY, ANYWAY...

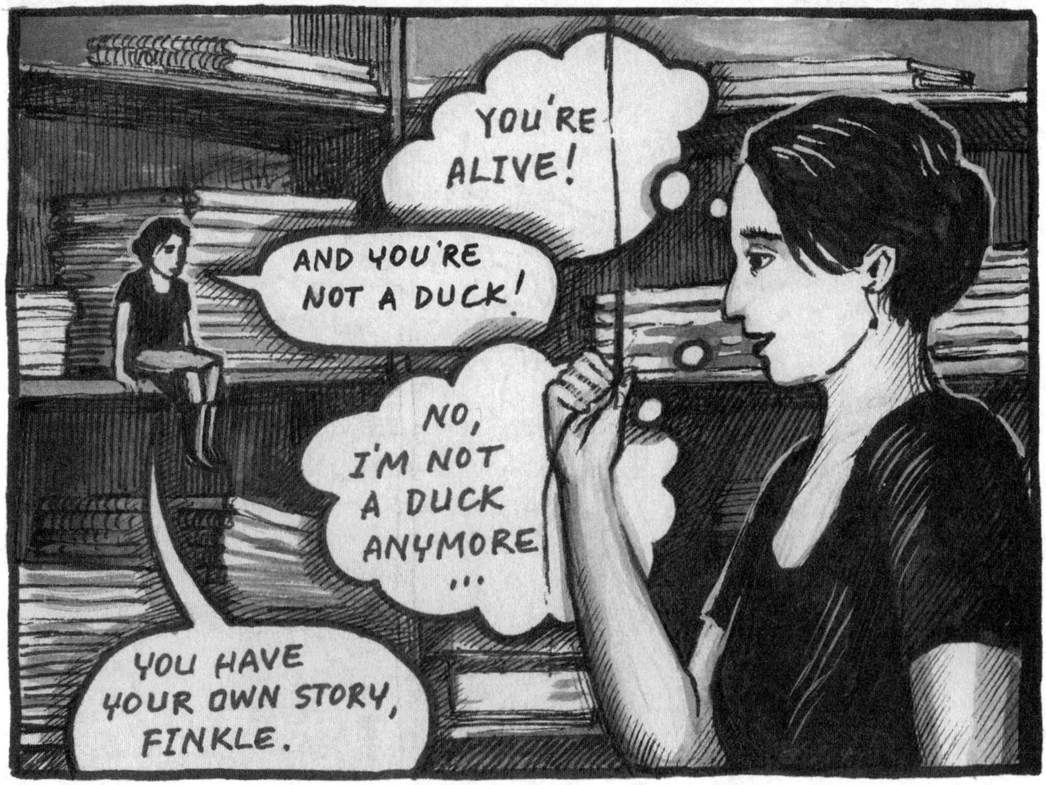
YOU'RE ALIVE!
AND YOU'RE NOT A DUCK!
NO, I'M NOT A DUCK ANYMORE ...
YOU HAVE YOUR OWN STORY, FINKLE.

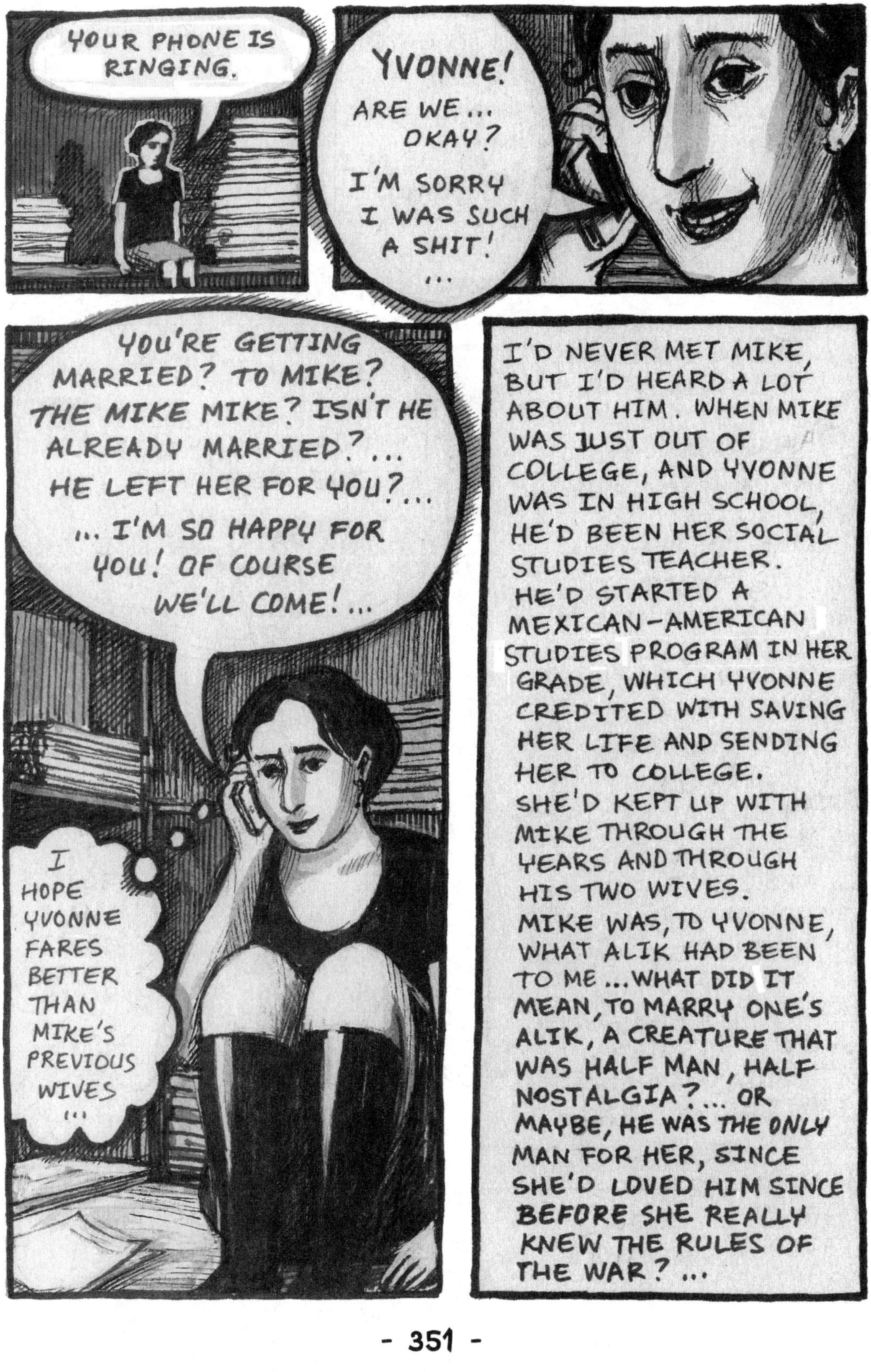
YOUR PHONE IS RINGING.
YVONNE! ARE WE... OKAY? I'M SORRY I WAS SUCH A SHIT! ...
YOU'RE GETTING MARRIED? TO MIKE? THE MIKE MIKE? ISN'T HE ALREADY MARRIED?... HE LEFT HER FOR YOU?... ... I'M SO HAPPY FOR YOU! OF COURSE WE'LL COME!...
I HOPE YVONNE FARES BETTER THAN MIKE'S PREVIOUS WIVES ...
I'D NEVER MET MIKE, BUT I'D HEARD A LOT ABOUT HIM. WHEN MIKE WAS JUST OUT OF COLLEGE, AND YVONNE WAS IN HIGH SCHOOL, HE'D BEEN HER SOCIAL STUDIES TEACHER. HE'D STARTED A MEXICAN-AMERICAN STUDIES PROGRAM IN HER GRADE, WHICH YVONNE CREDITED WITH SAVING HER LIFE AND SENDING HER TO COLLEGE. SHE'D KEPT UP WITH MIKE THROUGH THE YEARS AND THROUGH HIS TWO WIVES. MIKE WAS, TO YVONNE, WHAT ALIK HAD BEEN TO ME ... WHAT DID IT MEAN, TO MARRY ONE'S ALIK, A CREATURE THAT WAS HALF MAN, HALF NOSTALGIA?... OR MAYBE, HE WAS THE ONLY MAN FOR HER, SINCE SHE'D LOVED HIM SINCE BEFORE SHE REALLY KNEW THE RULES OF THE WAR? ...

... THE LAST TIME I SAW THE ORPHAN WAS THE NIGHT BEFORE HURRICANE SANDY. THE AIR ABOVE THE CITY FELT AS IF IT WERE BEING VACUUMED UP BY A GIGANTIC STEAM CLEANER.
A CHINESE BAKERY WHERE THE ORPHAN AND I USED TO GET LUNCH HAD BEEN REPLACED BY AN OVER-PRICED VODKA BAR, AND THE ORPHAN NOT ONLY ENTERED THERE, BUT WAS BUYING US BOTH TWELVE-DOLLAR VODKAS...

...WHAT DO YOU WANT? HORSERADISH? YOU'RE HARDCORE! I'M STICKING WITH PEACH. ~SIGH~ I DON'T EVEN LIKE VODKA!

WATCHING YOU PART WITH YOUR MONEY WITH SUCH EASE GIVES ME AN APOCALYPTIC FEELING.

ARE YOU SURE IT'S NOT THE WEATHER FORECAST?

THE ORPHAN WAS DEPRESSED. HE WAS BREAKING UP WITH HIS LATEST GIRLFRIEND, WHO (SURPRISINGLY ONLY TO THE ORPHAN) HAD BECOME UPSET ABOUT IT. HE WAS UPSET THAT SHE WAS UPSET.

THE VODKA WAS QUICKLY DOING ITS THING.
DO YOU KNOW WHAT MY SHRINK SAYS ABOUT YOU?
WHAT?
THAT YOU'RE SOME KIND OF A SEX ANGEL, GOING AROUND AND SHOWING THE WAY TO LOST SOULS LIKE MYSELF... AND THEN PUSH US OFF ROOFS, LIKE WE'RE SUPPOSED TO FLY! HAHA.
HE SAID THAT?
SHE... NO, NOT EXACTLY. BUT I THINK THAT'S WHAT SHE MEANT...
UH... THAT'S EITHER FLATTERING OR TERRIBLE. I CAN'T TELL...
ORPHAN, HAVE YOU EVER BEEN IN LOVE?
I DON'T KNOW... NO. I GUESS NOT. MAYBE.... AH, I SHOULD GET SOME WATER...

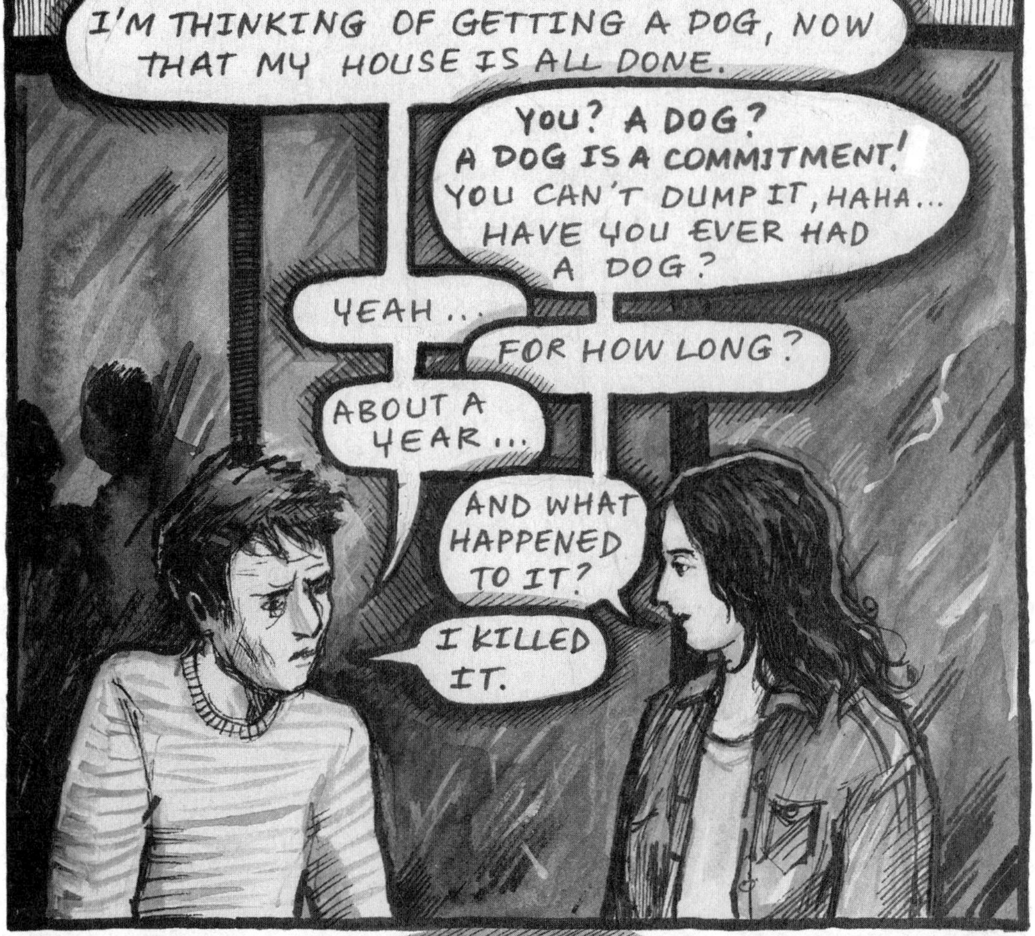
I'M THINKING OF GETTING A DOG, NOW THAT MY HOUSE IS ALL DONE.
YOU? A DOG? A DOG IS A COMMITMENT! YOU CAN'T DUMP IT, HAHA... HAVE YOU EVER HAD A DOG?
YEAH...
FOR HOW LONG?
ABOUT A YEAR...
AND WHAT HAPPENED TO IT?
I KILLED IT.

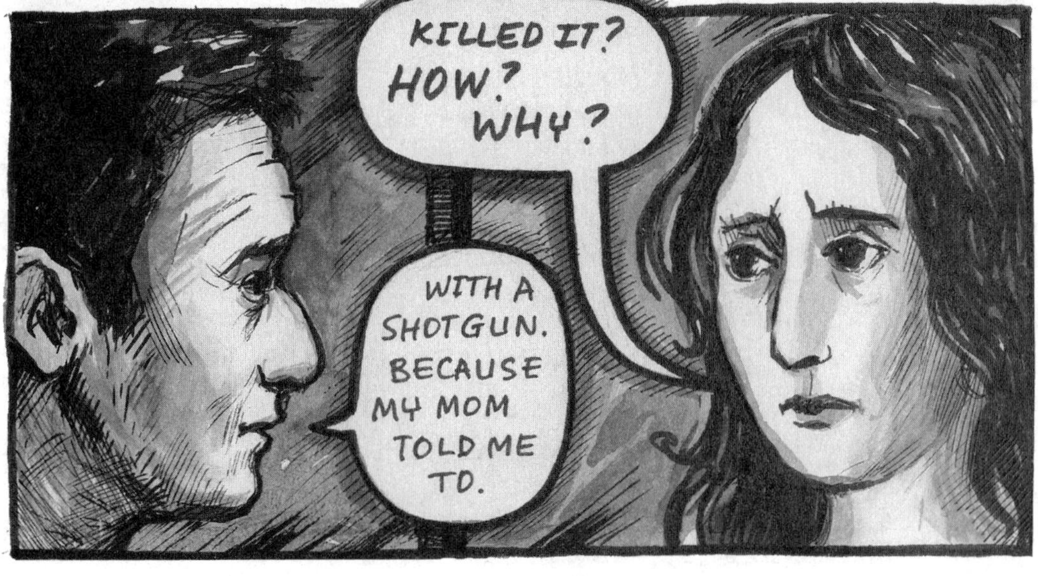
KILLED IT? HOW? WHY?
WITH A SHOTGUN. BECAUSE MY MOM TOLD ME TO.

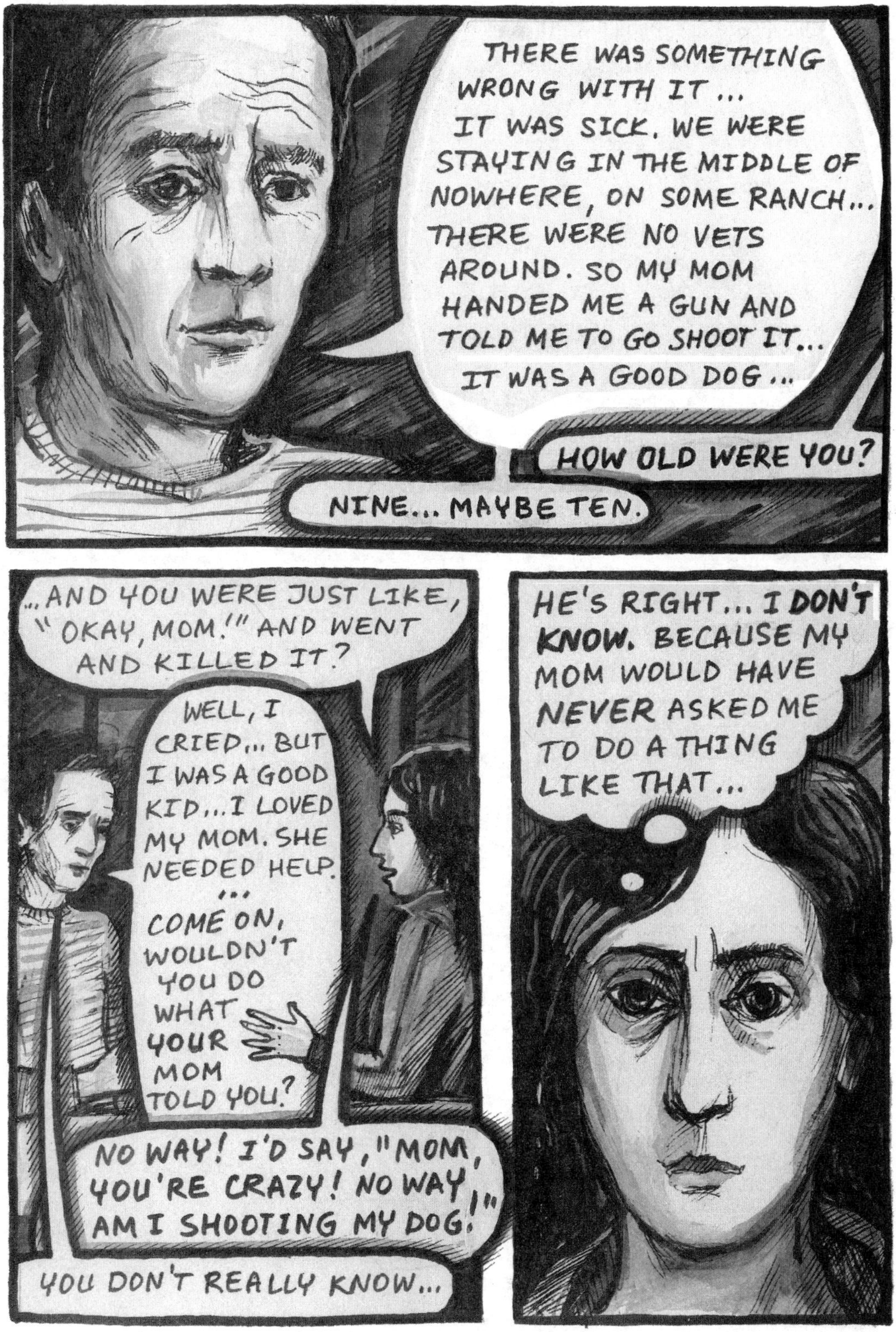
THERE WAS SOMETHING WRONG WITH IT... IT WAS SICK. WE WERE STAYING IN THE MIDDLE OF NOWHERE, ON SOME RANCH... THERE WERE NO VETS AROUND. SO MY MOM HANDED ME A GUN AND TOLD ME TO GO SHOOT IT... IT WAS A GOOD DOG...
HOW OLD WERE YOU?
NINE... MAYBE TEN.
...AND YOU WERE JUST LIKE, "OKAY, MOM!" AND WENT AND KILLED IT?
WELL, I CRIED... BUT I WAS A GOOD KID... I LOVED MY MOM. SHE NEEDED HELP. ... COME ON, WOULDN'T YOU DO WHAT YOUR MOM TOLD YOU?
NO WAY! I'D SAY, "MOM, YOU'RE CRAZY! NO WAY AM I SHOOTING MY DOG!"
YOU DON'T REALLY KNOW...
HE'S RIGHT... I DON'T KNOW. BECAUSE MY MOM WOULD HAVE NEVER ASKED ME TO DO A THING LIKE THAT...

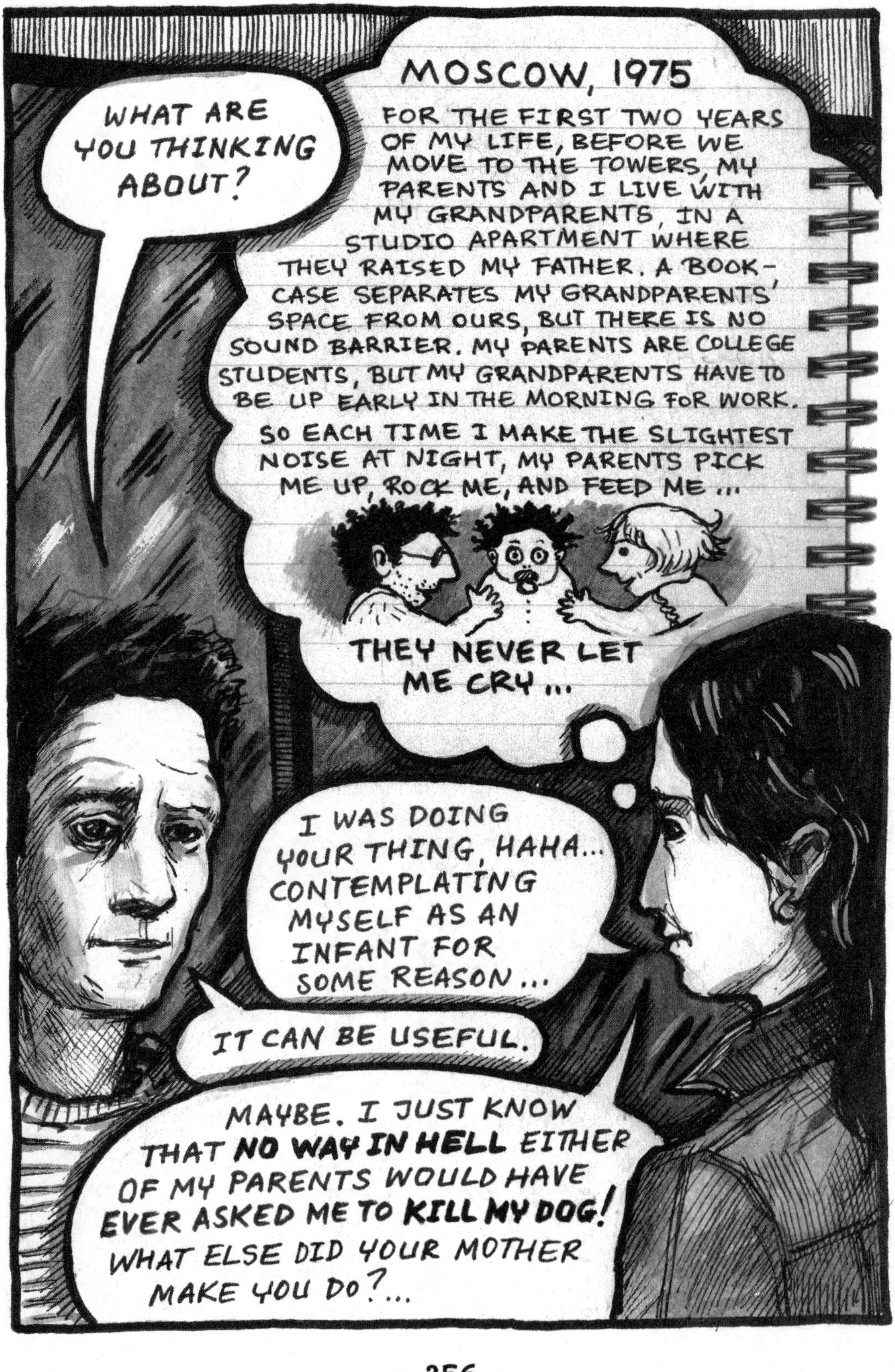

WHAT ARE YOU THINKING ABOUT?
MOSCOW, 1975
FOR THE FIRST TWO YEARS OF MY LIFE, BEFORE WE MOVE TO THE TOWERS, MY PARENTS AND I LIVE WITH MY GRANDPARENTS, IN A STUDIO APARTMENT WHERE THEY RAISED MY FATHER. A BOOK-CASE SEPARATES MY GRANDPARENTS' SPACE FROM OURS, BUT THERE IS NO SOUND BARRIER. MY PARENTS ARE COLLEGE STUDENTS, BUT MY GRANDPARENTS HAVE TO BE UP EARLY IN THE MORNING FOR WORK.
SO EACH TIME I MAKE THE SLIGHTEST NOISE AT NIGHT, MY PARENTS PICK ME UP, ROCK ME, AND FEED ME ...
THEY NEVER LET ME CRY ...
I WAS DOING YOUR THING, HAHA... CONTEMPLATING MYSELF AS AN INFANT FOR SOME REASON ...
IT CAN BE USEFUL.
MAYBE. I JUST KNOW THAT NO WAY IN HELL EITHER OF MY PARENTS WOULD HAVE EVER ASKED ME TO KILL MY DOG! WHAT ELSE DID YOUR MOTHER MAKE YOU DO?...

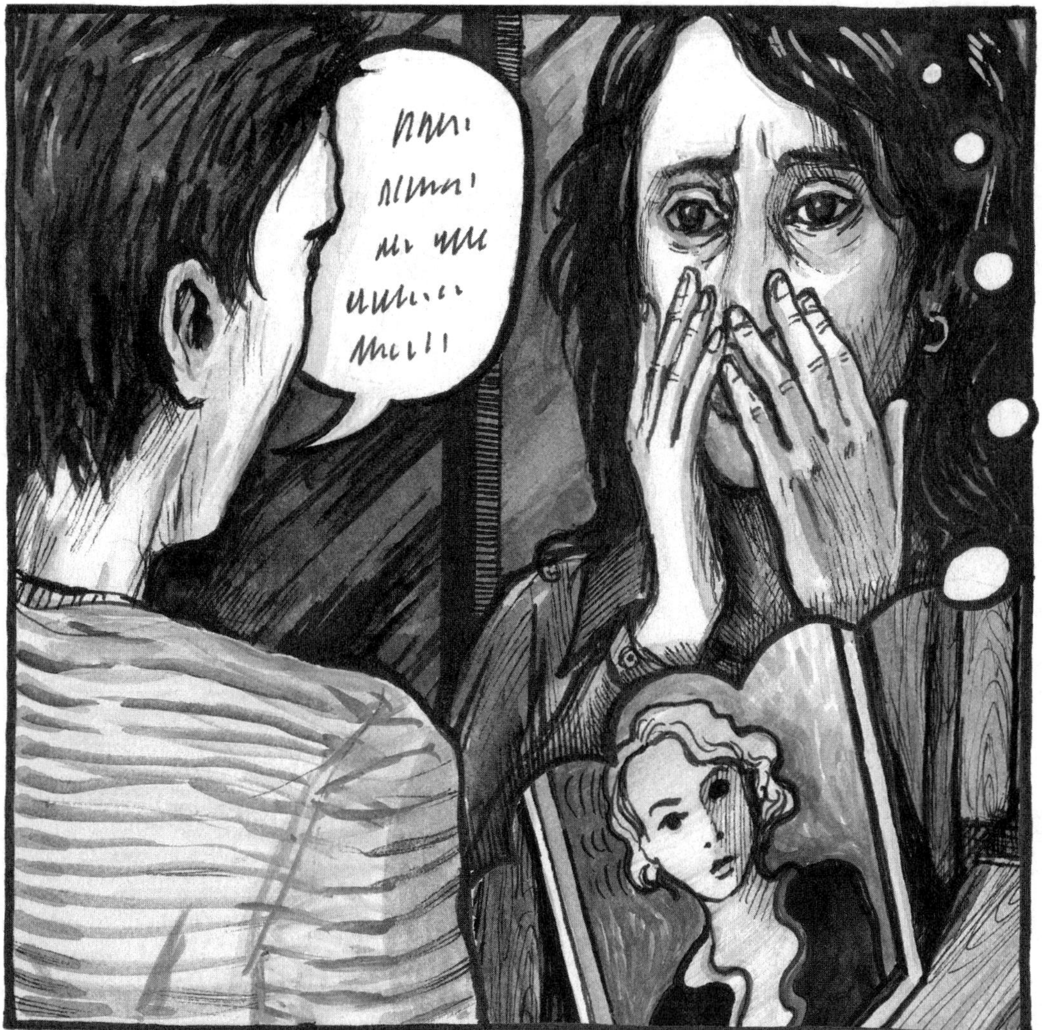

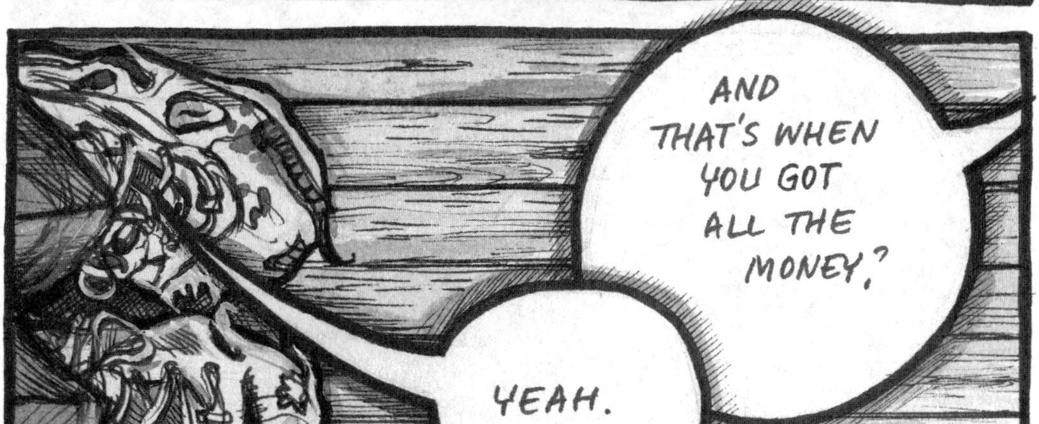
AND THAT'S WHEN YOU GOT ALL THE MONEY?
YEAH.

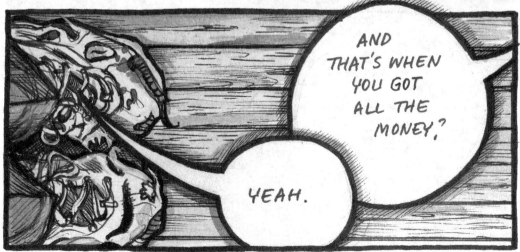

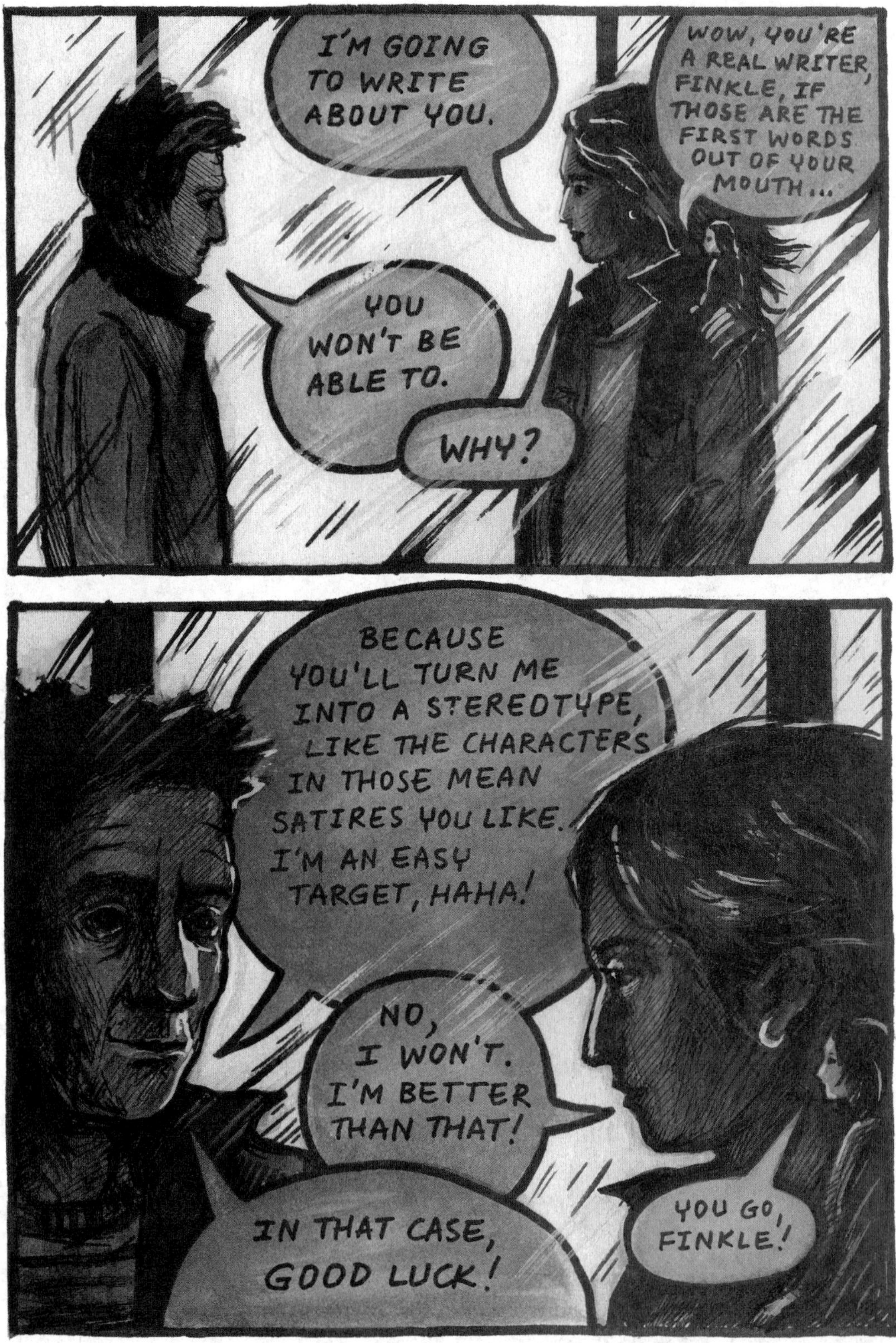
I'M GOING TO WRITE ABOUT YOU.
WOW, YOU'RE A REAL WRITER, FINKLE, IF THOSE ARE THE FIRST WORDS OUT OF YOUR MOUTH...
YOU WON'T BE ABLE TO.
WHY?
BECAUSE YOU'LL TURN ME INTO A STEREOTYPE, LIKE THE CHARACTERS IN THOSE MEAN SATIRES YOU LIKE. I'M AN EASY TARGET, HAHA!
NO, I WON'T. I'M BETTER THAN THAT!
IN THAT CASE, GOOD LUCK!
YOU GO, FINKLE!

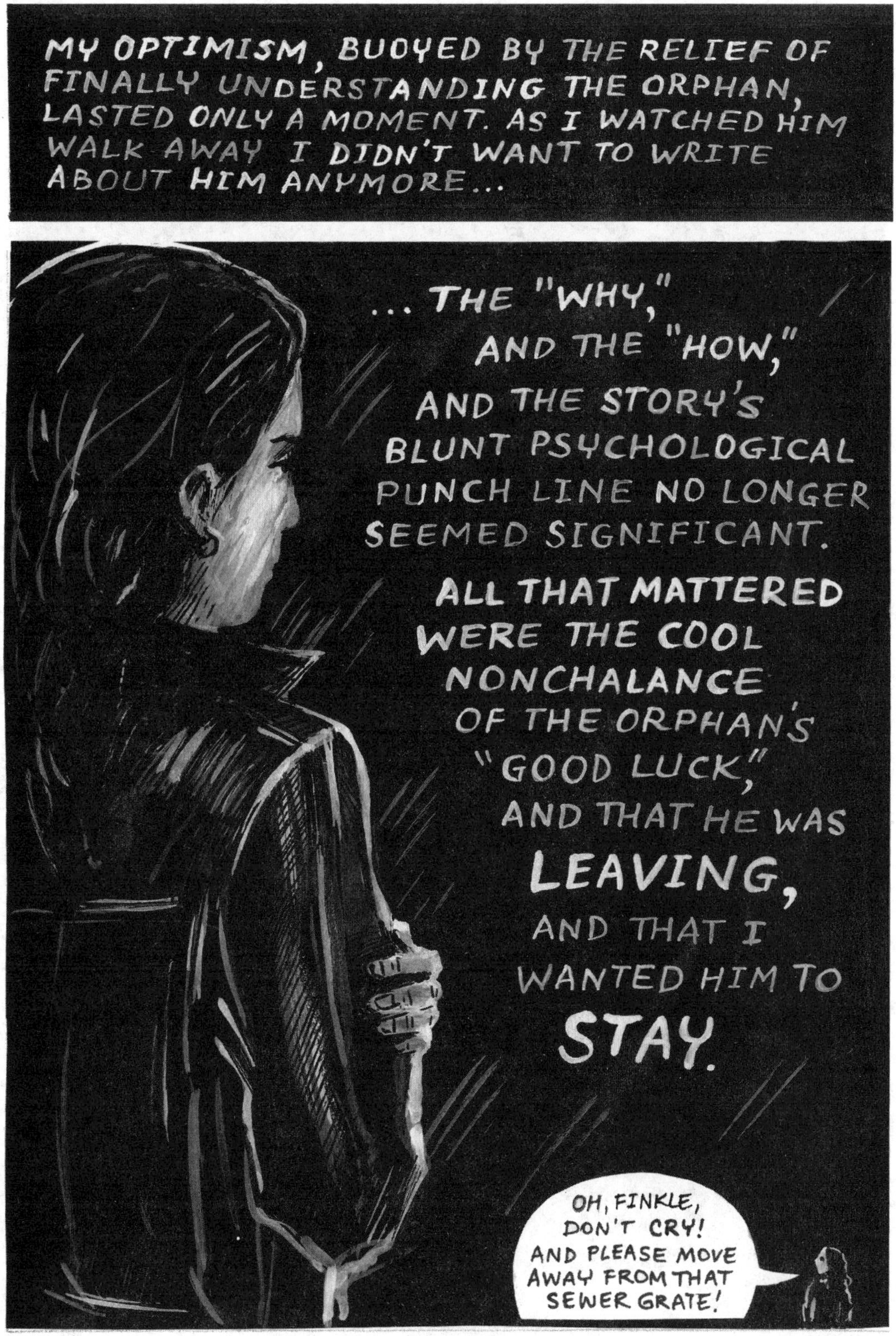
MY OPTIMISM, BUOYED BY THE RELIEF OF FINALLY UNDERSTANDING THE ORPHAN, LASTED ONLY A MOMENT. AS I WATCHED HIM WALK AWAY I DIDN'T WANT TO WRITE ABOUT HIM ANYMORE...
... THE "WHY," AND THE "HOW," AND THE STORY'S BLUNT PSYCHOLOGICAL PUNCH LINE NO LONGER SEEMED SIGNIFICANT.
ALL THAT MATTERED WERE THE COOL NONCHALANCE OF THE ORPHAN'S "GOOD LUCK," AND THAT HE WAS LEAVING, AND THAT I WANTED HIM TO STAY.
OH, FINKLE, DON'T CRY! AND PLEASE MOVE AWAY FROM THAT SEWER GRATE!

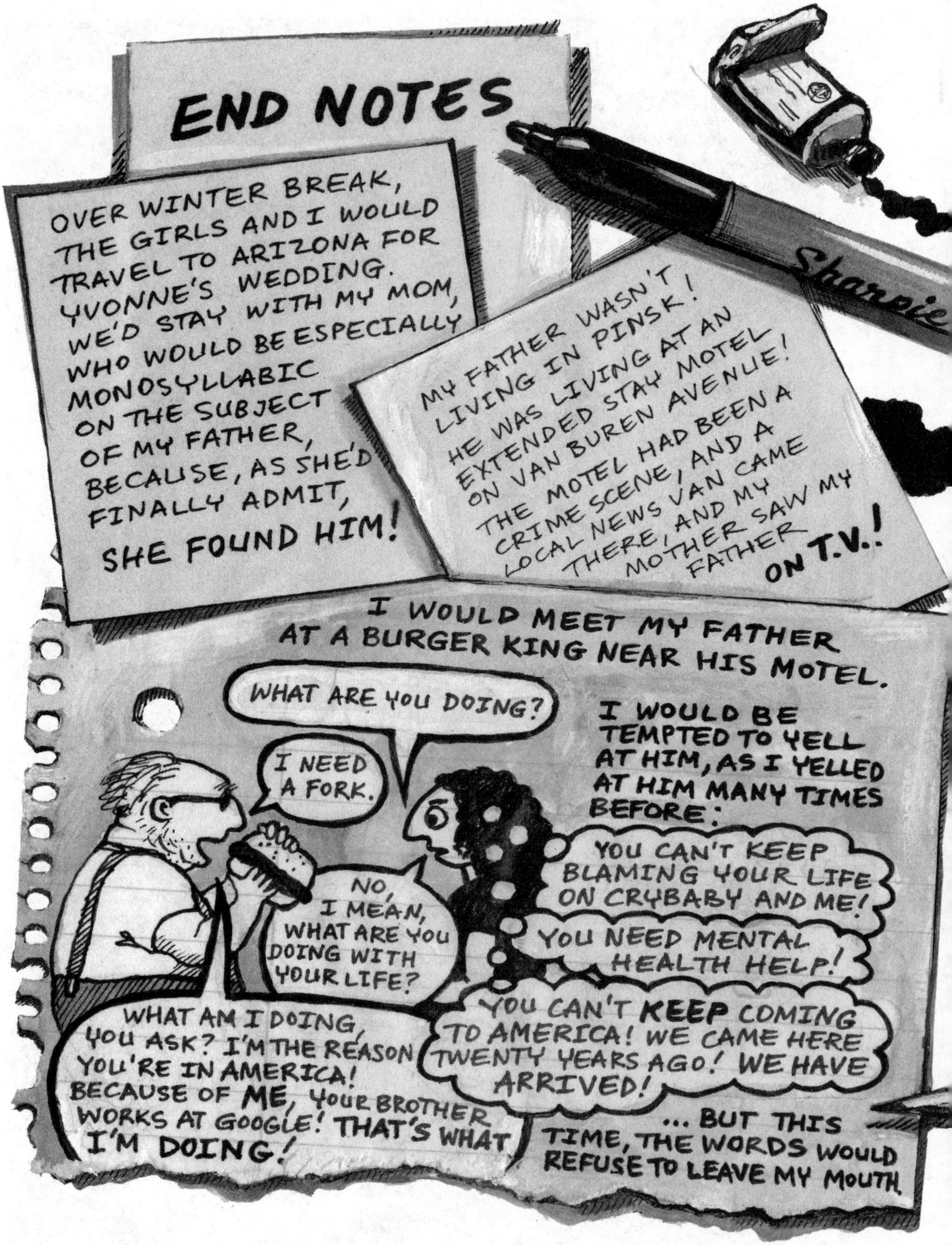
END NOTES
OVER WINTER BREAK, THE GIRLS AND I WOULD TRAVEL TO ARIZONA FOR YVONNE'S WEDDING. WE'D STAY WITH MY MOM, WHO WOULD BE ESPECIALLY MONOSYLLABIC ON THE SUBJECT OF MY FATHER, BECAUSE, AS SHE'D FINALLY ADMIT, SHE FOUND HIM!
MY FATHER WASN'T LIVING IN PINSK! HE WAS LIVING AT AN EXTENDED STAY MOTEL ON VAN BUREN AVENUE! THE MOTEL HAD BEEN A CRIME SCENE, AND A LOCAL NEWS VAN CAME THERE, AND MY MOTHER SAW MY FATHER ON T.V.!
Sharpie
I WOULD MEET MY FATHER AT A BURGER KING NEAR HIS MOTEL.
WHAT ARE YOU DOING?
I NEED A FORK.
NO, I MEAN, WHAT ARE YOU DOING WITH YOUR LIFE?
WHAT AM I DOING, YOU ASK? I'M THE REASON YOU'RE IN AMERICA! BECAUSE OF ME, YOUR BROTHER WORKS AT GOOGLE! THAT'S WHAT I'M DOING!
I WOULD BE TEMPTED TO YELL AT HIM, AS I YELLED AT HIM MANY TIMES BEFORE:
YOU CAN'T KEEP BLAMING YOUR LIFE ON CRYBABY AND ME!
YOU NEED MENTAL HEALTH HELP!
YOU CAN'T KEEP COMING TO AMERICA! WE CAME HERE TWENTY YEARS AGO! WE HAVE ARRIVED!
... BUT THIS TIME, THE WORDS WOULD REFUSE TO LEAVE MY MOUTH.

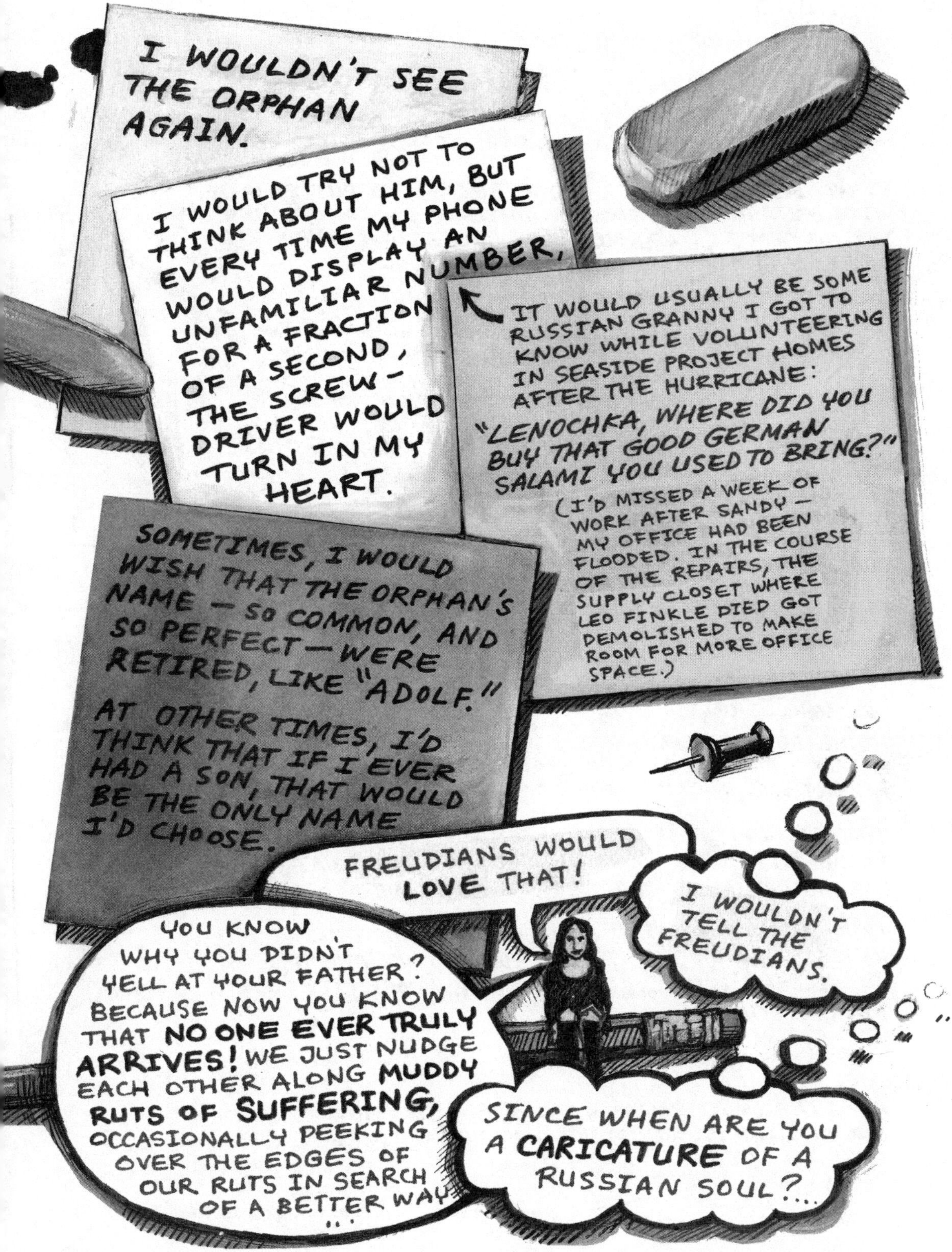
I WOULDN'T SEE THE ORPHAN AGAIN.
I WOULD TRY NOT TO THINK ABOUT HIM, BUT EVERY TIME MY PHONE WOULD DISPLAY AN UNFAMILIAR NUMBER, FOR A FRACTION OF A SECOND, THE SCREW-DRIVER WOULD TURN IN MY HEART.
IT WOULD USUALLY BE SOME RUSSIAN GRANNY I GOT TO KNOW WHILE VOLUNTEERING IN SEASIDE PROJECT HOMES AFTER THE HURRICANE:
"LENOCHKA, WHERE DID YOU BUY THAT GOOD GERMAN SALAMI YOU USED TO BRING?"
(I'D MISSED A WEEK OF WORK AFTER SANDY— MY OFFICE HAD BEEN FLOODED. IN THE COURSE OF THE REPAIRS, THE SUPPLY CLOSET WHERE LEO FINKLE DIED GOT DEMOLISHED TO MAKE ROOM FOR MORE OFFICE SPACE.)
SOMETIMES, I WOULD WISH THAT THE ORPHAN'S NAME — SO COMMON, AND SO PERFECT— WERE RETIRED, LIKE "ADOLF."
AT OTHER TIMES, I'D THINK THAT IF I EVER HAD A SON, THAT WOULD BE THE ONLY NAME I'D CHOOSE.
FREUDIANS WOULD LOVE THAT!
I WOULDN'T TELL THE FREUDIANS.
YOU KNOW WHY YOU DIDN'T YELL AT YOUR FATHER? BECAUSE NOW YOU KNOW THAT NO ONE EVER TRULY ARRIVES! WE JUST NUDGE EACH OTHER ALONG MUDDY RUTS OF SUFFERING, OCCASIONALLY PEEKING OVER THE EDGES OF OUR RUTS IN SEARCH OF A BETTER WAY...
SINCE WHEN ARE YOU A CARICATURE OF A RUSSIAN SOUL?...

HUGE THANKS:

TO MY PARENTS, LARISSA AND SERGEI, FOR THEIR LOVE.

TO MY CHILDREN, SOFIA AND REBECCA, FOR PUTTING UP WITH ME AND THIS PROJECT, WHICH BLEW INTO THEIR LIVING SPACE IN A THOUSAND PAPER SCRAPS AND REMAINED FOR TWO YEARS...

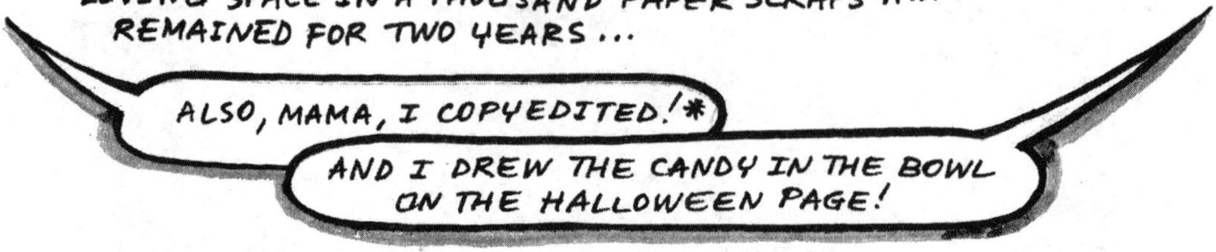
ALSO, MAMA, I COPYEDITED!*
AND I DREW THE CANDY IN THE BOWL ON THE HALLOWEEN PAGE!

TO MY EDITOR, MOLLY BARTON, FOR WHIPPING THIS MONSTER INTO SHAPE, AND TO CHRIS RUSSELL, FOR SEEING IT THROUGH TO COMPLETION.

TO MY AGENT, ANNA STEIN, FOR HER RELENTLESS CONFIDENCE IN ME EVEN WHEN I HAD NONE IN MYSELF.

TO EFFIE PHILLIPS-STALEY, FOR HELPING ME UNDERSTAND.

TO JOAN REILLY, FOR EARLY ADVICE.

TO MICHAEL BENNETT COHN, FOR TECH SUPPORT.

TO RACHEL EHRLICH, FOR SETTING ME FREE.

TO THE SUSTAINABLE ARTS FOUNDATION, FOR THEIR SUPPORT AND THEIR WORK TO ENSURE THAT ART AND PARENTHOOD NOT BE TWO SIDES OF A CHOICE.

TO MY SMART, EXCELLENT FRIENDS — BETTS BROWN, KATHLEEN HULSER, OLGA GERSHENSON, KRIS VAGNER, SARAH FERGUSON — WHO BELIEVED IN ME.

TO MY CRANKY RUSSIAN ART TEACHERS, FOR THEIR INSISTENCE ON THE CRAFT OF DRAWING, AND TO MY CHILDREN'S TEACHERS IN THE NEW YORK CITY PUBLIC SCHOOLS.

TO THE MEN WHO INSPIRED ME.

AND, FINALLY, TO EMILY WATERS, FOR JUST ABOUT EVERYTHING. I COULDN'T HAVE DONE THIS WITHOUT YOU.

* ONLY THE CHILD-APPROPRIATE PARTS.